JOURNAL FOR THE STUDY OF THE NEW TESTAMENT
SUPPLEMENT SERIES
210

Executive Editor
Stanley E. Porter

Sheffield Academic Press

A Continuum imprint

The Political Paul

Justice, Democracy and Kingship in a Hellenistic Framework

Bruno Blumenfeld

Journal for the Study of the New Testament
Supplement Series 210

For my father,
Broida (Boni) Blumenfeld,
1910, Botosani (Romania)—2000, Beersheva (Israel)

Copyright © 2001 Sheffield Academic Press
A Continuum imprint

Published by Sheffield Academic Press Ltd
The Tower Building, 11 York Road, London SE1 7NX
71 Lexington Avenue, New York NY 10017-653

www.SheffieldAcademicPress.com
www.continuumbooks.com

British Library Cataloguing-in-Publication Data

A catalogue record for this book is available from the British Library

Typeset by Sheffield Academic Press
Printed on acid-free paper in Great Britain by MPG Books Ltd,
Bodmin, Cornwall

ISBN 1-84127-187-X

CONTENTS

ACKNOWLEDGMENTS

This book owes much to few. Three friends became so involved in this work that they could justifiably be thought of as its co-authors: philosopher Lucia Lermond, who watched over the argumentation (I only wish I'd known how to answer most of her queries); writer James Waller, who questioned every word (I only wish I'd followed all his advice); and film scholar Gutsie Blumenfeld, who wondered 'Paul is a short story, why are you making it so long?' (I only wish I'd listened to her). I wish to share with them any interest this book might raise while obviously assuming the responsibility for all its failings myself.

Even more gratitude is owed Robin Scroggs, James Coulter and Holland Hendrix, who trusted me to produce a book where no one else saw one and who directed, encouraged and exhorted me in my waverings.

Although, sadly, neither of them is here any longer to thank, I feel I must acknowledge the influence on my thought and on my life of two men whom I had the privilege to know. Morton Smith and Paul Pavel were both larger-than-life figures, and my own life as a scholar and as a person would have been poorer without their guidance.

Karen Lyle, administrative assistant in the Department of Religion at Washington and Lee University, Lexington, Virginia, provided essential practical help in the preparation of the manuscript and has my sincere thanks.

I am also deeply indebted to the anonymous reviewers who endorsed this work and to Stanley Porter of Sheffield Academic Press, who accepted it for publication. Last but not least, I am thankful to the staff at Sheffield who worked on the publication of this volume.

ABBREVIATIONS

AGJU	Arbeiten zur Geschichte des antiken Judentums und des Urchristentums
ANRW	Hildegard Temporini and Wolfgang Haase (eds.), *Aufstieg und Niedergang der römischen Welt: Geschichte und Kultur Roms im Spiegel der neueren Forschung* (Berlin: W. de Gruyter, 1972–)
BAGD	Walter Bauer, William F. Arndt, F. William Gingrich and Frederick W. Danker, *A Greek–English Lexicon of the New Testament and Other Early Christian Literature* (Chicago: University of Chicago Press, 2nd edn, 1958)
BBB	Bonner biblische Beiträge
Bib	*Biblica*
BNTC	Black's New Testament Commentaries
BWANT	Beiträge zur Wissenschaft vom Alten und Neuen Testament
CAH	Cambridge Ancient History
CBQ	*Catholic Biblical Quarterly*
ClQ	*Classical Quarterly*
CRINT	Compendia rerum iudaicarum ad Novum Testamentum
CTM	*Concordia Theological Monthly*
DB	J. Hastings, F.C. Grant and H.H. Rowley (eds.), *Dictionary of the Bible* (New York: Charles Scribner's Sons, 1963)
Diels	H. Diels and W. Kranz, *Fragmente der Vorsokratiker* (Berlin: Weidmann, 5th edn, 1934)
DS	C. Daremberg, E. Saglio and E. Pottier (eds.), *Dictionnaire des antiquités grecques et romaines d'après les textes et les monuments* (Paris: Librairie Hachette, 1877–1919)
FGrHist	F. Jacoby, *Die Fragmente der griechischen Historiker* (Berlin: Weidmann, 1923–58)
FN	*Filologia neotestamentaria*
FRLANT	Forschungen zur Religion und Literatur des Alten und Neuen Testaments
GGM	C. Müller, *Geographi graeci minores* (Paris: Firmin-Didot, 1855–61)
HNT	Handbuch zum Neuen Testament
HTR	*Harvard Theological Review*
HUCA	*Hebrew Union College Annual*

HUT	Hermeneutische Untersuchungen zur Theologie
Int	*Interpretation*
JAAR	*Journal of the American Academy of Religion*
JAC	*Jahrbuch für Antike und Christentum*
JBL	*Journal of Biblical Literature*
JR	*Journal of Religion*
JRH	*Journal of Religious History*
JRS	*Journal of Roman Studies*
JSNT	*Journal for the Study of the New Testament*
JSNTSup	*Journal for the Study of the New Testament*, Supplement Series
JSOTSup	*Journal for the Study of the Old Testament*, Supplement Series
JTS	*Journal of Theological Studies*
LSJ	H.G. Liddell, Robert Scott and H. Stuart Jones, *Greek–English Lexicon* (Oxford: Clarendon Press, 9th edn, 1968)
Mitteis-Wilcken	L. Mitteis and U. Wilcken, *Grundzüge und Chrestomathie der Papyruskunde* (Leipzig: Teubner, 1912)
MM	J.H. Moulton and G. Milligan, *The Vocabulary of the Greek Testament Illustrated from the Papyri and Other Non-Literary Sources* (London: Hodder & Stoughton, 1914–29)
MNTC	Moffatt NT Commentary
NCB	New Century Bible
NHS	Nag Hammadi Studies
Nock-Festugière	A.D. Nock and A.J. Festugière, *Corpus Hermeticum* (Paris: Les Belles Lettres, 1945–54)
NovT	*Novum Testamentum*
NovTSup	*Novum Testamentum*, Supplements
NTAbh	Neutestamentliche Abhandlungen
NTD	Das Neue Testament Deutsch
NTS	*New Testament Studies*
OCD	N.G.L. Hammond and H.H. (eds.), *The Oxford Classical Dictionary* (Oxford: Clarendon Press, 2nd edn, 1979)
OGI	W. Dittenberger, *Orientis Graeci Inscriptiones Selectae* (Leipzig: Hirzel, 1903–1905)
PFay	B.P. Grenfell, A.S. Hunt, D.G. Hogarth and J.G. Milne, *Faŷum Towns and Their Papyri* (London: Offices of the Egypt Exploration Fund, 1900)
PTMS	Pittsburgh Theological Monograph Series
PW	August Friedrich von Pauly and Georg Wissowa (eds.), *Real-Encyclopädie der classischen Altertumswissenschaft* (Stuttgart: Metzler, 1894–)
RAC	*Reallexikon für Antike und Christentum*
RB	*Revue biblique*
SBLDS	SBL Dissertation Series
SBLBMI	SBL The Bible and Its Modern Interpreters

SBLMS	SBL Monograph Series
SBLRBS	SBL Resources for Biblical Study
SBLSBS	SBL Sources for Biblical Study
SBLSS	SBL Semeia Studies
SBT	Studies in Biblical Theology
SC	Sources chrétiennes
SIG³	W. Dittenberger, *Sylloge Inscriptionum Graecarum* (Leipzig: Hirzel, 3rd edn, 1915–24)
SJLA	Studies in Judaism in Late Antiquity
SJT	*Scottish Journal of Theology*
SNTSMS	Society for New Testament Studies Monograph Series
ST	*Studia theologica*
Str–B	[Hermann L. Strack and] Paul Billerbeck, *Kommentar zum Neuen Testament aus Talmud und Midrasch* (7 vols.; Munich: Beck, 1922–61)
SVF	H.F.A. von Arnim (ed.), *Stoicorum Veterum Fragmenta* (Stuttgart: Teubner, 1903–24)
TDNT	Gerhard Kittel and Gerhard Friedrich (eds.), *Theological Dictionary of the New Testament* (trans. Geoffrey W. Bromiley; 10 vols.; Grand Rapids: Eerdmans, 1964–)
TLNT	C. Spicq, *Theological Lexicon of the New Testament* (trans. J.D. Ernest; Peabody, MA: Hendrickson, 1994)
TLZ	*Theologische Literaturzeitung*
TTod	*Theology Today*
TWNT	Gerhard Kittel and Gerhard Friedrich (eds.), *Theologisches Wörterbuch zum Neuen Testament* (11 vols.; Stuttgart: Kohlhammer, 1932–79)
WBC	Word Biblical Commentary
WUNT	Wissenschaftliche Untersuchungen zum Neuen Testament
WW	*Word and World*
ZNW	*Zeitschrift für die neutestamentliche Wissenschaft*
ZTK	*Zeitschrift für Theologie und Kirche*

INTRODUCTION

Μηδὲν ἄναρχον εὑρὲν δύνασθαι.
('Nothing unruled can be found.')
Ps.-Ecphantus

Politeuesthe, 'Be citizens', Paul exhorts the Philippians (Phil. 1.27), placing himself in a long tradition of political reflection running from Plato through Aristotle to the political thinkers of his own Hellenistic milieu.

This study proposes to examine the *political* Paul, arguing that to neglect this dimension of Paul's thought decontextualizes him and falsifies our reading of his works. Pauline theology, in both its conservative and transformative aspects, cannot be fully understood or appreciated without knowledge of the political theories of Hellenism, most notably of the Hellenistic Pythagoreans.

My research naturally bridges two worlds, that of classical scholarship and that of New Testament studies, but directs itself more to the student of the New Testament. The classicist can learn here of continuities in the Western tradition that have not previously been suggested, but the presentation is geared to a reader less familiar with Greek political thought.

Interpretations of Paul can be divided, along the most visible fault lines, between the theological and the historical, between Judaizing and Hellenizing trends, and between the exegetical and social milieu studies. The hermeneutical borders are often seen as fluid, though even more frequently as impermeable.

Paul has always been at the crossroads. Was Paul a Jew or a Hellene? Was the prevailing influence on him Jewish or Hellenistic? The scholarly split between 'Judaizers' and 'Hellenizers' is periodically felt with unusual intensity. (Of course, the opposition Hellenizing/Judaizing is no simple polarity: for example, an eschatologist emphasizing Hellenistic Judaism is a Hellenizer in contrast to a theorist of Paul's continuity with rabbinical Judaism, but a Judaizer in contrast with a Hellenistic purist.)

Although the present study obviously falls on the 'Hellenizing' side of this divide, it also stands somewhat apart from the debate as it has been constructed thus far. Current scholarship has taken up again the exploration of the impress of Hellenistic culture on Paul's oeuvre. While the depth and abundance of Hellenistic-related studies throughout the history of Pauline interpretation justify the necessity of my inquiry and validate its orientation, this is of very limited direct import for my thesis, for the political-philosophical aspect of Paul's thinking forms the object of few, if any, of them.

I propose to show that Paul's views in general, and particularly in the letters to the Romans and the Philippians, are structurally, argumentatively and conceptually coherent with Classical and Hellenistic political thought. This involves a twofold task. The first objective is the examination of the question of sources, the external evidence for the perspective present in Paul's letters, and the outside support for arguing the case. The second goal is to trace this influence in Paul on the basis of internal textual evidence.

The debate itself proves that all scholarship regards Paul as heir to *some* tradition. I believe that he is most properly placed in a tradition of Hellenistic popular philosophy, a pastiche of political-theological theorization in which the latent force of Plato and Aristotle yet remains operative. Hence it is with these Classical thinkers that my study, after setting forth the parameters of contextualization of Paul in relation to Classical and Hellenistic political theory, properly begins. I emphasize those features of Classical political philosophy that bear most directly on Hellenistic and Pauline political reflection, and my detailed treatment of Aristotle's ethics and politics ends with a consideration of themes common to Aristotle and Paul.

In Classical political philosophy *oikos* and *polis* are clearly distinguished; Hellenistic thinking, exemplified in the theorists of the monarchic regime known as the Hellenistic Pythagoreans, overlaps the two. I find it useful, at this point, to explore the interplay *oikos*, *polis* and *ekklēsia* in Paul as well as to discuss political self-references in Paul.

I then go on to examine the writings of the so-called Hellenistic Pythagoreans, the school most fruitful for an appreciation of Paul's politics. This chapter divides into considerations of what I identify as a *polis* group and a *basileia* group of texts. Analysis of the *polis*-group fragments issues in a summary of themes crucial to Paul: *oikos* and *polis*; *sumpheron* in Paul's pneumatic politics; imitation; hierarchy and equality; distributive justice; and *nomos* and *dikaiosunē*. Christianity is deeply rooted in the politics of Hellenistic kingship, and analysis of the *basileia*-group fragments issues in a discussion of Hellenistic monarchy and Paul.

In the second part of the study, I turn to an analysis of Paul. Following the examination of Hellenistic sources, the book moves into a consideration of Paul's theorization of Rome—an interpretive nexus of profound significance for understanding the relation of the radical and the conservative elements of Paul's thought.

Moving to Paul's work proper, I first reflect on methodological questions generated by a search for the elements of Pauline politics, followed by an exegesis of political terminology in the Letter to the Philippians. I then present a cohesive reading of the Letter to the Romans, summarizing the Hellenistic Pythagorean evidence previously discussed. The concluding chapter focuses on the centrality of *dikaiosunē* in some interpretations of Romans, and puts the political charge of the concept into high relief. Finally, I reiterate the insights produced by this study as a whole. The most original result of my research is the argument that finds Christianity's roots in Hellenistic kingship theories. By grounding Pauline Christianity in Hellenistic political theory in general, and in the theory of Hellenistic monarchy in particular, the work also provides a new explanation for the success of Christianity.

At the end of this introduction, I shall have more to say on the particularities of the method I have used to connect Paul to this milieu. But let me first turn, briefly, to a description of the political-philosophical context to which, I believe, Paul belongs.

Hellenistic Popular Philosophy: The Context for Paul's Thought

It is a matter of near general agreement among scholars of Greek antiquity that the Hellenistic period saw the withering of the *polis* and the atrophy of the civic spirit.[1] Faced with 'large and distant political forms: monarchies, nation-states, federal leagues, and imperial dominions',[2] individuals retreated in befuddlement from participation in local politics, and the *poleis* became trinkets of Hellenistic kings.[3]

Yet, even at the peak of Hellenistic empires, the *polis* held its place

---

1.   For the content of this section I am indebted to Gruen 1993.
2.   Gruen 1993: 339.
3.   See, e.g., Tarn 1952, Préaux 1978, Walbank 1982.

as a focus of loyalty and affection, generated devotion and civic pride, enjoyed some autonomy and independent authority and even had an impact on the course of historical events.[4] The formulaic, equivocal and fatuous diplomatic language preserved in inscription after inscription records the monarchs' guarantee of *eleutheria, autonomia* and *dēmokratia*.[5] Yet these pronouncements were not always sanctimonious deceptions camouflaging despotism.[6]

Even more suggestive are the documents that illustrate the relations between Hellenistic *poleis*.[7] Most are accords and treaties concluded directly between city-states, which, even if of small significance internationally, reflect 'the continued vitality of the *polis*, its political and territorial integrity, and its autonomous posture'.[8] The *poleis* continued their existence alongside and within the Hellenistic superpowers.

Epigraphic evidence regarding how the *poleis* conducted their internal affairs is likewise vast. Although much of the information reveals dutiful functionaries and formulaic and threadbare functions of traditional and vacuous content, the inscriptions also provide proof of citizens' genuine, passionate fondness for their *poleis*—a persistent, vibrant cultivation of the significance of the *polis*.[9]

4. Gauthier 1984; Davies 1984; and esp. Gruen 1984, 1993.
5. See Gruen 1993: 340.
6. When Quinctius Flaminius defeats Philip V in the Second Macedonian War in 196 BCE, he proclaims, in Corinth, to great amazement and acclaim, the freedom of the Greeks to govern themselves according to their ancestral laws (Gruen 1993: 341).
7. See Gruen (1993: 342-44) for examples of agreements, peace-treaties, arbitration practices. Although the latter may actually help the thesis of the disintegration of the internal civic institutions of the *polis*, manifesting mistrust in the crumbling judicial system, Gruen shows that the roots of out-of-state arbitration go back to Classical Greece and that its use is chiefly in conflicts of economic nature; the foreign jurors are commonly responsible to the *polis* and not to royal appointees or to dynastic delegates (1993: 343-45).
8. Gruen 1993: 343.
9. See examples of oaths of allegiance, intercity exchanges of citizenship (*isopoliteia*), civic festivals, contribution of funds for public works or debt payment in Gruen (1993: 345-49). Although civic benefaction, the system of *euergeteia*, becomes by later second century BCE a means by which wealthy patrons virtually own the sycophantic and pauper city (349), Gruen prefers to emphasize the growth of private financing and investment of major municipal projects (350-51) in exchange for publicity and honors; recognition is also bestowed on philosophers, poets, athletes (351-52).

The view that emerges is that while the *poleis* declined in importance externally and deteriorated internally, the ideal of the *polis* remained undiminished.[10] Despite the ebbing of the *polis*'s political power, and despite social erosion, the power of the *polis* to mobilize devotion and civic emotion was little altered. Political theorists continued to reflect on the *polis* with fervor and longing, and it was precisely this sentiment that Paul tapped into.

Political reflection is a major dimension of Paul's thought. The Classical and Hellenistic background of political speculation must, by necessity, show in his work. While it cannot be irrefutably demonstrated that Paul knew any particular work of Classical or Hellenistic political philosophy, it can be convincingly argued that he was familiar with a tradition. The question with which to start is, What was the 'standard' political doctrine during most of the Hellenistic era? Answering this question requires, among other things, that we identify the authorities whose political views most likely prevailed in the nonprofessional philosophical circles of Paul's time.

Political thinking in Hellenistic times, for a period of about four hundred years before Paul and extending into the Roman era, was, for all the complexity of its hues, simple in design. Greek and Roman Hellenistic philosophers had little to work with beyond the Classical Athenian political writings—that is, the works of Plato and Aristotle, the latter justly credited with founding the field of political science. Whatever school's garb one wore, when it came to political theory the authority of the Classical philosophers was absolute, and it remained so even as their relevance was vanishing. Between Aristotle and Theophrastus, on the one hand, and Paul, on the other, practically[11] no new

10. For a study of the resilience of Hellenistic structures and of the politics of the *polis* under Rome, see Harris's 1980 study on Bithynia. On the vitality of the *polis* in Hellenistic and Roman times, see A.H.M. Jones 1940.

11. This obviously needs to be qualified. For all their veneration of the Classics, Hellenistic political philosophers, especially the Hellenistic Pythagoreans, made, within the Classical framework, theoretical advances that were important for subsequent thinking and that are visible in Paul. But they proved strikingly unwilling or incapable of formulating new ideas that would be genuine departures from the thought of Plato and Aristotle and not just subtle reworkings and agile consolidations. A certain coyness and diffidence seems to have dominated political discourse in Hellenistic times. The Romans *made* politics and thus produced great historians and generals, but political thought, as a field of intellectual exploration, recorded few major names before the success of Christianity.

political theory was elaborated. The same old teachings were used, tirelessly and uncritically; they were combined and extrapolated, abbreviated and annotated. In the process, political thought became increasingly artificial and incongruous, deplorably inadequate and woefully inappropriate to describe or explain, much less to stimulate and improve, political structures and proceedings.

The theories of the *polis* produced in fourth-century BCE Athens endured, and controlled political philosophy long after their usefulness was curtailed and far beyond the territory of their birth.[12] They were hardly suited for the large kingdoms and empires of Hellenistic times and even less so for the Roman political configurations, be these republican or imperial. When kingship became the order of the day, the Classics became largely irrelevant to political reality, yet Hellenistic historiographers and philosophers resolutely clung to the same antiquated, fatigued, yet magisterial canon. Rome's unparalleled expansion baffled the best Greek minds, and to understand it even Polybius (c.200–c.118 BCE), possibly the most original political analyst of the Hellenistic period, rushed back to the Attic masters (e.g. in his *Histories* 6.10). The mixed constitution—a fine theoretical construct whose life, outside Sparta, was mostly imaginary but which had haunted political thought for centuries—was retrieved again from the philosophical closet. Even Cicero modeled his *Republic* and *Laws* after Plato.[13]

Political theory is a sorry sight after Plato and Aristotle. The great Classical philosophers' riveting teachings ultimately engendered stilted handbooks, which, however, were cherished and enjoyed widespread circulation. It would be surprising indeed to encounter in the first century CE a wandering lecturer[14] who did not carry in his philosophical handbag the common fare of political reasoning: strips of Plato's *Republic*, bits of *Protagoras*, morsels of the *Laws*, scraps of Aristotle's *Politics* and tidbits of his *Ethics*.

Why should Paul be any different? Indeed, it would be amazing if he were. That political culture was badly adapted to reality and mostly frozen in the Classical Greek frame is, at least partly, to be explained by

12. 'Platonic interpretation has replaced historical reality', notes Burkert (1962: 84).

13. He does so, however, less in philosophical than in rhetorical terms (see Finley 1983: 128).

14. For good discussions of the popular, itinerant philosopher see Helm 1902, Friedländer 1921–23, Malherbe 1970, C.P. Jones 1986.

the system of education. The Hellenistic *paideia* stressed a relatively small and stereotyped body of knowledge, drawn almost entirely from the ancient Greeks, ancient even then: reading was learned on selections from Homer, Euripides and Menander;[15] rhetoric from compendia of Isocrates and Demosthenes; philosophy, mostly ethics and politics, from digests of Plato and Aristotle.[16]

The philosophy that Paul knew was of the 'popular' type. His infor-

15. Snippets from classical or 'modern' poets, which must have been found in school manuals, make it into the Scriptures. Acts 17.28 'quotes' Cleanthes or Aratus (*Phaenomena* was written between 276 and 274 BCE). Titus 1.12 has a line from Epimenides. Paul himself, in 1 Cor. 15.32 is thought to cite Menander: φθείρουσιν ἤθη χρηστὰ ὁμιλίαι κακαί, 'Bad company ruins good morals', though the case is pretty weak, for this must have been a current saying and Paul may have ignored its origin; he does not so much quote as betray his cultural background, the sociolect, as Riffaterre (1978) calls it. Nevertheless, Paul spoke Greek and his education could not have been different from what countless papyri shreds and ostraka shards from Egypt show to have been the homework of schoolchildren. Paul was a cultivated Hellenized Jew; he was a man of much learning (Acts 26.24, and variant readings).

It ought also to be mentioned that, beginning with Hellenistic times, education becomes subject to official control, and that the public schools are under the authority of the state; by state is meant the municipality, not the kingdom (Marrou 1956: 103). Municipal schools sprang up everywhere and the phenomenon continued under the Roman Empire. 'People had developed such a lively interest in education that every important city felt increasingly that it should have its own schools, and staff and maintain them and keep an eye on them at the public expense' (Marrou 1956: 305). Caesar and Augustus introduced measures to benefit the teachers, and many privileges and immunities were thus granted (Marrou 1956: 301-302). Caesar, for example, 'conferred citizenship (*civitas*) on all who practised medicine at Rome, and on all teachers of the liberal arts (*liberalium artium doctores*), to make them more desirous of living in the city and to induce others to resort to it' (Suetonius, *Caesar* 42.1, Rolfe trans.). Augustus, at a time of great scarcity, expelled from Rome 'all foreigners with the exception of physicians and teachers' (Suetonius, *Augustus* 42.3). Beginning with Vespasian the teachers would be exempted from *munera*, municipal levies, and would enjoy other considerable privileges all over the Empire (Marrou 1956: 301).

16. The best scholarly surveys of ancient education which are also relevant for Hellenistic *paideia* remain Marrou (1938, 1956, 1960) and Jaeger (1943–45, 1969). Particularly important for Paul are Wendland 1907, 1912, Cochrane 1957, Hatch 1957, Judge 1960, 1960–61, 1972, Unnik 1962, Hugedé 1966, C.P. Jones 1986, Neyrey 1990, MacMullen 1991, Anderson 1993, L.M. White 1995; for art and aesthetics see Bieber 1961, Giuliano 1965, B.H. Fowler 1989; for a good collection of sources see Newsome 1992.

mation was obtained mostly from general school instruction and by listening to the orators who traveled around lecturing. The vast majority of these speakers were themselves representatives of the class of 'popular philosophers', amateurs who lacked the expertise that comes from in-depth study of one philosophical school. Or, to put it the opposite way, the popular philosopher was not a professional; his very existence amounted to a resistance against the thoroughgoing profession-alization of virtually every aspect of Hellenistic society.[17] The Greek *ephēbeia* had become a professional army of mercenaries; the gym-nastics practiced by every (male) Greek in the palaestra had turned into professional athletics. In Plato's dialogues, Socrates inveighed against the Sophists, expressing the resistance of the *polis* to specialization and the professionalizing of philosophy,[18] but with Alexander and the *Diadochi*, the professionalization of politics, religion and education began in earnest. All fields of public life—legislation, magistracies, religion, politics—became professions, requiring special training and subject to remuneration. Philosophy may well have been the last field in which there was still room for the dilettante.

The term 'popular philosophy' covers a Hellenistic phenomenon that is as ambiguous as it is widespread. The affluent and education-in-fatuated urban environment of the eastern Mediterranean made an ideal setting for the activity of itinerant lecturers, well-spoken and eclecti-cally informed, of dubious resources but of opulent imagination, who because of their extensive travels could acquaint themselves with and carry around cultural trends, and who knew, probably through a scuttle-butt network, where they could find a public willing to listen to their stories and exhortations. The popular philosopher was a mixture of poet, philosopher and prophet, a product of political disenfranchisement who delivered hymns, moral lectures and visions in the marketplace or

17. Look, for example, at the city imagined by Onesicritus of Astypalaea, the Cynic, Alexander's seaman and historian: no politics, no science, except medicine, Spartan model of life. The inventors of outlandish locales show, in their fantasies, where it hurts: professionalization (of politics and sciences) and valuation of the body. The Cynic displays the strong nostalgia not for paradise but for freelance politics.

18. The Sophists, so much derided by Plato, are members of the professional class of philosophers. They are itinerant classroom teachers and paid lecturers. Plato certainly thinks, however, that philosophers should be specialists of a kind. Indeed, in the *Republic*, the basis of society is in division of labor according to aptitude.

at the city gates to an eager rabble pitching in their obols, or at a wealthy man's estate for a fee. Whatever their origin and whatever their message, popular philosophers all shared some features. They were wayfarers who often donned the Cynic pose and garb: long-haired; bearded; dressed in a coarse, mottled woolen cloak and carrying a wallet and a staff. They were people of wit, frequently wry, who offered speeches tailored to their audiences. They likely did not claim association with any established, formal philosophical school.[19] In effect, they often voiced a critique of established philosophical institutions and highbrow philosophers and challenged established wisdom. Diatribe and a protreptic style characterized their rhetoric. They advocated *parrēsia*, unrestrained freedom of speech. Their method was goal-oriented, focused on how life should be lived, and thus limited theoretically and speculatively. Their addresses were ethical in content, moral interpretation permeating most reflection on local, global and cosmic events. Their interest was in social, political and doctrinal issues. In their teachings they emphasized virtue, especially such traits as piety, patriotism toward the city, obedience to authorities, devotion to the family, hospitality to travelers and care of the poor, as well as self-control, moderation and rectitude.

The marked emphasis of the popular philosophers' homilies was *autarkeia*: not just 'self-sufficiency' but empowerment in the face of despotic politics—the ability to rule oneself in a world of alienating, self-serving tyranny. *Autarkeia* is a political challenge under the guise of a moral desideratum. This ideal called for cultivated detachment,

---

19. Conzelmann proposed that Paul had consciously founded a school, of the philosophical sort (1965: 233 and 1966: 307-308, *ap.* Meeks 1983: 82). E.A. Judge had already suggested that Paul established scholastic communities, a 'think-tank' we would call it today (1960; *ap.* Meeks 1983: 82). That 'the leaders of the Pauline circles were apparently acquainted with major topics current in Hellenistic *moral* [my emphasis] discourse and with some aspects of the style of that discourse' (Meeks 1983: 83) has been amply proven by such scholars as Malherbe (1968, 1970, 1976, 1987, 1988, 1989, 1991, 1992) and the 22 authors collected in the Malherbe Festschrift volume edited by Balch, Ferguson and Meeks (1990), Aune (1988, 1991), Stowers (1981, 1984b, 1988, 1994), Koester (1965, 1982), Balch (1981, 1990, 1992), Hock (1978, 1980), Betz ([1972] 1990a, 1975a, 1975b, 1977, 1979, [1987] 1990b), Judge (1968, 1972, 1980), Wuellner (1979). [In brackets, the original date of publication.] These scholars emphasize the importance of either ethical Hellenistic thought or its rhetoric on the New Testament moralists. For the relation of Hellenistic Pythagorean ethics to Paul, see esp. Balch 1992.

affirmed a turning-within, and redirected the responsibility due the *polis* and the political consciousness, which had long defined the Greek world, toward an individual ethic of unprecedented intensity and compass. The popular philosophers questioned *nomos*, conventional law, and exalted *phusis*, a natural code of thought and behavior. Finally, and possibly most important, they made an *exemplum* of their own lives. Poor, cherishing manual labor, valuing hardship, little interested in the comforts of family life, nomadic and fired by a consciousness of possessing a divine mission, speaking audaciously and uninhibited in conduct (*anaideia*), engaging in displays of supernatural powers, they were marginal characters at the center of Hellenistic social and religious life.[20] Few if any of these features would not apply to Paul. Paul of Tarsus was certainly perceived as, and promoted himself as, an itinerant teacher, a Hellenistic popular philosopher.[21]

Popular philosophy was, nevertheless, an intellectual genre. Although an amateur of philosophy, the popular philosopher was a professional of rhetoric. He was an expert in diatribe, a complex discipline implying a liberal education (which enabled him to quote philosophers and poets and to refer to historical events) while mixing ethics and religion, quackery and harangue.

The popular philosopher despised the intensely cultured, professionally qualified Sophist. For the popular philosopher, popularizing philosophy meant rendering it useful to the masses, even if this meant sacrificing context and argument for theatrics and quip. Manuals that assembled uplifting or chastising fragments of philosophers, repeatedly copied, increasingly jumbled and further and further removed from their original contexts, were used especially by Stoics and Cynics. It is quite likely that Paul either used such a handbook or himself assembled a *hupomnēma* (aide-mémoire) from notes he took while listening to popular philosophers' lectures or reading handbooks. The source for all

20. The distinction between religion and philosophy (either formal or popular) was minimal in antiquity. Philosophical schools were sometimes organized as 'a religious fellowship, *thiasos*, dedicated to the goddesses of culture' says Marrou (Marrou 1956, *ap.* Meeks 1983: 83), expounding on the Pythagorean school experience. On the notion that philosophical schools (such as Epicureanism, Pythagoreanism or Neoplatonism) were often organized as religious communities see Hadas-Smith 1965: 44 or Talbert 1978: 1646.

21. Many materials were used in writing this section. Most prominently, Adcock 1927: 102, Balch 1992: 390, Downing 1992, Muehl 1929: 118-19, 445-46, 463, Préaux 1976: 60, 62, Thesleff 1972: 95, and particularly Manning 1994.

the *digesta* was the isagogics, a literary genre of commentaries that functioned as introductions (εἰσαγωγή in Greek, *introductio* or *institutio* in Latin) to grammatical, rhetorical or philosophical works. They were produced in large quantities by scores of ancient writers over a period of seven hundred years. The most numerous were, as might be expected, the prefaces to Plato and Aristotle. These commentaries enjoyed a vast circulation; most of the time they formed genuine compendia; often they were used to write digests for students and amateurs.[22]

Lucian's treatise *Demonax*, written in the second century CE, provides an especially lucid picture of a popular philosopher in the person of the title character. A most respectable popular philosopher, Demonax is an original, with a inborn love (ἔμφυτος ἔρως) for philosophy; he does not derive his authority from any teacher but from his own impulse (οἰκεία ὁρμή). Demonax maintains his independence, refusing to identify with any particular philosophical school, though he is acquainted with all of them (*Demonax* 3). This eclecticism is one of the popular philosopher's most characteristic features. He flaunts professional jargon, the 'super-Attic' (ὑπεραττικῶς) (26). Demonax's philosophy is steeped in the empirical. He is a Socratic in the garb of Diogenes (5), that is, he stands for freedom from any form of slavery and for the right to speak freely (ἐλευθερία καὶ παρρησία) (3). He is

22. The isagogics, like much philosophical and literary production, became frozen in fixed patterns; the political treatises are a good specific example. This makes it possible, once a matrix is identified, to establish a chronological sequence of such documents based on variations and additions, and thus to date authors and to place anonymous compositions. The best treatment of the subject remains Plezia 1949.

Epitomes of the main tenets of ancient philosophers begin with Aristotle in the *Metaphysics* (on Pythagorean and Eleatic Schools). He is followed by Cicero in *The Nature of the Gods* and in *Academica*. Other major doxographers are Diogenes Laertius, *Lives of Philosophers*, and Plutarch(?), *De placitis philosophorum* (*Placita*). Whether by Plutarch, Ps.-Plutarch or Aetius, the latter collection is possibly the best illustration of ancient compendia, doxography or hypomnemata.

Many genuine philosophers use *digesta* for their discussions of Peripatetics: Seneca, on Aristotle and Theophrastus; Marcus Aurelius, on Theophrastus (Gottschalk 1987: 1140); Sextus Empiricus on Aristotle (Gottschalk 1987: 1139). Philo must have used second hand material in presenting the controversy between the Stoics and the Peripatetics (*On the Eternity of the World* and *On the Decalogue*, Gottschalk 1987: 1141, 1145-46 nn. 318, 319). Apuleius probably used a textbook, or some compilation, for his περὶ ἑρμηνείας (Dillon, quoted in Gottschalk 1987: 1149).

fond of asceticism (4).[23] His tongue is clever, his irony moderate. He is self-sufficient, virtuous and humane. Demonax does not shun human society, he participates in politics (ξυνεπολιτεύετο) (5). The principle of his life and action is expressed thus: 'It is of a human being to go astray, but of god, or of a divine man [ἀνὴρ ἰσόθεος], to set aright what has stumbled' (7). He claims to be divine (ἰσόθεος) but denies that he is a sorcerer (μάγος) although he is often so taken. His claim to equality with god stems from personal sanctity, not magical acts (67). Demonax exits life by choice (65). (Suicide is chic among Cynics.)

Little if anything of this picture would not apply to Paul himself or to his teachings. Like Demonax (and Socrates, for that matter), Paul repeatedly stresses that he teaches free of charge (ἵνα εὐαγγελιζόμενος ἀδάπανον θήσω τὸ εὐαγγέλιον) (1 Cor. 9.18; see also 2 Cor. 11.7). In fact, it can even be plausibly argued that Paul is not immune even to the thought of suicide. Important passages in Paul's letters express a preference for death over life (especially Phil. 1.22-23; Rom. 5.8). That Paul committed suicide is not more far-fetched than other solutions proposed to the silence maintained by Acts concerning Paul's death and to the growth of martyrdom legends. The anticlimactic finale of Acts, which has Paul in Rome awaiting his trial, is particularly vexing and leaves room for conjecture and speculation—which are not lacking either in early Christianity (e.g. *Acts of Paul*, in which Paul dies by decapitation while the rest of the prisoners brought to Rome are consigned to the pyre[24]) or in modern scholarship.[25]

The type has disappeared, and we can grasp the Hellenistic popular philosopher only with difficulty. The only modern term that comes at all close to describing this kind of person and his approach—though not

23. It should be noticed that, concomitant with the philosopher's withdrawal from the political field, another phenomenon characteristic of the Hellenistic era occurs: a change in the valuation of the body. The Hellenistic philosopher, turned away from politics, turns upon himself, as to the only world he can change and control. (Could it be that the process of body rejection and the realization of its irremediable imperfectibility began with the awareness of the philosopher's exclusion from politics and the dejection felt at, by then irreformable flaws, of human institutions? Historians remain baffled as to the causes of the rise of the ascetic craze.) In Hellenistic art, the burlesque and grotesque representations distort the body to the point of caricature, while, at the same time, it is shown vulnerable and humanized.

24. Hennecke and Schneemelcher 1963: II, 385.

25. See Cadbury 1979, esp. 326-28.

his influence—is 'humanist'. The human individual was at the center of the popular philosopher's concerns. The popular philosopher's emphasis is on morals,[26] and the feature that dominates each of the popular philosophers—and that is fully retained by Demonax—is a fierce attachment to freedom from any form of slavery. Demonax says about happiness, 'None but a free individual is happy' (μόνον εὐδαίμονα ἔφη τὸν ἐλεύθερον) (19). The point is momentous. Ἐλευθερία, 'freedom', is a political term par excellence.[27] *Eleutheria* is the condition of a citizen in the Greek *polis*.[28] Further, what makes a city a *polis* is its independence. *Eleutheria* describes precisely the position of a free city as compared to a dependent city and bespeaks the first's superiority. The opposite of political freedom is subjection; a subjugated city is servile (δούλη) or subject (ὑπήκοος).[29] As Hellenistic political discourse with-

26. Philosophical interests of popular philosophers were confined almost exclusively to ethics. Aristotelian ethics were excerpted or glossed in quite a number of handbooks of which some came to us. Of the first century BCE, Cicero's *De finibus* 5.9.24-26 gives a summary of Peripatetic ethics. His source was probably Antiochus of Ascalon. The same source may be behind at least part of Areius Didymus' compilation, although this writer has direct knowledge of Aristotle. Of the later compendia, the most famous are those of Diogenes Laertius 5.28-34 (first half of third century CE) and Stobaeus (early fifth century) (Gottschalk 1987: 1128 and n. 247). A score of others must have circulated.

27. 'l'éleuthéria appartient à l'essence même de la cité' (E. Lévy 1990: 56).

28. Freedom is what makes one a citizen in Athens. It is *eleutheria* that, in Greek terms, qualifies one to be a citizen. Servitude is the condition of the slave. Paul uses a terminology of slavery to refer to the Christians, an apparently polemical stance against this very conspicuous Greek view. Bondage to Christ is what makes the Christian. The free–slave dichotomy, however, bears the impact of the intervening Hellenistic monarchic politics. The concept of freedom has been debased during the despotic governments of Hellenistic times, yet retains an enduring potency and relevance due to the Hellenistic ideas of global statehood, at times extended to include the transcendental. Slavery as citizenship in Christ, freedom as enslavement to Christ, is a Pauline original of intense political significance, and understandable only against this background.

In Paul's society the mark of citizenship is *pistis*. But there is a major difference. While freedom was the thing shared in common in a Greek *ekklēsia* and allowed for no degrees, *pneuma*, the proof of citizenship in a Pauline society is also the differentiating factor.

29. Cf. E. Lévy 1990: 56. Lucian, again, translates the political into the moral and opposes individual freedom to slavery in the riotous satire *On Salaried Posts in Great Houses*.

drew into the ethical, the city became internalized.[30] Political liberty having long passed into oblivion, the world of popular philosophy found freedom in the provinces of morality and of the afterworld.

The Polis *versus the Ideal State*

Ancient political thinkers, more often than not, are drawn toward artificial constructs of ideal states. Plato's imaginary city, for example, is located in the *logos*, a heavenly paradigm (cf. *Republic* 9.592b). The *Republic* is an unusual text among Plato's writings, for in it he arrives at Form expressed as language, idea as discourse. The invention, with Plato, of the ideal state, the *idea* of the Republic, a purely discursive edifice, produces a political manifesto of philosophic disenchantment. That Plato's Socrates refuses to explain the source of his reluctance to tell the ψεῦδος γενναῖον (*Republic* 3.414d-415b) is almost a hypocrisy. He is deceptive, for while hiding he discloses a political defeat, and the defeat takes the form of a refuge in imagination. The recourse to myth here is not only a black hole of dialectics. It also stands for the end of the political as a valid choice for the philosopher. *Pseudos gennaion* has been variously and unsatisfactorily rendered. I think it is a double entendre, a 'high-minded lie'[31] but also a 'genesis fiction'.[32] What is lacking in Socrates' story is the *genos*, an actual community connected by shared blood and origin.

A *polis* is never a fiction. The fiction may describe a political unit and a form of government. It would, however, never incarnate, become *genos*. Socrates' embarrassment comes, I suppose, from his knowledge that the system he is about to present is stillborn.[33] There is nothing

30. For Aristotle, *eleutheria* is, politically, the very end of a city, ethically, the end of an individual. The Aristotelian path is walked *à rebours*.

31. Plato acknowledged that his ideal republic is a fiction, a lie, a dream, e.g., *Republic* 3.414d-415b.

32. ψεῦδος γενναῖον is a lie about the *genos*, a pun.

33. Yet, the accursed reality of the visible could never be an impediment to Plato's climbing of the epistemic ladder, even if the topic is politics. His investigation of the *polis* heads inevitably towards the ideal state. Plato did not expressly discount the possibility for attainment of his political ideal (*Republic*, 5.473a, 9.592b; *Politicus* ([*Statesman*] 300c; *Laws* 5.739e). Yet, he does refer to his ideal republic as a dream (*Republic* 4.443b; *Laws* 5.746a, 7.800a, 12.969b).

Utopia, a genre of political fiction, had a prodigious career. It became the sure mark of the political philosopher. Apolitical states are being furiously invented.

more alien to the notion of *polis* than speculation. *Polis* has as one of its basic meanings consanguinity (*genos*) and/or synoecism, geographical and political association. A *polis* is biologically and historically constituted; it does not admit of invention. Socrates, aware of this, attempts to compensate for the absence of this factor in his republic by appealing to the Athenian tradition of chthonic origin: his citizens must be made to believe that they are all brothers (*Republic* 3.414e).

The Socrates of Plato's *Republic* opens an age of comradeship of discontented philosophers, enamored of contemplation, living within the mind and outside the *polis*, even when they are not social recluses. The popular philosopher makes a different choice: in his fervor for virtue and ardor for the beyond, he instates a totalitarian regime of ethics in the service of rhetorical nowheres.[34]

Remarks on Method

This is a study of the Hellenistic Paul. More precisely, it is primarily concerned with the Hellenistic Greek perspective as opposed to the

Among the most famous cities of philosophers are: Diogenes' faceless state, Crates' island-city of Pēra ('Backpack'), Alexarchus's Uranopolis (all Cynics), Zeno's, Cleanthes', Chrysippus's or Diogenes (of Babylon)'s *megalopoleis*, *civitates* whose boundaries are the sun (all Stoics); Euhemerus's isle of Panchaia. (This to refer to the early Hellenistic period and to philosophers only. The genre went completely out of control in travel books and Hellenistic romances. These produce locations not so much ideal as idyllic, *loca amoena*.) For other examples see Aalders 1975: 39-93, esp. 75-93. Nothing of this is political thought and such speculations stretch unduly the notion of practical philosophy. The phenomenon belongs to political reflection only insofar as it witnesses the rupture between politics and philosophy. This literature continues, through Cicero and Augustine, to the Renaissance and More and to the nineteenth-century socialist utopians like Claude de Saint-Simon, Charles Fourier (whose 'phalanster' was a model for Christian socialism even in the US) and P.J. Proudhon. The twentieth century, with its passion for excess, gives it tragic forms, such as the Bolshevik state or the Jonestown commune.

34. Kristeller notes that the word *Utopia* is coined by Thomas More. Consisting of the negation *ou* and the term topos, 'noplaceness', the combination, despite its infelicity in Greek (which negates a noun with *alpha privativum*) acquired undisputed fame. This does not reflect badly on More's Greek, however, for *atopia* 'was preempted since ancient times' by meaning 'absurdity'. (Against Kristeller, I would argue that to make topos, a term eminently expressing concreteness into an abstraction, as the suffix *ia* indicates, is rather inspired.) But More got the idea from Plato's γῆς γε οὐδαμοῦ, *Republic* 9.592a (Kristeller 1985: 479-80).

Hellenistic Jewish one. My focus on the Hellenistic Greek milieu rather than Hellenistic Judaism is a matter of conscious decision. The possibility of a Jewish conceptual background to the Pauline political material is not ignored. It is simply not addressed. I do not presume to establish a ranking of cogency, whether the 'Greek' is more cogent than the 'Jewish'. I am fully aware that I am laying out only one option and so should the reader be. The analysis offered here means to show only that a Greek perspective is compelling in and of itself.

It may be argued that I disregard much of what we know about Paul. This book, however, proposes insights the Jewish Paul and even the Hellenistic Jewish Paul do not offer. A Hellenistic Greek Paul does not preempt a Hellenistic Jewish Paul. Even a Jewish Paul is not obviated by a Greek Paul. Paul could have sat at the feet of Gamaliel and still think like Hippodamos or Diotogenes. It is not impossible—it is indeed plausible—that Paul's knowledge of the sources discussed here already might have been filtered through Hellenistic Judaism. For example, Philo at times reflects awareness of the reasoning that drove Paul's political meditation. A detailed study of the relationship (assuming that there was one) between Philo and Paul is beyond the scope of this study, however.

My objective, in this work, is not to diminish traditional readings of Paul, though I do on occasion question their cogency and remark on their inadequacy insofar as they neglect the political dimension of Paul's thought. I admit that there are alternatives to the view I present, and I do not presume to rebut any interpretive approach—only to claim that mine is a legitimate reading and should be set alongside the others. My undertaking recognizes the complexity of Paul's mind and of his intellectual genealogy. It is to be hoped that my study, like any other serious attempt to decipher the Pauline conundrum, will enhance our appreciation of the apostle.

The method I use is best described as 'cultural focus', or 'cultural milieu'. It emphasizes the cultural repertoire to which Paul belongs, Paul's 'shared culture'. The cultural milieu approach relaxes the demand for proof of direct influence and makes possible the progress of the inquiry. Other interpretive techniques, such as the literary-critical or textual criticism as well as the historical, philosophical and archaeological approaches, have been assimilated to the cultural milieu method.

The method of estimating influence is to see whether a certain doctrine, tenet or attitude is not most naturally explained as a development from, an impression of or a reaction to a prior author's view. The question is not, How does Paul's position square with his knowledge of, for example, Aristotle? Rather, the question is, Is there anything in Paul that is best accounted for as a result of Aristotelian influence?[35] Pauline quotations from presumed sources may not be exactly identifiable; the origin of a detected influence may not be precisely pinpointed. The enterprise of estimating probable influence, however, has scholarly validity.

An investigation such as the one pursued here requires a constant effort at differentiation between the study of words and the study of concepts. The problem remains, however, that concept and word intersect, two systems of discourse systems bound in one textual structure. Each text effects an integration of terms and ideas to establish a particular set of relations between lexis and meaning, that is, between linguistic phenomena and philosophical or religious concepts.[36] For this reason, the critical word *dikaiosunē*, for example, remains throughout this work, for the most part, untranslated, in order to block the connotations of its various English equivalents and the theological baggage they bear along with them, thereby to avoid obscuring the political sphere to which the term belongs in Greek.

In an examination of this kind one is continually faced with the variability and versatility of words and meanings, of terminology and context. Similar vocabularies conceal incongruous meanings. Analogous or identical ideas are often expressed by dissimilar idioms. In the first case, it is the lexical constellation that makes possible the new meaning; in the second case, it is the conceptual matrix that renders the new term's significance intelligible.

Paul's originality can be understood as an attempt to reinvigorate and press to its logical limit political thought that emerges in Plato and especially, I contend, in Aristotle but that reached Paul mostly as a collection of platitudes, variously regurgitated and invested with venerable authority. On the question of Paul's knowledge of the Classical

35. This methodology is suggested by Sandbach 1985: 16, 24. See also Hahm's 1991 critique and the discussion of both Sandbach and Hahm by Sakezles 1996.

36. James Barr raised this issue in an exemplary fashion in his classical 1961 book. There he attacked, among others, *TDNT* which, thinks Barr, construed itself as a 'concept history' yet it actually is 'a dictionary of Greek *words*' (Barr's emphasis, 1961: 207).

philosophers, it is not necessary to claim that Paul had direct acquaintance with their works. Many of the first-rate philosophers and noted commentators on philosophical movements (themselves highly schooled in philosophy) who lived after Andronicus of Rhodes' edition of Aristotle's works was published in the first century BCE,[37] still used handbooks and anthologies for their information on Aristotle. It is not even necessary to claim that Paul read such remarkable compendia as those by Arius Didymus (first century BCE)[38] or Nicolaus of Damascus (late first century BCE).[39] (Paul might, however, have known the widely popular *De mundo*.[40]) True, an extensive scholarly literature debates the

37. Some of these were contemporary with Paul, some later, such as Philo, Sextus Empiricus, Seneca, Apuleius, Plutarch and Marcus Aurelius. See Gottschalk 1987: 1139-41, 1145-6, 1149.

38. Arius Didymus, a native of Alexandria, spends most of his life in Rome where he is a tutor in literature and philosophy to Octavian. His most famous work is the *Epitome*. The preface, on the parts of philosophy and their subdivisions, is followed by a summary exposition of the main doctrines of the major philosophical Schools (Academy, Peripatos, Stoa), organized under the heads of logic, natural philosophy and ethics. The ethical excerpts are preserved in Stobaeus 2.7 (Gottschalk 1987: 1125 and n. 233). The summary of Peripatetic ethics is very similar to that produced by Cicero in *De finibus* (5.9.24-26, cf. 4.7.16 -18), whose source may have been Antiochus of Ascalon (Gottschalk 1987: 1128; Moraux 1973: 333-35).

39. On Nicolaus of Damascus, see note 44 *infra*. He wrote, among many other works, Ἠθῶν παραδόξων συναγωγή, *Collection of Peculiar Customs*, probably derived from Aristotle, a genre much cultivated by the Hellenistic Peripatos (Gottschalk 1987: 1122 and n. 216).

The Stoics collected the maxims of poets, the *dogmata*, as digests and anthologies and circulated them as *Golden Verses*. These were manuals containing moral precepts drawn from all kinds of sources, with no connection between texts, widely used by itinerant preachers and educators (see Hugedé 1966: 69-70).

40. For the view that *De mundo* may be Aristotle's work, derived from his *Pragmateiai*, treatises that dealt with logical and metaphysical theory, see Gottschalk 1987: 1134-43.

Ps.-Aristotle's *De mundo* is a masterpiece of popular philosophy, an exceptional work of compilation of many major ideas and moods of Hellenistic times. The pieces are fitted together with such art and coherence as to make the whole an original writing of great significance and best-selling quality. The seven chapters of the composition each cover a revealing feature of Hellenistic speculation. Stobaeus' *Florilegium* preserves the greater part of the Greek text, with fragments extant in Latin, Armenian, Syriac, Arabic and Medieval Latin. The theme is cosmogony and the approach theological. The first chapter, written as an address to Alexander, speaks of philosophy as the science that allows for a unified view of the world and

question of the circulation of Aristotle's works.[41] Andronicus's edition restored to philosophy works from the class known as 'esoteric'.[42] I am concerned here, however, with two of the so-called 'exoteric', or common, works,[43] the *Politics* and the *Nicomachean Ethics*, about

---

permits the human soul to see god. The next two chapters depict the universe as divided in two spheres, supralunary and sublunary; the first, the *aither*, the seat of gods and of the celestial beings, the second, the world of the four elements, has the earth at the center; the latter's geographical description is included. The fourth chapter describes the phenomena taking place in the atmosphere, seen as the result of the tension between dryness and wetness. The leitmotif is that of change as the rule of the parts. Chapter five is concerned to the permanence of the universe as a whole, understood as the result of *harmonia* that holds together the opposing forces. All things have an *isomoiria*, an equality, vis-à-vis the whole, and all are permeated by a universal power. Chapter six discusses this power: god. His pure *ousia* resides beyond the highest celestial sphere, but his *dunamis* extends throughout the universe and sets each sphere in movement, by a domino-like effect. This single impulse is like one trumpet signal which moves to specific action the various parts of an army. (The same simile is used by Paul in his theory of music and of language in connection with glossolalia, 1 Cor. 14.8 [cf. Heb. 12.19].) God is called savior and creator. The last chapter emphasizes the singularity of god despite the multiplicity of names under which he is known. (See Gottschalk 1987: 1132-34; for an overview of the scholarly discussion of the question of authorship see 1135-39.) The work is such a dexterous combination of Aristotelian, Platonic, Hellenistic Pythagorean and Stoic elements as to defy attribution. Its increasing ascription to Aristotle is an aberration. It is a Hellenistic work reflecting the genius of Hellenistic popular philosophy.

Another well diffused work attributed to Aristotle but produced sometimes between first century BCE and first century CE was *De virtutibus et vitiis* that knows the tripartite psychology but not the notion of virtue as a mean (Gottschalk 1987: 1129).

41. See the discussions and the vast body of references in Moraux 1973, 1984, Tarán 1981, and Gottschalk 1987.

42. The ἐσωτερικά (also known as the epoptic or acroamatic or syntagmatic) writings were doctrinal lectures destined for the inner circle of Aristotle's disciples. Their plight after the death of Aristotle has been a matter of much conjecture and debate, both in late Hellenistic as well as in modern times. See Gottschalk 1987: 1172.

43. ἐξωτερικά. The expression goes back to Aristotle himself. According to an ancient source preserved by Gellius (*Attic Nights* 20.5), Aristotle lectured, in the morning (ἑωθινὸς περίπατος), to a select—esoteric—circle of intimates; these lectures treated more difficult topics such as philosophy, physics, dialectics. In the afternoon (δειλινὸς περίπατος), Aristotle spoke to a larger—exoteric—audience on topics of more general interest such as rhetoric, sophistic, and politics. As a result,

which the question of availability has never arisen. Still, even about these, Paul's knowledge was most likely derived from handbooks, lectures he attended or hearsay.[44] The same is true for Paul's knowledge

later writers referred to the first group as esoteric writings, and to the second as exoteric.

Aristotle uses the term ἐξωτερικοὶ λόγοι in *Nicomachean Ethics* 1.1102a26; 6.1140a3; *Politics* 3.1278b31; 7.1323a22, and four other times in other books (see Bonitz 1955, *s.v.* Ἀριστοτέλης, 104b44-105a48) to designate arguments and doctrines familiar in philosophic debates and writings not peculiar to a single school, disquisitions foreign to the matter at hand, or even writings of other authors (see Rackham, LCL ed. of *Nicomachean Ethics* 62, n. b; Stahr 1858: 322b). In the scholarly tradition concerned with the transmission of Aristotle's works, this phrase refers to Aristotle's lectures and treatises directed to a larger public, from outside the inner circle of the Lyceum. These employed a more popular method and style, were in the form of dialogue and covered mostly the domain of practical philosophy (Stahr 1858: 322b). The dualism esoteric/exoteric writings became a feature of philosophical discourse and entered into the popular image, as Cicero, Lucian and Aulus Gellius testify (Gottschalk 1987: 1172). These are well attested throughout the Hellenistic and Roman times, from the Stoic Chrysippus (Sandbach 1985: 15) to Cicero (Sandbach 1985: 93 and n. 65) and from Plutarch to Gellius (Stahr 1858: 322b), but the exoterics are now all lost. Cicero used Aristotle's *Politics* in *Republic*, especially in the distinction between tyrant and the ruler who pursues the public good only (Plezia 1966: 141). The *Ethics* and the *Politics*, as we have them, are course notes, ὑπομνηματικά. Diogenes Laertius' (5.22-27) list of Aristotle's works (that goes back to third century BCE) contains most of the popular published treatises, the exoterica. He lists both *Politics* and *Ethics* (Sandbach 1985: 10-11). Aristotle was read and studied under the Ptolemies, who collected his works for the library at Alexandria; there, it was his historical, political and rhetorical writings rather than the logical and metaphysical works that were mostly studied by the Alexandrine critics and grammarians (Stahr 1858: 323). Compilations and handbooks of Aristotle's works were available to a large audience throughout the Hellenistic times. Finally, there was an 'immense production of sub-philosophical tracts', a good example of which are the Hellenistic Pythagorean writings, that included Aristotelian and Platonic ideas, in a diluted and contaminated form (Gottschalk 1987: 1172).

44. If Tarsus, birthplace or not, was at all important in Paul's life, and I hold that it was (but any other major city of Asia Minor fills the bill as well), then there he might have had innumerable opportunities to listen to the vast fauna of itinerant lecturers or acquire cheaply a handbook that crammed together philosophical doctrines and literary excerpts.

Tarsus, in the heart of the Orient, boasts Argive, i.e. eminently Greek parentage. It attaches itself to Bellerophontes (and Pegasos), Perseus, and above all Herakles, it claims impeccable Greek pedigree. It looks at the Titans or to Triptolemos as

of Platonism and Stoicism. Because the focus of the present work is on Paul's practical philosophy and, especially, his politics and their possible sources, it is important to review the significant role of the Classics, Plato and Aristotle, for all subsequent practical philosophy and political reflection. It would be astonishing indeed had Paul, who was certainly conversant with Hellenistic ethical and rhetorical systems,[45] been ignorant of the other aspect of practical philosophy, politics.

father, i.e. it wants to pass, at all costs, for Greek (PW, *s.v.* Tarsus). This disease caught its citizens, it flared in its numerous philosophers (Semites, they take on Greek names), and it caught Paul as well.

Tarsus, particularly, although not a Peripatetic center, had a major Stoic school with many of its members versed in or even major commentators on Aristotle, the best example being Athenodorus (74 BCE?–7 CE?). He studied in Rhodes with Posidonius the Stoic; friend of Cicero (himself a governor of Cilicia, headquartered in Tarsus—who calls him Athenodorus Calvus, *To Atticus* 16.11); tutor of Octavian, whom he met and taught in Apollonia and whose counselor he later was (Dio Cassius, *Roman History* 52.36, 56.43; Zonaras, *Epitome* 544b, Zosimus, *New History* 1.6) and tutor of Claudius (Suetonius, *Claudius* 4); governor of Tarsus in old age (Strabo, *Geography* 14.674). Athenodorus returns (in 15 BCE?) with the backing of Augustus to a Tarsus misgoverned by Boëthus, friend of Antonius, to reform the government and make the *polis* famous for εὐταξία καὶ σωφροσύνη, 'order and good sense' (Dio Chrysostom 33.48); obtains from Augustus exoneration from vectigalia (land tax). He put Tarsus under the rule of the University (Strabo 14.14). Athenodorus was called Κανανίτης, from Canana? Cana? in Cilicia, the birthplace of his father. Son of Sandon, a Semite, he changed his name when he moved to philosophy (Strabo 14.674-75). It is against this background, i.e. as a philosophical custom, that I understand Paul's own change of name. This is evidence of an important practice that became a rule in Christian monastic circles, and that was widespread among philosophers in the Renaissance. Athenodorus died at 82 and was remembered with an annual festival and sacrifice (Strabo 14.674; Lucian *Makrobioi* [Octogenarians] 21; Cicero *Ad familiares* 3.7, *To Atticus* 16.14). Athenodorus wrote a commentary on Aristotle's *Categories* (Simplicius, *In categoriam* 159.32); an account of Tarsus addressed to Octavia; a περὶ σπουδῆς καὶ παιδείας; a περίπατοι; a work on the tranquility of the soul (see Seneca's *Dialogues, Ad Serenum* 9.34, for an extract). (See W. Smith 1858: 403b-404a; Schoeps 1961: 33, Gottschalk 1987: 1081, 1995-56, 1101-04, 1111-12.)

At the court of Herod lived the famed Nicolaus of Damascus, maverick and outstanding Peripatetic (64 BCE–4 BCE?). He described himself in terms of Aristotle's *Ethics* and in his self-praise stressed the Stoic *ponos*, endurance of toils (Gottschalk 1987: 1122-23). He also travelled extensively and lectured on the way.

These are examples of outstanding people and first-rate philosophers, known commentators of Aristotle's works, even if not themselves Peripatetics. Tarsus had

As a Hellenistic Jew, Paul participated in a distinctive 'shared culture' and partook of a diverse but definite cultural repertoire.[46] He questions its paradigms of meaning—and shatters many of them—without,
however, coming into conflict with the political institutions that support
and are supported by those cultural conventions. Paul produces a theory
larger than the cultural, social and political system from which it

established a reputation as a city where philosophy was at home, and Strabo notes
that philosophers played a prominent part in the affairs of Tarsus (14.14); he
presents Tarsus as above Athens and Alexandria in its excitement about education,
but out of the way (14.5.13). Yet, because the city was wealthy and the citizens
enjoyed a good talk, it was a favorite stop with traveling philosophers, such as Dio
Chrysostom, sure of a good honorarium albeit for castigating speeches. In Tarsus or
elsewhere, the throng of anonymous lecturers is sure to have far outnumbered those
whose names we know, themselves legion. The city-gates and market-place were
full of gangs of popular teachers and soap-box orators, as so many of Lucian's
satires stand proof.
    Paul's own extensive travels are consistent with the image of the vagrant popular
philosophers of his time. His journeys were not only occasions for speaking but
also major opportunities to listen to and debate with other philosophers, to acquire
knowledge of philosophical schools, to obtain philosophical digests.
    45. As scores of studies have demonstrated, some older but most of them quite
recent. Even the briefest summary must mention: Baur (1873–75 [German edition
1845]), the first to consider Greek influence on Paul's ethics; Holtzmann (1911),
who connected the Epistles to Greek culture; Deissmann (1901 [German 1895],
1926 [second German edition 1925], 1927 [German 1908]), who discovered that
many so-called Hebraisms are actually Greek expressions found also in papyri and
inscriptions; or Wendland (1895, 1907) and Bultman (1910) who saw in the
Epistles the Cynic and Stoic method of argumentation (see also Hugedé 1966: 16-
27). The contribution of Nilsson (1951–1960) and Nock (1938, 1972) to the subject
can hardly be overestimated. The works of M. Smith (1973, 1980), Koester (1962,
1965) and Betz remain landmarks of the importance of Hellenism in Christianity.
Newer scholarship has given again considerable attention to the Hellenistic
background of Paul's thinking. Aune, Malherbe and their followers have proven the
influence of Hellenistic, especially Stoic and Cynic ethics, on Paul. The relations
between Hellenistic and Pauline rhetoric has also received painstaking attention in
Stowers, Kurz, or Olbricht (see Balch 1990). Note also Scroggs's (1976) work on
Paul's rhetoric in Romans 1–11 and Coulter's (1964, 1976) comments on the
importance of Aristotelian rhetoric in Hellenistic and Roman times.
    46. This cultural background that makes and is disclosed by a literary work has
received any number of names: the cultural voice of the text (Barthes 1974: 17-18,
100); fusion of horizons (Gadamer 1975: 269-73); intertextuality (a successor text
plays off against a precursor) or hypogram (a covert word or text) (Riffaterre 1978:
12-13); 'misinterpretation' of a parent work (Harold Bloom 1975: 94).

derives—a theory large enough that the world can live inside it. To explain political experiences and concepts, Paul makes human society itself part of a metaculture,[47] Paul is not concerned with what is known but with the crisis introduced by a new knowledge, a crisis that questions the rules of knowing, the very principles of understanding. And this crisis that fractures epistemology is an experience and an empirical datum: a body. For at the beginning and at the center of Christianity lies a body, a dead body, an *absent* body. Jesus' dead, absent body lies at the intersection of household and *polis*, of family and political power, of Israel and Rome, of here and beyond. It spans human and divine natures, it transforms biology, it changes psychology, it alters metaphysics. Simply put, it throws all knowledge into disarray. That is the crucial new experience that requires explanation. Yet the missing dead body of Christ introduces a directness, an immediacy and an imminence that were never there before, into both the ontic and the epistemic structures. It is the nucleus and the ordering principle that will help reformat them. It is the cause of the change and the girder supporting its formidable burden. The syntax of this sweeping discourse is provided, however, by the *political*, its model being the theories that commenced with Plato and Aristotle, that were perpetuated and accommodated by the Hellenistic thinkers and that found their contemporary embodiment in the Roman State.

Hellenistic political philosophy retained from the Classical canon its theories about the *polis*, a concept that the Hellenistic thinkers employed slavishly but not in a sterile way, and its kingship theories, especially insofar as these show the transcendental foundation of monarchy and praise its merits. Paul has use for both concepts, the first within the Christian community, as a way of structuring and legitimizing it, and the second at the level of the empire, to accept and strengthen it.

The following points must be reiterated. First, Paul is heir to some tradition. In what follows, I shall pursue the Hellenistic Pythagoreans as the source of this tradition. Second, it is impossible to imagine this tradition, that of the Hellenistic Pythagoreans, without Plato and Aristotle. Plato and Aristotle are latent within this tradition, and this is

---

47. The term is an adaptation of 'metalanguage', which describes, in literary theory, a language about other languages.

why it is important to begin with the Classical philosophers. Finally, however, it should be remembered that Paul does not merely inherit; he also transforms.[48] My study addresses this play of continuity and transmutation.

48. As Nietzsche would put it, the will to power consists in the transvaluation of values.

Part I

CLASSICAL AND HELLENISTIC SOURCES

Chapter 1

CLASSICAL SOURCES: PLATO

Plato and Aristotle are the pre-eminent political philosophers of the West.[1] Of Plato's political texts, the *Republic* is by far the most important and it enjoyed a wide circulation both in antiquity and later.[2]

The *Republic*[3] is a formidably complex dialogue on justice (δικαι-οσύνη). *Dikaiosunē* is the supreme political excellence, (ἀρετή, *aretē*). The finale of the work, the Myth of Er (10.614b-621d),[4] concocts an afterlife in which justice is rewarded. Plato dispatches forever the Homeric underworld, a dull and dreary place that does not differentiate between the just and the unjust. Highly critical of disheartening representations of death and afterworld (3.386b-387b), Plato transforms Greek beliefs in the beyond.[5] From now on death will discriminate between baseness and virtue and will reserve different fates for them. The Myth of Er is necessary to, and demanded by, the question of *dikaiosunē*

1. 'Political reflection need not be systematic analysis and rarely is. In the realm of politics only Plato and Aristotle...may properly be labelled systematic thinkers. They were the first genuine political theorists of Antiquity and the last; the first and last to attempt a complete and coherent account of the ideal organization of society grounded in systematic metaphysics, epistemology, psychology and ethics' (Finley 1983: 123-24).

2. Besides the *Republic*, however, *Protagoras*, *Theaetetus*, *Crito*, *Gorgias*, *Politicus* and the *Laws* contain significant illustrations of Plato's political thought.

3. Πολιτεία, ἢ περὶ δικαίου, πολιτικός, *The Republic or On Justice, A Political Dialogue*.

4. This text is one of the most likely reasons for Plato's sanctification in the Eastern Orthodox Christian tradition.

5. It is one of the most interesting points of information that this dialogue preserves for us—the discovery that immortality of the soul is news for Glaucon (10.608d). This is no philosophical topic, but as Shorey tells us (and collects the relevant references), 'a pious hope and an ethical postulate' ('Introduction,' LCL trans. of the *Republic*, lxiv-lxv).

raised by the dialogue. It ties justice to redemption and thus extends the domain of the political to include the beyond. As I write of 'justice' (δικη, *dikē*, or *dikaiosunē*) and 'injustice', (ἀδικία, *adikia*), I must warn the reader against a moral reading of the terms as I use them. These sememes inhabit a vast semantic field. They belong, among other kinds of discourse, to political and to psychological language. In the political sphere, they refer to a society, its statutes, roles, norms, institutions and other structures. In the psychological domain, they describe desire, passion and intellectual functions. A fine example for the psychological meaning of injustice is given by Plato in the metaphor of the soul as a multiple being in human skin (9.588b-589d): a hideous monster, a lion, and a human all wrapped in human form (588d).[6] Injustice, in multifarious ways, feeds the brute and prevents the man, the divine (589d), from prevailing.

Aristotle believes that human beings cannot be perfectly just.[7] Absolute justice is reserved for god. This will be of critical importance to Paul, who, with a magisterial castling move, politicizes the divine and makes it the source and unique locus of *dikaiosunē*. It is interesting to note, however, that, in the Greco-Roman world, for all the circumscription of the divine within the human political sphere and for all the exhortation in Hellenistic political writings to imitation of the divine government of the cosmos, there is no instance in which a legal decision was ever issued claiming the backing of a god.[8] Before Christianity, justice remained a prerogative of the state.

Plato has a dual understanding of justice: on the one hand, political justice, which is the happiness of the state (4.420c); on the other, inner justice, which Plato formulates as the individual's being one instead of many (4.443d-e). The analogy state–individual, *polis–psuchē*, pervades the dialogue and gives originality and unity to the *Republic*. The two parallel motifs converge in their perfect conditions: the philosopher and Plato's republic. The soul of the philosopher becomes the locus of the ideal state (9.592b).

The first part of the dialogue[9] intends to determine that justice is an *aretē*. *Aretē*—that is, 'doing well' that for which one is made—is the

---

6. For an extensive discussion of the expression 'form of man' in Plato and Paul see Chapter 8 (below), the section on Romans 3.21–8.39, under 8.29.

7. *Nicomachean Ethics* 5.1137a26-30.

8. See also Finley 1983: 132.

9. Cornford's division, 1.327-354c.

source of happiness (1.352-354).[10] Things run somewhat amok, however, when Thrasymachus presents his view.[11] Thrasymachus defines
justice as the interest of the stronger (κρεῖττον, *kreitton*), that which is
useful to the master.[12] In the same breath, he enunciates a principle of
fateful relevance to political theory: justice as the political art of committing injustice with impunity. I call the consequences of this tenet to
Western political thinking 'Thrasymachus's curse'.[13]

Thrasymachus's argument is difficult. He shifts the ground without
warning, changing his terms as it suits him. In the end he defines *kreitton*
as the knowledge the ruler must possess in order to rule, and he shifts
its meaning from 'force' to 'qualification'. The ruler, as ruler, is infallible (340c-341a).[14] Thrasymachus ranks injustice with *aretē* and *sophia*,

10. *Aretē* is that state of the soul from which derives happiness (see Nettleship
1929: 42-3).

11. 1.336b-354c. The exchange between Socrates and Thrasymachus is one of the
most extraordinary pages of Platonic literature. Socrates is being scorned, abused,
laughed at, made fun of, and, incredibly, he responds to castigation with vulgarity. In
the game of imprecation, he is certainly the loser. The Socratic irony registers a re-
sounding defeat. More amazingly, his argument suffers a breakdown. He chooses
not to face his opponent's challenge. He develops subtle theories, advances difficult
ideas, i.e. engages in genuine sophistry only to distract attention from his inter-
locutor's confounding thought. The greater the audience's insistence on Socrates'
brilliance, the greater the reader's awareness that he uses diversionist tactics. The
conversation disintegrates and the fault is Socrates'. Yet, the text plays on the
reader's expectation and emphasizes the cleverness of Socrates' in turning Thrasymachus's view 'inside out' (1.343a). (This dialectical mechanism is of great importance in philosophy. Kant (*Religion Within the Limits of Reason Alone*) calls it
parergonality; Deleuze 1984, the *pli*, 'wrinkle'.) The careful reader cannot fail to
realize, however, that this turning inside-out, highly important as Socratic method,
is here operated not by means of dialectics but by those of exorcism, and is, at least
in this case, fictive.

12. *Republic* 1.338c, 339a, 341a, 2.367b, *passim*. The just is the advantage of
the stronger, τὸ δίκαιον...τὸ τοῦ κρείττονος ξυμφέρον (1.338c). Cf. *Theaetetus*
177d, *Laws* 4.714c.

13. See, e.g., 1.338d, e, 339a, 341b, 343c. This part of the dialogue (*Republic*
1.336b-347e) is the crux of Western political philosophy and has escaped the attention of no major political thinker since Plato.

14. τὸν ἄρχοντα, καθ' ὅσον ἄρχων ἐστί μὴ ἁμαρτάνειν (341a). (After all, this is
not at all unlike what Plato himself thinks of his philosopher-king.) Thrasymachus
produces a social discourse of unfathomable force. He concludes it with these words:
'Injustice on a grand scale is mightier and freer and more masterful than justice...
just is the interest of the stronger, unjust is the advantage and the interest of

'excellence' and 'intelligence' (348e).[15] Socrates finds this thesis 'tough and hard to refute' (348e). Injustice considered not only as useful but as good, as both *aretē* and *sophia*, is a striking idea. The ruler is above the law. Somehow this political idea is too large for practical philosophy.[16] Thrasymachus is the great promoter of professional politics. (It is also true that the professionalization of politics resulted in the split between ethics and politics.)

Thrasymachus's intervention is also important for understanding the Pauline tension δικαιοσύνη–ἁμαρτία, justice–error (*dikaiosunē–hamartia*). Paul's concern in the Letter to the Romans is similar to that of Plato in the first part of the *Republic*, and especially to the argument developed by Thrasymachus concerning the relation between the ruler and the metaphysical binary justice–injustice, *dikaiosunē–adikia*. Although Paul uses the dichotomy *dikaiosunē–hamartia*,[17] the paired terms are of the same conceptual order, and this is political. Thrasymachus's argument contains a passage (340c-e) that is essential for understanding the dialectical tension between the terms in each pair.

oneself' (344c) (modified trans.). The point is remarkable. Asks Thrasymachus: 'Are you so far out in your notion of just and justice and of unjust and injustice as not to know that justice (*dikaiosunē*) and the just (τὸ δίκαιον) (i.e., the right, the notion not the person) are the good of the other (ἀλλότριον ἀγαθὸν τῷ ὄντι), the interest of the stronger and also of the ruler; that that which is proper to the one who obeys and who serves is to take the loss; that injustice is exactly the reverse, asserting its authority over those naive and just; that the subjects work for the interest of the stronger; and that they work for the happiness of the stronger and not their own?' (343c, my trans.). What Thrasymachus shows is the identity between justice and injustice, the collapse of contradictions, the limit of the conceptual and logical framework in which the dialogue took place (which is not unlike Paul's language reversal technique). Socrates is constrained to accept that the thesis is 'tough and hard to refute', στερεώτερον, lit. a stiffer proposition (348e).

15. Justice is εὐήθεια, silliness, simple-mindedness; injustice is εὐβουλία, good counsel, wisdom. The unjust are ἀγαθοί and φρόνιμοι, excellent and practical (348c-d).

16. In Nietzsche's words, 'I ought not to have done that' must be changed by the one caught red-handed with '[H]ere something has *unexpectedly* gone wrong' (*On the Genealogy of Morals* 2.15, my emphasis).

17. These terms are often paired in the classical philosophical tradition. In *Epistle VII (to Dion)* 335a, Plato seems to equate ἁμάρτημα with ἀδίκημα: 'One must consider much less bad to suffer ἁμαρτήματα and ἀδικήματα than to do them.' Aristotle (*Nicomachean Ethics* 5.1135b18), refers to ἀδίκημα and ἁμάρτημα as harms, but from different causes: the first from knowledge, the second from ignorance.

Thrasymachus makes ἁμαρτεῖν, *hamartein*, the center of his demonstration that the ruler who rules as a professional, with complete skill and authority, rules infallibly. For Thrasymachus,[18] *hamartein* is to miss the mark; it is incompetence. It exposes want of credentials and is proof of mere pretense, of illegitimacy. In politics it identifies the one who is *not* fit to rule. The term belongs to the theory of knowledge; its burden is epistemological.[19] *Republic* 340e leaves little doubt about the meaning of *hamartein. Hamartein* is not a moral fault but a conceptual error, not a moral shortcoming but a mental incapacity; it points to a faulty perception of the true nature of one's lack. For, strictly speaking, one who has the right qualifications or talents simply cannot be wrong. This brief analysis is important for understanding Paul's opposites, *dikaiosunē–hamartia. Dikaiosunē*, in Greek political thinking and in Paul, describes 'justice'—that is, 'getting it', 'doing it right'. *Dikaiosunē* is term for the *professional. Hamartia* and its cognates mean 'not getting it', 'doing it wrong', 'having no business there'. It describes the action of a bungler. For Paul, as for Plato's Thrasymachus, these are epistemological concepts and belong to the lexicon of political philosophy and not that of ethics.

So also does *adikia*. In the *Republic* Plato calls *adikia* 'lack of concerted action' (1.351e-352a). The presence of injustice is marked by sedition and discord in a body, be this body a *polis*, an army or a family. It will have the same effect in an individual. *Adikia* traverses the entire political and psychological axis. The way Paul understands *adikia* is also congruent with the Platonic reading. In Paul, *adikia* retains the basic Platonic sense of 'division'; it is political factiousness that Paul condemns in Rom. 2.8. It is the dissolution of the body and the

---

18. 'But, I think, it is only a fault of language (λέγομεν τῷ ῥήματι οὕτως), to say that the physician was mistaken (ἐξήμαρτεν), or that the bookkeeper was mistaken (ἐξήμαρτεν), or the same about the grammarian. I think, however, that each of them, if worthy of the name we give each one (καθ᾽ ὅσον τοῦτ᾽ ἔστιν ὃ προσαγεύομεν αὐτόν) is never wrong (οὐδέποτε ἁμαρτάνει). To speak rigorously (ἀκριβῆ λόγον)…, no professional (δημιουργός) errs. He errs who is wrong (ὁ ἁμαρτάνων ἁμαρτάνει), and this if his knowledge (ἐπιστήμη) abandons him, in which case he is no longer a professional. Thus…the ruler (ἄρχων) is never wrong insofar as ruler, even if it may be *said* that he is fallible (ἄρχων οὐδεὶς ἁμαρτάνει τότε ὅταν ἄρχων ᾖ, ἀλλὰ πᾶς γ᾽ ἂν εἴποι ὅτι…ὁ ἄρχων ἥμαρτεν)' 340d-e.

19. Both Plato and Aristotle generally use ἁμαρτεῖν/ἁμάρτημα in a way consistent with this interpretation: *Republic* 336e: defect of method, error in the examination of a question. *Nicomachean Ethics* 5.1135b7: ignorance that lies in oneself.

soul that is indicated by this term in Rom. 1.18-32. By pairing *adikia* with ἀσέβεια (*asebeia*), 'impiety' (Rom. 1.18) Paul suggests the cosmic destructiveness wrought by this conglomerate. It includes rebellion against god the creator. *Adikia–asebeia* is the evil that splits being, *polis* and universe, and it is the very cause of irrationality, barbarism and chaos. *Adikia–asebeia* forms a continuum with *hamartia* (Rom. 6.12-13). The only force against injustice is *Dikaiosunē theou* (Rom. 3.5).

In the *Republic*, the argument that is next developed, by Glaucon and Adeimantus,[20] concludes with two themes that we can also recognize in Paul: no one possesses *aretē* of his own will[21] and no one knows what justice is—not in its effects, but in its essence, 'when it dwells in the soul unseen by gods or humans'.[22] Paul strikes a Hellenistic note of the same timbre when he says that the only thing that matters is what God sees, hidden and inward, irrelevant to outsiders (Rom. 2.29).[23]

For the next eight books of the *Republic* Socrates is practically the sole speaker. In 2.367e–5.471c Socrates investigates, in extensive detail, the meaning of justice, first in the *polis* (2.367e–4.427c), then in the individual's soul (4.427d–5.471c). In Socrates' long speech about the *polis*, Plato is constructing his ideal republic. His discussion of the Guardians' character, education and duties parallels, *mutatis mutandis*, Paul's instructions to his communities throughout his epistolary corpus.[24] A major principle is emphasized throughout this section of the

20. Plato's brothers, 2.358a-367d.

21. τῶν γε ἄλλων οὐδεὶς ἑκὼν δίκαιος, 2.366d. On *akrasia* see Chapter 2, Aristotle's Ethics section.

22. ἐν τῇ τοῦ ἔχοντος ψυχῇ ἐνόν καὶ λανθάνον θεούς τε καὶ ἀνθρώπους, 2.366e.

23. See Heckel 1993 for a comparison between Plato and Paul on the subject of the inner man. See also Chapter 8, section on Rom. 3.21–8.39, commentary on Rom. 7.22.

24. I am referring, first of all to the Guardians' two chief characteristics: spirited disposition towards the enemies and gentleness towards fellow citizens (2.375a-376e). Then, among others, the warning that the Guardians must be trained to be warriors not athletes, i.e. they are athletes with a cause (3.403c-404b), the mission of creating a 'communistic' economy, with no rich and poor, (4.422a), with meals in common (3.416e), to preserve the unity of their closed community (4.423a), to beware of innovation (4.424b), the need to respect the elders (4.425b), to cut their hair and dress decently (4.425b). See the entire section 3.416a-4.427c. See also 4.427c-434d, the transition passage between state and individual soul, where the four 'virtues', wisdom, courage, temperance and justice are discussed.

Republic: statesmanship is a profession,[25] a highly specialized field of expertise that depends on natural endowments[26] but also on education. A state so formed is called 'constituted on natural principles'.[27]

Plato, of course, is not building an actual state, an organic political community, but a stratified, pseudo-egalitarian social system containing few if any variables or bonds. It is a purely mental construct with no material record, a society that has no bond except in myth, a society in which citizenship is replaced by a caste system and that lacks anything like a constitution, if we do not count the infallibility of its philosopher ruler. The end result is a static military camp ruled by a godlike human. A dynamic, complexly configured, highly organized human political society like the Athenian *polis* is expected to resist this design, so, assuming that the appropriate ruler is found, the Platonic state would start with children of ten or younger who would be taken away from their parents and brought up in the Republic, while all others would be sent into the countryside (7.540e-541a).[28]

To the tripartite division of society in the Republic, grounded in the foundational myth (3.414b-415d), corresponds a trichotomy of the soul (4.436a-441c). The Platonic division will form the foundation of subsequent psychology:[29] at one end, the irrational appetites (impulse and desire) (437b-439d);[30] at the other, reason (439d, 441a).[31] The intermediary is the spirited or passionate element, θυμός (*thumos*), (439e-440a).[32] The soul is like the state, with its three classes: the productive

---

25. 'It is the science (ἐπιστήμη) of guardianship or government...' (4.428d).

26. In the metals allegory (3.415a-d), part of the 'noble lie' foundational myth (3.414b-415d), Plato suggests that each social class is naturally predetermined (yet promotion is by merit alone). Similarly, Paul introduces the Christ-factor to make us all naturally Christians.

27. κατὰ φύσιν οἰκισθεῖσα πόλις (4.428e).

28. They would be sent εἰς τοὺς ἀγρούς (7.541a).

29. See also Aristotle, *Nicomachean Ethics* 1.1102a31.

30. The irrational and the appetitive, ἀλόγιστόκόν τε καὶ ἐπιθυμητικόν (4.439d) is the general name for two types of ἐπιθυμίαι, one a craving, an instinct, an immediate need, ignoring pleasure, such as thirst or hunger, the other a drive proper, a desire, a qualified appetite, that seeks pleasure. Both, however, are engendered by external influences and abnormal conditions.

31. It is called τὸ λογιστικόν.

32. ὁ θυμός. The Story of Leontius (4.439e-440a) shows *thumos* on the side of reason.

order, the Warrior-Guardians and the Philosopher (440e).[33] Inner justice,[34] the 'well-tempered' soul (4.443d-e) and the harmony of its three parts, corresponds to justice, the supreme political virtue, which binds and harmonizes the state's three classes.[35]

Perfect justice, the main feature of Plato's happy state, elicits its prize: individual assertion, satisfaction and success (4.420a-b). Plato's philosopher is described, in the end, as a sort of mystical revolutionary. In 6.497a-502c, Plato shows how the philosopher, following a divine pattern, reproduces in his soul the world of unchanging harmonies and order. Becoming godlike, the philosopher refashions society and brings about a truly divine humanity. The language is less that of philosophy

33. Together with the Guardians, as the highest class.

34. Justice as a virtue of differentiation, as contrasted with *sophrosune*.

35. In *Crito* (50), the personified Laws remind Socrates that he engaged himself to obey them. It is assumed that Plato proposes there a contractarian view of the state, an exceedingly rare feature of ancient political theory. I read the same contractual aspect in Paul's concept of *pistis*, a *pistis* that requires suffering, as basis for the Christian state. The Sophists are also credited with an embryonic contract theory. They drew distinctions between the necessary, 'natural' elements, *phusis*, and the contingent, *nomos*, ones in the state machinery, and determined that the law appeared from an agreement (or a conspiracy) among the weak to curb the 'natural' power of the strong (Finley 1983: 132). (It is also true that some of the Sophists use the *phusis–nomos* contrast to elevate the *nomos*. See W.K.C. Guthrie 1977: 294-98.) This position is derived from Plato's view of justice as a set of provisions invented by the weak to limit the harm the strong can do (*Republic* 2.359a-b).

In *Protagoras* 320c-322d, Plato recounts, under the form of a famous μῦθος, the making of humanity. Having acquired, from Epimetheus and Prometheus, all σοφία περὶ τὸν βίον (321d) human beings still lacked political wisdom, the prerogative of Zeus, who, to save humankind from the losing battle against nature, Ἑρμῆν πέμπει ἄγοντα εἰς ἀνθρώπους αἰδῶ τε καὶ δίκην, ἵν᾽ εἶεν πόλεων κόσμοι τε καὶ δεσμοὶ φιλίας συναγωγοί (322c), sent Hermes to humans bearing shame and justice to be the ordering principles of cities, and the bonds of friendship, and togetherness (Jowett, modified translation). Αἰδώς is a political concept as it is made clear not only here but also by its use in Aristotle (*Nicomachean Ethics* 3.1116a18-29) in the context of the 'political courage' of the common citizen in battle: the sense of shame at incurring public disgrace, a virtue (3.1116a27-29). In *Protagoras*, the political *aretai* are bestowed upon all men, 'for cities cannot exist if only a few share in the [political] virtues, as [is the case with the talent bestowed only upon a few] in the arts' (322d). Notice the divine locale of political power and the universality of citizenship also in Paul. The speech Plato gives Protagoras in this dialogue is especially interesting for the tension between *phusis* and *nomos*.

and dialectics and more that of religion, of mysteries and mystical hope.[36] Plato produces less a political figure than a savior. Paul reverses the process and, starting with a savior, exploits his political potential.

36. It is in passages like this one that later Neoplatonism will find its inspiration.

Chapter 2

CLASSICAL SOURCES: ARISTOTLE

Aristotle's Ethics

Plato, aware that his ideal *polis* fails as *genos*, as kinship, has Socrates construct the myth of the metals.[1] For Aristotle as well, *genos* is a component of *polis*. As Adolph Stahr long ago wrote, 'The natural determining circumstance of birth is [for Aristotle] an essential element in the idea of freedom',[2] and hence of the *polis*. *Genos*, however, is not the only key component of the *polis*, as Aristotle sees it, that Plato's *Republic* lacks. Aristotle thinks of *polis* as a political structure in which the citizen participates in political power. For him—and this is one of Aristotle's central doctrines—the *polis* is a partnership of citizens in political life.[3] 'A human being is born for citizenship'[4] is, for Aristotle, a canon.[5]

In another major reaction to Plato, Aristotle insists that the essence of the *polis* is the principle of the equality and similarity of citizens, who hold office by turns. It is not the ruler who is the incontestable master possessing infallible knowledge, but the citizenry.[6] By this standard, the *polis* Socrates proposes in the *Republic* fails not only as *genos* but also

1. See Introduction (*The* Polis *versus the Ideal State*).
2. Stahr 1858: 341b.
3. κοινωνία πολιτῶν πολιτείας (*Politics* 3.1276b1-2). The *polis* is a corporation of *politai* in a *politeia*. *Politeia* means constitution, hence a form of political life.
4. φύσει πολιτικὸν ὁ ἄνθρωπος (*Nicomachean Ethics* 1.1097b11, Ross trans.). Henceforth, all references to *Ethics* are to *Nicomachean Ethics*.
5. In a certain sense, Paul thinks alike: everyone is born to be a christ, all are participants in the Christian *koinōnia*.
6. The best expression of this creed is *Politics* 3.1279a5-14, διὸ καὶ τὰς πολιτικὰς ἀρχάς, ὅταν ᾖ κατ' ἰσότητα τῶν πολιτῶν συνεστηκυῖα καὶ καθ' ὁμοιότητα, κατὰ μέρος ἀξιοῦσιν ἄρχειν... (3.1279a8-11).

as *politeia* (*civitas*), as the body geo-politic. It is essentially no *polis* at all.[7]

Aristotle conceives of politics as a science. In presenting his ideal state, which he relegates to the last two books of *Politics*,[8] Aristotle is merely being consistent with the tradition established by his master. Aristotle's interest is in data—analyzing and classifying, questioning and conceptualizing, recording and structuring data in order to understand the laws of political process and to formulate propositions. His sources are static and material—records and documents, including literature—although he does make allowance for opinion and for the experience of old people.[9] His task is theoretical: abstract explanations of the work of dynamic political systems. Aristotle created the instruments of political study. Long before he engages in a plan for an ideal state, Aristotle produces an 'ideal discourse', one that leaves nothing unanalyzed.

Aristotle's politics subsumes ethics; the interests of the parts are subsumed by that of the whole. For him, politics (ἡ πολιτική, *hē politikē*) is a grand practical science, 'the most authoritative art and that which is truly the master art'.[10] It comprises two undertakings. First is the theory of happiness, the knowledge of what the good and happy life is, 'the end merely for one person' (1.1094b7-12); this study of the human character is the region of ethics. Second is the theory of the *polis*, the constitution and social structure of a political system that can best ensure happiness, the end for a state. This is politics proper.[11] The end is the same for man and state, but securing the latter is by far superior.[12] Ethics and politics are related to one another as the particular is to the general, the happiness of the individual and that of the state being part

7.   On the triple meaning of *polis* as *urbs*, *civitas* and *respublica* see E. Lévy 1990.

8.   The theoretical formulation of the ideal state occupies no more than book 7. Book 7 is concerned with the training and education of the young in that state.

9.   The insight of the old is a secondary type of practical reason, which Aristotle calls 'the eye of the soul' (*Ethics* 6.1144a30).

10.   *Ethics* 1.1094a28-29, δόξειε δ'ἂν τῆς κυριωτάτης (lit. most lordly) καὶ μάλιστα ἀρχιτεκτονικῆς.

11.   *Ethics* 1.1094b7-12; cf. 10.1181b12-24.

12.   *Ethics* 1.1094b10, κάλλιον δὲ καὶ θειότερον, better and more divine. Such ascriptions of the political pursuit could very easily be read as falling into a sphere higher than man's, the work proper to a god. This is important for understanding Paul (as well as the Hellenistic Pythagorean Onatas).

of the same pursuit: 'The political philosopher...is the architect of the end'.[13]

For Aristotle, end is meaning. Meaning is rooted in growth, in becoming—that is, in the ἐντελέχεια, *entelecheia*, complete reality, that leads from potentiality (δύναμις, *dunamis*) to actuality (ἐνέργεια, *energeia*).[14] The term that Aristotle employs for meaning is 'the Good' (τὸ ἀγαθόν, *to agathon*). In politics (i.e. ethics *and* politics proper), the Good comes about through individual participation in collective values, social, political and cultural.

It comes as no surprise then, that Aristotle proceeds differently from Plato. He starts with the individual soul and moves to the state. This is Paul's way, too. Aristotle's psychology is logically derived from its connection with the soul.[15] It is informed by the then current Pythagorean and Platonic division of the soul[16] into the irrational and the rational.[17] The irrational is further split into the purely irrational, growth-nutritive faculty, common to all living things,[18] and the appetitive,[19] which

13. *Ethics* 7.1152b2, τοῦ τέλους ἀρχιτέκτων, lit. the master craftsman of the end, another figure easily transferable to god. Cf. 1.1094a2.

14. *Metaphysics* 12.1071b14-20: 'Nothing, then, is gained if we suppose eternal substances, as believers in the Forms do, unless there is to be in them some principle which causes change; nay, even this is not enough, nor is another substance besides the Forms enough; for if it is not to *act*, there will be no movement. Further, even if it acts, this will not be enough, if its essence is potency; for there will not be *eternal* movement, since that which is potentially may possibly not be. There must, then, be such a principle, whose very essence is actuality' (McKeon trans. and emphases). In other words, the Idea which cannot of itself actualize itself is impotent. It has only a potential existence, δύναμις, conceivable only, not perceptible. It becomes actuality, ἐνέργεια, perceptible *actus*, only by realizing itself, by completing itself gradually. The principle of transition from potential to actual is called ἐντελέχεια. The union of *dunamis* with *energeia* is a motion, κίνησις. Entelecheia is thus a principle of motion. (Buhle, in Ersch and Grüber's *Encyclopädie*, Stahr 1858: 337) Note that the substance in which *dunamis, energeia* and *entelecheia* are united is god, the absolute substance, eternal, unmoved, pure activity (12.1072b).

15. Aristotle is said to have thought that the soul is the form of the organic body. If this notion was, in some way, known to Paul, then it could be helpful for understanding Paul's idea of *sōma* in Rom. 8.10-13, 23 or his discourse on the resurrection body in 1 Cor. 15.35-58. Salvation of *sōma* is inherent to salvation.

16. *Ethics* 1.1102a26.

17. τὸ ἄλογον and τὸ λόγον ἔχον, or τὸ λόγου (*Ethics* 1.1102a27-30).

18. φυσικὸν-θρεπτικόν, commonly referred to as τὸ θρεπτικόν (*Ethics* 1.1102a34-1102b11).

human beings share with animals. This last, however, the seat of appetites and of desire in general,[20] belongs, not only to the irrational but
also to the rational part, thus giving both parts of the soul a twofold
composition. It can properly be called a rational-irrational element, a
thought-desire faculty,[21] and it may be dubbed the *nous-orexis* (νοῦς-
ὄρεξις) system.[22] What emerges, then, is a non-Platonic, actually an
anti-Platonic, psychology. The appetitive constitutes, for all practical
purposes, the intermediary part of the soul. In Aristotle ἐπιθυμία,
epithumia, not θυμός, *thumos*, as in Plato, describes this middle range.[23]
Since the function of man is 'an activity of soul which follows or implies
a rational principle',[24] only the last two parts of the soul, *epithumia* and
nous, can exhibit virtues (ἀρεταί, *aretai*), and thus virtues are both
moral and intellectual. Pure sciences pursue theoretical truth, the truth
about invariable, eternal, necessary things. The practical sciences examine the truth relative to a thought-desire (*nous-orexis*) system—that is,
the truth about variable, changeable things, a condition controlled by
choice (προαίρεσις, *proairesis*).[25] Hellenistic popular philosophy, to
which Paul is heir, focused on the intermediary, rational–irrational part,
the material for ethics.[26] In Romans, *epithumia* (1.24) and *orexis* (1.27)

19. Variously referred to, but generally called τὸ ἐπιθυμητικόν (*Ethics* 1.1102b12-
1103a4).

20. τὸ δ᾽ ἐπιθυμητικὸν καὶ ὅλως ὀρεκτικὸν (*Ethics* 1.1102b30).

21. See *Ethics* 6.1139a31-33: 'Now the cause of action (the efficient, not the
final cause) is desire and reasoning directed to some end' πράξεως μὲν οὖν ἀρχὴ
προαίρεσις (ὅθεν ἡ κίνησις ἀλλ᾽ οὐχ οὗ ἕνεκα), προαιρέσεως δὲ ὄρεξις καὶ λόγος ὁ
ἕνεκά τινος. See also *Ethics* 6.1139b5: 'Choice may be called either thought related
to desire or desire related to reasoning', διὸ ἢ ὀρεκτικὸς νοῦς ἡ προαίρεσις ἢ ὄρεξις
διανοητική.

22. The rational principle, the third component of the soul, is the τὸ λόγον or
the νοῦς (*Republic* 4.434d-441c).

23. This is a major issue since θυμός is a key term of Plato's psychology, and
hence of his political system. In Aristotle's sly reworking, Plato's *thumos* is dis-
carded; consequently, the same fate befalls the entire equalitarian society of Guardians (both Warriors and Guardians proper) that it had engendered, Plato's primary
claim to fame in his ideal republic.

24. *Ethics* 1.1098a7-8.

25. *Ethics* 6.1139a8. For the distinction between τὸ ἐπιστημονικόν, scientific,
and τὸ λογιστικόν, calculative or deliberative rational faculties, see 6.1138b18-
1141b23.

26. *Aretai* are differentiated according to the segmentation of the soul: to *nous*
belonging the dianoetic (intellectual) virtues; to the intermediary, the ethical ones,

describe precisely this median part of the soul, which is connected, as in Aristotle and the Hellenistic philosophers,[27] with morals.

The good (*to agathon*),[28] is for Aristotle the end (τέλος, *telos*) of any thing, yet certain ends are more desirable than others.[29] The Supreme Good,[30] the ultimate end or the end in itself,[31] is the end of the master art, politics.[32] The end of politics, therefore, is happiness,[33] the highest of all goods achievable by action.[34]

αἱ ἠθικαί (*Ethics* 1.1103a4-5).

27. Polybius, in his famous introduction to Book 3 of his *Histories*, in which he presents the purpose of his work and examines the Roman constitution, writes: '...I must also describe the driving forces (*hormai*, drives) and the dominant preoccupations (*zēloi*, ambitions) of the various people concerned, both in their public and in their private life' (3.4, Scott-Kilvert trans.). In other words, *hormē*, *zēlos* are political and psychological terms, and they could be *both* for a good life, τὰ καλά, but also for an immoral one (Polybius 31.25, on Scipio Aemilianus and his contemporaries). The moral implications of ancient psychology must always make us wary.

28. τὸ ἀγαθόν, in Aristotle, is not restricted to the moral good, as it is in the Stoics (see Sandbach 1985: 24).

29. *Ethics* 1.1094a4-7.

30. τὸ ἄριστον, lit. the best (*Ethics* 1.1094a22). The highest good is self-sufficient, αὔταρκες (*Ethics* 1.1097b9), in a political context, however, since 'man is by nature something political', ἐπειδὴ φύσει πολιτικὸν ὁ ἄνθρωπος (1.1097b11).

31. *Ethics* 1.1094a22.

32. *Ethics* 1.1094a26-1094b4.

33. *Ethics* 1.1095a15-16: the end of politics 'is the highest of all the goods that action can achieve', τὸ πάντων ἀκρότατον τῶν πρακτῶν ἀγαθῶν.

Happiness, εὐδαιμονία, is an activity of the soul, ψυχῆς ἐνέργεια, according to excellence κατ' ἀρετήν, the highest excellence, κατὰ τὴν ἀρίστην, in a complete life, ἐν βίῳ τελείῳ (1.1098a16-17). Happiness is not a static condition, *hexis*, but an activity, *energeia*.

For the Stoics, happiness is a state, *hexis*, that does not admit of degrees, διάθεσις. Long 1986 (*ap*. Sandbach 1985: 25) sees here a reaction to Aristotle. Sandbach thinks that they by-passed Aristotle and went to Plato; in *Philebus* 11d Plato writes: 'ἕξις ψυχῆς καὶ διάθεσις can make a man's whole life happy' (Sandbach 1985: 25). I disagree with Sandbach. *Hexis* is a technical term in Aristotle not Plato. *Diathesis* is polemic, and goes against Aristotle, the classical proponent for scaling *eudaimonia*.

34. The emphasis is on 'action', πρακτόν (cf. *Ethics* 1.1094a19), matter of moral action, and this is significant, for Aristotle will, in the end, when he compares it with contemplative life, think little of it. He sets a mood that will be long lasting, and that one finds, in a different form, in Paul's distinction between works and *pistis*.

Note also that Aristotle opposes Plato's idea of Good, Good-in-itself, the form, capable of *real* existence, of separate and independent life outside things. For Aris-

Aretē, which will form the basis for the best constitution, is first formulated by Aristotle with regard to the individual. *Aretē* is a state of mind, determining a choice, the choice consisting in a mean, a mean relative to us; this mean being determined by a rational principle, by the principle by which a person of practical reason would determine it.[35] This perhaps awkward rendering of Aristotle's definition—the sentence in the *Ethics* is highly compressed and difficult to unravel—nevertheless suggests the many directions in which uses of *aretē* branched in the long history of western ethics. Paul uses the term in the known writings only once, but this, significantly, occurs in Philippians, his eminently politics-in-action letter, in a catalog of civic qualities.[36] He would often,

totle ideas are only *nomina*, universals, but inseparable from composite things. This is the root of the medieval scholastic controversy between realists and nominalists. Human good is not a state or a disposition but an activity, a process.

35. *Ethics* 2.1106b35-1107a1: Ἔστιν ἄρα ἡ ἀρετὴ ἕξις προαιρετική, ἐν μεσότητι οὖσα τῇ πρὸς ἡμᾶς, ὡρισμένη (cf. 3.1114b26-30). The reader is prepared for this tough sentence by a detailed discussion of its parts (2.1105b19-1107a8).

The *genus* of the definition of *aretē* (2.1105b19-1106a13) is ἕξις, which is rendered alternatively as habit of mind, fixed disposition, state of character, state of will. Like the faculties (or capacities), δυνάμεις, ἕξεις are categories tied to passions (or emotions), παθή. Unlike the faculties, however, which describe capacity of responding to emotion (e.g. being angry), habits gauge the state of emotions (e.g. intense anger) (2.1105b19-27). Put in terms of linguistic morphology, I would say that passions are nouns (anger, fear, joy), faculties are verbs (feeling, becoming, being), states are adjectives (standing well or badly vis-à-vis emotions: intense, moderate, weak). Because habits, *aretai* are modes of choice, προαιρέσεις τινές, or involve choice (2.1106a3). *Aretai* are not by nature, *phusei*: 'we are not born good or bad by nature' (2.1106a10).

Choice is defined as deliberate desire of things in our own power, ἡ προαίρεσις ἂν εἴε βουλευτικὴ ὄρεξις τῶν ἐφ᾽ ἡμῖν (3.1113a.11).

The *differentia* is μεσότης (2.1106a14-b35), i.e. a disposition to choose the mean. The mean is the intermediary between excess and defect, τὸ δ᾽ ἴσον μέσον τι ὑπερβολῆς καὶ ἐλλείψεως (2.1106a29). The mean is, however, a variable insofar as relative to a human being, πρὸς ἡμᾶς (2.1106a32), i.e. the right amount. The mean rests with sense perception, αἴσθησις, not reasoning, λόγος (2.1109b22-23). That is why it is not easy to be good (2.1109a25). The criterion is the example of the prudent man, the man of practical wisdom, ὁ φρόνιμος.

Hexis is also a technical term for Stoic anthropology. The πνεῦμα (σωματικόν), corporeal breath, material even if fiery, is *hexis*, principle of existence, in inanimate beings; *psuchē*, principle of life, in living beings; and *logos*, principle of reason, in humans (Festugière 1932: 211 and n. 1).

36. Phil. 4.8. *Aretē* is an exceedingly rare word in the New Testament. Only the

however, insist on prudence and the example of the wise man, most notably in Rom. 12.3, where 'the mean relative to us' of *aretē* becomes, *mirabile dictu*, the measure of πίστις, *pistis*,[37] granted by God, unequal but appropriate in each.[38] In Aristotle, moral *aretē*, ἐθική, *ethikē*, is acquired by habit, repetition, example (ἔθος, *ethos*).[39] Throughout Paul's Letters, the importance of Paul's personal example, as well as the theme of the imitation of Christ, can hardly be overstated.

Moreover, after Aristotle, moral virtues are tied to psychology—pain and pleasure[40]—and so it is also in Paul.[41] Reductionist readings of such

pseudo-Petrine letters use *aretē*, three times: once, in tragic and dithyrambic mode, in what I see as personified attributes of God, 'tell out about the *aretai* of [him who]…' (1 Pet. 2.9), a possible counterpart of powers, authorities, and other dark aeons; a second time, also in connection with God, his '*doxa* and *aretē*' (2 Pet. 1.3); and finally, in a list of virtues that begins with *pistis* and ends with *agapē* (2 Pet. 1.5).

37. The meaning of *pistis*, usually translated as 'faith', is probably better conveyed by our words 'confidence' or 'trust'; I have intentionally left it untranslated throughout in order to emphasize its *political* function and to distance it from the theological meanings it has accrued.

38. ἑκάστω ὡς ὁ θεὸς ἐμέρισεν μέτρον πίστεως. The picture is the same, only the frame has changed. The whole pericope runs: ἐν ὑμῖν μὴ ὑπερφρονεῖν παρ᾽ ὃ δεῖ φρονεῖν αλλὰ φρονεῖν εἰς τὸ σωφρονεῖν, ἑκάστω κτλ. The language and the hermeneutics are remarkably close. *Aretē* is an unserviceable term to Paul, see Chapter 8, Rom. 11.25-36. For a development of this argument see section on Ps.-Archytas, Chapter 4, *analogia*.

39. ἡ δ᾽ ἠθικὴ ἐξ ἔθους περιγίνεται (*Ethics* 2.1103a15). Intellectual *aretē*, is produced by instruction, ἡ μὲν διανοητικὴ…ἐκ διδασκαλίας (*Ethics* 2.1103a15).

40. περὶ ἡδονὰς γὰρ καὶ λύπας ἐστὶν ἡ ἠθικὴ ἀρετή (*Ethics* 2.1104b9-10). Twice, in the *Ethics* there are excursus on pleasure (7.1152b-1154b and 10.1172a19-1176a29). They are consistent with each other. 'Pleasure, ἡδονή, is not a conscious (or perceptible) process, αἰσθητὴ γένεσις, but an activity, ἐνέργεια, of the natural state, τῆς κατὰ φύσιν ἕξεως; instead of αἰσθητή, ἀνεμπόδιστον, unimpeded (must be used)' (7.1153a13-15). Pleasures are not processes, γενέσεις᾽ but activities and an end, ἀλλ᾽ ἐνέργειαι καὶ τέλος᾽ (7.1153a10). Pleasure is a whole, ὅλον, and perfect, τελεία, at any time, like seeing, ὅρασις (10.1174a15). It is thus also no movement, κίνησις (10.1174a19), i.e., a process of change actualizing what is potential. It is the completeness of pleasure that makes it invaluable for the examination of suffering in Paul.

In *Protagoras* (351c-358b) Socrates finds that pleasure is a good, ἀγαθὸν τὴν ἡδονήν (354c), that the pleasant is the good, τὸ ἡδὺ ἀγαθόν ἐστιν (358b) and that the salvation of human life has been found to consist in the right choice of pleasures and pains, ἐπεὶ δὲ δὴ ἡδονῆς τε καὶ λύπης ἐν ὀρθῇ τῇ αἱρέσει ἐφάνη ἡμῖν ἡ σωτηρία

theories in a world that since Classical times had become increasingly adverse to the body and progressively dominated by ascetic ideals, have led to the simple idea that, for Paul, pleasure is an indication of moral want. But such a view severely misrepresents Paul's understanding of suffering, which I discuss below in Chapter 7, section Clues from Philippians, and Chapter 8.

Aristotle's treatment of ἀκρασία (*akrasia*),[42] the failure of the will, would acquire increasing significance as the fashion of questioning the body became widespread during Hellenistic times and into early Chris-

---

τοῦ βίου οὖσα (357a). This discussion leads to an analysis of *akrasia* and the notion that virtue consists in knowing how to choose the greatest pleasure, a conclusion with harsh implications (Tessitore 1988: 19 n. 12).

Aristotle makes it clear that pleasure, *hedonē*, only perfects the activity, as a *supervening* end, ὡς ἐπιγιγνόμενόν τι τέλος (10.1174b33), the end, *telos*, or the good of man, being the activity of the soul according to *aretē*, τὸ ἀνθρώπινον ἀγαθὸν ψυχῆς ἐνέργεια γίνεται κατ᾽ ἀρετήν (1.1098a16), an action, *praxis* (1.1095a5). The Peripatetics were, however, often criticized by the Stoics for lax ethics, for coupling pleasure and virtue as parts of the supreme good (Gottschalk 1987: 1140 and nn. 295, 296). In his ideal state, Aristotle again pairs *aretai* with χορηγία (*chorēqia*), extraneous equipment, health and wealth, for the best life of the individual (*Politics* 7.1323a-b). The Hellenistic philosophers had a hard time aligning pleasure and virtue. The Stoics denied that pleasure is 'supervening perfection' and activity. Pleasure is not a first impulse but an aftergrowth, not a *telos* but a result of its attainment (Sandbach 1985: 28). Paul does not go with the Stoics. Pleasure is no subsequence or consequence, but coincidence and concomitance; no parturition but superfetation (see the discussion of Paul's suffering and Christian suffering in the Epistle to the Philippians).

This topic is connected with the notion of happiness, εὐδαιμονία, which, similarly, is not a *hexis*, but an *energeia*, complete and autarchic, desirable in itself and an end (*Ethics* 10.1176a30-1177a12). Aristotle makes it very clear (1.1099a31-b3) that happiness requires external goods, τὰ ἐκτὸς ἀγαθά. *Eudaimonia* is a function of *aretē*, but there are degrees of *eudaimonia*. It is the higher degree that demands the external goods, (friends, wealth, political power; also, good birth, good children, beauty) mainly to facilitate virtuous action (Sandbach 1985: 24). The Stoics, who give *agathon* an exclusively moral value, deny that any externals are good, but are of value for leading a natural life, i.e. a life appropriate to human nature (Sandbach 1985: 24).

Note that for Paul suffering takes on the form of *agathon*, not as an external but as essential good for Christian *eudaimonia*.

41. E.g. Rom. 5.3 and parallels.
42. *Ethics* 7.1145a15-1152a35.

tianity. *Akrasia* is a central theme in Romans.[43] The question concerning how someone can do wrong knowingly was often asked in ancient Greece.[44] *Akrasia* describes precisely the doing of what one knows to be wrong. Socrates, in the *Republic*, denies that there is *akrasia* at all, for no one can do wrong while knowing that he does so. It only seems that he is doing what he knows to be wrong, while actually he does so through ignorance of right and wrong.[45] This leads to a difficulty, an aporia.[46] Some thinkers, writes Aristotle, while allowing that knowledge (ἐπιστήμη, *epistēmē*) is supreme, insist that no one acts contrary to his opinion (δόξα, *doxa*) of what is right.[47] Aristotle insists that the acratic not only *believes* that his act is wrong but *knows* it to be so.[48] Aristotle constructs an opposition between perceptual knowledge and a sovereign knowledge.[49] *Akrasia* can occur only in the realm of perceptual knowl-

43. Rom. 7.15-21.

44. Aristotle gives a review of the *status quaestionis* and its problems in *Ethics* 7.1145a15-1146b8.

45. *Ethics* 7.1145b25-30. Aristotle is drawing on Plato's *Protagoras*, from which he actually quotes (352b=7.1145b25). Socrates is adamant: 'no man voluntarily pursues evil, or that which he thinks to be evil. To prefer evil to good is not in human nature' (*Protagoras* 358c6-d1).

Euripides (431 BCE) has Medea wrest with this very notion: 'I understand the awful deed I am to do; but passion (θύμος), that cause of direst woes to mortal man, hath triumphed o'er my sober thoughts' (*Medea* 1078-80, trans. E.P. Coleridge). *Thumos*, anger, wrath, is here the irrational self, a pre-Platonic meaning.

46. This is how Aristotle describes ἀπορία: '[when] the resultant chain of reasoning ends in an *aporia*, ὁ γενόμενος συλλογισμὸς ἀπορία γίνεται; the mind is fettered, being unwilling to stand still because it cannot approve the conclusion reached, yet unable to go forward because it cannot untie the knot of the argument' (*Ethics* 7.1146a24-27).

47. *Ethics* 7.1145b32-1146a10.

48. *Ethics* 7.1145b31-1146b5 and 1146b24-1147b19 (R. Robinson 1977: 80). What Aristotle is essentially saying is 'that the acratic, at the time of his act, does not have fully in mind all the parts of the practical syllogism that ought to govern it' (R. Robinson 1977: 84).

49. αἰσθητικὴ ἐπιστήμη and κυρίως ἐπιστήμη (*Ethics* 7.1147b16-17). The homophonic play on words is interesting, 'sovereign knowledge' and 'lord [=Christ] knowledge'. Luke repeatedly uses the title ἐπιστάτης, an equivalent for κύριε or ῥαββί) for Jesus. In the New Testament *epistēmē* is used once, by Paul, and again in Phil. 4.8, ἔπαινος ἐπιστήμης, knowledge worthy of praise, an important variant reading, in the same list of virtues. The ἔπαινος ἐπιστήμης is obviously of the same kind as the κυρίως ἐπιστήμη.

The distinction between the two kinds of *epistēmē* is contextually connected with

edge, the domain of the rational-irrational soul and of moral principle, not in that of true knowledge. To avoid *akrasia*, knowledge[50] is necessary—the kind of knowledge that only the wise individual, the φρόνιμος (*phronimos*), would have. In Aristotle, the term *phronimos* acquires the meaning it will have for all subsequent philosophy: an 'ideal person', an individual with right desires and knowledge who is immune to *akrasia*.[51]

Socrates (7.1147b14-17), who embodies the sovereign knowledge. Socrates is not only the *phronimos* par excellence, but also the example of a life of radical inquiry. For Aristotle's treatment of Socrates in the *Ethics*, see Tessitore 1988.

The relationship between φρόνησις, prudence, and moral *aretē*, relevant for Paul as well, and the extent of the agreement and divergence between Aristotle and Plato on this, is a much discussed topic. To sum up its conclusions, Aristotle revises Plato's position (that *aretai* are rational principles, *logoi*, since they all are *epistēmē*), and holds that moral virtue is not knowledge yet it must be accompanied by a rational principle, λόγος; *aretē* cooperates with the right principle, ὀρθὸς λόγος (6.1144b21-30). Aristotle does not accept the paradoxical formula *aretē* = *epistēmē*. Further, prudence is not one and the same thing with virtue (Plato thought that all *aretai* are forms of *phronesis*), but it does presuppose all other virtues (6.1145a1-2). *Phronesis* is the right principle in matters of conduct (6.1144b1-20 and 6.1445a1-2). On the other hand, Aristotle acknowledges, with Plato, the existence of a still greater authority: that which belongs to the wise, σοφός, a god-like wisdom, σοφία, the highest and most authoritative human excellence (e.g. 6.1141a9-20, esp. 15-16). (See also Tessitore 1988: 17-18.)

Similarly in Paul, *phronesis* is the highest and leader of moral virtues. But above it, and of a different order, there is *pistis*. In regard to the relation between prudence and moral virtue (6.1144a6-1145a6), prudence gives the right means by which the good, the end of virtue, is reached (6.1144a7-8; 6.1145a5-6). Prudence enables the potential virtue to realize itself, in the one with a strong inclination towards virtue. Someone with natural excellence, ἀρετὴ φυσική, arrives, through prudence, at masterly, sovereign excellence, κυρία ἀρετή, these being the two aspects of the moral soul (6.1144b16-17). (See also Tessitore 1988: 14.)

50. σύμφυσις, according to *Ethics* 7.1147a22: δεῖ γὰρ συμφυῆναι, τοῦτο δὲ χρόνου δεῖται, [knowledge] has to become part of 'the tissue of the mind', and this takes time (Rackham). In Paul this integration of knowledge takes place via the death and the resurrection of Christ: σύμφυτοι (Rom. 6.5; cf. also Dio Chrysostom 12.28).

Aristotle begins his discussion of *akrasia* by introducing, without elaboration, a superhuman, heroic and divine *aretē*, the type of which is Hector, τὴν ὑπὲρ ἡμᾶς ἀρετήν, ἡρωϊήν τινα καὶ θείαν (7.1145a19-20). It prefigures the Christ-type in Paul (and, further down the road, Hegel and the Romanticism).

51. See N.O. Dahl 1984, the main argument for the second part of his book, *ap.* Hudson's (1988: 72) review.

The Stoics and Aristotle answer similarly the question how is virtue obtained. For

Aristotle clearly distinguishes between the *phronimos* and the *sophos*, between *phronesis* and *kuria aretē*, between moral (or practical) *aretai* and the intellectual *aretai*. 'For it is absurd to think that *politikē* or *phronesis* is the loftiest kind of *epistēmē*, since the human being (*anthrōpos*) is not the highest (*aristos*) thing in the world (*kosmos*)' (6.1141a20-22). Prudence is confined to humanity and is concerned with happiness: wisdom does not ask about generation; it is pure knowledge, contemplation of things yonder (6.1143b19-20). The distinction is carried into politics proper, where the good citizen is different than the good man, for the first complies with the laws of the state, the other follows the absolute virtue. This split between practical and theoretical reason would prove one of the most enduring results of Classical Greek philosophy, healed only with Kant and the Enlightenment.[52]

Aristotle, however, only wants to analyze the acratic act. Paul, in a stirring, agitated tirade (Rom. 7.14-21), displays the desperate, hopeless struggle of the will. For him *akrasia*[53] is explicable by ἁμαρτία (*hamartia*, error). At first glance, this might seem to follow the Platonic trend, but Paul's drama of the will depends on the Aristotelian notion that the wrongdoer knows that he is doing wrong. For Paul *hamartia* is this knowledge.

In Book 5 of the *Nicomachean Ethics*, Aristotle addresses the question of justice, *dikaiosunē*. Given Aristotle's usual method, one

---

Aristotle *aretē* is acquired by doing virtuous deeds, i.e., by acting as the good man would even if one lacks his virtuous disposition (*Ethics* 2.1105a31). For the Stoics, *aretē* is obtained by performance of καθήκοντα, appropriate actions. But while virtuous actions, κατορθώματα, in appearance, these are far from the good man's deeds, which are performed from complete and unshakeable understanding of what is consonant with nature, or, as Aristotle would put it, if the agent is in a certain condition when he does them (2.1105a31). (See also Sandbach 1985: 26-7.)

Paul would agree that it is not the work, but the state of mind of the doer of the work that matters. He does not condemn the work, but the work done without *pistis* (Rom. 12.6-8).

52. E.g. in Kant's paper *What is Enlightenment?*, where he makes the point that civic and intellectual freedoms, that is, the political and the philosophical minds, the practical and the contemplative faculties, are varieties of the same thing, one freedom, one state, one mind. In other words, two uses of reason (public and private) lead to two authorities (law and reason) and finally to two freedoms (civic and intellectual), each, however, two manifestations of the same thing: one mind, one state, one freedom.

53. He does not use this term in Romans, but knows it (cf. 1 Cor. 1.5).

would expect that his inquiry into the subject would turn first to the individual. Justice, however, elicits a modified approach dictated by the understanding of this virtue as a special kind of mean. *Dikaiosunē is* both a mean and the science of the mean, the determination of fairness ('particular' justice)[54] and lawfulness ('universal' justice).[55] As such, *dikaiosunē* is a political concept par excellence. This mean actually contains the *differentia* in the definition of justice. 'Universal' justice, justice in general, is complete virtue, perfect *aretē*.[56] Its loftiness makes it appropriate to the sphere of divine prerogative. It is the principle of law, of right; it is a form of infallibility. The domain of 'particular' justice, one of the *aretai*, is fairness and equality in issues of honor, money and safety.[57]

The *genus* of *dikaiosunē* makes it an even more peculiar *aretē*: a relation of one to another. 'Justice alone of the virtues is the "good of the other".'[58] The point is remarkable, for Aristotle quotes the very (even if ironic) words of Plato's Thrasymachus.[59] Also of the highest

54. I.e. in limited, or partial sense (of virtue), ἡ ἐν μέρει ἀρετῆς δικαιοσύνη (*Ethics* 5.1130a14), the other, is in the wide sense, the whole or universal, ὅλη ἀρετή.

55. 'Justice is a kind of mean (ἡ δὲ δικαιοσύνη μεσότης τίς ἐστιν), though not in the same way as the other virtues are, but because it is related to a mean (ἀλλ᾽ ὅτι μέσου ἐστιν), while injustice is related to the extremes (ἡ δ᾽ ἀδικία τῶν ἄκρων)' (*Ethics* 5.1133b34-35). Previously, Aristotle made it clear that the just is the lawful and the appropriate, while the unjust is the unlawful, the inappropriate: τὸ μὲν δίκαιον ἄρα τὸ νόμιμον καὶ ἴσον, τὸ δ᾽ ἄδικον τὸ παράνομον καὶ τὸ ἄνισον (5.1129b1). *Paranomia* (preserved by 2 Pet. 2.16) will be engulfed by Paul's *hamartia*. 'Universal justice', ὅλη ἀρετή (5.1130a10), has, as its counterpart 'universal injustice', ὅλη ἀδικία (5.1133a35); this is vice pure and simple, the whole of it, ὅλη κακία (5.1130a11).

56. ἀρετὴ τελεία (*Ethics* 5.1129b26). It is chief of virtues, more sublime than stars, sum of all virtues (5.1129b27-30).

57. ἡ μὲν περὶ τιμὴν ἢ χρήματα ἢ σωτηρίαν... (*Ethics* 5.1130b2). We recover here the Classical Greek meaning of *sōtēria*, to get safely to the destination, survival. What was a practical desideratum of everyday life and its enterprises would be translated into afterlife and its metaphysics.

58. ἡ δικαιοσύνη μόνη τῶν ἀρετῶν, ὅτι (ἀγαθὸν) πρὸς ἕτερόν ἐστιν (*Ethics* 5.1130a4-5).

59. *Republic* 1.343c: ὥστε ἀγνοεῖς, ὅτι ἡ μὲν δικαιοσύνη καὶ τὸ δίκαιον ἀλλότριον ἀγαθὸν τῷ ὄντι, τοῦ κρείττονός τε καὶ ἄρχοντος ξυμφέρον... 'wouldn't you know that justice and the just are literally the other fellow's good, the advantage of the stronger and the ruler', οἰκεία δὲ τοῦ πειθομένου τε καὶ ὑπηρετοῦντος βλάβη, 'but one's own harm, for the subject who obeys and serves' (Shorey trans.).

significance is the fact that justice, even if first treated in *Ethics*, is a purely political concept. Its political content is unavoidable and has been so ever since the fateful treatment given it by Thrasymachus in the *Republic*. Aristotle is fully aware of this. 'The good of the other' is the advantage of a ruler.[60] Aristotle makes the point unequivocally when he cites Bias's dictum 'rule will show the man'[61] 'for the ruler [ἄρχων]', continues Aristotle, 'is necessarily in relation to others and a member of the society [ἐν κοινωνίᾳ]'.[62] The indirect source of Paul's concept of *dikaiosunē* is found. Paul manages to preserve the notion that *dikaiosunē* is the prerogative of the ruler, while at the same time emptying that notion of the unseemliness of Thrasymachus's curse. Paul manages to retain the integrity of justice by deferring *dikaiosunē* to God, who alone is above suspicion and who alone can disburse justice equitably.

Another significant aspect of Aristotle's theory of justice reaches Paul. Aristotle contrasts[63] the two kinds of particular justice (μέρος δικαιοσύνη), namely distributive (or political) justice (τὸ ἐν διανομῇ or διανεμητικὸν δίκαιον)[64] and corrective justice (διορθωτικόν, i.e. penal and civil law). The comparison Aristotle employs is that of a geometrical versus an arithmetical proportion.[65] Although everyone agrees, says Aristotle, that distributive justice must be in geometrical proportion to one's worth (κατ᾽ ἀξίαν, *kat'axian*),[66] this is differently understood, according to the constitutional system (free birth, in a democracy; wealth, in a oligarchy; excellence, in a aristocracy). But whatever criterion is used, political justice is a kind of proportion (ἔστιν ἄρα τὸ δίκαιον ἀνάλογόν τι).[67] Distributive justice is also called the principle of 'assignment by desert' (Rackham trans.), or according to worth (κατ᾽ ἀξίαν).[68] Aristotle employs this major concept in his political theory

And, as a result, Thrasymachus proposes injustice as the solution.

60. ἄλλῳ γὰρ τὰ συμφέροντα πράττει, ἢ ἄρχοντι ἢ κοινωνῷ (*Ethics* 5.1130a5-6).

61. ἀρχὰ ἄνδρα δείξει (5.1130a2).

62. πρὸς ἕτερον γὰρ καὶ ἐν κοινωνίᾳ ἤδη ὁ ἄρχων (5.1130a3).

63. *Ethics* 5.1130b30-1133b29, 1134a25-1135a15, 1137a31-1138a4. He distinguishes distributive, corrective, economic, political, and household justice as well as equity.

64. *Ethics* 5.1131a10-1132b20.

65. *Ethics* 5.1132a1-2.

66. *Ethics* 5.1131a24.

67. *Ethics* 5.1131a29-30. See A. Delatte 1922: 104.

68. *Ethics* 5.1131a24.

when he tries to formulate a mean between aristocracy and democracy—that is, between the aristocrats' *aretē* (in effect, 'excellence of birth') and democrats' *eleutheria* ('free birth')—in regard to political participation. Distributive justice refers to awards in proportion to *axia*, worth.[69] Aristotle insists that the proportional is a mean and the just is proportional.[70] Distributive, proportionate justice is opposed to the absolute equality of the democratic constitution.[71] The topic naturally looms large in the *Politics*, where just distribution is that in which the relative values of the things given correspond to those of the persons receiving.[72] In other words, in a political society, a *polis*, award of honors and money ought to be in proportion to civic excellence (πολιτικὴ ἀρετή, *politikē aretē*). Thus, irrespective of free or noble birth, those who are superior in political excellence must have the larger share in the *polis*, and the principle of distributive justice gives them a greater recognition.[73]

Two observations must be made here. On the one hand, Aristotle's *axia* ('merit', 'worth'), when applied to political discourse, is identified with civic excellence and thus becomes a political term. On the other hand, his recognition that *politikē koinōnia* ('political association') is above *eleutheria* ('free birth') and *genos* ('pedigree') is remarkable, in that it preempts any claim that might be made for the superiority of either a democratic or an aristocratic government. The impact of these reflections can be seen in Paul's treatment of *pistis* as both moral and a political value and as the criterion for *dikaiosunē*, as well as in his

---

69. γεωμετρικὴ ἀναλογία (*Ethics* 5.1131a.25-26, 1131b13-14). Aristotle's geometrical proportion actually is, as his own demonstration attests (5.1131a29-1131b12), a simple proportion.

70. τὸ γὰρ ἀνάλογον μέσον, τὸ δὲ δίκαιον ἀνάλογον (*Ethics* 5.1131b12). In Paul justice is distributed by god according to one's *pistis* (Rom. 12.3).

71. Barker 1958: liii, 'Introduction' to Aristotle's *Politics*.

72. ὥστ' ἐπεὶ τὸ δίκαιον τισίν, καὶ διῄρηται τὸν αὐτὸν τρόπον ἐπί τε τῶν πραγμάτων καὶ οἷς... (*Politics* 3.1280a18-19).

73. πόλις δὲ ἡ...κοινωνία ζωῆς τελείας καὶ αὐτάρκους, τοῦτο δ' ἐστίν, ὡς φαμέν, τό Ζῆν εὐδαιμόνως καὶ καλῶς· τῶν καλῶν ἄρα πράξεων χάριν θετέον εἶναι τὴν πολιτικὴν κοινωνίαν, ἀλλ' οὐ τοῦ συζῆν· διόπερ ὅσοι συμβάλλονται πλεῖστον εἰς τὴν τοιαύτην κοινωνίαν, τούτοις τῆς πόλεως μέτεστι πλεῖον ἢ τοῖς κατὰ μὲν ἐλευθερίαν καὶ γένος ἴσοις ἢ μείζοσι κατὰ δὲ τὴν πολιτικὴν ἀρετὴν ἀνίσοις... (*Politics* 3.1281a1-9). Aristotle makes points similar to those detailed in this paragraph in his *Politics*. For discussion see Aristotle's Politics section.

valuation of *pistis* as an element of πνεῦμα (*pneuma*),[74] above social distinctions such as freedom or privilege.

A related theme, and one that further accounts for Paul's radical transferral of *dikaiosunē* to god, is Aristotle's analysis of the difficulty of being just.[75] The problem, as in Paul, derives from the argument that choice is the inner nature of justice.[76] Since justice is not a way of action but a fixed disposition, a condition of the mind,[77] Aristotle proceeds to a landmark correction of the meaning of being just. Humans think that being unjust is up to them and thus that it is easy to be just.[78] It is not so, retorts Aristotle. What is easy is the wicked *action*: seducing the neighbor's wife, harming another, bribery. But to *be* unjust, as a state of mind, as a habit, is neither easy nor in one's power.[79] This is why people wrongly think that the just man, no less than the unjust one, is perfectly capable of unjust acts. But doing contemptible things accidentally is one thing. Doing them from a certain state of the mind is another.[80] The condition of the just contains injustice as an aberration. Essentially, Aristotle posits two natures, the just and the unjust. The difference is one of kind, not of degree.[81] The two are irreconcilable.

74. No single translation of the critical term *pneuma*, a rational and supernatural agency, will do it justice. Its various meanings depend on the context, as will be seen throughout.

75. *Ethics* 5.1137a1-35.

76. *Ethics* 5.1135a15-1136a9, cf. 3.1109b30-1114b25. For an act to be just or unjust it must be voluntary, i.e. the moving principle is in the agent himself and he is aware of the circumstances of his action. τὸ ἑκούσιον (as opposed to τὸ ἀκούσιον) δόξειεν ἂν εἶναι οὗ ἡ ἀρχὴ ἐν αὐτῷ εἰδότι τὰ καθ᾽ ἕκαστα ἐν οἷς ἡ πρᾶξις (3.1111a22-23). It is a matter of choice, *proairesis* (3.1111b5), a desire involving deliberation, ἡ προαίρεσις ἂν εἴη βουλευτικὴ ὄρεξις τῶν ἐφ᾽ ἡμῖν (3.1113a11), i.e., based on λόγος and διανοία (3.1112a16). In Paul the mechanism of choice fails.

77. ὡδὶ ἔχοντας, just as one is (*Ethics* 5.1137a9). Rackham has 'disposition of the mind', Ross 'state of character'.

78. οἱ δ᾽ ἄνθρωποι ἐφ᾽ ἑαυτοῖς οἴονται εἶναι τὸ ἀδικεῖν, διὸ τὸ δίκαιον εἶναι ῥᾴδιον (*Ethics* 5.1137a5).

79. ἀλλὰ τὸ ὡδὶ ἔχοντας ταῦτα ποιεῖν οὔτε ῥᾴδιον οὔτ᾽ ἐπ᾽ αὐτοῖς (*Ethics* 5.1137a9)

80. *Ethics* 5.1137a17-24.

81. In speaking of the relationship between the ruler and the ruled (in the context of his theory of the household), Aristotle writes: 'The difference between ruler and ruled is one of kind, and degree has nothing to do with the matter, τὸ μὲν γὰρ ἄρχεσθαι καὶ ἄρχειν εἴδει διαφέρει, τὸ δὲ μᾶλλον καὶ ἧττον οὐδέν' (*Politics* 1.1159b38). In other words, the argument *a fortiori* does not hold. The moral case

Furthermore, Aristotle connects this issue with the law. Human beings think that to know what is just or unjust requires no great wisdom, for it is easy to understand the laws.[82] This is, again, false. The matters dealt with by the laws are just *per accidens* only.[83] To know how actions must be performed and distributions effected in order to be just is a remarkable thing indeed. Aristotle's conclusion is far-reaching: that which is human cannot be perfectly just. Just acts exist only between those who share in things good in themselves. The gods possess these things absolutely; the incurably bad have no share in them; and ordinary people participate in them to a limited extent.[84] Paul's dissatisfaction with human nature, his conviction about the fallibility of the human, and his essential distrust of the power of laws (even if divinely inspired) to reform humanity, situate him at the extreme end of a spectrum in the middle of which sat Aristotle.

Aristotle's central teaching is the science, or rather the art, of the mean.[85] He found nothing unusual in talking about the intellectual *aretai*[86] in the context of practical *aretai*, for one of these 'virtues',

---

of the just and the unjust is not susceptible of degree. This means also that the difference extends to the soul.

82. ὁμοίως δὲ καὶ τὸ γνῶναι τὰ δίκαια καὶ τὰ ἄδικα οὐδὲν οἴονται σοφὸν εἶναι, ὅτι περὶ ὧν οἱ νόμοι λέγουσιν οὐ χαλεπὸν ξυνιέναι (*Ethics* 5.1137a10-11).

83. ...κατὰ συμβεβηκός (*Ethics* 5.1137a12).

84. Ἔστι δὲ τὰ δίκαια ἐν τούτοις οἷς μέτεστι τῶν ἁπλῶς ἀγαθῶν, ἔχουσι δ' ὑπερβολὴν ἐν τούτοις καὶ ἔλλειψιν. τοῖς μὲν γὰρ οὐκ ἔστιν ὑπερβολὴ αὐτῶν, οἷον ἴσως τοῖς θεοῖς· τοῖς δ' οὐθὲν μόριον ὠφέλιμον, τοῖς ἀνιάτως κακοῖς, ἀλλὰ πάντα βλάπτει· τοῖς δὲ μέχρι τοῦ· τοῦτο δ' ἀνθρώπινόν ἐστιν (*Ethics* 5.1137a25-30). My reading differs from Ross's (1988: 132). The antecedent of τοῦτο, *touto* (1137a30) is not 'just acts' but the preceeding statement, 'to the rest, up to a point'. The assumption is not that 'justice is essentially something human', but that mortals fall short of perfect justice.

Plato's position in the *Republic* is different. Humans are capable both of perfect justice and, correspondingly, of the ideal state (the philosopher, *Republic* 5.471c-7.541b) and of perfect injustice and of the 'ideally' evil state (the tyrant, *Republic* Part 4, esp. 8.565d-9.579e). (Elsewhere in the *Republic*, however, Plato does say that the Republic is a fiction, a dream [3.414d-415b]). So also in the *Laws* he states that the ideal state is possible only for gods or the children of gods.)

85. In Rom. 14.17-23, Paul, when he opposes inordinate scruple as detrimental to the community, is in accord with Aristotle. In the same vein, Aristotle finds it vulgar, inconsistent with *megalopsuchia*, *summa virtutum*, to lord it over the weak, ταπεινοί, ἀσθενεῖς (*Ethics* 4.1124b23).

86. Book 4 of *Ethics*.

φρόνησις (*phronēsis*) provides the principle for determining the mean. (*Phronēsis* is practical reason; though usually rendered 'prudence', it actually means the wisdom of following the middle path, or mean.) *Phronēsis* is knowledge of how to *act* variables,[87] variables relative to a *nous-orexis* system.[88] The grasp of moral virtues lies outside ethics; the knowledge of political virtues lies outside politics. Similar in principle even if different in character, in Paul moral and political virtues are to

87. Science, ἐπιστήμη, is demonstrative knowledge of invariables, i.e., of things necessary and eternal, correct inferences from first principles (*Ethics* 6.1139b19-25). Everything existing of absolute necessity is eternal, τὰ γὰρ ἐξ ἀνάγκης ὄντα ἁπλῶς πάντα ἀΐδια, and what is eternal does not come into existence or perish, τὰ δ᾽ ἀΐδια ἀγένητα καὶ ἄφθαρτα (1139b23-24). Such ideas are common philosophical inheritance and even if it they are diffused through compendia amongst the popular philosophers, they pertain no less to philosophy. Paul uses precisely this terminology in Rom. 1.20-23: God is eternal energy, ἀΐδιος δύναμις (1.20), and incorruptible, ἄφθαρος (1.23).

Art, τέχνη, is concerned with coming into being, περὶ γένεσιν, of a thing the efficient cause of which is in the maker, not in the thing made, καὶ ὧν ἡ ἀρχὴ ἐν τῷ ποιοῦντι ἀλλὰ μὴ ἐν τῷ ποιουμένῳ (6.1140a14). It deals with variables, things made, ποιητόν. The domain of variables, τὰ ἐνδεχόμενα (6.1139a9) includes also actions done, πρακτόν (6.1140a1).

The latter kind of variables form the field of φρόνησις, practical reason. It is not a science, for actions are subject to change (6.1140a33-1140b1). Yet, it is neither an art (6.1140b2-4), since action has an end in itself, ἔστι γὰρ αὐτὴ ἡ εὐπραξία τέλος (6.1140b5). *Phronēsis* is (like *technē*) a reasoned state, ἕξις μετὰ λόγου (6.1140b6; cf. 6.1140a21) that reasons truly about *praktikē* (as opposed to *poiētikē*), about action concerned with the good and bad for human beings, περὶ τὰ ἀνθρώπῳ ἀγαθὰ καὶ κακά (6.1140b6-7). This definition is arrived at by theorizing about who it is that is the φρόνιμος (6.1140a24-25). Paul reveals the same approach not only in the common advice that one should follow the temperate man, but also, in a subtler instance, when, in Rom. 11.25, he refers to those who think of themselves as clever, [παρ᾽ /ἐν] ἑαυτοῖς φρόνιμοι.

88. I.e., the *aretai* of the *psuchē* that are called 'ethical' (*Ethics* 6.1139a1). Aristotle defines the right, ὁ ὀρθός, as the choice of the mean, τὸ μέσον, avoidance of excess, ὑπερβολή, and deficiency, ἔλλειψις; the mean is prescribed by the right principle, ὁ λόγος ὁ ὀρθός (6.1138b19-20). This principle, in the moral sphere, works conjointly with choice, προαίρεσις, and choice is deliberate desire, ὄρεξις βουλευτική (6.1139a24). *Proairesis* is the efficient (ἡ κίνησις), not final (οὐχ οὗ ἕνεκα) cause of action. It is *orexis* and *logos*; it involves both *nous* and *hexis* (6.1139a31-34). Choice is called thought related to desire, or desire related to thought, ἢ ὀρεκτικὸς νοῦς...ἢ ὄρεξις διανοητική; a human being as an originator of action is a union of desire and intellect, καὶ τοιαύτη ἀρχὴ ἄνθρωπος (6.1139b5-6).

be sought outside human subjectivity. For Paul, Christ is the mean, the right principle, the being at the crossroads between humanity and divinity, error and truth. Paul's *euangelion* is the expression of this objectivity.

Practical reason, *phronēsis*, has not only an ethical but also a political side—practical reason applied to the community, wisdom concerned with the city. Political *phronēsis* comprises two elements. One is the 'master art',[89] the *phronēsis* of the political professional (a legislator, a reformer). The other, the *phronēsis* of routine politics, is concerned with particular acts and consists of deliberation and execution, which, thinks contemptuous Aristotle, pertain to a lower class, the rank and file of politics.[90] These latter, the 'doers' of particular things, are those who

89. ἀρχιτεκτονική (*Ethics* 6.1141b25; cf. 1094a14). The actual meaning of this term, of overarching importance, is professional knowledge, the one who knows his stuff. Thus, in *Poetics* (19.1456b11), it is applied to the rhetorician. See also *Ethics* 6.1142a12-23, where Aristotle refers to mathematicians and metaphysicians, among others. In 1 Cor. 3.10 Paul applies it to himself, σοφὸς ἀρχιτέκτων, in this case meaning the knowledge of community building, i.e. (as I read it) of politics.

While knowledge of universals is acquired in universities, and is open to the young, *phronēsis* is not available to them. For particulars involve time-bound experience (6.1142a16-20). The object of practical reason is the ultimate particular, τὸ ἐσχάτον (6.1142a25), grasped only by *nous*, intuitive reason, not reached by *logos*, argument, reasoning (6.1143b1). *Nous* is the faculty that mediates between variables and invariables, things changeable and things eternal, it makes the transition from particulars to universals (6.1143a35-1143b5). For the difference *nous–phronēsis*, see 6.1142a25-30).

Aristotle admits also of a secondary intuitive reason, which consists of undemonstrated sayings and opinions of experienced *presbuteroi* and *phronimoi* (6.1143b11-14). He calls this experience and cleverness 'eyes of the soul' (6.1144a30), and it amounts to a surrogate form of practical reason.

Practical reason is closely related to σύνεσις, or εὐσυνεσία, understanding, the difference being that while *phronēsis* issues commands, its end being what ought or not to be done, *sunesis* only judges, 'critiques' (6.1143a9-10). It is also close to γνώμη, discrimination (6.1143a19-24), and all belong to the class of endowments that make somone wise, and this is a time related category.

Note, however, that while practical reason is a means for becoming good, it is not formal cause of happiness. Possession of philosophic reason, σοφία, of higher knowledge alone is happiness. No matter how hard Aristotle tries to place high practical wisdom, *sophia* comes first (6.1143b17-1144a6). *Eudaimonia* is the activity of speculative reason (6.1144a5-6). Contemplation, θεωρία alone produces perfect happiness (10.1177a17).

90. οἱ χειροτέχναι, handicraftsmen, manual artisans (*Ethics* 6.1141b30), involved

'take part in politics'.[91] The first kind of *phronēsis* belongs to the divine function of lawmaking; the latter fulfills deliberative and judicial functions. These are the functions of political participants proper, the citizenry, the political dilettanti.

At the core of Aristotle's ethical theory is the question of the individual's happiness. Happiness culminates in pure contemplation (θεωρία, *theōria*), and this is manifestly far above the capacity of ordinary human nature. The faculty of contemplation is identified by Aristotle with the object of contemplation, with god.[92] For Paul, too, politics is not an end in itself but a means toward the end. His citizens are christ-types, but the end is being with Christ, undergoing one's own rising from the dead. Activity is, ultimately, insufficient; *pistis* alone determines salvation.[93] In effect, *pistis* is Paul's name for *theōria*.

in βουλευτική and πρακτική (6.1141a26).

91. πολιτεύεσθαι (*Ethics* 6.1141b28). This is precisely the form of the verb used in Phil. 1.27.

92. *Ethics* 10.1177b26-1178a4. Life of contemplation is superior to human nature, κρείττων ἢ κατ' ἄνθρωπον (10.1177b26-27); if any being is to reach this life it would do so not insofar as human but insofar as divine, οὐ γὰρ ᾗ ἄνθρωπός ἐστιν οὕτω βιώσεται, ἀλλ' ᾗ θεῖόν τι ἐν αὐτῷ ὑπάρχει (10.1177b27-28). *Nous* is divine, and life according to *nous* is superior to mere human life (10.1177b30-31). Humanity must entertain thoughts higher than its own kind; it must, so far as it can, aspire to immortality, ἀλλ' ἐφ' ὅσον ἐνδέχεται ἀθανατίζειν (10.1177b34), 'and strain every nerve' (Ross) to live according to the highest nature (10.1177b35). This is, in fact, 'the true self of each' (Rackham), since it is the masterly and better part of each, δόξειε δ' ἂν καὶ εἶναι ἕκαστος τοῦτο, εἴπερ τὸ κύριον καὶ ἄμεινον (10.1178a1-2). (While it is true that *kurios* is the LXX translation of יהוה, it may also be granted, that for a Hellensitic Jew philosophically inclined, the technical meaning of the Greek adjective *kurios*, supreme, authoritative, helps bring the Scripture in line with philosophical thinking. His heart must have missed a beat every time he heard it in a Greek's discourse.) The section ends in what is the Aristotelian equivalent of Pauline paraenesis: it would be absurd indeed were one to choose to live another's life and not his own (10.1178a3-4)! (See also Fritz and Kapp 1977: 122.) Aristotle identifies the faculty of contemplation, θεωρητικόν, with θεωρία τοῦ θεοῦ, the contemplation of god, and simply with ὁ θεός, the object of contemplation (Defourny 1977: 106).

93. Hence Paul's concern with flesh, body, soul, spirit, σάρξ, σῶμα, ψυχή, πνεῦμα. This is not anthropology but soteriology.

In an excursus, Festugière (1932a: 196-220) attempts but fails to convince that *pneuma* comes from a Rabbinical source that stands behind both Philo and Paul. This in an essay in which he brilliantly argues that the Pauline trichotomy σῶμα–ψυχή–πνεῦμα [νοῦς] is solidly rooted in Greek philosophy. Festugière overlooks the

Aristotle's Politics

Although for Aristotle the zenith of *eudaimonia* is reached in *theōria*, pure contemplation—a happiness beyond most human beings' ability—Aristotle is the last philosopher before the Enlightenment to hold together the intellect, the life of contemplation and scholarship, and the moral and political life.[94] It is also true, however, that he brings them to a point at which cleavage is unavoidable.

What makes a human being is life in a community with other human beings.[95] It is this aspect of human life with which political science proper is concerned.[96] Aristotle's thesis that perfect happiness is theoretical activity[97] has a counterpart in political theory: the concept of the good life (τὸ εὖ ζῆν, *to eu zēn*).[98]

Aristotle calls the 'supreme good' (τἀγαθὸν καὶ ἄριστον, *tagathon kai to ariston*) an end of action that is desired for its own sake, while everything else is desired for the sake of it.[99] Not to have one's life organized with a view to this end is a sign of great folly.[100] It is this end that is the object of politics, for man's highest good is to be part of the political structure, the (Greek) *polis*.[101]

A treatise called *Politics*, one of the 'exoteric' writings, was pub-

fact that Philo, a ferocious assimilator, a χώρα, receptacle, as Plato would have called him (Festugière 1932a: 212 n. 4), does not need a rabbi to adapt and invent. Also, Festugière does not see that *pneuma* is a great example of the Pauline production of a new language. While it is true that *pneuma* is Paul's equivalent for *nous*, Festugière posits an unknown source where none is needed, and errs twice, once about the Alexandrine, once about the Tarsian. Paul rejects *nous* precisely because of its grand, central place in pagan philosophy.

Note that in the enduring Classical tripartition νοῦς–ψυχή–σῶμα, *psuchē* acquires, in Hellenistic times, the dubious eminence of an intermediary, torn between earthly body and celestial mind, a schizophrenic entity, incarnated as Gnostic Sophia.

94. For a development of the topic, see Mingay 1987.
95. *Ethics* 10.1178b5-7.
96. Aristotle deals with both disciplines, Ethics and Politics, as part of one comprehensive 'philosophy of human affairs' (*Ethics* 10.1181b15), and calls ethics too a 'political science' (*Ethics* 1.1094a27-b11). See also Fritz and Knapp 1977: 123.
97. *Ethics* 10.1178b7.
98. *Politics* 1.1252b30-34, 1253a18-30. See Fritz and Knapp 1977: 121-24.
99. *Ethics* 1.1094a19-22.
100. *Eudemian Ethics* 1214b6-7. See also Kenny 1977.
101. *Politics* 1.1253a1-2.

lished in various parts, with different names, by Aristotle himself.[102] As it has come down to us, the *Politics* is a collection of essays edited after Aristotle's death, but it was already set in the format and order we know by Theophrastus, Aristotle's successor as the head of the Lyceum.

The *Politics* can be divided in three general parts, which deal, respectively, with theories, institutions and the ideal state. Within the first part, Book 1 deals with social and economic theories; Book 2 with theories and approximations of ideal states; and Book 3 with the general theory of political constitutions. Books 3 and 4 are concerned with the morphology and pathology of real politics. Books 5 and 6 discuss practical politics, the theory of revolution and the mode of organizing democracies and oligarchies for maximum stability. The third part, comprising Books 7 and 8, elaborates Aristotle's ideal state.

The Political Game. Aristotle envisioned the theory of both the household and the *polis* as a game. He refers to people, insofar as they are political beings, as pieces in a game of draughts.[103] The game, as he sees it, has two participants, the player and the one played with—the first 'naturally ruling', the second 'naturally ruled'.[104] The political game itself is called 'the art of ruling and of being ruled'[105], and the purpose of the game is to ensure σωτηρία (*sōtēria*), the security of both.

The subject of the *Politics* is the Greek *polis*, of which Aristotle knew about 150 varieties. The *polis* occurs and develops 'by *phusis*'—that is, its essence is its growth from a potentiality to an end. The end of the *polis* is the nature of the *polis*,[106] and this nature is also the cause of its

102. As noted before, the expression, ἐξωτερικοὶ λόγοι, exoteric works, is found in Aristotle himself (e.g. *Ethics* 1.1102a26, 6.1140a3, *Politics* 3.1278b31, 7.1323a22: see Bonitz 1955, *s.v.* Ἀριστοτέλης, 104b44-105a27), but not consistently with the meaning given it later. A more useful distinction is that between the works published by Aristotle himself and those not prepared for publication but which probably circulated as course textbooks or lecture notes. To this latter class belong essentially all extant works. 'Exoteric' is also a term applied to books written by Aristotle for publication; of these none survived. See W. Smith 1858, *s.v.* Aristoteles, 319-24; *OCD, s.v.* Aristotle, 115-16.

103. *Politics* 1.1253a6-7.

104. ἄρχον καὶ ἀρχόμενον φύσει (*Politics* 1.1252a31).

105. τὸ ἄρχειν καὶ ἄρχεσθαι (*Politics* 1.1254a22).

106. In Aristotle, the state is based on nature not on contract. The contractual nature of the state is raised as an issue by the Sophists (Guthrie 1977: 6, 141-43). Plato too opposes this; indeed Glaucon's statement of this theory is in effect a refor-

beginning. The *polis* is for the Greek only; the non-Greeks (τὰ ἔθνη, *ta ethnē*) and the slaves are 'by *phusis*' incapable of making the *polis*.[107]

In Aristotle's method, which is informed by his concept of process,[108] *phusis* is the end proper to each thing,[109] that is, what each thing is when its growth is completed.[110] Not accidentally, this notion resembles Plato's understanding of *dikaiosunē*. For Plato, political justice is found in the determined and immutable station of every member of the city. In Aristotle, justice (or the determination of what is just) is an ordering of the political association; *dikaiosunē* is an element of the state.[111] While in Plato justice is the knowledge that one is in his naturally determined place, for Aristotle justice is inherent in the *polis*—that is, justice is the individual's growth toward his naturally intended end. The *polis* exists by nature,[112] among other reasons, because, as an end, as the completion of man and of his self-development and self-expression, it is natural in itself. The state is the highest self-sufficiency (αὐτάρκεια, *autarkeia*).[113] Moreover, the *polis* exists through human will and action. A human being, in Aristotle's famous dictum, is by nature a political being.[114] This means that the human aim is reached by sharing in the life of the (Greek) state. For Aristotle, the apolitical individual (ὁ ἄπολις, *ho apolis*)—that is, the individual who by misfortune (the exile, the outcast) or by nature (the political genius) is without a city—is either deficient in humanity or better than human.[115] Finally, the city is 'by

mulation of Thrasymachus's politics of egotism (*Republic* 2.358e-359c). Nevertheless, Socrates' argument in the *Crito* might be read as a positive use of a social compact theory.

107. When Aristotle discusses his ideal state, and looks at the ideal natural features of its inhabitants, he establishes that the North and the West are martial but dull, the East intelligent and refined but slavish. In other words, the ideal is represented, again, by the Hellenes (*Politics* 7.1327b18-40).

108. τὰ πράγματα φυόμενα βλέψειεν (*Politics* 1.1252a24).

109. ἡ φύσις τέλος ἐστίν (*Politics* 1.1252b33).

110. *Politics* 1.1252b34-35.

111. ἡ δὲ δικαιοσύνη πολιτικόν (*Politics* 1.1253a37).

112. πόλις φύσει ἐστίν (*Politics* 1.1252b31).

113. *Politics* 1.1253a2. Self-sufficiency of individual and of state, is, with a Stoic touch, also in Paul's mind in 1 Thess. 4.11. For *autarkeia* as enabled by God see 2 Cor. 9.8.

114. ἄνθρωπος φύσει πολιτικὸν ζῷον (*Politics* 1.1253a3). A passage (a8-18) explains the distinction of man from animals: language, that brings about the perception of good and bad. The same formula appears also in *Politics* 3.1278b19.

115. *Politics* 1.1252a5. Aristotle's *politikon zōon* is the counterpart of Plato's

nature' because it is prior—as the whole precedes the part in the order of nature—to both the family and the individual.[116] Politics dominates everything, even fashioning the system of religious belief. Religion always follows the state, and the temporal determines the faith.[117]

Aristotle continues by detailing various aspects of the 'game' of the ruler and the ruled. These are of relevance to Hellenistic thought, and eventually to Paul, and are therefore worth examining. The game is impossible among barbarians.[118] A uniform condition of slavery kills the political art, the art of ruling and being ruled. The barbarians' only way of entering the game is as slaves of the Greeks. Since there is no practical difference between barbarians and slaves,[119] the Greeks are naturally entitled to rule them.[120]

Among the Greeks, the game covers three cases: the *polis*, Greek war captives, and the household (οἶκος, *oikos*). Politics proper make sense only in the *polis* because statesmanship is the rule of men who are free and equal,[121] and, in its characteristic form, the political game is a rule by turns in a society of equals.[122] War, a mode of acquisition that is natural and naturally just,[123] leaves the prisoner Greek free even if he is legally a slave.

In examining these three cases—*polis*, the owner–slave relationship, and the household—Aristotle begins with the *oikos*. Aristotle's investigation of the household and of the art of household management

'noble lie'. Aristotle rejects Plato's 'noble lie' and his 'humans of gold'. Aristotle's critique of Plato's *Republic* is addressed primarily to all aspects in Plato's scheme that threaten the game. Plato's stand on property is such an example. Aristotle objects also to the state proposed in the *Laws*, again on the grounds of effacing the game. Plato does not explain, for example, how the ruler is to differ from the ruled. See *Politics* 1.1260b27-1266a30.

116. καὶ πρότερον δὴ τῇ φύσει πόλις ἢ οἰκία καὶ ἕκαστος ἡμῶν ἐστίν (*Politics* 1.1253a19). Also, the *polis* is part and end of a sequence of naturals (individual, household, village) (1.1252b32).

117. *Politics* 1.1252b25-29.

118. *Politics* 1.1252b6-8.

119. *Politics* 1.1252b9.

120. *Politics* 1.1252a35-b1.

121. *Politics* 1.1255b20.

122. *Politics* 1.1259b5. Note that the entire theory of game, and especially of a rule by turns is non-Platonic and anti-Platonic.

123. *Politics* 1.1256b24.

(οἰκονομία, *oikonomia*) is a landmark of political economics.[124] House-hold management entails the use of property[125] and involves the relations between the householder and his wife, children and slaves.[126] Unlike the political game, where the statesman is the ruler and his rule is political, in the domestic game the ruler is the master (δεσπότης, *despotēs*) and his government is of the monarchical type, the rule of one alone.[127] More precisely, the head of the *oikos* exercises a household power (ἀρχὴ οἰκονομική, *archē oikonomikē*) that takes three forms: despotic, toward his slaves; 'political', or marital, toward his wife; and royal, or fatherly, toward his children.[128]

Aristotle clearly distinguishes between domestic power and political power proper,[129] yet the relation between husband and wife is of a

124. Aristotle distinguishes between *oikonomia* and the art of acquisition of property, χρηματιστική (*Politics* 1.1253b14). He concludes that 'chrematistic', since it relinquishes good life for anxiety over livelihood, τὸ σπουδάζειν περὶ τὸ ζῆν ἀλλὰ μὴ τὸ εὖ ζῆν (1.1257b42), is not part of *oikonomia* and that, in the particular case of money-making, it is even unnatural, οὐ κατὰ φύσιν (1.1258a11, Barker's trans.). Chrematistic, accumulation, is a desire, ἐπιθυμία, and as such knows no limit, ἄπειρον (1.1258a1; cf. 1.1257b40). It is the nature of desire to be infinite, ἄπειρος γὰρ ἡ τῆς ἐπιθυμίας φύσις, he says elsewhere, repeating Plato's view (2.1267b4). The same analogy is made by Plato between the craftsman and desire.

125. *Politics* 1.1258a29-b15.

126. *Politics* 1.1259a37-1260b26.

127. ἡ μὲν οἰκονομικὴ μοναρχία (e.g. *Politics* 1.1255b20).

128. ἀρχὴ δεσποτική, ἀρχὴ πολιτική/γαμική, and ἀρχὴ βασιλική/πατρική respectively (*Politics* 1253b19-20, 1254b4-5, 1259a37-b17). Paul produces a formula that seems to combine the domestic *politikē*, internally, with a political *basilikē*, externally. In other words, a political type of government within the *ekklēsia*, with a universal metaphysical kingship.

129. Both Plato (*Politicus* 258e-259c) and Aristotle (*Politics* 3.1285b32, where kingship is compared with household rule) make the household/political power analogy. Aristotle, however, makes an explicit distinction between the two. He insists that the difference between *politikon, basilikon, oikonomikon* or *despotikon* is a difference in kind, and not a simple difference of numbers (of the rulers or of the ruled) (*Politics* 1.1252a7-9, 1253b19-23). See also Barraclough 1984: 518.

Aristotle, and the Peripatetics, make a clear differentiation between οἰκία and πόλις, household and city. The difference consists in that οἰκονομία (household rule) is monarchical, while πολιτική (politics, state government) is not. The crucial distinction (cf. also Plato's *Politicus*) is obliterated in Hellenistic times and the two become identified. Monarchy treats the state as its household. The motif is important also in Ps.-Aristotle's *Oeconomia* 1.1343a3-4, attributed to Theophrastus by Philodemus of Gadara, a first century BCE Epicurean (Aadlers 1975: 47).

'political' type,[130] in which the ruler and the ruled are equal yet distinct, and the distinction is established by ensigns, modes of address and titles of respect.[131] The master's rule is, however, permanent and the language of power permanently univocal. That is, while political rule proper allows for an interchange of roles and for a flexible language, the husband-wife relation is irreversible and the language that distinguishes the ruler from the one ruled is rigid. The relation between father and child is of the royal type (βασιλική),[132] marked by affection and seniority.[133] The relation of the master to the household slaves raises some complex issues.

Aristotle's Theory of Slavery. The theme of slavery looms large in Aristotle. He is among the earliest western thinkers to ask questions about slavery[134] and to deal with it on a rational basis and not just matter-of-factly. Aristotle argues that the difference between the master and the slave is a natural difference[135]—that is, a real disparity, not merely one, as some say, based on convention (νόμος, *nomos*) and relying on force and, as such, unjust.[136] The question of the dissimilarity between master and slave is set in the larger framework of the difference between the ruler and the ruled.[137] In this specific case the distinction is one of kind, not of degree,[138] which means that the difference extends to the soul, as well. Those who are ruled have reason (λόγος, *logos*) in common with the ruler, since they are all human beings,[139] but the ruled are otherwise deficient. Even if both ruler and ruled share in *arete*, their participation in it is different.[140] Thus, the deliberative faculty (τὸ βουλευτικόν, *bouleutikon*) (*Politics* 1.1260a13) is faulty in the ruled: inconclusive in the wife, immature in the child, absent in the slave. Consequently, their moral

130. *Politics* 1.1259b1.
131. σχήμασι καὶ λόγοις καὶ τιμαῖς (*Politics* 1.1259b8).
132. *Politics* 1.1259b1.
133. *Politics* 1.1259b12.
134. It is also through Aristotle that we know of divergent positions, against which he takes a strong stand (e.g. *Politics* 1.1253b15-23).
135. φύσει διαφέρειν (*Politics* 1.1253b22).
136. *Politics* 1.1253b20-23.
137. *Politics* 1.1259b22-1260a2.
138. τὸ μὲν γὰρ ἄρχεσθαι καὶ ἄρχειν εἴδει διαφέρει, τὸ δὲ μᾶλλον καὶ ἧττον οὐδέν (*Politics* 1.1259b37-38).
139. *Politics* 1.1259b28.
140. *Politics* 1.1260a3-4.

excellence[141] is different; while complete in the master, it is present in the others only in the measure necessary for the discharge of their proper functions.[142]

Aristotle constantly stresses the analogy between various forms of human community and the soul. In the game of ruler and ruled, it is always the *psuchē* that is the game-table. It is the psychological factor that frustrates equality and that explains the differences. If both master and slave, man and woman, partake in gentility,[143] why is there the distinction between ruler and ruled? The difference, a difference of kind, is imposed by nature[144] and is founded in the strict dichotomy of the soul: the soul's rational and irrational components (λόγον and ἀλόγον, *logon* and *alogon*), a ruling and a ruled part, to which different *aretai* belong.[145] This psychological fatalism makes it 'natural' for the free to rule the slave, the male the female, and the father the child (*Politics* 1260a10). Though all human beings possess the different parts of the soul, Aristotle insists that they possess them differently.[146]

The structural similarity between the *psuchē* and the *polis* was a given of Greek thought—an invariable, ruthless datum whose foundation lay in a rigorous philosophical system that liked to think in terms of perfect order, grand unifying theories and absolute truths. In Plato, the three powers of the state are the deliberative (βουλευτικόν, *bouleutikon*), the military (ἐπικουρικόν, *epikourikon*) and the economic (χρηματιστικόν, *chrēmatistikon*). These correspond to the three faculties of the soul: the rational (λογιστικόν, *logistikon*), the spirited (θυμοειδές, *thumoeides*) and the appetitive (ἐπιθυμητικόν, *epithumētikon*).[147] As Aristotle puts it, using a hysteron-proteron approach, it is in living beings that one can first observe both despotic rule (the power, in the

---

141. ἠθικὴ ἀρετή (*Politics* 1.1260a21). E.g. temperance, courage and justice. That women's foremost virtue is silence, is buttressed with a quote from Sophocles (*Ajax* 293, *ap.* 1.1260a31).

142. *Politics* 1.1260a2-20. Such notions of inequality within an essentially equalitarian domestic household, informed by cooperation and concern for each other's good, would be long lived, and in the form of distributive justice, also Aristotle's, would reappear with great force in Hellenistic political culture and in Paul's concept of *pistis*.

143. μετέχειν καλοκἀγαθίας (*Politics* 1259b35-36).

144. *Politics* 1.1259b37-38.

145. *Politics* 1.1260a5-8.

146. *Politics* 1.1260a11-12.

147. *Republic* 4.434a-d.

household, of the master over the slave) and political rule (of the statesman over the fellow citizens); likewise, the soul rules the body, with despotic power, and the mind rules the drives with the authority of the statesman or of the king.[148] The organization of the household and of the city is parallel to the constitution of the soul: the soul's authority over the body is despotic and absolute; reason rules over desires monarchically and constitutionally.[149] Soul and society are in an osmotic flow.[150]

148. *Politics* 1.1254b4-6.
149. See also A. Delatte 1922: 90; Erskine 1990: 196.
150. Note the absolute dominion of the soul over the body. Also, the position of desires: they are to be tempered and bonded as citizens, controlled not destroyed, made productive not repressed. Diogenes Laertius (5.31) informs us that Aristotle taught that the wise was not exempt from passions but indulged them in moderation, ἔφη δὲ τὸν σοφὸν ἀπαθῆ μὲν μὴ εἶναι, μετριοπαθῆ δέ. For the Peripatetics the passions should be restrained, *metriopatheia*, not eliminated, *apatheia*, as the Stoics would demand. (See also Gottschalk 1987: 1144.) Though a Peripatetic term *metriopatheia* is not found in the available Aristotelian corpus. *Metriopatheia* makes it into the New Testament (unlike *apatheia*), in Heb. 5.2, for describing the person and the teachings of Jesus the high priest. Tit. 3.2 expresses a view fully consistent with *metriopatheia*, '...be not contentious (ἀμάχους εἶναι); show perfect gentleness towards all people....' The context indicates that the author is less interested in the ethical aspect of passions (Tit. 3.3-8) than in the political one: obedience to political authorities (Tit. 3.1) and strict avoidance of factionalism (Tit. 3.9-11). Cf. also 1 Thess. 4.11, 2 Thess. 3.12, where Paul counsels for a disciplined and harmonious society, for living tranquilly, for minding one's own business and for being self-sufficient.
It should be also noticed that, in ethics, three Peripatetic theses gained wide currency among the Platonists: the notion that virtue is a mean, the notion that virtue is not sufficient for happiness without a measure of bodily and external goods, Aristotle's famous *chorēgia*, and the acceptance, in moderation, of passions. All three were prominent in the doctrine of Peripatos during the Hellenistic era. They featured in Antiochus of Ascalon's teaching and in Arius Didymus's handbook, and no doubt in many similar productions, now lost. Knowledge of these features cannot be taken as evidence of direct acquaintance with Aristotle's works (Gottschalk 1987: 1144). Given, however, that the second and third theses were violently opposed by the Stoics and by the rigorous Pythagoreans and Platonists, their endurance and circulation shows, I think, the acceptance of Aristotle's practical philosophy in large circles of popular (and even professional) philosophers.
Paul's approach to ethics shows acquaintance with all these three Peripatetic notions: he condemns both excess and defect in display of excellence; insists on the well-being of the body (his own or of others), so much so that *sōma* is included in salvation; and allows for a measure of weakness.

It must be emphasized, however, that Aristotle's argument about the naturalness of slavery applies to the household slave only, and makes sense within the distinction he works out between action and production.[151] The slave is concerned with the life of the household, with action (πρᾶξις, *praxis*), not production (ποίησις, *poiēsis*).[152] Action (doing) is complete in itself. Production (making) has an end other than itself. The slave helps in household living and in the performance of household activities, not in the manufacture of goods. Aristotle would have been hard pressed to justify slavery in the latter case. The nature (*phusis*) and quality (*dunamis*) of the slave are defined thus: a slave is any human being who, by nature, does not belong to himself but to another; who, while a human being, is, insofar as he is another's, an article of property;[153] and who, as an article of property, is an instrument of action, separable from his owner.[154]

By nature, a slave is a 'person-body' whose function is bodily service. The slave is a tool, but a tool of action. He and his master relate to one another as the part to the whole, as the body to the mind. In his totality, the slave is only a part, though a separable part, of his master.[155] A slave by nature is—and this point is essential—a person for whom slavery is the better and just condition.[156] And the further crucial qualification is that, for the natural slave, the relation between the master and the slave is one of friendship and reciprocal interest.[157] Recognition of the merit of their respective situations is the key factor of the master-slave relation. Slave and master are in a state of completion, best for each, and according to their proper ends.[158] A relation of obedience and willingness exists also between the ruler and the ruled in general.[159]

151. *Politics* 1.1253b23-1254a17.
152. *Politics* 1.1254a6.
153. ὃς ἂν κτῆμα ᾖ ἄνθρωπος (*Politics* 1.1254a16).
154. ὄργανον πρακτικὸν καὶ χωριστόν (*Politics* 1.1254a17).
155. *Politics* 1.1254a17-1255a2.
156. βέλτιον καὶ δίκαιον (*Politics* 1.1254a18). Aristotle extends the natural slave argument to war, which makes some masters over 'those who deserve to be slaves' (*Politics* 7.1334a2). See Erskine 1990: 197.
157. συμφέρον ἐστί τι καὶ φιλία δούλῳ καὶ δεσπότῃ πρὸς ἀλλήλους (*Politics* 1.1255b13). When slavery rests on legal sanction only, on mere superior power, the relation is one of enmity and conflict of interests (1.1255b15).
158. *Politics* 1.1254a17-1255b15.
159. This treatment of slavery, the most exhaustive until the age of geographical

The political theory that occupies Book 3 of the *Politics* concerns the rules of the game of ruler and ruled—that is, the constitution (πολιτεία, *politeia*). But this discussion first demands a clarification of what the game is (i.e. the nature of the *polis*), and this, in turn, requires three additional clarifications: who the citizen (πολίτης, *politēs*) is; who the ruler (i.e. πολιτικός, *politikos*, lit. the statesman) is; and how many kinds of games there are (i.e. how the ruler and the ruled are distinguished).

The citizen, according to Aristotle, is a participant in the political game, a man who shares in a deliberative or judicial office[160] for any period of time. Aristotle makes a far-reaching distinction between political *aretē*, the excellence of a good citizen, and the excellence of the good man. The first *aretē* is relative to a particular constitution[161] and hence has many varieties; the second is unique and perfect.[162] While these two species of virtue can never be identical for the ruled, even if they live under the ideal constitution, in such a state the statesman *can* achieve this equivalence.[163] The difference between the ruler and the ruled is only relative, however, for the *aretē* of the citizen is both to rule and to be ruled well.[164] In the political game proper,[165] each citizen, equal to all other citizens, must, as a ruler, know how to rule over free men and must, as one who is ruled, know how to be obedient.[166]

The theory of constitution, *politeia*, is probably the core of Aristotle's political thought. Here, Aristotle approaches the definition of 'constitu-

---

explorations, in the sixteenth century, would inform all thinking on the subject in antiquity, and it would be, by whatever routes, inescapable for Paul as well.

160. κοινωνεῖν ἀρχῆς βουλευτικῆς ἢ κριτικῆς (*Politics* 3.1275b18-20).

161. ἀρετὴν...πρὸς τὴν πολιτείαν (*Politics* 3.1276b31).

162. μίαν ἀρετὴν...τὴν τελείαν (*Politics* 3.1276b34).

163. *Politics* 3.1277a21.

164. ἡ ἀρετὴ εἶναι τὸ δύνασθαι καὶ ἄρχειν καὶ ἄρχεσθαι καλῶς (*Politics* 3.1277a27).

165. As distinguished from the domestic game, in which the ruler must know his prerogatives and how to use language and the ruled is inferior and servile (*Politics* 3.1277a34-1277b2).

166. *Politics* 3.1277b7-b13. Next, he alludes to the perfect political game, i.e. the situation under an ideal constitution (3.1277b14-33); this will form the matter of Chapter 7 of *Politics*. Aristotle discusses also the case of the 'bad people', hired workers and little entrepreneurs. As in Plato, they are out of the game, for, for want of leisure, they cannot pursue excellence. For Aristotle, they must not be citizens (3.1277b33-1278b5).

tion' in two ways: politically[167] and teleologically.[168] The political definition of constitution has to do with how the *polis* is organized with regard to all its offices but especially with regard to the civic body (πολίτευμα, *politeuma*) that is sovereign in a state.[169] This way of defining a constitution takes into consideration the fact that the end of the *polis* is the satisfaction of human beings' natural impulse for social life, together with the fulfilment of the common interest in the good life and the support of life pure and simple—the good that comes from the simple act of living.[170]

Polity and the Mean. Aristotle's classification of constitutions follows, as a fundamental principle, the common interest (τὸ κοινὸν συμφέρον, *to koinon sumpheron*).[171] Aristotle is clear that 'constitution' (*politeia*) is the same as 'civic body' (*politeuma*) and that the latter is the sovereign (*to kurion*) in every *polis*.[172] Aristotle identifies three right and three devious) forms of government,[173] which differ according to whether power is held by one, few or many. The three right forms are kingship, aristocracy and 'polity'; tyranny, oligarchy and democracy are their perverted correlates.[174] 'Right constitutions'[175] is the expression used by Aristotle to refer to those constitutions that aim at the common good.[176] 'Polity' (*politeia*), the generic name for 'constitution', becomes the type of constitution in which the masses govern for the common interest.[177] Yet Aristotle, first and alone among the ancient political philosophers, understands that the number of those who hold power is an accidental attribute of a constitution, and that the real determinant in

---

167. *Politics* 3.1278b5-1280a6 and 4.1290a30-1294b42.
168. *Politics* 3.1288a32-b6 and 4.1295a25-1296b11.
169. *Politics* 3.1278b9-11.
170. *Politics* 3.1278b20-30.
171. *Politics* 3.1279a29, 34, 37, cf. 1278b22, 1279a17; *Ethics* 8.1160a14.
172. *Politics* 3.1279a26-27.
173. ὀρθαί and παρεκβάσεις respectively (*Politics* 3.1279a18, 20).
174. *Politics* 3.1279a27-b10.
175. ὀρθαὶ πολιτεῖαι (*Politics* 3.1279a17-18).
176. τὸ κοινῇ συμφέρον σκοποῦσιν (*Politics* 3.1279a18). Plato calls these ὀρθοὶ νόμοι (*Laws* 4.715b). Paul uses a strikingly similar expression, ὀρθοποδοῦσιν πρὸς ἀλήθειαν τοῦ εὐαγγελίου, in an even more strikingly similar context, to refer to the *euangelion*: when he opposes his own constitution to the judaizing one of Peter, in Gal. 2.14. See also 2 Tim. 2.15, ὀρθοτομοῦντα τὸν λόγον τῆς ἀληθείας.
177. *Politics* 3.1279a38-39.

the classification of states is the distribution of wealth.[178] The socio-economic class of those holding power constitutes the real difference between democracy and oligarchy.[179] Aristotle takes up this subject again in Book 4,[180] where he critiques classifications that rely on the criterion of number, whether based on wealth, birth or occupation. He warns against the fallacy of argument from language and against generalizations. For example, descriptions of democracy as 'the greater number sovereign' or 'the free-born sovereign' or of oligarchy as 'the rich sovereign' are not necessarily true.[181] Aristotle insists that, for proper classification of states, three criteria must be fulfilled simultaneously: for democracy, the rulers must be freeborn and poor; for oligarchy, few, better-born and rich.[182] But, he notes, in practice there is only one division, that based on the socio-economic criterion.[183]

Aristotle goes on to discuss each form of constitution, the right constitutions and their depraved forms in all their variety. Since 'polity' and mixed constitutions[184] were to be extremely influential in Hellenistic and Roman times, they deserve special attention.[185]

Aristotle begins by treating 'polity' as a form of aristocracy. 'Polity' is actually called 'aristocracy' in most states;[186] language carries the biased assumption that culture and breeding belong to the wealthy; the rich alone are called gentlemen. Thus it is thought that the rule of law describes the government of the best and that 'the best' cannot refer to

---

178. Aristotle is absorbed by this question, as witnessed by the numerous passages where it appears. To take *Politics* alone, we see the rich–poor opposition, and the related problem of class, in 3.1279b6-40; 1281a12-19; 4.1289b29-32; 1290a30-b20; 1290b38-1291a40; 1291b2-13; 1292a30; 1296a22-32; 1296b24-34; 1299b38; 6.1315a31-33; 1317b2-10; 1318a31-32. Revealing are also the Greek terms available to describe the two classes. The rich: *chrestoi* (useful, worthy); *beltistoi* (best); *dunatoi* (powerful); *gnorimoi* (notable); *gennaioi* (well born). The poor: *hoi polloi* (many); *cheirones* (mean); *poneroi* (knaves); *ochlos* (mob). (This applies to Latin as well. Rich: *boni, optimi*; poor: *plebs, multitudo, improbi*.) See also Finley 1983: 2.

179. *Politics* 3.1279b10-1280a6.

180. *Politics* 4.1295a25-1296b11.

181. *Politics* 4.1290a30-b6.

182. *Politics* 4.1290b19-20.

183. *Politics* 4.1291b9.

184. *Politics* 4.1293b22-1294b42.

185. Although in the *Laws* Plato advanced a (tripartite) mixed constitution, it was Aristotle who, by his thorough investigation of the mixed constitution system, completed the canon of pagan political meditation for centuries to come.

186. *Politics* 4.1294a15-16.

the poorer sort. This problem will persist, Aristotle says, until it is realized that there are three elements to be equally considered in a constitution: not only free birth and wealth, but also excellence (*aretē*).[187] Once this third element is introduced it becomes possible to distinguish between aristocracy and polity. Both are mixed constitutions. Aristocracy is a blend of all three elements,[188] with pure aristocracy distributing offices strictly according to *aretē*.[189] 'Polity' is a mixture of two only: free birth and wealth (*Politics* 4.1294a23). Hence, 'polity' represents a compromise between democracy (where free birth is the defining criterion) and oligarchy (the rule of the wealthy). There are three possible ways to create this mix. First, there can be a state in which every political institution combines democratic and oligarchic features. Second, a state may find a mean between the two. Third, a state might take some elements of each.[190] Aristotle determines that the best result comes from taking two criteria into consideration: the criterion of proper mixture (a mean between extremes) and the criterion of inner strength (undesirability of change). In this way a good mixture between democracy and oligarchy is achieved.[191] In other words, the political definition of constitution arrives at the notion of the mean, and the name of this constitution is 'polity'.

    For the teleological definition of constitution, Aristotle uses the same method and means he employed when he spoke about the way an individual achieves goodness. In *Ethics*[192] and again in *Politics*, Aristotle declares that the happy life is the life without impediments (poverty and disease) lived according to *aretē*. *Aretē* is a mean—it is the mean that qualifies the best way of life, a mean attainable by each individual.[193] What is true for each citizen of the political body is also true for the sum, the constitution, for the constitution is the way of life of the *polis*.[194] By developing his argument in this way, Aristotle is led again, inevitably, to the notion of the mean. According to Aristotle, the social structure of most states consists of the filthy rich, the dirt poor and the

187. *Politics* 4.1294a19-20.
188. *Politics* 4.1294a24-25.
189. *Politics* 4.1294a9-10.
190. *Politics* 4.1294a30-b42.
191. *Politics* 4.1294b14-18.
192. *Ethics* 1.1101a14-22.
193. *Politics* 4.1295a36-39.
194. *Politics* 4.1295a39-b1.

middle class. Each of these classes has its specific psychology and role in the political game. The very rich, also called masters (i.e. those at one extreme, excess[195]), are violent and beyond the law. They are high-spirited and know only how to rule, not how to obey. The very poor, also called slaves (those at the other extreme, defect[196]), are rogues and outside the law. Poor-spirited, they know only how to obey, not how to rule. The middle class is the mean. Its members are ready to listen to reason, suffer least from ambition and are therefore the perfect players in the rule-ruled game.[197] Again, it is this game, as ruler-ruled balance, that describes a proper constitution. Willingness, friendship and exchange of roles are emphasized.[198] Under actual conditions, the constitution based on the middle class is the best, and the best form of political society is 'polity', whose existence depends on there being a sizable middle class.[199] Both the political and the teleological definitions of constitution arrive inexorably at the theory of the mean, Aristotle's *clef de voûte*, the first leading to 'polity', the second to the middle class.[200]

195. They are super-handsome, super-strong, super-noble, super-wealthy, ὑπέρκαλον, ὑπερίσχυρον, ὑπερευγενῆ, ὑπερπλούσιον (4.1295b6-7).

196. Super-poor, super-weak, exceedingly wretched, ὑπέρπτωχον, ὑπερασθενῆ, σφόδρα ἄτιμον (4.1295b8).

197. Note the striking terminology of masters and slaves, although Aristotle describes *poleis*, Greek states, not barbarian or abstract societies. Note also how he moves from social class to psychology, maintaining the firm analogy society–soul.

198. This extends to property as well. Aristotle begins his critique of other ideal-state theories (Book 2), with an analysis of the question of property. Starting with Plato's common property community, described in the *Republic*, he asks whether common property should be in all things or only in some (*Politics* 2.1261a37-39), and whether property should be in common at all or privately held (2.1262b37-40). He answers that, for the best political society, possession should be private, use common among friends (2.1263a21-40). See also A.C. Mitchell 1992: 262.

199. It bears emphasizing that polity is the best constitution under *actual* conditions. The middle class vanishes in Aristotle's ideal state.

200. In *Politics* 3.1281a39-1282b14, Aristotle assesses again the cumulative political and aesthetical excellence of the many. He ascertains that collective excellence of the mass surpasses both individual excellence and the sum of its parts. Aristotle notes that the deliberative and judicial functions, i.e. electing and checking on magistrates, is the proper domain of the mass' sovereignty. The Court, the Council, the Assembly, traditionally the offices of the mass, are properly sovereign on issues more important than those assigned to the better sort of citizens. The effort to achieve the best society under existent conditions characterizes Paul's political

Justice and the Law. Aristotle's theory of kingship[201] also reverberates through Hellenistic and Roman political theory. Having resolved that the middle class is the basis for the best constitution, he wonders about the case of the political genius in such a society.[202] Since such a man would be like a god among men,[203] Aristotle counsels that the political genius should either be ostracized or made king. This leads to the question of kingship (βασιλεία, *basileia*). The main problem that Aristotle has with monarchical varieties of constitution is the effect that they have on the political game. A *polis* with no game is a contradiction in terms. Yet, monarchy in the form of absolute kingship (παμβασιλεία, *pambasileia*)[204] is a very tempting constitution. The Platonic philosopher-king seems to haunt Aristotle, who is also obsessed by the specter of his pupil Alexander. Aristotle is enticed by the unlimited possibilities that the unconstrained person of a genius-king could unleash and control. It is especially the generality of law, whose practicality is always limited given the diversity of situations that arise in life, that recommends the *pambasileus*. Because such a king would be a law unto himself, he could tailor the law to suit the particularities of each individual case. Ever loyal to the *polis*, however, Aristotle restores the game through his emphasis on the law: whatever may be lost, because of the law, in spontaneity, more is gained by virtue of the law's impartiality. The king himself must be subject to the law, for even the best human is still a beast, subject to appetite and violence.[205] Law alone is impartial, intellect without desire.[206] Nevertheless, the case for an absolute king has been made. From here to a divine king is only a leisurely run.

Reflections about justice, *dikaiosunē*, play a part in both approaches to the definition of constitution.[207] As we have already seen, for Aristotle *dikaiosunē* is an ordering of the political association;[208] justice is inherent in the *polis* conceived as growth to a naturally intended end.

---

thought as well.
201. *Politics* 3.1284b35-1288b6.
202. *Politics* 3.1284a3-b34.
203. θεὸν ἐν ἀνθρώποις εἰκός (*Politics* 3.1284a10).
204. Politics 3.1285b33.
205. ἐπιθυμία...καὶ ὁ θυμός (*Politics* 3.1287a31).
206. ἄνευ ὀρέξεως νοῦς ὁ νόμος ἐστίν (*Politics* 3.1287a32).
207. *Politics* 3.1280a7-1284b34, 4.1292b22-1293a34.
208. *Politics* 1.1253a37.

What is the end (*telos*) of the state? For Aristotle the *telos* of any science or art is a good.[209] Since political activity[210] is the most lordly (κυριωτάτα, *kuriōtata*) of all sciences and arts, its *telos* is the greatest good. The name of the political good is justice.[211] Aristotle's reflections on *polis* are tied to the question of justice. That justice could be discussed outside the context of the political (and by extension, the psychological) was inconceivable to a Greek. Even when applied in the ethical—i.e. the psychological—sphere, the concept of justice makes sense only because of the charge it carries over from the political. A good, right, just human individual outside the *polis* is a preposterous concept. The political is the proper domain for a discussion of justice, and, outside it, the notion evaporates into thin air.

To understand a political system is therefore tantamount to investigating its understanding of justice. Thus, when Aristotle looks at a power system he looks for the significance justice has in it, the way in which it constructs and expounds justice. The interpretation of justice is the signature of a state, and the state itself is the expression of its conception of justice. Nothing makes a *polis*, not laws and not territory, but justice. This reminder is necessary only for the modern reader, sundered as we are from political reflection. For the ancient Greek it was a matter of course. Justice, however, was as tangled and controversial an issue for the Greeks as it remains for human beings today. The political was such a fundamental, innate component of the individual, the permeation of the citizen by power so complete, as to lead to an alteration, a mutation, in both the psychological and the rational functions, in fact and in theory. As psychic and conceptual life were configured by political form, so also their theorization was shaped by the particular political order that was their medium.[212]

It is the general opinion that justice is some kind of equality. But Aristotle's agreement with this truism stops here.[213] In analyzing the

---

209. *Politics* 3.1282b15-16.

210. πολιτικὴ δύναμις (*Politics* 3.1282b16). *Dunamis* is, in Aristotle's so-called esoteric writings, e.g. the *Metaphysics* or the *Analytics*, a technical term: potentiality, capacity for existence, capacity for activity, as opposed to ἐνέργεια, actuality. Here it is used in the somewhat less technical sense of faculty, capacity, activity.

211. *Politics* 3.1282b16-17.

212. See *Politics* 3.1280a20-23.

213. The issue of distributive justice, τὸ δίκαιον ἀνάλογον, and political justice, τὸ πολιτικὸν δίκαιον, was raised already in *Ethics* 5.1131a10-b24, 1134a25-b9, 1134b19-1135a15.

notion of power, Aristotle begins with the two extreme perceptions of power that hold sway in the opposite political anomalies known as democracy and oligarchy. These political systems codify justice differently. For democracy, the algorithm is, justice is equality; oligarchy has an equally simple formula: justice is inequality. That both positions are the result of *parti-pris*, that each is the consequence of a political knowledge and language that leaves no other choice to the adherents, becomes immediately apparent as Aristotle explodes the seemingly irreconcilable tension between the two.

Democrats and oligarchs agree that the essence of justice is equality, but both are in error about the meaning of equality, mistaking the part for the whole. Democrats, equal as to freedom of birth, wrongly think themselves to be entirely equal. Oligarchs, unequal in wealth to the rest of the populace, wrongly imagine themselves to be unequal in all other respects.[214] Both commit the fallacy of failing to consider full, absolute justice ,[215] and both fail to see the full reach of their principles.

Aristotle agrees with both, while disclosing their mistake. Justice *is* equality, but only for equals,[216] and justice *is also* inequality, but only for those who are unequal.[217] Justice, for Aristotle, is relative to persons.[218] Justice is the proportionate equality between the value of the things given and the value of the person receiving.[219]

Aristotle continues by reviewing opinions as to what constitutes the raison d'être of the state.[220] He refutes the view of the oligarchs that wealth is the foundation of a political community. He also denies that it is brotherhood that brings about alliances and contracts, as the democrats would have it. Aristotle is emphatic that a political entity is a state in name only if it is not concerned with political *aretē*.[221] The law (*nomos*) of the good *polis* is law that makes the citizens good and

---

214. See also A. Delatte 1922: 105.

215. πᾶν τὸ κυρίως δίκαιον (*Politics* 3.1280a11).

216. οἷον δοκεῖ ἴσον τὸ δίκαιον εἶναι καὶ ἔστιν ἀλλ᾽ οὐ πᾶσιν ἀλλὰ τοῖς ἴσοις (*Politics* 3.1280a12-13).

217. καὶ τὸ ἄνισον δοκεῖ δίκαιον εἶναι, καὶ γάρ ἐστιν, ἀλλ᾽ οὐ πᾶσιν ἀλλὰ τοῖς ἀνίσοις) (*Politics* 3.1280a13-14).

218. τὸ δίκαιον τισίν (*Politics* 3.1280a16).

219. Cf. *Ethics* 5.1131a14-24, distributive justice, to which Aristotle actually refers here.

220. *Politics* 3.1280a25-3.1281a10.

221. *Politics* 3.1280b7.

just.[222] The end of the *polis* is the good life.[223] Aristotle differentiates between law and justice: while laws are aimed at producing fine members of the state (i.e. fashioning citizens in the image of power), justice is a system of distribution of power that awards political rewards in proportion to civic merit. In other words, the laws of a state are a rule of life for the people who hold power. Justice is a universal political principle that describes and defines a properly constituted political structure. Law is distinguished from justice as means are distinct from end.

The law must rule, but laws must be rightly constituted,[224] for, by necessity, the laws only replicate the power system that created them.[225] There are good laws and bad, just laws and unjust. Only laws informed by the principle of distributive justice are good and just. Justice *is* the political good.[226] Justice is a principle of nature;[227] it is the very way the universe works. Justice might be thought of as 'pure' law: that is, law that is the structure of universal power, an absolute intelligence of value. Justice is the reason states—and laws—exist in the first place.

The theory of equality occupies a central place in Aristotle's detailed discussion of the distribution of power under different types of constitutions. It forms, as we have seen, the core of the critique of oligarchy and democracy.[228] It is those who contribute most to a properly constituted political association—a state whose end is good life—who ought to have a greater share in the *polis* and receive higher offices or honors, irrespective of birth or wealth. Civic excellence[229] is the criterion of equality as determined by justice.

Misunderstanding the nature of justice, as embodied in this type of equality, is the underlying origin of much political controversy and the main cause of dissension and resulting political ruin. Aristotle analyses this in the opening sections of his treatment of the general causes of constitutional shifts (στάσις, *stasis*) in Book 5.[230] *Stasis* means sedition

---

222. οἷος ποιεῖν ἀγαθοὺς καὶ δικαίους τοὺς πολίτας (*Politics* 3.1280b12).

223. τέλος μὲν οὖν πόλεως τὸ εὖ ζῆν (*Politics* 3.1280b40; cf. 3.1280a31, 3.1280b34, *passim*).

224. *Politics* 3.1282b1-2.

225. ὁμοίως ταῖς πολιτείαις ἀνάγκη...τοὺς νόμους (*Politics* 3.1282b8-9).

226. ἔστι δὲ τὸ πολιτικὸν ἀγαθὸν τὸ δίκαιον (*Politics* 3.1282b16-17).

227. See *Politics* 3.1287a11-19, 7.1325b6-12.

228. *Politics* 3.1280a8-1281a10, esp. 1280a7-18 and 1281a; cf. also 6.1317b, for democracy, and 5.1301a26-1301b4, for democracy and oligarchy.

229. πολιτικὴ ἀρετή (*Politics* 3.1281a8).

230. *Politics* 5.1301a19-1302a15.

and, in general, any sort of scheming with a view to effecting political change or any action that may disturb the stability of the state. Each imperfectly constituted state is based on a specific misunderstanding of justice, and each incomplete view of justice, while validating a particular constitution, is also, because a misinterpretation, the cause of its downfall. Democrats claim equal shares in everything; oligarchs press for increasing inequality. The moment arrives when the pressures on the existing state make it give way. The cause of sedition, determines Aristotle, is always and everywhere a perception of inequity, an impression of inequality in the constitution. There is no inequality, he insists, where unequals are treated in proportion to the inequality existing between them.[231] In general, it is passion for equality that is the motive of faction.[232] The whole difficulty, then, is the meaning of equality. And Aristotle recalls that there are two kinds of equality, arithmetical equality and equality according to worth.[233] It is the latter, the analogic *dikaiosunē*, that is the absolutely just.[234] This, however, eludes the arguers.[235]

Politics versus Philosophy. The task remains to look briefly at Aristotle's ideal state (Books 7 and 8). Overall, his republic represents a regress from some of the ideas expressed previously, in relation to actual conditions. He depicts a society that represents the last resistance to the inexorable Hellenistic political and social upheaval.[236] The feature in which this is most immediately evident is the social structure of the ideal state. In what looks like a departure from his earlier valorization of a large state resting on a sizable middle class, Aristotle insists on a limited, self-sufficient and self-enclosed state.[237] The citizenry of

231. *Politics* 5.1301b27-28.
232. *Politics* 5.1301b29.
233. ἔστι δὲ διττὸν τὸ ἴσον, τὸ μὲν γὰρ ἀριθμῷ τὸ δὲ κατ' ἀξίαν ἐστίν (*Politics* 5.1301b30).
234. τὸ ἁπλῶς δίκαιον (*Politics* 5.1301b36).
235. Aristotle continues, in the rest of Book 5, with a detailed examination of the particular ways in which each type of constitution degenerates. Psychological factors lead the train of causes for *stasis*; economic factors lag behind them; political ones come last. Book 6 elaborates a theory of political management, i.e. how to make democracies and oligarchies most stable.
236. In this sense, Aristotle, despite the charge of collaborationism with the Macedonian occupier, emulates Demosthenes, though without the defiant patriotism and insurgent pathos of the great orator.
237. Aristotle is careful to isolate as much as possible his *polis* from corrupting

this republic is non-specialized and differentiated by age groups. It is a propertied citizenry, able to enjoy leisure. The citizens, called 'parts' (μέρη, *merē*) provide a military class (to 35 years of age), a deliberative class (from 35 to 50) and a civic priesthood (in old age). Political action (and excellence) is denied the other sections of the population, the 'conditions' (οἱ οὐκ ἄνευ, *hoi ouk aneu*), the proletariat and specialized professional groups who are disfranchised, landless and propertyless.[238] Leisure (σχολή, *scholē*) is the factor that determines this social and political split. *Scholē* it is defined as activity for its own sake—the activity of the speculative faculty of the rational soul, performed for the cultivation of the mind.[239] Its opposite is not labor, but business, want of time for leisure.[240] This is an activity for the sake of something else and thus falls short of the best way of life and the good and cannot bring happiness.[241] The individual and the state share the same end: the best way of life. The goods of the soul (*aretai*) and the 'extraneous equipment' (χορηγία, *chorēgia*) are required both for the happiness of

influences. He even requires that the city be at some distance from the harbor, not only for security reasons, but also for purity of mores (7.1327a33).

238. Aristotle and Plato are in collision on the subject of ideal republic. Aristotle opposes the specialization of citizens and relegates this revolutionary element of Plato's thought to the 'conditions'. He rejects Plato's 'communism', and does away with the most original feature of Plato's republic. Aristotle gives all property to his equivalent of Plato's guardians. Plato, Aristotle contends, has denied them full happiness by impeding their access to the external goods. Aristotle's solutions are open to criticism: he creates a still-born ideal state, since his non-specialized citizens, for all their splendid chivalry and aristocratic pursuits, march towards their own undoing in a world increasingly professional, detailed and precise. Aristotle's ideal state appears, in Barker's words, as a torso (*Politics*, Barker's Intro. p. lii). It is both vulnerable (to *stasis*) and deficient in virtues, since the citizens undergo nothing of the elaborate tests Plato's guardians had to pass.

Aristotle's system reveals, at the same time, remarkable consistency. Aristotle's treatment of 'conditions' indicates not that he loathes work but the high regard in which he holds leisure. For Aristotle, it is obviously leisure (σχολή) that is the condition of all virtues (see also 7.1334a10-19). Aristotle's differentiation between citizens by age can be understood as specification of his theory of the game. He keeps the ruler and the ruled distinct in a society of equals. Aristotle, like Plato, conceives the best constitution as necessitating limitation of the franchise.

239. *Politics* 7.1334a10-19. It is precisely this term and this concept that are employed by Paul in 1 Cor. 7.5: prayer requires *scholē*.

240. ἀσχολία (*Politics* 7.1334a16).

241. *Politics* 7.1323b21-22.

the individual and for the happiness of the state.[242] Both the individual and the state have at their disposal two bests: for the person, either political or contemplative life; for the state, mastery over others (i.e. imperialistic pursuits) or mastery over itself (i.e. the best internal political and social life).[243]

Despite his coordination of the end of the individual and the end of the state, however, Aristotle actually achieves a split between private and public life, philosophy and politics, contemplation and action. This dichotomy was to prove enduring. The causes of the rift were complex and momentous, but, in simple terms, I see them as follows. The larger, Hellenistic world brought with it specialization and professionalization. With these, rejection of the physical world set in among the intelligentsia: they turned their backs to the world and looked elsewhere. Denial of the world and denial of the body go together; productive activity and the body became signs of coarseness; otherworld and asceticism became the new fashions. For all his interest in the political game, Aristotle's leaning is clearly toward philosophical life: 'thoughts with no object beyond themselves, speculations and trains of reflection followed purely for their own sake are far more deserving of the name of active'.[244] No one could be fooled by Aristotle's insistence that both kinds of life—political and contemplative—are best. If the best activity is not that of the political man, then the best *polis* provides only the second-best way to live. The political-philosophical equivalence reveals a lopsidedness, and the *polis* and the philosopher go separate ways.

Aristotle and Paul: Ekklēsia *as* Polis

Paul's attack on the Greeks, modeled on the language of handbook philosophy, is structured by a critique of ἀσέβεια (*asebeia*, Rom. 1.18; 4.5; 5.6). In Classical Greek and Hellenistic philosophy *asebeia* is related to *adikia* (cf. Rom. 1.18). The latter is injustice, disregard of another human; the former, godlessness, refusing god. For giving up the truth about god (1.18, 23, 25-27), the *asebeis* are given up by God to impure cravings (1.24), base passions (1.26), unnatural lusts (1.27), fatuous minds (1.21, 22) and an inventory of foibles (1.29-30).

Beneath its Stoic garb, Paul's stereotypical list of vices is rooted in

242. *Politics* 7.1324a1-23.
243. *Politics* 7.1324a23-1325b33.
244. *Politics* 7.1325b16-22.

Platonic-Aristotelian psychology. Paul's thought betrays the influence of a philosophical current inspired by an Aristotelian tradition. The Platonic tripartite division of the soul (*psuchē*) into appetites (*epithumia*), spiritedness (*thumos*) and reason (λογιστικόν, φιλόσοφον, *logistikon, philosophon*),[245] while professedly accepted by Aristotle, is actually reworked by him. Plato's most original construct, *thumos*, is scrapped, and with it goes its political progeny, the communistic society of Warrior-Guardians. (Spiritedness is the feature of this class.) Aristotle produces, instead, a two-tiered soul,[246] one of whose parts is irrational, the other rational. The irrational, however, extends beyond its proper sphere, the growth-nutritive faculty common to all animate beings, into the domain of the rational, in effect forming an intermediary part of the soul.

In Aristotle, *epithumia* describes this middle range of the soul. A composite faculty, *epithumia* may heed reason or disregard it. The seat of appetites and of desire in general,[247] to *epithumia* also belong *aretai*, qualities, in this case of the moral kind. These refer to a thought-desire system (*nous-orexis*), a system of variables controlled by choice (*proairesis*).[248] Hellenistic popular philosophy, to which Paul is indebted, focused on this intermediary rational-irrational part, the domain of ethics. In Romans, *epithumia* (1.24) and *orexis* (1.27) describe precisely this intermediary aspect of the soul, connected, as in Aristotelianism, with morals. The Greeks' *asebeia* is, in Paul, the uprising of the vices. Moreover, the Aristotelian origin of Paul's system of ethics receives a further proof in that the heart (καρδία, *kardia*) (1.21) is the seat of the soul. (For Plato, it is the brain.[249])

The way Paul employs the term *phusis* again reveals Aristotelianism as the source, while announcing the new, Christian meaning: what is not 'by *phusis*' is 'against nature' (παρὰ φύσιν, *para phusin*) (1.26)—that is, error, *hamartia*. *Hamartia* becomes the equivalent of the unnatural. It is uncontrolled desire, burning lust (1.27). It distorts the body, its nature and its function. The diatribe against the Greeks ends with another Aristotelian echo: to *do* evil is mostly incidental, but to *be* unjust—as a state, a condition, a habit, an approving of evil, as Paul

---

245. E.g. *Republic* 4.434d-441c.
246. *Ethics* 1.1102a27-1103a10.
247. *Ethics* 1.1102b30.
248. *Ethics* 6.1139b5-6.
249. The psychological construct has a strict parallelism in politics not only in Plato and Aristotle but also in Paul.

puts it (Rom. 1.32)—is abhorrent.[250]

Paul appeals to philosophical, Aristotelian-inspired terminology in a sensitive situation (Rom. 2.12-29). To be a Jew means at most to be part of the audience, the public of the law (ἀκροατής) (2.13). That someone is a Jew does not mean that he is necessarily *of* the law. Many of the Gentiles who do not have the law *do* the law *by nature*[251] (2.14). To do the law by nature is to be a law unto oneself (2.14). (The expression, 'they are a law unto themselves' [ἐαυτοῖς εἰσιν νόμος], known from Greek philosophy, is complemented by the scriptural 'law written in one's heart' [2.15].) But Paul, ingeniously, shifts the emphasis from the law to the work, the doing of the law (τὸ ἔργον τοῦ νόμου γραπτὸν ἐν ταῖς καρδίαις αὐτῶν) (2.15), or 'doers of the law' (οἱ ποιηταὶ νόμου) (2.13).

The way Paul thinks of law is audacious. It would seem as if a Jew should see in the Law the equivalent of what a Greek would mean by *phusis*: inherent quality, permanence, universality. For Paul, however, law is activity. Paul downgrades the law further by taking advantage of the ambiguity of the term *nomos* in the Platonic-Aristotelian tradition and rendering it as 'convention' (see also Rom. 3.20-31; 5.12-21; 7.12-25). The Gentiles work by συνείδησις (*suneidesis*) (2.15)—that is, by conscience, nothing other than moral sentiment. (This Peripatetic-Stoic term denotes a faculty of the soul that discriminates between right and wrong and prompts one to approve of and follow the former and to disapprove of and avoid the latter.[252]) The conflictual nature of the human (rational-irrational) soul (2.15) is resolved by this *suneidēsis*, and it is this that God judges. Uncircumcised 'by nature' (ἐκ φύσεως, *ek phuseōs*) (2.27), the Gentile may have an inward circumcision, a circumcision of the heart (2.29). What Paul is actually saying here is that the law-doing Gentile is naturally circumcised, that he is so in his inner naturalness. At the same time, only that which God sees, hidden and

---

250. *Ethics* 5.1137a5-9. 'Men think that acting unjustly is in their power, and therefore, that being just is easy. But it is not; to lie with one's neighbor's wife, to wound another, to deliver a bribe, is easy and in our power, but to do these things as a result of a certain state of character, τὸ ὡδί, is neither easy nor in our power.'

251. φύσει τὰ τοῦ νόμου ποιῶσιν.

252. Cf. also Rom. 9.1; 13.5; 2 Cor. 1.12; 4.2; 5.11; 1–2 Timothy; and Titus. *Suneidēsis* is the weak element in 1 Cor. 8.7, 10, 12; 10.28-29; yet food itself has nothing to do with it (1 Cor. 10.25, 27).

inward, matters (2.29).[253] There should be little doubt that, in the way of Greek philosophical tradition, Paul is making a distinction between *nomos* and *phusis*.

Paul also distinguishes between an outward, visible nature (ἐν τῷ φανερῷ) (2.28), which describes the uncircumcision of the Gentile (ἡ ἐκ φύσεως ἀκροβυστία) (2.27) as well as the circumcision of the Jew (ἡ ἐν σαρκὶ περιτομή) (2.28), and an inner nature, 'the Jew within' (ὁ ἐν τῷ κρυπτῷ Ἰουδαῖος), which is the pneumatic, or Spirit-induced, circumcision of the heart (περιτομὴ καρδίας ἐν πνεύματι) (2.29). It may also be noticed here that Paul, in what seems a direct strike at the notion of *phusis*, which by then was common philosophical baggage, amends the Peripatetic theory of *phusis*. God can oppose the Jew, that which is natural (*kata phusin*) but without *pistis* (*apistos*). He may favor the Gentile, that which is contrary to nature (*para phusin*) but has *pistis* (11.20-24).

Romans 7.15-21 contains the key to the Pauline conception of will. Will is good. It is, however, ineffectual: 'I do not do what I will' (7.15). 'That I do what I do not wish to do shows that *hamartia* controls me, possesses me' (7.17, 20). Paul's psychology sees man split between his rational and irrational sides. It is amazing to what extent the 'sarkic' and the unconscious can be identified. Paul's judgment of *sarx* (weakly rendered as 'flesh') is harsh: 'I know, with my reason [*nous*] that what is living in me, what is 'sarkic' about me, is not good. I can will but I cannot act according to my will' (7.18). 'This is what I find to be the principle [*nomos*] [of my being]: whenever I want to do the beneficial, the fine thing [τὸ καλόν], the malignant, the ugly one [τὸ κακόν] is at hand' (7.21). Paul is describing a dysfunction, and he does so with the clinical precision of a physician. There is a whole medical tradition that depicts such failures of the will. Aristotle, ever the scientist, the medical practitioner—the Asclepiad[254]—had recognized the phenomenon, assigning it to the middle register of the soul, and comparing it with a case of paralysis in the body in which willing to move a limb in a certain direction results in a contrary movement. Impulses (ὁρμαί, *hormai*) also disobey the command of reason, says Aristotle.[255] Will and action are divided against one another. The theoretical background of this

253. Just as Plato thinks of the essence of justice, *Republic* 2.366e.
254. A suggestive link: the earliest use of ἔκτρωμα, Paul's metaphor for abortion (and himself) in 1 Cor. 15.8, is in Aristotle (D.J. Williams, 1999: 73 n. 64).
255. *Ethics* 1.1102b19-25.

symptom is the *akrasia* concept.[256] *Akrasia*, weakness of the will, is the name Paul himself gives the disease that he describes in Rom. 7.15-21 (cf. 1 Cor. 7.5).[257] His anguished question is the cue for the cure (Rom. 7.24).

The Christian Polis. Borrowing amply from current popular philosophy, Paul constructs a political theory for Christianity. He conceives it as a two-tiered system, the first level based on the *oikos-polis* blend, politics proper, and a *basileia* level, which places a transcendental being atop the political structure.[258] Aristotle's complex theory of the *polis* had been reduced by Hellenistic and imperial Roman times to an Aristotelian politics of the master–slave relation. Paul follows, while reworking, this scheme. He elaborates a political philosophy that makes a new type of *polis*, the Christian *polis*, the basis of his system. Christ, the master (κύριος, *kurios*), has also been one of the ruled, himself knew the condition of the slave. He is Paul's solution to the demand of reciprocity in Aristotle's political construct. Christ saves the political game as well.

In characteristic Aristotelian style, Paul moves from the individual to the *polis*, from ethics to politics. In Aristotle, ethics and politics are related to each other as the particular to the general, and both belong to the grand practical science of politics (*politikē*), 'the most authoritative art and that which is truly the master art'.[259] Aristotelian politics subsumes a theory of happiness, the study of the human character that is the region of ethics, to a theory of the *polis*, the constitution and social structure of a political system that can best assure happiness.[260] The happiness of the individual and that of the state are continuous. Paul, too, connects the individual's proper end with the collective end, the good of the individual with that of many, ethics with politics. This relation is made plain in the list of admonitions in Rom. 12.9-21. As in one body there are many members (τὰ μέλη, *ta melē*), each with its own

256. *Ethics* 7.1145a15-1152a53.
257. As in Rom. 16.20, 1 Cor. 7.5 makes Satan not a theological or ethical concept but a political one: the metaphor for division, for rebellion. Also, *akrasia* as well as *scholē*, two Aristotelian concepts that went on to have a long career in Hellenistic philosophy, make it unnecessary to appeal in the interpretation of 1 Cor. 7.1-15 to Pharisaic purity laws as is often the case.
258. The background for this is Hellenistic Pythagoreanism. See Chapters 4 and 5.
259. *Ethics* 1.1094a28-29.
260. *Ethics* 1.1094b7-12, 10.1181b12-15.

function (πρᾶξις, *praxis*) (12.4), so we, the many (οἱ πολλοί, *hoi polloi*), are one physical body (σῶμα, *sōma*) in Christ but are parts (*ta melē*) in relation to one another (12.5). This is an example of the famous body-and-limbs motif that appears, for example, in Menenius Agrippa's parable in Livy.[261] Paul uses it repeatedly (Rom. 12.4-5, 1 Cor. 12.12-27) and so does his school (the writers of Ephesians and Colossians). The political nature of this parable, a topos of Mediterranean culture, leaves little doubt as to its political meaning in Paul. Body and body-politic stand in close relationship. Even more, Paul preserves the *psuchē–polis* analogy, the Greek mark of philosophy. Thus, he is ever watchful against psychological transgressions caused by desires, the cause of political *stasis*.[262]

For Paul, the natural end of the *polis* is to be a Christian *polis*. Each member of the society functions according to *charis* (κατὰ χάριν, *kata charin*) (Rom. 12.6), that is, according to what the will of God has decided about each individual in proportion to his *pistis* (κατὰ τὴν ἀναλογίαν τῆς πίστεως) (12.6). *Mutatis mutandis*, Paul's concept of justice comes close to that of Aristotle. On the one hand, Aristotle's 'universal justice', an *aretē* par excellence, is delegated, by Paul, to God. On the other, Aristotle's primary 'particular' justice, 'distributive justice', which confers award in geometric proportion to merit,[263] has its counterpart in Paul's concept (12.6) of a distributive justice that is a result of God's *dikaiosunē* and is disbursed 'in proportion [*kat'ana-logian*] to *pistis*'.[264] It has often been remarked that Paul is not always clear about what distinguishes the recipients of God's 'proportional justice'. I think that degree of possession by πνεῦμα is the distin-

261. Year 494 BCE, discussed by Ogilvie 1965: I, 312-13.

262. See more in the discussion of the *polis* group of Hellenistic Pythagoreans. Although *stasis* is not encountered in Paul, he develops a vast discourse on unity and conflict. See Chapter 7, Rom. 16.17-20, for a discussion of Paul's rhetoric of *parti-pris*.

263. *Ethics* 5.1129a1-1131b24; *Politics* 3.1280a7-25. Plato speaks of equality by geometrical proportion in *Republic* 8.558c; *Gorgias* 507e, cf. 483e, 488c; *Laws* 6.756e-757e. The geometrical proportion is great among both gods and men, ἡ ἰσότης ἡ γεωμετρικὴ καὶ ἐν θεοῖς καὶ ἐν ἀνθρώποις μέγα δύναται (*Gorgias* 508a). Interestingly, Plato advises, however, to revert to arithmetical distribution, 'equality of the lot', τὸ ἴσον τοῦ κλήρου, to appease the crowd (*Laws* 6.757e). See A. Delatte 1922: 99-102, 111.

264. The connection is mediated through Hellenistic Pythagoreanism and is, I think, striking.

guishing mark.[265] Thus, prophecy tops the nomenclature, with the rest of the gifts following by degrees.[266] The 'compassionate' (whom I assume to be the widow doing all the work in the association) is placed last. Both, however, prophet and nurse, are part of the same political body and both are partners in *pistis*. This throws light on the notion of ἔργα as well. *Erga* does not simply mean 'works', but activity lacking in *pistis*.

Aristotle's argument, in the *Ethics*, about ἔργον/ἔργα (*ergon/erga*)[267] is of interest here. He introduces his discussion with the observation that the statement 'the supreme good is happiness'[268] requires an account of what constitutes happiness. The question to ask, contends Aristotle, is, what is human work? That is, what is his activity or function (*to ergon*)? In his answer, he first remarks that 'good' or 'well', as this valuation applies to a flute-player, a sculptor or any craftsman who has any work or business to perform,[269] lies in the work each does.[270] Similarly, with regard to a human being as such, the good consists in his *ergon* as a human being. What then, asks Aristotle, is the work a human being is designed by nature to fulfill? As the eye, hand, foot and each of the various members of the body perform a certain *ergon*, so also a human being has a function, above and beyond his particular members. 'Living' (τὸ ζῆν, *to zēn*, i.e. nutrition and growth) is not sufficiently specific, as it also applies to plants. Similarly, humans share 'perception' (αἰσθητική, *aisthētikē*) with the animals. What is characteristic of human beings alone is the intentionality of their rational soul[271] in its active aspect.[272] Thus, the work of a human being is the activity of the soul's faculties according to reason.[273] Consequently, the human good, or happiness, is this activity performed in accordance with *aretē*

265. Paul's *pneuma* recalls the Aristotelian *scholē*, leisure: an activity for its own sake of the speculative faculty of the rational soul for the cultivation of the mind, *diagogē*. Its counterpart is occupation, *ascholia*, similar to Paul's 'works': an activity for the sake of something else (*Politics* 7.1334a10-19).

266. προφητεία, διακονία, διδάσκων, παρακαλῶν, μεταδιδούς, προϊστάμενος, ἐλεῶν (Rom. 12.7-8).

267. *Ethics* 1.1097b25-1098a20.

268. εὐδαιμονία τὸ ἄριστον ἀγαθόν (*Ethics* 1.1097b21).

269. ἔργον τι καὶ πρᾶξις (*Ethics* 1.1097b26).

270. ἐν τῷ ἔργῳ δοκεῖ τἀγαθὸν εἶναι καὶ τὸ εὖ (*Ethics* 1.1097b28).

271. πρακτική τις τοῦ λόγον ἔχοντος (*Ethics* 1.1098a4).

272. κατ᾽ ἐνέργειαν (*Ethics* 1.1098a6).

273. ἔργον ἀνθρώπου ψυχῆς ἐνέργεια κατὰ λόγον (*Ethics* 1.1098a6-7).

over a human being's entire life span.[274] Aristotle distinguishes between *ergon* in a particular sense, as professional proficiency or anatomic functionality (performing a work according to certain rules and objectives), and the *ergon* of a human being in the general, universal sense, and it is this latter sense that enters into the definition of supreme good and happiness.

The contrast between *erga* and *pistis* is Paul's most acclaimed dichotomy.[275] *Erga*, once the connection with Aristotelianism has been made, can be profitably understood as particular function or activity performed according to the peculiar demands of idiosyncratic law, while *pistis*, the real human *ergon*, is an enterprise that follows the exigencies of a universal power. Paul's *erga–pistis* contrast parallels Aristotle's contrast between particular and universal *ergon*.[276] I have little doubt that, as Paul uses *pistis*, it is his invention, and not an easy one to grasp.[277] I think, however, that his contemporaries had much less

---

274. *Ethics* 1.1098a16-18.

275. The opposition ἔργα–πίστις is conspicuous in Romans (3.27, 28; 4.5 [verbal forms]; 9.32) and Galatians (2.16; 3.2, 5). Also in 1 Tim. 3.1 (singular *ergon*) and Tit. 3.8.

Paul's use of *ergon* outside the dichotomy *erga–pistis*, almost always in the singular, falls into two neat groups that reinforce this approach. On the one hand, a negative charge, as in work of law, τὸ ἔργον τοῦ νόμου (Rom. 2.15; Gal. 2.16—plural), work that leads to condemnation (1 Cor. 3.13-15), work (such as immorality) that requires expulsion from the community (1 Cor. 5.2). On the other, a positive valuation, as in work of God or of the Lord (Rom. 14.20; 1 Cor. 16.10; Phil. 2.30), Paul's work (1 Cor. 9.1); good work, ἔργον ἀγαθόν (Rom. 2.7); in oppositon to strife; 2 Cor. 9.8; Phil. 1.6; 1 Thess. 5.13, cf. Gal. 6.10 [verbal form]), or 2 Tim. 2.21, 3.17; Tit. 1.16, 3.1); work of faith, ἔργον πίστεως (1 Thess. 1.3; 2 Thess. 1.11).

276. I made above the correspondence of Paul's *erga* with Aristotle's *ascholia*. *Ascholia* is the same as occupation, particular *ergon*, in Aristotle. Aristotle's universal *ergon* corresponds to Paul's *pistis*. Moreover, the similarity between Pauline *pneuma* and Aristotelian *scholē* suggests the identity between *pneuma* and *pistis*. I do not, however, claim a logical identity for these terms. They are not synonyms although they have the same extension.

The age of *pistis* begins with Christ. The concept of an age of *pistis* becomes intelligible only through affirmation of resurrection, the raising from the dead, Christianity's 'noble lie', or rather, 'good story', ψεῦδος γενναῖον (see *Republic* 3.414d-415b).

277. 'We must at times admit the existence of originality in authors and movements that have survived' wryly says Nock in a reference to Paul (1972: 939). Nock

trouble with it than we do. The concept of distributive justice, very popular with Hellenistic political philosophers, supplied the proper context, a political one, for making sense of it.

The hierarchy, then, in Paul's *pistis*-informed society, runs something like this (in descending order): cult leaders, cult officers, cult instructors, solicitors, givers, managers, social workers. The ranking descends from exemplary pneumatic faculties to exemplary *sōmata*, bodily faculties. In Paul, these officers are the magistrates of the state. Romans 12.4-8 allows an inside view of the organization and activity of the early Christian association, (ἐκκλησία, *ekklēsia*). While *ekklēsia* could loosely be read as being identical with *polis* (particularly in Christianity), here, as in the Greek world, it is, technically speaking, the *assembly* of the *polis*, the supreme power in a democratic constitution. Aristotle's double definition of constitution is relevant here. First, a political definition: an arrangement of offices in the *polis*.[278] Second, a teleological definition: constitution as a way of life.[279] What Paul does in his hierarchical scheme is to present a constitution of the Christian *polis* in the first sense. But, above all, and in most of the Letter to the Romans, he is concerned with the teleological definition, a constitution whose end is the happy life.

A Republic of Cheerful Slaves. As an arrangement of offices, Aristotle's *polis* is a 'polity'. As we have seen, polity, the generic name for constitution, also receives a technical meaning in Aristotle: the type of constitution in which the masses govern for the common interest, a mixed-type, democratic-aristocratic constitution.[280] As a way of life,

suggests, for example, Pauline originality on the concept of Son of God behind Phil. 2.6-11. Stead, to give another example, writes about the *avant la lettre* triad formula in 2 Cor. 13.14: 'St. Paul's language, then, is vivid, but essentially plastic and inventive' (1994: 152).

278. *Politics* 3.1278b5-1280a6; 4.1290a30-1294b2.
279. *Politics* 3.1288a32-b6; 4.1295a25-1296b11.
280. It is relevant that in Aristotle's ideal state as in Plato's republic, the sovereign civic body is the army. Christianity would follow this idea, making its citizens *milites*, an idea rooted in the Pauline contest metaphors, which rely on both athletic and battle images. A battery of military terms rank prominently in Paul: 'in proper battle order' (κατὰ τάξιν, 1 Cor. 14.40, cf. 14.33); 'putting (oneself) in line' (ἔταξαν, 16.15); '(military) ranks' (τάγματα, 1 Cor. 15.23); 'keeping in line' (στοιχέω, Gal. 5.25). See also 2 Cor. 7.5 (battles) and 10.3-6 (siege of the soul won by God's weapons); Gal. 5.17 (conflict); Phil. 2.25 and Phlm. 2 (fellow soldier);

Aristotle favors a 'middle-class' type constitution. These definitions converge in the concept of the mean. Paul's Christian *polis* is also a mixed constitution, an innovative mix to be sure, a blend of theocracy and democracy. We might call it 'doulocracy', a republic of cheerful slaves ruled by a saving, absolutely just God. To anticipate some of the main results of the present study: teleologically, Paul's polity emphasizes the christ-type class. Paul's definitions converge in the notion of *dikaiosunē*, where *dikaiosunē theou* is the notion of justice pertaining to God and *dikaiosunē pisteōs* is the concept of justice that describes the human community, the community of *pistis*.

The ultimate basis of Paul's the notion of δοῦλος (*doulos*) is the detailed Aristotelian discussion of the issue of slavery in Book 1 of *Politics*. One is the slave of him whom one obeys, reprises Paul (Rom. 6.16). In this system of relations, willingness is all important. In Aristotle, willingness characterizes both natural slavery (the Barbarian–Greek 'compact') as well as the Greek *polis* (the ruler–ruled political game). The same Aristotelian teleological thinking informs Paul. One cannot willingly be simultaneously a slave of two opposing masters: *hamartia* and God. Slaves of *hamartia* (6.17, 20) have as their end (*telos*) death (6.21). But now there is a new teaching (τύπος διδαχῆς, *tupos didachēs*) (6.17), and those whose hearts are in it, the slaves to *dikaiosunē* (6.18), have eternal life as their end (6.22, 23). With his characteristic love for rhetorical balance and intellectual consistency, Paul insists not only that the human being as a whole is a slave to whomever he chooses to obey but that each of his parts serves the selected master, as well.

We are presented, in the sixth chapter of Romans, with an occasion for observing the mechanism by which a specifically *Christian* language comes into being. Although Paul keeps the old terminology unchanged, he radically alters its meaning, and a language mutation occurs. 'Slave'—the despicable, the preposterous *doulos* of Greek social culture—receives an explicit and unqualified positive sense when Paul uses the word to mean the *doulos* of God. But this novelty has actually been

Rom. 7.23 (making war). D.J. Williams 1999: 211-44, esp. 213 and notes and 224. Martial imagery would prove enduring. At the end of the first century, a fast day is called a 'station', which is a 'day of military duty on the watch' (Chadwick 1967: 459). The *Shepherd of Hermas* confirms this usage. The very locution *missa*, from which 'mass' derives, originally referred to dismissal of soldiers (Chadwick 1967: 268 n. 1).

prepared for by the Aristotelian view of the natural slave, one for whom the better and just state is to be a slave. Paul also shares in the Stagirite's notion that a complete slave is but a part of his master—in Paul's case, part of God. No less than Timothy or Titus, the Classical Greek political thinkers, especially Aristotle, are Paul's *sunergoi*.

Chapter 3

EKKLESIA, *OIKOS* AND *POLIS* IN PAUL

The Polis *at Paul's Time*

The Hellenistic world is primarily a Greek world. The *locus classicus* for understanding what a Greek world is is Herodotus 8.144. There, Mardonius, Darius's son-in-law and Xerxes' commander in Greece after the Persians' naval defeat at Salamis, ineffectively attempts through emissaries to conclude a separate peace with Athens and thus to sunder it from the Greek alliance. The Spartans learn about this and send an embassy to Athens to dissuade the Athenians, with pledges of aid, from giving in to the Persian scheme. The Athenians have a field day. They contrive to have both the Spartan and the Persian delegations in Athens at the same time, and they bring both Mardonius's ambassador and the Spartan envoys to the same hall. After turning down Mardonius's offer, the Athenians speak to the Spartans, genially censuring them for their apprehension (and refusing their offer of relief) and presenting the reasons why an Athenian defection is inconceivable. First, the Athenians refer to their duty to avenge the destruction of the temples of the gods; then, they speak of 'the kinship of all Greeks in blood and speech, and the shrines of the gods and the sacrifices that we have in common, and the likeness of our way of life...' (Godley's trans.). The Greeks are united by blood, language and common sanctuaries, worship and traditions.[1] This became the basis of all subsequent understanding of what makes one Greek.

Consanguinity (ὅμαιμος, *homaimos*), was the foremost criterion on the list. But blood relation was not just genetic, but also 'eisegetic'—a matter of perception, a cultural issue. 'Within this general consanguinity there was a second level consanguinity, which tied more closely certain

---

1.   ὅμαιμόν τε καὶ ὁμόγλωσσον καὶ θεῶν ἱδρύματά τε κοινὰ καὶ θυσίαι ἤθεά τε ὁμότροπα (Herodotus 8.144).

communities on the basis of preferential relations attested by local traditions'.[2] Such relationships, expressed in terms of blood ties, took primarily political form and became part of the official language of decrees. Cultural openness made the Greeks occasionally extend consanguinity to peoples who were not Greek at all,[3] provided these were culturally attuned to the Greeks. The definition of a Greek city was extended to include, not only cities that are Greek by origin and blood, but also any community organized on the Greek model and using Greek as its official language.[4] Herodotus himself connected ethnicity with language. Adopting a Greek political structure and speaking Greek qualified one for consanguinity. Συγγένεια (*sungeneia*), the community of stock, was a basic motif used by the Greeks, especially in Hellenistic times, to define the relations between cities, between peoples and between the city and the sovereign.[5]

In Classical Greece, the *polis* distinguished the Greeks from the barbarians. The *polis* was not just an urban center but, above all, the political center of a surrounding area. The Greek *poleis*, whether democratic or oligarchic, were communities based on the government of the

2.   Giardina 1998b: 41.

3.   Giardina 1988b: 43.

4.   Greek language was the necessary, even if not sufficient, factor for Greek culture, and there is plenty of epigraphical and papyrological evidence to show that the urban poor and the peasants spoke it, and this even in the remotest parts of the East, where some native languages still enjoyed currency. (Aramaic survived even if the region was Hellenized; Demotic Egyptian also continued.) Jones 1940: 288-91.

5.   Giardina 1998c: 43. The Romans had little use for *cognatio*, or *consanguinitas*, which they rarely used and mostly for forging alliances in threatening circumstances, but then promptly ignored. Examples are the alliances with the Choni of Siris (Gulf of Tarentum) against the Samnites, with the Segestans of Sicily against the Phoenicians, with the Veneti for the Istrian campaign in 129 BCE, with certain communities of Troad and with the Lycian confederacy in actions in the Eastern Mediterranean, and with the Aedui, a Gallic tribe of Gallia Transalpina who received the title of *fratres consanguineique* during the campaign beginning in 125 BCE. Consanguinity remains foreign to the language of imperial politics. Rome did not countenance, among the people of its empire, any theoretical hierarchy, any ethnic advantage. It only recognized romanization, acknowledging as closer the people who were romanized first. Yet, romanization was 'alla portata di tutti' (Giardina 1998c: 45), available to anyone. The Romans were really unique in this sense: while for most people autochthony was the sign of a privileged and superior condition, the Romans made much of the category of citizenship only. See Giardina 1998c: 43-45.

citizens; they were self-governing entities: 'Slaves to no lord, they own no kingly power'.[6] Ideally, the *polis* was free, autonomous and autarchic and was ruled by the *nomos*, the law. Although the Greek states differed greatly, the typical political institutions were, in each case, the Assembly, the Council and the magistracies. Ἐκκλησία (*ekklēsia*), the Assembly, was the seat of power, the sovereign, τὸ κύριον (*to kurion*), in a democracy. The *ekklēsia*, the voting body of all adult, free, male citizens, decided on all matters of the government of the *polis*, in both internal and external affairs. Βουλή (*boulē*), the Council, was the main political body in an oligarchic or aristocratic constitution; in a democracy, it served as a 'rules committee', determining the Assembly's agenda and convoking and dismissing it. It also worked with the magistrates, whether chosen by lot or elected, who held most of the executive power.

A most remarkable development in Hellenistic times, rarely discussed, is the transference of the city organization to the countryside. While, in the cities, democracy falters as a result of the preponderant role of a wealthy oligarchy, the democratic ideal lives on in villages. The strength and intensity of democracy persisted even while taking ever innovative forms. The country-dwellers who even in the best of times participated in the Assembly only at important votes and on election day, achieved, by the Principate, and especially in western Asia Minor and central Syria, an active local political life, founded on a democratic type of constitution. The cities provided the inspiration and the model, but not the impetus. The magistrates' name reflect local traditions. Cities rarely interfered in village affairs. Occasionally villages have patrons (προστάται) from the city wealthy. Strong democratic village life is most prominent in areas with sparse and immature cities.[7] The history of the Hellenistic[8] age is, above all, the history of Hellenization.[9] The known

6. οὔτινος δοῦλοι κέκληνται φωτὸς οὐδ᾽ ὑπήκοοι (Aeschylus, *The Persians* 242, Robert Potter trans.)

7. Jones 1940: 271-74.

8. The term Hellenism and the idea of a Hellenistic Age were created by Johann Gustav Droysen (1808–1884) in 1836 in his *Geschichte des Hellenismus*. Hellenism is defined as the encounter and the fusion between the Greek and the Oriental civilizations.

9. Technically, the Hellenistic world comprises the period between the death of Alexander the Great (323 BCE) and the end of the last of the Hellenistic monarchic states, Ptolemaic Egypt (30 BCE), as a direct consequence of the battle of Actium (31 BCE).

world undergoes a process of becoming Greek in language, institutions and mode of life. Hellenization is the continuation of the traditions of the *polis*.[10] The Hellenistic socio-political system is binary: king and city, *basileia* and *polis*. Power rests with the king, who relentlessly gambles it: but the *polis* is the Hellenistic determinant; it signifies the age. Cities are asked to support the monarchs' military campaigns, which they resentfully do by housing garrisons, lodging and feeding soldiers and making contributions. Correspondingly, the kings lavish monumental buildings on the cities and sustain them with largesse, to the point of inhibiting the cities' own economies and stifling the citizenry's mercantile spirit. Hellenistic wars serve merely to redraw borders of kingdoms composed of *poleis* which are culturally similar though distinct in character. Philosophy, ethics, art, law, science and religion are parallel entities.

The life of the Greek cities changes little with Hellenism, except for the superimposition of a monarchic power structure; the king is the final authority and arbiter, savior and benefactor, who needs to be eulogized and flattered, swayed and persuaded, revered and obeyed. Internally, the citizen body continues to govern through assemblies, councils and magistrates. The intervention of the king, however, regulates the size and composition of the body politic.[11]

The Hellenistic city has been both exalted and besmirched. Alexander, who saw democracy as the normal constitution of the *polis*, tied the notion of a free city to that of a democratic city. Whenever a Hellenistic king (such as Antipater or Cassander) attempted to obstruct democratic government, this folly was immediately exploited by rival kings and proved the king's undoing.[12] While few contest that the *polis* formed the infrastructure of Hellenism, its commitment to democracy is still debated. In the Hellenistic *polis*, the citizenship criterion of free birth was relaxed to mean citizen descent on one side only, and

10. With a characteristic meiosis, *OCD* notes that 'the Hellenistic age owed much of its intellectual life to the traditions of the Polis (852b)'. See *OCD*, Victor Ehrenberg, 'Polis', 851a-52b.

11. For the relation of cities with the Hellenistic monarchic power see, among others, Jones 1940: 96-100, Préaux 1978: 414-40.

12. 'Whatever devices [kings] might invent to secure their control over their cities, there was one which they could not use, the formal limitation of political power to a small class' (Jones 1940: 157 and 334 n. 1).

residence was no factor. Alien residents,[13] manumitted slaves[14] and, for
a while, the *perioeci*, the conquered indigenous population, were, however, excluded from citizenship.[15] When the natives ('barbarians'), in
whose midst the Greeks ensconced themselves, adopted the institutions
of a Greek city, there should have been no reason to prevent them from
being included among the citizens. It is assumed, however, that the
Greeks snubbed them, along class lines.[16]

Foreigners were generally well received if they could contribute
positively to the well-being of the city. Desirable strangers were usually
organized either as a *politeuma*, a self-contained political and social
unit, a city within the city, or as corporations or fraternities. (The best-
known *politeuma* regime was that of the Jews of Alexandria.[17]) In their
organization, both *politeumata* and fraternities imitated the governmental structure of the city.[18] Both were means for preserving the laws
and culture of the newcomers, but also for keeping them separate from
the city, because they were regarded as culturally inferior.[19] Primary
Hellenization was acquired through the Greek language. Genuine attainment of Greek culture was reached only through the gymnasium, a

13. *Katoikoi*; *metoikoi* in Athens.
14. This was in contradistinction to Roman Law: n. 15, below.
15. Rome's imperial success, had, as a decisive factor, the openness of Roman
citizenship. All people of the world were 'romanizzabili' (Giardina 1998a: 39), 'ro-
manizable'. No considerations of race, of stock, of (ethnic) origin, were obstacles.
The condition of barbarian was a historical condition, because culture had precedence over blood lineage. Similarly, manumitted slaves of Roman citizens did
become, according to Roman Law, Roman citizens.
16. Jones 1940: 158-62.
17. Described by Josephus, Philo, Strabo, and other literary sources; see Préaux
1978: 453-56. The term is also applied to soldiers settled on royal domains (Préaux
1978: 456).
Burkert (1995: 202) notes that a *polis* not only makes decisions about religion,
but actually makes religion. Citizenship meant, among other things, κοινωνία ἱερῶν,
community of religious life. Jews and Christians, who excluded themselves from
this *koinōnia*, would call their own form of religion their πολιτεία, constitution
(Philo, Josephus, *1 Clem.* 54.4, cf. Eph. 2.19). Clear distinction must be made,
insists Burkert, between *sacra*, cults and rituals, and belief; the latter is a concept
which hardly existed in practical Greek religion (vs Wilamowitz's 'der Glaube der
Hellenen') (Burkert 1995: 205).
18. Préaux 1978: 456, 458.
19. Préaux 1978: 456, 459.

central and exclusive political institution.[20] Honorary citizenship was often granted to physicians, poets and philosophers by the cities through which they passed, and this led to the 'internationalization' of this intellectual class. In general, however, citizenship was closed to foreigners, and the right to citizenship remained closely guarded.[21]

'Democracy' meant that magistracies were open to all citizens, yet the Athenian custom of choosing most magistrates by lot was not embraced elsewhere. The Hellenistic *poleis* preferred to elect their magistrates and strictly to limit their terms of office, to make certain priesthoods hereditary and to auction others. All important magistracies were *collegia*, the equally empowered members being drawn from the tribes, commensurate with their numbers. Magistrates were reviewed at the end of their terms. A particularly intriguing office was that of the eponymous magistrate. His name was used in dating public documents, but his functions were mostly ceremonial. This suggests a vestigially great authority. More often than not the eponymous magistrate was a priest, a dynastic cult priest, or a *stephanēphorus*, a sacred office. As cities tried to downsize their bureaucracies, the eponymous magistrate was sometimes replaced by other existing magistrates.[22]

The critical power in a democratic *polis* was held by the Council. It had extensive financial and deliberative functions and it acted as a 'checks and balances' system on the sometimes reckless Assembly. In Hellenistic times, virtually no legislative item reached the Assembly before the Council 'passed a preliminary resolution' on it. The common formula declared that a law was enacted by 'the Council and the people'. No legislative initiative could bypass the Council, even if it chose to move it to the Assembly without any debate. The Council's *de facto* control over legislation made it imperative, if it were to be a functional institution in a democracy, that the Council represent the mood and leanings of the people. This Athenian blueprint[23] was imitated by many, but by no means all, cities. Rather, different cities experimented

---

20. Préaux 1978: 456, 459.

21. Préaux 1978: 459, 442.

22. Jones 1940: 162-64.

23. Athens provided the model for an effective council. The council had a large membership (about 500 citizens), divided equally between the city's tribes, selected by lot, and changed every year or even more frequently. One member of the presiding committee was chosen by lot to chair both the council and the assembly for one sitting. Jones 1940: 165.

with different organizational structures and chose what they thought worked best. Most significant was a tendency toward oligarchy,[24] in which a board of generally wealthy and well-born magistrates sorted out proposed measures even before they reached the Council. Cities were mindful of the fact that they had to deal with kings (and later with Rome), and that they would receive a more favorable audience if their institutions were staffed by notables. Also, the citizenry found in its interest to select as magistrates those who could contribute opulently to the public services entrusted to them. In the end, magistrates paid for providing the very services they had to oversee.[25]

A most remarkable development illustrates a preeminent political feature of Hellenistic age. Previously, a clear demarcation existed between magistracies and liturgies. Magistrates (at Athens, for example) incurred no expenses and may even have been remunerated. Liturgies were the duty of moneyed persons and were thrust on them by magistrates. In Athens, Demetrius of Phalerum ended the practice of coercive spending, and the elected magistrates began to use public funds for their tasks. This became the case for much of the Hellenistic world. Yet magistrates were usually elected precisely because they were able to cover the expenses of the public works their offices were expected to oversee. Magistracies and liturgies overlapped. Magistrates turned into benefactors; civic functionaries became patrons; public servants, philanthropists. The state increasingly relied on the wealthy. Determining the needs of the state became the prerogative of the rich, and state priorities were determined by personal priorities. Under such conditions, democracy became sycophancy. Legislative activity became eulogy. The *polis* lived off charity, and the citizen's role in the legislative activity of the city declined considerably. The city was thus enfeebled politically, and its intellectual and economic creativity stunted.[26] By Paul's time the city's fiber had softened dangerously.[27]

24. Here again, Classical Athens set the example when it tried to limit the power of the rabble.

25. Jones 1940: 164-67.

26. Jones 1940: 167-69.

27. Jones calls this political affliction 'a convention'. 'Democracy was then in the Hellenistic age tempered by a convention that the rich should have a virtual monopoly of office, provided that they paid for it liberally' (1940: 168). That it worked must have been felt, by the thoughtful citizen, as no less dismaying. A democracy surrendering its prerogatives to the moneyed class, no matter how democratically minded, remained a deplorable sight of terminal political condition.

A.H.M. Jones is emphatic: 'It would scarcely be an exaggeration to say that the history of Greco-Roman civilization is the history of the cities' (1940: 299). Democratic traditions defined the cities for a long time—that is, until the citizenry surrendered its political power to moneyed potentates. Still, most of these, while pursuing their political ambitions, were civically minded and worked for the effective management and good reputation of the city. Throughout most of Hellenistic times democracy was so entrenched in the political tradition of city life that the overthrow of democratic institutions was never an option for either the kings or the upper classes. The Hellenistic state is monarchic. Political power rests with it. The Hellenistic kings ruled the cities in their kingdoms not so much as subject political entities but as self-administered properties. This does not mean in the least, however, that the institutions of the Greco-Roman city-states were irrelevant to governance. Quite the contrary; internally, the political vigor of the *poleis* remained great, the institutions strong. As Dio Chrysostom remarked in the first century CE, the city is a political and moral reality: *polis* means 'people dwelling in the same place and governed by laws'.[28]

It helps to make a critical distinction between political history and the history of institutions.[29] Otherwise, the danger lurks that one will disparage the social and political reality of the Hellenistic *poleis* and focus solely on the monarchic states, as if these alone were politically consequential. *Euergesia*, the benefactor system, did not in and of itself depoliticize the citizens, enslave the city or cause the community to disintegrate. It is true that a small propertied class, acting out of ambition as well as a desire to maintain social peace, became the bearer of the burdens of the state. At the same time, the classical institution of the Assembly did more than simply consent to the Council's proposals and enact honorific decrees.[30] Philippe Gauthier reads the scholarly tendency to devaluate the Hellenistic city as 'Atheno-centrism', namely modern historians' proclivity to pit every ancient city against Athens, a

---

Hellenistic *poleis* sank into blissful irrelevance. The only gain, if gain it was, was that, in this state of affairs, class struggle burrowed indefinitely. Socially, this system reduced the tension between the rich and the poor and ended the class conflict. The civic sense of the well-to-do increased dramatically, and under the fawning language of decrees it is possible to sense genuine ardor. See Jones 1940: 168.

    28. 19.20, *ap.* Saïd 1994: 216.

    29. It is what Gauthier 1984 sets out to do.

    30. See Gauthier 1984: 83-85.

contest in which all others are fated to disappoint. Hellenistic cities neither aped Athens, nor were they just mirror images of each other.[31]

The history of Hellenism is not uniform, nor is that of *euergesia*. The role of the *euergetēs* and the relation between him and the community can be thoroughly understood from decrees, public subscriptions and dedications. The situation differs between the earlier Hellenistic period, up to about the beginning of the second century BCE, and the later Hellenistic period. The first is marked by the prosperity of the middle class that followed the cessation of the *diadochi* wars, the second by the ruin of the same class as a result of the Macedonian, Syrian and Achaean wars, and the concentration of resources in the hands of a minority enjoying Roman favor.[32] During the first period, benefactors are honored for their patriotism rather than their generosity, and for excellence in executing the functions entrusted to them. They are honored, as the decrees proclaim, for the services they render the community (and individual citizens), and not for their personal qualities.[33] Wealthy citizens often step in to fend off financial crises. At the same time they serve as elected magistrates, obeying the city laws and submitting to the citizens' review at the end of their office. Honors are bestowed on them according to rigorous procedures, which had become even stricter at the beginning of the Hellenistic Age.[34]

In the second period, city affairs change hands, being transferred from the Assembly to an often hereditary minority that pays for the services required by the state and is repaid by having honors piled on it—an urban aristocracy and a cultural elite at the same time.[35] Second-century BCE inscriptions document a change in the function and situation of the benefactor vis-à-vis the city. It is only now that one can see the transformation of *euergesia* into a form of government, and that the *euergetēs* begins to enjoy a stature above that of other citizens. The benefactions the *euergetēs* renders the city are vital to its survival, whether these are

31. Gauthier 1984: 86.
32. Rostovtzeff 1941: II, 617-18, quoted by Gauthier 1984: 88.
33. These receive either the praise and the crown, or the highest honors (*megistai timai*), a statue in the agora, meals in the *prutaneion*, and best seats at public shows. In the third century any number of magistrates are honored for their distinguished service, but also for money advanced to the city during a shortage of cash in the treasury. Cities always suffered financial difficulties, due to their fiscal system and tax-farming. Gauthier 1984: 88.
34. Gauthier 1984: 87-90.
35. Gauthier 1984: 88 (quoting Lucien Robert).

embassies to kings or to Rome or gifts in the form of grain supplies, games, new buildings or oil for the gymnasium. The *euergetai* repeatedly receive the traditional honors, but new ones also emerge: sacrifices for their recovery from illness, funeral pageants, cults and so on. Decrees acclaim the moral qualities of the benefactor: his piety, faithfulness to parents, loyalty to friends. His nature is of a distinct kind. His *aretē* is said to have been manifest since youth, his conduct is proclaimed to be equal to that of his ancestors. As patrons of the city, however, the *euergetai* do not displace the citizenry. Councils and assemblies continue to meet, deliberate and decide city policies. Nevertheless, salvation comes from the benefactors, because of their wealth and because of the favor they enjoy at the royal or imperial courts.[36]

There is something else here. The city is the medium for spreading the Greek way of life, for maintaining Greek supremacy in the new kingdoms and for asserting the kings' ideologies. Kings and local dynasts make the city a showcase of the new world order. Moreover, the city has facilities and amenities (walls, gates, public areas, religious buildings, recreation and entertainment facilities, streets, aqueducts and drainage and sewerage systems[37]) that provide a high level of comfort to most citizens. Thus, the Greek character of a *polis* is not restricted to its political institutions or its public life. The very fabric of everyday life is also Greek.

The city of Dor provides a good example of the day-to-day aspects of Hellenization. Dor, on the Levantine coast of the Mediterranean, was an Oriental town, with Phoenician fortifications and Persian residential areas. In the second and first centuries BCE, however, it became a Greek city, a Hellenistic *polis*. Not only did its inhabitants assume Greek names and the Greek political structure,[38] but the Greek way of life

36. Gauthier 1984: 91-92. For major changes in the Council's prerogatives, see Jones 1940: 170-191.

37. For a good discussion of the case of Asia, see Owens 1991: 75-93, 149-63. For Strabo (64/63 BCE–21 CE), the *polis* is synonymous with civilization; a genuine city cannot exist in Celtiberia on account of the country's uncivilized character (τὸ ἀνήμερον) (3.4.13). For Pausanias (second century CE), the city is its buildings: a place which 'does not include public buildings, gymnasium, theater, market-place, water conducted to a fountain' cannot not be called a *polis* (10.4.1). For these and other examples of the variety of views of the city in the Roman Empire, see Saïd 1994.)

38. One is reminded that even the nationalistic Hasmoneans spontaneously took Greek names, an instructive example of the compelling force of Hellenism.

became entrenched in the minutiae of daily routine. In Dor one finds fine tableware pottery (deep-black glazed Attic earthenware, 'Megarian' bowls, imported 'West-Slope' utensils, *terra sigillata* vessels); miniature eastern Mediterranean perfume and medicine bottles; Greek oil-lamps; wine amphorae from Chios and Samos; clay braziers of a type known in Italy, Asia Minor and the Aegean Islands; votive offerings and cult objects reflecting the Greek and Hellenistic pantheon (clay figurines of Aphrodite and Tyche, stone statues of Hermes, and incense altars of a type common along the streets of many Hellenistic cities); bronze and other metal artifacts with Greek engravings; weights inscribed with the name of the *agoranomos*, the market official; and a profusion of Ptolemaic and Seleucid coins. All these bits of material culture bespeak the depth of Hellenization of an Oriental town.[39]

Architecture betrays the same Greek influence. Synagogues from the first century BCE—at Gamla in the Golan and in the plains of Jericho near Jerusalem—are astonishingly similar in design. Besides the central assembly room (a rectangular hall with colonnade and benches) and the *miqvaot* (pools and basins for ritual purification), these complex architectural structures include a *triclinium*, dining room, kitchen, and large open courtyards. The designs can be traced to the *bouleuteria*, the public halls of the Hellenistic age, or to the *basilicae* of republican Rome.[40]

With the coming of the Romans, things changed only marginally. Throughout the Hellenistic and (republican) Roman periods, the Hellenic and eastern Greek city-states remained internally self-ruling, usually with a vigorous self-esteem. Even after regional affairs attracted fateful Roman military intervention,[41] encroachments leading to subjection were basically unknown.[42] Greece only became a province of Rome in 46 BCE, under Julius Caesar, and even then the triumviral conflagrations

---

39. Stern 1994: 201-60.

40. Netzer 1998: 37.

41. The worst was in 146 BCE, Rome's action against the Achaean Confederacy, which ended with the destruction of Corinth. 'But Hellenic institutions, once the Romans retired, had a way of slipping back into place. Nothing, even in the Achaean documents, indicates the existence of census requirements, and the democratic character of governmental forms seems to have remained in force' (Gruen 1984: 524, 525 and n. 216).

42. See Gruen 1984: 520-23. 'Only misdirected hindsight can find Rome engaged in ever-increasing encroachment leading to Hellenic subjection. Continuities and repetition prevail, rather than gradual disintegration and submissiveness' (Gruen 1984: 527).

changed things little until Augustus's administrative dispositions of 27 BCE. For quite some time, the Greeks, at least the Hellenic Greeks, preserved their *eleutheria*.[43]

City life and ideals received renewed impetus with Augustus's re-organization of the eastern provinces. The new provinces, senatorial or imperial, were insulated from the abuses of unscrupulous tax-collectors when the system of taxation based on farming was replaced with direct taxes assessed on the basis of the census. Such reforms, which led to a new confidence and economic prosperity, boosted the process of Hellenization and the success of the *polis*. Founding cities became one of the criteria for the good emperor,[44] and the superiority of Rome was measured in the multitude of its cities.[45] While Augustus, under the Principate, significantly reduced the number of free cities, first in Greece and then in the other eastern provinces, those that retained this status kept their privileges, except that court appeals were now heard by the emperor or the local governor.[46] At the same time, new types of privileged cities appeared in the East: colonies of settlers from the West[47] and, more rarely, *municipia*, Greek cities awarded Roman citizenship.[48] The imperial government found that in most cases it was

43. Jones summarizes almost 1000 years of the history of the city's relationship with the larger rulers: 'The cities changed gradually from political corporations to administrative districts. The Hellenistic kings made but sparing use of the civic governments as agents for their administration, preferring to keep taxation in the hands of their own officials and concessionaires, and to maintain mercenary armies with which not only to fight their wars but to police the cities. The Roman republic on the whole kept up the same policy, and it was not until the principate that the central government made any extensive use of the cities for imperial services. From now on the civic authorities took a predominant part in collecting taxation, in maintaining the post and, from the third century at any rate, the roads along which it ran, in policing the country, and in supplying recruits, remounts and provisions for the army. These functions they continued to fulfill as long as they retained sufficient vitality to shoulder the burden, and even in the sixth century A.D. their part was important, though by now the central government was obliged to intervene extensively through its own officials to goad the councils into action (1940: 274)'.

44. Dio Chrysostom 40.6; 45.15

45. Aelius Aristides, quoted in Jones 1940: 326 n. 78.

46. Jones 1940: 131, 134-35.

47. Although Roman emperors established some Roman colonies in the East, these were scant and too isolated to influence significantly the Greek culture in which they were immersed, and ended by following the lead of the prevalent and mature Greek culture.

48. Jones 1940: 131-33.

much more profitable to terminate the system of direct administration of certain regions and to relegate local government to cities, either existing cities or ones newly created for this purpose.[49]

Collusion between the *polis* and the *basileia* remains the conspicuous feature of political, social, economic, cultural and religious life at the time Paul arrives on the scene, and this will provide him with the model for his own grand unified political theory. In Paul, the *polis*, a fellow-ship that derives its raison d'être and its authority from a divine source but that retains Hellenistic institutions in its structure, is conjoined to a divine *basileia*. The point of contact between the *polis* and *basileia*, between humanity and divinity, is evinced in expressions such as 'God's fellow worker' (συνεργὸν τοῦ θεοῦ, describing Timothy in 1 Thess. 3.2), 'our fellow worker in Christ' (συνεργὸν ἡμῶν ἐν Χριστῷ, describing Urbanus in Rom. 16.9) and 'For we [Paul and Apollo] are God's fellow workers; you are God's field, God's building' (θεοῦ γάρ ἐσμεν συνεργοί, θεοῦ γεώργιον, θεοῦ οἰκοδομή ἐστε, 1 Cor. 3.9). These phrases also reveal the importance of the human constituent in the divine–human partnership.

Paul the Architect

There is an expression in Paul that, above all others, reveals the political nature of Paul's self-understanding and his understanding of his work. This is σοφὸς ἀρχιτέκτων (*sophos architektōn*) 'master builder' (1 Cor. 3.10). It is also one of the most direct evocations in Paul of Classical political sources.

Aristotle calls *architektōnikē* a master art or, rather, science, which subordinates all beneath as an *architektōn* does his workers,[50] and he makes politics such a science par excellence.[51] For Aristotle, politics is a grand practical science, 'the most authoritative art and that which is truly the master art'.[52] Politics include both ethics, 'the end merely for

49. Jones 1940: 60-74. Rome did keep, however, the system of direct administration in the cases of provinces like Egypt, Judea, Cappadocia, and Thrace where the centralized control was still effective, and capable of delivering vast revenues (Jones 1940: 74).

50. *Nicomachean Ethics* 1.1094a14, *Metaphysics* 5.1013a14.

51. *Ethics* 1.1094a27-28.

52. δόξειε δ᾽ ἂν τῆς κυριωτάτης [lit. most lordly] καὶ μάλιστα ἀρχιτεκτονικῆς (*Ethics* 1.1094a28-29).

one individual',[53] and politics proper. The latter is the theory of the *polis*, the constitution and social structure of a political system that can best ensure happiness, the end of the state.[54] 'The political philosopher', writes Aristotle, 'is the architect of the end',[55] that is, the builder of public happiness and political good.[56] In its political aspect, practical reason (*phronēsis*) is reason applied to the community, to the *polis*. Political *phronēsis* describes, first and foremost, the legislator, the reformer. This primary political reason is again called 'a master art'.[57] It implies a specialized knowledge that is characteristic of the professional.[58]

Politics is concerned with the human association and the power relations between individuals in a stratified society. The simile of the master builder is a natural trope for the activity of the legislator and community-founder, and 'building' became a topos of political vocabulary. If Christianity was to be a viable society, it had to take the principles of politics into consideration. Paul speaks of himself as an expert in the science of community-building, of politics, and he bears witness to the popularity of the 'building' trope. The master-builder metaphor is a favorite of Paul's. *Oikodomē*, the building of the community, appears in most of his genuine letters (1 Thess. 5.11; 1 Cor. 3.1-14; 8.1, 10; 10.23; 14.3-5, 12, 17, 26; 2 Cor. 10.8; 12.19; 13.10; Rom. 14.19; 15.2, 20); unsurprisingly, it is in Galatians alone that Paul describes himself 'more a wrecker rather than a builder' (Gal. 2.18).

The context in which the self-designation *sophos architektōn* appears in 1 Cor. 3.10-14 is indisputably political. In this passage, Paul speaks of working together with God, as God's *sunergos* (1 Cor. 3.9), to raise a structure (*oikodomē*) on a foundation (*themelion*) that is Paul's alone (1 Cor. 3.10, cf. Rom. 15.20). Paul constructs a political theory for Christianity. His central practical preoccupation is the community—the founding and building of communities. This is an inescapable aspect of

53. *Ethics* 1.1094b7-12.

54. *Ethics* 1.1094b7-12, cf. 10.1181b12-24.

55. τοῦ τέλους ἀρχιτέκτων, lit. the master craftsman of the end (*Ethics* 7.1152b2).

56. *Politics* 3.1282a3, *Poetics* 1456b11.

57. ἀρχιτεκτονική (*Ethics* 6.1141b25, cf. 1.1094a14).

58. In *Poetics* 19.1456b11, it is applied to the rhetorician; in *Ethics* 6.1142a12-23 to mathematicians and metaphysicians; cf. *Politics* 3.1282a3, *Metaphysics* 5.1013 a14.

Paul's activity. He draws borders, organizes crowds, sets rules, creates a government, gives a constitution.

Political Fellowship

A *polis* is a political partnership, a κοινωνία (*koinōnia*). *Koinōnia* is another political term that infuses the Classical[59] and Hellenistic political vocabulary and that is characteristic of Paul's thought, as well.

Aristotle's political *koinōnia* is based on the notion of end, *telos*, which for the *polis* is to live well (*to eu zēn*). Φιλία (*philia*), friendship, is the motive of social life and the *polis*'s means of existence.[60] A *polis* is a partnership (*koinōnia*) of clans and villages living a full and independent life, that is, a happy and noble life.[61] It must therefore be the case that political fellowship (*politikē koinōnia*) exists for the sake of noble actions, not merely for living in common.[62] Political fellowship is not merely a partnership, but a partnership for the good life, a community whose purpose is to foster *aretē*.

Although the term was also used by the ancient Pythagoreans and by Plato, the meaning of *koinōnia* deepens in Hellenistic times. For the Hellenistic Pythagoreans, *koinōnia* denotes not only a social group but also a political *aretē*, a defining attribute of the divine ruler. It integrates the *polis* and the universe, and, while not canceling the distinction between the two worlds, it emphasizes the harmony and synergy between them. At the same time, it conveys the sense that the king is a being with a social inclination and a political disposition, who can carry the state and the subjects he rules.[63] Because of the king's *koinōnia,* the people have a relation to the universe at large and a chance to achieve *aretē*.

---

59. E.g., Thucydides 3.10; Plato *Symposium* 182c, *Republic* 5.466c; Aristotle *Politics* 1.1252a7.

60. *Politics* 3.1280b39-40.

61. πόλις δὲ ἡ γενῶν καὶ κωμῶν κοινωνία ζωῆς τελείας καὶ αὐτάρκους, τοῦτο δ᾽ ἐστίν, ὥς φαμεν, τὸ ζῆν εὐδαιμόνως καὶ καλῶς (*Politics* 3.1281a1-2).

62. τῶν καλῶν ἄρα πράξεων χάριν θετέον εἶναι τὴν πολιτικὴν κοινωνίαν, ἀλλ᾽ οὐ τοῦ συζῆν (*Politics* 3.1281a2-4).

63. Cicero translates *koinōnia* as *communitas*, and designates by it the community of world and city but also the virtue that characterizes the king vis-à-vis his subjects (*ap.* L. Delatte 1942: 241). Hellenistic Pythagoreanism makes 'community' the virtue of one. This remarkable political enallage, that substitutes the singular for the plural, is fully consistent with the mystical-monarchical doctrine of Hellenistic Pythagoreanism.

Koinōnia is an intricate, pivotal concept in Paul. It is the best name
for the Christian society, for it describes the fellowship with Christ
(1 Cor. 1.9), the inclusion in his body (1 Cor. 10.16) and the partnership
in Christ's sufferings and resurrection (Phil. 3.10).[64] *Koinōnia* is a
pneumatic association (Phil. 2.1, cf. 2 Cor. 13.13), a partnership in the
euangelion (Phil. 1.5) and a co-sharing of *pistis* (Phlm. 6). It defines a
social and economic identity (Gal. 6.6, verb). Often, *koinōnoi* is the
name Paul gives to the citizens of this community (e.g., 1 Cor. 10.18;
2 Cor. 1.7; 8.23).[65]

64. Wick 1994 (ch. 6) considers *koinōnia*, understood as mutual service and
rejoicing, the leitmotif of the entire Letter to the Philippians.

Sampley (1980: 60-71) reads *koinōnia* in Phil. 4.10-20 as a technical, legal
societas between Paul and the Philippians. The emphasis is thus on partnership.
Sampley thinks that partnership would have made the Philippians understand better
the nature of their relationship with Christ: 'They joined with Paul as equal partners
in living and preaching the gospel. Paul became their representative, and periodically
they sent him support for his evangelistic endeavors in their behalf' (61). There are
many problems with this approach. The most obvious are that Paul serves no one
but Christ and that he accepts no payment for his teaching. Also, equality is
citizenship in the Christ *polis*, but qualified in a pneumatic hierarchy. I think that
the reading association, fellowship, community is more appropriate. Paul appears as
lawgiver and statesman, bearer of the *euangelion*. The reading I prefer is political,
not economical. Significantly, as he moves on with his analysis, Sampley comes
increasingly closer to the political meaning of *koinōnia*. *Auto phronein*, being of the
same mind, which Sampley takes as a feature of *societas* (62-70), is a political
injunction to unity and cooperation. The same is the case with *sumpsuchoi* (see 71).
Tapeinophrosunē, humility, which he presents as basic to *societas* (66), is actually
the quality that most uniquely describes the membership in the Christ *polis*; its
sense is best rendered by the now proverbial expression 'to carry the cross'. In
Philippians Paul does not present a *societas Christi* as Sampley thinks, but a *polis
Christi*, with its members not *socii* but *polites*. Paul does not need to use a concept
of Roman law to make his point, for he has one that is much closer and more
comprehensible to his Greek addressees, one which pervades their political culture.
Sampley agrees that in Romans, *koinōnia* and the verbal forms and *auto phronein*
cannot refer to *societas*; he calls these uses 'sententious', their purpose being 'to
describe how the believers should care for one another. [They are] dislodged from
[the] original social matrix' (96). In recognizing that in Romans Paul refers to
something other than *societas*, Sampley misses the point even as he hits it.

65. *Koinōnia* is also used to translate in Greek the Latin *societas*. (*Koinōnia* will
be used, however, in Byzantine Greek to describe any contractual type society—
Fleury 1963: 45, *ap.* Sampley 1980: 45 n. 26.) The *societas* is a legally binding,
reciprocal and voluntary partnership or association towards a shared goal or concern,

Paul extends the 'partnership' meaning of *koinōnia*, a word that evokes intimacy and inextricable unity,[66] to designate a contribution, donation or collection (Rom. 12.13 [verb], 15.26; 2 Cor. 8.4; 9.13; Gal. 6.6.).[67] This is also the sense κοινωνοῦτες (*koinōnountes*) has in Rom. 12.13.[68] Paul is the earliest source for this usage. With the benefit of hindsight, it can be said that the system of social assistance and support it put in place is probably the single most important factor in the success of early Christianity, and it is probably Paul who set its foun-

mostly economic in character. Sampley acknowledges that '[n]ot every appearance of *koinōnia* is equivalent to the Latin *societas*' (1980: 29). One convincing case, however is Gal. 2.9, where a *koinōnia* is entered by the giving of the right hand, an act often associated in Hellenistic texts with a binding agreement, a formal commitment. Paul forms a *societas* with the Jerusalem pillars for the purpose of partitioning the missionary territory (1980: 26-36).

66. A papyrus from the time of Augustus uses it for marriage (MM, *s.v.* κοινωνία). See also LSJ, *s.v.* κοινωνία.

67. A papyrus dated 140 CE uses the revealing expression κατὰ κοινωνίαν, belonging in common (MM, *s.v.* κοινωνία).

68. A large number of studies are devoted to the social and economic issues within, and between, the early Christian communities, as well as to the social and economic Hellenistic and Roman environment in which they developed. The seminal work on the subject is Harnack 1908. He surveys (I, 147-198) the social and economic services offered by the *ekklēsia* to its members. Other important newer contributions to the economic aspect of Pauline communities are: Hands 1968 (on charities and social assistance); Hatch 1972 (on the organization of early churches); Hock 1980 (on Paul's tent-making and social class); Meeks 1983 (on the egalitarianism ideal); Gielen 1990 (on the economics of the Christian household); A.C. Mitchell 1992 (on friendship across status divisions); Clarke 1993 (on the economics of power in Corinth).

A plethora of recent articles and monographs deal with the social structures of early Christianity. A short list should include MacMullen 1974, 1975; Gager 1975; Malherbe 1977, 1983; Scroggs 1980; Theissen 1982, 1992; Stambaugh and Balch 1986; Watson 1986; M.Y. MacDonald 1988; Hodgson 1989; Lampe 1989; J.T. Sanders 1993; Witherington 1994. On the *collegium* typology of the early Christian communities, with its patronage networks and partnerships, see Judge 1960, 1960-61, 1972, 1980; Fleury 1963; Sampley 1980; Chow 1992; Hendrix 1992; as well as the study of Waerden 1979 on Pythagorean fellowship. Winter 1994 covers the topics of civic benefactions in which Christians were encouraged to engage and of the Christians' activity as citizens in the Hellenistic and Roman *poleis*. Rostovtzeff's acclaimed studies on the social and economic history of Hellenistic and Roman times (1941, 1957) are unsurpassed. A more recent good collection of articles is Crawford 1985.

dations in the *ekklēsiai* he established. In the Christian association, *koinōnia* is the legal tender for *all* intercourse between its members. The expanding semantic field of the word *koinōnia* precisely reflects Paul's worldwide ambitions for the Christian community.[69]

Ekklēsia, Oikos *and* Polis

The interplay among *oikos, polis* and *ekklēsia* in Paul remains vexing, even after much discussion. In analyzing this interplay, one must first understand that Paul both uses Classical/Hellenistic political terminology, which he charges with new meanings, and employs new political terms with recognizably old meanings. In the first case, the lexical constellation makes possible the new meaning; in the second, the conceptual matrix that the term carries with it renders its significance intelligible.[70] Here, I will emphasize the microstructural aspect of the system, the human household-assembly, *oikos-ekklēsia* part of the project, referring only occasionally to its macrostructural aspect, *oikos* as *basileia*, which will be developed in Chapter 5.[71]

---

69. *Koinōnia* is part of political thought. See, for example, Plato (*Laws* 5.736d-e), Aristotle (*Politics* 6.1320b10-11), Ps.-Charondas (fragment 10) and Ps.-Ecphantus (fragment 4). Although the Classical inspiration cannot be discounted, the source for this new understanding of *koinōnia* should be sought in the Hellenistic kings' philanthropy. It became so much an attribute of royalty that a decree of the Ptolemies, the legal document itself, is called *philanthrōpon* (φιλάνθρωπον) (Préaux 1978: 67). See also Chapter 4, Ps.-Charondas, fragment 10, for a more detailed presentation of this issue.

70. A note on Paul's use of the vocabulary of practical philosophy. Paul's terminology is, often, not consistent with that of philosophy. I regard this as intentional. Paul rejects political and moral terms (such as *polis, politēs,* or *aretē, adikia*) rendered famous by their use in connection with pagan practice and reflection. He accepts, however, those he can transfer from the public order to God (e.g., *dikaiosunē*), or those that are so suitable for his communities that he finds useful (e.g., *ekklēsia*). Finally, and most importantly, Paul adopts lexemes that are compromised (e.g., *stauros, tapeinos, doulos, diakonos*) and thus sets in movement the mechanism for the formation of Christian language. A new sociolect comes out of an idiosyncratic lexis.

71. *Ekklēsia* and *oikos* are only two of the many Pauline terms operative politically, either in the more limited domain of the human *oikos* or in the considerably vaster one of the divine *basileia*. While the functioning of *ekklēsia*, at the human scale of the *polis* and its transformations witnessed in Paul, is sufficient to make explicit one dimension of Paul's political emphases, the coordinates it dis-

The natural, characteristic and familiar locus of the political institution known as *ekklēsia* is the *polis*. As the Classical Greek world mutates into the Hellenistic world, and then as the Hellenistic world coalesces with and gives way to the Roman Empire, the *polis*, while the basic unit of administration in the East, loses much of its freedom and importance. Although 'the Roman Empire was to become a commonwealth of self-governing cities', as M. Rostovtzeff put it,[72] the *polis* becomes a shell of its former self and is often little more than an instrument in the imperial politics of domination and expansion.[73] Even in a shriveled *polis*, however, the *ekklēsia*, the citizens' assembly, retains significant power over matters of local interest. It continues to express the old ideal of self-government.[74]

Simultaneously, as public political life shrinks and sheds its relevance, the *oikos* expands its sphere and increases in significance; it itself becomes a *polis*. The household, especially in Roman times, develops into a vast and complex system of inner and outer connections of allegiance and obligation, a 'network of relationships, both internal— kinship, *clientela*, subordination—and external: ties of friendship and

plays at a cosmic scale are less obvious. There are, however, many other political concepts whose works display much more symmetry in both spheres, such as *dikaiosunē* or *pistis*.

72. 1957: I, 49, *ap.* Meeks 1983: 11.

73. Externally, Rome could interfere in its constitution, could suspend unruly assemblies, and could curb clubs, the chief means by which lower classes could obtain political advantages by having their voting power organized and prioritized (Jones 1940: 134). Internally, with the conflation of magistracies and liturgies, the distinction between magistrates and benefactors is increasingly blurred and the city appears to be their client (see Jones 1940: 168-69).

74. One difference between Paul's *ekklēsia* and that of the *polis* is immediately significant. The *ekklēsia* in a *polis*, in a democratic constitution, is the voting body of all adult (at least 18 years old), free, male citizens. The only citizens excluded from the *ekklēsia* were the *atimoi*, persons who by law or sentence had lost their political rights. *Metoikoi* (resident aliens, including freed slaves), *xenoi* (visiting foreigners), slaves, and females were excluded from political rights. See Hansen 1987: 7. Paul's *ekklēsiai* are limited neither by free birth, nor by gender, nor by any particular citizenship. Property qualifications, introduced by Rome for membership in the *ekklēsiai* of the Hellenistic *poleis*, are not a factor either. *Atimia*, however, seems to be a criterion for exclusion in Paul as well, and describes Greek immorality (Rom. 1.24, 26) or Jewish inflexibility (2.23). Cf. also Rom. 9.21 and 1 Cor. 15.43. See also 1 Cor. 11.14. *Atimia* is also a test case for language reversal in Paul: see 1 Cor. 4.10; 12.23; 2 Cor. 6.8; 11.21.

perhaps of occupation'.[75] In the end, the *oikos* effectively substitutes for the *polis* in meaning and extension.

Paul is one of our chief witnesses to this phenomenon. In establishing local communities, Paul gives a new force to the *ekklēsia* and a new dimension to the *oikos*. Paul's invigoration of the tightly knit, self-governing, conscientious *ekklēsiai*, and, at the same time, his effort to integrate them into an empire-wide *oikos* characterized by intense and mutually beneficial exchanges and alliances, were major reasons behind Christianity's becoming the premier social and political power of the Roman world by the fourth century CE.

To schematize it succinctly, for Paul the *oikos* is, first, a public meeting place, a gathering site for an *ekklēsia*.[76] (There is no necessity that the head of the household, the *paterfamilias*, be a Christian nor that all the household members be Christians.) The original meeting place of an *ekklēsia* was a member's house. The phrase ἡ κατ᾽ οἶκον ἐκκλησία, 'the assembly at the household [of so-and-so]' (with a local sense of the preposition[77]), makes the *oikos* the location for the gathering of an *ekklēsia*. *Oikos* is also a form of *ekklēsia*, a partially or fully converted[78] household with a meeting place. In either case, whether as an unassuming image of the city's assembly building (ἐκκλησιαστήρον, *ekklēsiastēron*) or as a form of the duly summoned and regularly constituted Assembly, the *oikos* becomes the new locus of the *ekklēsia*. The *ekklēsia* becomes aligned with the household, becomes a household institution, finds its meaning as part of the *oikos*. Finally, *oikos* is a private home (in the trivial sense of the word), a place with no public function, a place where one is 'at home', where things not allowed in public are permitted. This usage confirms the distinction between the public, and thus political, meaning of *oikos* and the private employment of *oikos*, *oikos* as dwelling or estate.[79] By making this distinction, Paul operates an

75. Meeks 1983: 76. Together with the *oikos*, other associations such as the club, *collegium*, private, professional and cultic organizations, or philosophical coteries gain importance. Basically, all forms of private, corporate fellowship know an explosion in Hellenistic and especially Roman times, in essentially direct proportion with exclusion from and concentration of political power.

76. Rom. 16.5; 1 Cor. 16.19; Phlm. 2; see also Col. 4.15.

77. Smyth 1920: #1690.

78. Converted either by Paul (1 Cor. 1.16, cf. 1 Cor. 16.15) or by others; thus, there are the many *oikoi* mentioned in Rom. 16.10-11, 14-15 or 1 Cor. 1.11. A similar case is the ἐκ construction, οἱ ἐκ τῆς Καίσαρος οἰκίας in Phil. 4.22.

79. Thus, ἐν οἴκῳ one can indulge in excessive eating or a woman can speak

emphatic separation between the public and the private, the collective and the personal.

In Paul, *ekklēsia* (sing.) is (1) a household assembly, (2) a city-wide assembly, (3) a global assembly or (4) the Judean groups. The first meaning, that of *ekklēsia* as a household assembly, has been considered above. It is quite likely that in a large city Christians would meet in many discrete places, constituting separate *ekklēsiai*.[80] These are usually referred to as the assembly 'at the household' or 'in the household' (κατ᾽ οἶκον [*ekklēsia*] or [*ekklēsia*] ἐν οἴκῳ), the veritable cells of the earliest Christian movement. As he works with *oikoi*, Paul thinks, mostly, in small, local and discrete political units—numerous *oikoi* housing minute, motley and lively *ekklēsiai*. Occasionally, though, there are hints in Paul of a city-wide *ekklēsia*.[81] And, sometimes, Paul seems to contemplate an *ekklēsia* that encompasses the entire Christian movement. The ἐκκλησία τοῦ θεοῦ (*ekklēsia tou theou*), the worldwide *ekklēsia* of God, the *ekklēsia* of a universal *oikos*, is distinguished from and listed together with the Jewish and Greek *ethnea*.[82] (In the fourth, a peculiar use of *ekklēsia*, Paul is designating the inchoate Jewish-Christians of Judea whom he 'persecuted'.[83]) *Ekklēsiai* (pl.) are (1) specific provincial or regional clusters[84] or (2) generic assemblies, be these of Christ,[85] or of God,[86] or of the Greeks.[87]

(1 Cor. 11.34; 14.35). Οἰκία, home, is where one can get drunk or display opulence (1 Cor. 11.22). This is the non-sacramental *oikos*, the place devoid of collective, political significance.

80. Such is the case in Corinth (1 Cor. 1.11; 16.16), or Rome (Rom. 16.5, 14-15) or Colossae (Phlm. 2), cf. Col. 4.15 about Laodicea. See Meeks 1983: 76, 143.

81. In Corinth: 1 Cor. 14.23, cf. 1 Cor. 5.4; 11.18, 20; 14.19, 28, 35. The same may be the case in 1 Cor. 1.2; 2 Cor. 1.1. Or in Rome, Rom. 16.23—meeting at Gaius's villa. Or in Philippi, Phil. 4.15. See also 1 Thess. 1.1; 2 Thess. 1.1.

82. 1 Cor. 10.32.

83. Gal. 1.13; 1 Cor. 15.9; Phil. 3.6. Cf. the plural *ekklēsiai* in e.g., 1 Thess. 2.4; Gal. 1.22. This reference to the *ekklēsia* in Judea, 'persecuted by Paul', may also very well be a deliberate suggestion to a restricted, limited Christian movement before Paul came about.

84. Such are the *ekklēsiai* in Galatia (Gal. 1.2; 1 Cor. 16.1), of Asia (1 Cor. 16.19), in Macedonia (2 Cor. 8.1), and of Judea (1 Thess. 2.14; Gal. 1.22). See Meeks 1983: 108, Branick 1989: 29. The sense is that of an alliance of *poleis*.

85. Rom. 16.16: αἱ ἐκκλησίαι πᾶσαι τοῦ Χριστοῦ, all the *ekklēsiai* of Christ.

86. 1 Cor. 11.16, 22; 2 Thess. 1.4: αἱ ἐκκλησίαι, the *ekklēsiai* of God. This expression occurs more frequently.

87. Rom. 16.4: πᾶσαι αἱ ἐκκλησίαι τῶν ἐθνῶν, all the *ekklēsiai* of the Greeks.

The force of the notion of *ekklēsia* is such that even Christianized Latin-speaking people of the West, who translated many other Christian technical terms, preserve the word untranslated. The reason, according to Deissmann, is that for all its words for assembly (*contio, comitia*), there was the feeling that Latin possessed no word exactly equivalent with *ekklēsia*.[88] And how could it, since Roman political history knows nothing of the institution of the *polis*?

Even more, the Romans have no political theories to offer, and although the political issues are Roman in practical form, their theoretical substance is Greek. Dionysius (of Halicarnassus)'s complex ῾Ρωμαϊκὴ Ἀρχαιολογία, *Roman Antiquities*, first century BCE–first century CE, written in Augustus's Rome, and in which traditional Greek categories form the underpinning of Roman illustrations, is a good example of this. Deissmann shows that even non-Christian Latin speakers felt the inadequacy of Latin to express the *polis* concept. Thus Pliny, in one of his letters to Trajan, writes, in precisely the context that describes the political structure of the *polis*, 'bule et ecclesia consentiente', with the approval of the βουλή and ἐκκλησία.[89] A bilingual inscription of 103–104 CE, found in the Ephesus theater, cited by Deissmann, has C. Vibius Salutaris, a Roman official, presenting a silver image of Artemis/Diana and other statues 'that they might be placed on pedestals in every *ekklēsia* in the theater' (ἵνα τίθηνται κατ᾽ ἐκκλησίαν [cf. Acts 19.23] ἐν τῷ [sic] θεάτρῳ [sic] ἐπὶ τῶν βάσεων/*ita ut [om]n[i e]cclesia supra bases ponentur*).[90] Again, the Greek term is retained when used to describe a Greek political institution with no equivalent in the Roman political environment.

Ekklēsia is an eminently political locution and intelligible exclusively in a Greek context to the point that it became indispensable to the Latin Christians (and the Latin authors referring to the Greek political gathering) as well. Moreover, to remove it from its cogent and coherent setting and persist to see it as the counterpart of the Hebrew *beit Israel* (as common in New Testament scholarship) is preposterous.

I am aware that *ekklēsia* is the LXX term for the community of Israel, whether assembled or not. This itself reflects the Greek usage and meaning. Meeks confidently traces the roots of *ekklēsia* (or *ekklēsiai*) of

---

88. Deissmann 1927: 112; see also M-M *s.v. ekklēsia*.

89. *Letters* 10.3; Deissmann 1927: 112.

90. Incidentally, this is a confirmation of Acts 19.32, 41 that the *ekklēsiai* in Ephesus gathered in the theater. Deissmann 1927: 113 and 113 n. 1.

God, either local (1 Cor. 1.2), regional (1 Cor. 16.1, 19; Gal. 1.2; 2 Cor. 8.1; 1 Thess. 2.14) or global (1 Cor. 10.32; 15.9; Gal. 1.13), to the biblical phrase 'assembly of the Lord', *ekklēsia tou kuriou*, which translates *qehal yhwh*, 'a formal gathering of all the tribes of ancient Israel or their representatives' (Meeks 1983: 108). Although, as Meeks (1983: 80-81) observes, the diaspora synagogue was 'the nearest and most natural model' for the urban Christian groups 'it is surprising how little evidence there is in the Pauline letters of any imitation of the specific organization of the synagogue'. *Ekklēsia* is never used by Philo or Josephus to describe the Sabbath meeting of the Jews.[91]

In the same way, *oikos* and the related terms have nothing to do with the Hebrew *beit Israel*, a widely held view. Against the evidence that 'Israel was never called "the household of God"',[92] many persist in seeing the source of the expression 'household of God' in the limited and provincial sense of 'house of Israel'. This is Greek terminology and Hellenistic thinking, applied to the *oikos/ekklēsia* of the early Christians.

Tellingly, because it discloses the exact source of Paul's appropriation of the term, Paul often identifies the *ekklēsia* with the city in which it is constituted, and he calls it by the name of the city's residents. A *polis* was always designated by the name of its citizen body, the members of the *ekklēsia*.[93] Thus Thucydides: 'It is men who make

91. Meeks 1983: 222 n. 34, referring to Linton 1959 and K. Berger 1976.

92. Cf. Meeks 1983: 77; Branick 1989: 17.

93. Hansen (1996) notes that the usual way of naming a *polis* was to use the nominative plural of the adjectival form of the name of the city as the official name of the community itself, and to use the toponym as the name of the urban center. Thus a citizen of Ambrakia was called Ἀμπρακιώτας, and the name of his *polis* was (οἱ) Ἀμπρακιῶται, whereas the toponym Ἀμβρακία was mostly used of the urban centre of the community (169). Political communities are designated by the collective use of the adjective. Often, a Greek carries a name, *onoma*, and a patronymic, *patronumikon*, which identify him uniquely (170), and an ethnic. The ethnic, *ethnikon,* could refer to a *polis* or to a region, a regional ethnic and a city-ethnic (176). All ethnics are related to toponyms. Is the message primarily topographical or political? (181) A *polis* is both an urban center and a political community. Found mostly outside the *polis* and encountered for both men and women (esp. in private, mostly sepulchral inscriptions), and sometimes in manumitted slaves, a city-ethnic seems to suggest geographical rather than political origin (183). Yet, the epigraphic evidence shows that city ethnics are primarily political (182-87). Regional ethnics form a mixed group (187-90): those derived from toponyms are primarily topographical, those designating a people suggest national identity though not necessarily membership in a political community

the city'.[94] When Paul writes to his people, he addresses them as members of the body politic; in Phil. 1.1, the *polis* is the Φίλιπποι, the Philippians. He identifies the city as the citizenry gathered in the assembly: τῇ ἐκκλησίᾳ Θεσσαλονικεών (1 Thess. 1.1; 2 Thess. 1.1). He also refers to the *ekklēsia* by the name of the city in which it functions: the *ekklēsia* in Cenchreae (Rom. 16.1), Corinth (1 Cor. 1.2; 2 Cor. 1.1) or Philippi (Phil. 4.15).[95] In all these examples Paul replicates[96] the town meeting of Classical Greek, Hellenistic and Roman usage, the *polis ekklēsia*. Yet, Paul uses the terminology current in the *polis* to refer to the *oikos ekklēsia*.[97] In a Pauline community people conduct their business by coming together in an assembly: συνερχομένων ὑμῶν ἐν ἐκκλησίᾳ.[98] Obviously, in calling an *ekklēsia* 'the Philippians', or 'the Thessalonians' or 'the Corinthians', Paul does not mean the entire citizenry or the assembly of the Greco-Roman city of Philippi, or Thessalonica or Corinth, but he conceives his communities *as* those *poleis*. Wherever one of these corporate associations is, it has no political model other than the *polis*. The traditions of the *polis* inform the Hellenistic writers; the *polis* forms the intellectual infrastructure of their thought. This is inescapable for Paul, as well.

Increasingly, the designation *ekklēsia*, the political institution par excellence, jumps species and infiltrates the household. We see Paul making a vital and vibrant connection between *ekklēsia* and *oikos*, underscoring the withdrawal of *ekklēsia* from the larger sphere of the *polis* to the intimate sphere of the *oikos*.[99] At the same time, though the

(190). Greeks remain the only people in the West to use hereditary surnames (sub-ethnic, city-ethnic, regional ethnic) as an indication of political status (as opposed to habitation, place of origin). It reflects the importance Greeks attached to being members of a *polis*; sub-ethnics and city ethnics were a prerogative of citizens to the exclusion of foreigners and slaves (190).

94. ἄνδρες γὰρ πόλις (7.77.7).

95. See also Meeks 1983: 108 and 229 n. 159.

96. These 'mimics or parody' the Greco-Roman example, writes Meeks (1983: 108).

97. In the later Pauline-inspired literature the *ekklēsia* becomes the equivalent of the *oikos*: ἐκκλησία θεοῦ ζώντος, the *ekklēsia* of the living God, is οἶκος θεοῦ, the household of God (1 Tim. 3.15, cf. 1 Tim. 3.5; 1 Pet. 4.17).

98. 1 Cor. 11.18; 14.19, 23, 28, 35.

99. The most immediate and major consequences of an *oikos-ekklēsia* political unit at microstructural level are many and momentous. One outcome is the power opportunity this offers women. See Torjesen 1995 for an excellent discussion of

evidence for this is less frequent, in Paul the *oikos* tends to distend into a global, kingdom-like, imperial, even cosmic dimension and, concurrently, the *ekklēsia*, by now infrangibly tied to it, becomes worldwide. Its institutions desert the *polis* to retire into the niche offered by the *oikos* or to occupy the large space of the cosmopolis within a monarchic political framework.[100]

this issue. This process also explains the conspicuousness of family terminology and the profusion of household legal metaphors so characteristic of Paul's political thought and so distinctive of his epistolary style. See Banks 1994, esp. 47-58; Schüssler Fiorenza 1983, chs. 5 and 8; Lyall 1984.

100. The pull of the *polis*, though thus transformed, is never forgotten. In the Letter to the Philippians the verb *politeuomai* (1.27) and the noun *politeuma* (3.20) are used to render the civic and political content of the *ekklēsia* and of its membership in its original setting. Though sometimes thought otherwise, the meaning of these terms in Diaspora Judaism, among the Greco-Roman Jews, are not Paul's meanings. *Politeuesthai* appears in a decree from Sardis (Josephus, *Ant.* 14.259-61) in which the city council and the citizenry, the *boulē* and the *dēmos*, confirm the right of 'the Jewish citizens (*politai*) living in our city' to 'come together and have a communal life (*politeuesthai*) and adjudicate suits among themselves, and that a place be given them in which they may gather together with their wives and children and offer their ancestral prayer and sacrifices to God…' (quoted by Meeks 1983: 34-35). *Politeuma* is a political unit formed by Jews in those cities were they constituted a large segment of the population, a city within a city; a recognized, semiautonomous body of residents in a city who, though not citizens, shared some specific rights with citizens (Meeks 1983: 36). *Politeuma* also applies to non-Jewish communities such as Italians and Syrians at Delos or natives of an older city refounded as a Roman colony, such as the πολιτεύματα of Phrygians, Beotians, and Lycians in Alexandria, Cretans in the Fayyum and Caunians in Sidon (Meeks 1983: 36 and 207 nn. 169, 170). Cf. Meeks 1983: 35, 207 n. 163. The relation between *politeuma* and *dēmos* is a matter of controversy. Josephus refers to Jewish residents in Sardis as citizens, *politai*; in Antioch, he calls them resident aliens, *katoikountes* (*Against Apion.* 2.39); elsewhere they are referred to as both *katoikountes* and *politai* (Meeks 1983: 34, 36). Could the confusion and ambiguity derive from the same interplay between *polis* and *oikos*? Be it as it may, Christians cannot have inferior status in the heavenly city.

Chapter 4

HELLENISTIC PYTHAGOREANS: THE *POLIS* GROUP

Hellenistic Pythagorean Corpus

The Pythagorean pseudepigrapha are a collection of texts, a few of which are attributed to well-known Classical Pythagoreans who flourished from the sixth to the fourth centuries BCE, such as Pythagoras, Philolaus, Lysis and Archytas,[1] but the majority of which are preserved under the names of their probable authors, for example, Ocellus and Sthenidas of Locri, Damippos, and Callicratidas of Sparta.[2] These latter produced not so much forgeries of illustrious predecessors as textbooks, manuals of instruction and philosophical propaganda for nonprofessionals,[3] in circles where Pythagoreanism continued to be a cultural factor and to exert philosophical authority even after the closing of the original Pythagorean School in the fourth century BCE. This was especially the case in southern Italy, especially on the eastern coast of the peninsula, including the area of Tarentum (modern Taranto), the location of the most famous of the new Pythagorean schools, and in eastern Sicily. (Both areas had ports of major importance for the traffic of ships in the Ionian and Tyrrhenian Seas.) The Pythagorean teachers and manuals also certainly circulated in other areas of the Aegean and Mediterranean basins. The probable period for the production of many of these materials is between 270 and 168 BCE, that is, between the Roman conquest of southern Italy that resulted from the war with Pyrrhus—making avail-

---

1.   Most of our information about the Pythagoreans comes from Iamblichus's five-part collection: *On Pythagorean Life* (Περὶ τοῦ Πυθαγορικοῦ βίου), *Introduction to Philosophy* (Λόγος προτρεπτικὸς εἰς φιλοσοφίαν), and three treatises on mathematics, written at the end of third century CE; and from Philostratus' *Life of Apollonius of Tyana*, about a first century CE mystic with Pythagorean leanings, written in early third century.

2.   Thesleff 1961: 74-75.

3.   Bickel 1924, Wilhelm 1915, Ferrero 1955, *ap.* Thesleff 1961: 59, 72, 96, 101.

able an avid market and eager consumers for this kind of Greek knowledge—and the year when Macedonian power was destroyed in the battle of Pydna. The latter date marks the start of the great invasion of Rome itself by Greek learning and art, when the Doric South lost its importance and became a cultural backwater.[4] The texts continued to be known and used, however, not only in the late Hellenistic Era but also into the first centuries of the Christian Era. Stobaeus,[5] who preserved most of these fragments in his *Florilegium* (or *Sermones*), read them in the early fifth century CE, in itself an important testimony to the continued circulation and widespread appeal of these writings.

A word of caution must be inserted here. The dating and even the existence of Hellenistic Pythagoreans has been questioned by scholars, though less so of late. Such debates, however, are irrelevant to this study.[6] For the thesis being developed here it is sufficient to show that, preceding and around the time of Paul's activity, Hellenistic political theories of the kind manifest in Paul's writing were common and widely diffused.

The Hellenistic Pythagorean writings are characterized by conspicuous eclecticism. They rely extensively on Platonic and Aristotelian material even for the information they contain on ancient Pythagoreans.[7] Genuine

4.   See also Thesleff 1961: 97-99.

5.   Ἰωάννης ὁ Στοβαῖος or Στοβεύς, from Stobi, Macedonia. In early fifth century Stobaeus wrote four books, two of *Eclogues* (Ἐκλογαί), and two of ancient *fragmenta*, called the *Florilegium* (Ἀνθολόγιον), allegedly for the use of his son Septimius. Although bearer of a Christian name, Stobaeus preserves not a single Christian text.

6.   Since besides the Hellenistic Pythagorean corpus and the Roman Pythagorean texts there is not a single witness—no gravestone, no inscription, no papyrus—that points to the existence of a Pythagorean group with Pythagorean beliefs in the Hellenistic times, Burkert wryly writes that there is a flood of Pythagorean writings, but no Pythagoreans (1961: 234, *ap.* Balch 1992: 386-87). The literature is, he thinks, apocryphal. But, Burkert adds, this literature calls actual Pythagorean groups into existence; in place of the Pseudopythagorica appear Pythagoreans (Burkert 1961: 235, *ap.* Balch 1992: 387). I think, however, that most of the names attached to the so-called Pseudopythagorean corpus actually belong to real people; the prefix 'pseudo' ought to be removed from many of their names and the appellation 'Pseudopythagorica' changed to 'Hellenistic Pythagorean'.

7.   Praechter (1891) first noticed references to Aristotle's *Ethics* and *Politics* in Callicratidas and Hippodamos. For parallels to Classical Greek thinkers, particularly for the authors of the *polis* group, see esp. A. Delatte 1922. L. Delatte 1942 is especially important for the sources used by the writers in the *basileia* group.

Pythagoreanism is rarely the concern. The motley assortment of Academic, Peripatetic and some Stoic doctrines in these works has been noted ever since modern scholarship first paid attention to them.[8] Scholars soon observed that the late Peripatetic school is the most important source for Hellenistic Pythagorean literature.[9] Often the tracts appear to be regurgitated Academic and Peripatetic political philosophy masquerading as Pythagorean teachings. Hellenistic Pythagoreans, however, overcame the differences that splintered those schools and produced compositions for popular religious need,[10] philosophical propaganda for lay people.[11] This corpus is an outstanding case history of Hellenistic times—a significant cross-section of the popular political, ethical and religious feelings of the urban Hellenistic liberal individual. These works are also first-rate documents for revealing the state of Academic and Peripatetic ideas—their mingling, manipulation and shift of focus—during the heyday of the Hellenistic era, specifically the third and second centuries BCE. In general, we may say with confidence that the Pythagorean pseudepigraphical texts functioned as channels of transmission of Classical political philosophy into the Hellenistic culture at large.

Many of these works can be banded in groups with homogenous content, which indicates that common sources were used in their composition.[12] Their proliferation suggests the demand for these writings and the esteem in which they were held. For our purposes, the controversy surrounding the dating of the many scraps that form the available Hellenistic Pythagorean corpus has a reassuring side.[13] Paradoxically, the fact that the scholars' disagreements mark out so wide a compass of

---

8. From Praechter (1891) onwards.

9. E. Zeller 1923: III, 2, 126, 158, and Theiler 1926, *ap*. Balch 1992: 385.

10. Theiler 1926: 153, Burkert 1962: 85, Balch 1992: 385, 387.

11. Thesleff 1961: 27-29, 46, 72.

12. Thesleff 1961: 92-96.

13. Many scholars have tried their hand at dating Stobaeus' fragments: Praechter 1891 (first century BCE–first century CE), Wilhelm 1915 (first century BCE–second century CE), A. Delatte 1922 (early date, fourth century BCE), Theiler 1925, 1926 (first century BCE), Marcovich 1964, Burkert 1961 (beginning with third century BCE), 1962 (many after 150 BCE), 1972 (many about Augustus's time), Thesleff 1961 (after third century, most after second century BCE), 1972 (late second century BCE), Moraux 1984 (esp. 605-83), Huffmann 1985, Fiedler 1986. The tendency is to move the writings toward later dates, but rarely later than first or (even rarer) second century CE.

time—from the early Hellenistic period to the second century CE—gives us confidence that the political ideas that these fragments expound were 'at home' across hundreds of years and that these materials are representative of the spirit of Hellenistic and Roman times generally.

The issue of dating aside, there remains the question what to call these texts. Designating them 'Hellenistic Pythagorean' may be regarded as simply a matter of convenience (backed up by significant scholarly consent). I do not make the case that these writings represent a Pythagorean *tradition*. Perhaps a more accurate way of citing this mass of writings would be always to put Hellenistic Pythagorean between quotation marks, but this I have avoided for reasons of practicality. These texts repeat Plato and Aristotle and assume a southern Italian, Pythagorean pose and lexicon. The name given them is of no consequence for this investigation. Accurate dating and/or precise attribution are no critical matter here. What is really significant in the context of this study is the very existence of these texts, the incontrovertibility of their reality.

These are Hellenistic compositions. They are situated in a period that encompasses Paul's active period. They had widespread circulation. They are political in content and focus on the Hellenistic king. They may be sources for Paul (which I consider likely) or products of the same environment. This body of evidence is so pertinent to understanding Paul and early Christianity it cannot be ignored.

In the sections that follow I develop the following arguments: (1) that Hellenistic Pythagoreans relied extensively on Plato's and Aristotle's works, and (2) that the Hellenistic pseudepigrapha formed an important part of the cultural background for Paul's politics. Paul, as I have already begun to explain, produced a two-tiered political system. One layer focuses on the issue of divine rule and displays similarities with the Hellenistic Pythagorean writings associated with the names of Diotogenes, Sthenidas and Ecphantus. They are known as the '*basileia* group'. The other layer, though still imbued with what we would call religious concerns, emphasizes human institutions. This layer of Paul's political system shows likenesses with what I call the '*polis* group' of Hellenistic Pythagorean writings, which includes works of Ps.-Archytas, Hippodamos, Callicratidas, Ocellus, Damippos, Euryphamos, Ps.-Zaleucus and Ps.-Charondas. It is to the *polis* group that I first turn my attention.[14]

14. Greek spellings: *basileia* group: Διωτογένης or Διοτογένης, Σθενίδας

Ps.-Archytas: περὶ νόμου καὶ δικαιοσύνης
(peri nomou kai dikaiosunēs), On Law and Justice

The writer known to us as Ps.-Archytas appears to have lived in the western part of the Greek world at the middle or end of the fourth century BCE.[15] The available fragments of his work *Peri nomou kai dikaiosunēs*[16]—whose very title announces an issue of paramount importance for a political analysis of Paul and, specifically, of the Letter to the Romans—deal with the distinction between *nomos* and *dikaiosunē*. The treatise thus belongs to the tradition that places the two concepts at the core of political discourse—the tradition, that is, that connects Plato (*Republic, Laws, Politicus, Protagoras*) and Paul (Romans).

The question of the difference between law and justice implies two further issues: the distinction between written and unwritten law, especially the meaning of the latter), and the topic of divine, or natural, law (often represented by *dikaiosunē*). A very brief overview of the history of these questions in Greek political thought is therefore in order.

The Sophists—for example, Critias and many other fifth century BCE writers—posited an utter antinomy between the order of law and the tendencies of nature. Sophocles,[17] Plato,[18] the Pythagoreans—whose cult

Λοκροῦ, Ἔκφαντος. *Polis* group: Ἀρχύτας, Ἱππόδαμος, Καλλικρατίδας, Ὄκελλος or Ὄκκελος, Δάμιππος, Εὐρύφαμος or Εὐρύφημος, Ζάλευκος, Χαρώνδας.

15. Thesleff 1961: 114.

16. Stobaeus 4.1.135-138 pp. 82-88 and 4.5.61 p. 218 Hense = T 33.1-36.11; A. Delatte 1922: 71-124. *On Law and Justice* may be dated to the fourth century BCE, though this remains a matter of much dispute. A. Delatte thinks it is an authentic work of Archytas of Tarentum which influenced Plato and Aristotle (1915: 121-24). Thesleff thinks things were the other way around, but still places the work in pre-Hellenistic times (1961: 92-96). Theiler (1926), followed by Goodenough (1928), regards this treatise as compatible with second–first century BCE politics and considers it the work of an anonymous writer (*ap.* Thesleff 1961: 35). For the purpose of this study, it is sufficient to accept Ps.-Archytas as part of the Pythagorean pseudepigrapha, a Hellenistic corpus, a large part of which displays great interest in political theory.

NOTE: Henceforth, (1) Hense refers to the Wachsmuth-Hense 1884–1912 (reprint 1958) edition of Stobaeus' *Anthologium*; (2) sigla T refers to Thesleff's 1965 edition of the Hellenistic Pythagorean texts; (3) the numbering of fragments follows A. Delatte, not Thesleff, except where noted.

17. *Oedipus Rex*, 865-67.

of the law begins with Pythagoras himself—oppose the notion that the laws are products of art, that is, that they are created by the imagination of wise men. Thrasymachus, in my opinion, represents the Sophists' view when he speaks of the ruler as a political professional as opposed to an intellectual (i.e. Plato's philosopher-king).[19] Thrasymachus's 'right of the stronger' doctrine is also opposed by Plato on the ground that it is in conflict with the laws and conventions of human societies. Plato, in *Gorgias* (482-84), has Socrates and Callicles debate whether law and virtue oppose nature, whether nature condones passions, and whether the laws were invented for the benefit of the weak.[20] The two terms, justice and law, *dikaiosune* and *nomos*, are, more often than not, identified in the fourth and third centuries BCE,[21] but later, in Hellenistic times, are separated again.[22]

Furthermore, the relation between written and unwritten laws—that is, the question of where the laws as man's productions stand vis-à-vis traditions, or laws of nature, or laws of God—had a long history of debate among ancient philosophers, sometimes with the same author shifting sides over time. Three basic positions on what the unwritten laws are can be identified. For Thucydides, Plato, Isocrates, Aristotle[23] and many after them, unwritten laws are customs and traditions particular to one people. For another group, which includes Xenophon, Demosthenes, Aristotle and Anaximenes (of Lampsacus),[24] unwritten laws are customs common to all people. For Demosthenes and Aris-

18. E.g., Plato, *Laws* 10.

19. *Republic* 1.336b-347e.

20. A similar argument takes place between Archytas and Polyarchos in Aristoxenus (fourth century BCE), *ap.* Athenaeus (second/third century CE) 12.545-47; Aristoxenus' Πυθαγορικαὶ ἀποφάσεις, Pythagorean Maxims, is a major source for Pythagoras and Classical Pythagoreans.

21. Xenophon, Antiphon, Plato, not to mention the Pythagoreans, for whom 'la Justice consiste à observer la Loi' (A. Delatte 1922: 83).

22. Against A. Delatte 1922: 79. Aristotle discusses the distinction between natural and conventional, law-bound, justice, φυσικόν–νομικόν δίκαιον, in the context of political justice (*Ethics* 5.1134b18-1135a15).

23. Thucydides 2.37.2; Plato, *Republic* 4.425a-e, *Laws*, 6.773e, 7.788b; Isocrates, *Areopagiticus* 41; Aristotle, e.g., *Ethics* 10.1180a35, *Politics* 6.1319b40, *Rhetoric to Alexander* 13.

24. Xenophon, *Memorabilia* 4.4.19; Demosthenes, *Against Aristocrates* 61, 85; *Against Stephanus* 1.53; *On the Crown* 275; Aristotle, *Rhetoric to Alexander* 10, 15; Anaximenes, *Rhetoric* 2 (*ap.* A. Delatte 1922: 80).

totle,[25] 'right according to nature' (κατὰ φύσιν, τὰ τῆς φύσεως οἰκεῖα) is a common right (κοινόν) constituted by a uniform conception of right and by an ensemble of customs that are more or less invariable for all people. This right is the 'community of nature' of all human beings. Finally, for Antiphon and Alcidamas,[26] the laws of nature are what make us all equal and free. They are contrary to the written laws *and* to customs and have to do with human nature itself. Similarly, later Hellenistic writers, Philo and Cicero,[27] both influenced by the Stoic doctrine, speak of a unique unwritten law, the will of God or of nature. For the Stoics, as Cicero's case testifies, the law of nature is the foundation of human right, right reason, the divine rule of the constitution of the universe.[28]

Fragment #1.[29] The Hellenistic Pythagoreans continue earlier debates on the distinction between written and unwritten laws. Paul's identification of two modes of violating the laws—the Greeks' transgression and that of the Jews (Rom. 1.18-32 and 2.17-29, 3.21-30)—can be best explained by knowledge of precisely such a tradition of argument. For Ps.-Archytas (though fragment #1 may go back to the genuine Archytas), the unwritten laws are the fathers and the guides of the written laws.

Fragment #2a.[30] In characteristic Pythagorean fashion, Ps.-Archytas compares law with music. The law is to the soul and to human life as harmony is to the ear and to the voice (νόμος ποτ᾽ ἀνθρώπου ψυχάν τε καὶ βίον ὅπερ ἁρμονία ποτ᾽ ἀκοάν τε καὶ φωνάν) (T 33.3-4); the law educates the soul and organizes life (παιδεύει μὲν τὰν ψυχάν, συνίστησι δὲ τὸν βίον) (T 33.5); and harmony teaches (ἐπιστάμονα) (T 33.6) the ear and sets the ear and the voice in accord (ὁμόλογον) (T 33.6). In Paul, the importance of harmony, the stereotypical, unmistakable trope of the Pythagorean milieu, is overwhelming. As do the Pythagoreans, Paul mainly uses harmony as a political metaphor, for concord. But

25. *Rhetoric to Alexander* 13, 15 (*ap.* A. Delatte 1922: 92 and notes).
26. Rhetoricians of the fifth and fourth centuries BCE.
27. Philo, *Abr.* 5; Cicero, *Pro Milone* 10, *Philippicae* 11, 12, 28, *Laws* 2.9 (*ap.* A. Delatte 1922: 80).
28. A. Delatte 1922: 92 and notes.
29. Stobaeus 4.1.135 p. 82 Hense [not in Thesleff]; A. Delatte 1922: 79-82.
30. Stobaeus 4.1.135 p. 82 Hense = T 33.3-6; A. Delatte 1922: 83-84.

Paul's musical dissertation is rich in yet other Pythagorean undertones, amounting to a genuine theory of sound (φωνή) (1 Cor. 14.7-11, cf. also 1 Thess. 4.16), produced by both instruments (flute, lyre, bugle) and voice (languages). The ability to match sound (φωνή) with an instrument makes its message intelligible, just as knowledge (γνωσθήσεται) of a language (φωνή) gives that language meaning. Paul makes the point dramatically, by suggesting the dire consequences of the failure to sound a trumpet properly, or to understand its meaning, in battle. Paul parallels the distinctness in tones of instruments (διαστολή τοῖς φθόγγοις) with semantically intelligible speech (εὔσημος λόγος). One encounters here an unusually powerful instance of the characteristic Pauline dialectic. The tension between the emphasis on harmony and the importance of glossolalia as an atonal[31] expression of unity is beautifully illustrated. Glossolalia appears as a major, if not the highest, activity taking place in the Pauline assembly (ἐκκλησία), but it is in need of interpretation, of organization and discipline. No φωνή is meaningless (ἄφωνος), but speaking it is not enough; one also needs to interpret (διερμηνεύῃ) it (1 Cor. 14.13).[32] Glossolalia functions in Paul, and paradoxically so, in the same way that games, music and dance do in the didactic theories of Plato and Aristotle: it has a binding character and helps develop a social instinct just as it helps release pent-up energies.[33]

Fragment #2b.[34] Ps.-Archytas distinguishes between an animated law (νόμος ἔμψυχος, *nomos empsuchos*, i.e. the king, βασιλεύς), and an inanimate law (ἄψυχος, i.e. the written law, γράμμα).[35] This is a constant in Hellenistic Pythagoreanism.[36] The king-law identification is also known to Plato[37] and Aristotle,[38] in both of which there may be some Pythagorean strain. Aristotle calls the judge justice personified, δίκαιον

31. Or, to use Arnold Schönberg's term, *pantonal* style.
32. Paul would push this affinity between music and language, based on the common element of sound, to people, in showing that there is no distinction between a Jew and a Greek (Rom. 3.22).
33. Plato, *Republic* 3, *Laws* 2.653d, 659d, 664c; 7.797; Aristotle, *Politics* book 8; or the Hellenistic Pythagorean Diotogenes, in περὶ ὁσιότατος, T 76.1-2.
34. Stobaeus 4.1.135 pp. 82-83 Hense = T 33.6-12; A. Delatte 1922: 84-86.
35. See also Chapter 5, especially Diotogenes.
36. All the previous quotes T 33.8.
37. *Politicus* 294a-b.
38. *Politics* 3.1284a3-16.

ἔμψυχον (*dikaion empsuchon*).[39] *Nomos empsuchos* had a remarkable career all the way through the first and second centuries CE, in Philo, Musonius, Plutarch and Clement of Alexandria,[40] and even further into Byzantine and medieval times. For Paul, Christ alone would fill this role, as the connector between the two tiers of his unified political system.

In the same fragment, εὐδαιμονία (*eudaimonia*) (T 33.10) is understood as the ideal pursued in the organization of a political community.[41] In this, Ps.-Archytas follows Plato and Aristotle:[42] *eudaimonia* is the end of a political society. In the Hellenistic mind—that is, somewhat later than Ps.-Archytas—political *eudaimonia* is replaced by σωτηρία (*sōtēria*): not happiness, but preservation, security, deliverance. This is also the case with Paul. The end of *pistis* is *sōtēria* (Rom. 1.16).[43]

Fragments #3a-b.[44] According to Ps.-Archytas, the law must (1) conform to nature (ἀκόλουθος...τῇ φύσει) (T 33.20); (2) be effective for political actions (δυνατὸς τοῖς πράγμασι) (T 33.20-21), that is, be appropriate as political law; and (3) be useful to the political community (συμφέροντος τᾷ πολιτικᾷ κοινωνίᾳ) (T 33.21). Let us treat each of these conditions—and similar themes in Paul—in turn.

First, what does it mean for a law to imitate the justice of nature (μιμεόμενος τὸ τᾶς φύσιος δίκαιον) (T 33.23-24)? The justice of nature is proportional justice, justice κατ᾽ ἀναλογίαν, justice that apportions to each according to his worth (τοῦτο δὲ ἐστιν τὸ ἀνάλογον καὶ τὸ ἐπιβάλλον ἑκάστῳ κατὰ τὰν ἑκαστου ἀξιάν) (T 33.24-25). This Hellenistic text, which itself dwells on Aristotle, has strict equivalences in Paul. For Paul, gifts (χαρίσματα) are a measure of *dikaiosunē* and are distributed in proportion to *pistis* (κατὰ τὴν ἀναλογίαν τῆς πίστεως) (Rom. 12.6).[45] The similarity of Ps.-Archytas's text to Rom. 12.6 is

39. *Ethics* 5.1132a22.

40. Philo, *Life of Moses* 1.162; Musonius (in Stobaeus 4.7.67); Plutarch, *To an Unlearned Ruler* 780d; Clement of Alexandria, *Stromata* 1.26.151, 2.4.158 (A. Delatte 1922: 85).

41. A. Delatte 1922: 84.

42. Plato, *Republic, passim*; Aristotle, *Politics* 3.1280b33-35, 7.1323b30, 7.1324-a13.

43. For fragment #2c, Stobaeus 4.1.135 p. 83 Hense = T 33.13-18; A. Delatte 1922: 86-90, see Damippos, p. 160 below.

44. Stobaeus 4.1.136 pp. 83-84 Hense = T 33.19-28; A. Delatte 1922: 91-93.

45. Cf. Rom. 12.3, to each according to the measure of *pistis* that God allotted, ἑκάστῳ ὡς ὁ θεὸς ἐμέρισεν μέτρον πίστεως.

striking in yet another way. The Hellenistic Pythagorean fragment, apparently explaining κατ' ἀναλογίαν, says that many are not competent to receive the full natural right, what is good by nature and primary, but only what is convenient and acceptable to them (πολλοὶ γὰρ τὸ τᾷ φύσει καὶ πρᾶτον ἀγαθὸν [οὐχ] ἱκανοὶ δέξασθαι, τὸ δὲ παθ' αὐτοὺς καὶ τὸ ἐνδεχόμενον) (T 33.26-27). Right is that which is in harmony with those to whom it applies (δυνατὸς δέ, εἰ ποτὶ τοὺς νομοθετουμένους ἔχει τὰν συναρμογάν) (T 33.25-26). Ps.-Archytas's text makes it clear that this relativity is political, not moral. This helps us understand the Pauline passage, in that the *charismata* define not merely a religious but also a political community. (It is useful to remember that *dikaiosunē* itself is a political and not a religious concept.)

Fragments #4a-b.[46] In analyzing the second defining criterion of law, Ps.-Archytas uses an agricultural metaphor which is also dear to Paul (e.g., Rom. 11.21). The law must take into account soil (χώρα) and location (τόποι); as the terrain does not everywhere produce the same fruit (κάρπος), so the souls of humans are differentiated in *aretē* (T 34.1-3). Hence also the diverse kinds of constitutions and the various modes for the distribution of justice: aristocracy, where justice is apportioned 'analogically' (T 34.5) and the most is given to the greatest; democracy, where a 'geometrical' allotment apportions an equal quantity to everyone; and oligarchy and tyranny, both of which distribute justice 'arithmetically', giving the greatest to the smallest number (T 34.3-10).[47] Ps.-Archytas takes his lead from Aristotle. Aristotle contrasts the

46. Stobaeus 4.1.137 pp. 84-85 = T 33.30-34.14; A. Delatte 1922: 93-109.

47. The fragment, as preserved by Stobaeus, has dubious mathematics. But its meaning is unambiguous.

Harvey (1965) uses this doctrine of arithmetical and geometrical proportion to revise the dating of Stobaeus' fragments of Archytas, and, in the process, discusses the vexing issue of the apparent conflict in the meaning of these terms when compared with the Classics. He argues that the interpretation of 'proportion', τὸ ἴσον, in Archytas makes the work pseudonymous and late (first century CE?). In the early authors, including the authentic Archytas, democrats praised 'equality' in the sense of arithmetical proportion, while aristocrats valued geometric proportion. In later authors, Boethius and this Ps.-Archytas fragment, arithmetical proportion results in the men of greatest worth having power (aristocracy), and geometric proportion means that all men of whatever worth have power (democracy) (Harvey 1950: 124, 131-38 and nn. 89, 112, 116, *ap.* Balch 1992: 388). While the argument is exciting, such a reversal may be due to misreading or scribal error. Plutarch (second century

two kinds of particular justice (μέρος δικαιοσύνης)[48] as a geometrical to an arithmetical proportion. There are similar passages elsewhere, as in the discussion of the distribution of power in different kinds of constitutions,[49] and when Aristotle determines that persons alike according to nature (κατὰ φύσιν, *kata phusin*; or, as Paul would put it, with an equal share of *pneuma*) must have the same principle of justice[50] and that justice is contrary to nature (παρὰ φύσιν, *para phusin*) if it works any other way.[51] This view explains Aristotle's critique of democracy, which, he says, replaces the natural criterion of merit with that of numbers.[52]

Every time a notion of justice is presented in which the analogical principle is at work, a disdain for democracy is implicit.[53] So also in Paul. Inequality as the foundation of *dikaiosunē*, is, to express it fatuously, a major crux of Pauline thinking. Paul's subtle accounting is not dissimilar to that of other political theorists who emphasize justice as a type of equality of the analogical kind, corresponding to an aristocratic constitution. The Pythagoreans, when addressing a large public, buttress the mathematical considerations with an appeal to philosophy and religion, showing that in nature such a type of equality is the product of the God's will and urging that such a fine model be imitated. Paul, less rational than his pagan counterparts, starts with the model rather than the math.

Like Ps.-Archytas, with his preference for the analogic distribution characteristic of the aristocratic constitution, Paul is inclined toward a pneumatic constitution that follows a directly proportional relation to

CE) has things right. He comments (in *Table-Talk* 8.719b-c) that the political approximation of the natural, geometrical justice is aristocracy (lit. virtuous oligarchy) and legitimate kingship; the arithmetic equality is the feature of democracy (*ap.* A. Delatte 1922: 102.) (Plutarch goes on to call the geometrical proportion *dikē* and *nemesis*, an old Pythagorean binomial, not unlike the wrath and justice of the Hebrew God.)

48. Namely, distributive justice (τὸ ἐν διανομῇ or διανεμητικόν) and corrective justice (διορθωτικόν), i.e. penal and civil law (*Ethics* 5.1131a-1132b).

49. *Politics* 3.1280a8-25.

50. *Politics* 3.1287a.

51. *Politics* 7.1325b8-10.

52. *Politics* 6.1317b.

53. A. Delatte 1922 concludes a fine argument (104-106) with the remark: '[L]es éloges du système politique basé sur la proportion ou égalité géométrique sont inséparables des polémiques contre la démocratie' (106).

excellence (*pistis*, Paul would say). That God works according to mathematical principles, though likely a Pythagorean notion, is also found in Plato.[54] Plato regarded God as a geometer (and warned that no one who did not know geometry should approach his Academy, in an inscription over its gates) precisely because of the importance that geometric proportion has in his concept of justice. Geometric distribution characterizes both a virtuous oligarchy and a legitimate royalty, Plato's favorite forms of political organization. In *Gorgias* (507e), the Sages consider natural, or proportional, right to be the principle of justice that governs the universe. The invention of this kind of equality is attributed to Zeus's design in *Laws* (6.756e). It is a commonplace in pseudo-Pythagorean writings that there is a close relation between cosmic harmony and political concord and that the latter is an imitation of the former. The magistrates also copy the divinity.[55] The formula that Plato proposes for political justice is as follows: 'the natural equality given on each occasion to unequals'.[56]

Waxing even more Platonic, and identifying justice with a law of nature, Ps.-Archytas makes the principles of just distribution 'ideas' (ἰδέαι) and calls their application to politics 'images' (εἰκόνες) (T 34.10-14). Here, again, a Hellenistic Pythagorean provides a missing link between Classical and late Hellenistic political philosophy. Ps.-Archytas's use of εἰκών (*eikōn*) offers a major clue for understanding the significance of *eikōn* in the Pauline and deutero-Pauline corpus. In all instances in which the term is employed in Paul and the deutero-Pauline writings, *eikōn* describes, reveals or demonstrates something about the human level of existence that reproduces, emulates or even denies another—perfect or divine—level. In Rom. 8.29, the elect are the *eikōn* of God's son, who is the 'first-born' (πρωτότοκον), that is, the paradigm, or 'idea', for many images. 1 Cor. 15.49 makes man a dual *eikōn*, of things chthonic and things uranic. In 2 Cor. 3.18, all (πάντες) are metamorphosed into the *eikōn* of the lord, a change that, as I read it, knows degrees of *doxa*, just as the model knew.[57] No contrast between

54. *Gorgias* 507e; *Laws* 6.756e. Closer to Paul, Plutarch uses it (*Table-Talk* 8.2.2).

55. A. Delatte 1922: 166-67.

56. τὸ κατὰ φύσιν ἴσον τοῖς ἀνίσοις ἑκάστοτε δοθέν (*Laws* 6.757d; trans. Bury, modified).

57. καθάπερ ἀπὸ κυρίου, just as (we know) from the master. This reading also makes less surprising the so-called Philippians' hymn. In Col. 3.10, knowledge

image and idea, however, is more dramatic than that in Rom. 1.23, where Paul explains the error of the Greeks. These, although imbued with the knowledge that philosophy provided, are so debased as to prefer *eikones* of mortal beings, shadows of pale images, to the *doxa* of God. That the LXX material also employs this term is of only incidental relevance.[58] What is important is that Paul, reared in the general education of Hellenism, cannot fail to realize that his Greek or Hellenized Jewish audience would understand his statements in the light of current philosophical notions. Everyone had in the pocket, in the form of small change, Plato's idea-image antithesis. On every coin the effigy (*eikōn*) of the ruler sent the mind rushing instantaneously to the divine emperor and his cult.

Fragment #5a.[59] Continuing with the question of the efficacy of law for political actions, Ps.-Archytas, following the fourth century BCE tradition that credited Sparta with the most enviable political life and made it the examplar of a well-ruled *polis*, proposes, with Plato and Aristotle,[60] a constitution that, like the Spartan system of power, is composed of elements of all other constitutions. The Spartan constitution combined monarchy (the kings) with aristocracy (the *gerontes*), oligarchy (*ephoroi*) and democracy (the *hippagretai* and the *koroi*). The principle at work in the constitution proposed by Ps.-Archytas is reciprocity between its various parts (ἀντιπεπονθέναι τοῖς αὐτῶ μερέεσσιν) (T 34.21-22), an ancient form of checks and balances known to Plato and at the center of Aristotle's ideal republic. Reciprocity, or reciprocal equality (τὸ ἀντιπεπονθός τε καὶ ἴσον), is a Pythagorean commonplace, possibly inspired by a primitive law system; it becomes a central feature of Aristotelian political thought as rule-by-turn (ἐν

possessed by the initiated is the *eikōn* of the creator. Heb. 10.1 knows two removes from the prototype, not just *eikōn*, but also a lower level of perception, entirely consistent with Plato's ontological-epistemological scheme, the shadow, σκιά. The law, *nomos*, is the shadow of the good things to come, not their *eikōn*.

58. It may even be that the translator(s) of Genesis, Hellenized Jew(s), was already permeated by the commonplaces of Greek philosophy, for he consistently downgrades *eikōn* one step from its model; see, e.g., Gen. 1.26 (Adam the image of God), or Gen. 5.3 (Seth the image of Adam).

59. Stobaeus 4.1.138 pp. 85-86 = T 34.16-34.27; A. Delatte 1922: 109-14.

60. Plato, *Laws* 3.691d-692d, 4.712d. Aristotle, *Politics* 2.1265b33-1266a1, 4.1294b14-40; for mixed constitution, or 'polity', see esp. 4.1293b31-1294b40, 1295a25-1296b11, 5.1317a1-3; also book 7, *passim*.

μέρει), the ruler-ruled exchange of roles.[61] According to Aristotle, reciprocal equality preserves the *polis*.[62] Paul, too, is attracted by the promise of stability offered by a political construct that includes correlates and interchanges, in the form of a hierarchy-within-equality order in which *pneuma* is the operative agency. Throughout ancient political thought, the issue is the production of a constitution that is strong and durable (ἰσχυρὸς καὶ βέβαιος). In Paul, *bebaios* and its verbal cognates describe events or actions that relate to the ideal constitution (*euangelion*, Phil. 1.7) or that qualify its synonyms, such as divine promise (Rom. 4.16; 15.8), Christ (1 Cor. 1.8), God (2 Cor. 1.21)—and even Paul himself, as a witness to Christ (1 Cor. 1.6; 2 Cor. 1.21), and his hope for the community (2 Cor. 1.7). *Ischuros* has identical applications: in 1 Cor. 1.25, Paul ascribes it to God; in 2 Cor. 10.10, he applies it to his own Letters.

Fragment #5c.[63] Ps.-Archytas[64] insists on inculcating the constitution in the citizens so that they carry it in their mores (ἐν τοῖς ἤθεσι) (T 34.31) and do not just engrave it on walls and gates. This, I think, echoes a tradition found in Plato, Isocrates[65] and Aristotle. Aristotle is a staunch proponent of a system of education suited to the constitution,[66] which alone ensures the stability of the constitution.[67] It is habit or customs (ἔθεα, *ethea*) that secure a constitution and these take a long time to form.[68] In the time period framing Paul's activity, both Philo and Dio Chrysostom[69] emphasize the importance of planting the laws in people's minds. Paul's call for learning (ὑπακοή), especially loud in the fine rhetorical climax of Rom. 10.14-15, reflects precisely the same stance:

61. *Politics* 6.1317b20, 7.1325b8, cf. also 3.1283b40-1284a3.

62. *Politics* 2.1261a31. Polybius appeals to this theory in *The Rise of the Roman Empire* 6.10. Polybius thinks that the Spartan constitution of Lycurgus is the best one for it avoids pitfalls by having built-in a system of checks and balances in regard to the kings, the commoners and the elders. Fear (φόβος) appears to be, however, the functional element (see esp. 6.10.6).

63. Stobaeus 4.1.138 p. 86 Hense = T 34.30-35.1; A. Delatte 1922: 114-15.

64. And also Diotogenes; see Chapter 5.

65. Plato, *Republic* 3.412a, 3.412b-4.421c; Isocrates, *Areopagiticus* 39-41.

66. τὸ παιδεύεσθαι πρὸς τὰς πολιτείας (*Politics* 5.1310a14).

67. *Politics* 5.1310a12-13.

68. *Politics* 7.1334b6-13.

69. Philo, *Abr.* 5, *Omn. Prob. Lib.* 7; Dio Chrysostom, *Discourse* 76 (πέρι ἔθους, *On Habits*) (*ap.* A. Delatte 1922: 115).

'How are [people] to call upon him of whom they have not heard; and how are they to hear without someone to herald him; and how could there be envoys should they not be sent?'[70] For Paul, listening, hearing, paying heed are the equivalent of *paideia*, habit-forming.[71]

Fragment #5d.[72] On the third function of the law, usefulness to political society, Ps.-Archytas says that the common good, *sumpheron*, is ensured by law that does not allow for the tyranny of one individual or group (αἴκα μὴ μόναρχος ᾖ καὶ ἰδιοωφελής) but that enables the common advantage (κοινωφελής) of all citizens (T 35.1-3). The political connotations of *sumpheron* are unmistakable in Paul. Numerous and remarkable passages bear witness to this;[73] to give only one example: 'A sign of the *pneuma* is given everyone for the common good' (1 Cor. 12.7).[74] This is the Pauline passport, the proof of citizenship in his state. Paul's constitutional formula is a pneumatic *polis*, and Paul's political philosophy is pneumatic politics.

Another motif that Paul shares with Ps.-Archytas is that of public shame associated with the transgression of the law. It is a commonplace in Classical Greece that breaking traditions or customs (unwritten laws) inflicts shame on the offender, that it entails a loss of face. Many ancient writers report the phenomenon, sometimes considering it an outlandish punishment, sometimes taking matter of factly. Thucydides

70. Πῶς οὖν ἐπικαλέσωνται εἰς ὃν οὐκ ἐπίστευσαν; πῶς δὲ πιστέσωσιν οὗ οὐκ ἤκουσαν; πῶς δὲ ἀκούσωσιν χωρὶς κηρύσσοντος; πῶς δὲ κηρύξωσιν ἐὰν μὴ ἀποσταλῶσιν

71. The antithesis *hupakoē–parakoē*, terms usually translated as obedience and disobedience, is a central feature of Paul's rhetoric of hearing and deafness, the basis of the Christian *paideia*. See Chapter 8, section on Rom. 5.12-21, for discussion of Adam–Christ dichotomy; section on Rom. 10.14-21, for an analysis of *parakoē*; and section on Rom. 16.17-20, for an examination of *hupakoē*.

It is a commonplace of scholarship, when engaging in the generalities of the cultural contrasts between Jews and Greeks, to oppose the biblical religion of the word and hearing to the Greek religion of images and seeing. See Finney (1984, 1993) for a discussion and critique of the verbal–visual, Greek–Jewish dichotomy. Passages like the one in Ps.-Archytas above, that contrast epigraphical inscriptions with individual's habits, as well as the Classical texts that they rely on, stand proof to the fallacy of this mode of reasoning.

72. Stobaeus 4.1.138 pp. 86 Hense = T 35.1-8; A. Delatte 1922: 116-17.

73. E.g., 1 Cor. 10.23 (cf. 1 Cor. 6.12), 1 Cor. 12.7 (cf. 2 Cor. 12.1).

74. ἑκάστῳ δὲ δίδοται ἡ φανέρωσις τοῦ πνεύματος πρὸς τὸ συμφέρον.

makes Pericles remark, in his widely known funeral oration, 'We obey...[the] unwritten laws, which it is an acknowledged shame to break'.[75] Xenophon notes that those who incur the opprobrium of public opinion lead 'life of a pariah'.[76] Plato seems to accept public opinion as means of punishment,[77] though with much reservation. And Aristotle displays a very intricate psychology of shame.

Hellenistic writers of different schools continue this tradition. Ps.-Archytas considers that the best law is the one that, when broken, invites shame and dishonor as punishment (καὶ τὰν ζαμίαν ἐς τὰν αἰσχύναν καὶ τὰν ἀτιμίαν ἀμφέρῃ) (T 35.3-4).[78] Dio Chrysostom bluntly contrasts laws and customs: obedience to laws (νόμοι) yields a state of slaves, (δούλων πολιτεία); adherence to traditions (ἔθη) produces a state of the free (ἐλεύθερον [πολιτεία])—this because the laws' penalty extends only to the body while breach of customs dishonors the trespasser. Written laws, concludes Dio, are for the bad, oral laws for the good.[79] Paul and his disciples share in this tradition. In the deutero-Pauline Letter to the Ephesians (5.3-5, 11-12), shame is caused by moral offenses that directly and firmly reflect Greek and Hellenistic routine: scandalous sexual practices. In a Platonic vein, Paul's follower urges the citizenry, the imitators of God (μιμηταὶ τοῦ θεοῦ) (Eph. 5.1), to inform on the transgressors (μᾶλλον δὲ καὶ ἐλέγχετε) (Eph. 5.11). Paul himself is unequivocal that trespassing custom, especially violating gender distinctions (as when a woman prays with her head uncovered, or cuts her hair, or is inappropriately assertive) (1 Cor. 11.5, 6; 14.35), brings shame—community disapproval—on the transgressor.[80]

75. [νόμοι] ἄγραφοι ὄντες αἰσχύνην ὁμολογουμένην φέρουσιν. *History of the Peloponnesian War* 2.37.2 (trans. Warner). See A. Delatte 1922: 81 n. 3. Pericles' *epitaphios* is attributed to Aspasia the Sophist by Plato (*Menexenus* 236).

76. αἰσχρὸς βίος. *Spartan Constitution* 9 (*ap.* A. Delatte 1922: 116).

77. *Laws* 6.774c.

78. Other Hellenistic Pythagoreans concur. Diotogenes (third century BCE?), in περὶ ὁσιότατος (Stobaeus 3.1.100 = T 75.26-28) finds the foundation of a good life fear of shame rather than of fines. Ps.-Charondas and Ps.-Zaleucus (third or second century BCE) in their προοίμια νόμων also emphasize the importance of public blame and loss of face for breaking certain laws, especially those regarding the honor due the gods (*ap.* A. Delatte 1922: 116 n. 1, 116-17, 190).

79. *Discourse* 76 (*On Customs*), 76.4. For further discussion of this passage see Chapter 8, section on Romans 1.1–3.20, esp. Rom. 1.1-17.

80. For the more complex Rom. 1.24-32 (esp. 26-27), where sexual misbehavior is the cause of disrepute, see Chapter 5, section on Ps.-Ecphantus, and Chapter 8,

Paul goes beyond this tradition, however, actually reworking the concept of shame. This is a distinctive feature of Pauline thinking: to submit to, yet also to withstand, accepted practice; to invent a form of argumentation that recognizes influence while resisting traditional practice, thus confusing and disrupting channels of transmission. This is what Paul is doing, for example, in his resolute defense of the *euangelion* despite the scandal it provokes (Rom. 1.16)[81] or in his defiance of the contempt elicited by his excessive boasting about his authority (2 Cor. 10.82). So also in Rom. 6.20-21, where the very adherence to law itself is cause of embarrassment.

The language reversal in a 'shame' passage like 1 Cor. 1.27 epitomizes Pauline thinking and dialectical technique. By means of the rhetorical form of chiasm, Paul trains his readers to perform conversions of ordinary meaning and to walk with him into a new language. Paul's mind is so informed by chiastic logic that his audience grows accustomed to semantic shocks. In this case, as part of a chain of reversals, the stupid shame the wise, the weak shame the strong. The end of this dialectical process occurs in Philippians: shame describes the earthly city, whose *telos* is destruction (Phil. 3.19); antipodally to it stands the heavenly city, home of the *sōtēr* (3.20). What starts as paradox ends as norm.[82]

Fragment #5e.[83] In his excursus on the ideal physical conditions for a self-sufficient *polis*, Ps.-Archytas compares the state with a body

section on Romans 1.1–3.20, *ad. loc.* The point here is clearly a transgression of natural law, *phusis*.

81. See also Chapter 8, section on Romans 1.1–3.20, esp. Rom. 1.16.

82. It goes without saying that a good source for the language of shame employed by Paul is the Hellenistic document known as the LXX. Although in the Letter to the Romans Paul twice (9.33 and 10.11) paraphrases Isa. 28.16, it does not necessarily mean that the source of Paul's shame-language is Hebraic rather than Greek, since the translators of the LXX participated in, and were influenced by, the same, Hellenized Mediterranean culture from which Paul emerged several centuries later. As Deissmann (1926: 87) wrote, 'The Septuagint translation represents not only a formal, but also a material Hellenisation of Jewish monotheism. On some chief points this amounted to a considerable alteration. This Greek bible, in the light of universal history a book of the East and West, is an accommodation of the faith of the East to the Western world'. The view of the LXX as an East–West book is reiterated by C.H. Dodd, who notes that in the LXX the accent shifts from cultus to salvation (1935: 39). For a critique of this approach see Schoeps (1961: 27-32).

83. Stobaeus 4.1.138 pp. 86-88 = T 35.8-30; A. Delatte 1922: 117-20.

(σῶμα, *sōma*), a family and an army. Like the *polis*, these entities are well organized when free (T 35.14), that is, when the cause of their salvation lies within them and does not come from the outside.[84] Later in the same passage, Ps.-Archytas reiterates and unifies some of the major themes of his discourse: the need to interiorize the law in the morals and the customs of the citizens, for this process alone renders them complete; and the notion of distributive justice, for the law disburses to each according to his worth.[85] In other words, the Hellenistic Pythagorean identifies both law and justice, *nomos* and *dikaiosunē*, as equally essential, and equivalent, components of the perfect state. That this equation is operative is demonstrated by the simile in the next sentence, where the law is likened to the sun, which gives to each the part that is appropriate to it (T 35.24-27).[86] The seemingly inconsistent and confusing way in which Paul uses *nomos* in some sections of Romans (e.g., Rom. 3.31) may have a similar explanation. When Paul appears to use *nomos* and *dikaiosunē* interchangeably, he can do so, logically and consistently, by applying them to a *polis* under ideal conditions—which is precisely how he conceives the world under *pistis*.

The issue of *sōma* in Paul is too complex to be discussed in detail here.[87] What is significant is that, for Paul, *sōma* has an integrity that makes it particularly suitable to function as the image of the social and the political. That the body is the model of the *ekklēsia*—the 'assembly', that is, the political 'body' that is the church—is a commonplace in the Pauline literature. It is not necessarily the *personal* body of Christ that is the *tertium comparationis* for the church as the body of Christ; *any* human body[88] may serve as such. Therefore, no mystical unity or identity between Christ and church should be read into this imagery. The genitive 'of Christ' is to be understood as a possessive, not an

---

84. οὕτω γὰρ καὶ σῶμα καὶ οἰκία καὶ στράτευμα, συντέτακται καλῶς, τὸ ἐν αὐτῷ ἔχον τὰν αἰτίαν τᾶς σωτηρίας, ἀλλὰ μὴ ἔξωθεν (T 35.11-12).

85. τὸν νόμον ὧν ἐν τοῖς ἄθεσι καὶ τοῖς ἐπιτηδεύμασι τῶν πολιτῶν ἐγχρῴζεσθαι δεῖ· τοὺς γὰρ πολίτας αὐταρκέας Θήσει καὶ διανεμεῖ τὸ κατ᾽ ἀξίαν ἑκάστῳ καὶ τὸ ἐπιβάλλον) (T 35.21-24): 'It is necessary that the law is encrusted in the mores and the practices of the citizens; it is only thus that it will render them self-sufficient and that it will apportion each according to his worth and according to what is fitting him.'

86. As A. Delatte puts it 'La comparaison des effets de la Loi avec ceux de Soleil rappelle l'assimilation du droit politique au droit de la Nature' (1922: 119).

87. See Chapter 8 for a discussion of Rom. 8.10-13 and 12.1-3.

88. See Rom. 12.5; 1 Cor. 12.14-26.

explicative.[89] The political body that is the church *belongs* to Christ, and, as such, is necessarily the best example of a well-organized body!

Autarkeia ('self-sufficiency', 'contentment'), a Cynic and Stoic *telos*, is used by Paul to describe himself (Phil. 4.11). In 2 Cor. 9.8, *autarkeia*, an individual virtue par excellence, becomes a collective good. It is transferred (as in Aristotle) to the political sphere.[90] Moreover, one's completeness is God-bound; it comes, like *charis* or *pistis*, from a source outside oneself. In Aristotle it is essentially economical and political in content, and so also in Paul.[91] It is noteworthy that Paul, like Aristotle, makes *charis* and *autarkeia* near-synonyms. For Aristotle, the *telos* of the state is the good life (*eu zēn*), and the end of such life is *charis* and *autarkeia*.[92] In Paul, the community is presented by God with πᾶσαν χαρίν and πᾶσαν αὐτάρκειαν, two syntactically parallel constructions (2 Cor. 9.8). This is indeed a convincing affinity.

I have already referred to the importance of the theme of justice distributed according to worth (*pistis*) in Paul. Paul also clarifies the meaning he gives the term 'worthy' (ἀξίως, *axiōs*). The word *axiōs*, common in Paul, is often used in the phrase περιπατεῖν ἀξίως τοῦ [θεοῦ], 'to lead a life worthy of [God]'.[93] The major passage for the technical operation of the term is Phil. 1.27: 'Be citizens worthy of the constitution, the evangel' (Μόνον ἀξίως τοῦ εὐαγγελίου τοῦ Χριστοῦ πολιτεύεσθε). The political application and context are indubitable. Though expected, that identification is nevertheless striking. It discloses the mechanism and the concern of Paul's thought.

Fragment #6.[94] The last section of Ps.-Archytas preserved by Stobaeus reemphasizes the requirements of legitimacy (νόμιμος, *nomimos*) and competence for the ruler.[95] This, a major topic in Classical and Hellenistic political thinking, hearkens back to Plato's Thrasymachus. Paul's

---

89. Yorke 1991, quoted in Fee 1993: 358.

90. For Archytas, *autarkeia* has mostly moral implications, as it otherwise does for the Cynics and Stoics. This means that Ps.-Archytas cannot be taken as a line of transmission. There might have been, and in view of the fact that this is an Aristotelian overt locus, most likely there was, some other intermediary. As it stands, however, this reflects Paul's relation to Aristotle.

91. It is a matter of economy at least in 2 Cor. 9.8.

92. ζωῆς τελείας χάριν καὶ αὐτάρκους (*Politics* 3.1280b35).

93. Rom. 16.2; 1 Thess. 2.12, cf. 2 Thess. 1.11; Eph. 4.1; Col. 1.10.

94. Stobaeus 4.5.61 p. 218 Hense = T 36.1-11; A. Delatte 1922: 120-21.

95. The ruler possesses a science, ἐπιστήμη (T 36.3).

concern with affirming and proving his own legitimacy and authority looms large in his letters.[96]

Hippodamos: περὶ πολιτείας *(peri politeias),* On the Republic

Fragments ##1 and 2a.[97] Like Ps.-Archytas, Hippodamos lived in the western part of the Greek world; he appears to have been active in the third century BCE.[98] Hippodamos, whose indebtedness to Aristotle has been noted,[99] may himself be a source for later Hellenistic Pythagoreans. The fragments of his *Peri politeias* that are preserved in Stobaeus[100] are primarily concerned with a political system's hierarchy.

For Hippodamos, a state (πολιτεία) is made up of three classes (μοίρας):[101] the deliberative (βουλευτικόν), characterized by excellence (ἀρετά); the defensive (ἐπίκουρον), identified with force (δυναμή); and the productive (βάναυσον). The first two have leisure (ἐλευθερία); the third works for a living (βιοπόνος). The first is superior (ἄριστον); the second in the middle (μέσον); the third inferior (χερῆιον). The lower ranks in this hierarchy are ruled (ἄρχεσθαι) by the higher, who rule (ἄρχειν). Each class is further broken down into three groups, and the first military group, that of the officers, is further categorized according to the officers' ranks and functions.[102] The first class, the *bouleutikon*, is called κυβερνῶντες τὰ κοινά when it is first introduced (T 98.13-14). This is consistent with the Classical notion of the *polis* as a ship and of the rulers as its helmsmen.

There are a number of similarities between this passage from Hippodamos and Paul. First, there is a formal affinity. As Hippodamos is centrally concerned with the hierarchy of the *polis*, so Paul is consummately interested in the structure of the *ekklēsia*. Paul draws hierarchical lists time and again;[103] though these lists appear in various contexts, Paul

---

96. See esp. 1 Cor. 2.4; 2 Cor. 10.10; 11.6.

97. Stobaeus 4.1.93 pp. 28-29 Hense = T 98.11-22; and Stobaeus 4.1.94 pp. 29-30 Hense = T 98.23-99.15; A. Delatte 1922: 132-35.

98. Thesleff 115.

99. Praechter 1891: 50 n. 2, *ap.* Balch 1992: 385.

100. Stobaeus 4.1.93-94 pp. 28-36 Hense and 4.34.71 pp. 846-47 Hense = T 97.16-102.20; four fragments; A. Delatte 1922: 125-60.

101. In political language, parties, factions. Later, they are called, as in Aristotle, μέρεα (e.g., T 99.16, μέρος). Each class is called μέρος (T 98.25, T 99.5).

102. Fragment #2a, T 98.23-99.15.

103. E.g., Rom. 12.6-8; 1 Cor. 12.4-10, 28-29; 14.2-3. Paul's ecclesiastical organi-

140 The Political Paul

often places them within the framework of body imagery (Rom. 12.5; 1 Cor. 12.25). Paul's society may seem looser than Hippodamos's, but it is actually very precisely classified. There is also a certain resemblance of vocabulary between them. For example, the κυβερνήσεις (*kubernēseis*) and the δυνάμεις (*dunameis*) appear in the administrative configuration laid out in 1 Cor. 12.28-29. This parallel is arbitrary, however, and it shows that identity of terminology is rarely determinant. From Hippodamos to Paul, the 'power' has changed semantically, from referring to the army to applying to the miracle worker. Similarly, in Paul the 'pilot' no longer refers to the helmsman but to the bookkeeper. But, in both cases, the terms still denote functions in the state; they both belong to the civic structure of the *polis*. The army of the *polis* has become *militia Christi*.

Hippodamos's classification closely follows Platonic-Aristotelian solutions for the social and political structure of an ideal state, and may reflect not only the variations the masters underwent in Hellenistic times but also the consolidation of their respective systems. In Aristotle's *Politics* the essential social configuration of the ideal state is a duality between organic parts: *merē*, full citizens who wholly share in the good life of the state, and *hoi ouk aneu*, subordinate members of the state who make possible the good life of the true citizens. Any state must provide six cardinal services: farming; arts and crafts; defense, to maintain authority, repress disobedience and repel foreign aggression; land ownership; public worship; and political deliberation and public jurisdiction. Thus, the society needs farmers, craftsmen, a military class, a wealthy class, priests and judges.[104] The number of classes and their

zation, a hierarchical structure, is derived from the Hellenistic association (while the council of elders system follows that of the synagogue); see Merkel 1991: 12. (For a challenge to the traditional Protestant view that an 'elder' in the early Christian church was an office similar to that in synagogues, and that this role was the antithesis of the charismatic order of the Pauline churches, see R.A. Campbell 1994.) As this configuration is discussed in 1 Timothy, the bishop rules over a tighter congregation, as a leader with authority on theological decisions and with disciplinary powers over the elders (1 Tim. 5.19-21), though the bishop may have been recruited from among the elders as Titus seems to suggest (1.5-7). The details are less important here than the origin of the construct.

104. *Politics* 7.1328b1-1329a39, esp. 1328b20-24 and 1328b39-1329a6. This insofar as the ideal state is concerned. Elsewhere, when he critiques Plato's *Republic* and discusses the most common constitutions, democracy and oligarchy, Aristotle identifies eight such groups: οἱ γεωργοί, τὸ βάναυσον, τὸ ἀγοραῖον (merchants),

nomenclature remains flexible, however. Irrespective of the number of occupations providing essential services to the state, the body of those who enjoy the political rights of citizenship is formed of two groups only: τὸ ὁπλιτικόν (*to hoplitikon*) and τὸ βουλευτικόν (*to bouleutikon*), the army and the politicians.[105] They are differentiated by age, with the younger serving as soldiers, the mature in deliberative and jurisdictional capacities, and the old in religious functions. They are non-specialized, propertied individuals, enjoying free time to produce goodness and make politics. The rest, the working classes busy pursuing their manual and mercantile lives, are excluded from the citizenry because their lack of time for cultivation and political activity makes them incapable of *aretē*. The disfranchised are highly specialized, professional groups (τὸ βάναυσον, ἀγοραῖον, γεωργόν) or the lowly proletariat.[106]

In Aristotle, and by inference in Hippodamos as well, only the first two classes are enfranchised; no real political rights belong to the third class, for labor is incompatible with leisure. Granted, Paul's *ekklēsia* has given up the dramatic tripartition of citizenry for the interminable bureaucracy of the Roman empire. Like the Roman citizen, whose real participation in power was nil, the members of Paul's *ekklēsia* can only behold the power. Even so, Paul hearkens back to Hippodamos and his Classical predecessors in several important regards. First, Paul preserves the distinction between those who labor and the entity that, because it is above labor, rules. Second, as outlined above, Paul shares the Hellenistic, and to a lesser extent Classical, predilection for categorizing the forms of activity within the *polis*. There is, in Paul, a recapitulation of Classical and Hellenistic notions about the relation between classes who occupy higher and lower rungs in the hierarchy. For class superiority/inferiority, however, Paul substitutes countless occupational, *pneuma*-related skills; political unimportance is camouflaged by pneumatic relevance. In pure Hellenistic spirit, Paul professionalizes his *ekklēsia* and populates it with specialists differentiated by an exacting division of labor.

τὸ θητικόν (menial laborers), τὸ προπολεμῆσον (the army), τὸ ταῖς οὐσίαις λειτουργοῦν (the wealthy undertaking liturgies, i.e. expensive services), τὸ δημιουργικόν, the ruling group, which is made of the deliberative, τὸ βουλευόμενον, and judicial, τὸ κρῖνον, classes (*Politics* 4.1291a1-40).

105. *Politics* 7.1329a31, cf. 1329a3.
106. *Politics* 7.1328b1-1329a39, esp. 1328b39-1329a4.

Fragment #2b.[107] Hippodamos compares πολιτικὰ κοινωνία, political society, with a lyre (T 99.18) and briefly pursues the application of musical theory, especially the concept of harmony (συναρμογά, *sunarmoga*), to politics (T 99.18-22, cf. T 100.5-7). This is not just a Pythagorean trademark; it is favorite trope among political writers from Plato and Aristotle onward.[108] The motif is known to Paul (see esp. 1 Cor. 14.11) and to his school. For example, it is used twice in the Letter to the Ephesians. In Eph. 2.21, the συμπολῖται, the citizens, form a cosmopolitical οἰκοδομία, structure, that 'fits together'—συναρμολουμένη, a term peculiar to the author of Ephesians but derived from musical theory. In Eph. 4.16, the same expression is used to describe the body, itself a political cliché.[109]

The association between music and the well-run household or state likewise appears in Paul himself. Σύμφωνος (*sumphōnos*)—'harmonious', but also 'agreement', 'contract'—is what the family concludes in order to lay sex aside for a time and, presumably, also to renounce other household and professional activities to make time to devote itself to prayer (1 Cor. 7.5). (It is noteworthy that for cultivation of the spirit, one needs leisure, *scholē*, precisely the technical term used by Aristotle to describe those who enjoy the political rights of full citizenship.) In a strongly related passage in a different letter, Paul traces the whole compass from family to state to the whole creation. Each individual is responsible for avoiding marriage compacts with unsuitable people, for no state can be formed with unfit members. There can be no συμφώνησις, harmony, between opposing cosmic forces (2 Cor. 6.15). Paul is consummately concerned with unity and agreement within his communities and often speaks against division and strife.

Fragments ##2c1, c2 and 2d1, d2, d3, d4.[110] Hippodamos continues by enumerating the measures by which a political community can be 'harmonized': words (λόγοι), customs or mores (ἤθη, ἐπιτηδεύματα)

107. Stobaeus 4.1.94 pp. 30 Hense = T 99.15-22; A. Delatte 1922: 133-41.

108. *Republic* 4.443c, *Politics* 2.1263b35 (*ap.* A. Delatte 1922: 140-41). Shorey's LCL translation of Plato's *Republic* adds an example from Cicero (*Republic* 2.42) and quotes from Shakespeare and Milton, to show the extent of the commonplace analogy between music and government (*Republic*, LCL 414-15).

109. For the use of the state–body metaphor in Paul see discussion in Chapter 8, Rom. 12.5.

110. Stobaeus 4.1.94 pp. 30-33 Hense = T 99.22-100.23; A. Delatte 1922: 141-46.

and laws (νόμοι) (T 99.22–100.5). Discourse acts on drives (*epithumiai*) and directs them toward *aretē*. Laws restrain through fear of punishment and lure with the bait of honors and rewards. Customs work on the *psuchē* and build its natural character (φυσίωσις). Excellence can be acquired in three ways: by acting on desires, through shame and by fear; it is *logos* that commands desires; morals, as expressed in public opprobrium, that give rise to shame; and laws that work by fear (T 100.14-19). Further, Hippodamos proposes a few applications of these three means. Like his Classical models, he sees them securing the highest good of a political community, agreement and harmony, and warding off its direst dangers, sedition and contention (T 100.7-8). Like Aristotle, Hippodamos is concerned with finding the right measure, the mean vis-à-vis passions, wealth, ability and energy.

Like other Hellenistic philosophers, Hippodamos appears to fuse Plato and Aristotle, both of whom distinguish three elements in the formation of political *aretē*: *phusis, ēthē* (or *ethos*) and *nomoi* or, in Aristotle, *logos*.[111] In *Politicus*, Plato makes true and natural (*kata phusin*) that political science (*hē politikē*) that forms states from people of suitable nature only, people who would then be inculcated with the laws and educated to uphold the customs. The true statesman alone can produce the resulting divine bond, the bond that unites the eternal part of the soul, which knows what is honorable and good and just, with the divine.[112] For Aristotle, political *aretē* is the product of nature, habit and reason, the latter two subject to education.[113]

Fragments #3a1, 2, 3, 3b, 3c.[114] Hippodamos makes a detailed study of each one of the three measures. Traditions are evaluated according to whether they are indigenous, and therefore good, or imported and bad, an Aristotelian approach that Hellenism removed the relevance of, but that Hippodamos repeats in trite imitation of the Classical masters (T 100.24–101.16).

Discourse is divided between that which upholds universal human knowledge (κοιναὶ ἔννοιαι) and is common to all political society and political life, and that which opposes it (the cause of anarchy, ἀναρχία)

111. Plato *Politicus* 310a; Aristotle *Politics*.
112. *Politicus* 308d-310a.
113. *Politics* 7.1332a30-b10, *Nicomachean Ethics* 2.1103a14-34.
114. Stobaeus 4.1.95 pp. 33-36 Hense = T 100.24-102.20; A. Delatte 1922: 146-55. Fragments 3a1-3 deal with customs, 3b with discourse, 3c with the laws.

in regard to the gods and human institutions (T 101.17–102.6). Speech must be 'political', that is, solemn and patriotic (τῷ λόγῳ πολιτικῷ καὶ σεμηῷ καὶ οἰκείῳ) (T 102.4-5). Speech makes manifest the character of the speaker (ἁ λέξις ἐσσεῖται τὸ τῶ λέγοντος ἦθος ἐμφαίνουσα) (T 102.5-6).[115]

Finally, Hippodamos addresses the subject of the laws. An epigone of Plato and Aristotle, Hippodamos commends even as he warns against kingship, a form of government that imitates the divine but is inappropriate for easily corrupted human beings. Likewise, he embraces aristocracy and accepts democracy as a necessary evil. Hippodamos proposes an odd yet familiar-seeming constitutional formula made of a pinch of *basileia*, a large measure of aristocracy and some democracy.

Hippodamos' dependence on Plato and Aristotle is undeniable. Is any link with Paul detectable? In fact, there is such a link. The three elements of political *aretē*—rhetoric, customs and laws—are central to Paul's political thinking, as well.

The importance of speech in Paul is so great, so pervasive and so often discussed as to require little comment. Paul perceives his own mission as that of an ambassador of Christ, the broadcaster and teacher of the good news. Orating/preaching and listening/obeying are the two most stressed exigencies in the Pauline writings. In Paul, *euangelion* and its cognates—equivalents for speaking, a certain kind of speaking, a new rhetoric—are probably the most-used sememes. The title that Paul arrogates for himself is 'apostle for the *euangelion*' (Rom. 1.1). The combined anaphora and climax, rhetorical figures in Rom. 10.14-15, are probably the best expression of this idea in Paul: 'How then could they call on him [in whom] they did not trust? And how could they trust [him] of whom they did not hear? And how could they hear without there being a herald? And how could there be envoys should they not be dispatched?[116] The activity of the envoy is εὐαγγελίσασθαι, 'to proclaim good news' (Rom. 1.15). He not only announces the *euangelion* but also suffers for it—for its advance (προκπή) (Phil. 1.12) and for its defense (ἀπολογία) (Phil. 1.16). For all that is novel here, the rhetorical aspect of the envoy's function is not lost. The speech,

115. This is exactly what the deutero-Pauline Titus demands and thinks of speech, Tit. 2.7-8.

116. Πῶς οὖν ἐπικαλέσωνται εἰς ὃν οὐκ ἐπίστευσαν; πῶς δὲ πιστεύσωσιν οὗ οὐκ ἤκουσαν; πῶς δὲ ἀκούσωσιν χωρὶς κηρύσσοντος; πῶς δὲ κηρύξωσιν ἐὰν μὴ ἀποσταλῶσιν;

moreover, is political oratory. Paul admonishes his listeners to be citizens 'worthy of the *euangelion*' (Phil. 1.27). His challengers are sophists, those who speak 'clever words' (ἐν σοφίᾳ λόγου) (1 Cor. 1.17; 2.1, 4), scholars (παιδαγωγοί)[117] (1 Cor. 4.15) and super-apostles (ὑπερλίαν ἀπόστολοι)[118] (2 Cor. 11.5; 12.11). One of the outrages with which Hippodamos charges the Sophists is their teaching that the divinity either does not exist or that it is not interested in human beings (T 101.22-23). This, he says, is contrary to common sense (κοιναί ἐννοίαι) (T 101.22) and thus filled with anarchy (ἀναρχίας πλαρωθεὶς) (T 102.3) and productive of confusion in the public life (κοινὸς βίος) (T 101.24). Hippodamos's opinion prefigures Paul's critique of the Greeks.[119]

With Hippodamos, and squarely within the same tradition, Paul claims that his speech acts on his listeners' conscience (συνείδησις, *suneidēsis*), their faculty of discerning right and wrong (2 Cor. 4.2). What makes Paul's speech a new type of speaking, *euangelion*, is that his words come with the backing of a power, a holy spirit (1 Thess. 1.5). And that is what is new about the speaker, too. He is under compulsion to speak: 'Woe to me if I don't speak the message!' (οὐαὶ γὰρ μοί ἐστιν ἐὰν μὴ εὐαγγελίσωμαι) (1 Cor. 9.16).

The terms *ethos* and *ēthos* (ἦθος), both meaning 'custom', 'habit', 'tradition', 'law'), are conspicuously absent in Paul. He uses the latter term only once, in quoting a proverb, 'Bad company ruins good habits' (φθείρουσιν ἤθη χρηστὰ ὁμιλίαι κακαί) (1 Cor. 15.33). The usefulness of these terms is preempted by their visibility in expressions such as 'the customs of the fathers', 'the customs that Moses handed down', 'to live according to the laws' and 'customs of the Jews'.[120] In Paul's mind, the terms are compromised because of their association with Jewish law and tradition. The only instance in which Paul can use such a term is in repeating a Hellenistic cliché.

---

117. Leaders of rival political parties? See Plutarch's usage in *Aratus* 48, *Galba* 17.

118. Graduates of philosophical schools? A similar expression, ὑπεραττικῶς, 'super-Attic', a professional jargon, is used in Lucian's *Demonax* 26.

119. Rom. 1.18-32, Phil. 3.18-20, esp. 1 Thess. 4.5. *Asebēs* becomes a crucial issue in Rom. 4.5.

120. ...οὐδὲν ἐναντίον ποιήσας...τοῖς ἔθεσι τοῖς πατρῴοις... (Acts 28.17); ...τὰ ἔθη ἃ παρέδωκεν ἡμῖν Μωϋσῆς (Acts 6.14, cf. 15.1); ...τοῖς ἔθεσιν περιπατεῖν (Acts 21.21); ...πάντων τῶν κατὰ Ἰουδαίους ἐθῶν... (Acts 26.3).

Yet Paul *does* defend customs and mores as means of preserving the
unity of a political society. He just calls them by a different name:
παραδόσεις (*paradoseis*). With a characteristic twist, Paul identifies
'customs' with the new traditions that he has instituted. In 2 Thess.
2.15, for example, Paul tells this audience to 'stick to and hold fast the
traditions which you were taught by us, either by speech or by letter'
(cf. 1 Cor. 11.2; 2 Thess. 3.6).[121] These new traditions are over and
against the Jewish ones (Gal. 1.14). And Paul is quite close to Hippodamos in identifying one of the main causes for the usurpation of
traditions: pleasure. Hippodamos writes, 'Pleasures bring ills to men',
coupling this with the Stoic adage, 'Toils bring them good things'.[122] In
Paul's accusations against the Greeks—an indictment, in fact, against
the age—he finds them consistently at fault for the abandonment of the
good in favor of sensuality (Rom. 1.18-32; Phil. 3.18-20). Paul's theory
of suffering, quintessential to his politics and rooted in the Aristotelian
psychology of pain and pleasure, is only superficially Stoic. While
Stoicism is no resolute woe but rational accord with the changes of
fortune, suffering is not, for Paul, just wise resignation. For him,
predicament is achievement. Enduring difficulties and afflictions for the
euangelion amounts to its affirmation. Paul is not just cheerful 'inside
Phalaris's bull'[123] or happy on the rack, as the Stoic would be, Paul is
positively *creative* there.

Revealingly, when referring to the denotative area covered by the
terms for 'custom', 'mores', 'habit' (etc.), Paul prefers *phusis*. He
moves from the laws, customs and traditions of Jews to the nature and
the natural of Greek and Hellenistic speculation. What is authoritative is
not what one or another people holds as normative, but what nature
teaches (ἡ φύσις αὐτὴ διδάσκει) (1 Cor. 11.14). For example, in
Romans, which can be viewed as a doctrinal and philosophical treatise,
Paul uses the concept of *phusis* not only in his critique of the moral
offenses against gender that result from the capitulation to passions
(Rom. 1.26-27, cf. 1 Cor. 11.14), but also in the famous parable of the
natural branches and the wild olive shoot, to distinguish between Jews
and Greeks in regard to salvation (Rom. 11.17, esp. 11.21, 24). Nature

121. ἄρα οὖν, ἀδελφοί, στήκετε, καὶ κρατεῖτε τὰς παραδόσεις ἃς ἐδιδάχθητε εἴτε
διὰ λόγου εἴτε δι᾽ ἐπιστολῆς ἡμῶν.
122. ἐργατεύοντι δὲ τοὶ μὲν πόνοι τὰ ἀγαθὰ τοῖς ἀνθρώποις, ταὶ δὲ ἀδοναὶ τὰ
κακά (T 101.4-5).
123. Cicero, *Discussions at Tusculum* 5.26.76.

provides the criteria for distinguishing between man and woman or between Jew and Gentile (Rom. 11.21, 24). At critical moments, the antithesis *kata phusin–para phusin* is determinative in Paul's thought. Thus, it first helps evaluate and resolve an ethical argument (Rom. 1.26-27), then a political one (Rom. 11.21-24). In Paul's political discourse, the *phusis* distinctions ultimately become inoperative,[124] as Paul undoes the binaries.

I have already frequently referred to Paul's position on law and law's preeminence in his political system, and I shall further discuss these issues later. To the extent that laws are important in maintaining the unity of the state and in fending off discord and conflict within the *polis* (which, in Paul, is identified with *ekklēsia*), Paul might have been reluctant to eliminate them completely. But, in the available texts, there is no evidence of such reticence. In Paul as we have him, there is simply no room for Law or laws, but only for the pneumatic order and *pistis*. Paul counts on his epideictic rhetoric to counter threats of sedition and disharmony. The law is fine only insofar as one is law-abiding. As such, it is useless to the just and even more so to the criminal.[125]

Like Hippodamos and his Classical antecedents, Paul, too, is seeking a constitutional formula. As has already been mentioned, Hippodamos praises kingship while alerting against it, for it is a case of divine imitation (θεομίματον πρᾶγμα) (T 102.12). In Paul, imitation (μιμέομαι, μιμητής) becomes the highest desideratum.[126] Mimesis is the cry of the reformer, for the divine—and/or he himself—are the only possible examplars, not customs or laws. Paul's constitutional formula is, therefore, a *basileia*,[127] a system of metaphysical politics, where the citizens are *douloi*, slaves of the divine. But they are organized in *ekklēsiai*,

124. While God's saving act renders inoperative the distinction between male and female or between Jew and Greek, the first difference does not become inactive in his critique of gender relations; here the confusion is a sign that something has gone wrong, not a sign of transcendence.

125. Romans 7. See the deutero-Pauline 1 Tim. 1.8-10 for an intensifying gloss to Romans 7.

126. Imitation of God is Platonic. The *Politicus* is the best expression of Plato's view on the statesman's political science, systemic approach to state government, and imitation and reproduction of the divine. See also Goodenough 1928: 74.

For discussion and examples of the notion of imitation, see below, final section reviewing main themes, and Chapter 5, esp. section on Ps.-Ecphantus.

127. For more on this topic see the discussion in Chapter 5 of the treatises on kingship attributed to Ps.-Ecphantus, Diotogenes and Sthenidas.

assemblies, according to the *polis–oikos*, political structure. The people live in a political society, that of the *euangelion* (Phil. 1.27), but their commonwealth (*politeuma*) includes God (Phil. 3.20).

Fragment #4.[128] We possess only fragments of the Pythagorean document attributed to Hippodamos. The political reflections discussed above form a relatively coherent whole. But Stobaeus preserves yet another scrap, presumably of the same work, which I think also has a bearing on Paul. Hippodamos recalls the Stoic doctrine of the eternal return of the cosmos but gives it a political, Aristotelian twist and uses it to reflect on the particular fate of human institutions, families and states. The things that nature creates (τὰ μὲν ὑπὸ φύσιος γινόμενα) (T 97.22) know cyclical change. Human productions follow a similar fate, not by necessity of nature (δι᾽ ἀνάγκαν φύσιος) (T 97.18), however, but because of human stupidity, aroused by hubris and surfeit. Families, states and governments go through the stages of acquisition, enjoyment and oblivion (T 98.2-3). Things incorruptible, ruled by the gods, will be eternally saved (σῴζεσθαι); things mortal, under human control, undergo eternal change (ἀεὶ μεταβολάν) (T 98.6-8).[129]

This fragment also contains a tantalizing reference to what may well be a theory of internal social revolution and interstate war as products of change, but change that is valuated *positively*. The have-nots, unhappy, will go for the state; the haves, sated, will lose it (T 98.3-5).

---

128. Stobaeus 4.34.71 p. 846 Hense = T 97.17-98.10; A. Delatte 1922: 155-58.

129. The same notion of permanence of God's world and transitoriness of human institutions is present in Rom. 12.2: do not be formed like this age, but be transformed by the renewal of your mind, so that you prove what is the will of God, what is good and acceptable and perfect (καὶ μὴ συσχηματίζεσθε τῷ αἰῶνι τούτῳ, ἀλλὰ μεταμορφοῦσθε τῇ ἀνακαινώσει τοῦ νοὸς εἰς τὸ δοκιμάζειν ὑμᾶς τί τὸ θέλημα τοῦ θεοῦ, τὸ ἀγαθὸν καὶ εὐάρεστον καὶ τέλειον). A similar idea is expressed by Plato in *Politicus*, where he writes: I say that the opinion about the beautiful and the just and the good, and about their opposites, which is true and [which] has confirmation [in the mind], is a divine principle, and when bred in the souls, it is so, I say, in the nature of daimon [i.e. superhuman] (τὴν τῶν καλῶν καὶ δικαίων πέρι καὶ ἀγαθῶν καὶ τῶν τούτοις ἐναντίων ὄντως οὖσαν ἀληθῆ δόξαν μετὰ βεβαιώσεως, ὁπόταν ἐν ταῖς ψυχαῖς ἐγγίγνηται, θείαν φημὶ ἐν δαιμονίῳ γίγνεσθαι γένει) (309c). Σχηματίζειν, to configure, and cognates, is part of the astronomical vocabulary and is found in writings about the celestial bodies from Aristotle to Ptolemy, the astronomer (second century CE) and to Proclus (fifth century CE).

Surfeit and hubris attract ruin; lack and poverty bring bravery (T 98.8-9). Here, Hippodamos is consistent with the Classics: first, with Aristotle's theory of cyclically changing constitutions[130] and his war doctrine, which conceives of war as a natural, 'naturally just', mode of acquisition and a correction of nature's oversight;[131] also, Plato, who regards as 'natural' the acquisition of Greek property in war. Hippodamos is also in agreement with Aristotle's classification of constitutions on a socio-economic basis.

Developing a theme that was widespread in Hellenistic times among both philosophers and, especially, the people, this fragment I think expresses Paul's concern precisely. Such an attitude appears to be the very source of what I call Paul's *revolutionary conservatism*. Paul subverts only to remove the indeterminateness of political duration; he is a reformer only insofar as he wants to stop the wheel of change.[132] Paul endeavors to arrest political circularity, to stop the decadence and ruin inherent in human institutions. Passages such as this from Hippodamos provide us with the Hellenistic Pythagorean background of Paul's reasoning, revealing the suppressed part of Paul's political logic: duration, stability, perfection. At heart, Paul is a political idealist, a utopian in the tradition of Plato and Aristotle. His ideal, as we shall see, is to maintain the impermanent.

Hippodamos: περὶ εὐδαιμονίας *(peri eudaimonias),* On Happiness

There is yet another passage, from a different work by Hippodamos, also preserved in Stobaeus.[133] While it has elements in common with *Peri politeias* the accent here falls on *aretē*. One must not only learn *aretē* but also know how to possess it and how to exploit it, with the purpose of defending, increasing and remedying the households and the cities (οὐ μόνον μαθεῖν δεῖ τὰν ἀρετάν, ἀλλὰ καὶ κτήσασθαι καὶ χρήσασθαι αὐτᾷ ἤτοι ἐς φυλακίαν ἢ ἐξ συναύξασιν ἢ καὶ...ἐς ἐπανόρθωσιν οἴκων τε καὶ πολίων) (T 96.2-4). Everything is 'in' *eunomia,* ('good government') (ἐν εὐνομίᾳ γὰρ τὰ πάντα ἐστί), Hippodamos declares (T 96.8).

---

130. Aristotle's theory of *stasis* rests on arrestingly psychological explanations; the constitutions collapse, periodically, into each other (*Politics* Book 5).

131. *Politics* 1.1256b20-26.

132. Eschatology too is a possible answer, the permanence of the end. But it also ends the political game, humanity.

133. Stobaeus 4.39.26 pp. 911-13 Hense = T 96.2-97.12; A. Delatte 1922: 170-72.

A human being can acquire *aretē* only in a community, for a human being is a member of society (ὁ γὰρ ἄνθρωπος κοινωνίας μέρος ἐντί) (96.16-17). A person can achieve happiness and perfection of the soul (εὐδαιμονία καὶ ἀρετὰ ψυχῆς) (T 96.24) only in a group, either a family or a state, for the individual and the community are coterminous.[134] Happiness and perfection form the universe and are diffused, successively, in the political association, the family and the individual (T 96.24-28). The fragment concludes with a thrice-tripartite kinship: the *aretē* of the universe, the city and the body are, respectively, harmony, eunomy and health, while God, the citizenry and the individual wield power in each of the three domains (T 97.2-11). Thus does Hippodamos establish congruity and solidarity between the individual, the social group and the cosmos.[135] Such ideas are staple stuff in Hellenistic times,[136] and they go back to Aristotle.[137] The difference, and the mark of specifically Hellenistic political reflection, is the integration and the hierarchical arrangement of the various political levels. Hellenistic political reflection is also characterized by the fact that, while there is at the highest level a transcendent model for the governing of the subsequent political systems, each level retains its distinctiveness and can function as an interchangeable metaphor for the others. As measured against the gods (or deified proxies), human beings carry little weight in 'political' affairs, construed on the cosmic level. But human action is still a factor, as suggested by the presence of the individual and of the body in the political scheme. Moreover, that humanity has a role in the political game is evident in the fact that the

134. These statements obviously echo the Aristotelian formula ὁ ἄνθρωπος φύσει πολιτικὸν ζῷον (*Politics* 1.1253a2, 3.1278b20).

135. See also A. Delatte 1922: 172.

136. They may have been also a feature of Classical Pythagoreanism, cf. Aristotle, *Ethics* 1.1096b5-9.

137. Hippodamos's use of the tandem εὐδαιμονία καὶ ἀρετὰ ψυχῆς, and especially, the uncommon expression 'excellence of the soul', reminds me, again, of Aristotle, who, in one place (*Ethics* 1.1102a6-16), specifically connects *eudaimonia* with *aretē psuchēs*, and further, with *politikē*, the science of politics. Since, as we have seen, *psuchē* is formed of two parts, one *alogon* and one *logon*, there are also two genera of *aretē*, αἱ ἠθικαὶ ἀρεταί, and αἱ διανοητικαί or λογικαί, the ethical and the rational (*Ethics* 1.1102a23-1103a10). Happiness, or the good of man, the aim of every human activity, was defined as an activity of the soul, displaying *aretē*, over a complete lifetime, τὸ ἀνθρώπινον ἀγαθόν ψυχῆς ἐνέργεια γίνεται κατ' ἀρητέν....ἐν βίῳ τελείῳ (*Ethics* 1098a16-17).

good is attainable by individual effort (albeit only through membership in society and by emulation of the divine).

Paul shows a concern similar to the Hellenistic Pythagorean's for ranking and integrating individual, family, state and cosmos, but the balance is different. In Paul, *oikos* and *polis* are subject to cosmic government. Paul does not give us a sequence of layers, each autonomous even while it is a metaphor for the others. In Paul, each level surrenders to the cosmos. Though there is room in Paul for political self-determination, in the end politics, too, becomes the slave of God. The individual reaches happiness and the good through the extraordinary means of suffering (παθήματα, *pathēmata*) (Rom. 8.18; 2 Cor. 1.5-7; Phil. 3.10), humility and obedience—that is, *passively*. One cannot but surrender completely to the justice (*dikaiosunē*) of the only perfect judge, who dispenses the sentence and the reward according to a quantity called *pistis*, the new *aretē*. This political eschatology is the Hellenistic mood gone wild.

In another section of this fragment, Hippodamos explains the primacy of divine rule over political society and the soul by the preeminence of the whole over the part. The divine is the *first*, which, by its harmony and gaze (ἁρμονία καὶ ἐποψίς), keeps everything together. This can be discerned, says Hippodamos, from living nature (ζῷον), from the way the animal (and human) body is put together. For without the whole living body neither the eye, nor the mouth, nor the ear would exist (T 96.33-97). The body, the metaphor for political society, is also the paradigm of hierarchy within equality. The affinity between Hippodamos and Paul on this theme offers an excellent testimony of the unity of mood and the fraternity of thought in Hellenistic times. It is precisely the approach of Paul in 1 Cor. 12.14-26: 'If every part were the body where would the body be?' asks Paul (12.19). 'As it is, there are many parts but one body' (12.20). And then he goes on to discuss the treatment of the superior and the inferior parts, and emphasizes the latter: what seems weaker (ἀσθενέστερα) is indispensable (ἀναγκαῖά ἐστιν) (12.22); what seems less honorable (ἀτιμότερα) or inferior (ὑστερούμενος) is more interesting (περισσότερος) (12.23-24). In both Hippodamos and Paul, the context is political and the referent is God's rule.

Callicratidas: περὶ οἴκου εὐδαιμονίας *(peri oikou eudaimonias),*
On the Happiness of the Household

Stobaeus preserves four fragments from Callicratidas, who lived in
Sparta, possibly during the third century BCE.[138] The fragments, from a
work called *Peri oikou eudaimonias*,[139] all treat the family group.

Fragment #1.[140] Bringing together Platonic and Pythagorean terminologies without mixing them, Callicratidas transfers Plato's tripartite
psychology and the Pythagorean Table of Oppositions[141] to the family:
husband, wife and child correspond to *logismos, epithumia* and *thumos*
(T 103.1-10); the male becomes the monad, the female, the dyad (T
103.11-18). The household is the emulation (τὸ ἴχνος) of the soul.[142]
As might be expected, *logismos*, like other key words of Greek philosophy, is devalued in Paul. *Logismoi* are the Greeks' perplexities (Rom.
2.15) or the sarkic arguments of Paul's opponents, to be vanquished by
his weapons and to be made prisoners of Christ (2 Cor. 10.4).

Fragment #2.[143] The centerpiece of the available text is the theory
that makes the *oikos*, like a choir or a ship, 'an assembly of correlated

138. Thesleff 1961: 115. On dating Callicratidas and on his dependence on
Platonic and Peripatetic sources, see also Praecther 1891: 50 n. 2 and Wilhelm
1915: 163, 173, 179, 205, 210-12, 220, 222-23, *ap.* Balch 1992: 384 n. 31. Theiler
identifies a parallel to Cicero (*Cato Maior* 77, 1926: 152, *ap.* Balch 1992: 385).

139. Stobaeus 4.28.16-18 pp. 681-88 Hense and 4.22.101 pp. 534-35 Hense = T
103.1-107.11; A. Delatte 1922: 161-69.

140. Stobaeus 4.22.101 pp. 534-35 Hense = T 103.1-18; A. Delatte 1922: 169.

NOTE: Although the numbering of the Hellenistic Pythagorean fragments in this
study follows A. Delatte, not Thesleff, in Callicratidas's case it was found more
expedient to follow Thesleff.

141. A. Delatte 1922: 169. These Tables are characteristic of Pythagorean School
speculation and represent pairs of opposites (such as limited and unlimited, odd and
even, male and female, good and bad, and numerous others), considered basic elements or principles of the universe; they influenced both Plato's and Aristotle's
thinking.

142. In Paul, the same term, *ichnos*, footprint, footstep, track, is used to describe
an act of imitation, such as following the *pistis* of Abraham (Rom. 4.12), or walking
in Paul's footsteps (2 Cor. 12.18).

143. Stobaeus 4.28.16 pp. 681-84 Hense = T 103.19-105.9; A. Delatte 1922:
162-63.

factors…formed of contraries and dissimilars, organized around one element, 'the best' (τὸ ἄριστον), and geared toward the common good' (κοινὸν συμφέρον)[144] (T 103.21-23). In a household, 'the best', the central, privileged structuring element, is the οἰκοδεσπότης, the master. The name of the common good is ὁμοφροσύνη ('like-mindedness', 'common disposition', 'unity of feeling',—i.e. harmony) (T 104.3). A household, like a harp (ψαλτήριον) (T 104.4),[145] needs three things; fittings (ἐξάρτυσις), tuning (συναρμογά) and touch or musical know-how (ἁφά or χρῆσις μωσικά) (T 104.5).

In discussing the fittings (*exartusis*), Callicratidas determines that the parts of the family are, as in Aristotle, the people (T 104.13-24, 105.8-9) and the goods (T 104.24–105.8). The people (ἄνθρωποι) are blood relatives (συγγενέες) and familiars; legal relatives (οἰκῆοι); and friends. This is the conceptual background needed to properly understand such difficult passages as those in Romans 11. Jews, Greeks and barbarians are part of the same household, only some are blood kindred and some joined the compact by alliance.

Callicratidas divides the material goods (κτῆσις; Doric κτᾶσις) into necessary (ἀναγκαία) and 'bountiful' (ἐλευθέριος) (T.104.25-26). The latter, when beyond what is required for grooming and improvement, lead to political ruin (ὄλεθρος) by the following progression: delusion (τετυφωμένον), imposture (ἀλαζονεία), revilement (of relatives) (ὑπερηφανία), and outrage, paroxysmal excess (ὕβρισμα).[146] Callicratidas proposes surrendering the material surplus to the lawgiver (νομοθέτης).

Paul is cognizant of this process of deterioration, though not neces-

---

144. σύσταμα κοινωνίας συγγενικᾶς…ἔκ τινων ἐναντίων καὶ ἀνομοίων σύγκειται, καὶ ποτὶ ἕν τι τὸ ἄριστον συντέτακται, καὶ ἐπὶ τὸ κοινὸν συμφέρον ἐπαμφέρεταί.

145. The word for 'harp' (*psalterion*) is the same as that used by Aristotle in the *Problemata* (919b12), in a context that describes the means of producing an accord in the octave, and that leads to the reflection that, of all things that are perceived by the senses, only that which is heard possesses moral character (919b26-37, 920a3-5). It is harmony that makes the political. This household theory is very important for, as I contend, it is part of the foundation of Paul's political system. A. Delatte (1922: 162 n. 4) dismisses, and rightly so, Gruppe's argument (1840: 130) that the use of *psaltērion*, would indicate a Jewish author.

146. Opulence, *truphē*, and overindulgence, *koros*, lead to *apolausis*, *hubris*, *olethros* and end with political collapse also in Aristoxenus (a fourth century BCE Pythagorean), as well as in the Hellenistic Hippodamos and Ps.-Charondas (see A. Delatte 1922: 43, 158, 197).

sarily in the context of affluence. The dissolution of the *ekklēsia* brought
on by excess is a common theme in the Pauline letters. *Olethros*, ruin,
the sum product of societal fracture, stands in Paul for death, destruction and the power of Satan. Destruction is the wages of the sarkic
(1 Cor. 5.5); eternal destruction is reserved for the seditious (2 Thess.
1.9). In a remarkable and revealing passage, ruin is spawned by the very
attainment of the (Augustan) political ideal of peace and security
(εἰρήνη καὶ ἀσφάλεια) (1 Thess. 5.3). We have here, set in rare
apocalyptic tones, the very expression of Paul's political nightmare.
Human society, no matter how perfectly accomplished, breeds destruction if left to its own devices. It simply cannot endure. Its triumph
betokens the 'round-the-corner' apocalypse. Something is missing. The
political peace Paul aims at is the peace of God (εἰρήνη θεοῦ), the
trademark of Paul's introductions to his Letters. He is aware that the
concept is demanding, that this is a peace that baffles all understanding
(ἡ ὑπερέχουσα πάντα νοῦν) (Phil. 4.7). Yet this is the necessary
condition for a durable constitution and an enduring state.

The root of Callicratidas's sentiment can be found in the Classical
writers Plato, Isocrates and Aristotle.[147] Aristotle explains that it is very
difficult for humans who have reached affluence to maintain a state. The
greater the riches, the higher the need for *philosophia, sophrosunē* and
dikaiosunē.[148] The warning against desiring riches that appears in
1 Tim. 6.9 is very closely related to Aristotle and an almost exact
equivalent of the Hellenistic Pythagorean theme: love of money plunges
those afflicted by this *epithumia* into ruin and destruction (εἰς ὄλεθρον
καὶ ἀπώλειαν); the enjoyment (ἀπολαύσις) of riches, continues the
author of 1 Timothy with an apparent pun,[149] makes sense only if its
source is God (1 Tim. 6.17).

147. E.g., Plato's *Republic* 4.421, where the Guardians are refused the happiness
that is associated with possessions. Isocrates' *Areopagiticus* 1, where he laments
the decline of public morals because of wealth. In Aristotle's *Politics*, speaking about
politeia, the best constitution under real conditions, he warns against the political
risk inherent in wealth and extols the virtues of the middle class (4.1295b); and,
when constructing his ideal state, although critical of Plato's denial of property to
his citizens, Aristotle too censures luxury (7.1334a). The enjoyment of prosperity
and peaceful leisure makes people wanton [and the door is left open for political
insurgency], ἡ δὲ τῆς εὐτυχίας ἀπόλαυσις καὶ τὸ σχολάζειν μετ' εἰρήνης ὑβριστὰς
ποιεῖ μᾶλλον (*Politics* 7.1334a27-28).
148. *Politics* 7.1334a32.
149. Inspired by Aristotle (*Politics* 7.1334a27-28)?

Fragment #3.[150] In another fragment, Callicratidas identifies three types of power: despotic (δεσποτικά), professional (ἐπιστατικά) and political (πολιτικά). The despotic considers the interest of the ruler only; the professional (e.g., coaches, physicians, professors) pursues the advantage of the ruled (client); the political has in view the advantage of both ruler and ruled. It is the political type of authority that keeps together (συνήρμοσται) the *oikos*, the *polis* and the *kosmos* (T 105.22-23). 'Household and *polis* are imitations, according to the principle of analogy, of the administration of the cosmos' (μίμαμα δ᾽ οἶκος καὶ πόλις καττὰν ἀναλογίαν τᾶς τῶ κόσμω διοκήσεως) (T 105.23-24). This classification of governments may be a simplification of a similar passage in Aristotle, where the Stagirite, taking issue precisely with such reductionism, shows that in each of the three cases the lines between the interests of the ruler and the ruled are much more blurred than such theories would assume.[151]

In tracing this line of transmission from Aristotle through the Hellenistic Pythagoreans to Paul, it is important to observe three expressive examples of creative adaptation. First, Callicratidas does not distinguish between political rule (ἀρχὴ πολιτική) and household rule (ἀρχὴ οἰκονομική), as Aristotle so emphatically does.[152] This is a very significant modification, and we see it in Paul as well. That Paul makes no technical distinction between household rule and political constitution is, in fact, one of the lynch-pins of his political system. The association of *oikos* with *ekklesia* is present in almost every letter.[153]

Second, Callicratidas makes a sharp contrast between the despot and the professional ruler, while Aristotle treats the latter as a case of the former. This is revealing, for Callicratidas's placement of the *epistatic* in a category by itself shows the intense awareness of the status of professional classes and of the importance specialization and expertise acquired in Hellenistic times.[154] In my opinion—and I cannot emphasize

150. Stobaeus 4.28.17 pp. 684-86 Hense = T 105.10-106.13; A. Delatte 1922: 63-68.

151. *Politics* 3.1278b31-1279a16, or it may come from a source that antedates Aristotle, as A. Delatte thinks (1922: 164-65).

152. Moraux (1957) observes that in Callicratidas Aristotle's terminology is also modified. When Aristotle speaks of political rule (ἀρχὴ πολιτική) he refers to democracy, but for Callicratidas this term applies to monarchy. The form of government has changed (1957: 85, *ap.* Balch 1992: 391).

153. Rom. 16.5; 1 Cor. 16.19; or Col. 4.15; 1 Tim. 3.4; Phlm. 2.

154. Ἀρχὰ ἐπιστατικά, masterly rule (105.11-12, 14), central concept in

this enough—this difference is one of the clearest demarcations between Classical Greece and the Hellenistic era: the disparaging attitude toward skilled labor and technical craft is abandoned at the same time as the Greek gentleman, the *kalokagathos*, is vanishing. This radical change is most visible in politics and religion, where the amateur is supplanted by the disciplined specialist. As the world becomes increasingly less divided, knowledge gradually becomes territorialized; while political barriers fall, knowledge is punctiliously parceled.

Finally, Callicratidas offers the world (*kosmos*) as the model for political and household rule. A. Delatte (1922: 166) sees in this a revival of the old Pythagorean moral doctrine, whose central demand was to follow or to copy God, now applied to politics. I think, though, that this is a new phenomenon. The human cities become the city of gods. Religion changes from a voice in the chorus to the heldentenor. Religion converts from discursiveness to discourse. It presses history to move its weight from *politeia* to (what I would call a) '*polytheion*', from civil polity to a gods' world, from human to divine government. What the ancient Pythagorean Society applied to a small group of acolytes is now imposed on and extended to the whole world: political power, legislative and judicial authority, rests with the gods. Yet, neither Hellenistic nor imperial Roman ideology completed this transfer of power. For Hellenistic political thinkers and the theoreticians of the Roman state, imitation of God and the replication of universal harmony was only the desideratum. Thus was maintained a dividing line between the divine and the human, a separation that still allowed the latter a relatively large degree of self-determination. The transfer was completed by Christianity, and it may be that Paul singlehandedly accomplished it.

Kosmos is a favorite concept of Paul's, and its high frequency in his works points to where his interests focus. God, Christ, angels and human beings are its citizens.[155] The power that orchestrates them (συναρμολογέω), the master of the whole structure, is Christ.[156] The

Callicratidas' political theory, also designates the authority which aims at the benefit of the ruled by the ruler.

155. A fine example is 1 Cor. 4.9. The treatment of *kosmos* in Paul is a vast and complex issue, of Stoic and Gnostic parentage, which does not concern us here; the point I make is the unified political theory that characterizes Paul's thinking, his integrating the traditionally distinguished political units, family, state, universe.

156. See Eph. 2.21-22. Though Ephesians is a deutero-Pauline letter, the environment is Pauline.

idea that the family (in the traditional sense of husband-wife unit) and the city copy God's rule of the universe is also found in Paul.[157] The trite expression that 'all is from God' (τὰ δὲ πάντα ἐκ τοῦ θεοῦ) (e.g., 1 Cor. 11.12) is the Pauline equivalent of the Greek notion, emphasized in Hellenistic thought, that God is the beginning and the end of the order of the universe, that God's rule is the paradigm of proper administration, and that God's government is the test against which all other regimes are judged.

For Callicratidas as for his Hellenistic colleagues, the government of God is the model of all others, for God is 'the best' element in the universe. And this God is, according to received philosophical tradition (κατταν ἔννοιαν), a celestial being, incorruptible, the beginning and cause of the fine order of the universe (ζῷον οὐράνιον ἄφθαρτον, ἀρχά τε καὶ αἰτία τᾶς τῶν ὅλων διακοσμάσιος) (T 105.28–106.1).[158] Callicratidas's *zōon ouranion*, celestial being, recalls Aristotle's famous *zōon politikon*, political being,[159] which is also glossed here. The absolute political leader is a heavenly being. In Romans (1.20, 23), Paul's remark about the nature of God—that he is invisible, immortal and manifested in creation[160]—carries far more weight than the platitudes it reproduces: it anticipates and identifies the solution to the political questions raised in the letter itself.[161]

Fragment #4.[162] Domestic affairs, particularly the conditions for a proper balance of power between husband and wife, are the topic of the last of Callicratidas's preserved fragments. It is an unremittingly entertaining passage, in which practical rules for securing a harmonious family—the submissiveness of the woman and the authority of the

157. For the first, see 1 Cor. 7 and 11, and in particular 7.10, cf. 11.12, and 11.3. For the second, see Phil. 1.27, esp. 3.20 (cf. also Eph. 2.12). Note, that unlike the *ekklēsia* in a Greek city, Paul accepts women in it.

158. Callicratidas also discusses the notion of analogy, the natural principle of proportional justice, the meaning and the significance of which has been commented upon already.

159. *Politics* 1.1253a2, 3.1278b20.

160. In 1 Tim. 1.17 and 2 Tim. 1.10, Christ is so described.

161. God's *dikaiosunē* bestows on those found deserving God's own attributes, glory, honor, incorruptibility, eternity (Rom. 2.7). See also 1 Cor. 9.25 and esp. 1 Cor. 15.42-54, on the body of the resurrected that imitates God in that it does not degenerate.

162. Stobaeus 4.28.18 pp. 687-88 Hense = T 106.14-107.11; A. Delatte 1922: 169.

man—turn gender relations into sexual economics and politics. It is hard not to see in such texts the Hellenistic background to which Paul's dicta in 1 Corinthians 7 and 11 belong. Precisely the same kind of forces that govern the relationship between wife and husband in Callicratidas' family are operational in Paul, in the political rapport between humanity and the divinity (or his ambassadors).[163]

Ocellus: περὶ νόμου (peri nomou), On Law

Ocellus,[164] a fragment of whose work *Peri nomou*[165] is also preserved in Stobaeus, lived in the western part of the Greek world in the third or second century BCE. Ocellus's political system shows many similarities

163. In both Callicratidas and Paul, the same relation holds between the divine and human as holds between husband and wife. The husband/divinity is the guardian, lord and teacher (ἐπίτροπος, κύριος, διδάσκαλος) of the wife/humanity (T 107.4-6). The latter must be easily fashioned, easily led, easily taught, as well as fear (φοβηθῆμεν) and love (ἀγαπάξαι) the former (T 107.8-11). For *epitropos, epitropeuō* in Paul, in the family context, see 1 Cor. 14.34 (wives, authenticity disputed) and Gal. 4.2 (under-age individuals). *Didaskalos, didaskalia* is a pneumatic office or gift (e.g., Rom. 12.7; 1 Cor. 12.28-29) and divine instruction (e.g., Rom. 15.4) but also, sarcastically, a teacher in need of teaching (Rom. 2.21). Fear (both *phobeō, phobos*) positively valuated, is a Pauline mark; the theme it is particularly well developed in Rom. 8.15 and 2 Cor. 5.11 (fear and persuasion). (For a discussion of Rom. 8.15 see Chapter 8, ad loc., as well as below, section on Ps.-Zaleucus, frg. 13. For 2 Cor. 5.11 see also Chapter 5, section on Ps.-Ecphantus, frg. 3.3.) The issue of *agapē* (ἀγαπάω, ἀγάπη, ἀγαπητός) is too central even to be touched upon here. (See Rom. 13.11-14 and *passim.*)

It is very interesting to notice that in the Callicratidian triad *epitropos, kurios, didaskalos,* the usual δεσπότης is displaced by *kurios.* While *kurios* and (*oiko*) *despotēs* are synonyms and are sometimes used interchangeably to designate the master of the house (e.g., Aristotle, *Politics* 2.1269b10, plural form), the preferred term is *despotēs.* It is *despotēs* from which the name of the household authority derives, *archē despotikē* (as opposed to *archē politikē,* political authority). Exactly why Callicratidas favors *kurios* is not obvious. I think that it is consistent with his tendency to diminish the distance between the political and the household ruler, even to overlap the two, in accordance to the prevailing theories and truths about the Hellenistic monarchy. In Paul *kurios* is normative for both household and political authority.

While *despotēs* is absent in Paul, it reappears in 1 Tim. 6.1, 2; 2 Tim. 2.21 and Tit. 2.9 to express the (Aristotelian) slave–master relationship.

164. Also Okkelos or Ekkelos, Thesleff 1961: 115.

165. Stobaeus 1.13.2 p. 139 Hense = T 124.15-125.7; A. Delatte 1922: 172-74.

with those of Hippodamos and Callicratidas. Yet a few different and interesting things happen here. His thrice-tripartites are, first, body (σκᾶνος, a Pythagorean term), cosmos (κόσμος), and family and city (οἶκος καὶ πόλις) lumped together; these are sustained by life (ζωή), harmony (ἁπμονία) and concord (ὁμόνοια), respectively; the causes of each are the soul (ψυχή), God (θεός) and the law (νόμος), respectively (T 124.18-20). The cosmos is harmonized forever and never falls into disorder (ἀκοσμία), while cities and households are short-lived. All generated and mortal beings are formed of matter (ὑλή) and, as such, are, like matter, changeable (μεταβαλλόμενοι) and ever-passive (ἀει–παθείς). The salvation (σωτηρία) of matter is reproduction. The ever-moving principle rules; the ever-passive is ruled. The first rules the second by *dunamis*, might; the first is divine (θεῖον), rational (λόγου) and intelligent (ἔμφρον), while the second is engendered (γεννατόν), unreasoning (ἄλογον) and changing (μεταβάλλον) (T 124.20–125.7).

As we move along in the Hellenistic era, we notice, first, that the *polis–oikos* cluster forms an increasingly solid unit. The cosmos is emphasized as the model for both the body and the *oikos–polis* set. Next, the unified intricacy of the Aristotelian *psuchē*, partitioned between an *alogon* and a *logon* part, is externalized and ruptured, now used to describe the grand, irreconcilable dichotomy between matter and the divine. Third, the fatalistic view of human affairs becomes firmly planted in philosophy. Human institutions and creations have a hylic core. In Paul this is expressed by the *sarx* category. *Pneuma* and the *pneumatic* become the means of escape from matter.

The Gnostic mood must have had its origins in an increasingly acute awareness that the human world and God's world had drifted far apart, and this realization is first formally reflected in texts of political bent. In reaction to the ephemeral character of humanity's greatest achievement—political society—God is increasingly brought to bear on human affairs. It is for this reason that Paul produces his political system, which synthesizes the two worlds and leaves no room for any other political experiment, under threat of annihilation. A relation of the divine to politics had always been assumed by ancient political theory. It became increasingly inseparable from the civic political body. In Paul, it completely fills the upper tier of a unified two-tiered system, with, however, the lower tier evincing absolute servitude within meaningful human institutions.

Damippos: περὶ φρονήσεως καὶ εὐτυχίας *(peri phronēseōs kai eutuchias),* On Prudence and Fortune

Also preserved in Stobaeus are two fragments from Damippos, who lived in the western part of the Greek world in (probably) the third century BCE[166] and who therefore probably antedates Ocellus. The fragment from Damippos' *peri phronēseōs kai eutuchias*[167] that interests us is thematically consistent with those fragments from Hippodamos, Callicratidas and Ocellus just examined. *Kosmos,* in the sphere of the Universe (περιοχὴ τοῦ ὅλου), is the harmony (συναρμογά) of two natures (φύσεις), one perpetually moving (ἀεικίνατος) and divine, the other perpetually passive (ἀειπάθεια) and begotten (T 68.21-25). Similarly, *aretē,* in the human being (ἄνθρωπος), is the harmony of the the irrational (τὸ ἀλόγον) and the rational (τὸ λόγον ἔχον) parts of the *psuchē.*[168] Finally, mastery (κράτος) and concord (ὁμόνοια) in the *polis* are the harmony of the two groups of citizens, the ruled (ἀρχόμενοι) and the rulers (ἄρχοντας). To rule (ἄρχειν), the text continues, is proper to the stronger (κρείσσονος); to be ruled (ἄρχεσθαι) is proper to the inferior (χείρονος).[169] Mastery (τὸ κρατέν) and accord (τὸ ὁμονοέν), however, are common to both (κοινόν ἀμφοτέρων) (T 68.28–69.1).

This is a fine passage for understanding the Hellenistic Pythagoreans' use, manipulation and amalgamation of the Classical masters. A distinction is made between rule (τὸ ἄρχειν) and power (κράτος) that unfortunately is not elaborated on. It is worth dwelling, briefly, on this issue. Psychology and politics are juxtaposed in Classical and, as a consequence, in Hellenistic thought. The order of Socrates' exposition in Plato's *Republic* goes from the state to the soul. To rehearse: first Plato (speaking through Socrates) determines that the state is composed of three classes—economic, military (auxiliaries) and political (guardian rulers)—and buttresses his tripartite division of society with the 'noble lie' of the three metals. Next, he turns to the soul, presenting his tripartite *psuchē,* consisting of rational, spirited and appetitive elements. Plato then constructs the analogy between politics and psychology: the

---

166. Thesleff 1961: 115.
167. Stobaeus 3.3.64 pp. 215-17 Hense = T 68.19-69.19; A. Delatte 1922: 173.
168. Almost verbatim quote from Aristotle.
169. The Thrasymachus argument in Plato's *Republic* (1.338c, 339a, 341a. Cf. also 5.460c).

ruler is parallel to the rational faculty, the auxiliaries to the spirited, and the craftsmen to the appetitive. Finally, Plato presents the four virtues of the individual soul, in which inner justice is seen as the harmony among the three parts of the soul and is compared to the harmony among the three fundamental notes, or strings, of the octave. The comparison between the *polis* and the human individual is likewise transparent in Aristotle,[170] where he says that despotic and 'political' rule are first found in the living being: the soul rules the body as a despot, but the mind (νοῦς, *nous*) rules the appetites as a statesman or king.

While generally similar, the Hellenistic Pythagorean approach works differently. Damippos, in the fragment under discussion, finds a correspondence among the universe, humanity and the state. But the parallelism breaks on the third leg and the text is obscure. The question that Damippos does not answer is, essentially, What is it that the weak, like the strong, are masters over? *Homonoia* is a political term in the Classical authors. *Homonoia* has 'a purely political meaning, concord between conflicting groups of the community'.[171] As might be expected, with the loss of the political significance of the *polis* from the fourth century BCE on, the term came to describe an internal harmony within the individual. As the *polis* is internalized, its terminology is transferred by Hellenistic philosophies to the wise man, a detached, even misanthropic figure. In Plato, however, *homonoia* is concord, harmony or union within the *polis*, the army or the family, the opposite of *adikia*, injustice.[172] In Aristotle, *homonoia* is a form of friendship, *philia*, with political objectives.[173] Although Aristotle uses the more general *philia* even when he speaks politically, he prefers *homonoia*, the purely political *philia*, when he needs precision: 'friendship appears to be the bond of the state; ...lawgivers seem to set more store by *philia* than they do by *dikaiosunē*, for to promote *homonoia*, which seems akin to

---

170. E.g., *Politics* 1.1254b4-7.
171. Höistad 1948: 107.
172. *Republic* 1.351e-352a.
173. Political or civic friendship, πολιτικὴ φιλία, also called political partnership, πολιτικὴ κοινωνία, is what makes the state (*Politics* 4.1295b21-25). *Philia* and concord, ὁμόνοια, are identified (*Nicomachean Ethics* 1167b2-3). A political compact is, in fact, founded on *philia*, for it is friendship that makes cohabitation and intermarriage possible; it starts families, brotherhoods and religious and avocational clubs (*Politics* 1280b35-38). See also Mayhew 1966. For the idea that *philia*, friendship in Aristotle, is replaced by *agapē* in New Testament, and especially in Paul, see Hauck 1908.

philia, is their chief aim, while faction [*stasis*], which is enmity [*echthros*], is what they are most anxious to banish'.[174] Aristotle makes clear that, technically speaking, *homonoia* is the opposite of *stasis*, the force that breaks a political society. Plato too, in the Thrasymachus argument, puts *homonein* on the same level with justice, while its opposite, *stasiazein*, is the equivalent of injustice, *adikia*.[175]

'Mastery' (*kratos, kraten, kratein*) has weak political substance in the Classics, and as a political term it is a Hellenistic novelty. In Aristotle, only the verbal forms are known and are mostly used in non-political contexts.[176] When employed in political settings it is quite non-technical or at most ambiguously technical.[177] Most interesting, however, is a passage in Aristotle,[178] in which he aims his argument at the confusion that marks the debaters in the controversy about natural and legal slavery. Addressing the dispute whether the person superior in power (κατὰ δύναμιν κρείττονος) can turn the conquered into a slave and

174. *Ethics* 8.1155a23-26, cf. also *Politics* 5.1306a9-10, where the verbal form is used.

175. *Republic* 1.351e-352a. Pythagoras uses *homonoia* as the name for the numbers 3 and 9 (*ap.* Iamblichus, *In Nicomachi arithmeticam introductionem* 16.57). The term *homonoia* is also popular with the Stoics. (LSJ, *ad loc.*). Early Stoics, such as Chrysippus (of Soli in Cilicia, son of Apollonius of Tarsus), define concord as ἐπιστήμη κοινῶν ἀγαθῶν, knowledge of good things held in common, giving it a characteristically Stoic moral sense (Clement of Alexandria, *Stromata* 2.9; Stobaeus 2.93.19, cf. 2.7.105—*SVF* 3.72.9 [#292], 3.160.15 [#625], 3.166.17 [#661]). The science of the common good, a political concept *par excellence*, is given an ethical twist (cf. *SVF* 2.315 [#1076], where Zeus is described as possessing εὐνομία, δίκη, ὁμόνια, εἰρήνη, and nearly all other virtues—all politically charged ideas). These Stoics, however, prefer *homologoumenos*, as Zeno's or Chrysippus's ὁμολογουμέ-νως ζῆν, living in agreement with virtue (see *SVF* 2.39.5, 3.5.14, 3.6.9; see also Long and Sedley 1987: 394-95), or in harmony with reason, or, as their successors preferred, in concord with nature, as the end of life or the definition of happiness (see index to *SVF*, 4.104, and Long and Sedley 1987: #63). Dio Cassius (second/ third century CE) refers by ὁμονοεῖον to the Roman Temple of Concordia (49.18, etc.).

176. E.g., *Ethics* 7.1150a9-1151a27, mastery over pleasure and pain. There is one exception, the use of the noun in the treatise περὶ κόσμου, *On the Universe* (399b9).

177. In *Politics*, κρατεῖν is applied to a government that rests upon force (3.1276a13); or on prevailing in war (1.1255a7); about factitious parties gaining the upper hand over the other (4.1296a29), or in reference to defense-walls (1327a35) or about securing certain qualities in arts and sciences (1331b38).

178. *Politics* 1.1255a4-21.

subject (δοῦλος καὶ ἀρχόμενος), Aristotle finds the source of the difficulty in the dual meaning of ἀρετή (moral excellence and general excellence, or mastery), and determines that the strong party (τὸ κρατοῦν) always possesses superiority in something that is good (1.1255a15), so that no force is devoid of *aretē*. Similarly, in Plato, the meanings of *kratos/kratein* are the habitual ones: 'power', or 'prevail', or, in the passive mood, 'be overcome'.[179] An interesting and significant case, however, is presented by *Laws* (4.714c). The section (4.713a-714a) begins with a *mythos* by means of which Plato says that any well-ordered human society ought to be the μίμημα ('copy') of divine rule. He urges the governments of both houses and cities (οἰκήσεις καὶ πόλεις) to obey the law. Next (4.714b-714d), Plato launches a virulent attack against a false principle of government, namely, the belief that the best way of expressing the natural definition of justice[180] is that justice is the interest of the stronger (ὅτι τὸ τοῦ κρείττονος συμφέρον ἐστίν).[181] Although Plato and Aristotle address different questions and reach different conclusions, the language is the same. Damippos ought to be read against this background.

The Damippos excerpt is nearly identical to a fragment from Ps.-Archytas,[182] in which he writes that actions imply three principles: to rule (τὸ ἄρχειν), to be ruled (τὸ ἄρχεσθαι) and to master (τὸ κρατέν). In the *polis*, the first belongs to the stronger (κρείσσονος), the second to the weaker (χερήνος) and the third to both (ἀμφοτέρων). In the *psuchē*, the ruler is τὸ λόγον ἔχον, the ruled τὸ ἄλογον; to master (κρατοῦντι) again belongs to both (ἀμφότερα). Ps.-Archytas also explains what it is that these master: to wit, the passions (πάθεια). *Alogon* and *logon* command the drives. The harmony (συναρμογά) between the first two components of the soul is *aretē*. The parallelism with the psychology of Plato and Aristotle is inescapably here, but the presence of passions, *patheia*, in Ps.-Archytas's formula is Hellenistic. This *aretē*, freeing the soul from pleasures and pains (ἀδονᾶν καὶ λυπᾶν), brings it tranquility and imperturbability (ἀρεμία καὶ ἀπάθεια). This is exactly the view Aristotle attributes to 'some thinkers', a view with which he agrees with

---

179. E.g., *Symposium* 196c, mastery over pleasures and desires is self-control; *Phaedrus* 272b, mastering an art.

180. καὶ τὸν φύσει ὅρον τοῦ δικαίου λέγεσθαι κάλλισθ᾽ οὕτω (*Laws* 714c3).

181. See also *Republic* 1.338, 2.367.

182. In his treatise περὶ νόμου καὶ δικαιοσύνης, T 33.13-18.

one important correction: pains and pleasures ought to be qualified as
'the wrong' pains or pleasures.[183]

We may now conclude this long digression. Neither Ps.-Archytas nor
Damippos tell us what *kratein* corresponds to in *political* terms. In the
psychological sphere, it is clear that mastery means the overruling of
passions. Both thinkers, however, seem to have difficulty carrying the
reasoning into the political. This inability or unwillingness is by itself
remarkable. Their dependence on Plato and Aristotle would suggest that
kratein should be read as 'sovereignty', the ultimate power in the state.
To be sovereign belongs to both ruler and ruled, Damippos would seem
to say. (This also suggests the rule-by-turns of Aristotle.) But the ruler–
ruled dichotomy in the Hellenistic Pythagoreans, expressed as an
antithesis between the superior and the inferior, or between the strong
and the weak, is too strong to allow for this. The Hellenistic thinkers
fail to sustain the soul–state analogy. On the other hand, I can detect a
possible parallelism by pursuing the *aretē* theme. *Kratos* and *homonoia*,
in Damippos at least, correspond to *aretē*. The terms would thus
designate the participation of all citizens in something like political
aretē. But what is this? For Plato and Aristotle there is no doubt: justice
and law, *dikaiosunē* and *nomos*. But, precisely here, the Hellenistic
state fails the later thinkers, and the Hellenistic Pythagoreans stutter.

The examination of such texts, in which *kratos* and/or *homonoia*—
that is, a major element of power, whatever its name or meaning may
be—is common to both the ruler and the ruled is at least doubly significant for Paul. First, let us examine the case of *kratos* and *homonoia*
proper. We have seen that for the Hellenistic Pythagoreans, *kratos*,
while acquiring an increasingly central spot in their political terminology, loses its previous meaning, most probably because ideological
reasons demanded its modification. It is central yet meaningless. While
it still has the ring of genuine power, it nevertheless suggests that the
real locale of might is elsewhere, eluding the citizen. The concept of
mastery was never firmly planted in the political soil.

Paul has no use for *kratos*, for he has found his central and centripetal

---

183. *Ethics* 2.1104b3-1105a16, esp. 1104b21-26. Aristotle is for *metriopatheia*,
moderation, not eradication of passions. It is usually conjectured that the reference
is to Speusippus. *Apatheia*, however, in the doctrinal sense of freedom from passions,
is first introduced in Hellenistic times, by Stoicism. See also Rackham's note in
LCL trans. of *Ethics* p. 80 n. c. Although Ps.-Archytas may know the Stoic doctrine, the usage here is hardly specialized.

concept in *pneuma*, a force that connects all levels of Pauline society, both the strong and the weak, the higher and the lower. The term *kratos* and the idea it expresses persisted, however, in Paul's circles; when resurrected it becomes, as might be expected, an attribute (or an activity) of God.[184]

To *homonoia*, so important given the musical proclivity of the Pythagoreans, Paul prefers other political terms, more familiar to his less frequently concertgoing audience, among which the most important is εἰρήνη ('peace'). The rhetoric of political harmony is well represented in Paul. To take just a few examples of a theme that recurs often both in Paul and in this investigation: fellowship (κοινωνία) in the blood and body of Christ (e.g., 1 Cor. 10.16); one body (ἓν σῶμα) in Christ (e.g., Rom. 12.5; 1 Cor. 10.17; 12.25); partners, fellow-citizens (κοινωνοί), both in Paul's sufferings and consolations (2 Cor. 1.7). One might add the exhortations to peacefulness and meaningfulness when gathered together in the assembly (συνέρχομαι ἐν ἐκκλησίᾳ) (e.g., 1 Cor. 11.18, 20, 33); the deep affection both in suffering and joy informing the community members (συμπάσχει, συγχαίρει) (1 Cor. 12.26). Perhaps the best example of this motif is Phil. 2.1-5, an impassioned cry to concord, mutual tolerance, consent, unity, and humanity. Paul does not need to employ the same word to express the same idea as his Classical and Hellenistic forebears.

Moreover, such passages from Damippos and Ps.-Archytas may be seen as the intertextual environment for the major idea of equality-within-hierarchy that informs Paul's political theory. There are numerous instances, in all the Letters, that can be used to illustrate this point. While differences between the constituents of the community are not just voiced but even stressed, and while subordination is sometimes strict, parity, based on the notion of equality inherent in true justice, is the dominant motif. For example, although there are old and new members of the household *ekklēsia*, the first versed in fine points of reasoning (διάκρισες διαλογισμῶν) and the latter weak in *pistis* (τὸν ἀσθενοῦντα) (Rom. 14.1, cf. 1 Cor. 3.2-4), each and every member of this asso-

---

184. It is a favorite with the authors of Ephesians, Colossians and 1 Timothy, for example, in such tautological formulas as 'the force of his strength' (κράτος τῆς ἰσχύος αὐτοῦ) (Eph. 1.19; 6.10), 'the might of his glory' (κράτος τῆς δόξης αὐτοῦ) (Col. 1.11) and 'eternal power' (κράτος αἰώνιον) (1 Tim. 6.16). Could such expressions be Hebraisms, or echoes of magical invocations? Paul uses the verbal form in a paraenesis, with the trivial meaning 'stand firm', 'hold fast' (1 Cor. 16.13).

ciation is a household slave (οἰκέτης) of a master (κύριος) (Rom. 14.4). They are all brothers and sisters—Paul's preferred way of addressing his people (Rom. 16.1).[185] Despite their unequal stations, both men and women pray and prophecy (1 Cor. 11.4-5). A variety of gifts, services and powers are manifest, but all are produced by the same *pneuma* and all are for the common good, *to sumpheron* (1 Cor. 12.4-11). Rather, it is the magnitude of the gifts of the *pneuma* that determine the hierarchy in an equality-informed *ekklēsia* (1 Cor. 12.28-31; Rom. 12.6-8). In Paul, the power belongs to *pneuma*; *pneuma* distributes its rewards as it itself determines (βούλεται) (1 Cor. 12.11). There are weak and strong members of the community, superior and inferior offices—a rating is at work—but all are members of the same body (1 Cor. 12.14-27; Rom. 12.4-5) and all share in the *pneuma*. Citizens share in *agapē* (1 Cor. 13). Everyone needs and is dependent on the other (1 Cor. 14). The power that is *pneuma*, however, is common to all. Yet, just as the excellent ruler in the Classics and in the Hellenistic Pythagoreans does, *pneuma* rules by distributive proportion, *analogia* (Rom. 12.6). With the authors of the texts under discussion, Paul treads common Hellenistic cultural ground.

Ps.-Zaleucus: προοίμια νόμων (prooimia nomōn), Preambles to the Laws

There were presumably quite a few versions of these Preambles to the Laws, attributed to one or the other of two authors, Zaleucus and Charondas, namesakes of the famous Pythagorean lawgivers of Magna Graecia and Sicily.[186] The Hellenistic texts are collections of religious,

185. See Chapter 8, Rom. 14.1-23 for an elaboration of this theme.

186. The two Hellenistic Pythagorean authors are often mentioned in the many studies which focus on the *Haustafeln*, the household-duty codes, in the Pauline literature. For an important contribution to the *Haustafeln* topic and its relation to Paul see Balch 1992. This scholar determined numerous parallels between the Hellenistic Zaleucus and Charondas fragments and New Testament texts (Col. 3.18–4.1; Eph. 5.21–6.9; 1 Pet. 2.11–3.12; 1 Tim. 2.1-15; 5.1-2; 6.1-2; Tit. 2.1-10; 3.1). Balch concludes that 'Both [the New Testament and the Ps.-Pythagorean] groups of moralists were concerned about authority and subordination. In fact the Neopythagorean concern for proper household management is closer to the similar New Testament concern—in both form and content—than are the other [Stoic or Hellenistic Jewish] parallels usually suggested' (Balch 1992: 408). For other important studies on this topic see Adcock 1927, Muehl 1929, and the bibliography cited in Balch's article.

ethical and political prescriptions, general in character and possibly aimed at creating a civil religion. Ps.-Zaleucus, the first author whose Preambles to the Laws[187] we shall consider, lived in the West, possibly in Sicily. Different scholars have dated him differently.[188]

Fragment #1 (T 226.10-13 and 226.24-27). The inhabitants of cities and villages must be convinced and must believe (πεπεῖσθαι χρὴ καὶ νομίζειν) that the gods exist, since the beauty and order of the heavens and the cosmos prove it. This beauty and order cannot be the result either of fate or of humankind (οὐ γὰρ τύχης οὐδ᾽ ἀνθρώπων). Although this proof of the existence of the gods had already been presented by Plato in *Laws* (886a),[189] we have here the phraseology of Hellenistic religious credos. Though the Pauline formula retains the sacramentality of the Hellenistic formula, it is interesting to see what changes: one must trust and declare (πιστεύεται [καὶ] ὁμολογεῖται) (Rom. 10.10). In Paul, *pistis* holds pride of place. Although it has been pressed to fit a reversed, two-part, mouth–heart, Septuagintal quotation, Paul's formulation displays the same prescriptive urgency and hieratic feeling as that of the Hellenistic Ps.-Zaleucus.[190]

Fragment #3 (T 226.17-22 and T.226.29–227.1). All must keep purity of soul (δεῖ τὴν αὐτοῦ ψυχήν...καθαράν). Gods are honored by *aretē*, by *politai* showing *eusebeia* and *dikaiosunē*,[191] not by displays of wealth and bombastic speeches. *Eusebeia*, construed as purity of conscience, is a motif in the deutero-Pauline letters, First and Second Timothy and Titus.[192] Paul admonishes the Corinthians for displaying

187. Preambles to the Laws. Diodorus 12.20.1-3 = T 226.7-22; Stobaeus 4.2.19 pp. 123-27 Hense = T 226.23-228.21; A. Delatte 1922: 177-95.

188. Third-second century BCE (Thesleff 1961: 115); first century BCE (A. Delatte 1922: 179).

189. *Ap.* A. Delatte 1922: 189.

190. Dio Chrysostom (*The Third Discourse on Kingship*, 3.51) uses a similar formula: 'not only confessing, but also believing', οὐχ ὁμολογῶν μόνον, ἀλλὰ καὶ πεπεισμένος... See Chapter 8, commentary for Rom. 10.10, for further discussion of Dio's passage.

191. Diodorus's version, first century CE.

192. 1 Tim. 4.7-8 warns against the education of children that stresses [Homer's] myths and physical exercise against *eusebeia*! See Plato, *Republic* 2.376e–3.412b, esp. 2.377a–3.391e (objections against literary fiction); 3.400c-403c (aim of education in music); and 403c-411e (athletics).

opulence in the assembly. He often speaks against the high-flying speeches of opponents. The emphasis is the same.[193] Plato, according to whom the good person can, because pure, sacrifice and talk to the gods,[194] may lie behind both Ps.-Zaleucus and Paul. In 2 Cor. 6.6, purity (ἁγνότης) tops the list of virtues; in 2 Cor. 7.1 Paul urges, καθαρίσωμεν! ('Let us purify ourselves!').

Fragment #5 (T 227.5-14) All citizens and residents in the state whose souls, because of desires (ὁρμαί) are moved toward injustice (ἀδικία) must remember that the gods will judge them. As remedy, Ps.-Zaleucus proposes that one bring before one's mind's-eye the moment of life's end.[195] Fear of incurring the gods' judgment, at death, for one's injustice is nowhere to be met in Classical thinking.[196] Ps.-Zaleucus's sentiment is Hellenistic vernacular: at the appointed time (*kairos*, itself sometimes personified) the gods will mete out punishment for wrong-doing. *Kairos* emerges as a major theme in Paul, as well. When the *kairos* comes, God will judge (1 Cor. 4.5).[197] But in Romans, for example, Paul has the antidote to precisely such a fear: the *kairos* of

193. In the available 'genuine' Pauline corpus the term appears nowhere. *Eusebeia* and cognates abound, however, in the Septuagint, almost exclusively in the Hellenistic material, mostly in the Maccabees, Jewish national epics, of which 50 times in *4 Maccabees*, written about two generations before Paul, and in the wisdom literature, of which 15 times in Sirach. The notion of Jewish piety with which it was certainly associated made it unserviceable to Paul. *4 Maccabees* shows a real penchant for martyrdom, an idea repugnant to Paul, partly, I think, because of the political affront implicit in it, but cheered by the Stoics. Partly, also, because martyrdom as ransom for sin, expounded in *4 Maccabees*, goes against Paul's view that the act of salvation is singular and restricted to Christ, who, however, opened the floodgates to the society of christs. Paul uses, however, the opposite, *asebeia*, four times in Romans, mainly to express the paradox of Christ's death for the God-bashers. *Asebeia* is popular with 1 and 2 Timothy and Titus as well.

194. *Laws* 716d-e (A. Delatte 1922: 190).

195. καὶ τίθεσθαι πρὸ ὀμμάτων τὸν καιρὸν τοῦτον, ἐν ᾧ γίνεται τὸ τέλος ἑκάστῳ τῆς ἀπαλλαγῆς τοῦ ζῆν.

196. A rare, indirect reference may be a passage in Plato in which Cephalus expresses the view according to which possession of wealth is an advantage over the fear of death, for the rich dies knowing that he is in no debt to anyone (*Republic* 1.330d-331b, *ap.* A. Delatte 1922: 191). The myth of Er means not at all to terrify the citizens, it is actually a reaction to Homeric presentation of death as indiscriminately gloomy, but to enhance patriotism.

197. Also, wrath of God is revealed to all *asebeia* and *adikia* (Rom. 1.18).

Christ's death meant release for all ἀσεβεῖς (*asebeis*), the godless (Rom. 5.6, cf. 4.5).[198] When the *kairos* is at hand, one will 'put on Christ' (Rom. 13.11) as immunity from the *kairos* itself. Few themes dominate the popular culture of Hellenistic times more intensely than does the fear of death. All itinerant moral philosophers use this dread in their speeches. Philosophies rise by exploiting it. Savior gods incessantly multiply. Paul offers the most paradoxical of them all. It is on the strength of such a God that he can proceed to reform the world and upbuild it.

Fragment #6 (T 227.14-20). In a remarkable passage, an epitome of Hellenistic language and beliefs, Ps.-Zaleucus speaks of *adikia*, injustice, as possession in need of exorcism, either by means of apotropaic rites or by associating with good men. A good man can dispel *adikia* by conjuring the good daimon (εὐδαίμων) and by making speeches that describe how the evil are punished, deterring the *adikos* from evil actions through fear of the vengeful daimones (δεισιδαιμονῶν δαίμονας ἀλάστορας). The text assumes only the fuzziest line between the exorcist and the philosopher; while, on the one hand, speech has power to control desires,[199] magical actions are also recommended. This short precept is reflected in Paul in at least two ways, first in Paul's concern with *adikia*. *Adikia* is as prominent in Paul as in his predecessors. From heaven, God's wrath against it is revealed (Rom. 1.18; 2.9); it heads the list of vices (Rom. 1.29); it is the antithesis of truth (ἀλήθεια) (Rom. 1.18; 1 Cor. 13.6; 2 Thess. 2.10, 12); it not only obfuscates the nature of reality but it is the cause of dissension, a capital political offense (Rom. 2.9); it is the equivalent of *hamartia* (Rom. 6.13) and is ranked with *asebeia* (Rom. 1.18); it is incompatible with ὄνομα κυρίου (*onoma kuriou*), the name of God (2 Tim. 2.19)—that is, it disrupts the power of the name of God. Yet, with his characteristic contrariety, Paul declares that our *adikia* demonstrates God's *dikaiosunē* (Rom. 3.5, cf. 9.14).

Moreover, Paul repeatedly insists that he not only speaks—brings rhetorical arguments—but also, like Ps.-Zaleucus's exorcist, demonstrates (the power of) the *pneuma* and the power of God (δύναμις θεοῦ). He acts in word and deed, with the power of signs and miracles and with the power of the *pneuma* (Rom. 15.18-19; 1 Cor. 1.17; 2.4, cf.

---

198. *Asebeia* is, for the Greeks, a rational not a religious flaw; it is a debasement of the higher reaches of the soul. See *passim*.

199. See, e.g., Plato's *Gorgias* 493a.

2 Cor. 10.10).[200] 'We may seem quacks', says Paul in perfect elliptical style, 'yet we are true', (ὡς πλάνοι καὶ ἀληθεῖς) (2 Cor. 6.8). Once more, a Hellenistic text helps illuminate a Pauline thought.

Fragment #8 (T 227.22-25). In another interesting precept, Ps.-Zaleucus exhorts those who possess reason and want to be saved (παρ' ἀνθρώποις νοῦν ἔχουσι καὶ σωθησομένοις) to obey laws and officials (ἄρχοντες).[201] Reason and salvation are tied together. In Plato the identical phrase stops before 'salvation',[202] and thus reveals what is new in Hellenistic thinking. Paul's prodding his listeners to obey the establishment (Rom. 13.1-2) has raised many a critical eyebrow. It is, however, not only consistent with Hellenistic political thinking but is the very framework for Paul's political vision. Because all political power is from God (οὐ γὰρ ἔστιν ἐξουσία εἰ μὴ ὑπὸ θεοῦ) (Rom. 13.1) political disobedience is mutiny against God and will incur punishment. The association of reason and salvation is one of those amazing hybrids peculiar to Hellenistic thinking. It throws light on, and makes intelligible, paradoxical Pauline constructs such as rational worship (λογικὴ λατρεία) (Rom. 12.1) and unintelligible reason (μὴ εὔσημον λόγον) (1 Cor. 14.9).

Fragment #10 (T 227.29–228.1). Here, Ps.-Zaleucus postulates an important political rule that is encountered, albeit in different form, in Paul: do not reckon another citizen as an irreconcilable enemy (ἐχθρός ἀκατάλλακτος).[203] Paul uses a similar formula to explain the event by which human society enters God's political rule: 'While enemies [of God] we were reconciled with God [εἰ γὰρ ἐχθροὶ ὄντες κατηλλάγημεν τῷ θεῷ] by the death of his son' (Rom. 5.10). God himself does not hesitate to use radical means to turn his seemingly irreconcilable enemies back to him. The context is different, certainly, and the two

200. Also, the *euangelion* is both word and the power of the spirit called holy (Rom. 1.16; 1 Thess. 1.5).

201. Iamblichus attributes the same expression to Aristoxenus, *On Pythagorean Life* 196, 224 (*ap.* A. Delatte 1922: 192 n. 2).

202. *Crito* 51b (A. Delatte 1922: 192 n. 2). Plato's 'people of understanding', know that the country is above parents and forebears and more valued, higher and holier than they. It is to be obeyed, and whether in battle or in a court of law one must do what the *polis* and the country, πατρίς, order one (*Crito* 51a-c).

203. He who does so, says Ps.-Zaleucus, in whom passion, θυμός, is stronger than reason, λογισμός, is disqualified from magistracies and administration of justice.

passages are connected only by a linguistic thread, but, despite the complexity that the thought achieves in Paul, both passages convey the political idea of harmony and unity, ubiquitous yet noteworthy throughout the Hellenistic era. The likelihood that even the most radical, uniquely Pauline ideas may have been suggested by familiar and ordinary Hellenistic views cannot be discounted.[204]

Fragment #12 (T 228.4-10, 16-21). It is one of the most firmly grounded convictions of both Classical and Hellenistic political thinkers that changing the laws is worse than living under an unfair and inequitable law. Both Plato and Aristotle speak aggressively against attempts to change the law as a cause of anarchy and political ruin. Ps.-Zaleucus condenses this attitude in a memorable formula: he who proposes a modification of a law should make his proposal to the citizens 'with a rope around his neck' (εἰς βρόχον εἴρας τὸν τράχηλον).

This anathematizing of political change is of momentous significance for Paul. Paul does not touch the established laws and authority; he is careful to avoid even the suspicion of a challenge to power. But Paul's conservatism arises not only from a fear of retribution from Roman authorities; it is not just diplomatic surrender to officialdom. Rather, it is rooted in the highest precepts of ancient political philosophy: one should not dream of changing a political system, for tampering with the laws risks chaos and destruction. No idea, thought or intellectual creation can survive the destruction of the political context in which culture is created. Thus Paul not only accepts, but, more important, upholds the political structure that produced him. No matter how novel his approach, how many reversals he subjects language to, how many times he jolts his listeners' minds, the simple truth is that Paul would *never* touch the system. He would do only one thing 'against' it: he would nurture, fortify and bolster it, directing all his energy, originality and authority toward arresting its deterioration, halting its dignified disintegration and reversing the faltering cadence of its workings. Paul is downright reactionary, for he is bent on frustrating the self-destructive forces of history itself. Paul's vitality and confidence in his own construct is prodigious; the weight he throws against the inherent decadence of the system is formidable. Thanks to Paul, the Roman empire, which had hardly stopped mourning the death of Augustus, has yet to

---

204. The theme continues in the next dictum (#11, T 228.1-4), that prohibits slandering both city and fellow-citizen, the disunity motif, present in Paul as well.

reach its climax; in a sense, it will never fall. It may fragment itself, then coalesce again. It may change its center and axis, but it will endure, as a Christian empire, till our own days. No state has yet invented a punishment for excessive zeal for its survival. Over-enthusiastic patriotism, no matter how objectionable, is not punishable by law. For Paul's culpa is not that of having menaced society, but of having robbed it of the possibility of degeneration.

Fragment #13 (T 228.9-16). Finally, a reverberation can be sensed between Ps.-Zaleucus and Paul on the distinction between slavery and freedom vis-à-vis justice. Slaves, writes Ps.-Zaleucus, do what is just on account of fear, the free on account of shame and (knowledge of) the good.[205] Φοβος (*phobos*), fear, characterizes the slave, αἰδώς (*aidōs*) and καλόν (*kalon*), shame and propriety, characterize the free. One's identity is established according to where one stands in regard to submission to justice, laws and the constitution. Slavery is coercion into a political compact; freedom is setting store on one's reputation, vis-à-vis one's fellow citizens, and on the recognition of the good.

Paul thinks of *phobos* in some quite interesting ways. His variegated uses of *phobos* can be consolidated under three headings, each defining a specific degree of slavery. Fear of God, understood as awe, makes one a slave of freedom. Fear of human authority shows one as the slave of a slave. Fear of one's fellow citizens is largely understood as shame or loss of face and designates one as a slave to one's equals. We have, here, a version of an Aristotelian-Hellenistic classification of slavery. The first category is strikingly close to Aristotle's slavery by nature;[206] the second to the Stagirite's definition of legal slaves;[207] the third to Plato's, Aristotle's and the Hellenistic authors' notion of shame.[208]

Paul employs *phobos* in three distinctive situations: to define a relation to the divinity, to describe an effect of human institutions and to reveal the force of inter-human actions. The first instance finds its

205. τοὺς μὲν οὖν δούλους προσήκει διὰ φόβον πράττειν τι τῶν δικαίων, τοὺς δ᾿ ἐλευθέρους δι᾿ αἰδῶ καὶ τὸ καλόν (T 228.13-14).

206. *Politics* 1.1253b15-1254a13, 1254b20-21. Note that the natural slave, for all the unfavorable position of slavery in antiquity, is hardly a negative term. In Paul everyone is a natural slave of God.

207. *Politics* 1255a4-b31, cf. Plato *Republic* 5.469b-471c.

208. Discussed elsewhere, see above, sections on Ps.-Archytas (fragment 5d, esp. T 35.3-4) and on Hippodamos.

exemplary expression in Rom. 8.15: 'You did not receive the *pneuma* of slavery to fall back into fear, but you received the *pneuma* of sonship'.[209] It is precisely Ps.-Zaleucus's point, stated with the same language, less the *pneuma*. Fear and slavery are part of the same conceptual aggregate. Participation in the new association makes one a child of God, determines one as part of the divine household (Rom. 8.16).[210] The human condition vis-à-vis God is dual, freedom and slavery at the same time. All are natural slaves of God, are under his masterly power. Fear, when of God, becomes awe (Rom. 11.20; 2 Cor. 5.11); the formula is 'fear and trembling' (φόβος καὶ τρόμος) (1 Cor. 2.3; 2 Cor. 7.5; Phil. 2.12; see also Eph. 6.5), a psychic disturbance seemingly caused by *pneuma*.[211]

The second category of Paul's uses of 'fear' is well illustrated by the *phobos* cluster in Rom. 13.1-7, the notorious passage on the obedience owed human political institutions. In the same group belongs Gal. 2.12, where the fear spoken of is of the powerful 'circumcision party'. The third case, fear as shame, is best illustrated by the deutero-Pauline 1 Timothy: 'As for those who persist in wrong actions scold them in front of all, so that the others may be ashamed [to follow them] (5.20)'.[212] The notion (and the language) is similar to Rom. 12.17: 'Take thought for what is noble in the sight of all'.[213]

209. οὐ γὰρ ἐλάβετε πνεῦμα δουλείας πάλιν εἰς φόβον ἀλλὰ ἐλάβετε πνεῦμα υἱοθεσίας (Rom. 8.15). Remember the complexity of the term *pneuma*, which I called a supernatural and rational agency.

210. What Paul means is made clear in the next phrase: a possession by a power that makes one in a glossolalia fit howl 'Abba!' is interpreted by Paul as an admission of sonship to God.

211. See also *4 Macc.* 4.11. Also, fittingly, a poetical idiom, found in Horace as well: *timor et minae, Carmina* 3.1.27.

212. τοὺς ἁμαρτάνοντας ἐνώπιον πάντων ἔλεγχε, ἵνα καὶ οἱ λοιποὶ φόβον ἔχωσιν (1 Tim. 5.20). The term for 'shame' itself, *aidōs*, is used in 1 Tim. 2.9, in a command to women to adorn themselves modestly and wisely.

213. προνοούμενοι καλὰ ἐνώπιον πάντων ἀνθρώπων. *Aidōs* and *kalon*, writes Ps.-Zaleucus, characterize the free. The faculty to recognize the good, turns up in almost all of Paul's letters, at crucial points in arguments. Nothing good, ἀγαθόν, is in my *sarkic* self, I can will the good, τὸ καλόν, but I cannot do it (Rom. 7.18, cf. also Rom. 7.21). This oppressing discovery is the flagship of the concept. That good is to die is the seeming paradox in 1 Cor. 9.15. These, to refer only to the most dramatic instances. But they go far beyond what Ps.-Zaleucus intended.

Ps.-Charondas: προοίμια νόμων (prooimia nomōn),
Preambles to the Laws

Charondas, the twin of Zaleucus, is associated with a very similar set of texts, also known as *prooimia nomōn*.[214] The following fragments from Ps.-Charondas, who lived in the West in the third or second century BCE,[215]are preserved in Stobaeus.

Fragment #1 (T 60.10-13). When the citizens are assembled for deliberation and action, they take decisions with God (διὰ τὰν πρὸς τὸν θεὸν ξυμβουλίαν), so they must avoid any foul action, for God is part to no injustice (οὐδενός γὰρ ἀδίκου θεὸν κοινωνεῖν). In Paul, when the Christians are together in the *ekklēsia*, *pneuma* guides them. Doing things *with* God (Christ) is a major feature of the Christian *ekklēsia*; its very identity is derived from acting in concert with God. To mention only the most obvious references: Paul assumes the 'same form' with God (συμμορφιζόμενος, Phil. 3.10), Christ's followers 'suffer' and 'are glorified' with him (συμπάσχομεν, συνδοξασθῶμεν, Rom. 8.17) and 'grow together' with him (σύμφυτοι γεγόναμεν, Rom. 6.5). God's wrath at *adikia* is notorious (e.g., Rom. 1.18; 2.8; 3.5; 9.14). Even more important, these and similar texts can be seen as part of the background for the grand, central motif of God's *dikaiosunē* against the *hamartia–adikia* aggregate, developed primarily in Romans.

Fragment #2 (T 60.14-19). Ps.-Charondas exhorts involvement in political life: a man must participate in judicial matters and in public affairs, according to his worth (κατ᾽ ἀξίαν τῶν δικαίων μεταλαμβάνεν καὶ πράσσεν), so that when he undertakes things according to his stature and rank (κατ᾽ ἀξιαν τὰν ἑαυτῶ καὶ δυναμίαν) he will be honored and respected (ὅπως τίμιος ἧς καὶ σεμνός). The importance of activity according to value (*pneuma*, in Paul), the consummate interest in hierarchy-within-equality and the urge to political involvement are all pivotal in Paul's thought. Of particular interest is the case of πράσσω (*prassō*), 'to do'. The absolute, political use of the verb has an enlightening history and a major significance in Paul, who gives

214. Stobaeus 4.2.24 pp. 149-55 Hense = T 60.9-63.7; A. Delatte 1922: 195-202.
215. Thesleff 1961: 115.

πράττειν (*prattein*) a legal or political meaning in Rom. 1.32 (cf. Gal. 5.21; Rom. 2.1-3, 25; 7.15-19; 13.4).[216]

Fragment #3 (T 60.20-25). Ps.-Charondas advises against congregating with the *adikoi*, unjust men and women,[217] and in favor of associating with the good (*agathoi*, men only), for one resembles those with whom one keeps company (ὡς ὄντα ὅμοιον ᾧ ὁμιλεῖ). This injunction is linked to the claim that one is a perfect man (ἀνὴρ τέλειος) only if one is initiated in the greatest and most perfect initiation, self-mastery (τελεῖσθαι τε τὴν μεγίστην καὶ τελειοτάτην τελετήν, ἀνδραγαθίαν), imitating [the good] according to truth and acquiring excellence (μιμουμένος ἐπ᾽ ἀληθείᾳ καὶ κτωμένους τὴν ἀρετήν). A number of observations are in order.

Ps.-Charondas refers to a proverb that Paul also quotes:[218] 'Bad company ruins good morals' (φθείρουσιν ἤθη χρηστὰ ὁμιλίαι κακαί) (1 Cor. 15.33). Plato uses similar locutions.[219] The argument that partnership with the bad soils the soul is one that Paul makes in his diatribes against the Greeks. He, too, counsels thinking according to [*pistis*-dependent] wisdom (φρονεῖν εἰς τὸ σωφρονεῖν (Rom. 12.3) and gives himself as an example of the man who thinks soundly (σωφρονοῦμεν) (which, with typical Pauline logic, does not exclude going crazy [ἐξέστημεν] for God; 2 Cor. 5.13).[220] All this, however, is commonplace Greek and Hellenistic ethics. Another aspect is much more intriguing.

Ps.-Charondas's text operates a transfer of religious initiation language to morals.[221] This may be a characteristically Pythagorean feature, for Plato[222] attributes the 'body-as-tomb' (σῶμα-σῆμα) view to 'a Sicilian or Italian' and says that he called 'uninitiated' (ἀμύητοι) (493a) those ruled by desires (ἐπιθυμίαι) (493b1). Plato's pun-making here, as Socrates recounts the story of the 'sly Italian', is memorable. The Italian, he says, 'invented a tale in which, by playing with the word

216. For a more thorough analysis of the absolute use of *prassō*, see Chapter 8, section on Rom. 12.1–16.23, esp. Rom. 13.4.

217. Ἀδίκῳ δὲ ἀνδρὶ ἢ γυναικὶ κεκριμένοις... δὲ προκεκριμένους ἄνδρας ἀγαθούς... (T 60.20-22).

218. Either following Menander (fourth/third century BCE), or, more likely, lifting it, as the author of comedies probably did, from the common wisdom.

219. E.g., *Laws* 5.728b or 9.854c. See A. Delatte 1922: 196.

220. For more examples see 1 and 2 Timothy and esp. Titus.

221. *Ap.* A. Delatte 1922: 196.

222. *Gorgias* 493a-c.

[παράγων τῷ ὀνόματι], he called the soul a 'receptacle' because it is *spacious* and receptive [διὰ τὸ πιθανόν {*'specious'*} τε καὶ πειστικὸν ὠνόμασε πίθον]' (493a). The seat of desires in the soul of the uninitiated, or the 'leaky' (ἀμυήτοι, another play on words), is compared with a vessel full of holes, because never satisfied (493a-b). There are important instances in which Paul, too, applies initiatory terminology within a moral context.[223] He warns, for example, against being 'initiated in desires' (ἐπιθυμίαν σαρκὸς οὐ μὴ τελέσητε) (Gal. 5.16). The identification of the immoral with the uninitiated is further suggested in the mystery religion language of 2 Cor. 4.4-9.[224] The light that shines out of darkness—the light of the knowledge of the glory of God in the face of Christ that shines in the soul (4.6)—is a treasure housed in clay vessels (4.7). It is this light, a superlative power, that sustains us in affliction (4.8-9). Romans 9.19-29, further working the clay vessel/potter metaphor, differentiates between vessels of wrath and vessels of mercy. In Phil. 3.19-21, Paul distinguishes between, on the one hand, those whose God is the belly and who glory in their shame, who think of mundane things and whose end is destruction; and, on the other, those who are citizens of the city of God, whose bodies will be changed by a savior into glorious bodies like his own.

Fragment #8 (T 61.11-15). Each citizen should be prudent rather than rash (σωφρονεῖν μᾶλλον ἢ [μέγα] φρονεῖν).[225] This is a popular tune in both Classical and Hellenistic authors and the homophony *sōphronein-phronein* (some negative compound of *phronein*), a cliché. It is the same advice Paul gives the older members of *ekklēsia*: avoid arrogance. This is more than a moral injunction, however. It is a political exigency, a condition of the community's stability. For example, in Rom. 12.3, Paul exhorts each of the ἀδελφοί (*adelphoi*, Rom. 12.1), the 'brothers', as he calls the members of the *ekklēsia*, not to be overbearing but to be

223. Rom. 9.21-23; Gal. 5.16; 2 Cor. 4.4-9; Phil. 3.19-21. For further discussion of the vessel metaphor (*skeuos* and *python* are equivalent) see Chapter 8, section on Rom. 9.1–11.36; Rom. 9.21-23.

224. The language of mysteries Paul uses in the following passages is not specifically Pythagorean, nevertheless, the terminology is that of initiations.

225. μέγα is my addition, and it is certainly what the author intended, as seen in the next phrase: προσποιείσθω δὲ ἕκαστος τῶν πολιτῶν σωφρονεῖν μᾶλλον ἢ φρονεῖν· ὡς ἡ προσποίησις τοῦ φρονεῖν μέγα σημεῖον ἀπειροκαλίας καὶ σμικρότητος (T 61.11-13).

wise (*huperphronein-sōphronein*),[226] for they are all members in the body of Christ (Rom. 12.4-5), the well-known political metaphor. Paul and the Hellenistic thinker share the same paraenetical context, the same paraenesis, the identical language. *Phronein* becomes, in Paul, an equivalent for political concord, as in Rom. 15.5, 'to live in harmony with each other' (φρονεῖν ἐν ἀλλήλοις), or Phil. 4.2, 'I beg Euodia and Syntyche to agree' (Εὐοδίαν παρακαλῶ καὶ Συντύχην παρακαλῶ τὸ αὐτὸ φρονεῖν). Harmony, as we have seen, is politically laden; it is the basis of a state's endurance.

Fragment #9a (T 61.16-19). Ps.-Charondas urges good will toward, and obedience and veneration of, the magistrates (πρὸς τοὺς ἄρχοντας εὔνοιαν...εὐπειθοῦντας καὶ σεβομένους). They oversee the city's hearth and the salvation of citizens (ἄρχοντες γὰρ ἑστιουχοῦσι πόλεως καὶ πολιτῶν σωτηρίας). *Archōn* (pl. *archontes*) is, technically, the Greek translation for the Latin *consul* or *praefectus* (governor of an imperial province), as numerous inscriptions attest. In the two notorious passages in which Paul speaks about the established political powers (Rom. 13.1-7; 1 Cor. 2.6-8), *archontes* is the generic name Paul gives rulers, authorities and officials (Rom. 13.7; 1 Cor. 2.6, 8). Obedience is owed them as appointees of God and defenders of the laws (Rom. 13.1-4). Payment of taxes is due them as contractors of God (λειτουργοὶ θεοῦ) (Rom. 13.6). While Ps.-Charondas seems to recommend a cult of magistrates, however, no trace of that can be found in Paul. Rulers are subservient to God. But that their authority is from God, that they are God's stand-ins, are ideas that Paul shares with Western political thought as it developed from Classical antiquity on.

Fragment #10 (T 61.23-27). Ps.-Charondas urges the creation of a system of charity and social assistance. Political reasons underlie philanthropy. The money will go toward supporting the needy, those who find themselves in a straitened situation because of adverse fortunes, but whose children become defenders of the country. The system of social assistance and support it instituted is, as I have elsewhere contended, probably the single most important factor in Christianity's

---

226. μὴ ὑπερφρονεῖν παρ᾽ ὃ δεῖ φρονεῖν ἀλλὰ φρονεῖν εἰς τὸ σωφρονεῖν (Rom. 12.3). Paul indulges in the repetition of φρονεῖν even if produces an awkward construction: 'do not think more presumptuously than one ought to think but think as a wise one would think'.

success, and it may be Paul who laid its foundations. Social welfare, however, is not unique to Christianity; as the Ps.-Charondas fragment indicates, it had been a concern among earlier political thinkers. It is also encountered in Plato, who thinks that charity is the salvation of a state and basis of political order,[227] and in Aristotle, who attributes it to the Tarentines (Tarentum was a Pythagorean stronghold) who earn the good will of the multitude by providing for the poor and the destitute.[228] As we have seen, Paul uses a political term, *koinōnia*, for charitable contributions (Rom. 12.13; 15.26; 2 Cor. 8.4; 9.13; 1 Tim. 6.18).

Fragment #11 (T 61.28-35). In a context that makes it a social obligation to blow the whistle on anyone committing an injustice (*adikia*) and thus endangering the constitution, Ps.-Charondas differentiates between involuntary ignorance and intentional transgressions (ἐμφανιζόντων δὲ μὴ τὰ δι᾽ ἀκούσιον ἄγνοιαν γιγνόμενα, ἀλλ᾽ ὅσον ἂν ἐκ προνοίας τι ἁμαρτάνωσιν) (T 61.31-32). The same topic is continued in fragment #12 (T 61.36–62.4), where voluntary evil against *dikaiosunē* is a very grave offense. This distinction is made by Aristotle in his discussion of freedom of will and accountability. He distinguishes between unintentional actions, performed under compulsion or in ignorance,[229] and voluntary actions,[230] which make the agent responsible and introduce liability for action,[231] and he establishes degrees of responsibility for voluntary actions.[232] Paul shows knowledge of this distinction in 1 Cor. 9.17, where he contrasts ἑκών (*hekōn*) with ἄκων (*akōn*), willing with unwilling action. In Rom. 8.20, the creation is unwillingly ignorant (οὐχ ἑκοῦσα) of its plight.[233] This distinction is connected with the major theme of instruction, a dominant issue in each of Paul's Letters (e.g., Rom. 16.25, where the *euangelion* and the message [κήρυγμα] impart the mystery long kept secret).[234]

227. *Laws* 5.736d-e.
228. *Politics* 6.1320b10-11.
229. *Ethics* 3.1109b30-1111a20.
230. *Ethics* 3.1113a21-1113b1.
231. *Ethics* 3.1113b2-1114b25.
232. *Ethics* 5.1135a15-1136a9.
233. That intentionality is also a matter of intense debate in Judaism does not detract from the Hellenistic intertextuality of the idea.
234. Gal. 1.16; 3.23; Eph. 1.9; 3.3; 3.5; Col. 1.26; 2.2; 1 Cor. 14.2-5, which elaborates on the need for an interpreter; Rom. 15.14-15, instructing one another or through the letters of Paul.

Fragment #13 (T 62.5-7) Ps.-Charondas thinks that dying for the country (ὑπὲρ πατρίδος ἀποθνῄσκειν) is more dignified (σεμνότερον) than love of life (γλιχόμενον τοῦ ζῆν). The latter expression is also found in Plato[235] and Aristotle[236] to show the power of the instinct of self-preservation. Conventional rhetoric of patriotism becomes, in Paul's Christian *polis*, the revolutionary slogan, 'To live is [to die with] Christ and to die is to gain' (τὸ ζῆν Χριστὸς καὶ τὸ ἀποθανεῖν κέρδος) (Phil. 1.21), a transformative interpretation of political duty. The metaphysical sophistication of the Pauline phrase does not obscure the similarity of the underlying principle.

Fragment #17 (T 62.19-23). In this fragment, Ps.-Charondas commands that slave of riches must be despised, frowned upon (καταφρονείσθω). Paul phrases his attack on the Corinthians who display their opulence in the *ekklēsia* similarly: 'Do you despise the *ekklēsia* of God and humiliate those who have nothing?' (ἢ τῆς ἐκκλησίας τοῦ θεοῦ καταφρονεῖτε, καὶ καταισχύνετε τοὺς μὴ ἔχοντας;) (1 Cor. 11.22).[237]

Review of Main Themes

To claim, as I do, that Paul is a political thinker in no sense denies that he is a theologian; rather it adds a dimension to our understanding. Paul's pneumatic politics, while definitely original and inventive, can be seen to fit into a Greek tradition of political theory in which the relation to the divine is an integral element.[238] Before turning to what I call

235. *Phaedo* 117a.

236. *Politics* 3.1278b29. See A. Delatte 1922: 199 n. 1.

237. See also the charges against the slaves of desires. There is, finally, a set of exhortations against immorality, focusing on the unity of the family and on not offending the family gods, that recalls 1 Cor. 7, but the content of which is different from Paul's concerns, mainly the subordination of women to men.

238. Relations between Pythagoreanism and Christianity had often been noticed in antiquity. Thus, Clement of Alexandria viewed the affinity between the *akousmata* and the 'barbarian', i.e. Jewish and Christian philosophy (*Stromata* 5.5.27-31 esp. 5.5.27.12, *ap*. Thom 1994: 96). For him the Pythagorean teachings *depended* [my emphasis], in an inscrutable way, on the 'barbarian'. Hippolytus of Rome endeavored to demonstrate, by citing *akousmata*, that heresy was rooted in Pythagorean philosophy (*Refutatio* 6.26-27, esp. 6.28.1, *ap*. Thom 1994: 97). The same Hippolytus saw Gnosticism as having sprung from Pythagoreanism (Mansfeld 1992, *ap*. Thom 1994: 97 n. 19. For a good discussion of *Refutatio* 6 see also Mueller

the *basileia* group of Hellenistic Pythagoreans, it may be worth reviewing the points of connection that I have discerned between Paul and the members of the *polis* group.[239]

1992: 4326-32). Philosophy in general was often identified as the cause of heresies. That Pythagoreanism is cited as the source of Gnostic reflection by a man with as formidable a knowledge of Greek and Roman thinking as Hippolytus, and by so well versed a heresiologist, should give one pause. (On Hippolytus's reliability see M. Smith 1958). Gregory of Nazianzus recognized the similar fundamental attitude towards the cult founders in Pythagoreanism and Christianity (*Orations*, 4.102, *ap.* Thom 1994: 103 n. 55). The *Sentences of Sextus*, an anonymous work of Neopythagorean origin, was edited by a Christian around 200 CE to include gospel logia (Finney 1993: 644). Tertullian, recognizing two jurisdictions, Caesar's and God's in Lk. 12.15b-16, comments that the emperor's image on the coin is counterbalanced by God's image in a human and concludes that one should render the money to Caesar but oneself to God (*De idololatria* 15.3, *ap.* Finney 1993: 644). Carrying God's image in one's person, in a political context, is Pythagorean, although Finney (1993: 644) considers it a Stoic topos.

239. A growing force in the intellectual environment of late Hellenistic times, Pythagoreanism had an impact on the Early Christian writers. Modern scholarship has paid some attention to the contacts between Pythagoreanism and Christianity. Thus, I. Lévy (1927), Detienne (1963), Hemmerdinger (1972), Grant (1980), K. Berger (1984), Balch (1992) and Thom (1994) address the issue, but these scholars restricted their discussions to moral, didactical, or legal similarities (Lévy, Balch, Grant), or to philological points (Hemmerdiger), or to the *Gattungen*, formal genres common to the two movements (Berger), or to the influence of a particular concept, such as daimon (Detienne), or to the general echo left by the Pythagorean *akousmata* on the scriptures (Thom). The focus is on the gospels; little, if anything, of this seems relevant to Paul. The political significance of Pythagoreanism is missed.

Thom finds a confirmation of the importance of Pythagoreanism in the late Hellenistic and Imperial period in the widespread circulation of ἀκούσματα, 'secret teachings', also known as σύμβολα or αἰνίγματα, of which about 120 are known, and the numerous commentaries on them in Hellenistic writers (1994: 96-99). He attempts to prove, rarely convincingly, that many *akousmata* made their way, in form (definitions and precepts), content (rigorism, belief in *daimones*, eschatology), or in the allegorical mode of approach into the New Testament (99-112). Relevance for Paul appears marginal but not insignificant. There are some superficial similarities, e.g., 1 Cor. 12-14, on spiritual gifts being *malista*; or the saying 'Do not help remove a burden, but help put it on', being the uninteresting reverse of the trivial Hellenistic and Pauline 'bear one another's burden' (Gal. 6.2, but see also Gal. 6.5); or Pythagoras's 'When you go on a journey, do not turn around at the borders', seen as a factor behind the positive attitude about death in Phil. 1.20-24; 1 Cor. 15 (107-108, 111). (A more convincing case is the critique of what look like

Oikos and Polis. A series of Hellenistic Pythagorean texts sets the background for the first layer of Paul's two-tiered political society. In Hippodamos, Callicratidas and Ocellus, the *oikos* and the *polis* become fused together. In Hippodamos' *On Happiness* a person can achieve happiness and perfection (εὐδαιμονία καὶ ἀρετὰ ψυχῆς) (T 96.24) only in a group, either family or state, for the individual and the community are coterminous. Happiness and perfection form the Universe, from which they are diffused, successively, in the political association, the family and the individual (T 96.24-28). In a fragment of Callicratidas' *On the Happiness of the Household*, one observes that the Hellenistic Pythagorean does not distinguish between political rule (ἀρχὴ πολιτική) and household rule (ἀρχὴ οἰκονομική) a very significant modification of Aristotle that Paul will carry on. In Ocellus's *On Law*, we notice that, as we move forward in the Hellenistic era, the *polis-oikos* cluster forms an increasingly tight unit.

Oikos, used by itself to denominate 'household', 'family', is unexceptional in Paul.[240] What is outstanding and characteristic is Paul's consolidation of *oikos* and *ekklēsia*.[241] This is generally understood as a reference to house churches. What is less obvious is that this concept has its genesis in two pivotal Greek political units, the family and the citizens' assembly. Paul's politics centers on the notion of the household *ekklēsia* as *polis*, an innovation prepared for by Hellenistic political reflection.

Revealing, in this context, is the absence in both Paul and his circles of 'synagogue' (συναγωγή, *sunagōgē*). The glaring omission of the term the Jewish place of assembly suggests not only the unsuitable character of Jewish-related terminology for Paul's politics, but also the disassociation of his political system from anything Jewish. The case

Pythagorean ideas behind the excessive ritualism, asceticism and worship of angels in Col. 2.8, 16, 18, 20-23 (99).) Most interesting, however, seem to be the *akousmata* with a social and political character. 'Friendship is harmonious equality', recalls 2 Cor. 8.13-15 and the argument for Paul's collection for the Jerusalem church: 'it is a question of equality...' Or, 'Do not pluck a crown', read in the Hellenistic sources as 'Do not transgress a city's laws, which is her crown', similar to Rom. 13.1-7; 1 Tim. 2.1-2; Tit. 3.1 (111). Ironically and significantly, Hellenistic writers read 'the laws of the Hellenistic *polis*' in 'crown', the expression *par excellence* of royal and absolute power.

240. Especially in 1 Corinthians and in the deutero-Pauline 1–2 Timothy and Titus.

241. Rom. 16.5; 1 Cor. 16.19; Phlm. 2; also 1 Tim. 3.4; Col. 4.15.

may also be made that *sunagōgē*, as an eminently Jewish communal institution, would have been a misleading designation for Paul's *polis*-like Christian *ekklēsia*.[242]

Pneumatic Politics. Paul exhorts the Philippians: 'Be citizens' (πολιτεύεσθε) (1.27). Demosthenes knew that what the active Athenians do is to take part in politics and govern (πολιτεύεσθαι καὶ πράττειν).[243] Aristotle finds *politeuesthai* to be the function of citizens.[244] The Hellenistic Pythagorean Ps.-Charondas urges his readers in *Preambles to the Laws* to 'spur yourself to participate in the legal process and to take part in public affairs'.[245] Be politically active (in the Christ *polis*); be citizens of the *euangelion* of Christ, commands Paul. The *euangelion* constitutes a community, a community with the divine but also a human community—a state, a *polis*—maintained by concern for *to sumpheron*, the common good.

We find the concept of the common good expressed time and again in the *polis* group of Hellenistic Pythagoreans. Ps.-Archytas defines the common good, *to sumpheron*, in terms of the law—the law that inhibits personal or gang despotism and that champions the common interest of all citizens (T 35.1-3). The highlight of Callicratidas's preserved fragments is the household theory that views *oikos* as an assembly of connected elements, constituted of opposing and discrete forces crystallized around the privileged center of 'the best' and directed toward the common good (see T 103.21-23).[246]

242. K. Berger 1976 refutes the frequent assumption that Paul used *ekklēsia* to avoid the theological connotations of *sunagōgē* (*ap.* Meeks 1983: 222 n. 24). Berger's reasoning neglects the political implications of Paul's choice of terms.
    See Levine 1996 (and the bibliography he lists) for an excellent discussion of the synagogue, itself 'the result of sustained and intensive contacts with the Hellenistic world' (436, cf. 443), a place for communal functions and activities which included 'political meetings, social gatherings, courts, schools, hostels, charity activities, slave manumission, meals (sacred or otherwise), and, of course, religious-liturgical functions' (430, cf. 443). Paul distinguishes between the synagogue as a 'community center' (441) and the *ekklēsia* as *polis*.
243. *On the Crown* 18.45. The phrase *politeuesthai kai prattein* does describe the business of those actively involved in politics even if, in this passage, Demosthenes castigates their venality and corruption.
244. *Ethics* 6.1141b28.
245. βοηθεῖν δὲ ἕκαστον ἑαυτῷ καὶ ποτικελεύεσθαι κατ' ἀξίαν τῶν δικαίων μεταλαμβάνεν καὶ πράσσεν (T 60.14-15).
246. The texts echo Aristotle's own usage. Aristotle calls 'right constitutions',

Paul's use of *sumpheron* has conspicuous political reference. The Hellenistic context of Paul's thinking throws into relief the political import of a passage like 1 Cor. 10.23: 'Everything is allowed, but not everything is for the common good'; in other words, everything is allowed, but not everything upholds a political society. Then there is the Pauline political ID, the act of naturalization in his state: 'A sign of the *pneuma* is given everyone for the common good' (1 Cor. 12.7). One is marked for citizenship by the *pneuma*. The *pneuma* gives a sign, as when an oracle speaks (2 Cor. 12.1), that identifies one as of that society. The *polis* is pneumatic.

Imitation. The motif of imitation is integral to the political writings of the Hellenistic Pythagoreans. Hippodamos refers to kingship as θεομίματον πρᾶγμα (*theomimaton pragma*), a case of divine imitation (T 102.12). Euryphamos's[247] *On Life*,[248] not included in the previous discussion, emphasizes the notion of imitation. Humanity is an imitation (ἀντίμιμον) of the divinity's own nature. No human work imitates (ἐμιμάσατο) the Universe as well as the harmony of a *polis* that is well governed (εὐνομουμένας).

Imitation of the divine is the foundation of Paul's political system as well—though in Paul it is extended mean imitation of God's very death and resurrection. The pneumatics are the first fruits of the *pneuma* (Rom. 8.23), those marked out for a form similar to the image of God's son (προώρισεν συμμόρφους τῆς εἰκόνος τοῦ υἱοῦ αὐτοῦ) (Rom. 8.29). Christ is only the first born among many. He is slave and master (Rom. 8.30), the paradox that rescues the political game, the ruler and the ruled by turns. In Paul, imitation is the impassioned invitation to salvation.[249] It is the constant Pauline paraenesis: 'Imitate me who imitates Christ/the lord' (1 Cor. 11.1; 1 Thess. 1.6); 'Imitate me' (1 Cor. 4.16; 2 Thess. 3.7, 9); 'Be co-imitators of me' (Phil. 3.17); 'Imitate the *ekklēsiai* in Judea' (1 Thess. 2.14). The plethora of συν-compound

ὀρθαὶ πολιτεῖαι, a constitution that aims at the common good, τὸ κοινῇ συμφέρον σκοποῦσιν (*Politics* 3.1279a17-18), as opposed to debased ones, παρεκβάσεις (3.1279a20, cf. Plato, *Laws* 714b).

247. West, third century BCE.

248. περὶ βίου (*Peri biou*), Stobaeus 4.39.27 p. 915 Hense = T 86.4-11; A. Delatte 1922: 174-75.

249. See also section on Hippodamos, above, and Chapter 5, section on Ps.-Ecphantus, for more discussion of this topic.

words in Paul ties the theme of imitation to that of the community. From many dramatic examples, I select just a few: 'Fellow heirs of Christ, we should share in his suffering so that we may share in his glory' (Rom. 8.17); 'For if we have grown together in the likeness of his death we shall also [grow together in the likeness] of his resurrection' (Rom. 6.5); 'Assume the same form as Christ' (Phil. 3.10, cf. also Phil. 3.21).[250]

Hierarchy and Equality. Perhaps the conceptual complex that most strikingly places Paul's pneumatic politics in a Greek context is his elaborate emphasis on social hierarchy, even within a discourse of imitative union that involves equality.[251] There are innumerable examples in the Letters in which the equality of the members of the society is discussed, while hierarchy is the point. Thus, in 1 Cor. 12.4-11, a variety of favors (χαρίσματα), services (διακονίαι) and activities (ἐνεργήματα) (1 Cor. 12.4-6) are all produced by the same *pneuma*, and all for *to sumpheron*, the common good (1 Cor. 12.7), the signature of a political society. *Pneuma* is the energy behind all this, and it is *pneuma* that distributes the gifts, but the relative magnitude determines the hierarchy in the equality-informed *ekklēsia* (1 Cor. 12.28-31; Rom. 12.6-8).

Both Ps.-Archytas and Damippos focus their politics on the dynamics of hierarchical division (T 33.13-18). The main principle of Ps.-Archytas's constitution is reciprocity (ἀντιπεπονθέναι τοῖς αὐτῶ μερέεσσιν) (T 34.21-22). Callicratidas and Hippodamos show a profound and clearly Classically-influenced concern for hierarchical categorization (T 98.11-22), also characteristic of Paul. Callicratidas emphasizes the distinction between household rule (δεσποτικὴ ἀρχή) and that of the professional (ἐπιστατική). At variance with Aristotle, he gives an importance to the *epistatic* that demonstrates the focal positioning of the professional classes and of specialized and skilled labor in Hellenistic times. Hippodamos' analysis of function within civic structure has as counterpart the *pneuma*-related occupational skills ranked by Paul. Man of his times, Paul professionalizes his *ekklēsia* and staffs it with

250. See also the remarkable pseudo-Pauline ἐστὲ συμπολῖται τῶν ἁγιῶν καὶ οἰκεῖοι τοῦ θεοῦ, you are fellow citizens with the saints and the members of the household of God (Eph. 2.19).

251. Legal equality, often personified, is a major concept in Greek and Hellenistic times. (In Philo it is the counterpart of God.) It is correlated with *dikaiosunē*. See Georgi 1992: 84-86, 138-40, 154; Stählin 1964: 343-55.

specialists—*pneuma*-graduated experts—while cultivating distrust of crossovers.[252]

Distributive Justice. Distributive justice, correlate of social hierarchy, is one of the themes most often treated by the Hellenistic Pythagoreans. We find it, for example, in Ps.-Archytas: the law must conform to nature (ἀκόλουθος…τῇ φύσει). But what does it mean for a law to imitate the justice of nature (μιμεόμενος τὸ τᾶς φύσιος δίκαιον)? The justice of nature is proportional justice, justice κατ᾽ ἀναλογίαν (*kat' analogian*), justice that apportions to each according to his worth (τοῦτο δὲ ἐστιν τὸ ἀνάλογον καὶ τὸ ἐπιβάλλον ἑκάστῳ κατὰ τὰν ἑκάστου ἀξιάν) (T 33.23-25). This Hellenistic text, which itself closely follows Aristotle, has strict equivalences in Paul. For Paul, gifts (χαρίσματα), measures of *dikaiosunē*, are distributed in proportion to *pistis* (κατὰ τὴν ἀναλογίαν τῆς πίστεως) (Rom. 12.6).

Likewise, Callicratidas's treatment of analogy as the natural principle of proportional justice corresponds, in Paul, to *pneuma*'s rule by distributive proportion (ἀναλογία) (Rom. 12.6), also expressed in Rom. 12.3: 'According to the measure of faith assigned to each by God' (ἑκάστῳ ὡς ὁ θεὸς ἐμέρισεν μέτρον πίστεως).[253]

Nomos and Dikaiosunē. The available fragments of Ps.-Archytas's *On Law and Justice* treat at length the distinction between *nomos* and *dikaiosunē*. His treatise thus lies squarely within the tradition that places the two concepts at the core of political discourse, a tradition that ultimately connects Plato (*Republic, Laws, Politicus, Protagoras*) and Paul (Romans). The question of the difference between law and justice raises two further issues: the distinction between written and unwritten law, especially the meaning of the latter, and the topic of divine or natural law, often represented by *dikaiosunē*.

According to A. Delatte, law and justice function 'as the two poles of the majority of political discussions begun by Sophism'.[254] A dynamic of distinction and identification, of shifting emphasis on one pole or the other, characterized political theory in the Classical and, later, the Hellenistic world.

The related examination of the issue of written versus unwritten

---

252. Rom. 12.6-8; 1 Cor. 12.4-10, 28-29; 14.2-3.
253. Cf. 2 Cor. 10.13; also Eph. 4.7.
254. A. Delatte 1922: 79.

laws—that is, the critique of man-made legal systems, of positive laws, and the question of their status when compared with traditions or natural or divine laws—also has had a protracted history of debate in antiquity. The Hellenistic Pythagoreans were certainly party to this controversy. Paul, heir to this tradition, treats trespassing against the law in two divergent ways. First, in describing the error of the Greeks, he focuses on transgression of natural law. The Greeks have permitted abject pleasure to overcome lofty reason. Romans 1.18-32 best presents this case: the Greeks, though cognizant of divine law, betrayed it in fallacious arguments and lost the rational light that had guided them. Abjuration of philosophical insight led, morally, to physical debasement and to activities in direct violation of the law of nature, *para phusin* (Rom. 1.26). To moral lapse (1.24-27) corresponds the political folly of division (1.28-31).

Paul attributes the other form of transgression to the Jews: excessive confidence in the written law with the accompanying disregard of natural law (Rom. 2.17-29; 3.21-30). Paul opposes the *dikaiosunē* of God to the *nomos* of the Hebrews (3.21). This critique defies Judaism. A Jew would stress the equivalence, indeed, the synonymity, of the divine law and the written Hebrew law. Paul's ruling could come only from a Greek-cultivated mind, one familiar with the ongoing argument about the difference between written and unwritten laws.

The crucial distinction between *nomos* and *dikaiosunē* that Paul employs is Greek in source and development. The first term designates, in its technical use, the written law; the second describes the concept of divine—or natural—justice. Positing a sharp opposition between natural law (the *nomos* of *dikaiosunē*) and the various laws of political communities, as well as identifying Christ with a 'living law', are characteristic of Paul's thought. Similarly, the *dikaiosunē* of *pistis*, a cosmic universal, is contrasted with the *nomos* and its particular adherents (Rom. 4.13-14). The *dikaiosunē* of *pistis* is opposed to the *dikaiosunē* of *nomos* (9.30-31). One living under the law is bound to the justice of the law, but there is also another justice, one based on *pistis* (10.5-6).

Pistis, in Paul, is part of the binary *pistis-dikaiosunē*. Traditionally, *dikaiosunē* was paired with *nomos*. Paul discards (human) *nomos* and makes (God's) *dikaiosunē* absolute. He replaces *nomos* with *pistis* and in the process eliminates the tension between *nomos* and *dikaiosunē* of Classical and Hellenistic political philosophy. *Nomos* is retained in phases such as ἐκ/διὰ πίστεως/νόμος, but as an appendage, as the echo of what replaces it.[255] *Pistis* acquires attributes *nomos* formerly held. *Pistis* becomes a political concept: the degree of allegiance to a God who dispenses *dikaiosunē*.

Romans 10.4 makes Christ and *dikaiosunē* the end (*telos*) of the *nomos*. The proper nature of the law is *dikaiosunē*; Christ and *dikaiosunē* are associated, although not identical. In Gal. 2.21 the death of Christ is the living law (*dikaiosunē*). A master of diatribe, Paul uses a fine litotes and a chiasmus to indicate that (positive) law is death and that Christ-*dikaiosunē* is life. A similar effect is obtained by the hypophora and chiasmus in Gal. 3.21: the law that gives life is no law but *dikaiosunē*. Philippians 3.6-9 represents the apex of this idea. The climactic arrangement of clauses moves from (Jewish) law as gain, to counting this gain as loss when Christ is gained, to loss of the limited *dikaiosunē* of the *nomos* to gain of the universal *dikaiosunē* of *pistis*. The interplay between *nomos* and *dikaiosunē* and between written *nomos* and living *nomos*—Christ, equivalent to the *nomos empsuchos* of the Hellenistic Pythagoreans—is difficult and illuminating. What rules the *kosmos*, says Paul, is not *nomos* but *dikaiosunē* (Rom. 4.13). The *dikaiosunē* of the law amounts to little (Rom. 9.31; Gal. 2.21; 3.21; Phil. 3.6, 9). The Greeks, who do not have *nomos*, do the law—that is, know the principles of political and moral excellence—by nature (*phusei*) (Rom. 2.14).

Laws define infractions and prescribe penalties. The punishment for breaking customs is neither fine nor imprisonment but loss of face, dishonor, shame. In general Paul shares with the Pythagorean pseude-pigrapha the motif of public shame associated with transgression. It is a commonplace of Classical Greece that violating traditions or customs (i.e. unwritten laws) inflicts shame on the offender, that it causes a loss of face, and later writers often report or elaborate on this theme. Ps.-Archytas thinks that the best law is the one the breaking of which attracts shame and dishonor as sanctions (καὶ τὰν ζαμίαν ἐς τὰν αἰσχύναν καὶ τὰν ἀτιμίαν ἀμφέρη) (T 35.3-4). Similarly, the (probably) third-century BCE writer Diotogenes, in *On Piety*,[256] finds the foundation

---

255. See also D.A. Campbell (1992a), who shows that the prepositional phrases ἐκ/διὰ πίστεως/νόμος are simply reiterative, and that the *nomos* paradigm is only a negative expression of *pistis* and has no internal logic or content of itself.

256. περὶ ὁσιότητος (*peri hosiotētos*). See Chapter 5, Diotogenes.

of a good life in fear of shame rather than of fines.[257] Ps.-Charondas and Ps.-Zaleucus, in their *Preambles to the Laws*, also emphasize the importance of public blame and loss of face for breaking certain laws, especially those regarding the honor due the gods.

Paul shares in this culture of shame and confronts it directly. His test case is the *euangelion*, the message at the heart of Christianity, which occasioned fits of mass indignation. Paul meets the outraged sensibilities of his contemporaries with defiance: 'I am not ashamed of the *euangelion*' (Rom. 1.16). What others take as offensive Paul embraces, for he stands firm in his belief that the *euangelion* is a divine power, able to work salvation for everyone fortified by a similar certainty. Paul's *euangelion*, the law of his people, is not a written code of law but a natural or divine system rooted in *dikaiosunē*.[258]

If *dikaiosunē* is rendered in English as 'righteousness', the Hebrew Scriptures, together with the Rabbis' commentaries, are immediately called to mind. If one translates it as 'justice', however, the backdrop changes—to the Greek and the Hellenistic political treatises. None of Paul's listeners—Greeks, Romans, Hellenized Jews or barbarians—would ever have called a Hebrew prophet to mind when they heard the apostle speak of *dikaiosunē*.

257. See also A. Delatte 1922: 116 n. 1.
258. Two motifs coalesce here: that of shame, for the *euangelion* scandalizes the Greeks; and that of divine law, which Paul takes his *euangelion* to be. See also Chapter 8, Rom. 1.1-17.

Chapter 5

HELLENISTIC PYTHAGOREANS:
THE *BASILEIA* GROUP

Writings for Kings

So far we have examined the culture of the household–*polis*, the human layer of Paul's two-tiered political system. It remains to look at the cosmic, divine part. For the literary and intellectual background of this idea, we turn to a group of Hellenistic Pythagorean writers that I call the *basileia* group: Ps.-Ecphantus, Diotogenes and Sthenidas.

As the Hellenistic era progresses, politics becomes the territory of professional politicians, not of philosophers. It becomes not only irrelevant but even dangerous to philosophize about politics. Politicians are more effectively served by religion than by philosophy. As Ps.-Aristotle's *De mundo*, the epitome of Hellenistic popular philosophy, puts it, to 'theologize about the world' is the order of the day.[1] The business of the practical philosopher is now the panegyric. If it is infused with mystical effluvia, so much the better. Under this guise, however, political reflection does, in fact, endure.[2]

The Classical philosophers had understood kingship as a basic form of political constitution. Plato in *Politicus*, *Republic*, *Gorgias* and *Laws*; Aristotle in *Nicomachean Ethics* and *Politics*; Isocrates in *Euagoras*, *To Nicocles* and *To Philip*; and Xenophon in *Argesilaus* and *Cyropaedia*—all theorize about kingship. They[3] distinguish between monarchy (βασι-

---

1. Ps.-Aristotle, *De mundo* 391b4.

2. It must be said that Hellenistic Pythagoreanism was not just a philosophy. A neo-Pythagorean basilica was unearthed near Porta Maggiore, in Rome, beneath the railroad tracks leading to Stazione Termini, the central railway station. See Carcopino 1943 (first edition 1927) (accepted by Rostovtzeff 1927: 126-43). Burkert (1961: 226, 227 n. 2, 229) thinks that it was not a cult room for a Pythagorean sect, but a grave (*ap.* Balch 1992: 385-86 and n. 46).

3. I follow here Aristotle's classification and discussion of monarchy in *Politics* 3.1284b35-1285b33.

λεία)[4] and absolute kingship, law-abiding but hereditary (κατὰ νόμον καὶ πατρικαί)[5]: the first is a legitimate constitution, while the second is personal rule, a form of dictatorship most often identified with the barbarians or the 'Oriental' East. Absolute monarchy proper (παμβασιλεία)[6] is household-type mastership over a city, a regime in which the king is the law. There is a major difference between absolute kingship and (elective) tyranny (αἰσυμνητεία or αἱρετὴ τυραννίς),[7] as well. In the Greek world, the latter is distinct from despotism. All Greek tyrants, for example, struck coins in the name of the *polis*, not their own.[8] With Hellenism come absolute rulers and a need to justify personal autocratic power. A literature on kingship appears—and grows. The Hellenistic Pythagoreans of the *basileia* group provide the best examples of this genre.[9]

The Hellenistic genre of literature περὶ βασιλείας ('on kingship') was in part an attempt to ward off sycophancy or intended as an antidote to its corrupting effects. Aware that absolute monarchy breeds flattering courtiers who in their effort to please deprive the king of good advice, Demetrius of Phalerus, Aristotle's friend[10] and from 317 to 307 BCE governor of Athens under the Macedonians, advises Ptolemy I 'to buy and read books on kingship and on political leadership. For those things which the kings' friends are not bold enough to recommend to them, are written in those books'.[11] As time goes on, these books themselves become encomiastic, yet their original function is preserved.[12]

---

4. *Politics* 3.1284b36.
5. *Politics* 3.1285a19.
6. *Politics* 3.1285b32.
7. *Politics* 3.1285b25.
8. Aalders 1975: 17 and n. 48.
9. Ps.-Aristeas's *Letter to Philocrates*, written by a Jew of Alexandria is another relevant text (Aalders 1975: 19).
10. He was also the philosopher's nemesis, for this friendship was invoked by the Assembly as one of the causes for Aristotle's being accused of treason.
11. ...τὰ περὶ βασιλείας καὶ ἡγεμονίας βιβλία κτᾶσθαι καὶ ἀναγινώσκειν· ἃ γὰρ οἱ φίλοι τοῖς βασιλεῦσιν οὐ θαρροῦσι παραινεῖν. ταῦτα ἐν τοῖς βιβλίοις γέγραπται (Plutarch, *Sayings of Kings and Commanders* 189d). This saying is also preserved by Stobaeus 4.7.27=Hense 4.255.
12. I find it remarkable that, when Eusebius of Caesarea writes his panegyric for Constantine (*Laudatio Constantini*, actually two works, written in 335 and appended to *Vita Constantini* of 337), the thought and the language are those of the Hellenistic Pythagoreans. His theory of the divinity of the emperor is rooted in the Hellenistic

These texts allow expression of political thought—and thus participation in political life—that would not otherwise have been possible. Moreover, Hellenistic political reflection gave rise to a body of mystical literature displaying profound anxiety, esoteric interest and transcendental aspiration.

Ps.-Ecphantus: περὶ βασιλείας (peri basileias), On Kingship

The work of Ps.-Ecphantus, who probably lived in southern Italy during the second or first century BCE,[13] looks like a radically reactionary and unabashedly sycophantic defense of Hellenistic monarchy. His *Peri Basileias* is a demonstration of the extent to which political philosophy and metaphysical/mystical literature dovetail—and fuse—during this

basileia reflection. The 'pilot who saves the ship' terminology and particularly the 'gaze' doctrine are Diotogenes'; the analogy between the king on earth and the Logos in cosmos is drawn from Ps.-Ecphantus and Sthenidas. The centrality of these ideas for Eusebius' doctrine of the emperor as an image of Christ convinces me that they are not just stale recitations of trite formulas. I think that Eusebius found in the Hellenistic Pythagoreans' writings on monarchy the political arguments for defending his own (Arian-inspired) convictions regarding the divinity of the Christian emperor.

13. Ps.-Ecphantus's dating is wild. The authors of the *basileia* group are generally dated later than those of the *polis* group. These dates range from the first century BCE (Thesleff 1961), to first century CE (Harvey 1965: 138), to c. 200 CE (Burkert 1972: 48), with Ps.-Ecphantus drifting between both ends of the range.

There might have been a genuine and a pseudepigraphical Ecphantus. Hippolytus of Rome (170–236 CE), the Church father and anti-pope, knows an Ecphantus whom he places among the pre-Socratics. Hippolytus makes him a Syracusan, location at odds with Iamblichus's Kroton (*On Pythagorean Life* 267). Hippolytus devotes to him a brief, corrupt section in Book 1 of *Refutatio* (1.13). Ecphantus appears as the mystic we know: movement of a body is due to divine power, mind and soul, of which the world is the representation. But he is also a skeptic, holding that knowledge is impossible and that all definitions are relative. For further discussion of the Hippolytus passage on Ecphantus see Mueller 1992: 4369-70. Aetius's (?) *Placita* (896a5) associates Ecphantus with Heraclides Ponticus in their stand on the movement of planet Earth, and presents a theory recalling that given by Hippolytus in *Refutatio* 1.13. They both make him a citizen of the Corinthian colony of Syracuse. The discrepancy between Iamblichus and the Hippolytus/Aetius points to two authors claiming this name, the first a pre-Socratic, writing in Attic Greek, the second, writing in Doric, a Hellenistic writer from Kroton (Crotone). Kroton was the ancient Greek colony of the Achaeans, in Southern Italy, the hot-bed of Pythagoreanism, both ancient Greek and Hellenistic. For this reason I call him Ps.-Ecphantus.

period. This is precisely the kind of text one would expect in Hellenistic times, dominated as they were by despotic kings. Classical political philosophy's ambivalence about absolute kingship and its stress on rational discourse have given way to a panegyric approach to political reflection in which the autocratic royal patrons are instructed in the science of government while exalted to divinity status. Ps.-Ecphantus, in a manner both singular and characteristic, fuses a profound monarchic mysticism with genuine political philosophy.

Fragments #1 and #2.[14] According to Ps.-Ecphantus, humanity is unevenly split between the ruler—the king—and the ruled. The king is a mediator between the human and the divine modes of being. He is very close to, yet distinct from, God. The king alone is made in the image of God. A similar view is held in regard to knowledge. The king alone has a conception of God. The king is known to God. On the practical side, Ps.-Ecphantus elaborates on the legitimacy of the king and the imitation of the king by the subjects. Then he discusses the king's functions. In the end, what has been said about the king is extended to the state, and Ps.-Ecphantus walks an unnerving line where politics and theology, society and God, city and religion all come together. 'That which brings things together'—in other words, the common good—refers to the good of both the ruler and the ruled, and is the end of any Pythagorean system.

1.1. The first section[15] of fragment #1, among other points, alleges that the king alone among men shares in the image of God. The tone of the

14.	Fragment #1: Stobaeus 4.7.64 pp. 271.13-276.9 Hense = T (#2) 79.8-82.6 = L. Delatte 1942: 26-32 (Greek), 47-50 (French trans.), 164-84 & 195-27 (Commentary). Fragment #2: Stobaeus 4.6.22 pp. 244.13-245.1 Hense = T (#1) 79.1-7; L. Delatte 1942: 25-26 (Greek), 47 (French trans.), 184-95 (Commentary); Goodenough 1928: 75-83.

	NOTE: The texts of Ps.-Ecphantus, Diotogenes and Sthenidas, preserved by Stobaeus, are found in Hense (1884–1912, reprint 1958); L. Delatte (1942), with separate French translation and separate commentary; and Thesleff (1965). Comprehensive reference to all this information is given for each fragment discussed. All references to L. Delatte in Chapter 5 are to his 1942 work, unless otherwise indicated. H abbreviates Hense. T abbreviates Thesleff 1965. All references to Thesleff in Chapter 5 are to this work, unless otherwise indicated.

15.	H 271.14-272.14, T 79.9-80.4, L. Delatte 1942: 164-81; also Goodenough 1928: 75-76. The renderings of Ps.-Ecphantus's work are not intended as exact translations but as close readings of the meaning of the text.

entire preserved text is given in the opening line: the nature of every creature is in harmony with the cosmos and with everything in the cosmos.[16] This is a reiteration of a common Pythagorean tenet, a feature of musical theory extended to all other fields of philosophic investigation: politics, ethics, economics, medicine, psychology and physics. The nature of each being, continues Ps.-Ecphantus, breathes with the world and is bound to it; each follows the swing of the universe and is part of its revolution, participating in the common order while maintaining its own nature, its own particularity.[17] The Stoics had posited a universal breath (*pneuma*) enfolding all elements of nature and maintaining the bonds (*desmoi* or *sundesmoi*) between them. Here, the Stoic conception is coupled with specific Pythagorean elements such as the thrust or sway of a body in motion, caught in the whirling movement of the firmament.[18] The best a body can do is to obey this force, and it actually does so out of necessity.

An interesting passage in the deutero-Pauline Ephesians (4.1-3) associates *pneuma* and *sundesmos* in a context that recalls the same background. Paul, ὁ δέσμιος (*ho desmios*), the 'bound one' (cf. Phil. 1.7—the translation 'prisoner' obfuscates the pun), calls for the unity of the *pneuma* in the *sundesmos*, the bond, of peace. And the text continues, 'There is one body and one *pneuma*, just as you were called in one hope of your call' (Eph. 4.4), and it ends with a creedal fragment, 'One God and father of all who is above all and through all and in all' (Eph. 4.6). The sense of the sweep and cohesion of all in an all-permeating One—the idea *and* the language—point to a Stoic-Pythagorean environment.[19]

This Pythagorean 'irresistible sweep', which draws one into action with the force of ἀνάγκη (*anankē*, 'constraint', 'necessity', 'fate'), is known to Paul. Obeying political authority, as a necessity (and, one may add, as the *best* thing to do), is dictated by both ὀργή (*orgē*,

16. ἄπαντος ζώω φύσις ποτὶ τε τὸν κόσμον ἅρμοκται καὶ τὰ ἐν τῷ κόσμῳ (H 271.14-15, T 79.9-10).

17. συμπνείουσα γὰρ αὐτῷ καὶ συνδεδεμένα τὰν ἀρίσταν τε ἅμα καὶ ἀναγκαίαν ἀκολουθίαν ὀπαδεῖ ῥύμᾳ τῷ παντὸς περιαγεομένῳ ποτί τε τὰν κοινὰν εὐκοσμίαν καὶ ποττὰν ἴδιον ἑκάστω διαμονάν (H 271.16-18, T 79.11-13).

18. L. Delatte 165, 167. A harmonic universe as a whirling animal is known to Plato, *Politicus* 269c (*ap.* Goodenough 1928: 76 n. 74).

19. A (less suggestive) form of the 'creedal' piece is met in 1 Cor. 8.6 and Rom. 11.36 (cf. Col. 1.16). 1 Cor. 8.4-5 acknowledges the multitude of divine beings in the cosmos, yet the uniqueness of one God and one master.

'wrath') and συνείδησις (*suneidēsis*, 'conscience') (Rom. 13.5). Paul cannot resist the cosmic drive; he 'goes with the flow', because this is the best and the necessary thing to do. The most convincing statement of the necessity of his obedience is 1 Cor. 9.16: 'For if I bring the *euangelion* (gospel) I have nothing to boast about; for necessity is laid upon me; woe to me if I don't bring the *euangelion!*' (cf. also Phil. 1.24).

Ps.-Ecphantus then concerns himself with the division of the universe into the traditional celestial, sublunary and earthly regions, populated respectively by the gods (the celestial beings), the *daimones* and the mortals.[20] He repeats the platitude that the name of the world, *kosmos*, derives from its being well ordered (εὐκοσμία).[21] The world is a living being and is densely populated. Each area is ruled by a being that shares a natural affinity with it, a being whose share of divinity is greater than that of the rest of the (natural or supernatural) population of that area.[22] Thus, the divine world is headed by none other than God; God's retinue (ἀκολουθία) is formed by the stars and the planets.[23] The sublunary world is the realm of the *daimones*; they govern (διεξαγωγά) the souls.[24] On earth, the king leads the human beings; he is superior to all other human beings.

It would be bewildering indeed if Paul did not show familiarity with this stratified Hellenistic universe. There are celestial bodies and there are terrestrial bodies, but, as to glory, they are very different, says Paul (1 Cor. 15.40-41).[25] He uses *kosmos* 32 times in the 'genuine' letters, mostly in Romans and 1 Corinthians. *Kosmos* has as many meanings in Paul as it does in Hellenistic writings generally. The word often designates the orderly universe (Rom. 1.20; 1 Cor. 4.9; 8.4; Gal. 4.3; Phil. 2.15), but *kosmos* is also employed to describe the inhabited world, the Greek world, the non-Christian world, doomed space, the daily round, the distracting world, and so on. In Rom. 1.20, Paul seems aware of the *kosmeō–kosmos* etymology. And in 1 Cor. 10.4 Paul gives us an image

20. H 271.19-272.9, T 79.13-18. See L. Delatte 1942: 169-75.
21. H 271.19-272.1, T 79.13-14.
22. ἐξάρχει τι ζῷον κατ᾽ οἰκηότατα ἐγγενῆ... (H 272.4-5, T 79.16). For ἐξάρχω see also L. Delatte 1942: 101.
23. H 271.4-7, T 79.17-18.2.
24. For this noun, see also L. Delatte 1942: 94.
25. The Philippian hymn (Phil. 2.6-11), so called, makes the same distinction (Phil. 2.10).

very close to that of the Pythagorean celestial cortège: Christ, as pneumatic food and drink, following (ἀκολουθούσης) the Hebrews in the desert. The divine world mixes with the human not only in the person of Christ and his *euangelion* but also in the powers and works of the *pneuma*. The separation of regions is much less strict than in the older, Classical, strictly stratified model of the world, and a loosening of territorial distinctions occurs in the Hellenistic Pythagoreans as well as in the Gnostic and Hermetic literature. A most remarkable illustration occurs in Phil. 2.15, where the Christians are stars in the cosmos (φωστῆρες ἐν κόσμῳ).[26]

In the economy of Ps.-Ecphantus's text, the purpose of this introductory section is to place the king in the cosmic order. The fragment continues by presenting the special position of the king vis-à-vis other human beings.[27] Of all the beings on earth, humanity has the absolutely best nature.[28] The king, however, is more divine; though sharing in the human distinctiveness, he claims a larger share of the superior principle.[29] The king is like the others in his 'covering' (σκῆνος[30]), since he is made of the same stuff.[31] The king, however, is created by the best artificer, who made him by taking himself as the archetype.[32]

What sets the king apart from the rest of humanity is his privileged standing in regard to the divinity. He is κρείσσων (*kreissōn*, 'stronger', 'better') or the possessor of a superior principle (τὸ κρεῖσσον).[33] At the same time, he is created in the image (ἀρχέτυπον) of the divine. Thus, though his appearance is that of all men, his nature is distinct from all others. The king's 'ontological category'[34] is that of an intermediary

26. The expression recalls the final fate of the Dioscuri. By the same token, their story—sons of Zeus and a mortal woman, of a singular nativity (hatched from an egg), lived on earth, died, were resurrected, live as stars—may well feed (together with other sources) into the myth of Christ in the Philippian hymn.

27. H 272.9-14, T 79.19-80.4, L. Delatte 1942: 175-81.

28. ἀριστοφυέστατος, H 272.9, T 80.1.

29. θειότερον δ᾽ ὁ βασιλεὺς ἐν τᾷ κοινᾷ φύσει πλεονεκτῶν τῶ κρέσσονος (H 272.10-11, T 80.1-2).

30. σκᾶνος, lit. tent, H 272.11, T 80.2.

31. ὕλη (H 272.13, T 80.3).

32. τὸ μὲν σκᾶνος τοῖς λοιποῖς ὅμοιος, οἷα γεγονὼς ἐκ τᾶς αὐτᾶς ὕλας, ὑπὸ τεχνίτα δ᾽εἰργασμένος λώστω, ὃς ἐτεχνίτευσεν αὐτὸν ἀρχετύπῳ χρώμενος ἑαυτῷ (H 272.11-14, T 80.2-4).

33. As L. Delatte (1942: 175) reads it.

34. L. Delatte 1942: 175.

between God and human. Ancient philosophy knows well this class of beings, the *daimones*, to whom it also gave political office.[35] Ps.-Ecphantus's 'superior principle' (*to kreisson*) is rooted in (Plato's) Thrasymachus' definition of *dikaiosunē*.[36] In Western political reflection ever since, *kreitton* has been a tenet of political power and inseparable from the description of the ruler. By the time it reaches Ps.-Ecphantus, *kreitton* is firmly understood as a divine endowment of the divinely appointed ruler.[37] On the other hand, the king is made after the divine *archetypon*. The notion that humanity as a whole is created by a God who takes himself as model is not strange to Greek thinking.[38] The distinction, however, between a higher and a lower individual, between the ordinary individual and the divine king, can only evolve in Hellenistic political reflection. It is encountered in late Hellenistic writers, ranging from Ps.-Ecphantus to Philo[39] to Paul.

The contrast ψυχή–πνεῦμα is characteristic of Hellenistic philosophical-mystical writings.[40] Paul's *pneuma–psuchē* language is often strong evidence that a text is authentically his. Louis Delatte points to Paul as a primary example of the concept of 'two human types'. This double discourse of type proliferates in Paul into the view that opposes celestial, pneumatic or Gnostic type to the terrestrial, psychical or carnal type.[41] Delatte certainly has in mind, first of all, the opposition

35. From Empedocles, Pythagoras and Pindar, to Cicero and Philo. See L. Delatte 1942: 175-77. The best known text that makes this association is Plato's *Laws* 4.713d: God appointed *daimones* as leaders of human cities.

36. *Republic* 1.338c, 339a, 341a, 2.367b.

37. In Paul a similar thought is expressed in Rom. 13.1-7, where the ruler's supreme divine mark is his wielding of justice.

38. Plato's *Timaeus* 30d, 31b, 37c, 39e, 41d is the likely source for the doctrine that the world was made to resemble God. The concept that the human is created by God is quite common in Hellenistic Pythagoreanism, in Aisara, Crito, Euryphamos and esp. Eurysos. It is well-known to the writers of the *Hermetica*. See L. Delatte 1942: 178-79; Goodenough 1928: 76 and n. 75.

39. For the creation of the human being in the image of God (*Op. Mund.* 69, *Det. Pot. Ins.* 87, *Leg. All.* 2.4) and the distinction between the celestial and the terrestrial individual (*Leg. All.* 1.31, 88) in Philo, see Bréhier 1908: 121-23; Reitzenstein 1921: 104-106; Pascher 1931: 125-29; Heinemann 1932 (*ap.* L. Delatte 1942: 179-80).

40. Reitzenstein 1927: 70-71, 325-27, 333-35; Weiss 1897 on 1 Cor. 15.44a; *Hermetica* 4.105.25, 107.7 (*ap.* BAGD, *s.v.* πνευματικός, 685b).

41. L. Delatte 1942: 180-81, referring to Reitzenstein 1917, 1927, and Pfister 1930. L. Delatte does not indicate or discuss the relevant passages on this issue.

πνευματικός–ψυχικός.[42] The doctrine of two *anthrōpoi*, one earthly and one celestial, is elaborated in 1 Cor. 15.44-51 and is qualified as a *mustērion* (51). In Paul's eschatological scheme the psychical type comes first (46). The psychical type is from earth, the pneumatic from heaven (47). Some people are psychical, others celestial (48). We were first in the image of the earthly man; we shall be in the image of celestial man (49) in the kingdom of God (50). Elsewhere, Paul writes that the psychical type deflects the things of the *pneuma*; these seem foolish to him because certain things can only be grasped by pneumatic inquiry (1 Cor. 2.14-15).

The essential point is simple: surrender to the damned flesh or to the mortal *psuchē* has blunted knowledge of the everlasting divine (e.g. Rom. 1.19-23). The rupture can be repaired only by the irruption of the divine into the world. The pneumatic is the one who is able to perceive this foray. The theorizer of the *pneuma* is, then, the fusion of the Cynic preacher with the Gnostic or Pythagorean contemplator; he occupies the place where rhetoric meets the numinous and where practical philosophy conjoins hermetic speculation—a marriage only achievable in the disenchanted, lunatic world of late Hellenism. Possessing the *pneuma*, being *pneumatikos*, belonging to the fellowship of *pneuma* (κοινωνία πνεύματος) (Phil. 2.1) is the distinctive feature of the initiate. The distance between the pneumatic and the sarkic, its opposite, is mystifyingly short. One who avoids desire—the 'belly'—lands directly in the transcendental. The invisible leap, however, demands a fold, a crease, and this is the divine intermediary: the king in Ps.-Ecphantus, Christ or his emissaries in Paul.

The creation of the human being in God's image is not a crucial issue for placing Paul in either a Greek or a Jewish sphere of influence. Hellenistic, Greek-speaking Judaism has already brought the concept into the Greek world. Ps.-Ecphantus is particularly interesting because he uses this notion to glamorize the king. Most Hellenistic authors, however, take it for what it is: a relation between the human in general and the universal. The human split—the dichotomy between the lesser, carnal being and the superior, spiritual being, with the latter being somehow divine or becoming so with the help of an intervening otherworldly power—is already a widespread idea.

---

42. It appears in 1 Cor. 2.14; 15.44, 45, 46. In 1 Thess. 5.23, πνεῦμα, ψυχή and σῶμα form the human entity; similarly, in Phil. 1.27, the political community has one πνεῦμα and one ψυχή.

By late Hellenistic times, the world and the individual are too dejected for *aretē* to have any redeeming power. Moral instincts and precepts cannot be upheld when one is stalked by dread and despair. Though formal philosophers continue to cling to the authority of morality as the only resource against social decay and personal degeneration, the popular philosopher—closer to the marketplace—requires a more effective agency. And thus his preference for the irrational becomes progressively more lopsided. (Even so, Paul—himself a Hellenistic popular philosopher—constantly finds himself needing to use moral exhortation, even toward the pneumatics.[43] He is surprised and disillusioned by the moral defections from the ranks of the initiated. Time and again, he is forced to relapse into ethical admonition, and this exasperates him.)

Paul's soteriology of mysterious, *pneuma*-filled gesture and discourse stresses not moral impulse but being *snatched from death*. Before Paul, Hellenistic thinkers had proposed various solutions to the problem of how to bridge the chasm between the human and the divine worlds, the first the province of fate and death, the second of justice and life. In all of them some intermediary being is pivotal. In Ps.-Ecphantus the king plays the critical role in the drama of salvation. This is a rich vein of reflection, insofar as it ties the redemption of the individual to the state. And it is precisely this orientation that we find in Paul, as well. The Gnostics preferred to focus on the individual, the solitary and subjective creature detached from the social complex. Paul, like the Hellenistic Pythagoreans, grounds his people in a political system. He rebuilds the individual within the community, as part of a social and political fellowship. The Classical Greek tenet that there is no humanity outside the *polis* still holds. In Romans (where Paul ignores ethics but not the law), the individual's act of conscience (*suneidēsis*) refers to subjection to rulers or to submission to the law of the *polis*, a political conscience demanded by membership in the state (Rom. 13.5; 2.15).[44] For Paul as for the Hellenistic Pythagoreans, the state is the vital foundation for the operation of salvation. It structures and organizes the people, protecting

43. It has been often noted (see e.g., Meeks 1986: 13) that Paul preaches hindmost transformation yet uses the means of traditional morality.

44. Besides political conscience, Paul appeals also to a pneumatic conscience, Rom. 9.1. Moral conscience is addressed in 1 Cor. 8.7, 10, 12; 10.25, 27, 28, 29. The significance of the community for the endurance of the Jewish diaspora is not lost on Paul either.

their social and political anonymity. Soteriology thus becomes efficient. One rescuer can easily generate a mass of unnamed kings.[45]

In Ps.-Ecphantus the intermediary himself is the upper tier of a two-layered humanity. In Paul, the two-level system takes on a new dynamic, since all humanity is in the same plight; Christ alone heals the rift between it and God. Christ is in the station of the king. He is, with a difference, precisely in the position of being both human and divine.

In both Ps.-Ecphantus and Paul, the mediator is the critical object of imitation. But being on one side or the other of the *pneuma–sarx* divide[46] becomes in Paul a matter of choice, not of privilege. Paul uses the telling term *tupos*, immediately keying us into the *basileia* literature (and, less surprisingly, the Septuagintal *eikōn*). *Tupos* as divine model or as *exemplum* is a characteristic Pauline idea. Around this 'imitation of the king' concept, he creates a new typology, that of a christ. This is Paul's answer to the '*kreitton* principle'.[47] Who is the *tupos*, the model, the type of the Pauline human that makes everyone 'superior'? All humanity, without exception, begins with the Adam type (or rather 'antitype'), and Adam is the *tupos* of the future savior (Rom. 5.14). *Tupos* is also Paul himself as the *exemplum* for imitation (Phil. 3.17).[48] On what is this exemplariness predicated? What is the authority that authenticates the replication? In other words, who or what is the *eikōn* being imitated or resembled?[49] The *tupos* locution is common in Paul.[50] The *tupos–eikōn*

45. Note that while the multitude of rising and dying gods of mystery religions also promise salvation, the Hellenistic Pythagoreans and Paul move from the individuality of salvation in a mystery religion to a wholesale salvation of a people as *polis*. Schoeps (1961: 20) refers to this as 'a communal incorporation of believers in a saving body'.

46. *Sarx*, weakly translated as 'flesh', is, for Paul, the opposite of *pneuma*. *Sarx* is an earthy, inferior aspect of the soul, and often, by metonymy, the soul of the rejector of Christ.

47. See the detailed discussion of this issue in Chapter 4, section on Damippos.

48. Sometimes *tupoi* describe pneumatic experiences, such as the cloud and the sea entered with Moses, the pneumatic food and the pneumatic drink consumed in the desert (1 Cor. 10.6).

Tupos is transferred from life model to text prototype, as in *tupos didachēs* (Rom. 6.17).

49. Ps.-Ecphantus does not use the term εἰκών in the preserved fragments, but he does use ἀρχέτυπον. After first century CE, *eikōn* is often employed to describe the relation between *basileus* or *basileia* and God, e.g., Plutarch, *To an Unlearned Ruler* 780d; Themistius, *Orations* 9.30, 10.1, 170.22, 25, 232.11; Eusebius, *Praise to Constantine* 5.4; Synesius, *To Arcadius* 4, 5; the author of the eighteenth treatise

connection is revealed by the reference to Adam in 1 Cor. 15.49: 'As we bore the *eikōn* of the [man] of dust [Adam, cf. 1 Cor. 15.45; Rom. 5.14], we shall bear the *eikōn* of the celestial man'. Elsewhere we read: 'We shall be changed in God's *eikōn* from one degree of *doxa* to another, even as the lord who is the *pneuma*' (2 Cor. 3.18), and the 'light of the *euangelion* of the glory of Christ is the *eikōn* of God' (2 Cor. 4.4). Romans 8.29, a key passage, makes a handful of elect the first to conform to the *eikōn* of God's son.[51]

Finally, both Ps.-Ecphantus and Paul use the term σκῆνος (*skēnos*), whose association with Gnostic (and Hermetic) language cannot be doubted.[52] Its meaning in Paul is consistent with mystical, Gnostic language: the humble garment known as the body of our earthly appearance (2 Cor. 5.1, 4). *Skēnos* is a cardinal part of the glossary of all the mystical speculation of the Hellenistic age. In Ps.-Ecphantus, *skēnos* envelops the king, just as *sarx* does Christ in Paul (Rom. 8.3, cf. Phil. 2.7). It is a datum of earthly existence, as inescapable for divine (human) beings as for their more earthbound kin.

1.2 and 2. The second section of fragment #1 and fragment #2[53] continue the notion that the king alone is made in the image of God, concluding that he is the one and only creature 'who can conceive' the God on high.[54] Though disputable, this reading, preferred by Louis

of the *Hermetica* 8; Rosetta inscription (*ap.* L. Delatte 1942: 180). Paul's continuity with Ps.-Ecphantus here is thematic and not terminological.

50. There is, obviously, also a negative use of the term. The abhorrent image is the idolatrous one, a rejection of God, Rom. 1.32. In Paul it stands as the mark of the Greeks' wisdom. The other traditional use is to describe the male as the image and glory of God, 1 Cor. 11.7.

51. For further discussion of the meaning of *eikōn* and of the Pauline doctrine of *eikōn*, see Chapter 4, Ps.-Archytas section and Chapter 8, Rom. 3.21–8.39 section, especially Rom. 8.18-30.

52. It is common in the Hellenistic Pythagoreans, such as Archytas, Theages, Timaeus, Aisara, Ocellus, Eurysos, as well as in Ps.-Plato's *Axiochos* or in the authors of *Hermetica*. Also in 2 Pet. 1.13, 14, in Clement's *Stromata*, and in the *Sentences of Sextus*. See L. Delatte 181; Goodenough 1928: 76 nn. 75, 76. The *skēnos* view in *Axiochus* is the basis of the body–soul dualism. It is used ten times in Hebrews and five times in Acts.

53. H 272.14-16, T 80.4-5 and H 244.14-19, T 79.3-7, L. Delatte 1942: 181-95, Goodenough 1928: 76-83.

54. κατασκεύασμα δὴ ὧν ὁ βασιλεὺς ἓν καὶ μόνον ἐννοητικὸν τῷ ἀνωτέρω βασιλέως, H 272.14-15 (=L. Delatte 1942: 28). This is actually L. Delatte's emen-

Delatte, has parallels in many Hellenistic authors.[55] Essentially, Ps.-Ecphantus's doctrine of kingship emphasizes the incapacity of ordinary human beings by themselves to understand and imitate God.[56] This is possible only through the mediation of an intermediary—in Ps.-Ecphantus, the king. The rest of the people can, however, look up to and imitate the king. Paul expresses the same idea in 1 Cor. 13.12: Now one is incapable of beholding God face to face but sees him only obscurely,[57] as in a mirror. Present knowledge is only partial; future knowledge will be complete.[58] Similarly, in 2 Cor. 3.18 Paul speaks for the superiority of direct contemplation of God, and Christ is the model of this competence.[59]

dation. T 80.4-5 reads, with other authorities, including Hense, ἐντὶ οἷα τύπος for ἐννοητικόν. This makes the passage translate: The king is really the one and only creature who is the *tupos*, the image of the king on high. L. Delatte (1942: 182) finds this redundant.

55. Most, just as they believe that humanity in general was created in the image of God, also share the wider view that all humanity is capable of conceiving the divinity, not just the king: Hellenistic Pythagoreans like Euryphamos (H 914.15), Crito (H 158.6). Onatas (H 48.5), however, makes this the privilege of a few; also many treatises in the *Hermetica*, e.g., 3.3, 4.2, 5.2, 8.5, 12.19. See L. Delatte 1942: 182-83. Increasingly restricting human divinity and access to God in theoretical treatises goes hand in hand with the practical increase of royal privilege in actual political life.

56. This view is expressed most clearly in fragment #2: ἀδύνατον ἐκείναν θεάσασθαι (H 244.19, T 79.7). This fragment acknowledges, however, that man in general has God as father, γεννητήρ (H 244.18, T 79.7).

57. It is sometimes argued that the issue is indirectness not unclarity, see below. This may also be a reference to Plato, for whom the soul, while in the body, has only a blurred perception of reality. Only when unmixed and pure can it clearly apprehend the divine forms (*Phaedo* 65d-66a).

58. βλέπομεν γὰρ ἄρτι δι᾽ ἐσόπτρου ἐν αἰνίγματι, τότε δὲ πρόσωπον πρὸς πρόσωπον· ἄρτι γινώσκω ἐκ μέρους, τότε δὲ ἐπιγνώσομαι καθὼς καὶ ἐπεγνώσθην (1 Cor. 13.12). L. Delatte himself notes this filiation, and quotes Paul together with Philo and with Gnostic and Hermetic mystic texts, 1942: 185-86. Cf. 2 Cor. 4.3, the *euangelion* is veiled to those who perish.

59. I read καθάπερ ἀπὸ κυρίου πνεύματος (2 Cor. 3.18) 'just as (we know) from the Lord who is pneumatic'. Two provocative studies take the mirror metaphor to mean that knowledge is not 'imperfect' but 'indirect' (Hugedé 1957 and Danker 1960). They argue for an entirely positive meaning of the mirror image. 'The imperfection consists rather in this, that we now see the eternal splendors indirectly' (Danker 428). But as Jewett (1994: 100) notes, the problem with the Hugedé and Danker approach 'is that it takes insufficient account of the balance between the

Classical philosophers had attributed to *nous*, intellect, the function of instructing the soul and revealing God to it, of attaching it to God.[60] Late Hellenistic writers make this the work of the *pneuma*. In Ps.-Ecphantus, the king is entrusted with this function, and he is designated with the periphrasis θεομοιρὴς ἐμπνοίησις, 'God-partaking breath'.[61] Paul goes further, transforming *nous* from a generic into an individual power, Christ. Paul moves from a moral and soteriological discourse to a political and eschatological one. In Paul, it is Christ who brings knowledge of the divine to humanity, and his identification with *nous* and *pneuma* is unavoidable.[62] Christ-like people have the *nous Christou* (1 Cor. 2.16, cf. Col. 1.28).[63] Christ is the content of all pneumatic events (1 Cor. 10.4). Christ is designated son of God in power according to the *pneuma* called holy (Rom. 1.4, cf. Rom. 8.2). Having *pneuma Christou* (or *pneuma theou*) is the mark of election and the guarantee of salvation (Rom. 8.9; Phil. 1.19, cf. Rom. 15.30; 1 Cor. 6.11; 2 Cor. 3.3; Phil. 3.3).

The role of *pneuma* in Paul can hardly be overemphasized. What is remarkable in this context is the way in which Paul accounts for the necessity of both *pneuma* and *nous* in a *pneuma*-imbued setting. While speaking of glossolalia, one of the most stunning manifestations of *pneuma*, Paul in 1 Cor. 14.14-19 is willing to play down the ecstatic operation in favor of the edification of the mind: *nous*, just as much as *pneuma*, must participate in the conversation with the divine.

positive and negative elements in Paul's rhetoric (in 1 Cor. 13.8-10, 12)'.

60. Festugière 1936: 105-107 and Wetter 1915: 25, 30, 32, 87-89 note that, for the ancient philosophers, knowledge by sense perception is explained by the similarity between the subject and the object with which it enters in contact. Plato moved this doctrine to the metaphysical sphere: *nous* can know the divine only because of its resemblance and of its relation, συγγένεια, with God. From metaphysics this doctrine is transferred to religion: the illumination of the spirit is possible because it participates in the divine nature. *Ap.* L. Delatte 1942: 206.

61. L. Delatte 1942: 191-92. In Philo, *pneuma* is the imprint of God, the force that makes it possible for the soul to see its creator *Det. Pot. Ins.* 83, 86, *Leg. All.* 1.38. The Stoics also teach that the world is animated by a universal *spiritus*, as in Seneca's *On Mercy* 1.3.5, 1.4.1, 1.5.1 (L. Delatte 1942: 192-93). See also L. Delatte 1942: 207, for sources treating the transfer to the king of the functions of the *nous*.

62. Identification of Christ with *nous* is a major device of the second-century Christian apologists, for example.

63. Expressed in intensely mystical terms, they are the fragrance of the knowledge of Christ, τὴν ὀσμὴν τῆς γνώσεως αὐτοῦ (2 Cor. 2.14).

For if I pray in a tongue, *pneuma* prays, but my *nous* is barren. What then? I will offer a prayer with the *pneuma* and I shall do the same with the *nous*. I will pray with the *pneuma* and I will also pray with the *nous*... You may give thanks well but the other is not edified... In the *ekklēsia* I would rather speak five words with my *nous*, so as to instruct others, than ten thousand words in a tongue.'

Although an extraordinary language for the initiate, *pneuma* is less effective for conveying knowledge to the ἰδιώτης (*idiōtēs*) (1 Cor. 14.16), the one who is not a member of the assembly. *Idiōtēs* is a private individual as opposed to the individual who is active in the *polis*,[64] the one in a private station as opposed to one holding public office or taking part in public affairs.[65] But *idiōtēs* is also one who lacks professional knowledge or expertise—an unskilled or uneducated person.[66] The ambivalence of the term, simultaneously covering the language of politics and of the professional guild, is fully retained in this pericope.

In a different context, it is *nous* that reveals the will of God (Rom. 12.2).[67] Paul is the all-out advocate for *pneuma* who, paradoxically, is averse to the knowledge that circumvents *nous*. Both *nous* and *pneuma* have access to God. His transcendentalism does not discard the rational. Ps.-Ecphantus moves away from other Pythagoreans when he gives the king the characteristics of *nous*. Ps.-Ecphantus's humanity is two-leveled: the king and the rest of the people. So it is in Paul. Only Paul makes *all* those who embrace Christ, all the pneumatics, into kings. The 'sarkics'—the carnal—are the rest. The terminology changes, but the concept is virtually the same—except that Paul has gone even further than Ps.-Ecphantus by making the *nous* historical by identifying it with the person of Christ.

Returning to 1 Cor. 13.12-13, the Pauline text most strongly analogous to fragments #1.2 and #2, we note an affinity so pronounced that it can be denominated a 'thematic quotation'. The iteration of a complex of

---

64. Thucydides 1.124 cf. 3.10; Plato, *Symposium* 185b; in inscriptions it is also used as the opposite of γένος or φατρία (LSJ, *s.v.* ἰδιώτης, 819a).

65. Herodotus 7.3, where *idiōtēs* is opposed to *basileus*, Thucydides 4.2; Plato, *Politicus* 259b, opposed to *archōn*; Demosthenes, *Philippic IV*, 70, opposed to *politeuomenos*, etc. (LSJ 819a).

66. LSJ 819a.

67. μεταμορφοῦσθε τῇ ἀνακαινώσει τοῦ νοὸς εἰς τὸ δοκιμάζειν ὑμᾶς τί τὸ θέλημα τοῦ θεοῦ (Rom. 12.2). This passage has an affinity with Plato, *Politicus* 310a, and has also been discussed elsewhere. Cf. Rom. 7.23, where mind and body are in a excruciating war.

extremely similar thematic elements is only slightly short of direct textual quotation. I have already referred to the important parallelism this passage provides, in the metaphor of the imperfect knowledge conveyed by the hazy mirror, to Ps.-Ecphantus's notion of the flawed knowledge of God achievable under the 'present' human conditions. The parallelism goes further. Both texts end with a statement about God's absolute knowledge of the elect, whether king or apostle. 'I shall know completely just as I have been completely known', says Paul (1 Cor. 13.12). After concluding that the king alone can have a full perception of God,[68] Ps.-Ecphantus adds, 'By his creator he has always been known'.[69] Moreover, the close resemblance of the two texts gives additional ground to Louis Delatte's observation that although the term *mirror* does not appear in the available text of Ps.-Ecphantus, it is to be presupposed.[70] The faulty vision of God inherent in ordinary human nature demands the intervention of an intermediary.

Paul closes his reflection in 1 Cor. 13.8-13 with the thought that what are present 'now' are *pistis*, *elpis* and *agapē*, trust, hope and love, of which love is the greatest. The corresponding passage in Ps.-Ecphantus suggests that Paul has replaced the major Greek political concept of *philia*, friendship and bonding, with a concept that covers the same semantic range of affection and brotherhood but that further combines polity and deity, human empathy[71] and God's compassion, practical and transcendental friendship—that is, *agapē*, the surpassing road (ὑπερβολὴ ὁδός) (1 Cor. 12.31).

1.3.[72] God foreknows the king. In Ps.-Ecphantus as in Paul (Rom. 8.28-30), those who are set aside for an unusual calling are predestined by God for the task.[73] Ps.-Ecphantus intertwines this theme with a new but

68. Or, in the Hense reading, he alone is *tupos* of the celestial king.

69. H 272.15-273.1, T 80.5-6, τῷ μὲν πεποιηκότι γνώριμον ἀεί. On predestination see also below, H 273.1-17, T 80.6-19 and Rom. 8.29-30.

70. L. Delatte 1942: 195. *Mirror* is there, in related contexts: in Plato's (?) *Alcibiades* 134e, Alcibiades, the political leader, sees God reflected in the purest and most divine part of the soul. It is also in Cicero, *Republic* 2.42.69, Philo, *Leg. All.* 3.101, or in Eusebius, *Praise to Constantine* 5.4 (L. Delatte 1942: 195). I think, however, that the shadows in the allegory of the cave, *Republic* 7.514-515, are the most likely source.

71. For *agapē* as the Pauline equivalent of *philia*, see Hauck 1908.

72. H 273.1-17, T 80.6-19, L. Delatte 1942: 195-207, Goodenough 1928: 77.

73. See Chapter 8, Rom. 8.29-30, for discussion.

related topic: how the king appears to his people. The subjects see the king in his kingship as in a light.[74] It is by this light that he is judged and approved.[75] This is further tied to the motif of royal legitimacy. Kingship is divine and difficult to contemplate because of its transcendental brilliance, except by the legitimate claimant.[76] Kingship itself is pure, incorruptible and hard to reach for the ordinary man because of its excessive divinity.[77] The legitimate king has a pure nature.[78] The pretender is shown up as false by his many fulgurations and blindings.[79]

The key terms that describe Ps.-Ecphantus's king—light (*phōs*), tested (*krinō*), judged (*dokimazō/dokimos*), genuine (*gnēsios*)—are all present in Paul, in similar settings. *Phōs*, though useful to Paul because of its vivid Gnostic symbolism,[80] is of limited import to him, because of the potential confusion with Satan, who disguises himself as an angel of light (2 Cor. 11.14).[81] The context remains, as in Ps.-Ecphantus, legitimate and illegitimate claimants to rule, here the true and false candidates for the leading role of apostles. In this conspicuous parallel (2 Cor. 11.12-15), Ps.-Ecphantus's king is described as blinding in his light, brilliant, pure. Elsewhere, Paul refers to the children of God as lights in the cosmos, blameless and pure. He sharply distinguishes between them and the twisted and perverse (Phil. 2.15). The transcendental brilliance that marks the king in Ps.-Ecphantus has a corollary in Paul, as well. It was God, says Paul, who shone in our hearts to give the

74. τοῖς δ᾽ ἀρχομένοις ὡς ἐν φωτὶ τᾷ βασιλείᾳ βλεπόμενον (H 273.1-2, T 80.6-7).

75. τᾳδε γὰρ κρίνεταί τε καὶ δοκιμάζεται... (H 273.2-3, T 80.7).

76. ...τᾶς βασιλείας...θείας τε ἐάσας καὶ δι᾽ ὑπερβολὰν λαμπρότατος δυσοράτω αἰ μὴ τοῖς γνασίοις (H 273.4-6, T 80.8-10).

77. αὐτὰ μὲν ὧν βασιλεία χρῆμα εἰλικρινές τε καὶ ἀδιάφθορόν ἐντι καὶ δι᾽ ὑπερβολὰν θειότατος δυσέφικτον ἀνθρώπῳ (H 273.10-12, T 80.13-14).

78. βασιλῆα δὲ τὸν ὁμιλήσοντα φύσιός τε ἀχράντω δεῖ μετέχειν (H 273.17-274.1, T 80.18-19).

79. μαρμαρυγαί τε γὰρ πολλαὶ καὶ σκοτοδινιάσεις... (H 273.6-7, T 80.10-11). L. Delatte (1942: 196-202) finds a close parallel to this view in Dio Chrysostom, *Discourse* 1.50 (*First Discourse on Kingship*). Points of contact are established with Plato, Cicero, Seneca, Plutarch, Plotinus, Eusebius and Hermetic writings.

80. E.g., Rom. 13.12, armor of light; 2 Cor. 4.4, light of *euangelion*; 2 Cor. 4.6, light of *gnōsis*; 2 Cor. 6.14, the enmity of light and darkness; 1 Thess. 5.5, sons of light, cf. Eph. 5.8, 9, 14; Col. 1.12.

81. αὐτὸς γὰρ ὁ Σατανᾶς μετασχηματίζεται εἰς ἄγγελον φωτός (2 Cor. 11.14). This remark is part of an intricate monograph on the deception of magical results applied to deceitful apostles, 2 Cor. 11.1-15.

light of the knowledge of the glory of God in the face of Christ (2 Cor. 4.6). (Paul prefers the less deceptive *doxa*—'radiance', 'brightness'—to portray divine beings or human persons distinguished for their perfection and exemplariness.)

To judge (*krinō, katakrinō*)—God's prerogative as compared to fallible human judgment—is extensively treated in Romans 2 and 14.[82] All—whether Greeks or Jews—are judged and found wicked, whether judged by God (Rom. 2.12, cf. 3.7) or by Paul (1 Cor. 5.5, 12). God is a cosmic judge (Rom. 3.6; 8.3; 1 Cor. 4.5), and so are the saints (1 Cor. 6.2-3). Judgment carries a negative charge. It is inappropriate that humans judge; law courts must be avoided (1 Cor. 6.1, 6). No one stands blameless under God's judgment. God's elect, however, experience a judgment transformed by Christ's intercession (Rom. 8.33-34, cf. 1 Cor. 11.32).

Paul couples *dokimazō*, a characteristic locution, and *phōs* in Rom. 2.18-19. While he castigates the Jews for their pretensions he describes their claims in terms resonant of Ps.-Ecphantus's doxology of the king. The Jews affect to approve excellence (cf. Phil. 1.10) and be a light to others (cf. Phil. 2.15). Elsewhere, Paul exhorts his people to be proofs of the will of God (Rom. 12.2), or to test themselves to see that Christ is in them (2 Cor. 13.5).[83] Being tested or testing oneself is how one demonstrates one's election.[84] Paul himself is approved by God (1 Thess. 2.4, cf. 1 Cor. 9.27).[85]

Paul pairs *dokimazō* and *gnēsios* in 2 Cor. 8.8, where he speaks of the Corinthians' love being tested for genuineness (τὸ τῆς ὑμετέρας ἀγάπης γνήσιον δοκιμάζων) (cf. 9.13). In Phil. 4.3 Paul addresses an associate with the expression 'genuine yokefellow' (γνήσιε σύζυγε).

82. Rom. 2.1, 3, 12, 16; 14.3, 4, 5, 10, 13, 22, cf. 1 Cor. 3.32, 10.29.

83. ἑαυτοὺς δοκιμάζετε (2 Cor. 13.5). Also, 1 Cor. 11.28.

84. There are many other examples of the import of *dokimazō*, to test, in Paul. Everyone's work will be tested with fire (1 Cor. 3.13). The man approved is the one whom God commends, δόκιμος...ὃν ὁ κύριος συνίστησιν (2 Cor. 10.18). The 'unnamed brother' was tested by Paul and found excellent (2 Cor. 8.22). The *dokimoi*, the tried and tested, are those who come through clean from divisive rivalries (1 Cor. 11.19, cf. Rom. 16.10). The idea of being tested by hardships is a commonplace in the Hellenistic moralists. In Paul it sometimes also acquires eschatological overtones: 1 Cor. 9.27; 11.19; 2 Cor. 10.18; 13.5-7 (but not in 2 Cor. 2.9). See Meeks 1973: 67 and 219 n. 96.

85. On the other hand, in a celebrated passage, the Greeks' *nous* is disqualified by God, in a play on words, οὐ δοκιμάζειν-ἀδόκιμος (Rom. 1.28).

The question of the legitimacy of apostles emerges as a central one in Paul, and his concern is as urgent as is Ps.-Ecphantus's for the genuineness of the king.[86]

1.4. This section[87] details the king's mission: to contemplate those beings more divine than he, not only to offer a model to common mortals but also, through contemplation, to find the help that common mortals need.

1.4.1[88] The king must know that he is more divine that the rest of humanity.[89] In Paul, the pneumatic, the king's equivalent, examines all things but is himself examined by no one (1 Cor. 2.15). This, we find out, is because he has the mind of Christ (1 Cor. 2.16). Paul's text is in perfect concert with Ps.-Ecphantus insofar as divinity becomes the measure of knowledge.

Though divine, the king knows that there are other beings more divine than he is. By comparing himself to these superior beings—reasonably, and admitting of the difference [i.e. 'by analogy'[90]]—the king understands his own subjects' relation to him, and thus makes the best use of his person and his subjects.[91] The notion of a hierarchy in the universe, in which the lesser must imitate the better, is widespread in Hellenistic Pythagoreanism and rests on a doctrine of σύστημα (*sustēma*) according to which all cosmic, political, economic, moral and medical systems have their model in musical theory. The world, the *polis*, the family, the soul and the body are συστήματα (*sustēmata*).[92] *Sustēma* is composed of contraries, or dissimilars; it is ordered according to the better element; it is managed with a view to *sumpheron*, the common good. The theory has three parts. The ἐξάρτυσις (*exartusis*, 'fittings') adjusts and

---

86. In *Politics* 6.1319b9, Aristotle derides the inclusion of inadequate citizens among γνήσιοι πολῖται, the legitimate members of the state. Aristotle reluctantly admits, in a depopulated state, unsuitable people among the γνήσιοι πολῖται (3.1278a30).

87. H 273.17-274.20, T 80.18-81.9, L. Delatte 1942: 207-18.

88. H 273.17-274.3, T 80.19-22, L. Delatte 1942: 208-10, Goodenough 1928: 77.

89. ἐπιστάμεν τε αὐτὸν ὅσῳ τῶν ἄλλων ἐντὶ θειότερος ὅσῳ τε ἄτερα αὐτῶ (H 274.1-2, T 80.19-20).

90. L. Delatte (1942: 210), justifiably, reads κατὰ λόγον somewhat like κατ' ἀναλογίαν.

91. οἷς δὴ κατὰ λόγον ἀπεικάζων ἑαυτὸν ἄριστ' ἂν ἑαυτῷ τε χρῷτο καὶ τοῖς ὑποτεταγμένοις (H 274.2-3, T 80.20-21).

92. L. Delatte 1942: 208-209. The reference to the definition of *sustēma* was made in the discussion of Callicratidas, where it appears in its most developed form.

assembles the contraries, or dissimilars; the συναρμογά (*sunarmoga*, 'tuning')[93] harmonizes and subordinates them to the better; and the χρῆσις (*chrēsis*, the 'use of the system', the 'instrumentality'),[94] effects *sumpheron*, the common good—that is, it functions according to a political-type authority.[95] Politically, as Ps.-Ecphantus employs the term, *chrēsis*[96] means 'to imitate the government of the universe'.[97] Ruling his realm in this harmonious way brings the political leader the admiration and love of the subjects.

The issue of hierarchy versus democracy, so significant for Paul, has been referred to already. Just like Ps.-Ecphantus's king, Paul himself, while recognizing his privileged position, acknowledges beings superior to him. 'Be imitators of me', he tells the Corinthians, 'as I am of Christ' (1 Cor. 11.1).

The term *chrēsis*, 'the use to which the system is put', is encountered in Paul in Rom. 1.26, an intriguing and highly controversial passage. Greek women exchanged the natural *chrēsis* for one against nature. The Hellenistic Pythagorean concept of *sustēma* applies remarkably well to this text. The moral and physical order is so profoundly corrupted by desertion of the intelligible world order that *use* itself degenerates into its opposite and the principle of *sumpheron* is violated. Defying God, a fatal violation at the highest level of the *sustēmata* chain, disorders the cosmic system itself, resulting in utter deviance at all subsequent levels. This is seen clearly at the very bottom of the sequence, at the level of the body. Romans 1.26-27, the notorious Pauline passage, is only an illustration of the dire consequences of the rupture produced in the very being of the world. It is not meant as a direct criticism of homosexual life. It agrees with, and it can be understood by reference to, Hellenistic Pythagorean thought.[98]

93. συναρμογά is also called ἕνοσις, κρᾶσις and σύνταξις.

94. χρῆσις is also called ἀφά.

95. L. Delatte 1942: 208-209.

96. L. Delatte (1942: 208-209) sees its reflection in Ps.-Ecphantus's χρῶτο. I notice a similar term, χρῆσθαι, employed in an equally relevant context in H 273.9, T 80.13.

97. L. Delatte 1942: 209.

98. The overlaying of *phusis* with ethical *aretē*, the overlapping of morals with nature displayed in Hellenistic thought, be it Cynic, Stoic, Pythagorean, etc., is a step backwards from the Classical Greek philosophy. It marks a regress, in that moral becomes natural. Trespass of ethical codes is a violation of nature. We see this in Rom. 1.26-27. For all the setback this means philosophically, it nevertheless

Other passages in Paul also lend themselves to this approach. 1 Corinthians 7.31 and 9.12, 15 use the verb χράομαι (*chraomai*), to make use, in contexts that may be better understood if the Hellenistic Pythagorean view is considered. Interestingly, verse 7.31 is also set within an argument concerning sexuality. In the middle of a long homily on marriage and family life, Paul swerves for a moment from the topic at hand and reflects on its broader conceptual framework. After suggesting that those who have wives should live as though they had none (7.29), Paul continues, 'And those who mourn or who rejoice [should live] as if they were not mourning or rejoicing, and those who buy, as though they had no goods [7.30], and those who make use of the world, as though they did not use it. For the form of this world is passing away' (7.31). 'I want you to be free from cares' (7.32a). The world is radically changing, and its social, psychological and economic structures conceive it—use it—in ways that are utterly inappropriate in that they do not reflect the world's imminent transformation. Although Paul may seem to be affirming Stoic indifference, he is not recommending moral virtues that enable one to withstand the world as it is, but warning that a new *sustēma* is coming into being. In this new order, values mutate and *chrēsis* is fundamentally restructured for a genuine *sumpheron*. The choice of terms appears to warrant such a reading. In 1 Cor. 9.12, Paul resists the Corinthians' offer to pay for his upkeep[99] since this would go against the larger good of the *euangelion*, here understood as the ultimate *sumpheron*. Paul resembles Ps.-Ecphantus in two ways: he casts his ideas in political terms and sets them in the frame of a cosmic *sustēma* whose *chrēsis* is the common good.

1.4.2.[100] That imitation of the divine—whether moral, political or mystical—is a prolific topic in Classical and Hellenistic reflection has already been noted in this inquiry. This passage, however, introduces a point that is of special significance for Paul. According to Ps.-Ecphantus, when ordinary humans (ἄλλους) go astray (ἁμαρτάνωντι), they have a divinely sanctioned remedy: emulation of the ruler, whether this

---

allows a decaying, corrupt earth and its wretched, pathetic inhabitants to be reconciled with the euphonious universe, makes possible for them to merge again with the harmonious cosmos. The stress given to moral *aretē* rather than excluding states or individuals from the cosmic fellowship, actually enables this participation.

99. οὐκ ἐχρησάμεθα τῇ ἐξουσίᾳ... (1 Cor. 9.12), cf. also 1 Cor. 9.15.

100. H 274.4-9, T 80.22-26, L. Delatte 1942: 210-17, Goodenough 1928: 77.

be the law[101] or the king.[102] When a king, because of a failure of his nature, needs 'the stronger', he immediately finds help in contemplation of 'that which is appropriate', that is, God.[103]

When Hellenistic writers urge imitation of God, the reason is almost always given in positive terms: one is pursuing some form of *aretē*, and the absolute source or referent is God. Ps.-Ecphantus reverses this approach. Instead the stress falls on the *need* for imitation, the lack. All human nature is flawed by *hamartia* 'error'.[104] The king, too, fails (*amplakein*) because of his human nature,[105] and attention focuses on the deficiency. We find this in Paul, as well: the terms *hamartia, hamartēma, hamartanō,* and *hamartōlos* abound in Paul's Letters.[106]

---

101. The law appears here anachronistically, a vestige from the Classical type of constitution.

102. καὶ τοῖς μὲν ἄλλοις ἀνθρώποις, αἴκα ἁμαρτάνωντι, ὁσιωτάτα κάθαρσις ἐξομοιωθῆμεν τοῖς ἀρχοντεσσιν, αἴτε νόμος αἴτε βασιλεύς…(H 274.4-6, T 80.22-23).

103. οἱ δ'εἴ τῶ κρέσσονος δέοιντο διὰ τὴν φύσιν ἀμπλακόντες…οἳ χρὴ θεωμένως εὐθὺ <ἐντι> τᾶς ὠφελείας τυγχάνεν (H 274.6-9, T 80.24-26).

Contemplation as imitation is found in Plato, *Republic* 6.500c (*ap.* L. Delatte 1942: 212). The notion that man achieves perfection in moral and political life by imitating God, fully good and supreme ruler, is widespread in Pythagoreanism and has been encountered often in the Hellenistic Pythagoreans. See also L. Delatte 1942: 213-15. The Pythagorean principle of ὁμοίωσις θεοῦ is also taken over by the Stoics who interpret it cosmologically and apply it to man in general or to life ideals but also restrict it to great politicians or to the king; for the latter, e.g., Seneca, *On Mercy* 1.7.1, 1.19.8 (*ap.* L. Delatte 1942: 215). All theories of kingship duly emphasize the duty of the king to imitate God: Cicero, Musonius, Seneca, Philo, Plutarch, Dio, Aelius Aristides, Eusebius, Themistius, Synesius; see L. Delatte 1942: 216-17. In general, contemplation and imitation of God has as its aim to know God. In Paul, however, the purpose of imitation is not so much *gnōsis* as *sōtēria*. It is important to see that Ps.-Ecphantus, like Paul, expresses philosophical and moral issues in political terms.

104. For a discussion of possible translations of this quintessentially negative idiom (and its cognates) see Chapter 1, Plato, pp. 39-40, and *passim*.

105. In Plato and Aristotle, as earlier discussed, this imperfection, inherent even in the best of humans, is the basis of the argument against absolute monarchy.

106. Forty-six times in Romans alone. Deissmann 1927: 113-15 notes that ἁμαρτωλός is a common Greek word although in literary sources is found only once in Aristotle and once in Plutarch. It is quite frequent, however, in inscriptions, especially in Lycia. It is extensively used in South-West Asia Minor epitaphs in the formula against desecration of the tomb, ἁμαρτωλὸς ἔστω θεοῖς (κατα)χθονίοις, let him be as a *hamartōlos* to the chthonic gods (Deissmann 1927: 114). The sense

The misery of the human condition, not the beauty of the universe, is stressed. What matters is man's inability to pull himself out of his woes (depicted in such a desperate hue in Rom. 7.15-20), not his achievements; what counts is the failure of the will, not its audacity.[107]

There is yet something else in Ps.-Ecphantus that is of even greater import: the solution to *hamartia*. Ordinary human beings, when in *hamartia*, can undergo supernatural purification by becoming exactly like the rulers (ἐξομοιωθῆμεν τοῖς ἀρχόντεσσιν).[108] This conception impresses me as precisely Paul's message *in nuce*: to defeat *hamartia* one must conform to Christ and must imitate him or his emissaries, the true apostles. The ruler of the *ekklēsia* is no man—not Paul, not Apollo, not Cephas—but Christ alone (1 Cor. 1.12-13). Purification, baptism in Christ, brings about the defeat of *hamartia* (Rom. 6.3-4; 1 Cor. 1.13). This is the essence of Paul's kerygma ('message') the crux of his *euangelion*. Ps.-Ecphantus utilizes an analogous instrument of salvation from *hamartia*: become like the king, like God. This is hardly coincidental. Ps.-Ecphantus and Paul come from the same political and spiritual Hellenistic environment and address readers and hearers who are comfortable with this kind of ideology and discourse. In both,[109] imitation is not just following a model but replicating it, becoming it.[110] The logic of expiation in Ps.-Ecphantus, as it moves to the transcendental, does not differ from that in Paul.

1.4.3.[111] In this reiterative section of fragment #1.4, Ps.-Ecphantus remarks that the ruler who commands others can also conceive his own commander. This possibility derives from εὐκοσμία (*eukosmia*), the good

---

is 'a criminal, an offender in a religious matter'. According to Deissmann ἐπάρατος, cursed, and ἔνοχος, guilty, are parallel terms. Deissmann (114) solves the puzzle of the genitival use after *enochos* in 1 Cor. 11.27, not attested in papyri and inscriptions, by noticing the parallelism with *hamartōlos*, known to be employed with the genitive of the authority offended. The synonyms ἄδικος, unjust, and ἀσεβής, impious, are similarly used.

107. Acclaim of the power of the will, universal among the Stoics, rests in the conviction of Stoic philosophy that will alone averts calamity, that its proper cultivation is enough to suspend the power of misfortune. This makes so much more understandable the despair Paul feels at the discovery of its collapse.

108. H 274.5, T 80.23; ἐξομοιωθῆμεν is aorist passive of ἐξομοιάζω.

109. This is also true for Diotogenes and for Sthenidas.

110. That is the meaning of Ps.-Ecphantus's spontaneous transformation or of Diotogenes' gaze. See below, section on Diotogenes.

111. H 274.10-20, T 80.26-81.9, L. Delatte 1942: 217-18, Goodenough 1928: 77.

government of the world. *Eukosmia* teaches the king that there is nothing unruled, as well as how to rule.[112] The king who imitates *eukosmia* becomes dear, because of his *aretē*, to God and to his subjects. No one loved by God can be hated by human beings.[113] The obedience of the ruled proves the ruler; because he rules well, the ruled obey well.[114]

The great significance of this passage consists in Ps.-Ecphantus's formulation of the dictum, 'Nothing unruled can be found in the universe'—a grand unified theory of politics. This is an old Pythagorean adage: 'Everything that rules is ruled in its turn'. This unending circle of authority and subjection, potently germane to Paul, plays a decisive and still-perplexing role in the Pauline conception of Christ. It receives its most recondite expression in the so-called Philippian hymn (Phil. 2.6-11). God alone stands outside this orbit. Everything else is intermediary, a process of mediation, ending in Hellenistic thought with the king, and in Paul with Christ. This supreme mediator, the legitimate ruler, is *theophilēs* ('loved by God') and is obeyed by the ruled.

This view has yet further implications in Paul. Paul's insistence on the global *polis* that incorporates all people—his single most characteristic idea—reflects this position. The image of heaven, earth and underworld all bowing to Christ (Phil. 2.10)[115] is intelligible to Paul's Greek audience because of its familiarity with widespread Pythagorean (and similar) political views.[116] Obedience is one of the most important issues in Paul's Letter to the Romans, where terms for obedience appear no less than 14 times.[117] The theme is also encountered in 2 Corinthians, 2 Thessalonians and Philippians. The concept of obedience is most often developed in political terms or in a politically charged context. Christian duty, obedience of *pistis* (ὑπακοή πίστεως), frames the Letter to

112. ...οὔτ' ἂν ἀνόητος εἴη τῶ διέποντος αὐτὸν ὁ ἑτέρων αὐτὸς ἄρχων. ἃ δ' εὐκοσμία πολλὰ καὶ τῷ μηδὲν ἄναρξηον εὑρὲν δύνασθαι καὶ τῷ τρόπῳ τὰς ἀρχὰς διδάσκει αὐτόν (H 274.10-13, T 81.1-4).

113. ...ἂν ὁ μιμασάμενος δι' ἀρετὰν αὐτῷ τε φίλος ὂν μεμίμαται καὶ πολὺ πλέον τοῖς ὑπ' αὐτὸν τεταγμένοις. οὐ γὰρ ἂν τις θεοφιλὴς ὢν μισείοιτο... (H 274.14-16, T 81.4-6).

114. αἱ δέ κα ἐμίσει τὸν ἀγεμονεύοντα, οὐχ εἵπετο ἂν πειθόμενος αὐτῷ. τὸ δ' ἐκεῖνον ἄρχεν εὖ αἴτιον τῷ καὶ τόνδε ἄρχεσθαι καλῶς (H 274.18-20, T 81.7-9).

115. The line is embedded in a quote of LXX Isa. 45.23, cf. Phil. 2.10b-11a, Rom. 14.11.

116. Such views evolved from and were exploited by both the Hellenistic and the Roman ruler-cult doctrines.

117. Nine times *hupakoē* and *hupakouō*; five times *peithō*.

the Romans (Rom. 1.5; 16.26). The disobedience (παρακοή) of one human being toward God brought about much error for many; one man's obedience to him will make many just.

The juxtaposition transgression-submission takes epic form in Paul (see Rom. 16.19-20). Christ's very assumption of human form and his sacrifice on the cross result from obedience (Rom. 5.19; Phil. 2.8, cf. Rom. 8.3). Obedience to Christ is the purpose of Paul's fight, which he describes in the heroic terms of battle (2 Cor. 10.3-6). Christ himself and his celestial legions will inflict vengeance on those disobedient to the *euangelion* (2 Thess. 1.8). So voracious is Paul's appetite for obedience-conveying terminology that he also appeals to πείθω (*peithō*), which in its passive mood means 'obey'. The dissident, those who do not obey the good, or the truth, incur God's wrath and fury; the obedient receive glory and honor (Rom. 2.8-10, cf. Gal. 3.1 t.r., 5.7). The Hellenistic Pythagorean political dictum expressed by Ps.-Ecphantus as 'the ruler is well-obeyed because he rules well', makes obedience conditional on the character of leadership. In demanding obedience from his people and in demonstrating it himself, Paul actually proves not only the legitimacy of his mission but also the validity of his *euangelion*. By Paul's time, the test of obedience—from bottom up and from top down—imbued political reasoning.

The principle of 'nothing unruled', inherent in *eukosmia*, also has as a corollary in Paul—the theme of imitation. Paul, founder of the Corinthian community, is the exemplum of imitation (1 Cor. 4.16). The Philippian *ekklēsia* is prodded to imitate him (συμμιμηταί μου) (Phil. 3.17). Paul urges the Thessalonians to be his and the lord's imitators (1 Thess. 1.6; 2 Thess. 3.7). Paul is to be imitated, before he himself imitates Christ (1 Cor. 11.1), because he is indisputably Christ's (Phil. 12-13), because he has proved himself in both word and the power of the spirit (1 Thess. 1.5) and because his conduct when he was among the Thessalonians warrants it (2 Thess. 3.9).[118]

1.5.[119] The alliance between the human king and the heavenly king forms a cosmic state. The fragment ends with Ps.-Ecphantus applying what he says about the king to the state.

---

118. The notion of imitation is also rendered by terms like ὁμοίωμα or the verb ὁμοίοω. See, e.g., Rom. 1.23; 5.24; 6.5; 8.3, cf. Phil. 2.7. For further discussion see Chapter 8, Romans 3.21-8.39 section.

119. H 274.20-276.9, T 81.9-82.6, L. Delatte 1942: 218-27.

1.5.1.[120] In this section, Ps.-Ecphantus blends together two distinct ideas, that of the equality of the king's and God's *aretē* and that of the descent of a divine being to rule on earth. Ps.-Ecphantus writes that he thinks that the earthly king cannot be inferior in any *aretē* (μηδεμιᾷ τῶν ἀρετῶν ἐλαττοῦσθαι) to the king in heaven. The king on earth is an alien being, descended among human beings; his *aretai* are his only insofar as they are the works of God. These two, the king who rules on earth and the king of the universe, are part of the primordial association (κοινωνία πράτα) of all beings, and their fellowship is the one most necessary for the human race. To exist (συνεστάναι) is impossible without friendship and fellowship (φιλία καὶ κοινωνία).[121]

Equality of *aretē* between the king and God is a novel idea, with little precedent in Hellenistic culture,[122] and the notion is complicated by the Gnostic language in which it is couched. Equality between a divine political hero and God, however, is a staple of political mysticism, and it appears most dramatically in Paul in Phil. 2.6. In this line from the 'Philippian hymn' (Phil. 2.6-11), Paul employs the phrase ἴσα (εἶναι) θεῷ (*isa theō*), 'equality with God').[123] Ps.-Ecphantus does not employ

120. H 274.20-275.9, T 81.9-16, L. Delatte 1942: 218-24, Goodenough 1928: 77-78, 83.

121. Ἐγὼ μὲν ὦν ὑπολαμβάνω καὶ τὸν ἐπὶ τᾶς γᾶς βασιλέα δύνασθαι μηδεμιᾷ τῶν ἀρετῶν ἐλαττοῦσθαι τῷ κατ' ὠρανὸν βασιλέως· ἀλλ' ὥσπερ αὐτὸς ἀπόδαμόν τί ἐντι χρῆμα καὶ ξένον ἐκεῖθεν ἀφιγμένον πρὸς ἀνθρώπως, καὶ τὰς ἀρετὰς ἄν τις αὐτῷ ἔργα ὑπολάβοι τῷ θεῷ καὶ δι' ἐκεῖνον αὐτῷ... κοινωνία τοιγὰρ πράτα τε πάντων καὶ ἀναγκαιοτάτα τῷ τῶν ἀνθρώπων γένει, ἃς μετέχει μὲν ὁ παρ' ἁμὶν βασιλεύς, μετέχει δὲ καὶ ὁ ἐν τῷ παντὶ πάντα διέπων· συνεστάναι γὰρ χωρὶς φιλίας καὶ κοινωνίας ἀμάχανον (H 274.20-275.9, T 81.9-16).

122. L. Delatte (1942: 219) parallels it with the Stoic divinity of the sage, but notes, however, the major discrepancy: the virtue of the Stoic sage is due to no one but himself and there is no sense of a coalescing between king and God. Obviously, Ps.-Ecphantus is non-Stoic in his stress on the *koinōnia* as a fellowship of God and king.

123. ἴσα, neuter plural is used as an adverb, with the dative. BAGD, *s.v.* ἴσος, 382a, gives a number of interesting references from Thucydides to Philostratus. A few are particularly relevant. In Aeschylus's *Persians* 855-57, βασιλεὺς ἰσόθεος Δαρεῖος, King Darius 'extended like a God his awful power' (Robert Potter trans.). Nicolaus Damascenus, of first century BCE, speaks about Caesar as τὸν ἴσα καὶ θεὸν τιμώμενον (90 frg. 130.97). For the meaning of ἴσα in Phil. 2.6, the phrase ἴσα εἶναι as used in this passage from Thucydides 13.14.1 may be helpful: ἐν οὗ τῷ ἱερῷ ἴσα καὶ ἱκέται ἐσμέν, in [Zeus'] temple we stand as suppliants.

This image of Christ is obviously not limited to the Philippian 'hymn'. It is at the

the term ἴσος (*isos*) (nor any term from the same family), as Paul does, but there is contextual similarity. Ps.-Ecphantus's text may even help explain the nature of the equality between God and Christ spoken of in the 'hymn'. Both texts develop this motif in terms familiar from Gnostic material. A divine being descends from heaven to earth, and, though he appears in the form of man, he is no ordinary human. After accomplishing his mission below, the divine being returns to his rightful home in magnified glory.

The notion that religious founders, kings and/or wise men are heavenly beings and will return to heaven at death is widespread in Hellenistic and Roman times.[124] What Ps.-Ecphantus and his like make clear is that such ideas have a political background. Against expectation, the fellowship of the king and God is explained not in mystical but in political terms. The state constituted by the king and his subjects forms an alliance with the universe.[125] The two form a foundational community, a *prata koinōnia*, which brings together all beings. In Paul, a similar

---

very core of the *euangelion*. Each one of the main elements of Christ's story, his descent, mission, death and return to heaven is told, in virtuoso *variazioni*, countless times in Paul.

124. This mysticism of the ruler as an alien descended from heaven (probably rooted in Plato's *Laws* 4.712b-717) penetrates not only Hellenistic Pythagorean thought but also Stoic philosophy. It is encountered in numerous passages in Seneca's *Epistulae Morales*. See L. Delatte 1942: 219-21. That great politicians, famous generals or emperors came down from heaven to save cities or the world is a popular belief extremely common in Hellenistic times. It is reported in Asia by Cicero, about Pompei and Quintus, and is echoed by Manilius about Caesar, Calpurnius about Nero, Themistius about Gratian (L. Delatte 1942: 220). Popular belief and court sycophancy conspire to deifying the ruler.

L. Delatte (1942: 221) himself notes in Paul the descent of the divine *pneuma* on the soul in a operation of divine possession that transfigures and illuminates the initiate, a theme common to Hellenistic mysticism. The *pneuma* of Christ cancels the sarkic, and although the body is dead because of *hamartia*, the *pneuma* is alive because of *dikaiosunē* (Rom. 8.9-10, cf. 1 Cor. 3.16; Gal. 2.20). Other similar passages may be added to this list.

125. The idea is retraced to the ancient Pythagoreans through Plato. In *Gorgias* 507e-508a Plato credits certain *sophoi* with the teaching that *koinōnia* and *philia*, as well as κοσμιότητα καὶ σωφροσύνη καὶ δικαιότητα, order, temperance and justice, bind together heaven and earth, gods and humans, and from this unity and harmony is derived the origin of the word *kosmos*. It is also met in the Stoics, e.g., Cicero, *Laws* 1.7.23. See also L. Delatte 1942: 222.

relationship exists between God and Christ, and, as we have seen, *koinōnia* is a constant theme in Paul.

This fellowship between king and God is also necessary for human life, for nothing can subsist outside the state. The relationship between the two kings, earthly and celestial, extends to their states. The divine government transfers its political configuration to the human king's state. The pivotal verb in Ps.-Ecphantus, *sunestanai*,[126] appears in exactly the same political and mystical framework in the 'Colossian hymn' (Col. 1.17), which even if of disputed Pauline authenticity certainly belongs to the Pauline school and bears a resemblance to the 'Philippian hymn'. The Christ is before all, and all come into existence (συνέστηκεν)[127] in him (Col. 1.17); he is the head and the body of the *ekklēsia*, the beginning, the first-born from the dead (Col. 1.18); in him all fullness of God · dwells (Col. 1.19). The community that exists between the cosmic and the earthly, the *exemplum* and the imitator, the political and the transcendental are found in Paul as in Ps.-Ecphantus.

1.5.2.[128] The same mutuality can be observed in political compact (ἐπὶ τῶν συμπολιτευομένων), *koinōnia* in the ordinary sense. Inferior to the divine-royal *koinōnia*, which lacks for nothing and does not require anything, the human political community comes about so that the needs of its members may be satisfied by their reciprocal support. The divine and royal natures have the fullness of *aretai*; in the *polis*, the close association (φιλία), which has a common end (κοινῶ τινος τέλεος), imitates the concord of the universe (τοῦ παντὸς ὁμόνοιαν μεμίμαται). No city can survive without decrees and a government. The ruler and

126. Forced by L. Delatte (1942: 222) to recall *sustēma*.

127. The RSV translation is 'are held together'. The passive perfect of συνίστημι (like the passive second aorist) has the meaning 'exist' (LSJ, *s.v.* συνίστημι 1719a, IVd).

128. H 275.9-276.5, T 81.17-82.3, L. Delatte 1942: 224-26, Goodenough 1928: 83. Σκοποίη δ᾽ ἄν τις ταῦτα καὶ ἐπὶ τῶν συμπολιτευομένων, ἐξελὼν τῷ λόγῳ τὰν κατὰ συνάθηαν κοινωνίαν· ἐλάττων γὰρ αὖτα τᾶς τε θείας φύσιος καὶ τᾶς βασιλικᾶς· οὐ γὰρ δέονται τὰν τοιαύταν δέησιν ἀλλάλων, καθ᾽ ἅν συνευπορεῦντες τῶν ὑστερούντων, ἀναπλαροῦτι κοινὰν τὰν βοάθειαν; τέλειοι γὰρ κατ᾽ ἀρετάν. ἁ δ᾽ ἐν τᾷ πόλει φιλία κοινῶ τινος τέλεος ἐχομένα τὰν τοῦ παντὸς ὁμόνοιαν μεμίμαται (μιμᾶται): ἄνευ δὲ τᾶς περὶ τᾶς ἀρχὰς διατάξιος οὐδεμία ἂν πόλις οἰκοῖτο. εἰς δὲ ταύταν νόμων τε δεῖται καί τινος προστασίας πολιτικᾶς τό τε ἄρχον καὶ τὸ ἀρχόμενον. ἀποσῳζοι δ᾽ ἂν τὸ ἐκ τούτων κοινὸν ἀγαθὸν εὐαρμοστία τις καὶ τῶν πολλῶν ὁμοφωνία μετὰ πειθοῦς συνῳδοῖσα. ὁ κατ᾽ ἀρετὰν ἐχάρχων καλέεταί τε βασιλεὺς καὶ ἔντι, ταύταν ἔχων φιλίαν τε καὶ κοινωνίαν ποτὶ τὼς ὑπ᾽ αὐτὰυτὰν, ἅνπερ ὁ θεός ἔχει ποτί τε τὸν κόσμον καὶ τὰ ἐν αὐτῷ.

the ruled thus need laws and some political authority.[129] The ensuing common good (κοινόν ἀγαθόν), the harmony and accord of the masses, is preserved thanks to persuasion (or obedience). He who rules according to *aretē*—he who is a genuine king—has toward his subjects the same friendship and liberality (φιλία καὶ κοινωνία) that God has toward the world and its beings.

Ps.-Ecphantus's view of human political society draws heavily on Plato and Aristotle. As Ps.-Ecphantus moves from the cosmic fellowship to the political *koinōnia*, his work takes the form of a *Peri politeias* treatise, one dealing with the political compact and with civil polity, with the *polis* and not with the *basileia*. As in Paul, however, Ps.-Ecphantus's *koinōnia* has both a political and a transcendent component. Politics and metaphysics overlap. The ultimate term of any *sustēma* is the common good, and in a political system this is the stability and unity of the state; laws, constitutional leadership and persuasion of the masses contribute to this end. None of these elements is absent in Paul, where they are figured as *euangelion*, Christ and genuine apostleship, and *peithō* ('persuasion') and imitation, respectively.

1.5.3.[130] The good will (εὔνοια) between king and subjects is like that between a father and his son, a shepherd and his flock, the law and the law-abiders. These are all common motifs in antiquity.[131] The subject of the reciprocity of good will is a topos of political philosophy, and much is made of it by Aristotle. Paul constantly reminds his communities of the relationship between them and him. 'If I love you the more, am I to be loved less?' he asks the Corinthians in one of the most dramatic invocations of this motif (2 Cor. 12.15, cf. 8.8). The same rapport is established in the household between the husband and the wife (1 Cor. 7.3) and between the master and the slaves (Eph. 6.7, cf. 1 Cor. 7.22).

Finally, in reference to fragments #1 and #2, it must be said that

---

129. The text is corrupt here.

130. H 276.5-9, T 82.3-6, L. Delatte 1942: 226-27. ὅλαν δὲ τὰν εὔνοιαν χρὴ παρασκευάζεσθαι πρῶτα μὲν παρὰ τῶ βασιλέως ἐς τὼς βασιλευομένως, δεύτερον δὲ παρὰ τῶνδε ἐς τὸν βασιλέα, ὁποία γεννάτορος ποτὶ υἱέα καὶ ποτὶ ποίμναν νομέως καὶ νόμω ποτὶ χρωμένως αὐτῷ.

131. The Hellenistic king's *eunoia* is a commonplace. Comparison of the royal authority with the paternal one is trivial. The shepherd and the flock metaphor is used from Homer on. It is widespread in Plato *Republic* 3.416a, 4.440d, *Politicus* 265a, 268a, 275a (see L. Delatte 1942: 227, Goodenough 1928: 84-86, 84 n. 92). The king as law and his subjects, a Hellenistic Pythagorean locus, is elaborated in Diotogenes.

the transcendent's political manifestation renders both Ps.-Ecphantus's and Paul's thought more rational than, and distinguishes them from, Gnosticism, although a resonance of this powerful current in Hellenistic culture is present in both authors. The king (in Ps.-Ecphantus) and Christ (in Paul) have an acute consciousness of who they are at all times. The king (or Christ) *alone* comes down from heaven. Human beings always have a reliable example to imitate, that will guide them to truth and the good, and will never leave them completely lost and forgotten on a hostile planet. Man is never lonely so long as he gives in to his social essence. Ps.-Ecphantus's fragments and Paul's Letters alike are infused with a deep-seated belief in the *polis*, finding no tension between this ideal and that of God's rule. Submission to perfect autocracy appears to be the best insurance against anarchy. Consolidation of the two realms is seen as the solution: a human society with God as ruler, a *polis* that follows the universal governing principles. God's distribution of *pistis* and *charis* and the elimination of all the relativities of human bias and flawed judgment are the ultimate response to error.

Fragment #3.[132] This text concerns the pursuit of *aretē*. Ps.-Ecphantus assumes, in a Classical philosophical vein, that people naturally seek *aretē*. Here, *autarkeia* is the virtue elaborated.

3.1.[133] In this section, Ps.-Ecphantus raises the issue of self-sufficiency, *autarkeia*. He poses the question whether *autarkeia* is compatible with public life. Insofar as his private life is concerned, it is a given that the king is *autarkēs*, self-sufficient. The king, however, cannot rule without a government. God, of course, governs alone,[134] and God's *autarkeia*

---

132. Stobaeus 4.7.65 pp. 276.10-278.20 Hense = T (#3) 82.7-83.17; L. Delatte 1942: 32-35 (Greek), 50-51 (French trans.), 227-40 (Commentary). Goodenough 1928: 88-91.

133. H 276.11-19, T 82.7-14. μιᾷ γὰρ ἀρετᾷ πρὸς τὸ ἄρχεν ἀνθρώπων καὶ πρὸς τὸν αὐτῶ βίον χρήσεται, οὐδὲν ὡς δι' ἔνδειαν ποτιλαμβάνων εἰς ὑπηρεσίαν τὰν αὐτὸς αὐτῶ. ἀλλ' ὡς κατὰ φύσιν συνεργῶν· κοινωνίας γὰρ ἐάσας οὐδὲν ἔλαττον ἕκαστος αὐτάρκως βιώσει καθ' αὐτόν. δοκεῖ μὲν γὰρ ὁ αὐτάρκης μηδενὸς ἂν ἄλλω πρός γε τὰν αὐτῶ διεξαγωγὰν ποτιδεήσεσθαι. αἱ δ' ἄρα δεῖ βίον ἐνεργέα ζώεν, δᾶλον ὡς καὶ ἄτερα ἂν προσλάβοι, οὐδέν τι ἔλαττον αὐτὸν αὐτάρκεα ποιήσει·

134. Without διάκονοι and ὑπηρέται, writes Ps.-Ecphantus (H 277.5-6, T 82.17-18). These functions, drawn from political life, appear in Paul as well. The *diakonoi* are major players in the *ekklēsia* structure. The apostles appear as *hupēretai* of Christ (1 Cor. 4.1), a general term meaning subordinate or assistant but which was

alone is perfect. The deity is ideally self-sufficient. The king, despite his need of others in order to rule, only cooperates according to his nature (ἀλλ᾽ ὡς κατὰ φύσιν συνεργῶν) and remains self-sufficient in regard both to his personal and his political life. His perfection is not impaired by public office. First, because the king naturally resembles God, he shares intrinsically in the divine qualities—he cannot but be like God. Second, by the nature of his kingship, he makes himself a model for his subjects. He does this just as God does it: by being *agathos*, 'good'. *Autarkeia* is a condition of being *agathos*. Not only the king, but everyone who lives in the state needs to associate with other people. *Autarkeia* remains a desideratum in the case of the subjects as well, but these need the intervention of the *logos* to achieve it.

Paul speaks just like the Hellenistic Pythagoreans. Social existence does not destroy one's private excellence. One's *agathon* is not depreciated because of public-life compromise (see, e.g., Rom. 14.16). One's personal goodness is not affected if one pursues the collective good (e.g., Rom. 15.2). 'Know the good (τὸ ἀγαθόν)' is Paul's exhortation (Rom. 16.19).

The distributor of αὐτάρκεια is God, its source, writes Paul (2 Cor. 9.8), in full agreement with Ps.-Ecphantus. Ps.-Ecphantus's king's *autarkeia* is assured even in his political activity, for in his royal function he cooperates according to his nature (κατὰ φύσιν συνεργῶν).[135] That God and his people co-work is a widespread idea. It appears often in Paul. God works with his people for *agathon*, salvation (Rom. 8.28); his people work with God (θεοῦ συνεργοί) (1 Cor. 3.9, cf. 15.10).[136] Elsewhere Paul gives the Cynic definition of private *autarkeia*: 'to live quietly, to mind your own business, to work with your hands' (1 Thess. 4.11).[137]

---

used in at least one cultic environment, Mithraism, LSJ, *s.v.* ὑπηρέτης. Both *diakonos* and *huperetēs* are known cult titles (MM, *s.v.* ὑπηρέτης). Their presence in Ps.-Ecphantus suggest the negligible distinction between political and religious titles in Hellenistic times. The ambiguity seems to be retained by Paul who calls the apostles as ὑπηρέται Χριστοῦ καὶ οἰκονόμους μυστηρίων Θεοῦ.

135. H 276.13-14, T 82.10. The idea is encountered in the Hermetic literature, Philo, Christianity (L. Delatte 1942: 229).

136. L. Delatte himself observes this Pauline use (1942: 229).

137. ἡσυχάζειν καὶ πράσσειν τὰ ἴδια καὶ ἐργάζεσθαι ταῖς [ἰδίαις] χερσὶν ὑμῶν (1 Thess. 4.11). The pastoral 1 Tim. (6.6) advises εὐσέβεια μετὰ αὐταρκείας, i.e. it couples reverence towards God with self-sufficiency. 'To live quietly' would become the core of a mystical doctrine in Eastern Orthodox monasticism that takes its name from it: hesychasm.

And, just as Ps.-Ecphantus calls the king,[138] Paul calls himself *autarkēs* (Phil. 4.11).

Ps.-Ecphantus's whole approach to *autarkeia* makes sense only if one understands that *aretē* is the highest good, that it must be recognized as such and ardently pursued. This axiological datum, so alien to the modern interpreter, has its precise analogue in Paul. Although *aretē* is no longer a central concept for Paul—by his time what people want is salvation—the mechanism for achieving salvation is identical: imitation of the king. In both Ps.-Ecphantus and Paul the king (Christ, in Paul) is himself pushed so far into the divine sphere that he is indistinguishable from God.[139]

Ps.-Ecphantus's text shows the cultural context of the apostle's thinking, even as the dynamic of Paul's discourse itself reveals that context. Yet there is a difference. So long as *aretē* is the matrix of human participation in the divine, things keep their cool, their coherence and logical civility. When death slips the philosophical grip and becomes a stark horror, as it does for the Hellenistic popular mind, the passage between this world and the divine is marked by fear and loathing. With Paul the gentility of philosophy ends.

3.2.[140] That God is good (*agathos*) is a Platonic idea that is common currency in Hellenistic times.[141] In Ps.-Ecphantus it defines God and is

138. *Autarkeia*, writes Georgi about 2 Cor. 9.8, is stripped of 'all the glamour' of Stoic philosophy (1992: 97). It means self-sufficient livelihood. But is this what Paul has in mind in Phil. 4.11? I agree, however, with Georgi that 'God does not offer or command withdrawal into inwardness; on the contrary, God grants the possibility of empowerment for active involvement within the community' (92). *Autarkeia*, the very product of Stoic political powerlessness, is in Paul, as in the Hellenistic Pythagoreans, an element of the political.

139. King and God are quite similar, except that God has no court, has no *diakonoi* and *hupēretai*, and thus needs not give orders, offer incentives, or castigate the defiant (H 277.5-9, T 82.17-20). On the other hand, God is absolutely good, good in himself, ἔντι δὲ αὐτὸς μὲν ἀγαθός, and absolutely free (H 277.10-11, T 82.21-22).

140. H 277.5-11, T 82.17-22. χὠ μὲν θεὸς οὔτε διακόνως ἔχων οὔτε ὑπηρέτας οὔτ' αὖ προστάξει τινὶ χρώμενος οὐδὲ στεφανῶν ἢ ἀναγορεύων τὼς πειθομένως ἢ ἀτιμάζων τὼς ἀπειθέοντας, οὗτος αὐτὸς ἄρχει ποτὶ τοσόνδε μέγεθος ἀρχᾶς, ἀλλ' οἶμαι παρέχων ἀξιομίματον αὐτὸν ζᾶλον ἐντίθητι πᾶσι τᾶς αὐτῶ φύσιος. ἔντι δὲ αὐτὸς μὲν ἀγαθός καὶ τόδε μόνον τε καὶ ῥᾴδιον ἔργον αὐτῶ·

141. It pervades, for example, Hermetic literature and Neoplatonism (*ap.* L. Delatte 1942: 230).

the cause of his *autarkeia*. The good (*to agathon*) is a conspicuous concept in Romans. It describes God and his work (Rom. 8.28); it designates God's will and is used for those who undertake self-meta-morphosis by the renewing of their minds (Rom. 12.2). It is the greatest virtue, and a universal human virtue at that (Rom. 2.10).[142] Christians must cleave to the good (Rom. 12.9). In Ps.-Ecphantus the good is ultimately an element of the political. In precisely the same vein, Paul says that political authority serves God for the subjects' good (Rom. 13.4). Like the Pythagorean, Paul emphasizes the relativity of human good (Rom. 14.16) and expresses the view that the good, though it is the highest desideratum, is impossible for man (Rom. 7.18-19).

Ps.-Ecphantus sees the king's *autarkeia* as both cause and source of imitation. The king is *autarkēs* because he is image and example—the image of God and the example for his subjects.[143] The main attribute of the ruler, God or king, is that he is worthy of imitation (ἀξιομίματος).[144] On the one hand, the king resembles the deity; he is ὁμοίωσις θεοῦ (*homoiōsis theou*), God's image.[145] On the other, he 'models' for the people; he is *axiomimētos*. Moreover, the king, like God, because he is *axiomimētos*, inspires one to emulation (ζᾶλος).[146] Although the term *zēlos* is frequently used by Paul, the concept it names is more complex in his system of thought. Still, the notion of emulation of the divine indicates a Hellenistic topos. Zeal for God (ζῆλος θεοῦ) is a consistant Pauline theme. What is wrong with the Jews, says Paul, is not that they do not have zeal for God but that their zeal is not informed by knowledge that *dikaiosunē* is God's alone (Rom. 10.2-3). He urges the Corinthians to aspire (ζηλοῦτε) to the higher gifts (1 Cor. 12.31), the pneumatic goods, especially prophecy (1 Cor. 14.1, 39). It is good to have zeal for the good (καλὸν δὲ ζηλοῦσθαι ἐν καλῷ) (Gal. 4.18). And, like Ps.-Ecphantus's king, Paul himself excites this zeal. There are many more examples,[147] but one very revealing use of the term is when Paul

142. The term is also used in the argument against the antinomians (Rom. 3.8). In a poignant passage, Paul makes the startling observation that, in his world, death is conceivable for the sake of an *agathos*, while it is not expected for a *dikaios*, a just one (Rom. 5.7).

143. ἀπεικάζων τε γὰρ αὐτὸν ἑνὶ ἂν ἀπεικάσειε τῷ κρατίστῳ καὶ πάντας ἑαυτῷ πειρώμενος ὁμοιοῦν ᾧ θεὸς [αὐτάρκης] ἔσσεται (H 277.16-18, T 82.26-27).

144. H 277.9, T 82.20-21.

145. See discussion of Ecphantus 1.4.2.

146. H 277.9-10, T 82.21.

147. The Corinthians display zeal for him (τὸν ὑμῶν ζῆλον ὑπὲρ ἐμοῦ) (2 Cor.

describes his own misguided zeal when he had pursued the *ekklēsia* because of *zēlos* inspired by the Jewish law and Judaism (Gal. 1.14; Phil. 3.6).

Paul's prodding his hearers to imitation—of God, of Christ, of the Judaean *ekklēsiai* or of himself—is a major motif in most of the Letters. It is just as central in Paul as in the Hellenistic Pythagoreans. Imitation alone is the means to transcendence, to salvation. Ps.-Ecphantus introduces the view that imitation of God makes one better than one would otherwise have been—and this without impeding *autarkeia*.[148] What is notable here is that imitation, being like the God (or the king), does not interfere with personal *autarkeia*. Imitation of the king is the infallible means for achieving one's fullest potential. In the political dimension of imitation, membership in society and individual *autarkeia* merge.

The notion of imitation of the king practically ensures that the shared identity of all the constituents of the state takes precedence over individual difference. When, as in Paul's construct, a group of people come into the union with a strong, already formed identity, as the Jews do, their claims to specificity must give way to the commonality. Imitation of Christ (or of Paul) is the unique political *aretē* of this community. These features are lifted directly from the political reflections of the Hellenistic Pythagoreans of the *basileia* group.[149]

3.3.[150] While imitation of the king is warranted by the king's similarity with God, the human basis of this imitation is the king's εὔνοια

7.7). This zeal is implanted by the Godly grief (τὸ κατὰ θεὸν λυπηθῆναι), the remorse that Paul's letter has stirred in them (2 Cor. 7.9-11). Corinthian zeal about the collection also fires the Macedonians (2 Cor. 9.2). Paul's divine *zēlos* in regard to the Corinthians (ζηλῶ γὰρ ὑμᾶς θεοῦ ζήλῳ) is that they should stay pure for God, as fitting bride for Christ (2 Cor. 11.2).

148. οἱ δὲ μιμεύμενοι αὐταυτῶν κρέσσον τῷδε πάντα ἐργάζονται· ἁ δὲ ὁμοίωσις καὶ ἑκάστῳ τῶνδε αὔταρκές ἐντι (H 277.11-13, T 82.22-24). It is not clear whether he refers only to the king or to everyone.

149. An important point ought to be made here. Nowhere does imitation take, in Paul, the form of contemplation. (For *theōria* in Plato and later authors see Festugière 1936.) Imitation is an active process, the result of speech, writing, presence. Writing, discourse and *exemplum* are the store of imitation. The *euangelion* is the source of imitation. Paul's revelation of it, in lectures, letters and through his life and activity is what matters. Paul is no mystic but a popular philosopher, his tools are different. What he pursues is *sōtēria* not *autarkeia*.

150. H 278.12-20, T 83.11-17. τὼς δὲ ὥσπερ ὑπὸ μέθας διεφθαρμένως καὶ διὰ

(*eunoia*)—that is, his good will, the kindness that characterizes his relationship with his subjects.[151] Under ideal conditions, no coercion or pressure (βίας καὶ ἀνάγκας)[152] need be applied. Here, Ps.-Ecphantus reflects the Aristotelian notion of cooperation between ruler and ruled, whether in a household or in a *polis*.

Ps.-Ecphantus now launches into a meditation that has a pronounced Gnostic coloring. People may want nothing better than *arete*, but the human condition is steeped in ignorance and human beings are incapable of achieving *arete* by themselves. Persuasion and even force and coercion (*bia* and *ananke*) are necessary, but these remedies are deplorable. Had humanity not been degenerate, imitation of the king would have taken place without pressure. The beautiful (*to kalon*) would have been practiced spontaneously and naturally (αὐτοφυῶς), without persuasion or fear.[153] To absorb *to kalon* spontaneously, to practice it by one's own nature, is the culmination of the mystics' quest, be they Pythagoreans, Platonists or Paulines.[154] This is the apex of Ps.-Ecphantus's political-mystical reflection.

In the world as it is, however, persuasion and fear are indeed means

κακὰν τροφὰν ἐς λάθαν ἐμπεσόντας αὐτῶ παραλαφθεὶς ὁ λόγος ἐπέρρωσέν τε καὶ κάμνοντας ἰάσατο καὶ τὰν ἐκ τᾶς κακίας ἐνοικεῦσαν αὐτοῖς λάθαν ἐκβαλὼν τὰν μνάμαν ἐσῳκισεν, ἐξ ᾆς ἀπετέχθη ἁ καλεομένα πειθώ. καὶ τὰν ἀρχὰν ἐκ φαύλων σπερμάτων λαβοῦσα αὐτα τι σπουδαῖον ἐφύη τὰν ἐπίγηον οἰκεῦσα χώραν, ἐν ᾇ δι᾽ ἀσθένειαν τᾶς ἁμῶν φύσιος ὁ λόγος ἀνθρώποις ὁμιλέων ἀναπλαροῖ τι τῶν διὰ κακίαν ὑστερούντων.

151. H 278.1-2, T 82.29-83.1. In Paul it is the traumatic death of Christ that is the compelling factor in the relationship between people and the (intermediary) God. Interestingly, the Aristotelian rooted *eunoia*, willingness, appears twice in the Pauline and deutero-Pauline corpus in the context of household relations: between the husband and the wife (1 Cor. 7.3, t.r.) and between the slave and the master (Eph. 6.17). For the idea of willingness, as the distinction between the subjects of a king and those of a tyrant, see, e.g., Plato, *Politicus* 276e; Aristotle, *Politics* 1285a27, *passim* (Goodenough 1928: 90 n. 119).

152. H 277.18, T 82.28.

153. ὅσα δ᾽ αὐτοφυῶς τῷ καλῷ χρῆται, τούτοις οὐδεμία πειθοῦς αἰδώς, ἐπειδήπερ οὐδὲ φόβος ἀνάγκας (H 278.8-9, T 83.7).

154. Goodenough 1928: 91. Diotogenes (see next section) expresses this in his doctrine of the gaze, προσαύγασις (Doric, προταύγασις; H 268.10, T 74.16). Contemplation of the king purges all strident, false sound and brings life into the perfect harmony of *dikaiosune*. In Paul one finds an equally striking and characteristic locution: the fragrance (ὀσμή) of the knowledge of [Christ], the aroma (εὐωδία) of Christ to God (2 Cor. 2.14, 15).

for arriving at *aretē*.[155] The digression on persuasion that follows is cast in recognizably Gnostic terms. Corrupted by Drunkenness (Μέθη, *Methē*),[156] human beings fell into Forgetfulness (Λήθη, *Lēthē*).[157] *Lēthē* dwells in humans because of their vices. *Logos* casts out *Lēthē* restoring Memory (Μνήμη, *Mnēmē*),[158] and thus heals human beings and cures them of their illnesses. *Mnēmē* gives birth to Persuasion (Πειθώ, *Peithō*). *Peithō*, though it had its beginning in a base seed (φαῦλα σπέρματα),[159] grew up (ἐφύη) as something excellent (σπουδαῖος).[160] *Peithō* has value in the earthly region,[161] where *Logos* consorts (ὁμιλέων) with men because of the weakness (ἀσθένεια) of human nature.[162]

155. Hippodamos' περὶ πολιτείας (4.31.3) and περὶ εὐδαιμονίας (4.912.6) know a similar tripartite distinction for establishing political harmony: fear—of laws, persuasion—through discourse, and traditions. In Ps.-Ecphantus mores and customs are replaced by imitation. See L. Delatte 1942: 234-35. The importance of rhetoric, of speech in the civil and political society, is a constant of Greek, Hellenistic and Roman thinking. L. Delatte (1942: 235-40) finds a close agreement between Ps.-Ecphantus and Philo (*Migr. Abr.* 39, *Mut. Nom.* 98, *Congr.* 70) on the natural or spontaneous and education-mediated ways of achieving virtue, means discussed in both authors in language marked by a symbolism of longing for a transcendent, other world.

156. Drunkenness (μέθη), as simple vice not cosmic mythical character, appears in Paul in the catalogues of vices, in Rom. 13.13 and Gal. 5.21.

157. I think that 1 Peter and (especially) 2 Peter offer promise for a Hellenistic Pythagorean parallel. The importance that *aretē* plays there and the cosmic imagery, which includes *lēthos* (2 Pet. 1.9), *mnēmē* (1.15) and *truphē* (2.13), as well as the presence of a score of other important terms, such as *enkrateia* (1.6), supports the possibility.

158. *Mnēmē*, Memory, Recall, is similarly employed in 2 Pet. 1.15.

159. For an intriguing presence of *phaulos* in Paul in the context of seed, see Rom. 9.11. Φαυλός is used there in opposition to ἀγαθός, in a moral sense.

160. For *spoudaios* as antonym of *phaulos* see Plato, *Laws* 6.757a, 7.814e, Aristotle, *Poetics* 2.1448a2 (LSJ, *s.v.* σπουδαῖος).

161. Goodenough (1928) translates '*even* in an earthly environment', (emphasis mine). 'Even' is not only superfluous, but also obscures the point of the Logos–king parallelism; the king's sphere *is* the earth.

162. L. Delatte (1942: 238-39) sees an intimate connection between the treatment of the Logos in Ps.-Ecphantus and in Philo. There is a certain equivocation about the Logos in Ps.-Ecphantus, for his presence is demanded by human imperfection; it is only beyond Logos that rests the vision of God.

This is not the place to do a detailed examination of the function of Logos in Paul. Paul has no Logos theology. His is a theology of *stauros*. Logos, in the sense of divine reason, though never personified as a distinct force, does appear in Paul:

The two sections that constitute fragment #3.3[163] thus display a two-fold approach to salvation: imitation of the king and the intervention of *Logos* to rout oppressive worldly powers. The first leads to an immediate, theoretically instantaneous possession of salvation; the second promises a future transformation of the entire world order. The Pauline *euangelion* unifies the two strands: Christ's resurrection vanquishes the deadly authority of the sublunary rulers, even as it is also the *exemplum*, the salvation archetype for all other men.

Logos, understood in Ps.-Ecphantus as the power who awakens human beings from their drunkenness and forgetfulness, corrects, enlightens and perfects. *Logos* is the opposite of *Lēthē*, Forgetfulness. *Logos* is our companion because of our weak nature;[164] by his company and inter-

---

Rom. 9.6, ὁ λόγος τοῦ θεοῦ, implies reason, a model, a design, cf. 1 Cor. 14.36; 2 Cor. 2.17; 4.2; 5.19; Phil. 2.16; 1 Thess. 1.6, 8 (κυρίου), 2.13; 2 Thess. 3.1 (κυρίου). It must be noticed, however, that a logos ambiguity persists in Paul as well. While a personified Logos is nonexistent in Paul, *logos* as discourse, speech or spell, occupies a prominent place in Paul's letters. Λόγος σοφίας, speculative discourse, is opposed to λόγος σταυροῦ, the cross discourse. 1 Cor. 1.17-18; 2.1-4, where πειθοί σοφίας λόγοι, the persuasive learned discourse conflicts with the (λόγος) πνεύματος καὶ δυνάμεως, the spontaneous discourse of divine spirit and power, cf. 2.13; 4.19. (A similar point is made by Plato's Socrates in the *Apology*: poets write poetry not by wisdom but by some kind of 'nature', and inspiration, ὅτι οὐ σοφίᾳ ποιοῖεν, ἃ ποιοῖεν, ἀλλὰ φύσει τινὶ καὶ ἐνθουσιάζοντες, 22c. This inspiration has a negative valence.) Yet Paul can speak approvingly of a λόγος σοφίας or a λόγος γνώσεως if bestowed by *pneuma*, 1 Cor. 12.8. Λόγος θεοῦ can be spoken by spurious as well as by genuine lecturers, 2 Cor. 2.17. It is a question of competence, ἱκανός, vs inspiration, ὡς ἐκ θεοῦ 2 Cor. 2.16-17, cf. 4.2. The λόγος τῆς καταλλαγῆς, the word of reconciliation (or the *euangelion* of reconciliation, as other sources have it), divine revelation, λόγος θεοῦ, or ζωῆς, can be imparted only by God's emissaries, cf. Phil. 2.16; 1 Thess. 1.8; 2.13; 2 Thess. 3.1. The *logos* (some sources obviously feel the need to supply τοῦ θεοῦ) becomes an expression for immediate, unstudied imitation in Phil. 1.14. Precisely the same sense is found in 1 Thess. 1.6: the *logos* received through suffering, affliction, tribulation—Cynic/Stoic addition to Pythagorean ideas—is of the direct, natural kind, an imitation: καὶ ὑμεῖς μιμηταὶ ἡμῶν ἐγενήθητε καὶ τοῦ κυρίου, δεξάμενοι τὸν λόγον ἐν θλίψει πολλῇ μετὰ χαρᾶς πνεύματος ἁγίου. This *logos* of suffering, that functions as imitation, grants immediate access to God. It is exactly such a doctrine that gave impetus to the martyr rage: the promise of instantaneous vision of God.

163. H 277.18-278.12, T 82.28-83.10 and H 278.12-20, T 83.11-17.

164. By reverting to the first person the author suggestively emphasizes the urgency and breadth of the problem and moves from an abstract position to one which elicits his sympathy and compassion.

course *Logos* fills what is missing in us, that which we lack because of evil.[165] In a previous passage,[166] Ps.-Ecphantus had used the term *hamartia* for that which Logos restores. *Hamartia* was cured by imitation of the king. The two ideas are related. The identity of the king as logos and savior is demonstrated here by a mystical argument. As savior of his subjects from *hamartia*, the king is 'a dynamic and personal revelation of deity'.[167] (This pertains to the essence of the king as *nomos empsuchos* ['animate law'].)

Logos walks with human beings and is the catalyst for their awakening and their disposition toward persuasion; thus, ultimately, he brings about their return to *aretē*. This *Logos*, then, is the king's double. The mediating function of the king moves from the political sphere to that of the soul; his political role becomes fused with that of a redeemer. As Ps.-Ecphantus puts it, the king alone can energize the good (*to agathon*) in human nature so that the human, by imitating the superior being who is the king, follows him on the road to duty.[168]

This passage sounds an unmistakably late-Hellenistic note. There are

165. ...ὁ λόγος ἀνθρώποις ὁμιλέων ἀναπλαροῖ τι τῶν διὰ κακίαν ὑστερούντων (H 278.20, T 83.16-17).

Throughout Ps.-Ecphantus's fragment, *Logos* appears in a guise that can be called 'pleromatic'. He 'fills' (ἀναπλαροῖ) a lack, he corrects, enlightens and perfects. This hearkens back to Plato. (Goodenough [1928: 90] sees here Platonizing Stoicism, the Stoic λόγος σπερματικός transferred from God to king.) In what looks like an 'invisible' polemic or, rather a compressed argument, Paul seems to respond to a '*pleromatic*' *logos* theology in 1 Cor. 1.17-18. Paul is not sent 'to fill up' (as Ps.-Ecphantus puts it), with the *sophia* of the *logos* 'lest the cross be emptied of its power', ἵνα μὴ κενωθῇ ὁ σταυρός τοῦ Χριστοῦ. (In 2 Cor. 2.17; 4.2, however, Paul makes clear that there are *logos* peddlers and shams.) He opposes the *logos* of *sophia* to the *logos* of *stauros*, i.e. the *logos* of folly, μωρία (1 Cor. 1.18, cf. 1 Cor. 2.1, 13). He contrasts the *logos* of *sophia* with the demonstration of *dunamis*, supranatural power (1 Cor. 2.4; 4.19, cf. Rom. 15.19). He counters the *logos* of *sophia* with the *logos* of *pneuma* (1 Cor. 2.13). (Yet, in 1 Cor. 12.8 both kinds of *logos* are considered valid.)

Elsewhere (Rom. 11.25-36, cf. 11.12), Paul engages in a speculation about bringing to fullness (*plēroma*) the incomplete number of converts. Ps.-Ecphantus may be used to show the dissemination of the motif in mystical literature.

166. H 274.4, T 80.22.

167. Goodenough 1928: 91. In Paul it is also *hamartia* that cries for correction. So also the akratic will.

168. ἐνεργάσαιτο δ' ἂν μόνος ὁ βασιλεὺς ἀνθρώπῳ φύσει καὶ τόδε τὸ ἀγαθόν, ὡς διὰ μίμασιν αὐτῷ τῷ κρέσσονος ποτὶ τὸ δέον ἕπεσθαι (H 278.9-12, T 83.9-10).

thousands of religious-philosophical texts like it: Hermetic and Gnostic texts, mystery religion propaganda, some of Philo's works, and many mystical writings of the first centuries CE. The tone of these texts is also Paul's. Both Ps.-Ecphantus and Paul, however, exhibit a difference from these other rueful opera. Both bring to this discourse some affirmation of the earthly world that is alien to those other, more alienated writings. In Paul as in Ps.-Ecphantus, the terrestrial state remains relevant.[169]

Several of the terms used by Ps.-Ecphantus in this section have distinct parallels in Paul. *Astheneia*,[170] weakness *as the human condition*, is encountered in dozens of Pauline passages. Paul's most impressive, seemingly paradoxical, use of the concept is to make it a sign of election (e.g., in 1 Cor. 1.25; 12.22). (One can be certain that a term or idea taken from the Hellenistic environment has become a technical term in Paul, that it has been singled out for attention, when he subjects it to this reversal process.) Paul, like Ps.-Ecphantus, makes the weakness of human nature the very reason why *Logos*, God (in Paul), gives attention to human beings. For Paul, as for Ps.-Ecphantus, only a radical act of divine intervention can overcome the weakness of human nature. *Astheneia* was the peoples' state when Christ died (Rom. 5.6);[171] *astheneia* suffuses human understanding while in its sarkic envelope (Rom. 6.19); *astheneia* is relieved by the *pneuma* (Rom. 8.26).

In Ps.-Ecphantus, *Peithō*, Persuasion, is planted (*ephuē*) by the Logos. 'Planting' (*phuteia* and the many derivatives from φύω) is a favorite trope of mystical writers, and the expression is there in Paul as well.[172] In Paul the most dramatic instance of its use occurs in Rom. 6.5, where those planted with Christ (σύμφυτοι) in imitation (τῷ ὁμοιώματι) of his death will also rise with him. (Incidentally, the difficult expression τῷ ὁμοιώματι becomes intelligible when the Hellenistic, and especially the Pythagorean, background is taken into consideration: resemblance, likeness, similarity are variations of the concept of imitation.)

---

169. The lexicon, ideas, and the imagery of Gnosticism in Paul form the object of scores of scholarly studies, beginning with Reitzenstein 1904 and Bossuet 1907. Among the recent comprehensive studies of the manifold issues are Pagels 1975, A. Segal 1977, Fossum 1985, Burkert 1987, Maccoby 1991, Theis 1991, Wink 1993.

170. In the forms ἀσθένεια, ἀσθενέω, ἀσθένημα, ἀσθενής.

171. Among other examples drawn from Romans alone: the law weakened by the flesh (Rom. 8.3); the weak member of the *ekklēsia* in Rom. 14.

172. It would make little sense in an urban environment if it were not connected with σπέρμα, seed, and thus have a germinative, sexual meaning.

A final example: the verb *peithō*, with a variety of meanings determined by mood and tense, is so heavily employed by Paul as practically to become one of his marks. If one looks at just a few of these uses, even chosen randomly, one learns a revealing lesson. Disobedience of truth derives from mutinous spirit; against this, coercion—the wrath and fury of God—must be exerted (Rom. 2.8). Elsewhere Paul derides persuasion, as if aware of its low, human-contaminated origin (as he most likely was): he addresses the Corinthians not with persuasive (human) words of wisdom[173] but with the (instantaneously persuasive) proofs of the spirit and (magical) power: the first are of human origin, the second of God (1 Cor. 2.4-5). Notice how *logos* and *peithō* are both coupled and decoupled. Paul's *logos* works not by human persuasiveness but by divine *pneuma* and *dunamis*. Elsewhere (2 Cor. 5.11), persuasion and fear (*phobos*) are paired as human instruments, just as in Ps.-Ecphantus. For both authors, the persuasion imagery and vocabulary are similar. Persuasion, associated with coercion and fear, is an inferior aspect of the *logos*. The need for persuasion results from rebellion, vice and ignorance (cf. Rom. 2.19). The direct efficacy of divine power and spontaneous imitation are contrasted with it. Even if Paul is not consciously using the Hellenistic Pythagorean doctrine, the way in which he employs terms and makes associations shows his affiliation to a cultural background and inheritance mediated by Pythagoreanism.

Fragment #4.[174] In the last preserved fragment of 'On Kingship', Ps.-Ecphantus reiterates the most important political virtues of God and the king. First, κοινωνία (*koinōnia*): social disposition, liberality, fellowship.[175] Then, *dikaiosunē*, justice,[176] which has the determining role in

---

173. πειθός as an adjective is a hapax. This is, incidentally, an anti-intellectual attack in good Cynic vein. See Downing 1992: 32-39.

174. Stobaeus 4.7.66 pp. 278.21-279.20 Hense = T (#4) 83.18-84.8 = L. Delatte 1942: 35-37 (Greek), 51-52 (French trans.), 241-44 (Commentary); Goodenough 1928: 86-88.

175. οὐ μὰν ἀλλ᾽ ὅτι γε δίκαιος ἐσσεῖται κοινωνικὸς ὢν παντὶ τῳ δᾶλον (H 279.1-2, 19, T 83.21, 84.9).

In Plutarch, *Table-Talk* 9.746a, κοινωνητική is associated with πολιτική in a phrase meaning 'social and political science' (*ap.* L. Delatte 1942: 98). I may add that this science/art is overseen by a muse and maintained by Persuasion, Πειθώ, who calms down rebellious spirit.

176. ἰσότατι γὰρ ἁ κοινωνία καὶ ἐν τᾷ ταύτας ἀποδιανομᾷ ἐξάρχει μὲν ἁ δικαιοσύνα, μετέχει δ᾽ ἁ κοινωνία· οὐ γὰρ δυνατὸν ἄδικον μὲν ἦμεν, μεταδιδόμεν δὲ

the 'distribution of equality' (ἀποδιανομή ἰσότητος).[177] Third, ἐγκρατέα (*enkrateia*), self-restraint.[178] This is an important condition for *autarkeia*.[179] And, fourth, φρόνησις (*phronēsis*): practical wisdom, prudence.[180] They are all political *aretai*, and all are intertwined.

This text (together with Ps.-Ecphantus's earlier discussions of *koinōnia*) permits us to make a number of important observations. The Hellenistic Pythagorean understands *koinōnia* not just as a term for a social group but also as a political *aretē*, a defining attribute of the divine ruler. Although used by the ancient Pythagoreans and by Plato, the meaning of *koinōnia* deepens in Hellenistic times. It integrates the *polis* and the universe and, while not canceling the distinction between the two worlds, emphasizes the harmony and synergy between them. At the same time, it communicates the king's political role.[181] Because of the king's *koinōnia*, the people have the chance to achieve *aretē* and to establish a relation to the universe at large.[182] In Paul, too, *koinōnia*

ἰσότατος, ἢ μεταδιδόμεν μὲν ἰσότατος, μὴ κοινωνικὸν δὲ ἦμεν (H 279.2-6, T 83.21-24). *Dikaiosunē* is listed first in the final summary: ουδ' ὁ βασιλεὺς δὴ χωρὶς φρονάσιος ταύτας ἂν ἔχοι τὰς ἀρετάς, δικαιοσύναν φαμὶ καὶ ἐγκράτηαν καὶ κοινωνίαν καὶ ὅσα τούτων ἀδελφά (H 279.17-19, T 84.6-8).

177. H 279.2-3, T 83.21-22.

178. ἐγκρατέα δὲ πῶς οὐκ ἂν ὑπολάβοι τις τὸν αὐτάρκη; ἁ γὰρ πολυτέληα μάτηρ τᾶς ἀκρασίας, αὕτα δὲ τᾶς ὕβριος, ἐξ ἇς τῶν ἐν ἀνθρώποις κακῶν τὰ πολλά. ἁ δ' αὐτάρκηα οὐδ' ἂν τέκοι πολυτέλειαν οὔτε τὰ ἀπ' αὐτᾶς, ἀλλὰ αὐτῶ τις οὖσα ἀρχὰ πάντα μέν ἀγοῖ, ἀγοῖτο δ' ἂν ὑπ' οὐδενός· ὅπερ ἔντι μὲν τῶ θεῶ, ἔντι καὶ τῶ βασιλεῖ, αὐτῶ μὲν ἄρχεν (ἀφ' ὦπερ καὶ ὁ αὐτάρκης καλέεται), ἄρχεσθαι δ' ὑπ' οὐδενός (H 279.6-14, 19; T 83.25-84.3, 9).

179. *Autarkeia* is defined from its (surmised) etymology: αὐτῶ [=αὐτοῦ] ἄρχεν, to govern oneself (H 279.12-13, T 84.2-3).

180. ταῦτα δ' ὅτι μὲν φρονάσιος ἐκτὸς οὐκ ἂν γένοιτο, δᾶλον, ὅτι δ' ἁ τῶ κόσμω φρόνασις ὁ θεός ἐντι, φανερόν· συνέχεται γὰρ εὐκοσμία τε καὶ τάξει τᾶ δεούσᾳ· νόω δὲ χωρὶς οὐκ ἂν αὐτὰ γενοίατο (H 279.14-17, T 84.4-6).

181. Cicero translates *koinōnia* as *communitas*, and designates by it the community of world and city but also the virtue that characterizes the king vis-à-vis his subjects (*ap.* L. Delatte 1942: 241). Hellenistic Pythagoreanism makes 'community' the virtue of one. This remarkable political enallage that substitutes the singular for the plural, is fully consistent with the mystical-monarchical doctrine of Hellenistic Pythagoreanism.

182. For κοινωνία in this sense see 1 Cor. 1.9 (with Christ), 10.16-17 (with the blood and body of Christ); 10.18 (of the people of Israel), cf. 10.20 (with demons); 2 Cor. 1.7 (with Paul), 13.13 (with holy spirit), cf. 6.14 (of light with darkness);

assumes a dual role: it names the community while also denoting a quality of the community's members. It describes a political (and mystical-political) reality and a political quality.[183] This *aretē* is philanthropy. Paul is perhaps the first to use the term *koinōnia* in the sense of 'charity', 'donation' or 'contribution'. This meaning arises, however, from the social vocabulary of the *polis* and is prefigured in the Hellenistic Pythagoreans. It is an extension of the fellowship and liberality that are characteristic of life in the *polis*.[184]

In Ps.-Ecphantus, the king's *koinōnia* is tied with *dikaiosunē*, and thus establishes once more the political force of *dikaiosunē*. *Dikaiosunē* is at the same time a royal *aretē* and the inner mechanism of a political society. It is the gravitational force of the *koinōnia*. Society, says Ps.-Ecphantus, exists because of equality (ἰσότης, *isotēs*).[185] *Isotēs* is a political term drawn from the Classical lexicon of the *polis*, where it is tied with *dikaiosunē*.[186] *Isotēs* appears twice in 2 Cor. 8.13-14, where it refers to a democratic-type equality, in which burden and abundance are equitably shared between *ekklēsiai*.[187] For Ps.-Ecphantus, *dikaiosunē* is what determines the 'distribution of equality'.[188] In Paul, as we have

Gal. 2.9 (of Paul with other apostles), 6.6 (all Christians); Phil. 1.5 (*euangelion* fellowship), 2.1 (with holy spirit); 3.10 (with Christ's suffering).

183. 2 Cor. 1.7 and Phil. 3.10 makes *koinōnia* a quality akin to suffering, the mark of a true Christian.

184. Rom. 12.13 (verb); 15.26; 2 Cor. 8.4; 9.13; Gal. 6.6.

185. *Isotēs* is also a topos of Hellenistic moralists. In this case its meaning leans towards equity. In 2 Cor. 8, Paul's rhetoric could be read as depending on a series of antitheses leading to *isotēs* (but see below). See Stählin 1964: 354-55; Meeks 1983: 66.

186. The classical locus is Plato, *Laws* 6.757a-e. He discusses there the two kinds of *isotēs*, one 'simple', used by states in the distribution of honours, the other 'proportional', the 'judgment of Zeus' and the true political justice. See also Aristotle, *Politics* 3.1279a9, cf. 3.1280a10-22; 5.1302a7.

187 Georgi reads *isotēs* in this passage thus: 'legal equality of all citizens, realized in the democratic order of Greek cities. At the same time, ἰσότης is also the source of righteous activity in a general sense [presumably in relation to the good and just man], not just of that of the judge. The term is closely linked to *dikaiosunē*' (Georgi 1992: 85). Georgi traces the concept in Philo and notes how it moves from the idea of community in Greek thinking to becoming an ahistorical concept in the Hellenistic-Jewish Gnostic wisdom tradition (1992: 86, 138-40). It certainly has a different fate in Paul, where it is a political, community-based and historical concept. It is *dikaiosunē* that while keeping centerstage becomes disembodied.

188. ἀποδιανομή ἰσότητος (cf. H 279.2-3, T 83.21-22). Obviously, says Ps.-

seen, *dikaiosunē* is the prerogative of the divine; it is distributed according to *analogia*, and the *pneuma* and the *charis* of each member of the Christian state are dependent on it.

Ps.-Ecphantus binds together *autarkeia*[189] and *enkrateia*. Self-rule depends on self-control. In Paul, *enkrateia*[190] completes the list of *pneuma*'s rewards for those who will enter into God's *basileia* (Gal. 5.23). The opposite of *enkrateia* is *akrateia* (or *akrasia*), incontinence, intemperance. It is engendered by *poluteleia*,[191] sensual extravagance; it leads to *hubris*, rebellion, the source of all evils.[192] Ps.-Ecphantus enables us to confirm and clarify the political nature of Paul's accusation that the Greeks indulge the senses.[193] The fault with which Paul consistently charges them is incontinence or immoderation (ἀκράτεια, *akrateia*, or ἀκρασία, *akrasia*). *Akrateia* is the contrary of *enkrateia*, and though Paul does use *akrateia* (1 Cor. 7.5), he also expresses this concept through a variety of descriptive periphrases, including it in the larger category of *hamartia*. Conceptually, the Greeks' infamy is the result of *akrateia*. They violate a political *aretē, enkrateia*. Given the interlocking quality of these *aretai*, surrender to desire affects *koinōnia, dikaiosunē* and *phronēsis* and thus endangers the *polis*. The Greeks' defiance of the genuine God, revealed in nature as creator (Rom. 1.19),[194] is nothing less then political insurrection.

Ecphantus, *koinōnia* shares in this process, for no distribution can occur without the social inclination of the king (H 279.4-5, T 83.23-24).

189. Though brought to the fore by the Stoics, *autarkeia* as a primary characteristic of the king is known to Isocrates, *To Nicocles* 29, or Socrates, in the fragment preserved by Stobaeus 4.7.26, H 4.255 (*ap.* Goodenough 1928: 57, 70, 87 and n. 106). The equivalent of the kingly *autarkeia* is *sōphrosunē* in Plato, *Politicus* 267b, 275c; *Laws* 12.966e-968a, esp. 12.967e. This is precisely the term used by Diotogenes in a similar passage about the king (H 268.11, T 74.16). The fragment relates more strongly to Plato than to the Stoics. In general, Stoicism itself only transferred the notion that kings should be philosophers to the *sophos*, the wise man. See Goodenough 1928: 87 and nn. 107-108.

190. It must be possessed even by an athlete running for a perishable Olympic crown, says Paul (1 Cor. 9.25).

191. Synonymous with *truphē*.

192. The chain of defeats, πολυτέλεια-ἀκρασία-ὕβρις-κακία τὰ πολλά, excess-intemperance-outrage-all evils (H 279.7-9, T 83.25-27) is also known to Hippodamos.

193. E.g., Rom. 1.24-32; 8.5-8; Phil. 3.19.

194. Bultmann (1955: 135-37) reads Stoic natural theology. The idea that nature reveals God, however, would seem to predate the Stoics in Rom. 1.19.

Finally, Ps.-Ecphantus repeats the view that the reason (*phronesis*) of the universe is God, a fact that is evident in the fine arrangement and order (*eukosmia* and *taxis*) of the world. This is also implied in Paul's argument for the existence of God based on the beauty and order that can be seen in the things he has made (Rom. 1.20). For Ps.-Ecphantus, *phronēsis* is also the cause of bonding and unity.[195] This is exactly the sense in which Paul uses *phroneō* in Rom. 12.16: 'Live in harmony with one another' (τὸ αὐτὸ εἰς ἀλλήλους φρονοῦντες). Paul continues, 'Do not think conceitedly [μὴ τὰ ὑψηλὰ φρονοῦντες], but associate with the humble. Do not think that you are wise [μὴ γίνεσθε φρόνιμοι παρ' ἑαυτοῖς]'. This passage, remarkable for its use of the *phroneō* semantic group, represents the function of the term in Paul quite well. There is a sarkic *phronēma* mindset, inimical to God and his law, that leads to death, and there is a pneumatic one of life and peace (Rom. 8.6-7). Another revealing pericope is Rom. 12.3, where the opposites ὑπερφρονεῖν (*huperphronein*, 'to think arrogantly') and σωφρονεῖν (*sōphronein* 'to think prudently') are presented as forms of *phronein*, to great rhetorical effect. This paronomasia introduces a sequence of politically momentous passages: *pistis* is disbursed by God, just as *dikaiosunē* is in the Classical philosophers and the Hellenistic Pythagoreans, according to a certain measure (ἑκάστῳ ὡς ὁ θεὸς ἐμέρισεν μέτρον πίστεως) (Rom. 12.3c). This reference to the principle of distributive justice immediately leads Paul to a central topos of his political thought: the body metaphor (Rom. 12.4-5).

Ps.-Ecphantus's presentation of the connection between subjects and their relation to God, like his treatment of the ties between state and universe, emphasizes integration and consolidation, affinity and concord, parallelism and cooperation. In these fragments the distance between human and divine worlds is an ever-shrinking one. The dynamic certainly reflects real political developments of Hellenistic times. The rapprochement between the king and God is necessary not only to validate the increasingly extravagant claims of the state but also to guarantee its stability.

Transcendent politics brings the human and the divine together. The

195. H 279.16-17, T 84.5-6. L. Delatte (1942: 243) credits the use of *phronēsis* to the ancient Pythagoreans through Plato's *Philebus* 28c-e, 30d, where the cosmic order is due to a divine *phronēsis*, where intelligence and wisdom, *nous* and *phronēsis*, order and govern the universe (28d), and the *nous* is called the mind of a *basileus* (28c).

collapse of the king and God into one another is imminent, and it carries with it the promise that the human world will be absorbed into the divine. The ever-increasing (especially downward) traffic between the realms gives the feeling that God is ready to take over a messy, lost humanity, and this addresses the fierce need to bring God into one's own life and assuages the growing, implacable mood of alienation and loss of individual will and selfhood. Certainly, doctrines like Ps.-Ecphantus's give strength and stability to the state, but they also help stabilize and bolster the individual. In such doctrines the state finds its power infinitely expanded and made eternal; the individual finds his soul, whole and saved.

Mystical philosophies of Hellenistic times—Hellenistic Pythagoreanism and Christianity among them—have deep roots in the politics of Hellenistic kingship. Like many others, Ps.-Ecphantus realized that the common person's temper of alienation and dejection and the explosive distemper of the mob had to be addressed. It seems to have appeared to him, as it did to others, that the cause of psychological and social problems lay in the failure of politics to justify its absolutism with convincing religious trappings. What was needed was, first, a cult of the ruler—a heightening of the king's divinity to the point where the distinction between king and God is erased. (It bears noting that Ps.-Ecphantus is actually only reworking a process—a powerfully focused propoganda machine—that was already well established.) Ps.-Ecphantus (and the Hellenstic Pythagoreans generally) make God's universe one with the royal topography, and participation in a sacralized world as a king-emulator is open to everyone. (True, all become kings not in the *polis* but in the universe, not state administrators but cosmic citizens.) These authors explode the state's geography and duration to cosmic scale. While the expanded Hellenistic and Roman empires left less room for public life, the capacious and timeless universe restored political exposure to everyone. This distension absorbs any penchant for insurgency, any threat to the state.

The monarchic mysticism that develops—a royal mystique in which the king becomes the avenue to virtue and salvation—satisfies ruler and subject alike. Democracy and theocracy collude. In the Hellenistic Pythagoreans as in Paul, what is being produced is a universal household, a compact vastly removed from the structures of genuine political power but one that renders power as real as it is irrelevant. The household of God, the alliance of political authority and divine redemption, is the

234   *The Political Paul*

prolific, seductive framework in which to live, think, write, teach. One becomes a participant in the cosmic game having lost all say in the *polis*. And this construct possesses yet another outstanding feature. The re-invention of public life by the Hellenistic Pythagoreans means that the isolated lunatic or the misanthropic solitary, the obscure Gnostic or the self-sufficient Cynic, loses his appeal. The individual is incorporated into the universal household as a member of the state, as part of the constitutional arrangement; one is saved socially and collectively, not as a lonely wise man or recluse.

Paul intensifies this approach, giving it historical credibility and divine immediacy. In binding the universe in one bundle, both Ps.-Ecphantus and Paul retain one distinctive aspect of Classical political life, one to which ancient men were romantically attached and one that also happened to be very useful to the reformer: fondness for the *polis*. Despite democracy's Classical detractors, this feeling had always been, and continued to be, identified with democracy.[196] As democratic recollection becomes fainter, the deluded and the disillusioned—the illumination seeker, the wisdom devotee, the libertine, the magic dazzler, a host of respectable loners and enticers of the gasping rabble—incessantly splinter society with promises of spiritual delivery. Such divisions makes it harder to force people into orderly and organized—political—transcendence. Only this paradoxical promise of democracy—practically ineffectual yet ontologically redemptive—ensures the stability of the state and guarantees salvation to its citizens at the same time.

Diotogenes: περὶ βασιλείας (peri basileias), On Kingship

Diotogenes (most likely not a pseudonym) lived in southern Italy, perhaps around the first to second century CE.[197] Fragments of his *Peri basileias* are preserved in Stobaeus.[198]

196. Despite Plato's hatred for democracy, this was one of the most protracted features of ancient political feeling. Dio Chrysostom in his περὶ βασιλείας, *Third Discourse on Kingship*, probably delivered in front of Trajan on the emperor's birthday on 18 September 104 CE, suggests that democracy is the best yet least practicable human society because it rests upon the expectation that an equitable constitution based on law can come from the self-control and virtue of the mob, τρίτη δὲ πασῶν ἀδυνατωτάτη σχεδὸν ἡ σωφροσύνη καὶ ἀρετῇ δήμου προσδοκῶσά ποτε εὑρήσειν κατάστασιν ἐπιεικῆ καὶ νόμιμον, δημοκρατία προσαγορευομένη... (*Discourses* 3.47).

197. L. Delatte 1942: 108-109. Diotogenes' possible dates range, however, from

Fragment #1. According to Diotogenes, the king has a double aspect: as ruler and as human individual. Diotogenes begins by presenting the political persona of the king.

1.1.[199] The most just man would be king, the most lawful would be the most just. Without *dikaiosunē*, 'justice', no one could be king, and without *nomos*, law, there is no justice. For the lawful (τὸ δίκαιον) is of the law and the law is the cause of the lawful. The king is either the living law (νόμος ἔμψυχος, *nomos empsuchos*) or the lawful ruler (νόμιμος ἄρχων, *nomimos archōn*). This is why the king is the most just and the most lawful.

Diotogenes' reasoning goes as follows. Justice is a function of the law. The law necessarily results in true justice. The king is animate law.[200] As such he is most lawful and most just. The relation law—justice—king is the symmetrical reverse of animate law—most just—most lawful. The king is the bond. The king is the intermediary, the criterion of legality and the impartial agent of justice. Political and transcendental functions are combined in the king.[201] Diotogenes observes that the king is either *nomos empsuchos* or a constitutional ruler, the latter concept echoing Classical political theory.[202] Ps.-Archytas, Diotogenes' predecessor, had already characterized the king

Hellenistic times through the second century CE.

198. Stobaeus 4.7.61, H 263.14-265.12 = T 71.16-72.23, L. Delatte 1942: 37-39 (Greek), 52-53 (French trans.), 245-55 (Commentary); Goodenough 1928: 65-69.

199. H 263.15-20, T 71.18-23; L. Delatte 1942: 245-49; Goodenough 1928: 65-66. Βασιλεύς κ᾽ εἴη ὁ δικαιότατος, δικαιότατος δὲ ὁ νομιμώτατος. ἄνευ μὲν γὰρ δικαιοσύνας οὐδεὶς ἂν εἴη βασιλεύς, ἄνευ δὲ νόμω <οὐ> δικαιοσύνα. τὸ μὲν γὰρ δίκαιον ἐν τῷ νόμῳ ἐντί, ὁ δέ γε νόμος αἴτιος τῷ δικαίῳ, ὁ δὲ βασιλεὺς ἤτοι νόμος ἔμψυχός ἐντι ἢ νόμιμος ἄρχων· διὰ ταῦτ᾽ οὖν δικαιότατος καὶ νομιμώτατος.

200. This is a given, assumed known and not explained, a self-evident axiom requiring no demonstration.

201. The Stoics think much along these lines about the wise man; they drop, however, the critical political context. See Goodenough 1928: 65.

202. The third and last fragment (Stobaeus 4.1.133, H 79-81 = T 76.21-77.9) of Diotogenes' other preserved treatise, περὶ ὁσιότητος, *On Piety*, 'presents a picture of a city-state consciousness apparently undisturbed by any conception of a higher source of law than the will and conduct of the people as a whole. It could have been written and received with perfect propriety in any of the democratic cities of Greece', Goodenough 1928: 64-65. It is another instance of the perfect and unavailing assimilation of the political texts of Classical Greece and of its ideals.

as *nomos empsuchos* but had resisted the idea of absolute kingship.[203] The expression βασιλεὺς νόμος ἔμψυχος (*basileus nomos empsuchos*) has, of course, a long history,[204] but there is a crucial difference between the rational approach of Plato and Aristotle, followed by the more formal philosophical schools, and that of Hellenestic political theory, exemplified by Diotogenes. Diotogenes, like other Hellenistic mystical writers—and like Paul—elaborates a mystical monarchic theory that singles out the king as a being with a unique ontological status straddling the human and the divine. His prerogatives are not just God-sanctioned; rather, he *is* a God. (Not all Hellenistic Pythagoreans would put it precisely this way.)

Louis Delatte is, I think, incorrect in concluding that Diotogenes distinguishes between the law and the will of the prince. If the Pythagorean separates the *nomos empsuchos* from the *nomimos archōn*, kingship as animate law versus kingship as constitutional polity, this is only an atavistic political reflex, not the result of reflection.[205] Diotogenes' affirmations of law have no logical status in the unity of his thought, and thus are mere relics of an older, now alien, discourse of which Diotogenes has taken the impress. Where Paul praises the law, this is likewise a dim echo of older political discourse. Paul's restraint, however, has a further motivation. His concept of *polis* demands the inclusion of the Jews, and he is cautious not to rouse their zeal for the law. In Hellenistic and Roman politics, law is replaced by the authority of the divine king. Paul reflects this political reality in his metaphysical construct. Diotogenes is categorical: the rule of the king is 'unaccountable'

203. Περὶ νόμω καὶ δικαιοσύνας, *On Law and Justice*, Stobaeus 4.1.135, H 82.20; he contrasts the animate law to the written or inanimate one. His *nomos empsuchos* is subject to the written law.

204. Its softened version, 'sens adouci' as L. Delatte calls it, is encountered, in different formulations, in Euripides, Plato, Aristotle, Cicero, Philo, Musonius, Clement of Alexandria, Themistius and Plutarch. It becomes law and the ground for the claim of divine right of kingship in Byzantine (and later) times with its codification in Justinian's *Novellae*, 81.I (p. 473 Zacharia von Lingenthal ed.). See L. Delatte 1942: 245-48.

205. In the second of the three fragments of the treatise *On Piety* (Stobaeus 4.1.96, H 36-38 = T 76.1-20), Diotogenes writes that the one who is truly νόμιμος—lawful—will use the law-courts little and pay more heed to another's rights than his own; Goodenough 1928: 64. This goes back to Plato's *Republic* 3.405a-d, where lawyers and physicians are seen as the sign of the deterioration of the *polis*, the indication of the low state of education. Paul expesses a similar view in 1 Cor. 6.1, 6.

(ἀρχὰ ἀνυπεύθυνος).²⁰⁶ This does not mean, however, that it is inexpert or irresponsible.²⁰⁷

1.2.²⁰⁸ The king is commander (στρατηγός), judge (δικαστής) and priest (ἱερεύς).²⁰⁹ His functions are military (στρατηγεῖν), judicial (δικασπο-λεῖν) and cultic (θεραπεύειν θέως).²¹⁰ His duties are war, justice and religion.²¹¹

1.2.1.²¹² Like any supremely qualified professional—the pilot who saves the ship, the charioteer who steers the chariot, the physician who cures the ill—the king, as military commander, saves his subjects in war. Like the other specialists, he is the leader (ἡγεμών), manager (ἐπιστάτης) and initiator (δημιουργός) of a (political) system (σύστημα), the Pythagorean trademark par excellence.²¹³ These are all political terms.²¹⁴ In all these functions, the king *saves*—the state, the people, the

206. H 265.10, T 72.22.

207. Ps.-Ecphantus wrote that the king is tested and approved by God (H 273.2-3, T 80.7) also, that he is identical in *aretē* with God (H 274.21-275.1, T 81.9-10). See Chapter 8, Romans 2 and Romans 7, for discussion of *nomos* in Paul.

208. H 263.20-265.12, T 71.23-72.23, L. Delatte 1942: 249-55, Goodenough 1928: 66-69.

209. H 264.6-7, T 72.4-5.

210. H 263.21-264.1, T 71.24-25.

211. These are the functions of the king as far back as Homer, cf. Aristotle's description of heroic monarchy, *Politics* 3.1285b5-13.

212. H 264.8-12, T 72.6-9.

213. H 264.11-12, T 72.8-9. Goodenough (1928: 66-7 and n. 44) sees here, rather unconvincingly, a development of Plato's *Laws* 12.957c, on the universal saving *dunamis* of *nous*. I rather think that Diotogenes makes the most extreme and most logical application of the Hellenistic principle of skill and expertise. Politics become a professional field and the king is its supreme authority. The king displays βασιλικὴ ἐπιστήμη, the royal science, an idea found in Plato, *Politicus* 266c, and in Aristotle, *Nicomachean Ethics* 1.1094a27-28. (Goodenough is right only insofar *basilikē epistēmē* is based in *nous*, the analogue of the *sophiai* of other crafts.) Both consider the king a being closer to God than to human, *Politicus* 266c, *Politics* 3.1284a11, 1288a27-28. As such, the king replaces the law.

214. *Epistatēs* was a president in the *boulē* and the *ekklēsia* in Athens; it means also a military leader, and, since second century BCE, governor. *Dēmiourgos* was the name of a magistrate in many Greek states; here the sense is 'organizer', author of contingency plans, of organizational strategies and tactics. See also L. Delatte 250-51. *Epistatēs* is a term dear to Luke, Paul's companion, as a designation of Jesus; the verbal ἐπίσταμαι refers to a prerogative of the king as someone well informed, Acts 26.26. Ἐπιστήμη, knowledge, expertness is a Christian attribute in

mores. Beginning in Hellenistic times, the ability to save subjects' lives (σῴζειν, σωτηρία) is a key feature of political power, especially as wielded by the king. The title σωτήρ (*sōtēr*), savior, is given to numerous Hellenistic kings, and theoretical reflections often make salvation the first duty of the political leader.[215] Here, religion is ancillary to politics. The proliferation of savior gods in the Hellenistic age is a spinoff of the changing nature of kingship. Hermetica and mystery religions, while expressions of social and political dissatisfaction, found their inspiration and lexicon in political theory and reality.[216]

The savior and the theme of salvation are, of course, at the core of the Pauline *euangelion*, as well (e.g. Rom. 1.16; 1 Cor. 15.1-2). This is not the place to develop this topic fully, but I must point out a few instances where the political background of the term emerges especially vigorously. Paul's office (διακονία) is an instrument of salvation (Rom. 11.14); Paul applies whatever strategies are necessary to save men (Rom. 11.11; 1 Cor. 1.21; 10.33); sometimes even when Paul is absent, his *pneuma* saves (1 Cor. 5.5, cf. 2 Cor. 7.10; Phil. 2.12); Paul's own affliction works for the salvation of others (2 Cor. 1.6); the enemy is doomed to death, while those whom Paul leads are saved (Phil. 1.28, cf. 1 Thess. 5.9). Salvation is expressed in military terms in 1 Thess. 5.8, and, finally, there is the remarkable passage in Phil. 3.20 where *sōtēr* and *politeuma*, savior and body politic, are associated.

1.2.2.[217] As judge, whether he administers public or private law (ξυνός [or κοινός] or ἴδιος νόμος),[218] the king acts as God does in his leadership and command of the universe. In public matters, the king brings the whole kingdom into harmony by his sole rule; exercising the same leadership, he brings accord in private matters. The king is also a benefactor (εὐεργέτης), concerned with treating his subjects well (ποιεῖν εὖ) and benefiting (εὐεργετεῖν) them.[219] This is not possible without

Phil. 4.8, *varia lectio*. The author of Hebrews makes God the δημιουργός of the *polis*, Heb. 11.10.

215. So Cicero, *Republic* 1.35.54, 2.26.47, 6.13; Musonius (Stobaeus 4.280.7); Themistius, *Orations* 127.30, 210.17 (L. Delatte 1942: 49-50). See also Dornseiff 1929.

216. Certain well-known mystery religions, such as the cults of Sarapis, of Zeus Dolichenus, of Sol Invictus, as well as the innumerable Hellenistic and Imperial ruler cults, were political stunts, reflections and manifestations of political ploys.

217. H 264.12-265.1, T 72.9-14.

218. H 264.13-14, T 72.10.

219. H 264.19, T 72.14.

dikaiosunē and *nomos*, justice and law.[220]

Although the distinction between *koinos* law and *idios* law had been in use since Aristotle, the Stagirite had understood it as the opposition between natural and state law. Under the Hellenistic monarchies, writes E.R. Goodenough,[221] *nomos koinos* came to mean the king-made law that formed the constitution of the kingdom, while *idios nomos* or *idios logos* came to be associated with the 'private' law of local tradition. Cities could be guided by their own laws in local matters, but the law of the kingdom—that is, the law of the *king*—prevailed. This is consistent with the *nomos empsuchos* view of Hellenistic political treatises.[222]

We notice the same approach in Paul's legal language. On the one hand, there is the contrast between *idia dikaiosunē* and *theou dikaiosunē*. To refer just to some of the most conspicuous examples: Paul opposes the *dikaiosunē* of the Jews (a national, Mosaic, idiosyncratic law) to the universal, Christ-revealed, *pistis*-based *dikaiosunē* of God. God's justice not only takes precedence over Mosaic law—it is its demise (Rom. 10.3-6, cf. Rom. 3.21-22; 8.2; 9.30-31; Gal. 6.2). Paul discards his own, law-based *dikaiosunē* in favor of the justice of God based on *pistis*.[223] The *euangelion* is the paradoxical expression of God's law—a law that applies to Jew, Greek and barbarian alike; a *logos* of *stauros* (Rom. 1.15, 16; 1 Cor. 1.18, 24), a *dunamis* of *astheneia*, a power of weakness (2 Cor. 12.9).

On the other hand, Paul makes use of the stock *nomos-phusis* opposition in drawing the contrast between the human, particular law and the

220. H 265.1, T 72.15.
221. Goodenough 1928: 67-68.
222. L. Delatte gives this a different (but not contradictory) reading. He sees the judiciary work of the king as divided between the state as a whole, *koinos nomos*, and each individual, *idios nomos* (1942: 251). The disparity, I assume, comes from the different meanings of the pair *koinos-idios* in the political and nomological vocabularies of Aristotle. In the political context, the terms designate the opposition public-private, e.g., *Politics* 1265a26; see Bonitz, *s.v.* κοινός, ἴδιος. As part of Aristotle's legal theory, they stand for the natural law-state law distinction. The key passage is *Rhetoric* 1.1373b1-8. There, in the context of the theory of just and unjust actions, Aristotle observes that there are two kinds of law, *idios* and *koinos*, particular law and universal law. The first, partly written, partly unwritten, is that which each state makes for and applies to its citizens. The second is the law of nature, a natural justice and injustice, binding on all human beings.
223. Injustice (ἀδικία) too has a universal aspect; it describes all humanity and stands in counterbalance to the justice of God (e.g., Rom. 3.5, cf. 3.9, 23).

The Political Paul

law of nature, between positive law and divine law. Thus, the people who lack the law (of state) do by nature what the (universal) law requires (Rom. 2.14).[224] The written code of (Jewish) law is no match for inward (*pistis*-granting, *pneuma*-based) law, which for Paul is an analogue of natural law (Rom. 2.27-29, cf. Rom. 7.6, 8.2; Gal. 5.18).

'Benefactor' (εὐεργέτης, *euergetēs*) is possibly the most common epithet applied to the king—indeed, to any excellent man—during the Hellenistic era. 'Benefactor' is equally a title given to gods, especially divinities that function as political props, such as Sarapis, Osiris and Zeus.[225] The term often works in tandem with *sōtēr*.[226] In Diotogenes, however, *euergetēs* is a function of the king *as judge*. Similarly, it is from God's *dikaiosunē* that *charis*[227] and the pneumatic gifts originate in Paul.

As has been pointed out, the king–God analogy is a staple of Hellenistic Pythagorean political thinking. Diotogenes will later reiterate this again[228] in the conceptually and rhetorically best expression of this view: God and *kosmos* stand in the same relationship as do king and *polis*; king-god and state-world form a ratio. The complex chiasm affirms the divinity of the king and the consolidation of the *polis* and the universe. The equivalences bear distinct similarity to the outstanding features of Pauline political and transcendental thought: erasing human law while simultaneously elevating the state, exalting a human ruler to infallible judicature, placing the human state in the hands of a God and making the human a constituent of cosmic perfection.

1.2.3.[229] The cultic duty of the king depends on the notion that the best must honor the best and the ruler must honor the ruling principle. This establishes an indissoluble kinship between God and king and makes the king the pivotal character in the mystical movements of the Hellenistic age. The political and the transcendental form a continuum, and political theory plays a role in metaphysical knowledge. The corre-

224. Höistad reads in this verse the contrast between the law of *poleis* and the law of *aretē* (1948: 113-15). See Chapter 8, discussion of Rom. 2.14.

225. BAGD, LSJ, MM, *s.v.* εὐεργέτης; see also Préaux 1976. The same is stated by Luke, Lk 22.25, Acts 10.38.

226. Nock 1951.

227. *Charis*, another of Paul's terms difficult to translate, is discussed throughout. It essentially refers to God's liberality.

228. Fragment 1.2.4.

229. H 265.1-7, T 72.15-19. δεῖ γὰρ τὸ ἄριστον ὑπὸ τῶ ἀρίστω τιμᾶσθαι καὶ τὸ ἀγεμονοῦν ὑπὸ τοῦ ἀγεμονέοντος (H 265.3-4, T 72.16-18).

spondence between king and God leads to yet other ratios that likewise illuminate the cohesion between politics and divinity, king and universe.

1.2.4.[230] In this section, already referred to, Diotogenes states that king and *polis* are related in the same way as God and *kosmos*; *polis* and *kosmos* stand in the same relation as king and God. The state, a harmonious system of the 'many and diverse', imitates the cosmos, which is likewise well-ordered and harmonized. The king, because he holds 'unaccountable' power[231] and is animated law, appears to be (παρεσχημάτισται) a God among men. *Nomos empsuchos* is an eidetic expression, an eminently Hellenistic idiom, a daring phrase for someone who still embraces the severe ethos of the absolute primacy of the law. It may be argued that *paraschēmatizō* ('appears as', 'pretends to be') carries a derogatory connotation,[232] though the sense here may simply be 'imitation of' God or 'taking the form of' God. In any case, what is new with Diotogenes is that he assimilates king and God at least insofar as the royal office, if not the person, is concerned.[233]

The ambiguity notwithstanding, the rhetorical structure[234] boldly and deftly advances the case for the king as God. Rhetoric perfectly replicates the content; rhetorical strategy and political reality overlap. Diotogenes' theory replicates the political situation in the Hellenistic kingdoms, incessantly warring with each other yet in each of which the king

---

230. H 265.7-12, T 72.19-23. ἔχει δὲ καὶ ὡς θεὸς ποτὶ κόσμον βασιλεὺς ποτὶ πόλιν· καὶ ὡς πόλις ποτὶ κόσμον βασιλεὺς ποτὶ θεόν· ἁ μὲν γὰρ πόλις ἐκ πολλῶν καὶ διαφερόντων συναρμοσθεῖσαι κόσμω σύνταξιν καὶ ἁρνονίαν μεμίμαται, ὁ δὲ βασιλεὺς ἀρχὰν ἔχων ἀνυπεύθυνον καὶ αὐτὸς ὢν νόμος ἔμψυχος, θεὸς ἐν ἀνθρώποις παρεσχημάτισται. Harmony, imitation, ratios are Pythagorean fingerprints and are often found in the works of Hellenistic Pythagoreans. See L. Delatte 254-55.

231. Ἀνυπεύθυνος is rendered by the less subtle Latin mind with the blunt unambiguous term *dictator*. In Aristotle, it describes tyranny proper, as irresponsible rule, *Politics* 6.1295a20. Plato uses it for the kings' administration of justice: ἀνυπεύθυνος ἄρχειν, to rule unaccountably, *Laws* 6.761e.

232. See LSJ *s.v.* παρασχηματίζω, and L. Delatte 1942: 103, 255.

233. L. Delatte 1942: 255.

The term *paraschēmatizō* as used by Diotogenes recalls the difficult expression *morphē theou* in Phil. 2.6. What is less equivocal is that the terminology is Hellenistic and that it incorporates an ambiguity that may come from the awe and alarm that one feels when coming too close to either the God or the king.

234. A dual parallelism: *theos–kosmos* = *basileus–polis*, and *polis–kosmos* = *king–God*.

was at once God and animate law.[235] This text (1.2.4) marks a major moment in the identification of king and God and elaborates a political metaphysics that informs Paul's political-theological thinking.

Fragment #2.[236] In this fragment, Diotogenes produces a compendium for the education of a prince.

2.1.[237] First, Diotogenes focuses on the king as an individual and highlights his character. Three aspects are discussed: Diotogenes warns against pleasures and passions (ἡδονή and πάθος), greed (πλεονεξία) and arrogance (ὑπεροχή). He encourages manliness (ἀνδραγαθία); philanthropy, benevolence and defensive military expenses; and virtue-based authority. Diotogenes sums up the test of a true king thus: one who is moderate (σώφρων) in pleasure, generous (κοινωνητικός) with his goods and prudent (φρόνιμος) and fierce (δεινός) in power.[238] Then he presents a familiar, though modified, psychology. While the tripartite Platonic-Aristotelian division of the soul into ἡγεμονικόν (*hēgemonikon*) (or λογικόν, *logikon*), θυμοειδές (*thumoeides*) and ἐπιθυμητικόν (*epithumēti-kon*), i.e. rational, spirited and appetitive, seems to hold, a number of startling mutations occur. Good and evil (τῶν ἀγαθῶν καὶ τῶν κακῶν) are evenly mixed in each of these three parts. Diotogenes speaks only about the evils. *Pleonexia* ('excess', 'greed') is born in the *hēgou-menon*, the leading part of the soul, for this desire (ἐπιθυμία) is inherent in reason (λογική).[239] On a more common note, ambition and brutality (φιλοτιμία and θηριότης) belong to the *thumoeides*, the spirited element. Finally, love of pleasure (φιλαδονία) is part of the *epithumētikon*, the sensual element, for this constituent of the soul is female and moist.[240] Injustice, because a perfect and composite evil, encompasses the entire soul.[241]

235. Goodenough 1928: 69. He also refers to Kaerst 1968 (first edition 1901): 325-27, who described the personal character of each Hellenistic kingdom.

236. Stobaeus 4.7.62, H 265.13-270.11 = T 72.25-75.16, L. Delatte 1942: 39-45 (Greek), 53-56 (French trans.), 255-73 (Commentary); Goodenough 1928: 69-73.

237. H 265.14-266.19, T 72.25-73.15; L. Delatte 1942: 255-62; Goodenough 1928: 70-71.

238. H 266.7-10, T 73.6-9.

239. ἁ μὲν γὰρ πλεονεκτία γίνεται περὶ τὸ ἀγούμενον μέρος τᾶς ψυχᾶς, λογικὰ γὰρ ἅδ' ἐπιθυμία (H 266.12-14, T 73.10-11).

240. H 266.14-17, T 73.12-14.

241. ἁ δέ γε ἀδικία τελειοτάτα κακία καί σύνθετος ἐᾶσα περὶ ὅλαν γίνεται τὰν ψυχάν (H 266.17-19, T 73.14-15).

Diotogenes' associating *pleonexia* with *logikon*—his putting avarice and passion in the same league with the leading, rational element of the soul—seems impertinent and audacious. His phrase *logikē epithumia*—'rational desire'—strikes one as eccentric even for a Hellenistic mind,[242] but this is an outstanding example of how psychology was being pressed into the service of *Realpolitik*. *Logikē epithumia* is a magnificent example of the power of political interest over the academic discipline of psychology. Kings amass fortunes and are erotically extravagant, acquisitive and sensuous. Psychological theory must be made to fit monarchic practice and doctrine: these traits must be related to the rational and leading part of the soul, for it is the only one that befits the king.[243]

Further, Diotogenes' association of desire and reason is instructive as a sample of Hellenistic oxymoronic excess.[244] Paul provides two other, no less striking, identically patterned illustrations of this love for philosophical and emotional paradox: *rational worship* and *unintelligible reason*. In Rom. 12.1, Paul entreats his readers 'to present your bodies as a rational worship [λογικὴ λατρεία]'; in 1 Cor. 14.9, he refers to 'speech articulating unintelligible reason [μὴ εὔσημον λόγον]'. In Diotogenes, greed cohabits with reason; in Paul, the body is a form of worship engendered by the rational, inarticulate intelligibility. Paul, like the practical philosophers of Hellenistic times, needed to reconcile the

---

242. Goodenough (1928: 71) notes the obvious with unconcealed delight: 'no more shocking breach of Greek philosophic decorum could be imagined...' L. Delatte is not just perplexed, he is concerned. He assumes the text corrupt and undertakes an extensive search for an explanation, and finds one in the moral treatises of the Pythagoreans Metopus and Theages. These thinkers, apparently following Aristotle in a division of the soul into rational and irrational parts (the latter itself divided into the spirited, θυμοειδές, and the sensual, ἐπιθυματικόν), attach to each certain καλὰ (ἀγαθὰ) and certain κακά to produce a complex but coherent moral and psychological theory which may have inspired Diotogenes (1942: 257-62). While commendable for scholarship, L. Delatte's efforts are futile. Metopus (*On Virtue*, in Stobaeus 3.1.115) and Theages, too, connect *pleonexia* with reason, thus retaining the exoticism of the pair, even if *pleonexia* is the vice, κακία, of the rational, λογιστικόν.

243. Wisdom and virtue conspire with greed and folly and both poles are included in the portrait of the divine. Not since Homer have divine beings been so viewed. In a mode characterizing the Hellenistic mood, however, they are humane and cruel, at the same time confident and despairing.

244. For a discussion of a related figure, λογικὴ θυσία, rational sacrifice, in ancient mysticism and its reinterpretation in Christian liturgy see Casel 1924.

Classical notion of the rational pattern that underlies and constitutes the world with Hellenistic awareness of the devastating effects of fate and with the Hellenistic individual's anxiety about his temporal and eternal destiny.

It must also be noted that, for Diotogenes, *adikia*, injustice, is a pervasive evil that has access to all levels of the soul and also a perfect evil, thoroughly corrupting the soul. The analogy between the concept of *adikia* and *hamartia* again forcefully imposes itself. This association gives *hamartia* itself a political connection. For Paul, one is powerless against *hamartia*: its sarkic force annihilates individual action and will (Rom. 7.13-20). It is this *hamartia* that Christ, coming in the likeness of *sarx*, incorporates and vanquishes (Rom. 8.3). Its opposite is *dikaiosunē*, justice, which in Diotogenes as in all Classical political philosophy is the supreme *aretē* that includes all others.[245]

2.2.[246] In the long section that follows, Diotogenes elaborates on the king as public person and on the consequences of the king's being *nomos empsuchos*. This lengthy fragment reads like a manual for a prince, organized by Diotogenes into a series of brief chapters on major issues.

2.2.1.[247] The passage begins by stating the theory of the divine right of monarchy: leadership is from God (ᾧ δέδωκεν ὁ θεὸς αὐτῷ τὰν ἀγεμονίαν).[248] This doctrine is widespread in the imperial Roman period.[249] Paul shares exactly the same view in Rom. 13.1-7, where the

---

245. See fragment 2.2.4, on goodness. In Plato's *Republic* 4.443c-444a, for example, *dikaiosunē* is the foremost feature of both state and individual. This concept is derived from Pythagoreanism; *dikaiosunē* is a harmony in which each component performs its own function and the binding and harmonizing force compelling them to do so. (See Goodenough 1928: 71.) *Adikia* is a civil war, a *stasis*, among the parts that form the soul or the state (*Republic* 4.444b).

246. H 266.19-270.11, T 73.15-75.16, L. Delatte 1942: 262-73; Goodenough 1928: 71-73.

247. H 266.19-23, T 73.15-19. ὅθεν ὡς λύραν καὶ πόλιν εὐνομουμέναν δεῖ συναρμόσασθαι βασιλέα ὅρον δικαιότατος καὶ νόμω τάξιν ἐν αὐτῷ πρᾶτον καταστησάμενον, εἰδότα διότι τῷ πλάθεος...ἁ συναρμογὰ ποτ' αὐτὸν ὀφείλει συναρμοσθῆμεν.

248. H 266.22, T 73.18.

249. It is encountered in Philo, *Leg. Gai.* 50, Seneca, *On Mercy* 1.2, Aelius Aristides, *Orations* 102, Dio Chrysostom, *Discourses* 2.45, Pliny the Younger, *Panegyric* 1.10, Themistius, *Orations* 3.11; 10.3; 85.19; 87.12; 141.15; 142.1; 219.17; 277.20 (*ap.* L. Delatte 1942: 262). See also Chapter 8, Rom. 13.1-7.

rulers are described as deriving their authority from God.[250] The immediate and foremost implication of this claim is that a properly governed state is tuned like a lyre, as the king's soul itself knows the harmony and order reflected in his government.[251]

2.2.2.[252] Diotogenes produces a Hellenistic version of Machiavelli's *The Prince*, a treatise intended to groom the ruler for the part that he is destined to play. Indeed, Diotogenes and his Renaissance counterpart have the same objective: stability, the harmony (as Diotogenes puts it) of the state. The general principle is that, in order to play the political game convincingly and to appear to mean business, the good king's bodily dispositions and mental habits must seem neither harsh nor contemptible. The king must appear pleasant and ever-vigilant.[253] This is accomplished in three ways: by majesty,[254] by goodness[255] and by fierceness.[256] Diotogenes then expatiates on each of these facets of the king. In the discussion, Diotogenes exhibits impressive psychological subtlety, political acumen and metaphysical depth.[257]

---

250. οὐ γὰρ ἔστιν ἐξουσία εἰ μὴ ὑπὸ θεοῦ... (Rom. 13.1b). Other Christian authors appeal to it as well, e.g., Tertullian, *Apologeticus* 30, 33, Eusebius, *Praise to Constantine* (*ap.* L. Delatte 1942: 262-63 n. 1).

251. The analogy soul–state and the notion of *dikaiosunē* as harmony and order goes back to Plato and the Classical Pythagoreans.

252. H 267.1-16, T 73.19-74.5.

253. ...δεῖ καὶ διαθέσιας καὶ ἕξιας ἐπιπρεπέας ἐπιταδεύεν τὸν ἀγαθὸν βασιλέα, πολιτικῶς αὐτὸν πλάσσοντα καὶ πραγματειωδέως ὅπος μήτε τραχὺς φαίνηται τοῖς πλάθεσι μήτ᾽ εὐκαταφρόνητος ἀλλὰ καὶ ἁδὺς καὶ ἀμφιστραφής (H 267.1-5, T 73.20-23).

254. Σεμνός, in poise, speech and dignity of office, H 267.5-7, T 73.23-24.

255. Χρηστός. This goodness must be: in conversation, ἐντεύξιος; in appearance, ποτιβλέψιος; in benefactions, εὐεργεσίαι (H 267.7-8, T 73.25-26). In 1 Tim. 2.1-2, 4.5, *enteuxios* means intercession, i.e. conversation with God. In 1 Tim. 6.2, good behavior is required of Christian slaves towards Christian masters, especially since those who benefit by their service, *euergesia*, are brothers. Ignatius of Antioch uses the verb (προσβλέπειν) to say that one must 'look upon the bishop as the Lord himself' (Ignatius, *Eph.* 6.1, *ap.* BAGD *s.v.* προσβλέπω 719a).

256. Δεινός. Fierceness describes prompt reaction to evil and quick dispatch of enemies; it also refers to the king's craft, ἔμπειρος, and to his endurance, τρίβος (H 267.9-11, T 73.26-28). The king's μισοπονηρίας (H 267.9, T 73.26), hatred of evil, is the opposite of πονηρία, which figures in the Pauline lists of vices, following injustice (Rom. 1.29), or paired with κακία (1 Cor. 5.8).

257. There are many parallels to this triad in the Hellenistic age. L. Delatte (1942: 264-67) shows some of the most important: Cicero, *On Moral Duties*; Philo, *Praem. Poen.* 97; Seneca, *On Mercy* 1.13.4; Aelius Aristides, *Orations* 106, etc.

2.2.3.[258] The language and the ideas expressed in this section, on the kingly attribute of majesty, are tantalizingly similar to the 'Philippian hymn' (Phil. 2.6-11). Both texts are intensely Hellenistic in mood, originate in a political landscape, and display a mystical vista.

Diotogenes' fragment, which for the most part is didactic and prosaic, here abruptly turns vividly poetical and mysterious. *Dignitas* (σεμνότης) is an essential feature of the king.[259] He must do nothing base (ταπεινόν) but only things that elicit admiration and are appropriate to the royal prerogatives. He must not compete with inferiors or even with equals (τοῖς ἴσοις), but only with superiors. The king must not draw enjoyment from licentiousness[260] but from good and great deeds.[261] He must stay distant from the human passions and keep close to the gods (συνεγίζοντα δὲ τοῖς θεοῖς),[262] not in haughtiness but in nobility of soul and greatness of excellence. He must be distinguished and dignified in appearance, thought, words, habits, actions, bearing and attitude. Transfixed as they are by his majesty, moderation and distinction, those who gaze on him are made beautiful, able to transcend their own nature.[263] Contemplation of the good king affects the souls of those who contemplate him just as listeners are affected by the music of the flute and harmony.[264] Gazing (προσαύγασις [Dor. προταύγασις]) in awe (κατάπληξις) upon the king transfigures the soul of the viewer and instantly produces in it a perception of the divine. In other words, a numinous experience is produced through the mediation of a political personage; mystical ecstasy—common in all mystery and Gnostic-type religions—

258. H 267.16-268.14, T 74.5-19.

259. The attention accorded *semnotēs* in Pauline circles has been noted *supra*, under Ps.-Charondas. 1 Tim. 2.1-2 has been mentioned before for the use of *enteuxios*. In the same passage *semnotēs* appears, as the purpose of this intercession on behalf of the king: dignified life.

260. μὴ τὰς ἐπὶ τοῖς ἀκολάστοις (H 268.2, T 74.9).

261. This passage recalls Paul's ἀλλὰ ἀπειπάμεθα τὰ κρυπτὰ τῆς αἰσχύνης... (2 Cor. 4.2): 'but we have renounced the things hidden because of shame'. The context there has to do, however, with the office of *diakonos* (4.1) and the treatment of the λόγος τοῦ θεοῦ (4.2).

262. H 268.4, T 74.10.

263. ὥστε τὼς ποταυγασμένως αὐτὸν κατακοσμηθῆμεν καταπεπλαγμένως αἰδοῖ καὶ σωφροσύνᾳ διαθέσει τε τᾷ περὶ τὰν ἐπιπρέπῃαν (H 268.9-10, T 73.15-17).

264. οὐ γὰρ μῆον αὐλῶ καὶ ἀρμονίας <ἁ> τῶ ἀγαθῶ βασιλέως ποταύγασις ὀφείλει τρέπεν τὰς ψυχὰς τῶν ποταυγασμένων (H 268.12-14, T 73.17-19).

occurs in the context of a *political* initiation, with the king playing the role of hierophant.

Though born in an exalted estate, the cosmic hero of the Pauline myth does not take his divinity, his equality with God (τὸ ἐιναι ἰσα θεῷ) as a given. He is born a man, becomes a slave, humbles himself (ἐταπείνωσεν), endures the absolute degradation of the cross, and in this act of supreme, active obedience, he is raised to a station higher than the original one and receives recognition from the beings of all echelons of the cosmos. Though Diotogenes' king and Paul's Christ are apparently very different and often look like the very reverse of each other, their makeup is similar. They clearly appear to be drawn from the same Hellenistic pool of characters: divine, yet somehow incomplete, they undergo a very complex paedeutic discipline—a rigorous and sometimes excruciating formative process—and in the end achieve an exemplary and exalted status.[265] They are not only glorified but also provide a model that enables mankind to undergo a fundamental transformation and to achieve an otherwise unattainable transcendence. Moreover, even as they help others bridge the chasm between doom and salvation, they are making society and the world better. The renewal they offer is not just personal but also collective, expressed in mythical and political terms. Their mystical process of self-discovery and self-

---

265. A suffering savior does not appear in Hellenistic Pythagoreanism. Ps.-Ecphantus has *Logos* consort with men because of the weakness of human nature, a suggestion of *Logos's* apparent tribulation. Diotogenes' king (not unlike Paul's Philippian Christ) is, in some sense, incomplete and imperfect and needs to prove himself before he can take his place in the divine gallery. There is an intimation in both Diotogenes and Paul that full, unchallenged divinity requires an initiatory programme. Most mystery religions know a deity that undergoes itself or requires from its devotees a form of dismemberment (sometimes followed by assemblage) aimed towards a more perfect state. Persian Mithras, Egyptian Osiris, the Anatolian Cybele or Phrygian Attis, Syrian Adonis, Greek Dionysos, the Gnostic Savior or Hermetic Poimandres, the Christian Saviour, the Babylonian Mani, are only the best known examples of such Hellenistic divinities. Rites of passage everywhere involve suffering before attainment of a higher spiritual condition.

The archetypal Hellenistic *Sōtēr*, and a suffering savior at that, is Heracles. Dio Chrysostom has Zeus make Heracles king over the human race, Greeks and Barbarians alike, as one qualified to rule, κἀκεῖνος ἐπέτρεψεν αὐτῷ βασιλεύειν τοῦ σύμπαντος ἀνθρώπων γένους, ὡς ὄντι ἱκανῷ (*The First Discourse on Kingship* 1.84). Xenophon, *Memorabilia* 2.1.21, and Cicero, *On Moral Duties* 1.32, also give accounts of the choice of Hercules (Cohoon 45 n. *ad loc.* in LCL Dio Chrysostom). For Heracles as Cynic hero and king, see Höistad 1948.

creation is multipliable; it can be produced again and again. The two heroes mediate the restoration of man and of society at the same time. This is the trademark of the Hellenistic age, in which both person and *polis* lose their bearings and meaning and in which salvation must be both of the person *and* of the *polis*. To cope with loss and alienation, religious-political champions were produced—real and mythical, historical and imaginary, earthly and cosmic, civic servants and divine beings. At once kings and gods, they save soul *and* state, reestablishing order both within and without.

2.2.4.[266] The next section is on the king's goodness (περὶ δὲ χρηστό-τατος). The king's χρηστότης (*chrēstotēs*) is an aggregate of justice, equity and compassion. *Chrēstotēs* is also a Pauline term. In Rom. 2.4, in a passage about God's judgment, it is given as the first attribute of God (cf. Eph. 2.7; Tit. 3.4). It is again applied to God in the famous simile of the natural and the wild olive-tree branches, where *chrēstotēs* is opposed to ἀποτομία (*apotomia*, 'severity'), a pun on the latter's more common root meaning, 'cutting off' (Rom. 11.22). In 2 Cor. 6.6 it is part of a long list of attributes of the *diakonoi*, God's ministers. And in Gal. 5.22 (cf. Col. 3.12) it is listed among the gifts of the *pneuma* that counterbalance the works of *sarx*.

According to Diotogenes, the king must be just (δίκαιος), fair (ἐπεικής) and reasonable (εὐγνώμων).[267] Above everything else, *chrēstotēs* is associated with *dikaiosunē*. Justice maintains society and binds it together. Justice is to society as rhythm is to motion and harmony to voice. It harmonizes political society for the common good of ruler and ruled. Equity and benevolence are the attendants of justice.[268]

This formulation, the core of the *dikaiosunē* concept as understood in Classical and Hellenistic times, unites the reflections of Plato and Aristotle (and, most likely, the tenets of ancient Pythagoreanism that they receive and repeat) with the metaphysical monarchic theory of Hellenistic thinkers. Justice is the supreme political and moral virtue; it encom-

266. H 268.15-270.11, T 74.19-75.16.
267. H 268.16-17, T 74.21.
268. ἔντι γὰρ ἁ δικαιότας κοινωνίας συνεκτικὰ καὶ συνακτικὰ καὶ μόνα γε ὧν πρὸς τὼς πλατίον ἁ τοιαύτα διάθεσις ἅρμοσται τᾶς ψυχᾶς. ὂν λόγον γὰρ ἔχει ῥυθμὸς ποτὶ κίνασιν καὶ ἁρμονία ποτὶ φωνάν, τοῦτον ἔχει τὸν λόγον δικαιότας ποτὶ κοινωνίαν· κοινὸν γὰρ ἀγαθὸν ἐντι καὶ ἀρχόντων καὶ ἀρχομένων, εἴ γε δὴ συναρμοστικὰ ἐντι κοινωνίας πολιτικᾶς. ἁ δὲ ἐπιείκηα καὶ <ἁ> εὐγνωμοσύνα πάρεδροί τινές ἐντι τᾶς δικαιοσύνας... (H 268.17-269.7, T 74.21-27).

passes all others and is the king's basic feature, both as an individual (it is an aspect of his soul) and as a political persona.[269] Politically, *dikaiosunē* is the *harmonia* that gives concord to the multiple and disparate constituents of a political *sustēma*; psychologically, it is the *harmonia* that produces concord among the incompatible aspects of the individual soul.

Dikaiosunē functions similarly in Paul. For him, too, *dikaiosunē* indicates political cohesion (*dikaiosunē theou/autou*), a character of the soul (*dikaiosunē humōn/hēmōn*) and divine exemplarity (*dikaiosunē Christou*). For Diotogenes, justice is uniquely the king's, and it is the same for Paul. All three Pauline characterizations of justice express divine agency and articulate the prerogative of God.[270]

269. I have often noted that Plato makes justice the foremost attribute of both state and individual, and views it as the condition in which everything is in its proper place, the essential of political stability and individual unity. Justice is the force that binds and harmonizes the different parts in the *polis* and in the soul and compels each component to remain united (*Republic* 4.433c-434c and 4.441c-444a). Aristotle devotes to justice Book 5 of *Ethics* and section 3.9-13 of *Politics*. Both Plato and Aristotle refer to justice as a relation to one's neighbor (the argument in *Republic*, 1.327a-354c, or *Nicomachean Ethics* 5.1129b25-1137a30, esp. 1129b26.) *Dikaiosunē* is a relational, interactive concept, a political quality *par excellence*.

270. Δικαιοσύνη θεοῦ/αὐτοῦ appears in all of Paul's letters and most often in Romans. *Dikaiosunē theou* is revealed in the *euangelion* which is medium and result of *pistis*, ἐκ πίστεως εἰς πίστιν, 'through faith for faith'; *euangelion* is God's *dunamis*, the instrument of *sōtēria*, it is universal, applying to Jew and Greek alike (Rom. 1.16-17). *Dikaiosunē theou* is activated by and offsets human *adikia* (Rom. 3.5); it is the process that determines the just, *dikaios* (Rom. 3.26); it is distinct from local *nomos* (Rom. 3.21, 10.3). Δικαιοσύνη Χριστοῦ is also a common Pauline topos. It is Christ who singlehandedly counterbalances the rule of death introduced by Adam and who brings about the kingdom of life, a model to all persons (Rom. 5.17-18; 1 Cor. 1.30; Phil. 1.11, cf. Rom. 14.7-8); because of Christ *hamartia* is replaced by *charis* (Rom. 5.21); he is a new type, who taking the form of *hamartia* rescued us from *hamartia* and made possible for all to become like the *dikaiosunē theou* (2 Cor. 5.21); he is the end of *nomos*, Jewish law (Rom. 10.3; Gal. 2.21; Phil. 3.9). Δικαιοσύνη ὑμῶν (ἡμῶν) is a major motif not only in Romans but also in many of the other epistles. The connection of *dikaiosunē* and *pistis* is a constant throughout (Rom. 1.17; 3.22, 25, 26; 4.11, 13; 9.30; 10.6; Gal. 5.5; Phil. 3.9). Δικαιοσύνη πίστεως describes the circumcised and the uncircumcised, the Jew and the Greek (Rom. 3.22; 4.9; 9.30) and is radically different from the *nomos*, a particular law system (Rom. 4.13; 9.31; Phil. 3.9). The kingdom of God is a state of the highest soul (as opposed to the seat of appetites) and is located in *dikaiosunē*,

2.2.5.[271] In this section, Diotogenes treats the kingly attributes of equity (ἐπιείκεια) and benevolence (εὐγνωμοσύνη). Equity and benevolence accompany *dikaiosunē*. Helpful to those in need, the king must be beneficient (εὐχάριστος), and kind (ἀβαρής, lit. 'not onerous').[272] The king must avoid being oppressive toward anyone and must be especially *abarēs* toward the humble and those wanting in fortune,[273] for these, like those diseased in body, cannot bear any burden (βάρος). The king is beneficent (εὐχάριστος), not according to the magnitude of the reverence rendered him, but according to the conduct and intention of those revering him.[274]

Equity and benevolence are common virtues in both Classical and Hellenistic moral and political discussions.[275] Ἐπιείκεια (*epieikeia*) appears also in Paul: in 2 Cor. 10.1, Paul uses the term to describe Christ.[276] While Paul does not use εὐγνωμοσύνη (*eugnōmosunē*), he employs the term *charis* in the same way in which *eugnōmosunē* functions in Diotogenes' fragment. The semantic fields of the two terms overlap. *Charis*, especially as applied to God, is often used by Hellenistic writers, particularly in the first centuries CE.[277] Inscriptions and papyri of

peace, and joy (Rom. 6.13, 19; 14.17); the body is dead, the spirit alive (Rom. 8.10). Human *dikaiosunē* is part of a political-economic complex, it is distributed by God just as he does the seed of the sower and the bread for food (2 Cor. 9.10). *Dikaiosunē* is an intricate and pervasive concept. It is political and universal, exemplary and personal. It defines God, Christ and human.

271. H 269.8-270.1, T 74.28-75.8.2.

272. H 269.9-11, T 74.28-75.3; the point is emphasized again in H 269.15-270.1, T 75.6-8.

273. Reading καταδεεστέρως ταῖς τύχαις with T 75.7; L. Delatte amends it to ψυχαῖς (1942: 44.17), 'faiblesse de l'âme', for insufficiently convincing reasons.

274. H 269.13-15, T 75.4-5.

275. The companionship of equity and benevolence with justice is Aristotelian (*Ethics* 5.1137a31-1138a4, 6.1143a19-24). For these as royal virtues see, e.g., Themistius, *Orations* 141.23, 234, 277.26 or Seneca, *On Mercy* (*ap.* L. Delatte 1942: 272).

276. Ἐπιεικής, the adjective, is urged on the feuding Philippians (Phil. 4.5). In Acts 24.4 *epieikeia* is the attribute of Felix, procurator of Judea. It is a quality of the bishop (1 Tim. 3.3).

Epieikeia, a qualifier of *dikaiosunē*, should not be confused with ἰσότης, equity, equality, a political term drawn from the terminology of the Greek *polis*. See Ps.-Ecphantus, fragment #4.

277. It is used to describe God by Philo, Josephus, Dio Chrysostom, Aelius Aristides, Sextus' *Sentences* (BAGD *s.v.* χάρις 885b).

the same period apply it to emperors.[278] In the genuine Pauline letters, *charis* is often a mark of God's liberality, usually connected with God's *dikaiosunē*. The Christians are found to be just (δικαιούμενοι) by God's *charis* (Rom. 3.24, cf. Rom. 5.16, 17, 20, 21). *Dikaiosunē* comes not through law (*nomos*) but through *charis* (Gal. 2.21). Paul uses *charis* prolifically, and its set of meanings is therefore complex, but, even so, the term invariably expresses God's benevolence in judgment. It is conspicuously present in the formulas that open and close Paul's letters, where the apostle greets or takes leave of his readers by wishing that God be indulgent in his judgment of them, and that, finding them just, he bestow desirable powers on them.[279] Paul is likewise stressing God's benevolence when he cites *charis* as the source of his apostleship.

The passage in which Diotogenes credits the king with particular kindness toward the weak and the unfortunate is exceptional, for concern for social justice and the plight of the underprivileged is exceedingly rare in Greek antiquity.[280] There is, however, at least a bit of political

---

278. BAGD *s.v.* χάρις 885b. Schiavo 1993 translates *charis* as 'distinction'. He traces the cult of *charites* in Greece. *Charis* covered many areas, from personal adornment and grooming to the elegant demeanor at parties; from generosity in personal relations to liberal attitude in public life. A few chapters cover the concept of *charis* in public life, where it means sound balance of body and mind in the complete unity of the human being.

279. The opening formula is usually '*Charis* to you and peace...' In Rom. 14.17 the kingdom of God is *dikaiosunē* in peace and *chara*. Here, as often in Hellenistic usage, *chara* may not be differentiated from *charis*. See also BAGD *s.v.* χάρις, 885a.

Diotogenes connects equity and benevolence with *eucharistos*, and writes that the king is beneficent not according with the greatness of the homage paid but according with its purity. Interestingly, in 2 Cor. 8.1-5 (cf. 9.13-14), Paul reports on the effect of *charis* upon the Macedonians, and shows his gratefulness for a significant contribution to his collection that was so much more impressive as it came from poor people.

Eucharistos (like *Sōtēr* or *Euergetēs*) is a royal title in Hellenistic times. It was carried by Ptolemy V and VI (BAGD *s.v.* εὐχαρίσρτος; L. Delatte 272). Paul uses mostly verbal forms with the sense of giving thanks or being thankful, and makes God the recipient of the gratitude. Rom. 16.4 makes, however, Prisca and Aquila, a woman and her husband, the beneficiaries of thanks.

280. There may be an echo in Diotogenes of the Gracchi reforms of 133–132 and 123–122 BCE. In any case, one of the radically new features of some religious associations in Hellenistic times was the social services they provided to their members. The mushrooming of *collegia* in late Hellenistic and Roman times is another result of the need for social and economic support felt by the associates.

calculation behind Diotogenes' compassion. His interest in the political stability of the state is pre-eminent. The weak had to be drawn into the structures of power for the purpose of those structures' perpetuation. The same is the case in Paul. The desire to ensure the survival of the congregations he has founded determines his ethical injunctions. Exhortations against making judgmental remarks about one's neighbor (e.g., Rom. 2.1-3; 14.4, 10; 1 Cor. 4.5; 5.12) and perplexing the weak (e.g., Rom. 14.1, 13; 15.1; 1 Cor. 8.9; 9.22; 1 Thess. 5.14), warnings about the fallible nature of even the best (e.g., Rom. 7.15, 23; Gal. 5.16–6.10) and encouragements to his listeners to bear each other's burdens (e.g., Rom. 15.1-2, 7; Gal. 6.2) are not just common-sense moral proddings but sensible political strategies, as well. Anything that threatens the concord of the political corporation is to be averted.

2.2.6.[281] The preserved fragments of Diotogenes end with a grand pagan doxology. The attributes that the king should exhibit are the same as those of the gods (τὰς διαθέσιας τοιαύτας)[282] and especially of Zeus. Zeus, the ruler of all (ὁ κρατέων πάντων),[283] he who commands and rules all things (κρατὲν καὶ κυριεύεν πάντων),[284] is majestic (*semnos*) and awe-inspiring (*timios*) because of his superiority (*huperochan*) and the greatness of his *aretē*. He is good (*chrēstos*) because he is a benefactor (*euergetikos*) and a giver of goods (*agathodotas*). Zeus is frightening (*deinos*) because he punishes the unjust (διὰ τὸ κολάζεν τὼς ἀδικέοντας).[285] The final chord is the reiteration of the notion that kingship is an imitation of divinity (ὅτι θεόμιμόν ἐντι πρᾶγμα βασιλεία).[286]

Ever since Plato, Zeus had been regarded as the source of the political, or royal, science.[287] The name 'Zeus' was frequently given to Hellenistic kings[288] and to Roman emperors.[289] This imagery is useful in inter-

281. H 270.2-11, T 75.8-16.
282. H 270.3, T 75.9-10.
283. H 270.4, T 75.9.
284. H 270.8, T 75.13-14.
285. H 270.4-10, T 75.10-15.
286. H 270.10-11, T 75.15-16.
287. See L. Delatte 1942: 273. In *Protagoras*, Plato's Protagoras makes Zeus the keeper of political wisdom; it is he who gives αἰδώς and δίκη, public disgrace and justice, to men, the essential ingredients of political existence (322c). *Philebus* (30d) gives Zeus the soul and mind of a king.
288. Such as Seleucus I Nicator, in a second century BCE inscription, Dittenberger, *OGI* 245.10 (LSJ 754b).
289. E.g., Nero, in an inscription from Acraephiae, Dittenberger, *IG* 7.2713.41

preting texts such as the 'Philippian hymn' and for understanding the background of the picture of Christ developed by Paul—a portrait that conforms to the popular Hellenistic perception of the king. His own identification with Christ—his making himself a 'small-c' christ and linking his own activity to Christ's work—also fits this framework very well: Paul also becomes an exalted, merciful and just king who leads a stable and unified community.[290] The entire construct is grounded in two theses: the king *is* the law, the constitution; his person is the *exemplum*, the model for all. Paul consistently speaks not only about Christ but also about himself in ruler-language, a barely disguised political vocabulary that would have been easily understood by his Greek readers (though much less transparent in the provincial, insulated environment of Jerusalem).

Via Christ, the original model and living law, Paul is both *exemplum* and *nomos empsuchos*.[291] Christ *lives in him*: 'I have been crucified with Christ; it is no longer I who live, but Christ who lives in me' (Gal. 2.20) and 'To me living is Christ' (Phil. 1.21, cf. Rom. 8.10; 14.8; 2 Cor. 10.7). Kingship, says Diotogenes, is the business of imitating God. For Paul, 'christship'—assuming the spiritual *and* political authority of Christ—is also a matter of imitating the divine. Imitation remains the central, paradigmatic act, constantly demanded both by the Hellenistic Pythagoreans and by Paul.

(LSJ 754b). It is, as L. Delatte shows (1942: 273), a favorite theme with Dio Chrysostom, a generation or two after Paul.

290. See Préaux's (1976) portrait of a Hellenistic king. See also Goodenough's outline of Plutarch's *To an Unlearned Ruler* (1928: 95-97). There we have a king that directs into others the principle of rulership while diminishing himself, constantly conscious of himself being ruled not by a written law but by a law which is animate in him, a Logos which dwells in him and protects and guides him. Anyone who takes the king as a model and whose life is guided by reason may be represented as an Animate Nomos-Logos or king. The king is a minister of God for the care and safety of mankind. Justice, *dikē*, is the end of law. The ruler is the image of God; he makes himself into the closest likeness to God and dispenses God-like justice.

291. For Christ as the *exemplum* see, e.g., Rom. 5.17, 21; 6.4, 11; 8.2, 11; 1 Cor. 15.22; for him as law, see, e.g., 1 Cor. 9.21; Gal. 6.2. See also the *dikaiosunē* statements in Rom. 3.21-25.

Sthenidas: περὶ βασιλείας (peri basileias), On Kingship

Sthenidas[292] is probably the name of the actual author of this very short fragment of a treatise on kingship,[293] which therefore should not be treated as pseudoepigraphical. He may have come from Locri, in southern Italy; his dates are as widely fluctuating as those of his confrères—from Hellenistic to imperial times. The fragment, which despite its brevity is critical, expatiates on the relation between God and the king.

The text reads as follows: The king must be a wise man, for so he will be an imitator and a follower of the First God.[294] God, first, is king

292. Iamblichus (*On Pythagorean Life* 267) knows a Locrian pre-Socratic, Σθενωνίδας. Stobaeus, also used by Photius (*Bibliotheca*—or *Myriobiblion*—115a18), ascribes this passage to Σθενίδας, a Pythagorean from Lokroi (Locri); see also Goodenough 1928: 73 and n. 65; Thesleff 1965: 187. I see no reason why Sthenidas may not be the actual name of the Hellenistic author of this fragment.

293. Stobaeus 4.7.63, H 270.12-271.12 = T 187.9-188.13, L. Delatte 1942: 45-46 (Greek), 56 (French trans.), 274-81 (Commentary); Goodenough 1928: 73-75. Χρὴ τὸν βασιλέα σοφὸν ἦμεν· οὕτω γὰρ ἐσσεῖται ἀντίμιμος καὶ ζηλωτὰς τῶ πράτω θεῶ. οὗτος γὰρ καὶ φύσει ἐντὶ [ἐστὶ] καὶ <ὡσία> πρᾶτος βασιλεύς τε καὶ δυνάστας, ὁ δὲ γενέσει καὶ μιμάσει, καὶ ὁ μὲν ἐν τῷ παντὶ καὶ ὅλῳ, ὁ δὲ ἐπὶ γᾶς, καὶ ὁ μὲν ἀεὶ τὰ πάντα διοικεῖ τε καὶ ζωοῖ [ζώει] αὐτὸς ἐν αὑτῷ κεκταμένος τὰν σοφίαν, ὁ δ᾽ ἐν χρόνῳ ἐπιστάμαν. ἄριστα δὲ καὶ [κα] μιμέοιτο τοῦτον, εἰ μεγαλόφρονά τε καὶ ἅμερον καὶ ὀλιγοδεέα παρασκευάζοι αὐτόν, πατρικὰν διάθεσιν ἐνδεικνύμενος τοῖς ὑφ᾽ αὑτῷ [αὑτῷ] · διὰ τοῦτο γὰρ που μάλιστα <εἰκὸς> [καὶ] νενομίχθαι τὸν πρᾶτον θεὸν πατέρα μὲν θεῶν, πατέρα δὲ ἀνθρώπων ἦμεν, ὅτι ἤπιος πρὸς πάντα τὰ ὑπ᾽ αὑτῷ γενομενά ἐντι [ἐστὶ] καὶ ἀμελούμενος τᾶς προστασίας οὐδέποκα νοέεται· οὐδὲ ἤρκεσται τῷ ποιητὰς μόνον πάντων γεγονέναι, ἀλλὰ καὶ τροφεὺς διδάσκαλός τε τῶν καλῶν πάντων καὶ νομοθέτας πέφυκε πᾶσιν ἐπίσας. τοιοῦτον θέμις ἦμεν καὶ τὸν ἐπὶ γᾶς καὶ παρ᾽ ἀνθρώποις ἀγεμονεῖν μέλλοντα βασιλέα· οὐδὲν δὲ ἀβασίλευτον καλὸν οὐδὲ ἄναρχον. ἄνευ δὲ σοφίας καὶ ἐπιστάμας οὔτε μὰν βασιλέα οὔτε ἄρχοντα οἷόν τε ἦμεν. μιματὰς ἄρα καὶ ὑπηρέτας ἐσσεῖται τῷ θεῷ ὁ σοφός τε καὶ νόμιμος βασιλεύς.

NOTE: Pointed brackets indicate L. Delatte's additions or variant readings. Square brackets mark Thesleff's disagreement with L. Delatte's reading.

294. *Prōtos theos*, First God, is a Hermetic and Gnostic motif, present in mystical as well as in philosophical writings of late Hellenistic period. It is found not only in the Hermetic literature but also in the Hellenistic Pythagoreans, Onatas being another example, in the Neoplatonists Numenius, Albinus, Iamblichus, in the Stoicizing Cicero and Dio Chrysostom (see also L. Delatte 1942: 275-76). The concept of First God, opposed to an inferior creator God, gives cohesion to an otherwise vastly eclectic Gnostic genre. Such a distinction is absent in the Pauline literature. Could there be a polemical intent in Paul, who, in his proclivity for

and ruler by nature, the king by birth and imitation.[295] God rules all and the universe, the king rules on earth. God lives forever and manages all things, possessing wisdom in himself; the king is temporal and has a science, a system, of [political] knowledge. The king best imitates God by being high-minded, gentle and modest in needs, displaying a paternal disposition toward those under him. Precisely in these respects is the First God perceived to be father of gods and father of humans: that he is gentle (ἤπιος) to all under him that he has made, is never neglectful of rulership (τᾶς προστασίας), and, never content to be just the creator of all things, he is also sustainer (τροφεύς), teacher of everything that is good, and legislator equally to all. It is right that he who is destined to be king on earth and among men also be like this. Nothing unlike a king or unruled is good. Without wisdom and a system of knowledge, there is neither king nor ruler. In conclusion, the king who is wise and legitimate will be an imitator and servant of God.

reversal, inverts the first/second progression? His soteriology works a conspicuous wise/foolish shift. His ontology positions the physical (Adam) first and the pneumatic second (1 Cor. 15.46). His eschatology has apostasy, anomy and destruction come first and then the return of Christ (2 Thess. 2.3).

Antimimos theou, the expression used by Sthenidas, has a new force. It probably derives, as L. Delatte suggests, from the doctrine that makes man in general, not just the king, the imitator of God (1942: 276). Euryphamos (Stobaeus 4.915.10) and Philo (*Vit. Mos.* 2.65) apply *antimimos theou* to all humankind. Ignatius of Antioch uses the verb ἀντιμιμέομαι in a negative paraenesis, 'do not imitate [the persecutors]' (Ignatius, *Eph.* 10.2). This trajectory is most important for understanding Paul's theory of Christ-type. In Paul access to God is open to all who imitate and follow Christ.

295. Limited in time, indirect and imitative, the king's rule only replicates God's life of contemplation and happiness. As Aristotle puts it, the entire life of the gods is blessed, that of humans is so only to the extent to which it has some resemblance, ὁμοίωμα, to divine activity (*Nicomachean Ethics* 10.1178b26-27.) Elsewhere, when speaking of justice, Aristotle emphasizes again the imperfection of the human: just acts exist only between those who share in things good, which the gods have in unlimited measure, in which the incurably bad have no share, and in which the ordinary people participate to a limited extent (*Ethics* 5.1137a26-30). The human condition is, at its best, a paltry imitation of God.

Because of the special nature and activity of Christ, however, Paul can see it transfigured beyond any limitation. Paul recognizes that God as the model for things created is a common Greek idea (Rom. 1.19-20). Paul ties God with *phusis* as well and disqualifies actions and beings that are not natural (e.g., Rom. 1.26; Gal. 4.8).

Sthenidas's text is clearly Hellenistic Pythagorean, consistent with all the main doctrines of Pythagorean *basileia* writings, and, while reliant on Plato and Aristotle, it shares in the Hermetic-Gnostic taste of Hellenistic times. The fragment draws together the most important themes of monarchic mysticism and can help us redraw our understanding of some Pauline motifs.

1.1.[296] Sthenidas systematically matches king and God even as he distinguishes between them. They share much in common yet are two distinct entities, dissimilar primarily in the extent of their spheres of power and length of tenure, the foundation of their authority and, less clearly, the nature of their knowledge. God rules all creation and the whole universe,[297] while the king rules men on earth. God has eternal dominion, the king temporal command. God rules by nature, as First God and King; the king governs by birth, imitation and emulation. God's rule occurs as a result of *sophia*, wisdom; the king's because of *epistēmē*—that is, a body of knowledge, a science that he acquires as a trained professional.[298]

296. H 270.13-19, T 187.10-188.2.
297. L. Delatte (1942: 277-78) traces the history of the expression ὁ μὲν ἐν τῷ παντὶ καὶ ὅλῳ; it seems to begin with Plato and acquire force in Aristotle. It is Aristotle who defines and distinguishes πᾶν and ὅλον (*Metaphysics* 4.26.1024a1). Note also that the Stoics do not associate *pan* and *holon* (L. Delatte 1942: 278).
298. The fragment's Stoic flavor, due particularly to the use of the *sophos* concept, turns out to be specious. The king mimics God and as such is *sophos*. As Goodenough has proved, the idea that the *sophos* imitates God is 'definitely at variance with Stoicism' (1928: 74). Replication of God is conceivable only by philosophers for whom God is 'a moral existence ruling a world objective of himself. If God is all, as in Stoic pantheism, one may live in conformity with God's legal nature, but can hardly imitate him' (1928: 75).
    Although L. Delatte (1942: 274-75) upholds a Stoic influence upon Sthenidas, his argumentation in favor of this view is unconvincing. In emphasizing the doctrine of late Stoicism, according to which the good king is also, necessarily, a philosopher, while the philosopher is also a king, proofs of which he finds in Musonius as well as in Dio Chrysostom, Aelius Aristides, Eusebius and Themistius, L. Delatte misses the concern in Sthenidas: it is not philosophy but divinity. For Sthenidas imitation of the divine is at issue. (Paul will call this *pistis*. It is *pistis* that is required of the 'king'.) Later, in reference to Sthenidas's affirmation (H 271.9-10, T 188.11-12) that no king or public official can perform that function without *epistēmē* and *sophia*, L. Delatte (1942: 280) thinks that Sthenidas attempts gauchely to harmonize two different influences, the Pythagorean and the Stoic. If not a

God has *sophia*, the king *epistēmē*. The difference, however, is not all
that neat, either in Sthenidas or in Paul. Paul's use of the term *sophia
theou* (see esp. Rom. 11.25) is undoubtedly a by-product of the
abundant Hellenistic Gnostic and sapiential literature. Sometimes Paul
identifies *sophia theou* with Christ (1 Cor. 1.24, 30); sometimes, Paul
himself imparts the mystery called *sophia theou* (1 Cor. 2.7). *Pneuma*
bestows *sophia* on human beings (1 Cor. 12.8), but, more often than
not, the *sophia* Paul talks about is human and, as such, fallible (1 Cor.
1.17; 2.1, 4; 3.19). Paul also calls it 'sarkic' *sophia* (2 Cor. 1.12). To it,
he opposes *dunamis* (1 Cor. 1.17; 2.5). In his characteristic paradoxical
style, Paul finds the folly of his message—the cross—and the foolish-
ness of God to be far superior to human rhetoric and human wisdom
(1 Cor. 1.17, 21, 25). In short, *sophia* does not appear to have a
technical meaning in Paul, and such loose use of this term by someone
indubitably knowledgeable about the Hellenistic Wisdom literature and
the Gnostic genre must be deliberate.[299] This refusal on Paul's part to
accept the received meaning of the term may be explained precisely by
reason of familiarity: the idiom is unserviceable and therefore is dis-
credited. The problem seems even less ambiguous insofar as the term
sophos ('wise') is concerned. It, too, is compromised. Paul's consistent
critique of the wise, rooted in the affirmation of a unique divine
epistemology that defies human wisdom and learning, is aimed at the
School philosopher in general and especially at the Sophist.[300] The

scribal error, and I do not think it is, this is the result of ingenuous semantic consistency. *Sophos*, the king has also *sophia*. (L. Delatte himself makes this observation, but does not see Sthenidas's naive logic.) The author is innocent of any
Stoic constraint.

299. I agree with Stead (1994: 140) that the intelligible light terminology of
Rom. 13.12-13 may be a *logos-sophia* philosophical reflection, an inevitable effect
of the *sophia* motif.

300. Paul, just as other popular philosophers (Demonax or Apollonius are good
examples), inveighs against the ostentatious stance of high-brow philosophers, as,
for example, 1 Cor. 2.1. In the next verse (1 Cor. 2.2) he declares: 'All I care about
is Christ'. As the larger context shows (1 Cor. 2.1-14), Paul's *sophia* rests not with
the *nous* but with the *pneuma*. His philosophy is pneumatic and sensible, not noetic
and abstract. See also 2 Cor. 10.4 (discussed by Betz 1975b: 68, 140-41). For a
good treatment of Sophism in imperial times see Anderson 1986, 1993, 1994 (esp.
the last). An example of a more subtle anti-philosophical attitude is 1 Cor. 13.12 ('I
know in part', γινώσκω ἐκ μέρους). The latter appears to stand in contradiction to
Aristotle's definition of knowledge: 'the Mind's identity with its object' (*On the*

Stoic, is a target too, of this polemic. Stoicism emphasized the self-sufficiency of the *sophos*, and asserted the wise man's exclusive claim to kingship, and this would have generated Paul's opposition on both religious and political grounds.

Epistēmē had been the mark of the professional ever since Plato and Aristotle. In Sthenidas it specifically characterizes the king,[301] but in Hellenistic times all statesmanship had become professionalized. Paul has no use for *epistēmē,* for obvious reasons. Paul would have nothing to do with a learned skill, a discipline acquired in school and taught by philosophers. As we have seen repeatedly, Paul reviles the 'wise' person, be he the educated Greek speaker or the law-steeped Jew (e.g., Rom. 2.20). Paul can refer to himself as a 'professional' *polis*-founder, as when he calls himself (using a term rich in Classical political connotations) an *architektōn* (1 Cor. 3.10), but even in this case his skill is the result of God's *charis,* benevolence, not learning. As such, he is an apostle, an agent of God, someone sent on an ambassadorial mission for the supreme God, carrying the message of the *euangelion.*[302]

Soul 3.429b6-10, 3.431a1-5, 3.431b20-432a1; *Metaphysics* 12.1072b21; 12.1074 b38-1075a5; Stead 1994: 133 n. 10), i.e. knowledge is complete or perfect knowledge. Paul's formula opens the way to negative knowledge (Stead 1994: 133).

301. Plato elaborates this concept in the *Politicus.* The science of rule or command is called both royal and political, βασιλικόν καὶ πολιτικόν (267c), and is developed in the dialogue. Essentially, this royal knowledge enables the statesman to harmonize the state and secure the happiness of its citizens (311b-c). Aristotle makes *sophia* the combination of *nous* and *epistēmē,* of intuitive reason and scientific knowledge (*Nicomachean Ethics* 6.1141a19). Politics, or practical reason, is the most authoritative of sciences (*Ethics* 1.1094a27; *Politics* 3.1282b15-16).

302. See M.M. Mitchell 1992, who approaches the question of the origin of the institution of the apostle from the point of view of social and diplomatic conventions.

Paul may take literally the manuals on how to be a king, which try to sell a product by showing that God uses it. The king must be this and do that because so is and does God, a good slogan for the upper classes. Paul, however, can do away with the earthly teacher and the school and, in a purer Hellenistic Pythagorean tradition, learn directly from God. This way he also bypasses the temporality of knowledge. Paul's legitimacy comes from God not human persons. His persuasive powers derive from *pneuma* not from an academy. It is not *epistēmē* but *gnōsis* that he pursues, not science or a craft but illumination and revelation, *gnōsis theou* or *Christou* (e.g., Rom. 11.33; 2 Cor. 10.5; Phil. 3.8). Or, even more so, *agapē,* the great political upholder, the community builder (e.g., 1 Cor. 8.1; 13.4).

1.2.[303] The king is like God when he is noble-minded (*megalophrōn*), temperate (*hēmeros*) and moderate (*oligodeēs*). This triad of virtues recalls and corresponds to the Classical tripartite division of the soul into reason (*nous*), spirit (*thumos*) and desire (*epithumia*), a psychology encountered in most Hellenistic Pythagoreans[304] as well as in Paul.[305] The feature that most decisively identifies God and king is the fatherly disposition (*patrikē diathesis*) both show toward their subjects. The title 'father of gods and father of humans' (actually a quotation from Homer), as applied to God, is of central importance in Sthenidas's fragment. That the ruler is a caring 'father' to his people is a genuine topos of ancient Mediterranean culture generally. The paternal identification of God and ruler is prominent in political treatises—and particularly in the monarchic theories—of Hellenistic and Roman times, and it can be traced all the way back to the Classical period.[306] Of course, the ruler-as-caring father topos is not just a Greek, Hellenistic and Roman idea; it is also compellingly present in the Hebrew Scripture. Still, Sthenidas's fragment gives us reason, I think, to re-evaluate Paul's preference for this appellation of God[307] *as a political statement* whose origins may be as much Hellenistic as they are Jewish Hellenistic.

What makes God a father is that he is gentle (*ēpios*), watchful in his protection (*prostasia*)[308] and never just a creator but also a nourisher

303. H 270.20-271.12, T 188.2-13.
304. See L. Delatte 279.
305. Tilted in favor of an Aristotelian *nous–orexis* system, as esp. in Rom. 1.18-27.
306. It may have originated with Aristotle, who compares kingship with the relationship of father to sons, a relation which he calls royal. This is why, according to Aristotle, Homer calls Zeus 'father', for the ideal kingship is paternal government, πατρική ἀρχή (*Nicomachean Ethics* 8.1160b25-27). L. Delatte (1942: 279) finds this notion extensively in the Stoics (quoting Berlinger, *Beiträge zur inoffiziellen Titulatur der römischen Kaiser* [diss., Breslau 1935]: 77-79), who influenced Cicero, Seneca, Philo, Dio Chrysostom, Pliny the Younger, Themistius. For more references see also BAGD 641.3a, c, *s.v.* πατρική.
307. Such as the *abba* cry (Rom. 8.15; Gal. 4.6), or the references to God as *patros hēmōn* in the greetings of his epistles. See Chapter 8, Rom. 8.15, for further discussion.
308. The terms *ēpios, tropheus, didaskalos* and *nomothetēs* in Paul will be discussed below.
Prostasia, a term related to this complex of functions, occurs in Paul as the feminine *prostatis*, 'patroness', a revealing use. It is applied to Phoebe (Rom. 16.2) and suggests the *collegium*, the clublike environment in which early Christianity functioned.

(*tropheus*), teacher (*didaskalos*) and legislator (*nomothetēs*). God's fatherhood covers the entire developmental cycle of the human being and of the *polis*—from the nursery to political maturity and from foun-

---

The club, *collegium*, is structured thus: the patron or the benefactor, a man or a woman (sort of chairperson of the board, the president *ex officio*); the officers, with different administrative functions; the regular members. The last two groups together formed the full Assembly, *ekklēsia*. Within the club, all members of the Assembly have equal standing. In a *collegium*, commitment is to service, not to status. (For more on this issue see Chow 1992, Clarke 1993.)

The feminine *prostatis*, 'patroness', 'protectress', is not found in archaeological sources: the masculine is common (see MM 551a-b). The title is applied to the office-bearer in Hellenistic and Roman religious associations (Foucart 1873: 202, *ap.* MM 551a). Women's associations, whether religious or professional, were normal (see Lefkowitz-Fant 1982: 244-47). Women as *patronae* in men's *collegia* are not uncommon either. Five percent of known patrons during the empire were women (Waltzing 1895-1900: I, 348-49, IV, 254-57; Clemente 1972; *ap.* Pomeroy 1975: 200-201). Women patrons are well attested in Christian Gnosticism.

According to Meeks (1983: 78) '...collegia preserved at least the semblance of democratic internal governance, imitating the classical *polis* in organization and procedures for elections and decision-making. It is arguable that such democratic procedures were also at work in the Pauline congregations...' The structure of the democratic *polis* is captured in *collegia*, in the *ekklēsia* format of their functioning. Meeks downplays the similarity between the club and Paul's society. In Paul, notes Meeks, the *collegium* terminology, either about the group itself or about its leaders, is completely absent (Meeks 1983: 79). Common *collegia* names such as *thiasos, factio, curia, corpus* are applied to Christianity in the second to fourth centuries, but not in Paul. The internal hierarchy follows not municipal nomenclature but a pneumatic criterion. Of the names Paul gives his societies' members: 'the holy ones', 'called' (or 'elect'), 'beloved of God', none appear in the titulature of clubs. Of the names of civic offices often adopted by the club, such as *prutanis, decuriones, quinquennales, episkopos, diakonos, prostatēs (patronus)*, only the last three are used by Paul, but rarely and apparently non-technically (Phil. 1.1 *episkopos, diakonos*; Rom. 16.1 *diakonos*; Rom. 16.2 *prostatis*, about *diakonos* Phoebe [Meeks 1983: 79]). While Paul's understanding of the Christian *ekklēsia* goes far beyond club camaraderie and lodge fraternity, the *collegia* remain important case studies for Paul's communities. (See also Brandis 1905; Hands 1968; Judge 1972; Hendrix 1992.) Nevertheless, Paul's associations are created as the underlying tissue and muscle of the state, while rank and rewards are determined by a suprapolitical entity, *pneuma*. Paul is working consistently on two levels, political and metaphysical, and uses the terms of practical and speculative philosophy respectively. Paul is a politician of souls.

The Jewish synagogue community in Rome was recognized by Caesar as a *collegia* (Josephus, *Ant.* 14.10.8-12). See Wiefel 1977: 103, 111.

dation to law reform. The most remarkable finding here is the nexus *ēpios–tropheus*. Precisely the same connection is made in 1 Thess. 2.7, where Paul describes his own nurturing of the Thessalonian congregation: 'But we were gentle with you, as a nurse caring for her children'.[309]

In one sense, the similarity of Paul's words to Sthenidas's is unsurprising: Paul's phrase had already achieved the status of an aphorism. Nurses of antiquity were proverbially gentle.[310] Abraham Malherbe, one of the major re-discoverers of Hellenistic Paul, sees Cynic influence and anti-Sophistic polemic here.[311] But Sthenidas expands the background of Paul's metaphor considerably. *Ēpios* describes the king and is a political term. Sthenidas extends the concept of gentle nurturance from the Stoic–Cynic rhetorical and moral domain into a political and cosmic sphere and shifts the weight of the issue from morals to politics. The context in which the phrase 'gentle...like a nurse taking care of her children' (1 Thess. 2.7) occurs in Paul makes a political reading inevitable, though the text remains a polemic against charlatan preachers and retains an apologetic timbre. At issue is not so much Paul's form of address, a matter of rhetorical method, as the position of the speaker and his end. Paul appears in order to carry authority from God to speak

309. ἀλλὰ ἐγενήθημεν [ν]ήπιοι ἐν μέσῳ ὑμῶν, ὡς ἐὰν τροφὸς θάλπῃ τὰ ἑαυτῆς τέκνα (1 Thess. 2.7). The *lectio* ἤπιοι has an impressive manuscript attestation. Νήπιοι ('infants' or 'children') may be the result of the transfer of the ending consonant of the preceding word onto the next one, common confusion in dictation.

310. Tomb inscriptions testify to this. See Herzog 1937 (*ap.* Malherbe 1989: 43). This was before Grimm Brothers' times.

That God or the king, the Father *par excellence*, is nurse-like, is eminently provocative. It is cause for scandal in feminist theory. Having transformed the maternal generative power into a nursery, the passive *locus* of generation, the Greeks males are then appropriating even the nurturing function and bestowing it on men. See Cavarero 1990: 71-72.

311. Malherbe 1970=1989: 35-48. The gentle, *ēpion*, type of philosopher evokes 'the figure of the nurse crooning over her wards' (1989: 43). Malherbe finds the simile in Ps.-Diogenes, c. first century BCE, Dio Chrysostom, Plutarch, Epictetus and Maximus of Tyre, all late first and/or second century CE Stoic writers (1989: 43-45). The reference to the amiability of the nurse occurs in the context of the philosophers' assessment of the varied speech the orator must use in addressing his fellow men. Dio Chrysostom's criticism of the Cynics (*Discourse* 32) and his portrayal of himself in opposition to them (32.11-12), including the divine commission, is emphasized by Malherbe (1989: 45-47). He finds striking verbal similarities between Dio and 1 Thess. 2 (1989: 47-48).

on behalf of God (1 Thess. 2.4, 13), to make people ready for God's *basileia* (2.12), to make them *mimētai*, imitators of God's *ekklēsiai* in Judea, the exemplary casualties for truth (2.14-15). The stakes are political, and Paul presents himself, like God, as a father (2.11), a gentle sustainer of his people.

Paul's 'fatherhood' extends to his role as teacher of his people (1 Cor. 4.15). As such, he exhorts them to imitate him (4.16). He teaches the *euangelion*, a revelation, not a scholastic discipline (Gal. 1.11-12; 1 Thess. 2.13). Its teaching requires, however, a didactic, human approach, given the limitations of men (Rom. 6.17-19). The *didaskaloi* (teachers) represent a pneumatic appointment, and even if the apostles and the prophets come before them (1 Cor. 12.28; 14.6) in the hierarchy of the *ekklēsia* (Rom. 12.4-7), the important point is that the *didaskaloi* are so endowed by God, not by humans (Gal. 1.12, cf. Rom. 15.4), and that they perform a major function within the Christian corporation.

Nomothesia, the lawgiving function, in Paul belongs to God as well (Rom. 9.4). But this is not the point. In Paul, God's *nomos* is *dikaiosunē*. The essence of *dikaiosunē* is a principle of equality, as we have often seen, and this is exactly what Sthenidas has in mind when he writes', God [and the king as well] is a natural lawgiver, dispensing justice 'equally to all' (καὶ νομοθέτας πέφυκε πᾶσιν ἐπίσας). The *nomothetēs*, as Sthenidas understands him, frames no written code of law but legislates as a *nomos empsuchos*, which the phrase 'doing so by nature' suggests. Although Sthenidas does not use the expression *nomos empsuchos* in the brief extant fragment, the semantic logic requires this conclusion. Sthenidas's consistency with the other writings of the *basileia* group leads one to expect it. Moreover, God's (or the king's) equitable distribution of justice recalls the Hellenistic Pythagorean *analogia* standard. For Paul, God alone is capable of this.

The king is imitator and servant of God. That the king is *hupēretēs* is an important idea.[312] The notion of imitation has as a logical consequence the inferior status of the king vis-à-vis God. This is sometimes emphasized and sometimes effaced. But the assertion that the king is a servant of God, and the use of a term that indicates a clearly subservient position, is a rare occurrence in the political literature of antiquity. One is struck by the resemblance of Sthenidas's characterization to the Pauline idea, expressed in Rom. 13.4, 6, that the ruler is *diakonos* and

---

312. Ecphantus remarked that God has no need of *diakonoi* and *hupēretai*, attendants and servants (H 277.5-6, T 82.17-18).

leitourgos, judge and tax collector of God. Paul's styling of himself, routinely and elatedly, as *doulos Christou*, 'slave of Christ', belongs to the same category.[313] Slavery was regarded in antiquity as the most abject human condition, and its application to a figure of influence and power must have been astonishing indeed. One can uncover, however, a few instances in political contexts of positive evaluation of servility.[314] In Plato's *Laws*, the true magistrates, who conform themselves to the laws, are called 'servants of the laws' (τοὺς δ' ἄρχοντας λεγομένους νῦν ὑπηρέτας τοῖς νόμοις) (4.715c-d). Aware of his metaphor's punch, Plato explains that he does not mean it as a novelty (καινοτομία) but uses it because he honestly believes that the salvation (*sōteria*) of the state (*polis*) depends on this service. And, Plato concludes on a even more striking note, the state in which the law is master of the rulers and the rulers slaves of the law has salvation (ἐν ἧ δὲ ἂν δεσπότης τῶν ἀρχόντων, οἱ δὲ ἄρχοντες δοῦλοι τοῦ νόμου, σωτηρίαν...) (715d). Isocrates, in *Areopagiticus* 26, describes the magistrates as 'domestics' (οἰκέται) of the state. The phrase is at least as shocking as Plato's, for he applies this term to the people of leisure and means (σχολή and βίος ἱκανός). They are the servants of the 'household' of the state. Sthenidas and Paul represent a new approach, an increasingly prevalent view, which places the king in servitude to God. This reflects the pronounced propensity toward the notions of *nomos empsuchos* and imitation in the political reflection of late Hellenism.

313. He even uses the term *doulos* for Christ (Phil. 2.7).

314. It is Antisthenes, Socrates' devotee and father of the Cynics, who is credited with first finding intrinsic worth in slavery in the sense that individuals have worth despite being slaves.

It is assumed (Höistad 1948: 87-88, 202-203) that Dio Chrysostom goes back to Antisthenes' portrayal of Cyrus when he redefines the concept *doulos*: a man who lacks free spirit and has a servile nature, ἀνελεύθερος καὶ δουλοπρεπής (*Discourses* 15.29). 'For of those who are called slaves...many have the spirit of free men, and that among the free men there are many who are altogether servile' (15.29, Cohoon trans.). Dio also illustrates the extreme of making slavery a requirement of kingship: Dio shows Diogenes thinking that Alexander, to become a real king, must don the tunic with one sleeve, ἐξωμίδα λαβών (*Discourses* 4.66), the dress of the slave and the poor. See Höistad 1948: 218. But even before and outside the Cynic and Stoic sphere the notion that the ruler must be slave of the law is encountered in Plato and Isocrates. The king as slave of God, the theme that we pursue here, is Hellenistic Pythagorean.

Finally, Sthenidas gives us one of the most impressive political statements of the Hellenistic age: 'Nothing unruled by a king and without a
leader is good' (οὐδὲν δὲ ἀβασίλευτον καλὸν οὐδὲ ἄναρχον).[315] 'Nothing unruled is good' (οὐδὲν ἄναρχον καλόν) is a key idea of Pythagorean political thinking from Classical through Hellenistic times.[316] But
Sthenidas's monarchic theory adds *abasileuton* ('not ruled by a king')
and his dictum is much more than a simple reaffirmation of kingship.
Sthenidas actually defines the good as being like—sharing in, imitating
the qualities of—the king. Not only is the good of a political nature, it is
attained by all who are kinglike. This incremented formula claims objectivity and universality, provides humanity with a status in the political
nexus, and gives each individual a representative membership in the
legislation of the ideal kingdom. This kind of idea germinates in Paul.
In Paul it is the political—the *ekklēsia* that is founded for the common
good of its constituents and is part of the cosmic kingdom of God and
ultimately ruled by him—that is the cadre of the good, identified by
Paul with salvation. Each individual is a christ-type by his *pistis*. In
both Sthenidas and Paul the logic and emphasis are similar. Monarchy
and kingly *aretē* define the good. *Basileia* is the political regime;
basileuton the suitability for membership in it. 'Nothing unruled is good'
is the old political formula; 'nothing unlike the king is good' is the new
mystical monarchy. This conclusion of Hellenistic Pythagoreanism
infuses Paul's thinking.

Hellenistic Kingship and Paul

'Alexander abolished the political animal, ended the significance of the
polis, and made the temporal government monarchy pure and simple':
so wrote T.R. Glover in 1933.[317] Monarchy, as a practical or expedient
polity, had long been a form of government described by Classical political thinkers. True, kingship would occupy center stage in the political
philosophy of the Hellenistic and Roman periods, but little new was
added to the basic political theory of kingship after Plato and Aristotle.

315. H 271.9, T 188.10-11.
316. Aristoxenus, *Pythagorean Maxims*, according to Iamblichus, *On Pythagorean
Life* 175 = Stobaeus 4.1.49; L. Delatte 1942: 280. Ps.-Ecphantus put it: 'Nothing
unruled can be found' (H 274.12, T 81.2).
317. Glover 1933: 163-64.

The received text, however, has often enough been put to quite creative use.

A constant motif of Classical (and Hellenistic) period political philosophy is that the man of *aretē* is above the written law since he is steered by the ideal, or natural, law. In Plato, the reformer is above the very laws he makes for the people. He has knowledge of the ideal law, which the laws he makes approximate for others of less than perfect abilities.[318] The statesman of true political competence, like the skilled pilot of a ship, is superior to the laws.[319] To the law, Plato prefers a man with wisdom and royal power, for he can render justice appropriate to the particularities of a case.[320] Government is κατὰ τέχνην (*kata technēn*, 'expertise'), not κατὰ γράμματα (*kata grammata*, a written manual).[321] The divinely gifted man who has the knowledge to rule over himself needs no laws to rule him; he is naturally free. There is no law that is above knowledge.[322] Kings need give no account of their decisions, and their determinations are final.[323] The Sophists, in the spirit of Thrasymachus, advocate personal power and the downfall of the law, the weak's protection against the strong.[324]

Aristotle likewise considers the king a member of a race superior in virtue and political talent, above the law.[325] A king's judgment is more precise than the law, for it takes the specificity of events into account.[326] The ideal judge is the 'animate justice' (*dikaion empsuchon*),[327] a remarkable description that seems to bestow divinity on the magistrate. Plato's theory of *basileia* and, probably even more so, Aristotle's systematic analysis of the *pambasileus*, the absolute monarch, would control Hellenistic political thought and, translated into Christian language, dominate royal doctrine of modern Europe, Eastern and Western. Monarchy is the driving political force of Hellenism to such an extent that a letter, *Peri basileias*, dated to 330 BCE and written by a spirit with a profound grasp of Alexander's colonization projects (and, in fact,

318. *Politicus* 300c.
319. *Politicus* 297a.
320. *Politicus* 294a.
321. *Politicus* 296e.
322. *Laws* 9.875c.
323. *Laws* 6.761e. See also Goodenough 1928: 62.
324. Plato, *Gorgias* 482e-484a.
325. *Politics* 3.1288a.
326. *Politics* 3.1287b.
327. *Nicomachean Ethics* 5.1132a22.

The Political Paul

sometimes attributed to Aristotle), has been called the birth certificate of Hellenism.[328]

Following Plato and Aristotle, other philosophers developed the monarchical themes we have been discussing. Isocrates had hailed Philip of Macedonia as savior and legitimate ruler of Greece.[329] Though their political remarks rarely went beyond constructing utopias,[330] the Cynics and the Stoics gave the wise man the prerogatives of the king, internalized politics by proclaiming the kingdom within and stretched the polity by conferring cosmic citizenship. The (Classical or Hellenistic) Pythagorean Archytas of Tarentum (Taranto)[331] opposed the laws of the gods to the laws of men and maked the former the fathers and guides of the written laws. A community, Archytas wrote, consists of the ruler, the ruled and the laws. Laws are of two kinds: the animate law (*nomos empsuchos*)—that is, the king—and the inanimate, written law.[332] By announcing that state and universe share the same principles of government and morality, Archytas deepened Pythagorean interest in the king's office.[333] The Pythagoreans established political power, the system of right and legislation, under the authority of God.

328. Plezia 1969–70.

329. *To Philip* 114, 116 (*ap.* Goodenough 1928: 57).
Isocrates approves of absolute power and voices the popular beliefs according to which (1) the kings are equal in power with the gods (ἰσόθεοι), though fallible as humans (*To Philip* 5); (2) they must be the apex of virtue and models (παράδειγμα) to others; (3) the mores of the entire state are imitations of the rulers (τὸ τῆς πόλεως ὅλης ἦθος ὁμοιοῦται τοῖς ἄρχουσιν, *To Philip* 31); (4) to rule over oneself (ἄρχε σαυτοῦ,...κρατῆς τῶν ἐπιθυμιῶν, *To Philip* 29) is the sign of the true king; and (5) his pronouncements are laws (καὶ γὰρ πρέπει καὶ συμφέρει τὴν τῶν βασιλέων γνώμην ἀνικήτως ἔχειν περὶ τῶν δικαίων, ὥσπερ τοὺς νόμους τοὺς καλῶς κειμένους, *To Philip* 18).

330. Crates' *Pēra* poem describes a Cynic society (Diogenes Laertius 6.85-86). It is an example of political gastronomy. Thyme, garlic, figs and bread attract no stupid parasite, glutton or lecher. The highest good is liberty. Onesicritus' Gymnosophists (*FGrHist* 2.723-25, *ap.* Höistad 1948: 135-36) or Maximus of Tyre's theory of the Golden Age (*Oration* 36) are only a few from many possible examples.

331. As discussed in Chapter 4, the dating of Archytas is ambiguous. A. Delatte places him before Plato and Aristotle, while Theiler (1926a: 150 ff.) after them but outside the Stoic sphere of influence (*ap.* Goodenough 1928: 60).

332. Fragment #1, Stobaeus 4.1.135 p. 82 Hense [not in Thesleff]; A. Delatte 1922: 79-82; and fragment #2b, Stobaeus 4.1.135 pp. 82-83 Hense = T 33.6-12; A. Delatte 1922: 84-86.

333. See also Goodenough 1928: 61.

As the theory of absolute monarchy became the norm in Hellenistic political thought, it infiltrated Classical constitutional theory.[334] With the advent of imperial Rome, the process came full circle, with the emperor himself cast in the role of the leader of a true democracy[335] and a popular government.[336]

Paul is proposing a two-layered society, with corresponding dual politics. First, there is the *ekklēsia*, the political association proper. Within this *polis*-type community, the political game, as Classical and Hellenistic political philosophy had conceived it, applies. The supreme power belongs to the deity. Looked at one way, there is really nothing new here. Examined more closely, however, there is a difference between Paul's politics and that of any other ancient political philosopher, and this difference is overwhelming. The first-layer state actually lacks a ruler; it is a constitution *manqué*. This state is not only incomplete, it is not even a state, for it is not legally constituted unless joined to the second layer. The divine validates and governs it. Without this, the compact is nothing. The political transcends the human not just in the person of the ruler, as was common in both Classical and Hellenistic political philosophy. The divine does not just offer a political blueprint for human affairs, as any Hellenistic political writer would think. Human government is no longer just an imitation of God's rule of the *kosmos*. Paul explodes the distinction between human and divine affairs.

For all the difficulty, if not impossibility, of distinguishing between the two layers, the separation is both possible and necessary. The need for definition, unavoidable in any Western intellectual undertaking, directs me to the divisions operated by Aristotle. The first layer is a *politikē* rule of the *oikos–polis* type. The second is a *basilikē* order, a father–children relationship, an *oikos–basileia* political formula that turns the Classical fiction into normative reality. Paul creates an entity that he assumes exists objectively, but that may be analyzed solely in its fractured mode, split into its parts. Even if Paul thinks that the first layer is not politically viable if fractured from the transcendental, political discourse can examine it alone.

---

334. Aalders 1975: 3.

335. δημοκρατία ἀληθής (Dio Cassius, *Roman History* 52.14.4).

336. κοινὸς δῆμος (Philostratus, *Life of Apollonius of Tyana* 5.35). See Aalders 1975: 3 n. 4.

Political philosophy and metaphysics form a continuum, nowadays as in Greek antiquity. The relationship among concepts such as soul, reason, God and the government of the state is firmly established throughout Western philosophical speculation. According to Plato, the three powers in the state are *bouleutikon, epikourikon* and *chrēatistikon*: the political, the military, and the economic. These correspond to the three faculties of the soul, *logistikon, thumoeides* and *epithumētikon*: the rational, the spirited and the sensual.[337] For Aristotle, the organization of the city is parallel to the constitution of the soul. The *nous* ('mind') rules the drives with a political rule of the royal kind.[338] The Hellenistic Pythagoreans strike the same note. Diotogenes asserts that the same order observed in the universe is established in the soul.[339] For him, the king rules the state as the *logos* or *nous* rules the soul.[340] Most strikingly, discord is eliminated and life brought into the perfect harmony of *dikaiosunē* by the people's gazing upon the king.[341] Similarly, Ps.-Ecphantus alleges that imitation of the king redeems his subjects from their *hamartia*.[342] *Logos* (another name for the king), consorting with human beings, eradicates their evil, awakens and perfects them.[343] Remarkably, under ideal conditions the king spontaneously (*autophuōs*) transfers his virtues to his people. Ps.-Ecphantus's 'spontaneity' and Diotogenes' 'gaze' (*protaugasis*) restore the soul to a harmonious condition and align life with infallible *dikaiosunē*. This tradition of extending the domain of the political to include the beyond is of critical importance to Paul, who, with a stately maneuver, politicizes the divine and makes it the source and unique locus of *dikaiosunē*.

However 'transcendental' or 'irrational' Pauline political thought seems as compared with the political philosophy of Classical Greece, the continuity of the divine with the human community and the relationship of *dikaiosunē* with divinity are already strongly present in Classical political theory. The primacy of religion in any political system is a datum of Greek thinking. Aristoxenus the Pythagorean taught it.[344]

---

337. *Republic* 4.434a-d.
338. *Politics* 1.1254b5.
339. H 266.13-19, T 73.9-15.
340. H 268.17-269.6, T 74.21-26.
341. H 268.10, T 74.16.
342. H 274.3-5, T 80.21-23.
343. H 278.19-20, T 83.16-17.
344. Πυθαγορικαὶ ἀποφάσεις, *Pythagorean Maxims* (*ap.* A. Delatte 1922: 42-56).

Plato wants to call the government of a new colony by the name of the God ruling it.[345] Independently and working from a different perspective, the Romans followed a similar approach. In Rome, legal and political functions were always combined with religious ones, as is shown by the importance the *pontifices* ('priests') and the augurs retained throughout Roman history. The head of the *collegium* of *pontifices*, *pontifex maximus* ('high priest', actually a magistrate living in the *regia* and armed with the *auspicium*, 'authority'), was such an important personage in the state that in 12 BCE Augustus decided that this title could be claimed by emperors only.[346]

The centrality of the deity in traditional Western metaphysics[347] is intertwined with a politics of 'nuclear' power, whoever may be at its core. With the intensification of the tyranny of this deity, absolute monarchy finds its program validated. The proof of God's existence by the argument from creation, one of the most common in antiquity and one to which Paul subscribes (Rom. 1.20), is interlocked not only with an orderly universe but also with an orderly political society.

The pivotal concept in the dialectic between politics and metaphysics is *dikaiosunē*. From Plato on, *dikaiosunē* always has a divine or quasi-divine matrix. The individual 'in charge of' *dikaiosunē*, the lawgiver, is always seen as being in some way divine. *Dikaiosunē* can only derive from a source above the human, and the administrator of justice is consistently accorded suprahuman endowments. Moreover, the lawgiver always stands in an ambiguous relation to the law. Paul's source of *dikaiosunē*, his dispenser of justice, has no need of law, and in this sense Paul belongs squarely within the entire political tradition of *basileus* and *basileia*, rooted in Aristotle and lavishly applied in Hellenistic times.

345. *Laws* 4.712b-717b. 'But if states are to be named after their rulers, the true state ought to be called by the name of the God who rules over the wise' (4.713a). See A. Delatte 1922: 44-49. Plato uses a myth, μῦθος, to explain the best polity. The best ruled states are an imitation, μίμημα, of the rule of cosmos (in the time of Cronos). Since no human nature is qualified to hold supreme power without insolence and injustice, Kronos appointed *daimones*, a higher and more divine race, to be kings and rulers of the cities (4.713a-c).

346. Sandys 1925: 153.

347. In contrast to the resistance of the postmodern thought to the pull of onto-centrism. See Flynn 1992.

In Hellenistic political writings, imitation of the ruler is identified with *sōtēria*, salvation. By copying the king's virtues one attains moral salvation. The lawgiver is often called *nomos empsuchos*, living law. From Diotogenes' affirmation that the king is personified law, it follows that justice, the supreme *aretē*, is his paramount attribute; as God harmonizes the universe and its parts, so does the king effect the concord of the state and the harmonizing of each of its elements.[348] Justice is the common good—the good of both the ruler and the ruled— and the unifying principle in political society.[349] The force of the term *dikaiosunē* is political whether applied to God or to the king. *Dikaiosunē* describes the inner mechanism of a political society. It is, in Ps.-Ecphantus's terms, the gravitational force of the *koinōnia*. Society, says Ps.-Ecphantus, exits because of equality (*isotēs*). *Dikaiosunē* is what determines distributive justice.[350] In Paul *Dikaiosunē* retains its Classical/ Hellenistic essence: it is divine in origin and political in nature. God is author of the 'distribution of equality' that maintains the state as a whole and establishes the place of each of its actors.

In the Classical tradition, Plato's philosopher-king is a Godlike man who follows a divine pattern and reproduces in his soul the world of unchanging harmonies and order.[351] The philosopher-king is Plato's major contribution to the Classical constellation of political ideas. It is rooted in his 'like state, like soul' doctrine, which makes the aspects of the soul closely correspond to the classes of citizens in the *polis*. This implies that he who arrives at the mastery of *theōria*, he who contemplates the Forms and has knowledge of the intelligible order, is not only the obvious choice to lead[352] but must even be compelled to rule.[353] In Aristotle, the political genius is 'God among humans';[354] the individual in complete mastery of himself is the equal of God;[355] the legislator has high, superhuman endowments.[356] The ruler's difference

348. H 264.12-18, T 72.9-14.
349. (δικαιοσυνά) κοινὸν γὰρ ἀγαθόν ἐντι καὶ ἀρχόντων καὶ ἀρχομένων, εἴ γε δὴ συναρμοστικά ἐντι κοινωνίας πολιτικᾶς (H 269.5-6, T 74.25-26).
350. 'Distribution of equality', ἀποδιανομή ἰσότητος (H 279.2-3, T 83.21-22).
351. *Republic* 6.497a-502c.
352. *Republic* 6.484a-487a.
353. *Republic* 7.519c-520a.
354. *Politics* 3.1284a10.
355. *Politics* 3.1284b30-34, 3.1288a17-19.
356. *Politics* 7.1334a10-34; *Ethics* 5.1132a22.

from other people (e.g., heads of households) is one of nature.[357] Hellenistic and Roman monarchic theories abound in Godlike kings. Archytas, the early Hellenistic (or Classical) Pythagorean, introduces, besides the ancestral customs or natural law,[358] a new type of unwritten law: the monarch. He himself is not only a law but the vivid representation to men of *the* law—the will of the gods to which all local state laws must conform. The king himself *is* law. Archytas' king produces law for his subjects out of his own nature. He is so superior to the local codes that his legality is tested not by them but by his conformity to higher natural law.[359] Diotogenes writes that the king exercises unaccountable power (*archa anupeuthunos*),[360] is animate law (*nomos empsuchos*) and prefigures (*pareschēmatistai*) God among men.[361] The king is united to the state by the same ratio as God to the world; the king is to God as the *polis* is to the universe.[362] Diotogenes believes that the king's *aretē* is the same as God's[363] and that the king imitates God.[364] In the administration of justice, the king acts as God does in his leadership and command of the universe.[365] In Sthenidas, the *basileus* is a God by birth and by imitation, *genesei kai mimasei*.[366] For Ps.-Ecphantus the king's divinity is superior to that of all other beings, and he alone is capable of forming a conception of God.[367] The king is difficult to behold because of his excessive divinity.[368] By assimilation with divine beings superior to himself, the king best rules his subjects.[369] The earthly king is equal in *aretē* with God.[370] The king–God alliance is a fellowship that is most necessary and best for humanity, for

---

357. *Politics* 1.1252a7-18.

358. These may be the same.

359. Goodenough 1928: 60-61. Note that according to Xenophon's Socrates, the king must follow the laws of the *polis* (*Memorabilia* 4.6.12; *ap*. Goodenough 1928: 60-61).

360. The same expression, ἀνυπεύθυνος ἄρχειν, as in Plato's *Laws* 6.761e.

361. H 265.10-12, T 72.22-23.

362. H 265.6-8, T 72.19-20.

363. H 270.3-4, T 75.8-9.

364. H 270.10-11, T 75.15-16.

365. H 264.12-15, T 72.9-11.

366. H 270.16, T 187.13.

367. H 272.10, 14-15, T 80.1, 4-5.

368. H 273.11, T 80.14.

369. H 274.1-2, T 80.20.

370. H 274.21-275.1, T 81.10.

nothing can subsist outside society.[371] Ps.-Ecphantus sees the king as light and savior.[372] The king is the synonym of the *logos*.[373]

This political philosophy of kingship is by no means restricted to the Hellenistic Pythagoreans. E.R. Goodenough has shown that the 'philosophy of royalty was known and accepted in the Hellenistic age'.[374] Cicero conceives the good ruler as one who puts his own life as law before the citizens,[375] and since for Cicero true law is right reason in agreement with nature, the ruler thus almost becomes an incarnate *logos*.[376] In Philo the monarch is a divine image.[377] In Seneca, as in Plutarch, the good ruler is the incarnation of divine reason, or *logos*.[378] Hellenistic and Roman political theorists repeat *ad nauseam* the precept that the king is to the state as God is to the world and that the state is to the world as the king is to God.[379]

The continuity of the development is manifest. There is an ongoing effort to show the king as superior to all other humans: a noble-minded benefactor (*euergetēs*) of his subjects; living law (*nomos empsuchos*); *logos*; savior (*sōtēr*) of the people. And, of course, the portrayals of the king as a dispenser of justice are particularly interesting to the present study.[380]

371. H 275.5-10, T 81.13-16.

372. H 273.1, T 80.6-7.

373. H 278.12-20, T 83.11-17. Chesnut (1978: 1320) is mistaken to think that *Logos* is 'planted like a seed...' It is *Peithō* that is *ephuē*. Also, *Logos* is not 'in the king's mind', it *is* the king.

374. Goodenough 1928: 91. He demonstrates this by a survey of six texts representing a variety of genres and authorships: the Ps.-Aristotelian *Letter to Alexander*, *3 Maccabees*, Philo, the eclectic Stoic Musonius, Plutarch, Mithridates' speech preserved by Justinus, and Hellenistic dedicatory inscriptions (1928: 91-102). Particularly interesting is Plutarch's *To an Unlearned Ruler*. Just the enumeration of topics suggests the relevance of this text for some of Paul's teachings and for the image Paul creates for himself: on descent, on rulers, on animate law, on *dikaiosunē*, on suffering, on imitation (1928: 94-98).

375. *Sed suam vitam ut legem praefert suis civibus* (*Republic* 1.34.52).

376. *Est quidem vera lex recta ratio naturae congruens...* (*Republic* 3.22.33). See Chesnut 1978: 1326.

377. Migne (*ap.* Chesnut 1978: 1328). For an excellent, extensive treatment of the political-metaphysical complex in Philo, see Goodenough 1938.

378. Chesnut 1978: 1326.

379. Diotogenes, H 265.6-12, T 73.19-23. For Ps.-Ecphantus, friendship in the state imitates the concord of the universe, H 275.15-16, T 81.21-22.

380. The importance of this political virtue reflects the Classical Greek back-

The Hellenistic Pythagoreans succeeded in keeping their philosophical bearings even in the midst of turgid mystical affectation. Paul has to deal with a similar problem, the age's fixation on salvation-talk. Yet, like his Hellenistic colleagues, and precisely because of his grounding in the Hellenistic reflective environment, Paul manages to maintain a significant philosophical rigor even while steeped in irrational language.

The political and the metaphysical, the practical and the speculative, always formed a unity in ancient philosophy. Systems differ according to how the continuity is established. The Hellenistic Pythagoreans provide an elegant solution: it is the king's duality that bridges the two realms. For Paul, a scandalous, preposterous experience—the cross event—stands at the center of the dynamic, and this event explodes the narrow passage of kingship between the two worlds and opens the floodgates of heaven. Christ is the *exemplum* and archetype, yet everyone can not only imitate and reproduce him but can also identify with and *be* him, become one of many anonymous kings. The Godhead is open to all. Through his crucial act—the excruciating experience of the cross—Christ forces the hand of nature and makes all naturally kings. The replication of Christ in christs, as well as of the King in kings, is a powerful motif in Paul, a striking example of the mechanism for the creation of a new typology and a new type. Paul's sarcasm notwithstanding, in 1 Cor. 4.8, the Corinthians 'have become kings' (ἐβασιλεύσατε). Galatians is rife with similar references, most notably: 'Christ has been formed [μορφωθῇ] in you' (Gal. 4.19) and 'being a new creation' (καινὴ κτίσις) (Gal. 6.15, cf. 2 Cor. 5.17).

Every citizen of Christ's state is the king's subject, but he can be a king as well. The thirst for the irrational is satisfied, the world is turned on its head, and yet for the most part everything is done according to accepted philosophical procedures. Paul's continuity with Greek political theory makes his transformation a not completely surprising development. The distinction between Paul and his Hellenistic antecedents is most emphatically *not* in the role of the divine in human political affairs. Rather, the break has to do with the significance of reason, a breach in the assessment of rationality's relation to the divine.

ground of Hellenistic political ideas (Aalders 1968: 21); the king is law incarnate, νόμος ἔμψυχος, a notion rooted in the Classical theory of the king as above the written law (27). Although the king is well above ordinary humanity, however, Aalders remarks that 'straightforward deification of the king does not occur in our remains of Hellenistic political theory' (26).

The most striking and imposing aspect of the *basileia* group of writings is how really unsurprising they are. Ingenious and effective, they display, after all, the conventional, the normative political thought of the times. Paul is an impressive thinker, to be sure, but the infrastructure of his thought shares this undercurrent of normalcy. The *basileia* texts display the common level of reflection in Paul's Hellenistic milieu—an ordinariness of which Paul partakes and which he transgresses. He enforces the system—even as he disables it.

Part II
THE POLITICAL PAUL

Chapter 6

ROME AND PAUL

Paul is in agreement with the Classical view, inherited through Hellenistic Pythagoreanism and Stoicism, that political society is inherent in human nature and is grounded in objective, immutable principles. The Hellenistic Greeks had, however, little feeling for Roman political subtleties, including the emperor's efforts to represent himself as *primus inter pares*. Imbued with so many sycophantic and apologetic dicta about the transcendental procession of power, they perceived the Roman government as an absolute kingship, with the emperor as autocrat.[1]

A most revealing example of the Hellenistic Greeks' view of the Roman state is offered by the *Monumentum Ancyranum*.[2] The celebrated inscription *Res Gestae Divi Augusti* is known from the walls of the temple of Rome and Augustus at Ancyra (Ankara), capital of Roman Galatia. The original Latin text appeared on the inner walls of the pronaos.[3] The Greek translation—actually an *interpreted* version of the Latin—was inscribed on the temple's southwestern outer walls, fully visible to the passing crowd. In both its fidelity to the original (style, vocabulary correspondence) *and* its divergence from it (omissions, insertions, rearrangement, altered semantic context), the Greek version consistently carries out a 'program of monarchizing Augustus, discounting the people while glorifying the state of Rome and matching the Greek text to the linguistic, political, and cultural sensibilities of its eastern readership'.[4]

A few of the most interesting modifications of the Latin are worth recalling. First, in the Greek version, *polis* is used for five different Latin

1. 'The principate is viewed by the Greeks as a theocratic regime dominated by a living God' (André 1987: 9).
2. The following discussion is indebted to Wigtil 1982.
3. For archaeological details, see Akurgal 1993: 3.
4. Wigtil 1982: 636.

terms;[5] the complex Roman administrative system is thereby reduced to a term that would make sense to a Greek of Asia Minor and one that gives a false sense of the preservation of Greek institutions. Second, the Greek distinguishes between δῆμος (*dēmos*), used to describe the Roman people, and ἔθνος (*ethnos*), used for the Germans, where Latin uses *populus* in both cases.[6] Thus is created a Platonic–Aristotelian contrast—alien to the Latin original—between a traditional Greek political entity (now embodied and furthered by Rome) and a foreign political structure (embodied in the loose congregation of barbaric tribes) as well as an opposition between master and slave races. Further, the Greek displays no awareness of the significance and substance of two crucial Latin political terms, *princeps* and *imperium*,[7] translating them variously (and at variance with the standard Greek equivalents) and thus suggesting their irrelevance to the Greek reader. In the Greek version, person and office are one and the same, and no distinction is made between a merely honorific title and a term denoting absolute authority. Augustus's unnamed enemy at Actium, 'the enemy in war', becomes in Greek 'the adversary against whom I prevailed' (ὁ ὑπ' ἐμοῦ καταγωνισθεὶς πολέμιος),[8] implying that the fight was a moral competition won by Augustus because of his superior moral excellence.[9] The phrase *priusquam nascerer* ('before I was born') is rendered as 'before me' (πρὸ ἐμοῦ), making Augustus's own person the pivotal marker in the measurement of time.[10]

Practically all of Augustus's republican pretensions would have been lost on the Greek, who would have read the inscription as depicting an absolute, divine monarch ruling over an immense collection of pathetic

5.   Wigtil 1982: 632.
6.   Wigtil 1982: 633.
7.   Wigtil 1982: 637.
8.   Paul is very fond of related expressions with a very similar message. Ἀγών, ἀγωνίζομαι indicate his struggle, against great odds, with an evil adversary for the *euangelion* (Phil. 1.30; 1 Cor. 9.25; 1 Thess. 2.2; see also Col. 1.29; 2.1 [4.12]; 1 Tim. 4.10; 6.12; 2 Tim. 4.7).
9.   See also Wigtil 1982: 636.
10.   Wigtil 1982: 636. In the celebrated Priene inscription (*OGI* 458), of 9 BCE, the birthday of Augustus becomes the day of the New Year, the beginning of the calendar for the cities of Asia. The preserved Greek text opens with the words γενέθλιος τοῦ θειοτάτου Καίσαρος, the birthday of the most divine Caesar. The Latin original, fragments of which were found in Apamea, has here simply: *principis nostri*. The Greek fawning sycophancy is, as always, at work. See Penna 1984: 157.

subjects. The Greek text enhances the person of Augustus, boosts the emperor's character, makes his life exemplary. Augustus was an admirer of Alexander and certainly emulated him,[11] and the Greeks had no trouble seeing in Caesar the culmination of the Macedonian's long monarchial dynasty. The translator, a well-educated Greek with a good knowledge of Latin and someone deeply moved by the importance of his task, understood, however, the political essence of Augustus's literary masterpiece and made sure that neither Roman power nor the Greek audience was shortchanged.

A different kind of example shows, in a remarkably suggestive way, how Roman power borrowed from Greek political symbolism while at the same time voiding it, and how the Romans simultaneously pre-empted and impugned Greek tradition. When Augustus and his friend Agrippa resolved to begin an intense building program in Athens, they set their eyes on, among other places, the Athenian agora, a vast area dedicated to political debate, a Greek political space par excellence. Under the pretext of beautifying it, the Romans dismembered the agora, filling the plots with new, stately buildings.[12]

When the eastern Mediterranean fell to the Romans and Greek liberty became an entirely academic issue, political discussion focused on Rome—mostly expressing admiration and amazement. The Romans, however, had no political theory of their own. The political questions of the late Hellenistic period are, as practical matters, strictly Roman, but discussions of their theoretical dimensions are conducted in terms that are Greek.[13] The filiation between Rome and Greece came first; the defense of absolute monarchy followed immediately after. Virgil[14] brought the fable of Rome's Trojan origins to literary apex. The Greek descent of Rome was also embraced by Dionysius of Halicarnassus, who in his *Roman Antiquities* (2.3.1-8) has Romulus speak on the three forms of government, the fundamental Greek political discourse. Philo, in his *Embassy to Gaius* (147), regards Roman imperialism as the

11. See Hogarth 1897 (quoted by Glover 1933: 119). Paul thought that what the Roman emperors imitated, imperfectly, was God.

12. See Tufi 1993, esp. 94.

13. A good example of this is Dionysius of Halicarnassus's complex Ῥωμαϊκὴ Ἀρχαιολογία (*Roman Antiquities*, first century BCE–first century CE) written in Augustus's Rome, and in which traditional Greek categories form the underpinning of Roman events.

14. 70–19 BCE.

logical continuation of Greek rule. It was the Greeks themselves who
were the foremost apologists of Roman imperial power.[15]

15. The political and military power of Rome is variously interpreted by the
Greek authors. The Greek Polybius (second century BCE) sees it as a global vision
of Mediterranean history. Timagenes of Alexandria (first century BCE); Nicolaus of
Damascus, Herod's teacher (first century BCE); the Pontic Strabo (middle of first
century BCE–first quarter of first century CE); and the Alexandrian Jew Philo (end
of first century BCE–middle of first century CE): all see Rome as the conclusion of
the Hellenistic historical process. (For Philo, Rome joins 'other Greeces' to
Greece.) Appian of Alexandria (second century CE) positively assesses both the
period of Hellenistic monarchies and the Roman regime. The Carian Dionysius of
Halicarnassus (fl. c. 20 BCE) represents a milestone in this process: he disengages
Rome and its empire from the Hellenistic tradition and connects it to Classical
Greece. Dionysius, however, is the culmination of a tradition that begins with the
Sicilian Timaeus of Taouromenium (356–260 BCE), who turned Greek historiography about Rome around. See also Gabba 1994: 40-45.
    'Le soutien des penseurs grecs a renforcé chez les Romains la bonne conscience
impériale' writes André (1987: 65). André (59-70) also notes the support given the
imperial policies of Rome by Josephus (*War* 7.71) and Pliny the Elder (*Natural
History* 7.95), as well as by later writers such as Plutarch, Aelius Aristide, Fronto
and Apuleius. Christian writers, too, such as Tertullian and Origen (*Against Celsus*
2.30) emphasized the Roman peace and the greatness of Rome's people. Hash-
monean propaganda also was favorable to Rome; Rome is seen not just as a
superior military power but also as loyal to its allies (1 Macc. 8.1-32).
    The reversal of this process begins, however, with the Christian theologians—
ironically, Western ones, not Greeks. Hippolytus of Rome (170–235 CE, who, however, wrote in Greek) and Augustine (354–430) display an anti-Roman approach;
Rome begins to be seen as destructive of the national character of provincial popu-
lations (Gabba 1994: 45).
    Before the Romanocentric intellectual movement, the Greeks, while acknow-
ledging Rome's growing might, are more inclined, at least until Panaetius (second
century BCE), to rank Rome, culturally, with the Barbarians. See Gabba 1994: 42.
    Politically, republican Rome presented a special case. The Romans were not bar-
barians, for they were not a monarchy but an autonomous city, with popular
assemblies and a council (the Senate), with magistrates elected by the citizens.
Rome was, from the Greek point of view, a genuine *polis* (Giardina 1998b: 43).
This is, I suggest, what Heraclides Ponticus meant when, already in the fourth century BCE, he called Rome a 'Greek city' (Plutarch, *Camillus* 22.2)—a recognition
that Rome is a Greek-type political entity, a πόλις Ἑλληνίς, and not an example
of 'literary imperialism', as Gruen thinks (1984: 318). In the age of the kings, Rome
had already opened itself to Greek culture, as archaeological and epigraphical dis-
coveries attest. The Romans preferred, however, a Trojan ancestry for themselves,
'within the Greek reach but without identifying themselves as Greek' ('nella sfera

Hellenistic absolute kingship caused mutations in political reasoning and fundamental semantic changes in the language of political power. Absolute monarchy entered the 'Classical' tradition of constitutional theories.[16] Later, in imperial Rome, even the emperor's rule would be called a 'true democracy' (δημοκρατία ἀληθής) or a 'popular government' (ἡ ἑνὸς ἀρχὴ δῆμός…ἐστιν), as we see in Dio Cassius's *Roman History* (52.14.4) and in Philostratus's *The Life of Apollonius of Tyana* (5.35), respectively.[17]

In Dio Cassius,[18] the politician and financier Agrippa tries to persuade Octavian not to renounce the monarchy. The text, which places the speech in the year 29 BCE, has Agrippa urging the future emperor to pay no heed to the critics of monarchy, to quell their dissent by limiting free speech and to take the reins of public affairs unhesitatingly into his own hands while accepting 'the prudent' (i.e. those of similar persuasion) as counselors. Agrippa argues that only thus will the state be properly ordered and the services proper to its station be disbursed to each class of citizens. Only thus can true democracy be established and unfailing freedom acquired (ἡ δημοκρατία ἡ ἀληθής τε ἐλευθερία ἡ ἀσφαλής). In Philostratus[19] the sage and magician Apollonius of Tyana[20] delivers a speech in which he strengthens Vespasian's resolve to keep to monarchical policy, already a fact. While he sees himself as governed only by the gods, Apollonius acknowledges humanity's need for constitutional government; Vespasian's excellence makes him best suited to assume the leadership: 'For just as a single man preeminent in virtue transforms a democracy into the guise of a government of a single man who is the best, so the government of one man, if it provides all round for the welfare of the community, is popular government' (ἡ ἑνὸς ἀρχὴ πάντα ἐς τὸ ξυμφέρον τοῦ κοινοῦ προορῶσα δῆμός ἐστιν).

These instances represent only the end of the process by which the Roman empire and absolute monarchy were justified—a program just

greca senza per questo definirsi Greci' [Giardina 1998b: 44-45]). They blended the Trojan myth of Aeneas with another indigenous myth, of Romulus and Remus, the latter, ironically, itself betraying Greek mold and genre (H.J. Rose, *OCD* 936). According to Suetonius (*Claudius* 25.3), the people of Illium were declared *consanguinei* of the Romans. See also Gruen 1984: 64-65, 612-13.

  16. Aalders 1975: 3.
  17. See Aalders 1968: 120-21; Larsen 1973: 45-6 (*ap.* Aalders 1975: 3 n. 4).
  18. Second–third century CE.
  19. 170–c. 245 CE.
  20. A historical person, fl. first century CE.

as abject and just as buoyant as the earlier endeavor to uphold the Hellenistic kings. The modus operandi of any apologist for imperial autocracy was, as we have seen above, first to establish that the emperor was morally better than his subjects and/or opponents and, second, to prove that he ruled in his subjects' interest.[21]

Cicero, in *Republic* (3.36-37), has Laelius begin his address with an account of law in accordance with nature, a Classical motif that here takes on a Stoic coloring;[22] like a Hellenistic political writer, Laelius then compares the relationship between the imperial power and its subjects to the master-slave relationship (drawing on Greek, especially Aristotelian, theory of the household) and also to the kinship between the rational and the irrational parts of the soul, the Platonic–Aristotelian psychology. Laelius is not simply revising Aristotle's defense of slavery,[23] however, but is revamping it to apply to politics per se, to the relation between the ruler and the ruled.[24] This is remarkable: the Greek *topoi* receive the Roman imperial purple, thus becoming a 'new' politics and a 'new' psychology.[25] This 'new' political view is also Paul's, though with a twist.[26] The inadequate *logos* of the Aristotelian slave,[27]

21. Yet, Rome remains throughout its imperial period a tyranny. 'Le régime impérial n'a jamais été ni une dyarchie ni un régime de liberté, ce fut toujours un régime de tyrannie' (Le Gall 1990, *ap.* Nicolet 1990: 174).

22. This means, as Zeno, Cleanthes and Chrysippus are said to have taught, that true law is common to all things, ὁ νόμος ὁ κοινός, both to humans and to the universe; the law is identified with right reason, ὁ ὀρθὸς λόγος, pervading all things, and the same as Zeus, ὁ αὐτὸς ὢν τῷ Διί, i.e. unchanging and eternal (Diogenes Laertius 7.88).

23. Cf. also Strasburger (1965: 45) and Astin (1967: 300-301), *ap.* Erskine (1990: 196) who wrongly calls them to task for this view.

24. The theme is transmitted through the Hellenistic Pythagoreans. I fail to see anything Stoic here, against Erskine (1990: 196), but with the authors he criticizes. Amazingly, Erskine rejects the Aristotelian source precisely on the ground that, in Aristotle, the master–slave relation is absolute and despotic, and thus at odds with the reason–desire status, which is monarchic and constitutional. The oddity had long been removed by Hellenistic political reflection.

25. Laelius's approach also reflects the stance of later Stoicism, for the Early Stoics could not have disagreed more with both illustrations: for them the empire was unnatural and unjust and the soul was a unity, undivided between rational and irrational parts. Lack of excellence was only a defective rationality; the standard rationality is represented by the wise man (Erskine 1990: 194-95).

26. It will be taken over, practically unmodified, by the Early Church, and used for its internal organization. 'How natural and normal monarchy seemed with its

his incomplete humanity, in Hellenistic times becomes the common condition of all humanity. Hence the special, privileged place of the king.
For Cicero, men differ according to their ability to govern. Repeating a
Hellenistic stereotype, Laelius says that it is a principle of nature that
the best rule the weaker in the interest of the latter. In Plato and Aristotle, God directs man, mind steers the body, reason commands desire.
By the time we reach Cicero, a monarchic government rules its subjects
despotically—that is, as if they were slaves. Laelius's subtle sycophancy
makes it the emperor's duty to maintain his imperial power; to abandon
it would be an abrogation of his responsibility.

The intellectual critique of the empire is as feeble as it is venerable.[28]
(Armed resistance, suicidal, is confined to remote borders and religious
zealots.) There is really the feeling that there is no substitute for Rome.
Paul loves Rome. He falls within a compelling tradition of apologetics
for Roman power. His interests are not revolutionary. Yet his ends are
different from those of other apologists of empire. Paul both concentrates
and diffuses power. In Paul's system, power is not diluted by sharing.
Everyone who participates in it actually *adds* to Christ; the more of
them there are, the more absolute God's rule. By extending shares to
all, Paul augments what is expected from each. On the other hand,
Paul's reiteration of the theology of power is excessive: God is not just
the source of authority—of the king's legitimacy—but is alone the
ruler. Kings like commoners partake in power through Christ.

My view of Paul's relation to the Roman empire finds a suggestive
confirmation at the archaeological site of Caesarea, in Israel.[29] Here, a

hierarchy of graded civil servants, is proven by the swiftness with which the same
conception was adopted by the Church' (Glover 1933: 122).

27. *Politics* 1.1253a17-1255a2.

28. There are glimpses in literature of an opposition to the empire. Polybius's
Isocrates (*Histories* 31.33.5, 32.2.4-8); Agatharchides of Cnidos, after the destruction of Carthage (GGM I 189-90, section 102, Fraser 1972: I, 545, 550; II, 786);
Carneades, head of the Academy, in his discourse of 155 BCE for and against
justice (Cicero, *Republic* 3.8). Erskine 1990: 183, 189. It appears, veiled, in Dio
Chrysostom, in the conventional treatment of the opposition between Greek freedom and the Persian Empire (*Discourses* 14 and 15); and in Tacitus, who calls *pax
romana* the peace of emptiness (*Agricola* 30.4) and who reflects on the fragility of
the empire (*Histories* 1.3). André 1987: 68-69.

29. Caesarea was founded by Herod the Great (37 BCE–4 BCE) who was granted
the ancient Sidonian anchorage by Octavian Augustus in 30 BCE. It remained the
capital of Roman (and Byzantine) Palestine until the Arab conquest in 640. Paul

few steps west of the northern end of the *cardo maximus*, were found
the remains of a Byzantine-period administrative building. An inscription helped identify the edifice as the tax archive.[30] The mosaic floor of
Room 3 of the sprawling facility[31] displays a quote from Romans
(13.3): 'Would you not fear the authority? Do good and you will
receive praise from it'. By the time this floor was laid, Paul was firmly
embedded in the structure of Christian imperial power; his words were
official imperial propaganda. He was used to support, justify and
legitimize the Byzantine imperium's policies and the world order it
instituted. Paul's words encourage the subject to obedience and civic
duty. The Christian's reward for good citizenship is the commendation
of the monarch's officials.

Paul, in other words, is the ideological guardian of the processes and
structures of imperial power. Paul's political objective was to make the
empire endure, to ward off its decay by steeling it with a Christian
ribband. Paul understood the political advantages of Christianity and
used them to strengthen the Roman political system he admired and
endorsed.[32] He and later apologists (including the gospel writers) made
Christianity comfortable for the ruling authority.[33] Outspoken accep-

finds himself time and again in Caesarea, he leaves from or lands in Caesarea (Acts
9.30; 18.22; 21.8, 16), and was detained in the praetorium two years before being
taken to Rome, at his request, to have his case heard by the emperor (Acts 23–26).
Peter converted there the first Gentile, Cornelius, a centurion of the Roman garrison
(Acts 10). The first Revolt (66–70 CE) had one of its causes the Romans'
desecration of a Caesarea synagogue, probably at the incitement and certainly with
the consent of Florus, the abusive procurator (Josephus, *War* 2.285-92). A powerful
Rabbinical School functioned there from the third century CE, and its anti-Christian
polemic found the most redoubtable opponent in Origen, who lived 29 years in the
city (231–250 CE). See Murphy-O'Connor 1992: 213-14.

30. The inscription is now in the small Sedot Museum nearby. It reads: 'Christ
help Ampelios, the keeper of the archives, and Musonius, the fiscal secretary, and
the other archivists of the same depository.'

31. A courtyard around which are eight rooms.

32. Paul seems aware of the importance of social factors, esp. the weight of copy-
cat phenomena in determining political trends or religious fashion. He knows that if
enough people from any community and particularly enough wealthy or politically
prominent members of a society embrace his system, most, and eventually all, will.
And here the essential factor is concord among those already won.

33. The concept 'power through weakness' has often been applied to Paul's
strategy of power, most recently by Savage 1995. This power was understood, however, in ethical or theological terms, rarely political. 2 Cor. 10–13 is the *locus* of

tance of taxation is the most blatant kind of submission to the political regime. The implications of Rom. 13.6-7 as reiterated on this mosaic floor are momentous and fateful. Paul upholds political sovereignty and reaffirms the authority of the state while making it fully compatible with faith. Following the Hellenistic Pythagoreans, Paul actually turned political sovereignty into religious dogma.

What is new about Paul's political thinking is not the means but the end. He uses the same rhetorical techniques of moral exhortation, the same political and religious concepts as other popular political philosophers. Not even the formula of salvation he proposes is original, though he does seize on the tremendous novelty of Jesus' death and resurrection, which he develops and exploits in remarkable ways. Paul's ambition is to integrate the death of Jesus into a political plan. He unfreezes the common political stereotypes of the time and, while retaining the individual, egoistic character of salvation, he produces a soteriology that is collective and political, guided less by moral precepts than by his two-tiered constitutional formula.

Paul works consistently and concurrently in two registers: *polis* and empire, community and kingship. To ground the first, he needs the fusion between household and *polis*, secured from the Hellenistic theorists; to this *oikos–polis* structure Paul applies the name *ekklēsia* and makes the community an equality-within-hierarchy. For the second, he takes over the Hellenistic monarchical ideas and applies them to God. He thus produces a *polis intra imperium* political edifice that is not unlike the Hellenistic kingdom[34] and quite similar to the Roman administrative apparatus.

Paul constantly pursues parallelisms between the *ekklēsia* and Rome. Rome proved itself: military might and discipline brought *pax romana*.[35] God proved himself: he raised Christ from the dead. Rome conquered

Paul's presentation of this issue, and its characteristic expression is 2 Cor. 12.10, ὅταν γὰρ ἀσθενῶ, τότε δυνατός εἰμι. *Charis* is an expression of God's *dikaiosunē*, and its political force is strengthened by such contexts. I would qualify Paul's approach as 'power without the threat of power'.

34. In a Hellenistic monarchy, a *polis* is, constitutionally, only a part of a kingdom (Aalders 1975: 8).

35. The Roman peace is sung by Greeks and Romans, by pagans, Jews and Christians alike: e.g., Strabo (*Geography* 14, 144, 186, 204, 288); Philo (*Leg. Gai.* 21); Pliny the Elder (*Natural History* 14.2; 27.3; 36.118); Tertullian; Origen (*Against Celsus* 2.30); Prudentius (*Against Symmachus* 1.287; 2.582). *Ap.* Glover 1933: 120-22.

the world through the might of its army and the strategy of its generals; *militia Christi*, disciplined soldiers of Christ led by inspired coaches, make the vast Roman empire Christ's courtyard. Rome has organized its world into colonies, cities, peoples, nations according to a distributive justice based on cultural criteria.[36] Paul structures the empire in *ekklēsiai* and organizes these assemblies according to a distributive justice dependent on possession of *pneuma*.[37] Rome realizes the *cosmopolis* that escaped Alexander's Diadochi. Paul's Christianity fortifies it. Rome created ideological structures that while stimulating local and regional democratic practices excluded the multitude from political power. For Paul, organization and discipline give force to his communities. Power, however, is not of this world; it is of God. Rome gradually aligns *civitas* and *imperium*.[38] Paul anticipates it by identifying Christianity with *imperium*. The Christian is the *civis*.[39] While Roman historians of the first century reflect on the fragility of the empire, Paul conceives power without weakness, rule without decay, universalism without opposition.

M.I. Finley[40] identifies four areas that were rarely if ever questioned by the Greeks or the Romans: the legitimacy of the current ruler (except in cases of tyranny); its corollary, political obligation; the political and human nature of justice; and the notion that legitimate rule is by law, not by human beings. It is Paul who raises the question of a political constitution's legitimacy—an axiom in modern social-contract political theory—and he answers it with the principle of divine right. He actually bestows divine legitimacy on the imperial regime and on Roman law. While the Greeks and Romans had formerly used legendary characters to validate a system of justice,[41] Paul employs an explicitly historical hero to sanction a political system. Christ's method (as laid out by Paul) is unique. On the one hand, he gives a new constitution, the *euangelion*; on the other, he legitimizes the political organism that is already in

36. Pliny the Younger pleads for the privileged status of the Greek world based on its cultural superiority (*Letters* 8.24). *Ap.* André 1987: 60.

37. Obviously, this idea is borrowed by both from the Greek and Hellenistic political theories.

38. Caracalla's *Constitutio Antoniniana* would make it an equation when, in 212, he granted Roman citizenship to all Roman subjects.

39. These complementarities and harmonizations could continue indefinitely. See also André 1987: 62, 68-69, 72-73.

40. 1983: 131-40.

41. Theseus in Athens, Lycurgus in Sparta, Romulus in Rome.

place. Paul harnesses Rome to a dual yoke: Romulus and Christ. (Paul
also replaces the Jewish claim of antiquity, based on the 'laws of their
fathers' principle,[42] with divine sanction.) But, to make Rome work for
Christianity, Paul must first apply the concept of divine sanction to the
emperor and the Roman government. Further, Paul emphatically
stresses the notion, new with Christianity, of a political obligation that
goes far beyond simple allegiance. Paul's citizens are Christ-like people—are, in fact, christs. Paul gives a new twist to the Classical political
tradition that identifies citizenship with freedom by wiping out social
and legal distinctions in Christ.[43] Membership in the state, citizenship,
is acceptance of the hero, *pistis*. That is the contractual crux of Paul's
society. The sacral content of power becomes part of the political.

Throughout Hellenistic and Roman times, especially during the Principate, politics took the form of ideology. The pragmatic test of ideology
was stability, its success at warding of *stasis*, revolution,[44] and maintaining the status quo by concealing conflict. Ideology, like religion, belongs
to the category of the symbolic. One major feature of the symbolic is its
ability to expand and disperse beyond initial, specific locales and to
become universal (what we would today refer to as a 'world order'). Is
Paul an artificer, party to a process of ideological alteration and modu-
lation, or is he a restorer of genuine political thinking? The latter would
involve him in fostering meaningful participation in the governing
process and not merely urging acceptance (conscious or unconscious,
fatalistic or enthusiastic) of what is disseminated as an inexorable social
system (but which is only intent on preserving its stability).

Paul's approach is, I think, double-handed. He reinforces and justifies
the existing order by applying a new, highly effective symbolic to it; at
the same time, he produces a new constitution, effecting a reinterpre-

42. Πάτριος πολιτεία, ancestral constitution, the likely source of Josephus's
expression, is not uncommon in Greek antiquity, e.g. Aristotle (*Athenian Constitution* 34.3), the presocratic Thrasymachus of Chalcedon (*Republic* frg. 1), although
more common is πάτριοι νόμοι (e.g., Aristotle, *Athenian Constitution* 29.3). Plato
has πάτριαι καὶ ἀρχαῖα νόμιμα (*Laws* 7.793b), another possible source. Josephus
uses both πάτριος Ἰουδαίων (*Ant.* 12.253.2, cf. πάτρια Ἰουδαίων, *Ant.* 13.397.3;
20.41.5) and Ἰουδαίοις πάτριον (*Ant.* 20.35.1); and πατρίοι τῶν Ἰουδαίων νόμοι
(*Ant.* 14.117.1). In the formula πατρίως Ἰουδαίοις (*War* 1.477.3) the adjective
becomes an adverb, 'according to the laws of their fathers', i.e. 'by Jewish custom'
(cf. also ὑπὸ Ἰουδαίων πατρίως, *War* 5.51.3).
43. Stoic humanism and mystery religions perform similar operations.
44. Finley 1983: 136.

tation of power as every individual's call to take control of his own destiny actively and directly. Paul accomplishes this in a most astounding way: he makes the symbolic literal, he renders the imaginary real. He returns to a political society through ideology. He thrusts the empire not back to the Greek *polis* but upward to its utmost limit—to include God. This is possible only because of Christ, the man who crosses the border between becoming and being, the God who walks the boundary between life and death. Paul transfers the instrument of power, *dikaiosunē*, from man to God. Yet he means to do all this without conflict and contradiction. The *imperium* is God's, and by this Paul effectively renders the human ruler and the human ruled one. Among such Pauline binaries as free–slave, Greek–barbarian and man–woman, the binary powerful–powerless is conspicuously absent. For Paul, the last set of opposites is not only meaningless, it is unthinkable. He reinstates the cherished principle of direct participation, the mark of a true *polis*, while he reduces everyone to a redrawn status of *doulos*, slave. The real power is elsewhere.[45] Paul strengthens the empire while disempowering it. He empowers the christs while enslaving them. In doing so, he makes full use of Classical Greek political language and institutions. Paul uses religion for a profoundly political end. He makes politics and religion interchangeable. Paul changes the realm of change. The model and the analysis of this transformation remain political. He removes the state from history and posits an ontological continuity between two epistemologically different worlds, humanity and divinity.[46]

45. The Greek city, even at the time of its deepest enslavement, kept alive a political life and deceived itself into believing itself still free. Dio Chrysostom, Paul's younger contemporary (c. 40–after 112 CE) reflects this fantasy very well in his Thirty Fourth (or Second Tarsic) *Discourse* when he ridicules the vociferous city Assembly: '[you fight over] an ass's shadow, περὶ ὄνου σκιᾶς...for the right to lead and to wield authority that belongs to others (i.e. to the Romans), τὸ γὰρ προεστάναι τε καὶ κρατεῖν ἄλλων ἐστίν (34.48). He calls them 'fellow-slaves, ὁμοδούλοι, quarreling with one another over glory and pre-eminence' (34.51). These are dramatic, cruel and lucid statements, describing a situation common to all Greek cities at the peak of imperial times. Paul must have been intently aware of it and thought he found a way of changing it without colliding with the Romans.

46. Is Paul, then, an ideologue? After all, the human factor is, for Paul, no factor. Christianity came about through a process of self-alienation and suffering by a God completely foreign to the divine universe as conceived not only by Paganism but by Judaism as well, and for this reason a God both personal and accidental. This is, it seems to me, the great lesson of the Philippian hymn, so-called. It introduces incoherence, eccentricity, unpredictability in God.

Chapter 7

PAUL'S POLITICS

To secure imperial permanence, a political work of unprecedented magnitude, Paul fell back on Plato and Aristotle; for what they had to say was inescapable for the ancients. These two thinkers permeated all discourse, and no political, ethical or metaphysical discussion was possible outside the terms they had dictated.

My reading of Paul emphasizes the influence of Classical political philosophy, although direct textual influence on Paul from Plato or Aristotle cannot be found.[1] My argument therefore does not attempt to posit a direct connection between Classical Greek philosophy and Paul. Rather, my reading seeks to demonstrate that Paul's thought in the Letter to the Romans is grounded in Greek political theory. Hellenistic political concerns, imbued with Platonism and Aristotelianism, form the immediate background of Paul's political reflection. A vast mass of Hellenistic Pythagorean manuals, reduced by time to a small heap of miserable scraps—a defunct collection of boring or trivial cogitation of only archival interest—is brought back to life to bear witness to a Pauline project of unique intellectual sweep: that of restoring, all over the Roman Mediterranean world, a Greek political culture in the service of a Jewish resurrected God. This part of my work has, I hope, now been accomplished. But the undertaking further demands that we have a look at how it all works from Paul's *own* perspective. In what follows, I shall reflect on how the data presented in Part I can be used to clarify some of the most controversial aspects of the Letter to the Romans.

---

1. If my research has not been able to identify it, it probably does not exist. I must observe, however, that citations or even similarities between Paul and the Gospels are hard to come by, and yet the continuity and integrity of the two types of documents can hardly be discounted. This relationship has resisted many challenges ever since Wendt 1894 and Goguel 1904 endeavored to prove the complete break between Jesus' kerygma and Paul's *euangelion*.

The 'Revolutionary Reactionary'

To this point, this study has been a textual and historical analysis of a particular aspect—Classical and Hellenistic Pythagorean echoes—of Paul's general cultural milieu and of the political assumptions that underlay Paul's community-founding activity. Paul does not invent Hellenistic Christianity; it was already there, and he works on its soil, Hellenism.[2] Paul is not interested in Jesus the Galilean, but in Christ as *kurios*, master, ruler, lord.[3] Paul's missionary activity among the Greeks is the source of his theology. It is his work that feeds his thought. Paul's views of the law, of God's *dikaiosunē* and of *pistis* are contingent on his fellowship-building struggle. Paul's mission is to disseminate the *euangelion*, not to engage in tangled intellectual speculation. Paul's understanding of the *euangelion* in the political context of his *ekklēsia*-establishing work—not any particular dogmatic design—is the focus of his thought.[4] Paul starts his project with a message and with knowledge of political principles. But the venture raises issues on which he must reflect. His stand on the law, for example, changes and develops as the task requires.[5] The political character of his undertaking controls even

2. The idea of Hellenistic Christianity is introduced by Heitmüller (1912: 325-26). He proposes that Hellenistic Christianity predates Paul and that the sequence of the development of Early Christianity is: Jesus–primitive community–Hellenistic Christianity–Paul (*ap.* Kümmel 1972: 330). So also Bousset 1970 (German 1913): 'Between Paul and the primitive Palestinian church stand the Hellenistic congregations in Antioch, Damascus, Tarsus...'

3. Wrede 1907 (German 1904) is the first, intensely articulate proponent of the view that 'Paul believed in...a divine Christ before he believed in Jesus'. He overlapped the two at conversion. Bousset 1970 is the most prominent tracer of the *kurios* concept. Bultmann's (1969 [German 1929], 1964b: 20 [German 1960]) entire kerygma concept, the single most essential concept of his thinking, assumes this approach. It is the kerygma and the *Dass* of Jesus, Jesus as Christ, not the kerygma and the *Was* of Jesus, the historical Jesus, that matters for Paul. See Furnish 1989a: 24, 32, 44; Kümmel 1964: 172.

4. So also Jewett 1971; Beker 1988.

5. On this, I agree with E.P. Sanders's view 1977, 1983, who posits a flexible Pauline approach to the law, against Paul's categorical, irrevocable rejection of the law maintained by Bultmann 1951 or Bornkamm 1971. Paul's critique of Jewish law, thinks Sanders 1977, dwells on its impotence to connect people with Christ, which only faith can. Sanders 1983 insists that Paul's interest in *pistis* and *nomos* is reduced to the need to elucidate the conditions for acceptance in the Christian

such intricate, seemingly central Pauline theological topics as *pistis* or
the *dikaiosunē* of God. Paul's God is a people's God; he is for all humanity, and his leadership is political.[6] *Dikaiosunē* is a concept rooted
in Paul's missionary and pastoral context, a political notion that is
inseparable from his work and not a doctrinaire assumption behind it.[7]

Whatever the nature and origin of Paul's metaphysical thinking, in
practical matters his models are Greek, not Jewish. He is particularly
drawn to the idea of the *polis*. But Paul must not upset—and, more
important, does not wish to upset—the Roman political establishment.
After all, Rome provided the ideal setting for the infusion and diffusion
of a religious movement. The Roman empire united the world politically, culturally, socially and economically. This unity had to be preserved, and Paul's genius is conservative. He understands the potential
of the growing Jesus movement and quickly assembles a set of credentials to support his leadership role (the mystical call on the road to
Damascus, his change of name,[8] his superb *Erziehung*—including his
Pharisaic schooling and his initial persecution of the Christians).[9] He

community; the point is taken against extreme Jewish-Christians and not against
Jews as a whole. 'Far from favoring an anti-Jewish outlook, Paul was involved in
creating cross-cultural communities, "the body of Christ, in which all—Jew and
Greek, male and female, slave and free—become one person" ' (1983: 209). But
this approach also leads Sanders to wrongly downplay the importance of *dikaiosunē
pisteōs* in Paul.

    6.   Here, in concord with Bultmann 1951, who thinks that God in Paul is sig-
nificant not in himself but insofar as significant for human beings, i.e. that his
importance rests not in his metaphysical attributes but in his political ones. For
Bultmann *dikaiosunē* of God has mostly an anthropological weight.

    7.   See Furnish 1989b: 332-36.

    8.   Strabo, *Geography* 14.5.14 alludes to the proclivity of Semitic philosophers
in the Greek cities of Asia Minor for changing their names into Greek ones. Athenodorus, pupil of Posidonius, adviser of Octavius Augustus and tutor of Claudius, is
the son of Sandon, called Cananites, from Tarsus. It is not only a fashion but also
an initiation ritual, a form of conversion.

    9.   Credibility requires a lot of fiction. In the case of Paul, rhetoric is often
confused with character and invention with biography. Paul is the least elusive
figure of first century Christianity and yet very difficult to capture. He left many
drawings of himself, but no complete portrait. As we know it, Paul's life has all the
elements of the sensational: madness (visions, ascents), exotic voyages on land and
sea, dangers (vicious plots, narrow escapes), encounters with famous people (politicians, religious leaders, philosophers), perverse sexuality (celibacy), violent and
mysterious end (imprisonment, torture, disappearance). Paul's life is a juncture of

starts an effort of consolidation that makes the *telos* (the 'end'), of the Roman state that it become a Christian empire, and the *telos* of the emperor that he become a Christian ruler.[10]

To be sure, Paul's relation to the empire is paradoxical. Not only does Paul need the empire as the support infrastructure for his message, but he defends the power system with unabashed pride.[11] And yet, the defense of Rome that he mounts is that of a usurper, a pretender. Rome can survive and its stability be ensured only if Christ, or rather a christ-type, takes over. Paul usurps the power system in two ways. First, he challenges the system from within: he forces on his hearers a new language, which, although it mirrors the concepts and categories of the existing system, subverts them either by occluding them with new idioms or by reinterpreting them while keeping the old terminology. This produces an unsettling intellectual space in which disorientation is mixed with a feeling of privilege, of having a claim to the prerogatives of power. The second mode of subversion is radically transgressive: the introduction of the irrational. By 'the irrational', I don't mean God. The irrational is not god-talk, which was intimately and profoundly already part of the normative structure. I refer instead to a whole class of marginal phenomena: a crucified, law-breaking savior; glossolalia; a whole ontology of resistance, a whole epistemology of the inarticulate. What has always amazed me is that Paul got away with it; he did all this without arousing the suspicions of the very alert Roman praetorian guard. This seems to suggest that the groups he addressed were never perceived as dangerous by the imperial authorities.

I would call Paul a revolutionary if he were not so much of a reactionary. Paul erases ethnic, social and political binaries: Jew–Greek,

---

genres, a genre, and itself engendered genres. As Räisänen puts it 'This naive trust on a man's testimony about himself is a curious fundamentalistic survival within critical scholarship' (1983: 232).

10. This is the likely reading of the prominent place given conversions of Roman officials in Acts and of Paul's mentioning notable functionaries in his epistolary greetings (e.g., Erastus in Rom. 16.23).

11. 'If, as Renan justly observes, anyone had told the Roman Emperor in the first century that the little Jew who had come from Antioch as a missionary was his best collaborator, and would put the empire on a stable basis, he would have been regarded as a madman, and yet he would have spoken nothing but the truth' (Adolf von Harnack, *The Founder of Christian Civilization*, selections, in Meeks 1972: 303). So also Chadwick: 'What was wrong with the State was its old paganism. Change its religion and all would be well' (1967: 24).

Greek–barbarian, free–slave, wealthy–poor, ruler–ruled, and so on. Paul makes each individual body the image of the whole community,[12] and transforms each and every member of the group into a christ-type. Yet, even while he decentralizes power and circulates it, he emphasizes the contradictory notion of *analogia*. (The root of the contradiction, however, is the two-layered political structure he builds.)

Paul's status quo position is also revealed by his standing on sexual deviance. Throughout Classical antiquity, soul and society, psychology and politics, the individual and the political body were intimately connected. By Paul's time the parallelism of the body and the state is firmly in place. A corrupted body is not only a reflection but also a cause of a distorted community. Perversions signal political dissolution; gender transgressions indicate public disorder. Body and body politic are alike. The best illustration of this in Paul is his use of *sōma* as the image for *ekklēsia*, of the human body for the human assembly. Sexual excess, obscenity and depravity[13] are reflections of political subversion. And this, to Paul, is unacceptable.

What makes Paul a politician—and a good one at that—is his deep understanding of the human factor. In antiquity, formal philosophers dissertated eloquently about the essential rationality of this world and constructed exalted systems in which mind and idea occupied the loftiest places. But Paul knows, from the Hellenistic political professionals, that politics is the management of the irrational, the manipulation of human passions, fears and prejudices. Politics is the exploitation of human volatility and the control of human drives, and Paul manipulates human passions with feeling and fervor.

The Letter to the Romans, on which I focus in the next chapter, shows most clearly Paul's application of political thinking to Christian society, and one could fancy it as a contribution to a *Festschrift* for Nero, to celebrate the emperor's *quinquennium aureum*.

Clues from Philippians

Before turning to Romans, I wish to briefly engage in some exegetical considerations regarding Paul's politics that emerge from the Letter to the Philippians.

Philippians contains some provocative clues to Paul's political pre-

12. An excellent insight detailed in Yorke's 1991 study.
13. See, e.g., Rom. 1.23-32; 1 Cor. 5.

occupations: *politeuesthe* ('be citizens') (1.27) and the reference to a Christ-*polis* it implies; the *antikeimenoi* (the 'enemies') (1.28) and the reflection on the extension and limits of the Christian *polis* this term suggests; and *tapeinophrosunē* ('humility') (2.3) and the case it helps build for a Christian political vocabulary.

Christianity begins with a new *type*. Paul's genius is to bring together the inchoate Jesus movement—a first century expression of Judaic messianic and apocalyptic tradition—with the political aspirations of the cities of Asia Minor, themselves heirs to Greek political philosophy. He thus produces a new, viable and enduring social and political model, not only congruent with but even a reinforcement of Roman political theology. Paul and his disciples spread this model throughout the Roman world by means of both metaphor and conceptual exposition, that is, by diegetic *doxa* and philosophical *epistēmē*.[14]

Politeuesthe, the imperative form of *politeuomai* ('act as a citizen'), is used by Paul only in the Letter to the Philippians. Martin Dibelius[15] tried to show that *politeuomai* can be substituted for *peripateō* ('walk'), a favorite term of Paul's.[16] The interchangeability of these terms is, however, not at issue. What is relevant is precisely that *peripateō* is *not* employed in this instance. The sphere from which the verb *politeuomai* is drawn gives it its unique poignancy. Instead of appealing, stereo-typically, to a word long divorced from its roots in Hellenistic philosophy and ethics, Paul prefers this once to use a word that still preserves its power as an expression of the ideal of the *polis*.[17] *Peripateō* would fail to convey Paul's idea; *politeuomai* leaves no room for equivocation.

---

14. Nietzsche's lecture notes to a course on ancient rhetoric for the University of Basel, a course that he never taught, provide a succinct elucidation of the issues involved here. Summarizing the notes, rhetoric is (1) mythic image (vs rational argument), (2) play (vs the seriousness of intellect), and (3) *doxa* (vs *epistēmē*). See Blair 1983: 99.

The centerpiece of the letter is the so-called hymn (2.6-11), striking in its import for a theory of type, in the sense of an essentially Nietzschean theory of type. For Nietzsche, *type* is 'a determinate relation in the subject itself between the different forces of which it is made up…a reality which is simultaneously biological, psychical, political, historical, social and political' (Deleuze 1983: 115).

15. I used the 1937 edition of the commentary on the Philippians; the first edition was published in 1913.

16. Thirty times, according to my count, in the Pauline corpus.

17. MM, *s.v.* πολιτεύομαι, confirms that the basic meaning of *politeoumai* is 'to live the life of a citizen body'.

Paul conceives the Christian community as a distinct social, economic and political entity. Its constitution is not a democracy, nor a polity nor the rule of a philosopher-king, but *to euangelion tou Christou*, the evangel of Christ. For Paul, the Christian group in Philippi is a *new type* of society, a radically new *polis*, and this is what *politeuesthe* indicates. The *hoti* ('that') clause that follows redundantly emphasizes this point, in agonistic terms and by means of the body language that Paul uses to express both psychological individuality and political partnership.

The force of the term *politeuomai* is underscored by the occasion for this letter. No dogmatic or liturgical errors are at issue in the Philippian *ekklēsia*. Rather, the Philippians need to acquire a theoretical knowledge, a metaphysical understanding of the mode of life they already represent. This is what, in my opinion, distinguishes this letter from others Paul wrote. This is also how I explain the abundance of *hapax legomena* in this treatise. In Philippians, Paul lays the groundwork for a Christian metaphysics: faith, suffering, humility. *Politeuomai* differs essentially from *peripateō*, I think, especially in the complete absence of ethical connotations. It just says, 'You are the new order'.

Is the *ekklēsia* at Philippi itself the example of this new *polis*? Are the Philippians the inspiration for Paul's theories? Not necessarily. One is reminded that in 1 Thess. 2.2, Paul does not recall his experience in Philippi fondly. Moreover, epithets like φωστῆρες ἐν κόσμῳ ('lights in the world', Phil. 2.15) do not refer to the Philippians themselves. Neither are they empty rhetorical phrases. Such locutions express Paul's genuine belief about the Christians as type. In writing to the Philippians he describes the new *polis*.

A confirmation of this approach is found in Phil. 3.20, where the expression τὸ πολίτευμα (*to politeuma*, 'political community', 'state') appears—another instance of a term that occurs only once in the Pauline literature.[18] Many (πολλοί) live (περιπατοῦσιν[!]) as enemies

18. It is unseemly to read Alexandrian citizenship meanings into the Pauline *politeuma*. In the heavenly city, wherever its location, Christians cannot be resident aliens, second-class citizens. Even on earth Christians are members of a heavenly community. Paul's *politeuma* should be translated as political community, or, as Banks (1994: 40) parenthetically proposes, the 'place of citizenship'. He suggests that Paul is 'probably echoing the privilege of citizenship conferred upon the whole Roman colony of Philippi' (1994: 39). *Politeuma*, most likely a reference to *colonia*, is best translated here as 'state' or 'kingdom' (see Williams 1999: 161 n. 69). Philippi was settled by Mark Anthony's veterans after his and Octavian's battle against Brutus and Cassius, which took place there in 42 BCE. Philippi

of the cross of Christ, and their end is destruction (3.18-19). Paul's main accusation against such people is that their minds are set on perishable desires (τὰ ἐπίγεια) (3.19).[19] Unlike this impure crowd, we (ἡμεῖς) have our state in heaven (τὸ πολίτευμα ἐν οὐρανοῖς) (3.20).[20] While the political meaning of *politeuma* here can scarcely be in doubt, it could be argued that Paul speaks about the *polis* on high, a *civitas dei*.[21] To this one may reply that, as there is a sharp contrast between 'they' (the many) and 'we', so is there an opposition between 'their' *peripateo* and 'our' *politeuma*. Paul's ontological formula 'to live is Christ' (τὸ ζῆν Χριστός, *to zēn Christos*) (1.21)[22] undercuts the distinction between a Christian *polis* here and a Christian *polis* there. Although the citizens of this latter *polis* will have assumed new bodies, the foundational transformation into Christians has already taken place. *Politeuma* could be construed as the city of God, but it is also a political community, a place on high but also a political locale. As I shall demonstrate in even greater detail in my discussion of the Letter to the Romans in Chapter 8, Paul unites two strands of political discourse, the

becomes a colony with the title *Antoni Iussu Colonia Victrix Philippensium*. It is refounded by Octavian after Actium (31 BCE) and after 27 BCE bears the name *Colonia Iulia Augusta Philipp(i)ensis*. The settlers enjoyed Roman citizenship and the *ius Italicum*, i.e. exemption from land and personal taxes. See Murphy-O'Connor 1997: 212.

19. It is usually the Greeks who, in Paul's patterns of thought, are accused of adhering to the inferior sector of the soul and turning their back to reason. The Pauline attack, however, is directed here against 'the enemies of the cross of Christ' (τοὺς ἐχθροὺς τοῦ σταυροῦ τοῦ Χριστοῦ) (Phil. 3.18), a possible reference to a Judaizing party which devalued the significance of the cross by emphasizing practices demanded by the Law, such as circumcision and dietary rules. Whatever the case, I think it significant that the exalted *politeuma* of those 'in Christ' is set in contrast with either a debased Greek *polis* or a similarly depreciated Jewish *politeuma*.

20. From this heavenly *politeuma* comes a σωτήρ, a savior (Phil. 3.20). I cannot emphasize enough the political weight of this terminology. First *politeuma*, now *sōtēr*. *Sōtēr*, a common title for Hellenistic or Roman rulers, is used by Paul as a title for Christ *only* here—a remarkable point in itself. See also Williams 1999: 161 n. 69.

21. I find it odd that Augustine does not refer to this passage in his collection of sources for the title of his opus *De civitate dei*. Augustine's *civitas dei* is on earth, and intermingled with the city of the sinful.

22. It is inevitable to recall that *to eu zēn*, to live well, is Aristotle's political banner.

polis and *basileia*, to which he will assign two aspects of *dikaiosunē*. Thus the city on high and the present political community are distinct aspects of the continuity of Christian *polis*.

One is faced here with an incontrovertible instance of the creative thinking of a man who writes *occasional* documents. One fallacy that any New Testament scholar must be wary of is the argument that begins, 'Nowhere else in Paul...' Paul does not standardize his vocabulary.[23] *Politeuomai* has a peculiar and intentional force in Phil. 1.27.

For Paul, the *antikeimenoi* (Phil. 1.28) mark the extent and the limit of the Christian *polis*. The use of this term in Philippians can be subjected to a detailed analysis. Here, let me remark only that the *antikeimenoi* are improperly interpreted as adversaries external to Christianity.[24] Rather, they are believers, but believers who do not fulfill the true *type* of Christian believer, for whom suffering is integral to belief.[25] The language in Phil. 1.29 gives a valuable grammatical clue to the identity of the *antikeimenoi*. An anacoluthon occurs after ὅτι ὑμῖν[26] ἐχαρίσθη τὸ ὑπὲρ Χριστοῦ ('it has been granted to you that for the sake of Christ') (1.29a). The peculiar syntax strongly suggests that Paul intended to write (or dictate) *paschein* immediately after *Christou*. But as he got there he changed his mind. Paul felt that *paschein* was not enough. It might have been taken by the Philippians as a derivative of *pisteuein*—that is, Paul did not wish to leave any room for the inference that suffering derives from believing in the sense that believers will suffer attacks by others who do not share their beliefs. He interrupts himself. The middle clause οὐ μόνον τὸ εἰς αὐτὸν πιστεύειν ἀλλὰ καί ('not only to believe in him but also') is inserted. Paul does this because the *antikeimenoi* go only so far as belief but not so far as suffering. Paul adds the middle clause because he wants the Philippians to know that *paschein* is *built into*

23. 'Paul has neither the time nor the temper to be analytical and his thought and knowledge show kaleidoscopic range of variety' (Nock 1972: 805).

24. Lohmeyer (1961; first edition 1928) thinks that they are the eternal persecutors, the cosmic evil. Collange (1973) sees in them the Pauline equivalent for the later 'heretic'.

25. Collange regards the *antikeimenoi* as itinerant Jewish-Christian preachers who substitute for suffering an alluring miracle or a pneumatic experience as sign for salvation. (His hypothesis self-destructs: if these account docetically for the crucifixion then they belong to a gnosticizing trend; if they omit the cross altogether, they are Jewish-Christian missionaries of a different kind. They cannot belong simultaneously to both parties.)

26. Important manuscript evidence has ἡμῖν.

their *pistis*. For it is to *paschein* that Paul is obviously leading. After this middle clause, he picks up where he left off (τὸ ὑπὲρ Χριστοῦ) with τὸ ὑπὲρ αὐτοῦ ('for his sake') and ends with the thundering *paschein*. The Philippians' suffering is not derivative. They are not suffering because of some natural, social or political catastrophe. Nor is their suffering the involuntary consequence of *pistis*. The relationship between faith and suffering is not casual. They are one and the same. The believer suffers for Christ, not as a consequence of his believing. The *antikeimenoi*, therefore, are of no concern at all, because they are not, after all, Christians—even if they call themselves believers—because they do not suffer for Christ.[27] They fail the new type.[28]

A paradoxical teleology, characteristic of Paul, is suggested by the ἥτις (*hētis*, 'that') clause in 1.28b: ἥτις ἐστὶν αὐτοῖς ἔνδειξις ἀπωλείας, ὑμῶν δὲ σωτηρίας. Paul has just posited an irreconcilable difference between the *antikeimenoi* (believers or not) and the Philippians, the chasm between those who do not suffer for Christ and those who do. The *hētis* clause contains an expected antinomy between αὐτοί ('they') and ὑμεῖς ('you')[29] in terms of the ends of each of these groups: *apōleia* ('destruction') for the former, *sōtēria* for the latter. What is the basis for this distinction? Grammatically, *hētis* takes its gender, by attraction, from the predicate nominative in its own clause.[30] Knowing, when composing (or dictating) this passage, that this would

27. I thank J. Louis Martyn for the discussion leading to this argument.

28. Notice also the connection between 1.29, the passage in our attention, and 1.12-14, Paul's predicament as progress for the *euangelion*, Paul's equating faith and suffering in his own life. These verses suggest that the suffering built into *pistis* is the *visible* aspect of election: it induces wonder, initiates conversions, instills *parrēsia*—frees language.

29. Or ἡμεῖς, we, on good manuscript evidence.

30. Morgenthaler's *Statistik* (1958) confirms that attraction occurs often in Paul. There are other solutions: *hētis* may have *pistis* as its antecedent, or the antecedent may be omitted, as in general statements. A likely possibility is the following: the antecedent of *hētis* may be *endeixis*, by incorporation. In this case the clause would read: 'the sign which is one of destruction for them is one of salvation for you/us'. *Endeixis* acquires magical overtones: identical activities lead to opposite results according to the God invoked or served. What is, after all, this *endeixis*? A similar passage in 2 Thess. 1.5 suggests that it is Philippians' endurance. This is what Dibelius 1937 (1913), Lohmeyer 1961 (1928), Michaelis 1935, and Gnilka 1976 think.

be *endeixis*, Paul selects the feminine pronoun.[31] The feminine pronoun does not, however, make *endeixis* its antecedent. I think it is more likely that *hētis* functions here as the word 'this', without any accompanying noun. This approach sees everything that precedes *hētis*, and not any individual word, as its antecedent; here, then, the entire *hoti* clause is the antecedent: 'the struggling for the faith of the gospel and not being frightened in any way by the adversaries' (1.27b-28a).

Philippians 1.15-18 adds to the teleological perplexity. What is obviously unacceptable to Paul in the *hētis* construction seems agreeable here. In Phil. 1.15-17, in a classic chiastic construction, Paul identifies two classes of people (in Rome[32]) who do the same work but for different reasons: some teach Christ from envy and rivalry, others from good will.[33] 'So what?' (Τὶ γάρ) is Paul's reaction to this. What matters is that Christ be proclaimed (1.18). Does Paul, then, deny Philippi what he grants Rome? *Endeixis*, in 1.28b, determines and qualifies both genitives, *apōleias* and *sōtērias*. The same contest[34] will lead some to exaltation, others to annihilation. Is Paul really reversing himself when shifting from Rome to Philippi?

What changes first, in a magisterially orchestrated show of consistency and restraint, is the referent. In Phil. 1.15-18, those whom Paul is accepting, in great diatribe style, are his *personal* enemies. The cause, the ambassadorship for Christ, is served equally well by foe and friend alike. When addressing the Philippians (1.27-30), however, Paul does not speak of suffering as the result of a personal offense, nor is he willing to consider someone a Christian merely for acknowledging Christ. Rather, Paul is now speaking typologically. He is plowing the boundaries of the Christian *pomerium*. The suffering is Christ's. To be his is to suffer. The question is constitutional, and Paul is the lawgiver, legislating for the *polis*. Who the *politai* (the 'citizens') are makes all the difference. In building his society, Paul begins by eliminating those who fail the criteria for entering the compact.

---

31. This instance displays careful elaboration of Paul's thoughts. Had he improvised more freely, he would have used the much more common ὅστις or ὅτις, which by virtue of the rule of deviation or variation work with any antecedent.

32. Or in Ephesus, where this letter may have been written and Paul imprisoned.

33. Τινὲς μὲν καὶ διὰ φθόνον καὶ ἔριν, τινὲς δὲ καὶ δι᾽ εὐδοκίαν τὸν Χριστὸν κηρύσσουσιν (Phil. 1.15-17).

34. The battle, competitive, athletic game imagery dominates Phil. 1.27b-28a: στήκετε ἐν ἑνὶ πνεύματι, μιᾷ ψυχῇ συναθλοῦντες τῇ πίστει τοῦ εὐαγγελίου καὶ μὴ πτυρόμενοι ἐν μηδενὶ...

What changes next is the imagery; in Phil. 1.27-30, the motif is agonistic,[35] the imagery describing a competition, a power struggle between two parties. Both the imperatives[36] and the participles[37] show that there is only one group whom Paul is exhorting. The *antikeimenoi* are, syntactically, out of line with the paraenesis. The menace they represent is of concern but not of consequence.[38] The exhortation has only one addressee: the new type, the christ-type.[39] The life to which Paul calls his listeners is *agōn* ('struggle'), viz. *pistis and* suffering. Christ is the type, the archetype. Yet Paul reserves no mean role for himself. His *agōn* is the incarnation of the progress of the gospel (1.12), the *pistis* of the *euangelion* (1.27c), constitution of the *polis*. The body language that Paul uses,[40] its idiomatic character,[41] is a political metaphor, an appeal for unity among individuals who have made the choice to suffer for Christ.

Paul moves next, in Phil. 2.1-4, to a related theme, perhaps the most original contribution of this letter to Christian (and Western) thought. The value that describes the Christian *polis*, above all else, is humility.[42] Here, Paul changes the paraenetic style to a deeply affective language, taken from a wide body-language register, from φρονέω to σπλάγχνα

35. The verbs belong to the vaunting language of battle, the game of taunts proper to contests. In a way characteristic to human psychology, language can dispose of action. In action, it removes brutality from force. The Mesopotamian *Enuma Elish* or *Gilgamesh*, or the Greek *Iliad* show that the Near-East or the Aegean have long known the active force of rhetoric.

36. πολιτεύεσθε, στήκητε.

37. συναθλοῦντες, πτυρόμενοι, ἔχοντες ἀγῶνα.

38. In 1 Cor. 22, for example, Paul takes pains to identify the factions and the strife within the community. This was ostensibly a major concern in the Corinthians' letter to him in the first place. If the case of Philippi had been the same, we could have expected a similar careful diagnosis of the situation. Little, if any, of this is present. When addressing the Philippian community, while he knows that there must necessarily be dissensions within and enemies without, he nevertheless focuses his attention elsewhere: on what a Christian society should be.

39. Lohmeyer (1961 [1928]) demonstrated already that 1.27-28a and 1.30 are examples of the *agōn* theme, i.e. they do not refer to any external conflict.

40. ἐν ἑνὶ πνεύματι, μιᾷ ψυχῇ.

41. Formulas are the first metaphors, hence the earliest poetry. The import of this inchoate poetry latent in Pauline rhetoric is still insufficiently studied.

42. For the Greeks is *eleutheria*, freedom—as opposed to slavery; for the Jews, the recognition of the oneness of God—as opposed to divine multiplicity. In either case, Greeks or Jews saw themselves as repositories of special privilege.

(*phroneō* to *splanchna*), from mind to guts. The *polis* reaches the depths of physicality. The production of the new *tupos* touches the innards.

At the center of this passage stands ταπεινοφροσύνη (*tapeinophrosunē*) (2.3), an otherwise common concept, which Paul, however, uses in a way unknown before him. In the form employed by Paul the word is absent from the known papyri, inscriptions, ostraka, defixiones and other literary archaeological sources. Josephus's *The Jewish War* and Epictetus' *Diatribes*, both written just a little later than Paul's Letters, attest the word. Paul remains, however (until the contrary is proven), chronologically the first to use *tapeinophrosunē* in writing. After Paul, the term receives currency in Acts (2.9) and in the deutero-Pauline letters,[43] as well as in 1 Pet. 5.5.

But it is not the lexical form alone that is novel. The meaning is new as well. *Tapeinophrosunē* acquires a *positive* sense. The whole gang of related words had conspicuously negative connotations in Hellenistic literature. Both Josephus and Epictetus use *tapeinophrosunē* in a deprecating manner. The word is a derivation from the adjective *tapeinophrōn*. Well documented in late Hellenistic writings (from Plutarch to Iamblichus),[44] *tapeinophrōn* means 'stupid' or 'cowardly'. The adjective ταπεινός (*tapeinos*), which also enters into the composition of the noun *tapeinophrosunē*, has an unenviable set of meanings in non-Christian sources (the Septuagint included): 'poor', 'boorish', 'lowly', 'abject', and the like. The person Epictetus despises is 'servile [*tapeinos*], bitching, vengeful, wretched',[45] a veritable catalogue of Stoic vices.

Beginning with Paul, the adjective *tapeinos* as used in the New Testament consistently describes a positive quality. With Christianity the meanings of words, their chains of signification, often change. Christianity speaks a new language with old words and builds its vocabulary from *skandalon* to *skandalon*. Christian writers select their terms by the amount of outcry they cause. The cross (σταυρός, *stauros*) is the best such example, the topos, the word that started it all. The test of sense is the offense. 'Cross' is derogatory—it horrifies the Greek and the Roman—hence it is exactly what is clung to. Christian language develops at the expense of the Greek's perplexity. Language itself is thus crucified and resurrected.

---

43. Eph. 4.2; Col. 2.18, 23; 3.12.

44. E.g., Plutarch, *About the Fortune and Virtue of Alexander* (336e) or *About the Peace of the Soul* (475e); Iamblichus *Protrepticus* (21.5).

45. Epictetus, *Enchiridion* 3.2.14.

Such is also the case with the *tapeinos* family. 'Humility' describes the condition of the slave, the despised, the outcast. The cross changes its connotation and its value. In the Letter to the Philippians, no other designation is more representative of Christ, the prototype. What others reject the Christian embraces. What is contemptible becomes respectable. The issue is not moral vices and virtues, however. After all, the Greek placed even ἐριθεία (*eritheia*), labor for wages, among the vices, as it described an inability to participate in political activity because of lack of leisure.[46] By praising humility Paul is not commending a 'moral' virtue. He is articulating the character of political excellence in the new *polis*.

The Philippians knew what *tapeinos* and *tapeinōsis* and probably even *tapeinophrosunē* meant long before they had ever heard of Paul. He employs words that were there in their pre-Christian vocabulary. Yet, Paul uses this family of words in a topsy-turvy way. What is more, Paul expects the Philippians to understand *tapeinophrosunē* just the way he means it, and we may safely assume that they did.[47] In generating a new system of discourse, Paul renders intelligible a *tapeinos* of positive valence.

The Letter to the Philippians provided certain key ideas and terms that cued me to the notion that Paul thinks politically. It impelled me to seek in Paul a coherent theory that might inform his usage. This I found in Romans—a definite patterning of ideas that reminded me of constellations of concepts from Classical and Hellenistic political theory. Now, in the final portion of this book, I turn to a political reading of that letter.

---

46. Working for wages was, after all, regarded as akin to slavery even by Abraham Lincoln, not least because it left no room for spiritual life.

47. *Tapeinophrosunē* or *stauros* are only two, albeit the most remarkable examples, of the formative process of the language of Christianity. Other illustrations were given throughout this study. Many more can be added. Language bespeaks the power of the movement. As Thucydides wrote in the fifth century BCE, καὶ τὴν εἰωθυῖαν ἀξίωσιν τῶν ὀνομάτων ἐς τὰ ἔργα ἀντήλλαξαν τῇ δικαιώσει, 'to fit with the change of events, words too had to change their usual meanings' (*History of the Peloponnesian War* 3.82.10-11 [Civil war with Corcyra]; trans. R. Warner).

Chapter 8

ROMANS: A POLITICAL READING

The purpose of this extensive chapter is to review the argument of Romans in terms that can be described as philosophical and political. Like Moses, Akhenaton and Demetrios of Phaleron (a pupil of Aristotle and instrumental in connecting the cult of Sarapis with the Ptolemies), Paul was a practical visionary, political first and then religious.

It is true that the divine has a key position in Paul's rhetoric and in the ideology of Paul's community. It is not generally argued that, for example, Plato's political philosophy is theology in the same way that this is said about Paul. But, as with Plato, many of Paul's theological concepts can be equally well described as pertaining to the organization of human community and the structure of power.

Paul's interest in politics is consummate. Paul's central practical pre-occupation is with founding and building communities. To organize a group of people into a society, to bring individuals into a commonwealth, is necessarily a political undertaking. This is an inescapable aspect of Paul's activity. He draws borders, organizes crowds, sets rules, creates a government and gives a constitution.

For his basic assumptions, Paul relied on the political tradition of the Classical and Hellenistic world, on the political background of the Greek-speaking cities of Asia and Europe. Throughout his works, but especially in the Letters to the Philippians and the Romans, Paul shows that his mind works politically, that he is aware that his course is political and that he is informed by the political culture of his time. And Paul is not just mirroring or reproducing recognizable fragments from Classical and Hellenistic political theorists. Rather, his polemical strategy utilizes the very categories of Classical and Hellenistic political thought, often giving them new meaning. Paul adapts and adjusts, changes and reverses terms and concepts according to a program that, while distinctive in conception, yet shows a recognizably traditional configuration.[1]

For Paul, politics, while a human activity par excellence, is not inherently human. Humanity fails in *dikaiosunē*. Human *dikaiosunē* is possible only as an extension of God's *dikaiosunē*, yet it is distinct from God's. Paul produces a formula that combines the domestic *politikē* with a political *basilikē*—a constitution for the *ekklēsia* coupled with a universal metaphysical kingship. *Dikaiosunē pisteōs* characterizes human government, the *ekklēsia* (the term, again, technically denotes the assembly of the *polis*,[2] the supreme power in a democratic constitution). Since Paul accords citizenship, the criterion of participation in the *ekklēsia*, to all who have *pistis*, *ekklēsia* and *polis* become practically indistinguishable. In a Greek *ekklēsia*, it is freedom that is shared in common; in Paul's society—where distinctions of ethnicity, gender and intellectual status do not apply—*pneuma* is the common mark of citizenship. (*Eleutheria* allowed for no degrees, while *pneuma*, the proof of citizenship in Pauline society, is also the factor differentiating the citizens.[3]) This view of (mystical) citizenship is consistent with the Hellenistic Pythagoreans' view of the king's justice. Paul gave it universal validity by tying it with Christ. What is new in Paul is Christ. Christ moves *dikaiosunē* from the temporal and the particular into the permanent and the universal. In other words he brings *dikaiosunē* home, to God. The 'Philippian hymn' is, in a way, a story of how this happened. The Greeks, Paul says, knew God intellectually, but they abjured the intellect. The Jews knew God by revelation but appropriated

---

1. Also, while the theology of the letters is in no way programmatic, Romans may be in a special position, as Bornkamm 1977 and Karris 1977 argue.

2. *Ekklēsia* is the union of the entire people by Solon. It produced a divinity of its own, Aphrodite Pandemos (Πάνδημος) (Apollodorus—second century BCE—*ap.* *DS, s.v.* Venus 727b n. 20) 'the Goddess of the whole people', a collective, political deity, at Athens (and also at Erythrae, Thebes, Kos and Megalopolis, *ap. OCD, s.v.* Aphrodite 80b). (Pausanias, *Description of Greece* 1.22.3 places it at the time of Theseus' union of the demes. Only later it becomes 'common' Aphrodite, of Platonic fame.)

3. *Eleutheria* remains, however, in Paul, a major political component. The member in his *polis*, even if a *doulos*, a slave, is ἐλεύθερος of Christ (1 Cor. 7.22). (Conversely, Paul, *eleutheros* from all, is a *doulos* to all (9.19).) As Nygren (1949: 32, 38-39, esp. 206-229, and *passim*) persuasively and insightfully comments, in the community that exists under *dikaiosunē* of *pistis* the constituents share in the freedom from *hamartia* (Rom. 6.18, 20, 22), freedom from the law (7.3) and from death (8.21).

the revelation as exclusively theirs. The Greeks did not know how to keep him; the Jews did not know how to give him. They both exemplify the fate of *dikaiosunē* in human hands. Paul's Christ changed all this.

Romans has been taken as a 'cover letter'—Paul's introduction of himself to the Rome *ekklēsia*[4]—or some other kind of presentation piece.[5] It has been read as an elocution rallying the support of the Gentiles in Paul's confrontation with Jerusalem.[6] The intended audience of Romans is not necessarily specifically the Christian community of Rome.[7] It is, however, significant that Paul's magnum opus goes to the imperial capital.[8] Rome is not only a springboard for further work in the West, which makes writing to the Romans a 'demand of missionary politics',[9] but it is also the center of politics, and it is telling that this political-theological tract, 'disguised' as a letter, is sent there.[10] In

4. A popular position faulted by Manson 1977 (article originally published in 1938); he calls Romans a 'manifesto' (15).

5. Scroggs 1976 regards it as a sample of preaching. Nygren (1949: 7) refutes the view of Romans as example of missionary preaching: 'The Epistle is anything but an exhibition.' Stowers 1981 considers it a summary of teaching activity. For a review of Romans as an exposition of Paul's gospel see N. Elliott (1990: 21-23).

6. Jervell 1977 and Karris 1977 emphasize Paul's own life-situation as the underlying motif in the composition of this letter.

7. Following Jervell's argument for the letter's recipient, but disagreeing with his claim that Jerusalem is the actual audience (1977: 71).

8. Is Paul, in Romans, addressing the Christians of Rome, Rome itself or the Romans—as Acts (17.22-30) produces an address to Greece and the Athenians? Nygren (1949: 3) notes that Romans is the only letter Paul wrote to a congregation that was strange to him, in a certain sense a community not unlike the Athenian philosophers (Acts 17.18) who challenged him in the Areopagus (17.19-20) and disputed with him (17.18, 32), not necessarily out of opposition but out of curiosity. In any case Paul needed to make clear to the Romans who he was and what he stood for, before arriving in Rome and enrolling their support in preparation for work westward. See also Bornkamm 1977, who sees in Romans the crowning of Paul's message and theology (esp. 25). In Romans Paul appears *sub specie aeternitatis*. Wiefel 1977 makes an impressive case for Roman Christianity at the time of Paul.

9. Kümmel 1975: 312.

10. Nygren (1949: 7) notes that it has often been deplored that Romans has so little the character of a real letter. Romans takes the form of a philosophical letter, in which the personal is ancillary to the disquisitional. For a discussion of the Greek letter-essay see Stirewalt 1977, 1993. According to Stirewalt a letter-essay is normative, public and fictitious (1993: ch. 1), in other words an epitome, a textbook, and a doctrine. This fits Romans nicely, but see Wuellner's (1977: 156-57) critique

choosing a topic for his lecture to the Romans, Paul is deciding on the central concept of his *euangelion*, and he settles on *dikaiosunē*. *Dikaiosunē* is, of course, also the core of political discourse in Classical and Hellenistic times.[11] This treatise of Paul's is, therefore, not polemic or apologetic[12] but disquisitional,[13] and it has many of the features of a protreptic, a Hellenistic genre notably connected with philosophy.[14]

of this epistolographical genre, as slippery as that of diatribe.

The modern rhetorical approach to Romans begins with Wuellner 1977 (originally published in 1976) who considers the Pauline letters 'argumentative discourses' in the sense of both Greek and Roman rhetoric and of the new view of rhetoric as persuasive discourse, universal and not relegated to speech only. Wuellner proposes argumentative rhetoric as the best explanation of the Romans situation. Rhetorically, thinks Wuellner, the letter divides as follows: 1.1-15 *exordium* (which includes the prescript and the thanksgiving), projecting an *ethos* for the orator; 1.16-17 *transitus*; 1.18–15.13 *confirmatio*, central argumentation, of which 1.18–11.36 is general argumentation, the 'body' of the letter and 12.1–15.13 the *probatio*. The *probatio* includes: various *topoi* (12.1–13.14), emphasis on unity (14.1-23), personal *exemplum* (15.1-6) and appeal to unity (15.7-13). Finally, 15.14–16.23 *peroratio*, conclusion, consisting of: 15.14–15 recapitulation of thesis; 15.16-29 review of themes; 15.30–16.23, *pathos*, emotional appeal. This last section is subdivided in: call to intercessory prayer (15.30-33), recommendation of Phoebe (16.1-2), greetings (16.3-16), warning (16.17-18), summary conclusion (16.19-20), *sungeneis* character of associates (16.21-23).

11. *Dikaiosunē* remains, rhetorically, one of the 'special topics for ceremonial discourse' (Corbett 1965: 139-42, *ap.* Wuellner 1977: 160 n. 41, 172).

12. The bulk of Paul's letters appears to be *responsa* to queries—often trivial but always anxious—raised by communities he founded, or to reports about these groups—often routine but always disturbing—informing him of internal troubles and outside threats. In a few cases, however, Paul seems free from the constraint of practical questions or from the necessity of warnings, and then his concern is primarily with political theology and less with ethics.

Polemical reading of Romans was central to the ancient commentators of the letter (see Stowers 1986). This tradition is still strong. For example, Stowers 1984a reads Rom. 3.1-9 as a dialogue with a fellow Jew; Elliott 1990 considers that the rhetoric of Romans is dictated by Paul's dialogue with Judaism. Betz 1991 suggests that Paul attempts in Romans to define Christianity as a religion, by means of a debate between religions. The implication is that Paul conceives Christianity (which he never calls so) as discrete from and preferable to Judaism.

13. Black (1973: 18) agrees with Michel (1955: 5) in his characterization of Romans as 'epistolary catechesis', a *Lehrbrief*, an epistle for the instruction of its readers in general points of doctrine, with *dikaiosunē* as its central theme.

14. Guerra 1995, following Aune 1991 and K. Berger 1984, regards Romans as a specimen of the classical genre of *protreptikos logos* which 'functions as an

Paul's stance is not, however, philosophical—that is, a highbrow or pensive pose—for his subject is fraught with immediacy, full of loose ends and open to challenge, and it is addressed to people not ordinarily given to theorizing. Romans, from whatever range of genre models it may draw, is essentially a political treatise developed through (re)definition of key political terms, which, while composed with urgency and immediacy, reflects on universal and enduring themes. It is a political discourse[15] in the form of a letter.[16]

Paul begins his opus on *dikaiosunē* with a review of the two contemporary political structures in which *dikaiosunē* is active—the Jewish and the Greek *poleis*. Paul finds them both deficient. Romans constantly counterposes Paul's concept of *dikaiosunē* with both the Hebrew and the Greek concepts. This simple approach gives the letter a rhetorical unity and integrity.[17] (Paul will eventually split the *dikaiosunē* vector in two component forces, corresponding to the *polis* and the *basileia* tiers of the Hellenistic Pythagoreans, and then reintegrate them.) Paul does not engage in a debate with Judaism.[18] He is not writing 'about' Jews to the Greek-speaking Christians of Rome (cf. Rom. 1.13).[19] Rather, he is

invitation to a way of life, espousing a comprehensive world view, setting forth its advantages, and replying to objections' (1995: 170). More to the point, however, is Berger's definition of *logos protreptikos*, with its emphasis on the connection with philosophy: 'an advertisement which primarily attempts to win adherents to the pursuit of a certain discipline, especially philosophy' (*ap.* Stuhlmacher 1994: 13). Guerra, against Aune, considers Romans integrally as a protreptic, not three or four protreptics independently written with Rom. 9–11 as a digression, as Aune contends. Aune places Romans in the context of ancient religious and philosophical propaganda. According to Aune the basic structure of protreptic writings is: ἐλεγτικός, a critique of ways of living or schools of thought that reject philosophy; a positive section in which the truth, claims, and ways of living of the philosophical school are presented, praised and defended; προτρεπτικός, an optional section, a personal appeal to the hearer inviting immediate acceptance of the exhortation. Σύγκρισις, comparison, and ἀπόδειξις, probative evidence, are important instruments in a protreptic (*ap.* Guerra 1995: 184).

15. A very common genre in the first century CE, and of which Dio Chrysostom's orations are the best known examples.

16. Again, a genre popular at the time of Paul, esp. in the Latin literature, from Cicero to Seneca.

17. See Wuellner 1977, Beker (1984: 59-108), Jewett 1986, Aune (1987: 219-21), Malherbe 1989, Aletti 1990, and especially N. Elliott 1990.

18. Against Kümmel (1975: 312, 314).

19. Contra Kümmel's (1975: 309) 'double character approach'.

arguing (on the political side) against *any* manifestation of nationalism and (on the psychological side) against the abandonment of reason. Judaism is rejected, but so is Hellenism. Paul has no patience for ethnic or local sensibilities; like Rome itself, he works in large sweeps. What he seeks is concerted, consolidated order. The sweeping goal of Romans is to bring together the various Christian groups in the imperial capital and to set them all under the aegis of his *euangelion*—to teach them all how to become citizens of Christ and to show them why they must surrender their cultural and ethnic allegiances.

In a nutshell, the argument of Romans goes something like this.[20] Paul begins (1–3.20) by asking about the world he lives in, how it has been up until now. His focus is collective subjectivity—ethnic or cultural psychology, the ethnic, cultural aspect of the *psuchē*. (In this he follows Classical models;[21] Paul has little interest in psychology as we understand it today.) A critique of the Jews, of the Greeks and of humanity in general, ensues. This opening section, on the world as it is, the world of *hamartia* ('error'), dwells on the reign of *epithumia* ('desire') and *nomos* ('law'). Paul then (3.21–8.39) begins an inquiry into what the world ought to be. He moves from the *psuchē* to the *polis*. In a discourse on objectivity he demonstrates, by means of *exempla* (Abraham, Christ), that transcendence of mere humanity is possible. In this part of Romans, Paul sets the world straight. The rule of Christ has begun, and the operative justice is *dikaiosunē pisteōs* ('justice of trust'). Next (9.1–11.36), Paul lays the groundwork for his political metaphysics. This, the *basileia* part, is the central part of the letter. By series of binaries both disjunctive (*sarkic–pneumatic, parakoē–hupakoē*) and

---

20. I follow the common division of the Epistle (e.g., C.H. Dodd 1932, Nygren 1949, Käsemann 1980, Stendahl 1963, Stuhlmacher 1994): 1.1–3.20 [introduction; *dikaiosunē theou* vis-à-vis the Greeks and the Jews]. 3.21–8.39 [*dikaiosunē theou* and *dikaiosunē pisteōs*]. 9.1–11.36 [*dikaiosunē theou* and Israel]. 12.1–16.27 [*dikaiosunē theou* and the *polis*; conclusion]. Black 1973 (with C.H. Dodd 1932, N.A. Dahl 1951–52, Feuillet 1950, Dupont 1955) favors the division at 5.11-12 thus: 1.17-5.11 [theme of *dikaiosunē*]; 5.12–8.39 [theory of Christ-*polis*]. (Dahl, Michel, Dupont see chs. 6 and 7 [*hamartia, nomos*] as a digression from ch. 5, resumed in ch. 8.) 9–11 [the case of Israel]; 12–15 (paraenesis, i.e. Christian homiletic instruction) [practical aspects of Christ-*polis*]; 15.14–16.27 [conclusion]. The headings in the brackets are mine, and they suggest that although these sectionings of Romans are made from a theological viewpoint, they adequately serve my approach as well.

21. See, e.g., Plato, *Republic* 4.435e-436a: high-spirited Thracians and Scythians, money-loving Phoenicians and Egyptians, among others.

conjunctive (*dikaiosunē–pistis, hamartia–sarx, dikaiosunē–pneuma, dikaiosunē–sōtēria*), Paul painstakingly constructs a system of thought in which God is the central *datum*, the privileged signifier, the inescapable reality. Here, Paul presents the world at large, as dominated by the reign of God. The spotlight is on *dikaiosunē theou* ('justice of God'). Finally (12.1–16.23), Paul focuses on practical matters of organization—that is, on how to configure the Christian community in the context of a Roman empire whose perpetuation and stability are made possible by Christianity.

These divisions are, of course, rough. Paul's progress is not neat and linear, but convoluted and iterative. Strains of thought converge and separate unexpectedly, and the structure of the thesis conforms less to the laws of philosophical argumentation than to those of dramatic diatribe.[22]

Romans 1.1–3.20: Hamartia, *or the World As It Is*

The first part of Romans focuses on the world of *hamartia* (error), a world governed by *nomos* (law) and *epithumia* (desire).

1.1-17. Paul introduces himself as slave of Christ and carrier of the *euangelion. Doulos Christou Iēsou* is his credential: he is a slave, a slave of Jesus Christ.[23] While the term shocks, the meaning enlightens. Slavery

---

22. Diatribe is the most characteristic of epideictic rhetoric in antiquity (Reid 1992: 261 and n. 30). See especially Stowers 1981, 1988. Precise identification between Paul's letters and diatribe failed ever since Bultmann's 1910 well-known dissertation. Diatribe as literary genre, a *Gattung*, is a precarious proposition. While there are sufficient formal elements for recognizing diatribe (primarily rapports such as speaker–public, teacher–pupil, expressed position–anticipated objection, phrases coordinated paratactically, as well as display effects such as puns, alliterations, parallelisms, paradoxes, interjections, metaphors, the diatribe remains above all a rhetorical style, itself flexible and variable, rather than a genre. (See Donfried 1977: 133-40 for a diatribe against Bultmann's thesis.) *Diatribē* is the style of philosophical conversation favored by the popular, itinerant lecturer of Paul's time Black 1973: 61 (who refers to C.H. Dodd).

23. When Paul makes this assertion he refers to a well-known principle of the law of slavery. The slave is in the *dominium*, the ownership, of his *dominus*, owner, i.e. he has no proprietary rights, not even in his own body. The *dominus* has full legal power over the slave, the right to use it and dispose of it as he pleases. See A. Berger 1953, *s.v. dominus* 441b. As Plato puts it, 'we humans are chattels of Gods' (*Phaedo* 62b), with κτῆμα, chattel, the same as *doulos*. See A.E. Taylor 1927: 178-79.

to Christ stands in opposition to slavery to drives; it is harmony as opposed to discord, truth as opposed to deceit (16.17-20). The concepts are drawn directly from Hellenistic psychology: the *logon–epithumia* (reason–desire), *homonoia–stasis* (concord–faction) dichotomy of the soul.[24] Paul teaches slavery. Slavery connotes submission. Paul's mission is to bring the obedience of *pistis* (ὑπακοή πίστεως) to the nations (τὰ ἔθνη) (1.5).[25] (This is also precisely how he ends the letter [16.26].)

It is sometimes observed (e.g., D.B. Martin 1990) that metaphorical slavery to a deity is a common expression of Hellenistic mystery religions. This explains little, however, about the meaning Paul gives it, for *doulos* is not merely a soteriological ekphrasis but a political designation: it names the *politēs* of the Christian state. It is a complex concept that goes far beyond anxious submission to dubious, half-trusted cumulative divinities. The example of a certain Fabia Falconia Paulina, pluri-initiate and multiple divine slave is a case in point. *Mustēs* of Eleusis, Lerna, Aegina, Isis, recipient of the Taurobolium, hierophant of Hecate, she undergoes one initiation after another, while she knows that here excessive insurance is no deterrent to doom. For other remarkable cases of multiple initiations, common in Hellenistic and Roman times, see Nock (1972: I, 33-44) 'Studies in the Graeco-Roman Beliefs of the Empire'. For an interesting multiple priesthood see Nock (1972: I, 233). See also Nilsson (1951–60: 106-16), 'Greek Mysteries in the Confession of St. Cyprian', and Festugière (1932: 87-169). As Nock explains (1972: I, 39), the phenomenon is possible because the interest is on divine power rather than on a divine personality. A mystery is not primarily a union with God but *sōtēria*, salvation adds Festugière (1932: 133). In typical Pauline manner, a sharp distinction between the old and the new meanings of the word is operated: from a base, contemptible station to that of the willing, self-conscious citizen. *Douloi* of Christ are the antithesis of the *douloi* of passions (Rom. 16.18-20). The difference is between understanding and urges, between self-examination and instinct, between knowledge and libertinism, ultimately, between a solid, well-founded, permanent constitution and flashy, narcissistic, incoherent desire.

24. I use the word 'psychology' in the Greek philosophical sense: the nature and meaning of consciousness, for in antiquity psychology was a branch of philosophy. A number of distinct theories of *psuchē* are found in the Greek philosophers, but following Plato and Aristotle a strong tradition of soul as in essence immaterial and in some manner continuous with the divine marks Western psychology. The ancient soul also had a political aspect: when properly working was a harmonious whole in which the lower parts submitted to the rule of the higher. For the Greeks, the well-adjusted soul engaged in the pursuit of reality as purest subjectivity, the world as stripped of materiality. It formed the model and took its example from the well-ordered, unified society.

25. *Ethnē* is the way LXX refers to the non-Jews. The Greeks applied this term to the non-Hellenes, and meant the barbarians who did not live in a *polis*-type structure. Greek political documents of Roman time used *ethnos* for *provincia*. Its

For Paul, *doulos* indicates deferential equality. It indicates Paul's parity with Christ, that he is devoted to Christ and is himself a christ. *Doulos*, similarity with Christ, becomes part of the vocabulary of power, membership in the Christ-*polis*. The following parallels become intelligible: Paul is marked for the gospel (1.1, cf. 1.5-17); Jesus is marked as son of God (1.4); Paul serves God with his 'spirit' (1.9); Jesus is God's son by his 'spirit of holiness' (1.4).[26] Because he is *doulos*, Paul is free and equal to everyone else. Because he is *doulos* of Christ, Paul is in the service of all, Greek and barbarian, wise and fool (1.14).[27] Romans 1.16-17 sets the major themes of the work.[28] The *doulos* brings

meaning in Paul, an actual reversal, is devoid of disdain or distaste. Its most likely sense is urban people, the populace of the provinces of Roman Empire, less Judea, that lived in *poleis*. To make too much of Jewish contempt for the outsiders will not do, since Paul adopts this very term of discredit to apply to those who became his people. See MM, *s.v.* ἔθνη. Deissmann (1926: 98) thinks that Paul's use of the term does reflect a certain distaste for the non-Jews, just as the Romans applied the same word to the provincials. I am not convinced. It would be quite odd, certainly a faux-pas, for Paul to use it in the letter to the people of the imperial capital. It is indisputable, however, that whatever the word meant for Paul, his readers had no reason to suspect ridicule. And there was none.

26. *Pneuma, pneuma hagiōsunēs*, is not a thing, an attribute, but a person, a power. As the creedal formula Paul quotes puts it (1.3-4), it is possession of this 'spirit of holiness', πνεῦμα ἁγιωσύνης, which allows Jesus to perform the feat of coming back to life from the dead and thus be named son of God. As Christ, as legislator, Jesus does not dispense laws, but *pneuma*.

27. *Sophos* is an important concept of philosophy. Paul stands in an apparent polemical relation to the *sophos*. His mission is to the wise and the foolish indistinguishably (Rom. 1.14). The relation wise/fool proves often reversible (e.g., 1.22; 16.19; 1 Cor. 1.27; 3.19). *Sophos* is God alone (16.27). Paul lays claim to the politically laden title *sophos architektōn* (1 Cor. 3.10). He is not at variance with Sthenidas (frg. 1.1), for whom man is *sophos* insofar as he imitates God. There is, however, no hint in Paul of the *sophos* of Stoicism, for whom God as 'the all' allows for no imitation, only for conformity (see Goodenough 1928: 74-75).

28. This is generally agreed upon by commentators. Rhetorically it is the *propositio* of the letter. (See, e.g., Wuellner 1977, 1979, Siegert 1985, Jewett 1986, Aletti 1990). It must be noted here that although Wuellner cites N.A. Dahl and Betz as strong representatives of the rhetorical approach to Paul (vis-à-vis Galatians) (1977: 155), Wuellner is the first to apply it to Romans. He suggested that the Pauline letters are 'argumentative discourses' in the sense of traditional (i.e., Greek and Roman) and new (i.e., universal patterns of persuasion found in all types of speech and discourse) rhetoric. He proposes that Romans illustrates epideictic

the *euangelion*, a message that, like the carrier, recalls infamy. Yes, the *euangelion* makes public resentment soar; Paul's *cri de guerre* in Rom. 1.16, 'I am not ashamed of the *euangelion*',[29] obviously implies that the *euangelion* has been a source of public reproach. Paul, however, is willing to assume this opprobrium because of his knowledge that the *euangelion* is a power, the *dunamis* of God for salvation of everyone who has *pistis*.[30] This suggests that *euangelion*, the constitution of Paul's communities, is not a written code of law but a natural or divine system rooted in *dikaiosunē*.[31] The theme of shame belongs to a discourse of unwritten law. On this basis I claim, first, that *euangelion* is regarded as shameful for it contains violations of customs of the Hellenistic world and, second, that it itself constitutes unwritten law. The first claim has direct backing; the second is supported by my reading of *euangelion* as constitution. Paul's conviction relies on Hellenistic Pythagorean tradition, itself of Classical parentage.

As we have seen, ancient authorities long debated the issue of written versus unwritten law. The Hellenistic Pythagoreans followed their Classical forebears in this regard. Like many of his predecessors, Ps.-

rhetoric. (*Epideiktikon*, demonstrative rhetoric, treats the subject of praise and blame, the present condition of things [Aristotle, *Rhetoric* 1.3.3]).

29. Οὐ γὰρ ἐπαισχύνομαι τὸ εὐαγγέλιον (Rom. 1.16).

30. Käsemann and Bultmann *querelle d'Allemand*, which they are willing to push to warfare, makes a lot of the *dunamis* here, the *Macht–Kraft* quarrel. Bultmann reads Rom. 1.16 as 'The possibility of salvation is the Gospel' (1964a: 14 and n. 5). Käsemann interprets it to mean that Giver and gift are in a causal relationship, God as the *auctor* (1969c: 173). For Käsemann 'everything depends on the Gospel's being the manifestation of this God...' (1969c: 173) (If I see it correctly it is the clash between Hegelianism—Käsemann views everything in Paul as 'power [that] is always seeking to realize itself in action and must indeed do so' (1969c: 175)—and Existentialism—Bultmann emphasizes the individual and the anthropological anxiety, the *Dass* (the 'thatness') of Christ the anti-hero—transplanted in theology.) As I understand it, for Käsemann the *euangelion* is a personification of God; for Bultmann it is an enactment, a 'constitution', the allegiance to which grants salvation. I take *euangelion* as the power-text about the embodiment of Christ, the testament of the religious reformer, the creed of *dikaiosunē pisteōs*. At the same time the *euangelion* operates the (magical) transformation of the believer into a christ, for in its letter is the God (best expressed in Gal. 2.20, cf. Rom. 8.10; 2 Cor. 13.5). The *dikaiosunē* of God is his justice, disbursed as *charis* unto the holder of *pistis*.

31. Even Roman law was distinguished by the Roman jurists themselves from natural law; the former was of vast, yet not universal application and validity.

Archytas declares the preeminence of the unwritten over the written laws (frg. 1). For him, the best law is the one the breaking of which attracts shame and dishonor as sanctions.[32] Other Hellenistic Pythagoreans concur.[33] Diotogenes finds the foundation of a good life to be fear of shame rather than of fines.[34] Ps.-Charondas (frgs. 3, 16) and Ps.-Zaleucus (frg. 13) also emphasize the importance of public blame and loss of face for breaking laws.[35] In his *Discourse* 76 ('On Customs') Dio Chrysostom, a Stoic-Cynic itinerant philosopher and a younger contemporary of Paul's, distinguishes sharply between laws and customs (οἱ νόμοι–τὰ ἔθη) (76.4). The laws produce a state of slaves (δούλων πολιτεία), while traditions create a state of the free (ἐλευθέρων [πολιτεία]). 'For the laws inflict punishment upon bodies; but when the customs are violated, the consequent penalty has always been disgrace' (τὴν ζημίαν εἶναι συμβέβηκεν αἰσχύνην) (76.4). Therefore, for Dio the written laws are directed to the bad (φαῦλοι), the oral laws to the good (ἀγαθοί) (76.4).

Paul (and his disciples[36]) share in this tradition. Women—for example those who during (spirit-filled) meetings allow their hair to become disheveled or their veils to drop (1 Cor. 11.5-6)[37]—are most prone to incur public disgrace and censure. More important, however, are a series of situations that turn this concept of shame on its head. The powerful confluence of (1) the assimilation of the traditional concept of the relation of shame to the free citizen and (2) the aggressive reversal, which valorizes the shame of the crucified Christ and his slave-citizen in the nexus oral law–shame, argues for the influence on Paul of Classical and Hellenistic reflection on shame. The inversion of the traditional canon and the offense to venerable public opinion is characteristic of Paul's thought, illustrating the dialectical tension between Paul's

---

32. T 35.3-4.

33. See Chapter 4, section on Ps.-Archytas, for a sketch of the argument, and frg. 1 of Ps.-Archytas for details of his view.

34. Περὶ ὁσιότατος, Stobaeus 3.1.100, T 75.26-28.

35. Ps.-Zaleucus identified slavery with fear, and freedom with shame. He makes the entire moral order of a society depend upon the nature of laws one obeys. A state of slaves seems to be defined as one in which the citizen's obligation is to written laws, a state of the free is described as one in which accountability is to one's neighbors. See Chapter 4, section on Ps.-Zaleucus, frg. 13.

36. See Eph. 5.3-5, 11-12.

37. Even Rom. 1.24-32, esp. 26-27, fits here: this time it is sexual transgression, a transgression of natural law, *phusis*, that is the cause of disrepute.

conservative and his subversive tendencies. Statements that proclaim allegiance to the *euangelion*, for all its scandalous and disturbing content, execute a reversal and displacement of meaning that stand in conflict with influence and line of transmission. Its very shamefulness is the *euangelion*'s power. It is *pistis* in this power that guarantees salvation, *sōtēria*: for the Jew first and then for the Greek (Rom. 1.16, cf. 2.10). This order of citation identifies the dual cultural sources that hold the *euangelion* in disgrace.

Euangelion is God's *dunamis*, the instrument of *sōtēria*. *Pistis* in the disreputable *euangelion* brings release, *sōtēria*. *Sōtēria* is a political term in Plato and Aristotle. Its political meaning is 'best course' (commonly it means 'survival', a nautical metaphor). In Classical times it was *eudaimonia* ('happiness'), not *sōtēria*, that one sought, an ideal pursued in the organization of a political community, as Ps.-Archytas has it (frg. 2b). For Plato and Aristotle,[38] *eudaimonia* is the end of a political society. *Eudaimonia* is devalued with Hellenism and replaced by *sōtēria*, delivery from the ills of this life and release from death. In the Hellenistic Pythagoreans one finds *sōtēria* by imitation of the ruler. What both Hellenistic Pythagoreanism and Paul reflect is the political grounding of the concept: *sōtēria* is achieved by imitation of the ruler, and is obtained by an individual only insofar as he is part of an organized corporation, as a member of the state.

The *euangelion* is a universal polity, applying to Jew and Greek alike (1.16). The *euangelion* is a revelation in the same sense in which a code of law is a revelation. Paul believes, with the Greek *polis*, that legislating is not a function of the state legislature but of a founder or reformer of the constitution, who himself receives the constitution from God. This is legislative science, *politikē* proper. Statesmanship includes a deliberative and judicial aspect, and the people participating in it are said to be taking part in politics, *politeuesthai*.[39] God alone can hold the universe together.[40] The lawgiver is often *nomos empsuchos*, living law, in the Hellenistic Pythagoreans as in Philo, the Stoic Seneca and the middle Platonist Plutarch.[41]

38. *Politics* 3.1280b33-40, 7.1323b30, 7.1324a13.

39. Aristotle, *Nicomachean Ethics* 6.1141b24-30.

40. *Politics* 7.1326a32.

41. Not surprisingly, Philo too reflected the same thought that, I argue, drove Paul. Philo recognizes the king's divine nature in *Leg. All.* 3.82 and in a fragment preserved by Antony (Goodenough 1938: 99-100 and notes). The formula *nomos*

The locution *euangelion*, however, betrays its appearance of simplicity. It is an 'oddball' term in Paul's cultural setting, and the meaning he gives it is not necessarily obvious. In the singular it is exceedingly rare before Paul, in either the literary or the epigraphical and papyrological sources. In the plural, it bears a religious semantic charge mostly as a description of a class of offerings and sacrifices, those for 'good news'. The notorious exception—and the confirmation of what was to become a technical meaning—is the Priene inscription, where the birth of the God is *euangelia*, a religious-political-rhetorical name. The God there is Augustus. What is important here is that *euangelion* is a term that makes sense without having to appeal to transcendence—that the word has already been used in a primarily political way.⁴²

*Euangelion*⁴³ uncovers *dikaiosunē theou*, the medium and result of *pistis* (ἐκ πίστεως εἰς πίστιν) (1.17).⁴⁴ Immediately, Paul links (via a

---

empsuchos appears in Philo in *Vit. Mos.* 1.162 (A. Delatte 1922: 85). Abraham was 'himself a law and an unwritten statute' (*Abr.* 275-76; Williamson 1989: 202).

42. Priene was a major Hellenistic city on the Aegean coast of Asia Minor, between Ephesus and Miletus. The inscription, dating from 9 BCE, contains the words of Paulus Fabius Maximus, proconsul of Asia, and established that the cities of Asia would start their calendar year on 23 September, the birthday of Octavius Augustus. *OGI* 458 has, in l. 37, εὐαγγέλια πάντων, the good news among all (those who preceded and who will follow him); l. 40: ἦρξεν δὲ τῷ κόσμῳ τῶν δι᾽ αὐτὸν εὐαγγελίων ἡ γενέθλιος τοῦ θεοῦ, the birthday of God was the beginning, for the world, of the good news relating to him. Note the plural use of *euangelion*, always singular in the New Testament. The singular *euangelion*, besides its meaning 'reward for good news', is first employed in the sense of 'good news' in Josephus (*War* 2.420), δεινὸν εὐαγγέλιον, awesome news (on things going bad in Judea). See Penna 1984: 156-58.

43. Paul produces technical vocabulary even as he speaks. *Euangelion* often comes packaged in the idioms *euangelion tou theou* or *euangelion tou christou*. But it is also *euangelion mou* (2.16; 16.25), or plainly *euangelion* (1.16). It has enemies (11.28). Its main attribute is truth (e.g., Gal. 2.5). It is the foundation of the Christians' *koinōnia* (Phil. 1.5). Paul's mission is its *apologia* (Phil. 1.7, 16) and *bebaiōsis* (Phil. 1.7), he is its defender and its guarantor, both legal terms. He fights for its *prokopē* (Phil. 1.12), progress, a term from the social vocabulary. There are also competing *euangelia*, the *heteron euangelion* (Gal. 1.6). Paul brings the true gospel (2 Cor. 11.4, cf. Gal. 1.6, 8, 9; 2.5; 2 Thess. 2.13), *euangelion* not of man but of Jesus Christ (Gal. 1.11-12, 16; 2.2); Paul's *euangelion* consists both in word and demonstrations of power (1 Thess. 1.5) and only Christ's guarantees salvation (2 Thess. 2.14).

44. Aletti calls this expression a prepositional brachyological syntagma, and

modified Habakkuk) the *dikaiosunē* of God with the *dikaiosunē* of *pistis*: 'but the just shall live out of *pistis*' (ὁ δὲ δίκαιος ἐκ πίστεως ζήσεται) (1.17); the *dikaiosunē* of *basileia* is identified as the source and the force of the *dikaiosunē* of *polis*.[45] *Dikaiosunē theou* is almost personified; this is how salient a feature it is in Paul. Paul's entire political theory (and theology) derives from it.[46] *Euangelion* is the basis of the new compact (*diathēkē*), of the *kainē ktisis* (Gal. 6.15), of the new institution (see esp. Rom. 8.19-22). The political name of this constitution is *basileia (tou) theou* (14.17; 1 Cor. 4.20), a monarchy. This kingship is elsewhere described as *dunamis*, action (1 Cor. 4.20). *Euangelion* is an image of God (2 Cor. 4.4), a political document, a constitution (Phil. 1.27). Paul calls himself the founder, the father of his communities, which he has engendered through the *euangelion* (1 Cor. 4.15). The political force of such statements cannot be easily discounted. *Euangelion*, the story of Paul's Christ (the dead, raised and redeeming Christ) is the 'constitution'; there is very little of a sense of revelation, of irrational disclosure, in the way Paul uses the term. *Euangelion* is a model and a constitution according to which Paul is organizing the people, the foundation of the community that he forms. The *euangelion* is the paradoxical expression of God's law, a law that

reads it as the modality ('le "comment"') of divine justice in its maximal extension (1992: 359, 363).

45. The (semi)literal citation from LXX Hab. 2.4 in Rom. 1.17 is much made of by Feuillet 1959-60. Hab. 2.4 reads: ὁ δὲ δίκαιος ἐκ πίστεώς μου ζήσεται; this renders the words of the Lord, *kurios*, to the effect that while the Lord does not answer the prophet's question when the persecution of the faithful by the faithless will end, he warns that meanwhile the *dikaios* shall live by *my pistis*. As Hays understands it, 'it is a response to the problem of theodicy… The faithful community is enjoined to wait with patience for what they do not see: the appearing of God's justice' (1989: 40). I think it is no accident that Rom. 1.17, Gal. 3.11 leave out *mou*. (The important C witness—Codex Ephraemi Rescriptus, dated the fifth century, dissents from the Majority Text and restores it, in a transposed location: ὁ δὲ δίκαιος μου ἐκ πίστεως ζήσεται—the transposition of *mou* is attested in LXX manuscript tradition). What Paul actually does is to respond to Habakkuk. Through Paul, the prophet finally receives the answer he has been so agonizingly and waiting for so hopelessly long; out of faith against faith God's *dikaiosunē* is manifest, and its power works in Paul's *euangelion*. This is a dialogue across centuries, and the answer sought is finally found. In this process of historical recognition, Paul changes both the impact of the question and the breadth of the given answer.

46. So also Käsemann, who thinks it appears in this context 'in personified form as Power' (1969c: 169).

applies to all—Jew, Greek and barbarian; wise and fool (Rom. 1.16); slave and free; male and female (Gal. 3.28)—a *logos* of *stauros*, the logic of the cross (1 Cor. 1.18, 24), a *dunamis* of *aestheneia*, a power of weakness (2 Cor. 12.9).

1.18–2.29. Paul prefaces the sweeping diatribe against the errors of humanity,[47] of Greek and Jew, with a review of the nature of divinity (1.18-23): invisible, eternal *dunamis*,[48] divine, making himself visible to perception by the *nous* (1.20), incorruptible (1.23),[49] manifested in creation (1.19, 20). God is creator of *kosmos* (1.20); Paul's argument for the existence of God based on the beauty and order that can be seen in the things he has made (1.20) suggests his awareness of the traditional *kosmos–eukosmia*, world–order etymology.[50] Paul is here on well-

47. Witherington 1994, who highlights the grounding of '*all* Paul's ideas, all his arguments, all his practical advice, all his social arrangements' (2) in a story, identifies four principal plots for this story, the first being the story of the world gone wrong. This is precisely how the Romans begins. The other three are: the story of Israel in the wicked world, the story of Christ, and the story of the Christians.

48. Paul holds widespread and popular views of deity, which were, nevertheless, rooted in Classical philosophy. That God is eternal energy, ἀΐδιος δύναμις (1.20), and incorruptible, ἄφθαρος (1.23), recalls Aristotle's statement that everything existing of absolute necessity is eternal, ἀΐδια, and what is eternal does not come into existence or perish, τὰ δ᾽ ἀΐδια ἀγένητα καὶ ἄφθαρτα (Aristotle, *Nicomachean Ethics* 6.1139b23-24).

49. See also 1 Cor. 9.25 and esp. 1 Cor. 15.42-54, on the body of the resurrected, that imitates God in that it does not degenerate. On the importance of *eikones* in this verse see discussion at Rom. 8.29.

50. The proof of the gods' existence drawn from the beauty or order of the universe is already found in Plato (*Laws* 10.886a). Ps.-Zaleucus (frg. 1) repeats it. The derivation of *kosmos* from its being well ordered, εὐκοσμία, is a cliché (e.g., Ps.-Ecphantus, frg. 1.1). Callicratidas (frg. 3) invokes received philosophical tradition (καττὰν ἔννοιαν) for the notion that God is a celestial being, ζῷον οὐράνιον, incorruptible, beginning and cause of the fine order of the universe, ἄφθαρτον, ἀρχά τε καὶ αἰτία τᾶς τῶν ὅλων διακοσμάσιος. The absolute political leader is a heavenly being. In Paul, *kosmos* is primarily, as expected, the harmonious universe (Rom. 1.20; 1 Cor. 4.9; 8.4; Gal. 4.3; Phil. 2.15). Inhabited world, Greek world are other regular meanings. The Hellenistic gnostic mood had already transformed the word and reversed its valence; Paul also uses it to mean an accursed place.

Stead notes (1994: 115) that for the proof of the existence of God by the argument of beauty and order in Rom. 1.20, Paul is drawing on Hellenistic popular

trodden Classical and Hellenistic ground.[51]

The argument from creation, one of the most common in antiquity, relates not only to an orderly universe, however, but also to an orderly political society. Hellenistic Pythagoreans never tire of emphasizing that God is the beginning and the end of the order of the universe, that his rule is the paradigm of proper administration and that his government is the test against which all other regimes are judged. Paul's remarks remind the reader of the principles governing the universe. This is important: to Classical and Hellenistic political thought, household rule and state constitution are imitations of God's administration of the cosmos; moreover, the household head, the magistrate, the ruler are 'personified law', Godlike, *nomos empsuchos*. This notion of imitation anticipates and identifies the solution to the political questions raised in the letter itself. God's rule is tied with *phusis*; it is natural. Human politics is, at best, an imitation of this. In Sthenidas the natural rulership

---

theology. He thinks the source is the Stoics. I am convinced that Paul's source here is most emphatically Pythagorean.

51. God's deity, θειότης (1.20), points to yet another contributor to the bric-à-brac Hellenistic theology: Jewish Wisdom tradition. For the ambiguous and non-technical use of *sophia* by Paul see Chapter 5, section on Sthenidas, frg. 1.1.

For Paul as a partner in and revisionist of the Wisdom tradition as evinced in 1 Cor. 1.18–3.4 (esp. 1 Cor. 2.6-16), see Theis 1991, esp. Chapter 3. One strong evidence of an influence on Paul by the Hellenistic Jewish Wisdom literature, that Theis does not seem to notice, is the use of the term *theiotēs* in Rom. 1.20. This locution applied to a divinity is not encountered before, the Wisdom of Solomon 18.9, most likely written in Alexandria between 100 BCE and 50 CE, and Philo (*Op. mund.* 172 *Varia lectio*), c. 30 BCE–45 CE. After Paul the term is seen in the *Hermetica* (9.1c), Plutarch (*The Oracles at Delphi* 398a; *Table-Talk* 4.665a), Lucian (*Slander* 17) or in an inscription for Artemis at Ephesus (SIG[2] 656.31; SIG[3] 867.31), all second century CE. See L. Delatte 1942: 94-95; MM *s.v.* θειότης; BAGD *s.v.* θειότης.

The attributes of God listed in the letter's opening provide a reminder of another kind, as well. The nature of the universe is eternal and incorruptible. In contrast to it, human nature and creations are ephemeral and perishable, a Hellenistic motto.

This is particularly well articulated by Hippodamos (Chapter 4, section on Hippodamos, frg. 4). He reflects on the particular fate of human institutions, families and states and finds the cyclicality present in nature also in human activities and productions, this time because of innate human inanity. Eternally changing, the human world is contrasted with the divine one, eternally 'saved' (σῴζεσθαι), recycled. The same notion of the permanence of God's world and the transitoriness of human institutions is present in Rom. 12.2.

of God is the model for the acquired rulership of the king (frg. 1.1). Diotogenes, too, opposed the *phusis* of God to the *mimeisthai* (μιμεῖσθαι, 'imitation') of the human.[52] Paul disqualifies actions and beings that are not natural—for example, the unnatural morality resulting from abandonment of God (Rom. 1.26) and the so-called gods, those who are not so by nature (Gal. 4.8). As Paul will say later in Romans, every single citizen of the Christian society, each individual of the *ekklēsia*, is Christ-like, a christ-type figure, an imitation of God. God's *dikaiosunē* bestows God's own attributes, glory, honor, incorruptibility and eternity on those found deserving (Rom. 2.7).

Paul now undertakes a critique of two modes of violating the laws (Rom. 1.18-32 and 2.17-29; 3.21-30), a critique that can be best explained by reference to Ps.-Archytas' argument about written and unwritten laws (frg. 1). One mode, the Greeks', involves the transgression of the unwritten, divine or natural, law. It is the attitude that allows desires to obliterate reason. Romans 1.18-32 presents this situation: the Greeks, who possessed knowledge about God, turned to empty argumentation, and their 'incoherent heart was obscured' (1.21).[53] Having given up right thinking about God, they lapsed, ethically, into immorality (1.24-27) and, politically, into dissension (1.28-31). The Jews' failing—their over-reliance on the written law—is the counterpoint. The Jews boast of the written law and, absurdly, uphold it to the point of defying natural law (2.17-29; 3.21-30). Paul castigates the Jews for their pretensions (2.18-21) in terms resonant of Ps.-Ecphantus' doxology of the king:[54] the Jews affect to approve (δοκιμάζεις) excellence (2.18, cf. Phil. 1.10) and to be a light (φῶς) to others (2.19, cf. Phil. 2.15). By disclosing the vanity of the Jews' claims in terms similar to those usually used to apotheosize the Hellenistic ruler, Paul makes his ridicule devastating: the Jews attempt to fill shoes that are much too large for them, and they fail lamentably.

52. H 265.5-10, T 72.18.22. Late Hellenistic writers like Cicero and Seneca do the same; see L. Delatte 1942: 277.

53. For Paul's indebtedness to Aristotelian psychology see note below. Barrett also stresses the importance of *kardia* in Pauline psychology: 'one of Paul's most important psychological terms' (1957: 37), not necessarily good (1.24), nor necessarily evil (2.15; 5.5; 6.17), the organ of thought (10.6) and of feeling (9.2), essentially inward, hidden (2.29; 8.27).

54. Frg. 1.3. See also Chapter 5, section on Diotogenes, frgs. 1.2.1 and 1.2.2, where the king is leader, manager, initiator, benefactor and savior of his subjects.

The language of this passage makes it clear that Paul addresses the educated Greek and Roman.[55] Paul's vocabulary is that of handbook philosophy, imbued with Platonic, Aristotelian and Hellenistic philosophical terms.[56] Paul associates the Greeks (1.18-32) with immorality, the Jews (2.1-29) with inflexibility.[57] Both Jews and Greeks resist reason and God[58]—the Greeks by indifference, the Jews by intransigence. The Jew is ἀμετανόητος (*ametanoētos*, 'remorseless', 'unrepentant') (2.5). The Greeks' *asebeia* ('sacrilege', 'impiety') and the Jews' 'ametanoia' (lack of *metanoia*, 'change of heart') are equally severe disorders of the *psuchē*. Anthropologically and psychologically, the Jews can claim no privileged nature, neither for the bad nor for the good (2.10, 12). Notice how Paul puts it: there is no προσωπολημψία (*prosōpolēmpsia*, 'obeisance') in God (2.11). He uses a reference to an 'Oriental' custom—prostration, part of the political etiquette of Eastern despots—to declare that God shows no particular deference to the Jews. At the same time, the issue moves from the psychological to the political. *Asebēs* and *ametanoētos* are, in Pauline thinking, sarkic epithets. Essentially, they describe the failure to grasp the nature of the relation between human and God. This translates, in the Pauline system, into political subversion, treason against the sovereign power, *lèse majesté*.

While I do not wish to make too much of *asebeia* as Greek-specific, the larger context of the letter suggests it. The way I read Rom. 1.18–2.29, Paul opposes two types of political offenses, one characteristic of the Greeks (the Gentiles), the other of the Jews. I understand *asebeia* as

---

55. There is a long-standing thesis, from Munck 1959 (German edition 1954) to Gaston 1981–82 to Elliott 1994, that surmises that Romans, if not all of Pauline letters, was addressed first and foremost to the gentile Christians. I cannot think that the literate Jewish-Christian could be excluded from the Romans' audience.

56. Stowers 1994 (Chapter 2) remarks that Paul draws here on Greco-Roman decline-of-civilization narratives to present a caricature of loss of self-mastery. This theme, essential for understanding Paul's rhetorical strategy in Romans, according to Stowers, is the correct reading of Rom. 1.18–4.2, and especially 2.17-29.

57. I am puzzled by Stowers's notion that Paul uses in Rom. 2.17-29 the rhetorical device of speech-in-character (προσωποποιία) to present an imaginary Jew poised to cure 'the moral and religious malaise of Gentiles' (1994: 151). This intensely original scholar seems here dazzled by his own zeal for rhetorical proof. The passage reads clearly and consistently like a critique of the Jews and best reflects Paul's own thinking.

58. The Greeks' knowledge of God is by reason alone, philosophically. The Jews had the benefit of revelation, prophetically.

applying to the Greeks. In Classical Greek and Hellenistic philosophy *asebeia* is paired with but carefully distinguished from *adikia*. The latter indicates the basest form of relationship between humans, that is, injustice, while the former refers to hostility toward the supernatural, defiance of God. Hellenistic literature is replete with accusations hurled at the Greeks for having abandoned reason for the senses—precisely the strategy Paul uses against the *asebeis* in Romans. Paul's invective against the Greeks is dominated by the notion of *asebeia* (Rom. 1.18; 4.5; 5.6).

If humanity were a unified whole, its problems everywhere the same, much in Romans would make little sense. It is a near-consensus that Paul in this letter does not address internal divisions within the community; the epistle raises larger, more general concerns. These concerns take a dual form: on the one hand, the conflict between the Jew and the Greek; on the other, the divorce between *each* of the two cultural entities and God. (The latter appears also as the cause of the former.) Paul's distinction between the Greeks and the Jews is ethnically determined; his critique is not simply directed at humanity at large. Paul initiates the process of integration by disclosing to each of two groups that constitute his world where it primarily fails. What are the points of breakdown between each group and God, and, consequently, what is the reason for the disunity between the two groups? While it is true that Jews and Greeks stand united in *hamartia*, that humanity's common feature is *akrasia* (failure of the will) and that *adikia-asebeia* forms a continuum with *hamartia* (6.12-13), the two groups retain their distinctness. Each needs to understand its peculiar source of ruin before a rapprochement can be attempted.

The Greeks sold out the political, ethical and metaphysical ideals of Greek philosophy: *asebeia* is the debasement of the rational and the concentration on the lower parts of the soul, the passions.[59] The results

---

59. Paul's psychology is indebted to Aristotle. To briefly summarize: essentially, Aristotle produces a two-tiered soul, one part irrational, the other rational. The irrational reaches from the growth-nutritive faculty all the way into the rational, effectively constituting a middle layer of the soul. Aristotle calls this *epithumia*. *Epithumia*, given its mixed nature, has an unusual property: it may listen to or ignore reason. *Epithumia* is the locus of appetites and desires but also of moral qualities, *aretai*. These *aretai* describe a desire–thought nexus, *nous–orexis*, a volatile, unstable complex, determined by choice, *proairesis*. *Epithumia*, the province of ethics, is the favorite range of Hellenistic popular philosophy. Pauline *epithumia* (1.24) and *orexis* (1.27) point to the intermediate feature of the soul. The

of *asebeia* (1.18, 23, 25-27) are desires (1.24), ignoble passions (1.26),⁶⁰
lust (1.27), senseless hearts (1.21, 22) and a whole catalogue of vices
(1.29-31).⁶¹ Rejection of God contaminates both mind and propriety
(νοῦν καὶ καθήκοντα) (1.28).⁶² In a play on words, οὐ δοκιμάζειν-
ἀδόκιμος (1.28),⁶³ Paul says that the Greeks' *nous* is disqualified by
God. This in a world that sets a great prize on God's approval as the
mark of legitimacy.⁶⁴

The extensive catalogue of vices in Rom. 1.29-31 includes all the

---

Aristotelian inspiration of the system of ethics to which Paul and Hellenistic
popular philosophers subscribe is also illustrated by their preference for the term
heart, *kardia* (1.21), to name the soul. (Plato called it brain.) The psychological
construct has a strict parallelism in politics not only in Plato and Aristotle but also
in Paul.

It is significant that *logismos*, the rational, the highest element of the soul (see
Chapter 4, section on Callicratidas, frg. 1, esp. T 103.1-10), becomes devalued in
Paul. *Logismoi* stand for perplexities (Rom. 2.15); they are the sarkic arguments of
Paul's antagonists, defeated by his ammunition and made captives of Christ (2 Cor.
10.4).

60. Rom. 1.26 is remarkable for the employment of the term *chrēsis*: [Greek]
women exchanged the natural *chrēsis* for one against nature (αἵ τε γὰρ θήλειαι
αὐτῶν μετήλλαξαν τὴν φυσικὴν χρῆσιν εἰς τὴν παρὰ φύσιν). *Chrēsis* is a component of the *sustēmata* chain (see Chapter 5, section on Ps.-Ecphantus). *Chrēsis*
(use), serves to produce *sumpheron*, common good; *chrēsis* submits to a political-
type authority. Politically, as Ps.-Ecphantus employs the term, *chrēsis* means 'to
imitate the government of the universe'. To rule his realm in this harmonious way
brings the political leader the admiration and love of the subjects. The Hellenistic
Pythagorean concept of *sustēma* applies well to this text. Abandonment of reason
so perverted the perception of the sensible world that *chrēsis* works in contradiction
to *sumpheron*, the very principle it is designed to serve. As this applies to Paul,
abandonment of God, an outrage at the very top of the *sustēmata* sequence, throws
into disarray all its other layers. The confusion only increases as one descends the
sustēmata ladder, and it is most manifest at the body level. The so-called
homophobic passage in Rom. 1.26-27 only evinces the outcome of the initial upset.
Acting against nature, *para phusin*, is synonymous with rebellion against God.

61. Among these, κακοήθεια, malignity, goes back to Aristotle who defines
it 'taking everything for the worse' (*Rhetoric* 2.13.3, *ap.* Barrett 1957: 40).
Ἐφευρετὰς κακῶν (Rom. 1.30), contriver of evil, is traced by Barrett (41) to
Odysseus, esp. as described by Virgil: *scelerum inuentor* (*Aeneid* 2.164).

62. I can hardly see how this critique applies to the Jews.

63. *Adokimos* refers also to a counterfeit coin. Paul uses its opposite, *dokimos*,
genuine, for Apelles, in the list of greetings (16.10) (see Barrett 1957: 284).

64. See discussion of Rom. 6.17, on the issue of the authority of apostles.

Hellenistic Pythagorean moral abominations: *hubrisma, alazoneia, huperēphania* and so on.[65] Paul denounces the Greeks' abandonment of wisdom for desire. Nothing is more threatening a source of political downfall than moral dissolution. (Although couched in the language of ethics, the vices are the vitals of political *stasis*, for behind seemingly 'moral' lapses lie—as we learn from background sources[66]—the forces that shred family fabric and abet public disintegration. Paul does not name the specific source of the list of vices he recites. He does not have to. The people of Hellenistic times would have been only too familiar with them and their causes. Corruption of the soul, the immediate cause of *asebeia*, has manifold grounds. It is not the specific list of moral offenses that is the issue; such lists are unremarkable in Hellenistic and Roman times. It is the threat these offenses pose to the political nexus that is significant.

This moral-political connection has its root in the Classical writers Plato, Isocrates and Aristotle. But it is in Hellenistic thought that it achieves the form with which Paul is familiar. The Greeks' refusal to follow the true God, whom they knew from nature as creator (1.19),[67] amounts to political treason. *Hubris*[68] ('insurgency') is one of the many allegations against them (1.30). (Intriguingly, it is the same charge that Paul, at another time, raises against the Philippians [1 Thess. 2.2], who revolted against him in an act tantamount to political disobedience. The Philippians, of course, are those whom Paul exhorts *politeuesthe*! [Phil. 1.27]. This may help explain the political focus of the Letter to the Philippians.)

Paul's reproof of the Greeks concludes with yet another Aristotelian reverberation: the contrast between *doing* injustice and *being* unjust— the first fortuitous and excusable, the second a habit and odious.[69] To

---

65. See also Chapter 4, section on Callicratidas, esp. frg. 2, cf. 1 Tim. 6.9.

66. In Callicratidas, *hubris, alazoneia, huperēphania*, also listed by Paul, derive from excessive wealth. Overindulgence leads to political ruin, *olethros* (cf. 1 Cor. 5.52; 1 Thess. 1.9). In Ps.-Ecphantus, *hubris*, political rebellion, is the result of sensual cravings and of *akrasia*, intemperance.

67. Bultmann (1955: 141-42) reads in Rom. 1.19 Stoic natural theology. See also Stead 1994: 115. The idea goes far back, however, to Plato and even to the pre-Socratics.

68. As ὑβρίζω, ὕβρις, in the list of sufferings in 2 Cor. 12.10, ὑβριστης in the list of vices in Rom. 1.30, cf. 1 Tim. 1.13.

69. *Nicomachean Ethics* 5.1137a5-9. For discussion of this idea see Chapter 2.

approve of evil, says Paul, is to deserve to die (Rom. 1.32). Paul's use of the term 'to do' (πράσσω) is consistent throughout and entirely compatible with the political meaning it has in the Hellenistic Pythagoreans. Used eight times in Romans, it never just means 'to do [something]' but always figures in a direct or implied legal or political context: here (1.32, used twice, cf. Gal. 5.21), it refers to actions that violate God's decrees and thus incur death.[70]

Later (Rom. 3.5), Paul will call the Jews' outrage *adikia*. *Adikia* is rooted in the political, and when Paul applies it to the Jews he attacks their national exclusivism. *Adikia*, however, has greater breadth for Paul, essentially following the Platonic paradigm: it is synonymous with discord.[71] It devastates the political body and the individual soul. Paul denounces it as political dissent (2.8) or as disintegration of the body and the soul (1.18-32). (In the first case, *adikia* points, by and large, to the Jews, in the second to the Greeks.) The *adikia–asebeia* fusion in Rom. 1.18 indicates an all-embracing power of destructiveness that permeates the entire universe, dissolving the state and the self and rendering the people Godless. It infects this life and the next.[72]

The Jews can claim no advantage vis-à-vis the law. The traditional Classical/Hellenistic distinction between *nomos* and *phusis* helps us understand the lashing that Paul gives the Jews.[73] A Jew is ἀκροατής

70. It also covers actions attracting God's judgment (Rom. 2.1-3, used twice); it applies to 'doing' the law (2.25). For discussion of the use of *prattein* in absolute sense see discussion below, Rom. 13.4.

71. *Republic* 1.351e-352a. On discord as a political term see Welborn 1987, 1997. So far as I am aware, Welborn is just about the only published Pauline scholar who seriously endeavors to connect Paul with the political categories in use in Paul's time. As A.H.M. Jones (1940: 144-45) points out, following a sentiment well known in antiquity (e.g., Plutarch, *Precepts of Statecraft* 805a, quoted in Welborn 1987: 111), the martial sense of civic pride of Greek cities, practically eliminated by imperial control, becomes negatively internalized as σχίσματα ('divisions'). Welborn reads 1 Cor. 1–4 as an example of a function that associations must generally have had in the Roman empire, that of 'provid[ing] scope for the exercise of the political instinct…' (1988: 111).

72. See also Chapter 1, as well as the discussion of Rom. 3.15, below.

73. The antithesis *nomos–phusis* is an ancient Greek commonplace, which Höistad 1948 traces back to the fifth century Antisthenes, Antiphon and Hippias, according to whom codified, city laws are for the bad, the good are in no need of them, for they obey the laws of nature, *phusis*, laws that virtue alone, *aretē*, knows. See Diogenes Laertius 6.12; Aristotle *Politics* 3.1284a-b; Philodemus of Gadara (Höistad 1948: 113-14). 'The wise will act in politics, πολιτεύσεσθαι, not according

(*akroatēs*) (2.13), 'in attendance to', the law. Nations that do not have the law (the written law, that is) do the law *by nature* (φύσει τὰ τοῦ νόμου ποιῶσιν); they are a law unto themselves (2.14), explains Paul—that is they follow natural law.[74] On the basis of the traditional opposition *nomos–phusis* (the human, particular law versus the law of nature), Paul affirms that the people who lack the law (of states) do by nature what the (universal) law requires (Rom. 2.14). Paul shifts the emphasis from the law to the doing of the law, the 'doers of the law' (οἱ ποιηταὶ νόμου) (2.13, cf. 2.25). He annuls the much-vaunted privilege of a written code of laws and instead stresses lawful activity. Paul's thinking is provocative. Since the Jews' law is, *de jure*, the same as the Greek's natural law, the Jews have no special claim to distinctiveness. And since, in regard to the law, what matters is its actuation, the Jew who ignores the law is, *de facto*, in a wanting position vis-à-vis the Greek who acts according to it.

It is not *nomos* but συνείδησις (*suneidēsis*), a universal aspect of human consciousness, that matters.[75] The nations work by *suneidēsis*

to established laws, οὐ κατὰ τοὺς κειμένους νόμους, but according to *aretē*, ἀλλὰ κατὰ τὸν τῆς ἀρετῆς (Diogenes Laertius 6.11)' (Höistad 113). The *nomos–phusis* distinction is developed as a concept of two types of law: νόμος τῆς πόλεως and νόμος τῆς ἀρετῆς (Höistad 113). It is the latter *nomos* that functions 'as the only possible adequate expression of *dikaiosunē*' (Höistad 1948: 167). This is consistent with Plato's *Politicus* 300c and *Laws* 875c, Aristotle's *Politics* 3.1284a and also with the concept *nomos empsuchos* of the Hellenistic Pythagoreans (see also Höistad 1948: 168 n. 3). This is obviously both a dominant and a constant of Greek political thought.

For Antisthenes and his followers, determines Höistad, *dikaiosunē* 'is not bound up with the changeable laws of the state, but with an unchanging principle common to all humankind', with *phusis* (1948: 115). *Dikaiosunē* becomes part of a political critique. Antisthenes identifies it with καλοκἀγαθία, above wisdom and courage (cf. Xenophon, *Symposium* 3.4). In Antiphon, it punishes even the secret transgressor (Höistad 1948: 115). See also the note on this topic in Chapter 4, section on Ps.-Archytas.

Paul's concept of *dikaiosunē* follows this line of thought. In his system, where *pistis* replaces *phusis*, *nomos*, in the sense of positive law, has only very limited room.

74. Höistad reads in this verse the contrast between the law of *poleis* and the law of *aretē* (1948: 113-15).

75. Barrett recognizes that 'This inward nature of things [i.e. doing what the law requires "by nature", *phusei*] Aristotle distinguished from law (νόμος), law being for him convention'. He tends, however, to relate Paul to the Stoics who 'taught that true law was rooted in nature' (1957: 51-2).

(2.15), that is, by conscience. *Suneidēsis* is a term with a rather discontinuous history.[76] It is knowledge of right or wrong, in relation to past or future acts, committed by oneself or by others, with the accompanying elation or remorse.[77] Paul himself explains *suneidēsis*: it is the practical equivalent, among the Greeks, of the Law among the Jews (2.14). His formulation is clear: natural law, law written in the heart, compares well with the written law of the Jews (an incendiary remark under the circumstances) (Rom. 2.14-15).[78] Greek conscience is equated with natural law.[79] (In Rom. 2.14-15 Paul brings together the philosophical ἑαυτοῖς εἰσιν νόμος ['they are a law to themselves'] an expression of natural law and an allusion to the Hellenistic Pythagorean *nomos empsuchos*, with the scriptural 'law written in one's heart' [Jer. 31.33].[80]) All told, the written code of (Jewish) law is no match for inward (*pistis*-granting *pneuma*-based) law, in Paul an analog of the

76. The term's history begins with Democritus (Diels, frg. 297b) (see *TLNT*, III, 332 *s.v.* συνείδησις). It is sparsely used before first century CE (Chrysippus, Menander, Periander, Diogenes Laertius, Bias), only to explode afterwards, from Philo and Josephus to Plutarch and Lucian, as well as in many papyri (*TLNT*, III, 332-35). In Latin it produces *conscientia*, found often in Cicero and a favorite of Seneca's (*TLNT*, III, 335 n 8).

77. Pierce's 1955 analysis of the concept in Greek and Hellenistic tradition as well as in Paul, finds it to apply to an awareness that is universal and personal, which refers to past actions and which induces contrition. Maurer (*TDNT s.v. suneidēsis*) and Stacey 1956 determine that in Paul *suneidēsis* is evaluative, reflective and prescriptive, thus contradicting Pierce's conclusions. Thrall 1967 critiques Pierce and she too finds that, in Paul, conscience can suggest 'a course of action which lies in the future' (120); it provides 'the stimulus to moral action in the future' (124), based esp. on Rom. 13.5; can pass 'judgment upon the conduct or actions of another person' (124), cf. esp. Rom. 2.17-25; 1 Cor. 10.28-29; can express 'approval rather than condemnation' (125), cf. 2 Cor. 4.2; 5.11.

For a discussion of the rabbinic *halakha* on this, see Tomson (1990: 208-16). Tomson attempts to show, not entirely convincingly, that the interface between the Greek, Latin, and Hebrew meaning of the term is individual responsibility (213). In *suneidēsis* 'individual responsibility' is fused to a shared aspect: the very connection of the prefix συν to εἴδησις points to the collective constituent of the knowledge characteristic to *suneidēsis*.

78. 'Paul has come to regard conscience as performing in the Gentile world roughly the same function as was performed by the Law amongst the Jews', writes Thrall (1967: 124).

79. Hoïstad (1948: 113-15) reads Rom. 2.14: 'When Gentiles who have not the law of cities do by nature what the law of *aretē* requires...'

80. See also discussion of *nomos empsuchos* in Diotogenes frg. 1.1.

universal, natural law (Rom. 2.27-29, cf. 7.6, 8.2; Gal. 5.18).

In Rom. 2.15 the conflictual nature of the human (rational-irrational) soul is resolved by this *suneidēsis*, and it is this that God judges. (In Rom. 13.5, the individual's act of conscience, *suneidēsis*, refers to subjection to rulers or to submission to the law of the *polis*, a political conscience demanded by membership in the state. The move from soul to state is seamless, as in Paul's Hellenistic models.) Uncircumcised 'by nature' (ἐκ φύσεως) (2.27), the Greek may have an inward circumcision, that of the heart (2.29). That is, the law-doing Gentile is 'naturally' circumcised; he is so in his inner naturalness. Paul distinguishes between an outward, visible nature (ἐν τῷ φανερῷ) (2.28), which describes the uncircumcision of the Gentile (ἡ ἐκ φύσεως ἀκροβυστία) (2.27) as well as the circumcision of the Jews (ἡ ἐν σαρκὶ περιτομή) (2.28)—a sarkic mark—and an inner nature, the 'Jew within' (ὁ ἐν τῷ κρυπτῷ Ἰουδαῖος), the pneumatic or *pneuma*-induced circumcision of the heart (περιτομὴ καρδίας ἐν πνεύματι) (2.29). 'He is a Jew who is so unapparently, secretly [ἐν τῷ κρυπτῷ], the circumcision of the heart based on the *pneuma* not upon a scroll [οὐ γράμματι]'.[81] The letter of the law is opposed by the *pneuma*. Law and justice live in the soul; the pneumatic is their personification.[82]

3.1-20. The Jews' *adikia* rendered the law impuissant but did not detract from its validity (3.1-2). Their injustice only showed that humanity is incapable of *dikaiosunē*, which is the prerogative of God alone (3.5, cf. 3.3, 7). (This matches one of the perennial observations of both Classical and Hellenistic political philosophy: that human nature is incapable of *dikaiosunē*.) This deficiency makes God's perfection much more conspicuous (3.3, 5, 7), yet this does not mean, as some libertines and antinomians claim Paul says, that by doing evil the good comes forth (3.8). Similarly, this also does not mean, as some sophists may be

81. As Plato puts it, only that which God sees, hidden and inward, irrelevant to the outsiders, matters (*Republic* 2.366e).

82. Rom. 2.29 is a star witness for the identity between the concept of *nomos empsuchos* and *nomos pneumatos* and for the adaptation of the former to Paul's pneumatic political system (see 8.2). See also Rom. 7.6: the transformation operated by Christ rendered the antiquated law-code worthless, substituted for it the newness of the *pneuma*. Καινότης πνεύματος supplants παλαιότης γράμματος, a newness of *pneuma* contrasts with the outdatedness of law. The opposition living law–written law is evidently implied in this statement. Rom. 8.2: The *nomos* of the *pneuma* of life released me from the law of *hamartia* and death.

inferring, that, given the weakness of human nature, God's wrath is unjustified (3.5). It is absurd, remarks Paul, to call the possessor of *dikaiosunē* unjust (3.6). *Dikaiosunē theou* is activated by and offsets human *adikia* (3.5); it is the process that determines the just, *dikaios* (3.26).

Injustice, *adikia*, is applied to the Jews in 3.5. Its sphere of action, however, is much larger. *Adikia* has a universal aspect; it describes all humanity and stands in counterbalance to the justice of God (3.5, cf. 3.9, 23). In Classical and Hellenistic writers, *adikia* traverses the entire political and psychological axis. As noted, Plato calls *adikia* lack of concerted action,[83] whether in a social or an individual body. *Adikia* is a civil war, a *stasis*, among the parts that form the soul or the state.[84] According to Diotogenes (frg. 2.1), *adikia* is a pervasive evil that has access to all levels of the soul, and it is also a perfect evil, which thoroughly corrupts the soul. The pervasive view throughout Western history is that moral lapse is a political threat. In antiquity the logic was primarily psychological: excessive attention to the lower layers of the soul through arrogance and violence or sensuality and passions leads to withering of the rational, leading part, to the turning away from God and the world of ideas and to the abjuration of lofty political and moral excellence. This approach is operative in Rom. 1.18-32[85]: *adikia* indicates dissolution of the body and of the soul. Paul, however, goes further, using *adikia* in his critique of Jewish *nomos*.

Adikia is contrasted to truth.[86] Paul teaches that all must obey the truth (2.8; Gal. 5.7, cf. also Tit. 3.1). Disobedience of truth (i.e. obedience of *adikia*) stems from factious spirit; against this, coercion—the wrath and fury of God—must be exerted (Rom. 2.8).[87] The corrective of *adikia* is *dikaiosunē*. In Diotogenes (frg. 2.2.4) as in Classical political philosophy, *dikaiosunē* is supreme *aretē* that includes all others. In

83. *Republic* 1.351e-352a.
84. *Republic* 4.444b.
85. In Paul's accusation against the Greeks, in fact an indictment against the age, he finds them consistently at fault for the abandonment of the good in favor of sensuality (1.18-32; Phil. 3.18-20). Hippodamos writes: 'pleasures bring ills to human beings' (frgs. 3a1-3, esp. T 101.4-5).
86. According to Plato, truth is always the primary objective of any investigation, regardless of its chance of realization (*Republic* 5.472c-d).
87. Need for coercion, because of the deficiency of human nature, is a common place in the Hellenistic Pythagoreans, from the mystical Ps.-Ecphantus (frgs. 1.5.2, 3.3) to the didactic Ps.-Zaleucus (frg. 1).

The Political Paul

Plato's *Republic*, for example,[88] *dikaiosunē* is the supreme mark of both state and individual. Plato's concept of *dikaiosunē* is derived from Pythagoreanism: *dikaiosunē* is a harmony in which each component performs its own function, and it is the binding and harmonizing force compelling them to do so.

The only force against injustice is *dikaiosunē theou* (3.5). As Paul anticipates here (he will treat the issue extensively in 9.1–11.31), *dikaiosunē* applies not just to the government of God but also to the exercise of his function as judge. No one stands blameless under God's judgment.[89] To judge (*krinein, katakrinein*), in Paul as in the Hellenistic Pythagorean writers, is God's exclusive prerogative, and the inerrancy of God's judgment is contrasted with the fallibility of human judgment.[90] All are judged and found wicked, whether Greeks or Jews, whether judged by God (2.12, cf. 3.7) or by Paul (1 Cor. 5.5, 12). Though God may exercise wrath against the unjust, for the elect God's judgment is marked by kindness (χρηστότης[91]), moderation (ἀνοχή[92]) and patience (μακροθυμία) (Rom. 2.4)—Hellenistic fundamentals of justice.

Drawing further on the legal vocabulary, Paul 'charges' (προῃτιασά-μεθα) both Jew and Greek; they are both under error (ὑφ' ἁμαρτίαν) (3.9).[93] In an epic interlude (3.10-18) assembled from extracts from several Psalms, the forcefulness of which comes from the physical realism of the language, Paul dramatizes the biological dimension of human injustice: not only as a unified whole, as organically integral, has

88. *Republic* 4.443c-444a.
89. God's elect, however, experience a judgment transformed by Christ's intercession (8.33-34, cf. 1 Cor. 11.32).
90. This topic is extensively treated in Rom. 2 and Rom. 14 (2.1, 3, 12, 16; 14.3, 4, 5, 10, 13, 22), cf. 1 Cor. 3.32; 10.29. See also Ps.-Ecphantus frg. 1.3, esp. H 273.2-3, T 80.7.
91. In Diotogenes (frg. 2.2.4) the king's *chrēstotēs* is the sum of justice, equity and compassion. *Chrēstotēs* is also used by Paul: to designate the first attribute of God (Rom. 2.4, cf. Eph. 2.7; Tit. 3.4); to describe a divine trait (Rom. 11.22); to refer to one of the characteristics of the *diakonoi*, God's ministers (2 Cor. 6.6); to name one of the gifts of the *pneuma* (Gal. 5.22).
92. *Anochē*, holding back, restraint, allowing for a respite. It suggests truce, not, as Stowers thinks (1994: 105), delaying of punishment. 2 Macc. 6.14 that he quotes is the very reverse of Paul's intent; the two texts stand in a polemical relationship.
93. Stowers calls this 'rhetorical hyperbole' (1994: 81), though I miss the hyperbole. Few Pauline statements sound more factual.

humanity deserted God, but each human being has done so with every part of the body.[94] *Sarx* ('flesh') (3.20)—that is, every human individual, Jew no less than Greek—can say nothing in its own defense (3.19). Law itself—*written* law, that is—is questioned. The law is only knowledge of error (ἐπίγνωσις ἁμαρτίας) (3.20), and, while itself just, it only prescribes accountability; it reveals human fallibility. (There is also the implication here that the law is applicable only to those who recognize it, that it is for a limited group only.[95] Paul again seems to refer to the Greek *nomos*, with its dual, law-convention ambiguity.) One stands starkly culpable before God, with no recourse anywhere.

Paul's position vis-à-vis the law, *nomos* of the Jews (or *nomoi poleōn*, the decrees of the Greek city), is unequivocal. *Nomos* is of no importance; its usefulness is marginal at best. Paul's interest in *nomos* is dictated by its traditional dominance in civic and political life. His critique of the legal edifice of the Jews is intense. He finds a political structure that rests on laws to be inadequate and is dissatisfied with the justice laws engender. But although he questions the law, Paul is no antinomian. He is actually very careful to fend off such accusations (3.8). The issue is the inefficacy of the law for a humanity under *hamartia*.[96] The law is not *hamartia*, yet it is an instrument of *hamartia*, the consciousness of *hamartia* (7.7). A valid political construct cannot rest on this law, no matter how inspired the lawgiver. For genuine *dikaiosunē* something else is needed.

We find a parallel to this line of argument in the Hellenistic Pythagorean Ps.-Archytas, who, following Classical sources, differentiates between law and justice, *nomos* and *dikaiosunē*. He questions human *nomos* and speaks for divine, or universal, law. The Sophists[97] insisted on the contradiction between the precepts of law and the order of

94. Origen would write a paschal homily, apparently inspired by and in answer to this powerful poetry, in which he describes a reversal of this process of decay by a process of identification of human body parts with Christ's body.

95. ὅσα ὁ νόμος λέγει τοῖς ἐν τῷ νόμῳ λαλεῖ (Rom. 3.19). Boyarin (1994: 136), following Dunn 1990, suggests that 'the ultimate inadequacy of the Law stems from its ethnic exclusiveness…'

96. Paul employs *hamartia* in a sense that contradicts the Hebrew usage. As Rengstorf remarks (*TDNT s.v.* ἁμαρτωλός), the word sinner, *hamartōlos*, is characteristic Jewish language: רשע refers to the one guilty of sin, the wicked, and is more or less synonymous with the Gentiles. Paul changes this. For him, Jew and Greek alike succumbed to it.

97. E.g., Critias, in the fifth century BCE, long before Ps.-Archytas.

nature. The separation between *nomos* and *dikaiosunē* is likewise a feature of Hellenistic political theory. Commentator after commentator criticizes the laws of cities as being opposed to human nature.[98] Hellenistic Pythagoreans (of both the *polis* and *basileia* varieties) distinguish between the animate law, *nomos empsuchos*, and the written, inanimate law, and identify the king with the living law. Overall, the political background in which I anchor Paul consistently questions the efficacy of law for genuine political activity and for the common good, *to sumpheron*.

Romans 3.21–8.39: The World Set Straight[99]

This section develops the theme of the *polis* and the principle of *dikaiosunē pisteōs* that characterizes it.

3.21-26. The solution to human *hamartia* is God's *dikaiosunē*. God's justice, *dikaiosunē theou*, is apart from law (χωρὶς νόμου) (3.21).[100]

98. See Chapter 4, section on Ps.-Archytas.

99. The fracture between Rom. 1–2 and Rom. 6–8 has long been a scholarly quandary. In the first case *hamartia* is wrongdoing and *sōtēria* is due to principled behavior; in the second case *hamartia* is a power and *sōtēria* is the outcome of Jesus' crucifixion and resurrection. Seeley, who reviews this difficulty in a recent provocative study (1994, ch. 5), reaches a baffling conclusion: that Paul's gospel was a summation of ethical injunctions derived from Hellenistic Jewish apocalyptic and that in Rom. 6–8 Paul attempts, but fails, to couple his *euangelion* with a theory that would confer on the Greeks full membership in the *ekklēsia*. I think that political philosophy, in the structuring of such treatises as the *Republic* or the *Politics*, suggests a solution to this problem. Following the strategy used by his philosophical models, esp. Aristotle, Paul looks first at the world as is, and proposes a remedy operative under 'real conditions'. But then the Christ event allows the world to be contemplated under 'ideal conditions'. Both the agent behind the world's downfall and the power that saves it are seen in a different perspective. Now Paul discourses about the ideal world, the forces at work are on a different scale. For Paul, the ideal world is the one which integrates Jew and Greek, man and woman, wealthy and poor, wise and fool. This was rendered possible not by personal moral effort but by Christ. The difference is that between individual improvement and cosmic transmutation. The application, however, is in the real, human world. Rom. 4 expresses the same perspective as Rom. 1–2; Rom. 3 and 5 point to Rom. 6–8.

100. D.C. Campbell 1992b objects to the prevalent scholarly opinion that the lexical, grammatical and syntactical difficulties with this text spring from Paul's indebtedness to the tradition. Campbell focuses on rhetorical figures to resolve

The *dikaiosunē* of God is contrasted with the *nomos* of the Jews. This critique can hardly come from within Judaism. A Jew would insist on the identity of divine justice and the written law, even if only for the Jews themselves. It is only a Greek-educated, Hellenistic mind that can draw such a distinction—one that knows the antithesis between written, positive or human, law and unwritten, natural or divine, law. Universal *dikaiosunē* is distinct from Jewish *nomos* and is *pistis*-bound (3.21-22). *Nomos* is demoted by *dikaiosunē theou* via *pisteōs Iēsou Christou* (3.21-22). In Paul, Christ—royal and divine ruler—naturally and logically fills the position of the Hellenistic Pythagorean *nomos empsuchos*.[101] One can be reasonably confident, I think, that the *nomos empsuchos* model plays a role in configuring the Pauline Christ. Indeed, Paul would have had to have tried hard to have avoided this concept: *nomos empsuchos* is a well-documented motif[102] from Ps.-Archytas to Clement of Alexandria and beyond. This ubiquity makes quite defensible the thesis that Paul fashioned Christ as a *nomos empsuchos* type; Christ is ideally positioned in Paul to bridge the two distinct levels of a unified political system.

To *dikaiosunē*, the paramount political concept of the Greeks, Paul gives a reading that is consistent with the political transformations operated by Hellenistic Pythagoreanism. *Dikaiosunē* divides into two, and while it retains its full characteristics in each aspect of its divided state, a certain hierarchy is nevertheless being produced: *dikaiosunē theou* and *dikaiosunē pisteōs*. The second finds its source in the first, even as it has an autonomous integrity.[103]

---

structural and syntactic quandaries posed by 3.21-26. He unravels the tangle of 3.24 by splitting it. He construes 22c-24a, οὐ γαρ ἐστιν...χάριτι, as a self-contained parenthetical statement. By bracketing this section, Campbell obtains a neat phrase formed of three διά clauses, a rhetorical devise called epanaphora. He considers 25b-26, though lopsided, the result of isocolic reduplication. The epanaphora 21-25b reads: the *dikaiosunē theou*, *through* the *pistis* of Jesus Christ, for all who have *pistis*, *through* the ransom which is in Christ Jesus, whom God put forward as a sacrifice, *through* the *pistis* in his blood.

101. For *nomos empsuchos* see Chapter 4, section on Ps.-Archytas, frg. 2b; Chapter 5, section on Diotogenes, frgs. 1.1, 1.2.4, 2.2; and section on Sthenidas, frg. 1.2.

102. See Chapter 4, section on Ps.-Archytas.

103. The correlation of the two kinds of *dikaiosunē* enjoys increasing attention in recent scholarship. That God's *dikaiosunē* is a salvation concept has long been a commonplace. That from human perspective *dikaiosunē* is tied with *pistis* is also

In Plato, *dikaiosunē* gives the individual unity and makes the *polis* possible; in the Hellenistic Pythagoreans, the king's *dikaiosunē* harmonizes the state and makes it like the cosmos. In Paul, *dikaiosunē pisteōs* makes humanity equal (by the award of *pistis*, according to the formula of analogic *dikaiosunē*, the ideal justice) and the whole world one state (because of God's impartiality to Greek and Jew alike);[104]—a Hellenistic, but not a Jewish, concept. Only God can recognize merit and properly reward it; people simply clamor after their own interests. God's *dikaiosunē* underwrites both politics and metaphysics. *Dikaiosunē theou* is Paul's political–transcendental signature.

This perfect justice is disbursed on account of the *pistis of* Jesus Christ (διὰ πίστεως ᾿Ιησοῦ Χριστοῦ, read as subjective genitive[105]), which functions as a model for all human *pistis* (3.22c-24a), a christological *pistis* leading to a soteriological one.[106] Jesus Christ sets the paradigm of *pistis*. *Dikaiosunē pisteōs* describes the circumcised and the uncircumcised, the Jew and the Greek (3.22; 4.9; 9.30), and is radically different from *nomos*, a particular system of law (4.13; 9.31; Phil. 3.9). The universality of *dikaiosunē pisteōs* counterbalances *adikia*, which is the other universal characteristic of humanity (e.g., Rom. 3.23, cf. 3.5; 3.9).

One is rendered right as a gift of *charis*, God's benevolence (3.24a), and, since all have wronged God (3.23), no one is excepted from *charis*.

well understood. What links them together, summarizes Nebe (1992: 147), is the 'free gift' and the 'by grace' (Rom. 1.17; 3.21-24) '[G]iver, gift and the power that generates salvation' are connected. Nebe (147) also sees that *dikaiosunē pisteōs* retains the structure of a forensic judgment and allows that, among other influences, the Hellenistic and syncretistic environment must have played a role in it (148). I think that what separates the two is equally as important as what binds them. It is their distinction that explains their continuity, and this can only be seen from a political perspective.

104. οὐ γάρ ἐστιν διαστολή (Rom. 3.22, cf. 10.12).

105. For the growing literature on the reading of the genitive see the recent discussions in Keck 1989, Gagnon 1993, Heckel 1993, D.A. Campbell 1994, B. Dodd 1995, as well as Käsemann 1971a.

106. The perfectly just individual is ἀμετάστατος μέχρι θανάτου, 'unchangeable even unto death' (*Republic* 2.361c), a powerful expression that is reflected not only in the Hellenistic tradition of the suffering just man, but also in the famous Pauline phrase ἐταπείνωσεν ἑαυτὸν γενόμενος ὑπήκοος μέχρι θανάτου, θανάτου δὲ σταυροῦ, 'he humbled himself and became obedient unto death, even death on the cross' (Phil. 2.8). Epaphroditus, worthy imitator of Christ, nearly dies for the work of Christ,...διὰ τὸ ἔργον Χριστοῦ θανάτου ἤγγισεν... (Phil. 2.30).

(As usual Christ is both the operative factor and the *exemplum*: *charis* is obtained 'on account of the redemption [ἀπολύτρωσις[107]] which is Christ Jesus' [3.24].) In Paul's Letters, *charis* is often a mark of God's liberality, the result of his *dikaiosunē*.[108] (*Dikaiosunē* is not through law, *nomos*, but through *charis*, proclaims Paul [Gal. 2.21, cf. Rom. 3.21; 10.3].) Christians are found just (δικαιούμενοι) by God's *charis* (3.24, cf. 5.16, 17, 20, 21).[109] Christ's propitiatory sacrifice,[110] which

107. *Apolutrōsis* is often, since Deissmann (1927: 327-30), attributed to the ceremonial formulary of manumission of slaves. Stuhlmacher (1965: 88) considers it part of the legal glossary. Against this legal and Hellenistic background, Käsemann (1980: 96) places it in the liturgical vocabulary.

108. See Diotogenes on *eugnōmosunē* (frg. 2.2.5), for a sense in which the king's judicial generosity is conceived by the Hellenistic Pythagoreans.

109. *Charis* is prolifically used by Paul and its meaning is therefore complex, but the term invariably expresses God's benevolence in judgment. It is conspicuously present in the formulae that open or close his epistles in which the apostle greets his readers by wishing that God be indulgent in his judgment of them, with the result that finding them just he bestows desirable powers upon them. Paul's usage stresses God's benevolence also when he cites *charis* as the source of his apostleship. Most significantly, *charis* is part of the great political formula in Rom. 12.6: it describes how each Christian functions in the political body, a position bestowed in proportion to *pistis*.

Charis (pl. *charites*, and related terms, *charismata*, *chara*) has a vast semantic field, from erotic pleasure to a philtre—a love charm, and from favor and thanks to legal grant (LSJ *s.v.* χάρις 1979b). A political meaning can also be associated with it. In Greece *charis* is personified; the *Charites*, the Graces, attendants of Aphrodite and companions of the Muses, had city cults in Orchomenus (Boeotia), Athens and Sparta. A first-century CE inscription refers to αἱ τῶν Σεβαστῶν χάριτες, imperial grants (*OGI* 669.44, *ap.* LSJ 1979b). In Paul *charis* is from God and his *par excellence*. It is a pneumatic gift; as such, it belongs to the Hellenistic mystery religions. At the same time it is the instrument for rendering the world just, for setting it straight, the counterpoise of *hamartia* (5.12-19, 21). Criterion of election (11.5-6), *charis* is at the heart of the concept of 'power through weakness' (recently studied by Savage). Here, its political connotation comes forth with increasing force. *Charis* is the principle that makes visible the symmetry between the human state and the divine world, between *polis* and *basileia*. (See also Käsemann 1969b: 199.) It is the procedural form taken by God's *dikaiosunē* (Käsemann 1971b: 102). *Charis* is the power transforming the *asebēs* (4.5). It is the source of the superiority of the *pistis*-system over against the *nomos*-system (5.13, 20). *Charismata* are dispensed analogically (12.6-8), according to the formula of distributive justice; this is the *dikaiosunē* which describes in Classical and Hellenistic theorists the ideal constitution. (See esp. Chapter 4, section on Ps.-Archytas.) *Charismata* are the sources of community leadership, the very criteria for occupying magistracies in the Christ-

occurred by God's design (ὅν προέθετο ὁ θεός) (3.25), was a sign of God's justice in that God decided to bypass (πάρεσις) all former wrongs (ἁμαρτήματα) (3.25), to dismiss all charges. Here, with the first appearance of the idiom *dikaiosunē theou* in Romans after the enunciation of the theme of the letter in 1.17, we already have a tantalizing clue to the derivation of the concept *dikaiosunē theou* from the Classical and Hellenistic notion of distributive justice.[111] *Dikaiosunē*

polis. (See also Käsemann 1969d: 195.) *Charismata, diakoniai, energēmata* (12.4-6) are all for *sumpheron*, the common good, the mark of the political association. *Chara*, a related term, describes the *basileia theou* (14.17). In the imperial vocabulary, it is the joy at the emperor's accession (*PFay.* 207[1] third/fourth century CE, *ap.* MM *s.v.* χαρά 683a).

D. Zeller 1990 devotes a study to comparing *charis* in Philo and Paul. He discusses the Greek and Hellenistic background of the term, rooted in the Aristotelian notion of *charis* as an act the performance of which does not arise from self-interest (*Rhetoric* 2.7.1395a). The importance of the concept in Hellenistic Judaism and the connection with Hellenistic philosophy is studied in detail.

110. For a discussion of ἱλαστήριον see Käsemann 1980: 97-98. Few terms in Paul have been more closely linked with Jerusalem Temple practices. I agree, however, with Kümmel (1952: 160) that it would have been practically unintelligible to the community in Rome. Even Käsemann agrees that the meaning of the word should be looked for in the Greek cultic vocabulary of expiation (1980: 97).

111. This reading receives qualified support from no less expected a quarter than Bultmann. Taking issue with Käsemann 1969c, whom Bultmann understands as having expressed perplexity at the inconsistency in the use of the phrase *dikaiosunē theou* in Paul, Bultmann (1964a: 13) observes that Paul naturally uses *dikaiosunē theou* with various meanings, just as this concept is variously used in the Old Testament, Paul's model (12). Bultmann opposes human *adikia*, injustice (3.5), to *dikaiosunē theou*, the justice of God, and interprets it as distributive justice (subjective genitive). Bultmann then proceeds to discuss 3.25-26, to show how in 25b Paul speaks of a 'richterliche Gerechtigkeit', judicial righteousness, while in 26a he refers to God's 'Gabe der Gerechtigkeit an die Glaubenden', gift of righteousness on those who believe (1964: 13). See Käsemann 1969c: 169 and n. 1, for the rebuttal. Bultmann gives *dikaiosunē theou* a forensic-eschatological meaning, grounded in the Old Testament, while I view distributive justice as a political principle rooted in Greek Hellenism.

Rom. 3.25 yields to a wide range of hermeneutic strategies at the hands of a diverse range of commentators who yet share a theological orientation. For Käsemann, 3.25 describes the 'triumphant faithfulness of God', which faithfulness maintains the covenant and expresses the divine nature as true and consistent (1969c: 169 n. 1). Bultmann criticizes this reading and defends his distributive justice approach. Stuhlmacher 1994, who assays Käsemann, takes 3.25 as the very proof that righteousness of God is a pre-Pauline Jewish-Christian concept, that it 'was already

theou is activated by and offsets human *adikia* (cf. 3.5); it is the process that determines the just, *dikaios* (3.26).[112] Romans 3.26 rings taut and incisive: 'It is now, at the present critical season, at this historical time [ἐν τῷ νῦν καιρῷ[113]], that, through the *exemplum* of Christ's *pistis* [ἐκ πίστεως 'Ιησοῦ] to everyone who follows it, God disburses justice [δικαιοῦντα] according to the principles of *dikaiosunē* that he alone can properly apply [τῆς δικαιοσύνης αὐτοῦ...εἰς τὸ εἶναι αὐτὸν δίκαιον]'. Again, Jews have no claim to special treatment. Paul is emphatic on this: *pistis* alone, the law of *pistis* (διὰ νόμου πίστεως), makes one just (3.27).[114] Jew and Greek become just by *pistis*. 'I affirm the law' (νόμον ἱστάνομεν) (3.31), is Paul's famous antiphrasis, but it is a *new* law, a law that derives from *dikaiosunē theou* and is extended through *dikaiosunē pisteōs* via Christ.

understood in the Christian tradition which existed before Paul to refer at the same time both to God's own salvific activity (Rom. 3.25-26) and to its effect in the form of the righteousness which is allotted to those who, in faith, confess Christ (2 Cor. 5.21)' (1994: 31, cf. Käsemann 1969c: 177-78).

112. The Christians themselves become *dikaiosunē theou*, through Christ (2 Cor. 5.21). Δίκαιος is a title adopted by Hellenistic and Oriental kings. Antiochus I of Commagene and most of the Mithridates if Armenia and Parthia used it. Mithras, the Persian God, traditionally carries the name θεός δίακιος. See L. Delatte 1942: 249. Justice is a political function; ἡ δὲ δικαιοσύνη πολιτικόν, 'justice is political' wrote Aristotle (*Politics* 1.1253a37).

113. On *kairos* see also 5.6. That political identity is an instrument of history, though mostly associated with the notion of sovereign modern states (and, currently, taking the extreme form of nationalistic drives), goes back to Greece, Hellenistic times and Rome. A *polis* understands itself in terms of its history. Paul works within a tradition of such politico-historical interpretation; he only adds a pivotal new element: an *exemplum* of such force that it is capable of anticipating history, thus giving it strength and purpose. In antiquity, history often refers to the imaginary memory of a golden age, to be always longingly remembered and deplorably approximated. Paul's history is a history with a future. History has been theologically idealized as 'salvation history'. Salvation history as a theological issue was bitterly and buoyantly analyzed by Käsemann 1971a, his attitude well summarized by this phrase: 'It is only from a great distance that we can read salvation history without being aware of its catastrophes' (69).

114. Stowers (1994, ch. 7) makes 3.21-26 the key text for his theory of 'the messiah who delayed' and consequently an expression of the central moral and religious paradigm of the letter, the message of adaptability. At the heart of one of the major *dikaiosunē* constructs, where Paul is carefully splicing in its political and metaphysical components, *dikaiosunē pisteōs* and *dikaiosunē theou*, Stowers reads perplexity, an *aporia*.

The privileged, exemplary role of the king and the imitation of the king as the instrument of salvation—these comprise the most conspicuous topic in the political writings of the Hellenistic Pythagoreans. So also with Christ; although his preeminence and saving power are legitimized somewhat differently, the operative forces are the same. The full mechanism of salvation is exposed here. For all the distinctiveness of Christ,[115] the significance of the act of incarnation or that of expiation (depending on the scenario one follows) is as described by the Hellenistic Pythagoreans: the production of a model. The 'solid' *dikaiosunē* of Classical and Hellenistic theorists becomes 'fluid'—it flows through Christ. While *dikaiosunē theou* retains *analogia* as its essence, as elaborated by the *polis* group of Hellenistic Pythagorean writers, the essence of *dikaiosunē pisteōs* is imitation, as developed by the *basileia* group. *Dikaiosunē pisteōs* is what fastens humanity to God while also allowing humanity to retain its dignity. *Dikaiosunē theou* alone is perfect. The former is ancillary to the latter, derives from it, and yet, because of Christ's own duality, *dikaiosunē pisteōs* has its own integrity. In the end, because *dikaiosunē pisteōs* cannot exist without *dikaiosunē theou*, *dikaiosunē* is reunified, restored to its vectorial force. For the Hellenistic Pythagoreans, *dikaiosunē* is an indivisible concept. They distinguish between the human *polis* and the divine *basileia* by emphasizing the different ruling powers, king and God, respectively, and by stressing, in political terms, the concept of human imitation of the divine world.

3.27-31. The contrast between *erga* ('works') and *pistis* (3.27-28) is Paul's most acclaimed dichotomy.[116] As I have already observed, Aristotle makes a sharp distinction between a particular *ergon*, the competence of the expert who pursues a certain task with professional discipline, and the universal *ergon*, a component of the definition of highest good and happiness.[117] This tradition reaches Paul, who uses

115. Paul's treatment is not entirely unique. Ps.-Ecphantus has *Logos* undertake a traumatic incarnation as well. (Hermetic and Gnostic characters do the same.) The mythical terms of this operation, becoming Christ, as well as the suggestion of Paul's Hellenistic source, are best expressed in the Philippian hymn.

116. The opposition ἔργα–πίστις is conspicuous in Romans (3.27-28; 4.5 [verbal forms], 9.32) and Galatians (2.16; 3.2, 5). Also in 1 Tim. 3.1 (singular *ergon*) and Tit. 3.8.

117. *Nicomachean Ethics* 1.1097b25-1098a20.

erga to denote a specific endeavor or duty executed in accordance with the appropriate exigencies of a particular law; *pistis*, the true *ergon* of humanity, is a project that submits to the demands of a divine principle (cf. 1 Thess. 1.3). Paul's *erga–pistis* dichotomy corresponds to that which Aristotle draws between particular and universal *ergon*. In effect, as Paul will later make clear in his great political formula (Rom. 12.6), each member of the public body functions in this society *kata charin*, according to *charis*—that is, according to what the will of God has decided about each individual in proportion to one's *pistis* (κατὰ τὴν ἀναλογίαν τῆς πίστεως). And Paul will then go on (12.6-8) to itemize the different ways in which people participate in the community. The many functions of the different community members are, after all, all *pistis*-filled *erga*. When Paul critiques *erga* he does so insofar as they take the form of *pistis*-lacking activities.[118]

4.1-25. Paul knows that *pistis* is a difficult concept, and he uses a simile to introduce and explain it. To him who works, wages are reckoned as his lawful due (ὀφείλημα) (4.4). *Pistis*, however, is a grant, *charis*. Between works and *pistis* there is a difference in kind. Work is justifiable (4.2), but only *pistis* makes one just (4.3). *Charis* counterbalances *opheilēma*; *pistis* offsets *erga*. *Pistis* is the outgrowth of *dikaiosunē* (of *dikaiosunē theou*, that is) and is itself the ground for *dikaiosunē* (*dikaiosunē pisteōs*).

Paul now focuses on *dikaiosunē pisteōs*, the foundation of his *polis*. *Dikaiosunē* is what determines and defines the nature of a political system, and *dikaiosunē pisteōs* is the form of justice that describes the Christian community, the *ekklēsia*. *Dikaiosunē pisteōs* is the determination of what is just in that *polis*, the ordering of that political association. It designates the type of equality operative in the Christ-state; it forms the inner mechanism of the Christian society. The *dikaiosunē*

118. Further support for the view that Paul is not against *erga*, the works, is offered by Boers's 1994 study. Applying semiotic methods to Romans and Galatians, Boers determines that the epistles are unified at the level of 'deep structures'; they affirm two incommensurable value systems, each belonging to a different 'microuniverse': an 'existential' one in which the polarity 'life–death' is operational, and a 'social' one dominated by the polarity 'good–evil'; justification of faith belongs to the first, affirmation of judgment and justification by works belongs to the second; justification by faith is *not* (my emphasis) about negation of justification by works, since it relates to the existential not the ethical microuniverse (*ap.* Cosgrove 1996: 368.)

through which Paul's association is constituted is a justice based on *pistis*, trust in God. As has been suggested, Paul splits Classical political *dikaiosunē* into two vectors: *dikaiosunē pisteōs* and *dikaiosunē theou*, the first describing the Christian society, the second God's rule. With Paul, *dikaiosunē* is no longer the unique center of a simple *polis*. The world has dual dimensions, each with its characteristic *dikaiosunē*: a human and a divine vista. They are complete only when united, yet they are politically discrete. This duality-in-unity makes a unique causality imperative: Christ, the new type. A test is provided for *dikaiosunē pisteōs*: one whose *pistis* (trust) allows that even the *asebēs* (the ungodly) can be reckoned right by God (4.5).[119] This is a blow to both Jewish election and Greek reasoning. *Asebēs* is often understood as one of Paul's most remarkable descriptions of the power of *charis*, but I think this is to understand it with an Augustinian, predestination bias; it is to over-read it. From another point of view, the notion that God renders the *asebēs* just suggests the relativism of antinomianism; this is to under-read it. It is God, not man, who redefines the law. What happens to the *asebēs* tests both human and God. The redemption of the *asebēs* defines the ultimate human possibility even as it manifests the ultimate nature of the divine. The *pistis* that wins God's favor for the ungodly gets the prize of *dikaiosunē*. The divine *dikaiosunē* withdraws judgment as its judgment justifies the unGodly. *Asebeia*, in Pauline thinking, is a sarkic quality. It is the failure to understand the reach and grip of God's *dikaiosunē*—that *dikaiosunē* extends even to that condition of humanity that despises God. In effect, God relinquishes the claim to awesomeness—and becomes more awesome.

The *asebēs* becomes the indicator of the extreme power of *pistis*. The source of *pistis* lies elsewhere. To get there, Paul takes a step back. Abraham is father of many nations not because he is of the law (νόμου) (4.13) but because of *dikaiosunē pisteōs* (4.11, 13). His circumcision is only the mark of this *dikaiosunē pisteōs* (4.11). He is the forefather of the new politics, the politics at the center of which stands *dikaiosunē pisteōs*. The connection between *dikaiosunē pisteōs* and the *polis* appears most forcefully in 4.13: 'Inheritance of the world', control of human political power, comes through *dikaiosunē pisteōs*. It is not, as commonly thought, the result of wielding *nomos*.

---

119. In the disputation against Candidus in Athens, Origen's statement—so disturbing to the Egyptian bishops—that 'even the devil can be saved' seems to be inspired by this passage. See Chadwick 1967: 110.

This argument leads Paul back to law. It is the moment, Paul feels, to show in unequivocal terms law's invalidity for the new world order. The domain of the law is crime, trespass, *parabasis*. Paul expresses this aphoristically: 'Where there is no law, there is no crime' (οὗ δὲ οὐκ ἔστιν νόμος οὐδὲ παράβασις) (4.15). This radical idea, however, must not be read (as it had been by antinomians) as an invitation to anarchy. Instead, Paul is indicating an order that transcends law, in which the law's guardianship is overcome by other forces. Criticism of the Jews rests on critique of the law. (Paul well understood, and often had to confront, the seductive appeal of the Jewish law; it could have provided—as indeed it did for the Corinthians or the Galatians—an alluring organizing structure for a new community, a sometimes onerous but always unambiguous guiding principle.) Paul concludes the complex and difficult study of the Jewish constitution by insisting that the law is simply no longer of any consequence, not because there is anything wrong with it, but because it is superseded (see also 5.12-21). Here we again see *dikaiosunē pisteōs* in its full import. The human end is *pistis* as *justice-in-itself*: not a matter of law or of external tokens but of inner transformation, interiorization, what Paul calls *pistis Abraam* (4.16). *Pistis* produces a conversion of the human into a being that transcends the subjectivity of mere humanity. The source and end of this *pistis* is next made clear: God's power over death (4.17). This *pistis* defines the type. Even more, it points to a society. Paul describes the followers of the *pistis* of Abraham as those 'walking in his footsteps' (τοῖς ἴχνεσιν) (4.12). (Elsewhere [2 Cor. 12.18], the walking is in *Paul's* footsteps.) Imitation is so described by Callicratidas (frg. 1): the household is the emulation (τὸ ἴχνος) of the soul.

God can make the dead live. He can call into existence things that have no being (Rom. 4.17). The 'body' of Abraham and the womb of Sarah were deadness (νέκρωσις) (4.19). God brought them to life. God raised Jesus from the dead (4.24). Jesus, we learn from another bit of early *credo*, 'was given to death for our failures and…was raised from the dead', in order, adds Paul, 'to determine us just' (4.25). The Hellenistic Pythagorean notion that the king is incarnate law, *nomos empsuchos*—this forceful intensification of the idea that the lawgiver is somehow 'above' the law—is the background of Paul's thinking here.

5.1-21. Dikaiosunē pisteōs makes one supremely confident of having access to God. This is where the model provided by Christ is essential.

The central feature of this model is the notion of suffering (5.1-11).[120] Sufferings must be sought and indulged in, for they form character (5.4). Paul, however, goes far beyond this in his affirmation of suffering as a condition for the *euangelion*. Sufferings, in Paul, are marks of success and triumph. (Thus, Paul boasts of his labors, his imprisonment, his beatings, his near-misses [2 Cor. 11.23-28, cf. Rom. 5.3]. Even Paul's own, presumably physical, affliction is the price he must pay for the prodigality of revelations he receives [τῇ ὑπερβολῇ τῶν ἀποκαλύψεων; 2 Cor. 12.7].) The full development of this theme occurs in Philippians, where suffering is not 'because' of any external cause (from a neighbor's malice to organized persecution) but is intrinsic to being 'in Christ'.

These entirely new moral effluvia have been released by Christ, who, at the appointed season (καιρός), when the world was at its nadir, died for the Godless (5.6). There is a remarkable passage in Ps.-Zaleucus[121] that vivifies Paul's *kairos*—showing it to be at once response and reversal. The Hellenistic Pythagorean proposes anticipation of one's appointed time of death (*kairos*) as prophylaxis for injustice (*adikia*), which, caused by the power of desires (*hormai*), leads to damnation. Horror of a formal divine judgment at death is a philosophical novelty

---

120. Suffering, affliction, hardship are sometimes read by commentators as a reference to persecutions. Sometimes these are regarded as replicas of Stoic tenets. The views that see the Christians actively seeking martyrdom or rejoicing in affliction are an oversimplification of Greek and Hellenistic moral philosophies and the related psychological pain and pleasure theories, with the result that pleasure becomes an indication of moral want. In Paul, as in Aristotle and the Peripatetics, moral virtues belong to the psychology of pain and pleasure. Pleasures—writes Aristotle—are not processes, 'but activities and an end' (*Nicomachean Ethics* 7.1153a10). Pleasure is a whole and perfect, at any time, like seeing (*Ethics* 10.1174a15). It is the completeness of pleasure that makes it invaluable for the examination of suffering in Paul. (For a fuller presentation of Aristotle's view of pleasures see the section on Aristotle's Ethics in Chapter 2.) The Peripatetics were often criticized by the Stoics for lax ethics, for coupling (like Aristotle) pleasure and virtue as parts of the supreme good (Gottschalk 1987: 1140 and nn. 295, 296). The Stoics denied that pleasure is 'supervening perfection' and activity. They thought that pleasure is not a first impulse but an aftergrowth, not a *telos* but a result of its attainment (Sandbach 1985: 28). Paul does not go with the Stoics but with Aristotle. Suffering is integral, organic to his *euangelion*. For Paul suffering is not Stoic resignation. It is fulfillment, victory. Suffering for the *euangelion* are part of the essence of being Christ's. It does not merely accompany the condition of being Christian; it is intrinsic to it.

121. See Chapter 4, section on Ps.-Zaleucus, frg. 5.

during Hellenistic times.[122] Ps.-Zaleucus is suggesting a complicated game of *memento mori* with a therapeutic effect—a cathartic terror. In Paul, too, at one's *kairos* one will meet God's judgment (1 Cor. 4.5). And Paul, too, offers a cure for this, but a more extraordinary one: one will defeat this *kairos* with *kairos*, the *kairos* of Christ's death (5.6, cf. 4.5). All one will have to do when his own *kairos* is at hand is to 'put on Christ' (13.11). To stave off fear of death—the impulse that generated so many Hellenistic mystery religions and ethical philosophies—Paul promotes yet another God, but one who outdoes all others and on whose power Paul relies to rally the world.

The condition of those requiring the remedy of Christ's death is *astheneia*, 'weakness' (5.6). *Astheneia* is a sarkic affliction that dims the intellect (6.19). It describes the situation of *nomos* under *sarx* (8.3). Its antidote is *pneuma* (8.26).[123] Both Paul and Ps.-Ecphantus[124] consider this state of humanity to be the principal cause for the intercession of a divine agency. *Logos* (in Ps.-Ecphantus) and Christ (in Paul) step in to vanquish *astheneia*. Ps.-Ecphantus presents two modalities of recovery from subjugation by hostile powers: imitation of the king, an effective technique but hampered by human weakness, and direct intervention of an otherworldly being, the *Logos*. Paul's Christ is at once salvific presence and redeeming example, the unified and unique instrument of salvation.[125]

In an arresting pericope, Paul condenses the contemporary view that dying for the sake of an *agathos*, a good man, is acceptable, while it is not expected for a *dikaios*, a just man (Rom. 5.7). Everyone, he rightly assumes, knows the distinction between just and good (δικαίος and

---

122. The contrast life–death is of little concern to Plato and Aristotle. In a rare, qualified reference, old Cephalus remarks (*Republic* 1.330d-331b) on fear of death. He alludes to (popular) stories particularly frightening to the elderly about punishment in Hades for those who have committed *adikia* (ἀδικήσαντα) (330d). (Plato's mythologies of judgment, as in the *Republic* itself, offer a critique of popular presentations of death.)

123. Of course, a reversed, positively valenced *astheneia* is present in Paul: as attribute of God (1 Cor. 1.25) or as vital element in the physical and political body (12.22).

124. See Chapter 5, section on Ps.-Ecphantus, frg. 3.3.

125. It must be said, however, that the process of integration of the two savior figures is already hinted at in Ps.-Ecphantus. Political charisma and spiritual power come together in the person of the king. He alone not only leads the state but also awakens the individual to the good (H 278.9-12, T 83.9-10).

ἀγαθός). A good man is not only just, he also excells in all virtues.[126] No one would die for the merely just, some may die for the good, but Christ, *mirabile dictu*, died for the impious (ὑπὲρ ἀσεβῶν) (5.6), for the flawed (ἁμαρτωλῶν...ὑπὲρ ἡμῶν) (5.8). The idea is indeed novel, disquieting, perplexing. The wrong are made right and the hostile are reconciled with God in Christ's blood (5.9-10).[127] Now, this is reason for boasting (5.11), *ecce homo*! Master and slave, ruler and ruled, Christ is Paul's solution to the demand for reciprocity in Aristotle's political construct. Christ saves the political game as well.[128]

The fall of the first man, Adam, extends to all humanity (5.12-21).[129] Paul, a lover of Greek symmetry, is obviously very pleased with his discovery: the reconciliation of all humanity with God also happens with one man, Jesus Christ. The difficulty that remains pertains to the role of the law, and Paul solves it magisterially. Sedition against God—absolute folly, primordial crime, *hamartia* par excellence—happened before the law. With death operative, law regulates the world. The law is only posterior to the fall; it is given to deal with the whole range of consequences of the fall. In effect, the law only deals with ever-multiplying offenses (5.20, cf. 4.15). The violations law attends to are of a different order than Adam's (5.14). Adam is at once the prefiguration of Christ and his opposite. When Christ comes, he overcomes

126. Good, *agathos*, is firmly understood in Classical and Hellenistic philosophy (including Hermetism and Neoplatonism—see L. Delatte 1942: 230), as a divine attribute. In Ps.-Ecphantus (frg. 3.2) it describes God and is the source of his *autarkeia* (H 277.5-11, T 82.17-22). As does the Pythagorean, Paul stresses the volatile character of human good (Rom. 14.16), and thinks that the good is un-achievable by man, though it is to be intensely pursued (Rom. 7.18-19).

127. See Chapter 4, section on Ps.-Zaleucus, frg. 10) for a possible similarity between the notion of God's reconciliation with his enemies, expressed by Paul in Rom. 5.10, and the Hellenistic Pythagorean's exhortation not to consider a fellow citizen an irreconcilable enemy.

128. Paul follows, while reworking, this scheme. He elaborates a political philosophy that makes a new type of *polis*, the Christian *polis*, the basis of his system. Christ, the master, κύριος, has also been one of the ruled, himself knew the condition of the slave. He is slave and master (Rom. 8.30), the paradox that rescues the political game, which the ruler and the ruled play by turns.

129. Such a view would seem to be possible only on the basis of a generic creationism. Both the Greek, rooted in Aristotle, and the Near Eastern anthro-pologies readily provided such a generative theory of immutable genera and species. If Adam's fall extends to all, then Adam was created as much species as individual.

death and, necessarily, annuls the law that describes the world-order under death. The qualitative difference, the very possibility of *charis*, comes with Christ. The law, continuously itemizing and establishing punishments for ever-growing transgressions, only leads to a quantitative increase of God's *charis* (5.20). The abuses listed by the law are, in the new world order, occasions for *charis* (5.13).

Adam and Christ are contrasting 'types'[130]—both *sui generis* antitypes, opposing principles. Paul's use of the telling term *tupos* (5.14) immediately keys us to the *basileia* literature.[131] *Tupos* as divine model, as *exemplum*, suggests its derivation from the 'imitation of the king' concept; around this Paul creates a new typology, that of Christ. All humanity, without exception, begins with an Adam type; Adam was a *tupos* of the future savior (5.14).[132] The notion of imitation is made explicit by use of ὁμοίωμα (*homoiōma*) (5.14), though here imitation is not a matter of choice but the reenactment of Adam's offense.[133] Adam brought *hamartia* into the world, and thus death as a condition of being (5.12); Adam was judged and condemned, and his guilt spread to all human beings; disobedient, Adam turned all into transgressors. *Hamartia* becomes a technical term in Paul. Christ opens the world to *charis*; renders all human beings just; obedient, he introduces the reign of life for all, brings acquittal for all (5.12-19, 21). The core of the Adam–Christ antithesis is the *parakoē–hupakoē* (disobedience, 'failure of hearing' vs obedience, 'hearing') dichotomy. The same proliferation of humanity that meant multiplicity of *hamartia* because of Adam's *parakoē* led to increase of *charis* because of Christ's *hupakoē* (5.19; see also 10.14-15 and discussion at 16.19, below). *Parakoē* brought humankind the law of *hamartia*, a derivate of which is the law of Moses, paradoxically the instrument of *hamartia* (5.20, cf. 5.14; 7.12; 10.5). *Parakoē* was the cause of the Fall; *hupakoē* brought *sōtēria* (salvation) (10.10). God has confined all to *parakoē* (11.32, cf. 5.19) so that he may exercise his *dikaiosunē* and pronounce his *charis* over all (11.32,

130. Adam is referred to as a τύπος in Rom. 5.14.

131. Also, to the Septuagintal *eikōn*. See discussion for 8.29.

132. *Tupos* is the pattern that the Thessalonians set by their faith (1 Thess. 1.7). *Tupos* is also Paul himself as the *exemplum* for imitation (Phil. 3.17).

133. Or it may be a question of having suppressed God because of the passions, of having turned from immortal God to human and animal resemblances (Rom. 1.23). For the positive treatment of *homoiōma* see discussion of 6.5.

cf. 5.21).[134] *Charis* reigns (ἐβασίλευσεν) on account of (God's) *dikaio-sunē*. It is Christ who singlehandedly counterbalances the rule of death introduced by Adam and who brings about the kingdom of life, a model to all men (5.17-18; 1 Cor. 1.30; Phil. 1.11, cf. Rom. 14.7-8); because of Christ, because of his *dikaiosunē*, *hamartia* is replaced by *charis* (5.21).

Paul lived in a world in which ethics was the only field of intellectual speculation left to the philosopher. Yet Paul transcends morals and makes his way into the political. (Conceptually, Paul moves from ethics to politics, while discursively he progresses from a moral to a metaphysical language.) Finding inspiration in the Hellenistic political theories of his time, with their Platonic-Aristotelian moorings, Paul outlines a political theory for Christianity (6.1-23). He does so in two stages: the citizen (6.1-15, on which he elaborates further in 7.1-8.39) and the *polis* (6.16-23, to be applied to the empire in 12.1-16.23).

6.1-15. Christ is both unique and model *politēs*. He is treated as *type*, paradigm, the beginning of a new typology. All others share Christ's nature, both in the image of his death and in the image of his resurrection (6.5). This is the central formula, and it functions as a theme with variations: one is baptized in Christ's death (6.3) and buried with him (6.5); having crucified the old human (6.6), one is dead to *hamartia* (6.2, 6). Also, one is living a novel life (καινότητι ζωῆς περιπατήσ-ωμεν) (6.6), having been acquitted of *hamartia* (6.7);[135] one is alive with Jesus Christ (6.11), not being lorded over by *hamartia* (6.14). It is a mystical, mysterious process in which ritual death is affirmative and the beginning of renewed life.

In Rom. 6.3-4, Paul recalls the fundamental feature, the act of 'naturalization' in his fellowship: imitation of the death and resurrection of Christ

---

134. *Parakoē–hupakoē* axis is an expression of *paideia*, as we encounter it also in Ps.-Archytas (frg. 5c). See Rom. 10.14-15 and 16.17-20 for further discussion.

135. Scroggs (1963: 104-105) challenges the interpretation (Althaus 1959, Leenhardt 1957, Michel 1955) that reads δικαιόω as 'to be free' and ἁμαρτία as 'obligation to the Torah', and makes 6.7 read as a general legal maxim, identical to 7.1. He also criticizes (105-106) Kuhn's 1931 proposal according to which 6.7 is quoting a rabbinic maxim: 'all who die receive atonement through their death'. Scroggs argues that as the death in Rom. 6.1-11 is that of Christ, it is this death alone which justifies; ἀποθανών is the believer who dies with Christ in baptism (106). The concept may derive from the Jewish (Hellenistic) notion that the death of the righteous, viz. a martyr, has atoning power (107-108).

(see also 5.14; 6.5; 8.3, cf. Phil. 2.7). Paul goes beyond traditional models of imitation in the scandal of his *exemplum*, but his technique and that of the Hellenistic Pythagoreans remain congruent insofar as imitation is a path to salvation in both. The expression of imitation takes its epic form in Rom. 6.5 (a fine syllepsis and an ellipsis): 'For if we have been cultivated [cf. 6.4: συνετάφημεν, 'buried together'] with Christ in the *homoiōma*, the likeness of his death, we shall also [grow together in the likeness] of his rising up'.[136] (Conversely, God's son came in the resemblance of offensive flesh; he was born in the *homoiōma* of human beings [8.3, Phil. 2.7]. The ambivalence of this concept in Paul reflects the increased complexity of his system, which allows for two-way traffic along the fault line.)

Imitation is, as we have seen, a central motif in the language of mysticism that pervades Hellenism. One escapes death by dying with a God. In Paul, one escapes death with Christ—as if planted (or growing) together with him, as if 'co-natural' (*sumphutos*) or conjoined with him. This operation is τῷ ὁμοιώματι (*tō homoiōmati*), not just 'in the likeness' of, but, as we learn from the Hellenistic Pythagoreans, 'in imitation'—as a replication—of Christ's death and rising. Planting (*phuteia* and the numerous cognates), deeply rooted in the death-and-rebirth, fertility vocabulary of mystery religions, is present even at the heart of Ps.-Ecphantus' political treatise.[137] There (frg. 3.3), *Peithō* (Persuasion), is planted (*ephuē*), with *Logos*. The conundrum usually associated with the phrase *tō homoiōmati* (Rom. 6.5, cf. 8.3) becomes less challenging in the framework of Hellenistic Pythagorean political thought, for its link with the widespread and focal concept of imitation becomes apparent.

Both Ps.-Ecphantus and Paul produced similar answers to the question of *hamartia*, a first-magnitude topic. Any commoner, writes Ps.-Ecphantus (frg. 1.4.2), can escape *hamartia* by a mystical purification

---

136. εἰ γὰρ σύμφυτοι γεγόναμεν τῷ ὁμοιώματι τοῦ θανάτου αὐτοῦ, ἀλλὰ καὶ τῆς ἀναστάσεως ἐσόμεθα (Rom. 6.5).

137. It may be observed how even terms that seem so decisively derived from the mystical idiom have a philosophical heritage. *Sumphusis*, with the technical meaning 'integrated knowledge', is important for the Aristotelian analysis of the akratic act; only the wise man, the *phronimos* possesses it (*Nicomachean Ethics* 7.1147a22). In Paul, it is integration with the death and rising of Christ, being *sumphutoi* (Rom. 6.5), that produces this harmonization of knowledge.

Dio Chrysostom uses the same verb, *phuō*, on the first human conception of God (*Discourses* 12.28 [the Olympic], BAGD *s.v.* φύω).

that consists of assimilation to—becoming exactly like—the rulers (ἐξομοιωθῆμεν τοῖς ἀρχόντεσσιν).[138] This is the quintessence of the Pauline *euangelion*: *hamartia* is erased by one's becoming the image of Christ (or by bearing the impression of his envoys, the genuine apostles). Romans 6.3-11 is the consummate expression of this message; its leitmotif is dying and rising with Christ. The systemic transformation envisaged by both authors is similar—a similarity born of their shared background of Hellenistic political mysticism and of the fact that they both address the Greek-speaking citizen of the *polis*.

The pivotal point of Paul's theory is that Christ made it back to life from death, and cannot die again (6.9)—*and* that this is a *certainty*. The resurrection of Christ, while not an original concept per se—it is, after all, similar to common popular magical beliefs—takes on an irresistible power because *tested*. The transforming, transcendental power of contemplation of an exquisite, flawless exemplar is a topos of philosophy. It receives political charge with the spontaneous transformation produced (in Ps.-Ecphantus) by the contemplation of the king or (in Diotogenes) by gazing upon the king; but, in keeping with their Classical models, the Hellenistic Pythagoreans perceive this as an ideal. Paul delivers certitude.

This entire approach centers on the notion of the body of Christ and indicates the nature of the political association in Paul. Christ is the measure according to which one shapes one's being. Through the power of divine activity one becomes empowered to shape oneself according to this model. This is the norm that is structuring the new personality, the new way a person should work in the community. The relation between the members of the community as members of the body of Christ (plainly expressed in 12.4-5) and their taking on the nature of Christ, becoming Christ, is clarified not only here, in 6.1-15, but also in 7.1-11. Unique Christ is identical in all: the *pneumatics* are similar to the (living) image of Christ; Christ is the first-born among many (8.29).

6.16-23. The new type of *polis* is slavery to God. While slavery to God is a common religious metaphor in the ancient Near East (including the Hebrew Bible) as well as in Hellenistic times (including the LXX), the term bears a political charge in Paul. For its meaning one needs to look at ancient theories of slavery. Aristotle's theory of slavery posited that

138. H 274.5, T 80.23.

the *ethnē* (the non-Greeks) and the slaves are 'by nature' incapable of forming a *polis*[139]—this is because politics is the art of ruling and being ruled, and the uniform condition of slavery kills the political art. Since by Paul's time slavery is part of the normative political vocabulary, Paul's extending the condition of slavery to all humanity is not startling.[140] *Hamartia*, king of the body (Paul's political metaphor par excellence), makes all obedient to appetite (6.12). The importance of psychological factors in Paul's politics cannot be underrated. The role which desires, *epithumiai* of the *sarx*, play as a threat to the society that Paul establishes is incessantly recalled (6.12; but also, e.g., 1.24; 6.12; 7.7-8; 13.14; 1 Cor. 10.6; Gal. 5.16-24). *Adikia-asebeia* forms a continuum with *hamartia* (Rom. 6.12-13). Paul shows how contemptible slavery—slavery to *hamartia*—is abolished in favor of its opposite, blessed slavery—slavery to God.[141] In Aristotle's view, one is slave of the one whom he obeys, and the same Aristotelian teleological thinking informs Paul (6.16). One cannot simultaneously be a slave of two opposing masters: *hamartia* and God. Slaves of *hamartia* (6.17, 20) have as their end (τέλος) death (6.21). But now there is a new type of teaching (τύπος διδαχῆς) (6.17), and those who have their hearts in it and who have become slaves (ἐδουλώθητε) to *dikaiosunē* (6.18) have eternal life as their end (6.22, 23).[142] The kingdom of God is a state of the highest soul (as opposed to the seat of appetites) and is located in

---

139. *Politics* 1.1252a35-b1, 7.1327b18-40.

140. All that remains, by Paul's time, of Aristotle's elaborate political theory is the household politics of the master–slave relation. Hellenistic and Roman writers make no secret of this. Aristotle must have turned in his grave to hear that his argument for slavery (*Politics* 1253a17-1255a2) has become so successful as to leave no free people.

141. In a peculiar way, Paul is a close pupil of Aristotle. In his defense of the natural slave, Aristotle maintained, essentially, that for this kind of creature slavery is the better and just condition (*Politics* 1.1254a18, 1255a2); also, that the relation between the master and the slave must be one of friendship and mutual interest (1255b13). Obedience and willingness characterize the relation between the ruler and the ruled in general. Willingness informs both natural slavery (the Barbarian–Greek 'compact') as well as the Greek *polis* (the ruler-ruled political game).

142. Michel 1955 (*ap.* Black 1973: 99) suggests an interesting reading of verse 6.23 that enhances its political underpinning. Τὰ ὀψώνια may be derived from the military vocabulary, and mean the daily 'provision-money'. It is contrasted with τὰ χάρισμα, the bounty (*donativum*) distributed to the army on the accession of a new Emperor. *Hamartia*'s pay is death; God's largess is life.

dikaiosunē, peace and joy (6.13, 19; 14.17), political terms denoting harmony and concord.[143]

Paul continually plays *eleutheria* and *douleia*, freedom and slavery, the Greek political antinomies, against one another, in a rhetorical form whose chief purpose is to stress the content of the *polis* of Christ. Thus, *eleutheros* from *hamartia*, free from error, one is *doulos* of *dikaiosunē*, slave of justice (6.18). Once slave of *hamartia*, one was 'free' from *dikaiosunē* (6.20). You, writes Paul, set free from *hamartia*, have become slaves of God (6.22).[144] Paul is boldly and brilliantly playing against the ideal of *eleutheria* in the Greek *polis* and thus revealing the changes he operates: a super-valuation of *douleia* as the condition of membership in the Christ-*polis*.[145]

Tupos encompasses not only the life model but also the text proto-type, *tupos didachēs*.[146] As a teacher Paul teaches the *euangelion*, a

143. Käsemann makes energy, love, peace, wrath personifications of divine power (1969c: 173), divine attributes.

144. ἐλευθερωθέντες δὲ ἀπὸ τῆς ἁμαρτίας ἐδουλώθητε τῇ δικαιοσύνῃ...ὅτε γὰρ δοῦλοι ἦτε τῆς ἁμαρτίας, ἐλεύθεροι ἦτε τῇ δικαιοσύνῃ...νυνὶ δὲ ἐλευθερωθέντες ἀπὸ τῆς ἁμαρτίας δουλωθέντες δὲ τῷ θεῷ ἔχετε τὸν καρπὸν ὑμῶν εἰς ἁγιασμόν, τὸ δὲ τέλος ζωὴν αἰώνιον.

145. Against the Jews, Paul would sing the freedom from the law (cf. 7.3); for humanity in general he celebrates the freedom from ὀργὴ θεοῦ (1.18, cf. 5.9); and, in cosmic terms, he will oppose the *douleia* to decay to the *eleutheria* of glory (8.21). Nygren 1949 cannot emphasize enough the importance the series of *eleutheria* in Rom. 5, 6, 7 and 8 have in the great divide between the two aeons, of Adam and of Christ, antithesis that he regards as the key to the interpretation and the integrity of Romans. I place an equally high stress on the notion of *douleia* as defining the outrageous quality and inherent scandal of the Christ republic.

146. Philo is sometimes called upon to solve Rom. 6.17b and the verse becomes: 'you obeyed from the heart the imprint stamped by teaching, to which [imprint] you were handed over' (Gagnon 1993). A Pythagorean connection, however, can also be made. To what this *tupos didachēs* refers, however, remains a mystery. Gagnon notes that *tupos* is well attested in Greco-Roman philosophical writings in the sense of 'outline' (Plato, Epicurus), 'general character' (Plato, Isocrates, Iamblichus). He mentions but does not see the relevance of the Pythagorean usage τόν τύπον τῆς διδασκαλίας, 'general character of teaching', employed by Iamblichus (*On Pythago-rean Life* 23.105) when ready to give examples of teachings from Pythagoras' school (1993: 681 n. 46). This points to a teaching deriving from an absolute authority, which is, as to its nature, an enigmatic, symbol-ridden, secret teaching (cf. Eph. 6.19). Some saw it as possibly in contrast with, or rather different from Paul's own teaching (Weiss 1899, Kühl 1913), or 'as opposed to non-Pauline

political revelation and not a speculative scholastic discipline (Gal. 1.11-12; 1 Thess. 2.13). Paul's repeated invective against sham apostles, charlatan missionaries and bogus teachers is notorious (1 Cor. 1.17-2.13, cf. Rom. 1.22; 2 Cor. 1.12; 11.1-15; 12.11). Equally often, he demonstrates his veritable apostleship, his authentic leadership by possession of the power of the *pneuma* (Rom. 15.19; 1 Cor. 2.4; 1 Thess. 1.5). Why the vehemence? The crackpot is a political menace. He threatens the unity and stability of society by challenging authority and fomenting anarchy. The pressing topic appears in most of Paul's letters, and it is often the reason why a letter has been written at all. According to Ps.-Ecphantus (frg. 3), the impostors' troubles prove their ineligibility to rule. In Paul, the impostors (the false apostles) will be undone by their works (2 Cor. 11.15).[147] Given human limitations, however, teaching the *euangelion* requires a cautious, allegorical approach (Rom. 6.17-19).

Is Paul again attacking Jewish law? Or is he once more blasting the Greeks for their passions? Romans 6.19-21 uses language that (intentionally?) can be read both ways. (*Astheneia* [6.19], in any case, unifies both.) In a maneuver that looks as if Paul is carrying the position expressed by Dio Chrysostom in *Discourse* 76 (that laws produce a state of slaves while customs make for a state of the free, the latter because of the instrumentality of shame [76.4]) to the utmost logical extreme, and in language arrestingly similar to Dio Chrysostom's, Paul makes everything the law stands for a source of shame: 'When you were slaves of *hamartia*, you were free in regard to *dikaiosunē*; but then, what gain did you have from the things of which you are now ashamed? For their end is death'.[148] The Letter to the Philippians offers

teachings'; some read it 'opposed to the teaching of the law' (Lietzmann 1933: 70, *ap.* Gagnon 1993: 678 n. 35).

147. ὧν τὸ τέλος ἔσται κατὰ τὰ ἔργα αὐτῶν. The appeal to *telos*, end, is significant. In Ps.-Ecphantus failure proves fraud. In Paul, Stoic influence makes trials and tribulations a positive element. They become marks of success and triumph. Thus, Paul boasts of his labors, his imprisonment, beatings, near misses (2 Cor. 11.23-28, cf. Rom. 5.3), his (presumably physical) affliction (2 Cor. 12.7).

148. ὅτε γὰρ δοῦλοι ἦτε τῆς ἁμαρτίας, ἐλεύθεροι ἦτε τῇ δικαιοσύνῃ. τίνα οὖν καρπὸν εἴχετε τότε; ἐφ᾽ οἷς νῦν ἐπαισχύνεσθε, τὸ γὰρ τέλος ἐκείνων θάνατος (Rom. 6.20-21). καθόλου δὲ τοὺς μὲν νόμους φαίη τις ἂν ποιεῖν δούλων πολιτείαν, τὰ δὲ ἔθη τοὐναντίον ἐλευθέρων. ἐκεῖνοι μὲν γὰρ ποιοῦσιν εἰς τὰ σώματα κολάσεις· παραβαινομένους δὲ ἔθους τὴν ζημίαν εἶναι συμβέβηκεν αἰσχύνην (Dio Chrysostom 76.4).

the finale of this transformation: shame is the defining attribute of the earthly city things (τὰ ἐπίγεια), and the members of this city glory in their shame. Their *telos*, end, is destruction (Phil. 3.19). To this Paul opposes the heavenly city (πολίτευμα ἐν οὐρανοῖς) from which a *sōtēr*, a savior, comes (Phil. 3.20).

7.1–8.39. Paul's view of humanity, his theory of type, emerges in 7.1–8.39. This is a very difficult, yet unambiguous, portion of the letter. It takes the form of a diatribe on law, followed by the presentation of a new concept of humankind. This section consists of two parts: 7.1-11 (continued in 9.1-18), a theory of type; and 7.12–8.39, Pauline psychology. The first can only be understood in the light of the second.

In the spirit suggested in 6.19-21, Paul ties together law and psychology. Paul's human being has a sarkic-pneumatic soul (7.12–8.39). In the most general sense, the soul—'heart' in the popular philosophy of late antiquity—is understood as and identified with the rational-irrational composite, the middle register of the (Aristotelian) soul. It is the object of that branch of practical philosophy called ethics. But even in the form most widely favored by popular philosophy, moral philosophy can be quite subtle, and Paul bears witness to this. The rational-irrational, intermediate aspect of the soul only *seems* to fill the place of the entire soul. Paul also recognizes the irrational component, the sarkic, 'carnal', or 'fleshly' (7.5, 14), which is represented by the members, or limbs (τὰ μέλη) (7.5, 23). The rational element—the pneumatic, spiritual, refined—is expressed by the νοῦς (*nous*) (7.23, 25). *Nous* is a difficult term in Paul, but it covers most of the technical meanings it has in philosophical speculation: intuitive reason, mind and intellect but also moral state or disposition, sentiment, design; it can be identified, for all practical purposes, with the rational soul, with all its faculties, powers and affections. The sarkic is the body of death (7.5, 24), which does not listen to the will (7.15-16); it is lust, passions (7.5), the dwelling place of *hamartia* (7.17, 23) and the slave to the law of *hamartia* (7.25). Any individual under *hamartia* is sarkic (cf. 3.20). The pneumatic, by contrast, is the body of Christ (7.4), the inner human (7.22), the slave to the law of God (7.25). The sarkic and the pneumatic are governed by different laws or principles (νόμοι) (7.22-23, 25). The law of the sarkic is called the 'other law' (ἕτερος νόμος) (7.23), or the 'law of *hamartia*' (7.23, 25), or the 'law of the members' (7.23). The law of the pneumatic is named the 'law of God' (7.22, 25) or 'the law of *nous*' (7.23). (This is the new law, the *nomos* of *pistis* derived from *dikaiosunē theou*.) In the fallen state, the condition to which the 'disobedience' of the first man brought humankind, the law of *hamartia* is the only law. It governs the whole of humanity. The code of Moses, the Law, only acknowledges this state of affairs. It is the instrument of the irrational-rational part of the soul; it identifies an offense and warns against it, but, given the state of human nature, it is otherwise powerless. It only discloses the moral burden of fallen humanity. The law is holy, and its injunctions are just (7.12). It feeds, however, on *hamartia*. By the very commandment against it, *hamartia* is rendered exceedingly vicious (7.13). For Paul, one is powerless against *hamartia*; its sarkic force annihilates individual action and will (7.13-20). *Hamartia* is increased and multiplied by the law itself.[149] The law discloses it to me but precisely because I know it I do it: this is the power *hamartia* holds. The law is good, it is pneumatic—that is, it is rooted in the rational— but it is of no use to the sarkic human being. I am sarkic, I am sold to *hamartia* (7.14). The law cannot help; the knowledge of *hamartia* that the law provides only increases the torment (7.7-9).

Romans 7.14-21 is the key to the Pauline conception of will. Here, Paul focuses attention on the misery of the human condition, on the human inability to pull himself out of his agony, essentially because of failure of the will. The will that the law addresses is, like *nomos* itself, ineffectual, akratic (as the Greek philosophers refer to it;[150] cf. 1 Cor. 7.5). Will and action are sundered. 'I [that is, sinful humanity, of which I am a member[151]] do not do what I will. I do what I hate' (Rom.

---

149. As Nebe (1992: 138) remarks when Paul speaks of law as power he understands that the law leads further into *hamartia* or its knowledge, that the law empowers *hamartia* (cf. 1 Cor. 15.56) both individually/anthropologically and collectively/cosmically. For Paul 'the law is no longer the way to salvation, and thus neither is it the way to righteousness. And this what Paul places over against the conceptions of Judaism' (Nebe 1992: 138).

150. See esp. Aristotle, *Nicomachean Ethics* 7.1145a15-1152a35.

151. With Kümmel 1929, I read ἐγώ in this section as a rhetorical device, though not thoroughly *uneigentlich*, figurative; the condition described, however, does apply to Paul too (cf. 7.7; Gal. 2.15-21); also, the passage has nothing to do with Paul's Jewish past, but it describes the current condition of all humanity. See Seifrid 1992: 314-18. (For Seifrid, Rom. 7.14-21 parallels penitential prayers and confessions of the Hebrew Bible [1992: 322].)

Hellenistic Pythagoreans too commented on the flaws of the will. All aspire to

7.15).[152] This realization proves that the law that tells me what not to do is good (7.16). Even more, doing what I do not will shows that it is not my rational self that does it but the *hamartia* that dwells in me (7.17, 20). Paul's psychology sees the human split between rational and irrational sides. God, his law, inhabits the innermost self (κατὰ τὸν ἔσω ἄνθρωπον) (7.22).[153] My actions, however, obey not the *nomos* of *nous* (7.23); they are hostage to the *nomos* of *hamartia*, to passions. In Ps.-Ecphantus, a similar rupture between the human soul and the royal model it should imitate makes it necessary to coerce *Peithō* (Persuasion), the offspring of *Mnēmē* (Memory), a base seed (φαῦλα σπέρματα, cf. Rom. 9.11) that grew up (ἐφύη, cf. Rom. 6.5) into something excellent (σπουδαῖος).

The sarkic and the unconscious (to employ a term of modern psychology) are one. Paul's judgment is harsh: the sarkic is no good (7.18a). It overpowers the will. I can will but I cannot act according to my will; I cannot make the will act on its will, and, as a result, the good willed evades me and what remains is the bad done (7.18b-19).[154] 'This

aretē, yet ignorance makes unlikely the attainment of this goal, says Ps.-Ecphantus (frg. 3.3). Because of this violence and compulsion are needed, no matter how regrettable. The Stoic assurance that will alone wards off adversity, that it is able, when properly cared for, to withstand suffering, contrasts with Paul's discovery of its collapse.

152. Paul is diagnosing an affliction in the Aristotelian medical usage (see below). Ovid (*Metamorphoses* 7.20-21—*video meliora proboque, deteriora sequor*) and Epictetus (*Enchiridion* 2.26.4—[the thief] does not do what he wishes) (see Barrett 1957: 147) may reflect the same tradition.

153. 'The inner man' becomes part of the psychological vocabulary from Plato on, e.g., *Republic* 9.588a-89b. Heckel 1993 is the first book entirely devoted to tracking a Pauline idea to Plato. Heckel traces the Pauline language of the 'inner man' (2 Cor. 4.16; Rom. 7.22; Eph. 3.16; 1 Pet. 3.4) to the tradition of Plato's *Republic* 9.588a-589b, the 'beast-lion-inner man' metaphor of the soul. (The image is also found in Philo's commentaries on Gen. 1.26 and 2.7, *4 Maccabees*, Hermetica and Nag Hammadi.) The drawback of the study is that Heckel resists his own analysis and refuses to read Paul Hellenistically. While he shows that Paul borrowed this concept from Plato and left it essentially unchanged, Heckel is at pains to protect Paul's thought from the contamination of the Classical or Hellenistic culture. The Platonic connection of Paul is one that I long suspected and defended. I maintain that even the rather similar language of Rom. 2.29 or 1 Cor. 4.5 is Platonic, and comes from the *Republic*'s soul–state analogy and the discussion of the inner justice of the soul (Book 4, esp. 4.443d-e).

154. τὸ γὰρ θέλειν παράκειταί μοι, τὸ δὲ κατεργάζεσθαι τὸ καλὸν οὔ· οὐ γὰρ ὃ

is what I find to be the principle, *nomos* [of my being]: whenever I want to do the beneficial, the fine thing [τὸ καλόν], the malignant, the ugly one [τὸ κακόν] is at hand' (7.21). 'Who will snatch me from the vortex of sarkic rule, the law of *hamartia*?' asks Paul (7.24, 25). The way Christ does this is ingenious.

To answer this frantic call Paul develops a typological theory (7.1-11, cf. 9.1-18). Dying with Christ, described in Romans 6, deals the death blow to law.[155] Law is valid only while I am alive (7.1); dead, with a death like that of Christ (7.4, cf. 6.5), I am free from subjugation to the sarkic, of fleshly *hamartia* defined by law, by becoming Christ-like, through Christ free at once of *sarx* and of law. Planted (Paul is using the language of Hellenistic mysticism) with Christ in the likeness of his death (6.5), the Christians bear fruit for God (7.5). One is released from the age-old, fossilized, written law and becomes a slave to a brand-new spirit (7.6). Law and justice live in the soul; the pneumatic is their personification. The newness of *pneuma* (καινότης πνεύματος) contrasts with the outdatedness of law (παλαιότης γράμματος) (7.6).[156] Here, Christ unambiguously assumes the function that the Hellenistic Pythagoreans designated *nomos empsuchos*.

The notorious difficulty of understanding *nomos* in Paul is due mainly to Paul himself, who displays an elusive astuteness and underhanded subtlety in his treatment of this issue. He confounds both friend and foe. There is little doubt in my mind that Paul execrates the law. Doing this is so daring, however, that he immediately moves the diatribe to a defense of the law. Romans 7.7-14 is one of the most striking examples of this maneuver. Here, he jumps from condemning the law to exalting it. What he unequivocally denounces is written, external law. What he extols is the *euangelion*, pneumatic law. The passage is sly, its intent barely noticeable, interpretable but still perplexing.[157] Essentially, I

θέλω ποιῶ ἀγαθόν, ἀλλὰ ὃ οὐ θέλω κακὸν τοῦτο πράσσω (Rom. 7.18b-19).

155. The nonchalance with which Paul maneuvers between (Jewish) law and law of *hamartia* is terrific. It often sounds like Paul has no idea where he stands on law. The hesitation comes not from any unclarity on the law, he has no use of it, but from deference to the Jews, an essential component of his community, who identify with it. What he needs and uses is tact and euphemism, not moral and political integrity.

156 The concepts of living law as opposed to written law are evidently implied in this statement (see 2.13-14).

157. It is usually assumed, in the words of E.P. Sanders (1991: 117), that Paul's dilemma is 'how to hold together the two dispensations, one being God's election

believe that Paul recognizes a tragic incongruity between the promise of the law—that is, life—and its unperformable, unachievable demands, which lead to death (7.10). This is because a divine, pneumatic law is given to a sarkic human (7.14); this insufferable discrepancy makes the law torture (7.17-24, cf. Phil. 3.6). It is not pneumatic law that dwells in the human, but *hamartia* (Rom. 7.20, cf. 9.31). The human being is, if anything, a '*hamartia empsuchos*' (cf. 7.23-24). This contradiction can be mitigated only by an intermediary who is himself law and human at the same time. It is the intervention of Christ, embodied as man, that relieves the tension (8.3-4). With this pivotal transformation, *pistis* politically supersedes *nomos* (cf., e.g., Gal. 2.21; 3.2, 5, 11, 21, 24; 5.18).[158]

Law is not *hamartia*, yet it is an instrument of *hamartia*, the 'consciousness' of *hamartia* (7.7). As law has become invalid, *hamartia* is dead (7.8). If one looks for a metaphor here, one misses Paul's mean-

of Israel and his gift to them of the law, the other his offer of salvation to all who have faith in Christ'. This may be so, theologically. Paul the missionary has no such quandary. For him the law of the Hebrews lost its validating authority. Law is only the most conspicuous item to go. Not only the law but also circumcision is reviled and viewed in opposition to Christ himself and to *charis* respectively (Gal. 5.2-5). Jerusalem itself is reneged upon (Gal. 4.24-26). Above everything, however, law is a curse (Gal. 3.10). (See Dunn 1993: 459, 466.) Even granted that Paul is beyond himself with rage in Galatians, such statements are no accident. It is also assumed that Paul's quandary with the Jewish law is that for him this law differed from all other peoples' law by being of divine origin; it is precisely because of this, it is argued, that Paul is at pains to show why a law which came from God was no longer binding on the Gentiles (e.g. Schreiner 1993: 725-26). I cannot believe that Hellenistic Paul was not fully aware and quite persuaded that any Hellenistic *polis* claimed divine origin for its laws, or that the Hellenes of Classical Greece before them made similar claims. The Jews would just believe that much more fervently than any Greeks; of that Paul is fully and painfully aware, and he knows he has to deal with it. *But not because he himself thinks so.* He enters into a special critique of Jewish law because a compact that begins by making it impossible for certain people to join in is rightly inconceivable to him. Not only that Paul has enough political knowledge to see that clearly; much more importantly, (God's) impartial *dikaiosunē*, the quoin of his entire political theory and of much of his theology excludes it as madness.

158. While, in Paul's thought, *pistis* displaces *aretē*, a rhetoric of moral and political *aretē* is still useful. The beings of *pistis* retain, while living on earth, a sarkic envelope, and are in need of admonition against vice and discord and exhortation to moral integrity and political unity.

ing. He reveals a secret: the recipe for release from the sarkic, the technique for turning into a pneumatic: die with Christ, become Christ-like, be a christ. Paul's interest in the law is only incidental. That death is freedom is a philosophical platitude. Paul knows better: freedom is a Christ-like death. Relentless reflection went to the problem of spanning the chasm between human and divine worlds, the former the theater of fate and death, the latter of justice and life. The Hellenistic solution was to interpose an intermediary being. For the Hellenistic Pythagoreans, the king is the central actor in the drama of salvation.[159] Individual *sōtēria* is ineluctably linked to one's existence in an organized, political structure. This is also Paul's train of thought. The Classical dogma that one achieves freedom only in the *polis* continues to hold. The state, for Paul as for the Hellenistic Pythagoreans, is the precondition for salvation. It reinforces people's expectations and relieves their apprehension. It makes soteriology effectual even while preserving its personal character. In Ps.-Ecphantus, for example, the mediator inhabits the upper tier of a two-layered humanity. In Paul, who portrays all humanity as being in the same bind, Christ occupies the station of the king. Like Ps.-Ecphantus's king, Christ is both human and divine, but there is a difference, too: Christ not only assumes a complete identity with both realms, but does so by means of abasement and death. Still, in both cases the mediator is the imperative object of imitation for a congregated people, a political persona.

8.1-17. Humanity, in Paul, is strictly divided along the line separating pneumatic from sarkic. This divide is metaphysical and mystical as well as moral and political. As in Classical and Hellenistic writings, the dichotomy revolves around *aretē* or, rather, its negative aspect, the passions (or, more cardinally, *hamartia*). Lack of *aretē* (i.e. *hamartia*) becomes synonymous with loss of an eternal kingdom. The slightest

---

159. Ps.-Ecphantus (frgs. 1.5, 3.3) combines the separate notions of the king's parity of *aretē* with God and of the ruler's origin in heavens. The equivalence of royal and divine *aretē* is a new feature in Hellenistic politics. It is based, I believe, on the rather common similarity between some (lower) divine champion and God (motif used by Paul in the Philippian 'hymn'). See esp. Phil. 2.6, ἴσα (εἶναί) θεῷ, and discussion in Chapter 5, section on Ps.-Ecphantus, frg. 1.5.1. While Christ is the hero of the *euangelion*, Ps.-Ecphantus helps one understand the political milieu of such motifs. The divinity of great public figures (traceable to Plato's *Laws* 4.712b-717) is a widespread aspect of Hellenistic and Roman thought (be it Pythagorean or Stoic). For references, see Chapter 5, section on Ps.-Ecphantus, frg. 5.1.

disruption of *aretē* entails the cataclysmic desertion of God by human beings. Moral lapse and political breakdown destroy the human perception of God and lead to doom. The border between the two realms is nearly invisible: overindulgence of the body and the mental deterioration that inevitably follows bring alienation from the divine. Earthly slippage forfeits the heavens.[160]

To the law of *hamartia* and death (νό[μος] τῆς ἁμαρτίας καὶ τοῦ θανάτου) (8.2), the law of Adam, Paul opposes the law of the *pneuma* of life (νόμος τοῦ πνεύματος τῆς ζωῆς), the law of Christ Jesus (8.2), the law of God (νόμ[ος] τοῦ θεοῦ) (8.7). 'Law of *hamartia*' is a catachresis for the *nomos* of the Jews, now applied to the sarkic domain. The condition of law is actually *astheneia* (8.3). The bane of *nomos-sarx* is broken by Christ: what the law could not do because of the sarkic, God did by sending Jesus, in the *likeness* of *hamartia-sarx* (ἐν ὁμοιώματι σαρκὸς ἁμαρτίας) and for *hamartia* (8.3). There is no question of docetism here;[161] this is a technique of salvation (cf. also Phil. 2.7). Christ, coming in the likeness of *sarx*, incorporates and vanquishes *hamartia* (Rom. 8.3). Christ is *the* type. He brought about a division of humanity: κατὰ σάρκα (*kata sarka*, according to *sarx*) and κατὰ πνεῦμα (*kata pneuma*, according to *pneuma*) (8.4). This is a distinction of kind.

The sarkic–pneumatic split attacks φρόνημα (*phronēma*), practical reason, the traditional moral-political guide. The difference is that between death and life (8.6).[162] No more radical departure from passions is possible than being ἐν πνεύματι (*en pneumati,* in, or possessed by, the *pneuma*) (8.9). Paul puts it in political terms, another reference to the Hellenistic Pythagorean political origins of the idea: the belly-God, the shame-glory of the worldly, is contrasted with the celestial *politeuma* of the Christ-minded (Phil. 3.19-20). The passage from the carnal and psychological to the pneumatic and transcendental is made in one breathtaking dash.

Sarkic *phronēma* ('thought', 'purpose', 'desire') ends in death; pneu-

---

160. See also Gal. 5.19-21, cf. 3.3; 6.8 and Phil. 3.19-20, where a severe critique is made of moral and political failing in long lists of vices.

161. Christ takes on the 'form' of man (Phil. 2.7) as *skēnos* covers the king (H 272.11, T 80.2, cf. also 2 Cor. 5.1, 4). (See Chapter 5, section on Ps.-Ecphantus, frg. 1.1 for further discussion.) This is a fact of life on earth that applies to heavenly beings as well in their earthly transience.

162. τὸ γὰρ φρόνημα τῆς σαρκὸς θάνατος, τὸ δὲ φρόνημα τοῦ πνεύματος ζωὴ καὶ εἰρήνη (Rom. 8.6).

matic *phronēma* leads to life (8.6).[163] The *sarkic phronēma* is hostile to God; it is not, and indeed cannot be (οὐδὲ γὰρ δύναται), subject to the law of God (8.7). It cannot (οὐ δύναται) please God (8.8). Paul's psychological and anthropological distinction between 'we' (or 'you') and 'they' (ἡμεῖς/ὑμεῖς-αὐτοί), between 'us' and 'the many', is characteristic. The choice,[164] adherence to the outrageous *euangelion*, rests with the human being, not God. Even more remarkable, the pneumatic reaches his chosen state through the extraordinary means of suffering, of passions (παθήματα) (8.18; 2 Cor. 1.5-7; Phil. 3.10), humility and obedience.[165] One cannot but surrender completely to God's *dikaiosunē*. (Romans 8.19-25 places things in cosmic and apocalyptic perspective and recalls the myth of Christ in Phil. 2.6-11. The entire creation was voided so as to be recreated [Rom. 8.20-22]. The creation is unwillingly ignorant [οὐχ ἑκοῦσα] of its plight. Futility, however, engenders hope [8.20]. Now creation anxiously looks for a sign of the children of God [8.19], which will also signal its own deliverance [8.21]. The pneumatics themselves eagerly await full admission to sonship and bodily redemption [8.23]. The hope for unfathomed things requires patience [8.25].[166]) The definition of the pneumatic follows: the

163. Paul, whose entire career, message and reputation is built on the notion that there are no divisions within humankind based on ethnic group, legal status, gender or mental ability, breaks humanity at a level deeper than any of these, that of ontology. What constitutes the essence of the species, being human, is speciated into pneumatic and sarkic. The Christ event cleaves the very distinctness and uniqueness of the human category; anthropology is divided. Thus, human biology and common psychological makeup (*skeuos*, the envelope of flesh [Rom. 9.21-23], *sōma*, the body [8.10-13], *phronēma*, mind [8.5-8]) nonetheless describe two mutually incompatible states according to the group they qualify. There are two sorts of humans. The critical difference is due not to destiny or *telos* but to allegiance, social identity, an affiliation that has also a political dimension. Choice extends to the whole of the individual, the biological as well as the psychological. For other examples of such antithetical applications of the same function, quality or predicates, see Phil. 1.28; 3.18-20.

164. My exposition attempts to develop to maximum coherence the tensions among choice and chosenness, choice and universal *hamartia*, characterizing Romans.

165. I have little doubt that Paul deliberately sets himself here in opposition to the ubiquitous Stoics. For them (and in general for the Greek philosophers) *pathēmata* were anathema. For humility, the 'passion' *par excellence*, see Chapter 7, Clues from Philippians section.

166. Paul's language here is reminiscent of that of the gnosticism and astrology of his period (see Barrett 1957: 166).

pneumatic possesses/is possessed by the *pneuma* of God (8.9, 14), or
the *pneuma* of Christ (8.9), or the *pneuma* of him who raised Jesus from
the dead (8.11), or Christ (8.10). The virtual equivalence, if not the
identity, of these terms is thus emphasized.

   In Paul, the descent of the divine *pneuma* upon the soul is an operation
of divine possession that transfigures and illuminates the initiate, a common theme in Hellenistic mysticism.[167] The *pneuma* of Christ cancels
the sarkic, and although the body is dead because of *hamartia*, the
pneuma is alive because of *dikaiosunē* (8.9-10, cf. 1 Cor. 3.16; Gal.
2.20). If one has Christ, one cannot be sarkic. Paul is very explicit about
the distinction between the sarkic and the pneumatic. The dichotomy is
dramatized by the role the body (σῶμα) plays in his thinking. The
bodies of the pneumatic and of the sarkic meet different fates: the
former is saved, the latter destroyed. The pneumatic, though he still has
a mortal body (θνητὰ σώματα) (8.11) because of *hamartia*, is a living
pneuma because of *dikaiosunē* (8.10, 11). He who lives *kata sarka*,
according to *sarx*, will die; he who lives by the pneuma (πνεύματι), will
live (8.13). The *pneuma* puts to death the deeds of the *sarx* (τὰς
πράξεις τῆς σαρκός) (8.13), the very cause of body's death.[168] The
point is that Paul distinguishes carefully between *sarx* and *sōma*, the
first a drive, an expression of the unconscious, of the 'irrational'; the
second the physical aspect of being, of life. Thus, while the *sarx* of the
pneumatic is destroyed, his *sōma* is saved. The *sōma* of the sarkic ends
as the body of death (σῶμα τοῦ θανάτου) (7.24; see also 7.5, cf. Phil.

---

   167. L. Delatte 1942: 219-21. Delatte notes that the descent of the divine *pneuma*
in the soul of the devotee, a genuine divine possession which results in trans-
figuration and divinisation, is encountered in the mystical writers of Hellenistic
times. He gives Paul as an example of its presence in the first century writers. He
also refers to Aratus (*Phaenomena* 5) (and other 'poets') quoted in the Acts of the
Apostles (17.28). Plotinus (*Enneads* 6.7.34.13) also speaks of the identification
between the one who contemplates and the one contemplated (Delatte 1942: 121-
22). While it is not *pneuma per se* that effects the mystical union, Paul belongs,
when he expresses such sentiments, to the larger current of Hellenistic mysticism.
What is eminently significant is that, in Hellenistic and Roman times, mysticism
takes, more often than not, the form of the motif of the ruler as an alien descended
from heaven, possibly following Plato (*Laws* 4.712b-717).
   168. The reading σάρξ instead of σῶμα in 8.13 is attested by the manuscript
evidence: D, F, G, 630 as well as by Old Latin-Vulgate (latt). This is important for
Paul's consistency in the use of *sarx*.

3.19),[169] but the redemption of the pneumatic's *sōma* (ἀπολύτρωσις τοῦ σώματος) is proclaimed in 8.23. Salvation of *sōma* is inherent to salvation (8.10-13, 23).[170]

The pneumatic, because the *pneuma* is of God (8.9, 11, 14), of Christ (8.10), is in a son-father relation with God. (The pneumatics are defined as those who are led, carried off [ἄγονται] by the spirit [8.14]. They form the cortège of *pneuma*.) The pneumatic's *pneuma* is called the 'spirit of sonship' (υἱοθεσία) (8.15).[171] The pneumatic shares in God, partakes of Christ. He is a son of God (8.4), a child of God (8.16, 21), an heir of God, a co-heir with Christ, a sufferer with Christ; he is glorified with Christ (8.17).[172]

---

169. The body of death is sarkic *sōma*, for which he simply uses the term *sarx*. The body of death reaches its complete development in Augustine, where a part of the divided humanity gloats in delight at the other that never ceases dying. With medieval iconography this will turn into an aesthetical ideal. Sadism receives an inviolable license to practice its craft. Luther, intensely aware of the sarkic–pneumatic conflict, resolved the tension between Rom. 7 and 8 by observing that the believer is at once pneumatic and sarkic, and phrased it in the famous formula *simul iustus et peccator*.

170. The question is intriguing, as to whether Paul knew in some form the notion that the soul is the form of the organic body, as attributed to Aristotle by the later Peripatetics and certainly familiar to the 'Old Commentators' (first century BCE to first century CE). Athenodorus of Tarsus, the Stoic familiar with Aristotle, might have heard of it too (Gottschalk 1987: 1113-18 and notes). Paul's discourse on the resurrection body (1 Cor. 15.35-58) may go back to controversies that grasped the fractured world of Judaism in the first century, before Titus' destruction of the Second Temple.

171. *Huiothesia*, a Hellenistic term and a concept essential to Paul for describing the relation between the pneumatics and God, refers to a practice unknown in Judaism (see Barrett 1957: 163). The notion of *huiothesia* (cf. Rom. 8.23), the category of adoption (8.12-17; Gal. 4.4-7) and the terminology of inheritance and wills (Rom. 8.17; Gal. 4.7) belong to Roman jurisprudence, esp. to *patria potestas* (see Ball 1901, Lyall 1969, 1984, and the remarks and bibliography in Sampley (1980: 2, 8 nn. 7-12). *Huiothesia*, as the right to inheritance, is also known in Hellenistic Greek law (Black 1973: 118, who refers to Egyptian papyri in the Mitteis-Wilcken collection; Lyall 1969).

172. συγκληρονόμοι δὲ Χριστοῦ, εἴπερ συμπάσχομεν ἵνα καὶ συνδοξασθῶμεν (Rom. 8.17). It is God or the reformer who are the objects of mimesis, above customs or laws. See, e.g., 1 Cor. 4.16; 11.1; 1 Thess. 1.6; 2 Thess. 3.7, 9; Phil. 3.17. Also, the multitude of *sun-* compound words that point to group imitation; in Romans alone I notice 6.4-5; 8.17, 29. Imitation is the single most important topic

Christ is the *eikōn*, the image,[173] being imitated or resembled. His position is similar to that of Ps.-Ecphantus' king and that of other Hellenistic writers.[174] The *tupos-eikōn* connection is revealed by the reference to Adam in 1 Cor. 15.49: 'As we bore the *eikōn* of the dust-man [Adam, cf. 1 Cor. 15.45; Rom. 5.14], we shall bear the *eikōn* of the celestial one'. Elsewhere we read: 'We shall be changed in God's *eikōn* from one degree of *doxa* to another, even as the lord who is the *pneuma*' (2 Cor. 3.18). And, 'The light of the *euangelion* of the glory of Christ is the *eikōn* of God' (2 Cor. 4.4).

8.18-30. In other words, the pneumatic is a Christ-type. The pneumatics are the first fruits of the *pneuma* (8.23), those who love God (8.28); those called (8.28, 30), are those of whom God has the foreknowledge (8.29), those marked out for a form similar to the image of God's son (προώρισεν συμμόρφους τῆς εἰκόνος τοῦ υἱοῦ αὐτοῦ) (8.29).[175] Romans 8.29, a key passage, indicates that there are (or will be) a multitude of those conforming to the *eikōn* of God's son. Christ is only the first-born among many (εἰς τὸ εἶναι αὐτὸν πρωτότοκον ἐν πολλοῖς ἀδελφοῖς).[176] The content of this *eikōn* is described by the apposition

in the Hellenistic Pythagoreans: a society imitates God's world (the *polis* group), an individual imitates the king (the *basileia* group).

173. The world Paul inhabits is saturated with images which fill temples, theaters and forums: gods, emperors, generals, benefactors. The εἰκόνες βασιλικαί, *imagines imperatorum*, must have been the most visible (LSJ *s.v.* εἰκών 485b).

174. In Ps.-Ecphantus (frg. 1.1), the king has a special place among human beings. Pinnacle of human nature, the king partakes in the divine; identical biologically with any other human being, the king is made, however, by the highest artificer who uses himself as model. The term *eikōn* is not in the known Ps.-Ecphantus, but the similar *archetupon* is. After first century CE, it is often employed to describe the relation between *basileus* or *basileia* and God, from Plutarch to Eusebius and from Hermetica to the Rosetta inscription. See Chapter 5, section on Ps.-Ecphantus, frg. 1.1, for discussion.

175. I read προώρισεν, in 8.29, the aorist of προ-ορίζω, as a reference to the topographical measurement of land. God marked them out like boundaries, all with the same image of Christ, just as farm-plots were measured with the same measuring tape. This image is consistent with that of planting (6.5), and bearing fruit (7.5).

176. τῆς εἰκόνος τοῦ υἱοῦ αὐτοῦ (Rom. 8.29) is identical syntactically and semantically with the expression εἰκόνα...τοῦ ἀνθρώπου, used by Plato (*Republic* 9.588d), 'form of human', lit. the likeness of the human. Plato's text offers an important control for the understanding of the Pauline line. The translation 'form' for εἰκόνα is confirmed by a passage in Plato, only a few lines earlier: Εἰκόνα πλάσαντες

θάνατος–ἀνάστασις (*thanatos–anastasis*), death and resurrection, a typically Pauline correlate (6.5; 1 Cor. 15.21; Phil. 3.10). The argument is charged and complex; it can be comprehended, however, because it is being disseminated in the Hellenistic environment. Putting this in the context of Hellenism and, especially, of Hellenistic Pythagoreanism, one sees that there is really very little that is original here—except, that is, for the destiny of the mediator, the celestial man.

Romans 8.28-30, so important for the doctrine of *eikōn* it contains, has another salient feature in common with Ps.-Ecphantus: the notion of foreknowledge and calling. Ps.-Ecphantus (frg. 1.3) elaborates on the topic of God's foreknowledge in a vein foreshadowing Rom. 8.28-30. Paul says that God calls certain people to work together with him and that only those whom he has foreknown has he predetermined, to conform to the image of his son. Those whom he has predetermined, he

τῆς ψυχῆς λόγῳ (9.588b), 'imagining a form of the soul in [at the level of] language'. What Paul is saying is 'the form of his son;' he uses εἰκών and not μορφή for stylistic reasons. In fact the terms συμμόρφους and εἰκόνος express a paradigmatic relation, repeating the same thing in different ways. One is an *eikōn* of an original (see also Cornford's commentary *ad loc.*, 323-24). This 'original' is no longer a Form but a pattern, a paradigm for any of the natural or humanly crafted things.

The full impact of this notion will be encountered in Philippians, in the notorious crux μορφὴ θεοῦ (2.6), 'form of God'. Rom. 8.29 and Phil. 2.6 are interchangeable. 'Form of God', means neither God nor a hierarchical stratification implying inferiority (two solutions preferred by most commentators, though not by the same ones) but an attempt to produce meaning with the crude means of language. Gooch emphasizes that Plato and Paul 'locate full reality beyond the physical world and make that reality the object of complete knowledge' (1987: 187). It is unlikely that Paul read Plato, but quite plausible that he knew about this issue in the *Republic*. The Hellenistic Pythagoreans give this form to the king and his imitators.

The issue in both Paul and Plato is one of representation, of *mimesis*—not, however, in the larger sense of imitation of an original, as encountered in Plato's parable of the Demiurge with the Mirror, a satyrical metaphor for the *mimetēs*, the artist (*Republic* 10.596d-e). The representation here is of a Form, of Idea itself. Plato produces, in 10.595a-602b, the famous debate on reality vs. art, a systematic theory of language. The difficulty is to translate Idea into discourse, to find appropriate signifiers for what the contemplative intellect sees. Plato's reality is pure language, the signifier shaking off its chain, the word as univocal certainty and precise location, as center. Plato strives for the word uniquely and unvaryingly defined and the Form is precisely this: the end of change, of relativity, of becoming; it is real, self-existing, unchanging in space and time, unique (cf. 5.474b-480, where opinion and knowledge are contrasted).

has also called, judged and glorified. Similarly, in Ps.-Ecphantus, God has always known the king, his creation.[177]

Christ's slavery and mastery prefigure the new type. The slave/master notion is a supreme Pauline discovery, one that proclaims the new type. The pneumatic is Christ-like, a christ himself. 'Christ' is practically the name for the citizen.[178] Christ functions as a *nomen*, common to an entire *gens*, and Jesus is the *praenomen*, the founder of the house of Christos. But there are also a Christ Paul and a Christ Phoebe. One is made just, is glorified (8.30), is made the elect of God (8.33), is supervictorious (ὑπερνικῶμεν) (8.37)—Paul's fervor is unbridled. Paul intends to praise the *pneuma*, yet, while doing so, he himself falls into a trance. He is carried away by the spirit, the mark of the pneumatic (cf. 8.14).

The ecstasy extends to language. The *pneuma*'s first words are a recognition of the pneumatic's sonship. When *pneuma* inhabits and possesses the elect, if this takes the form of speech, he emits inarticulate cries: *abba(abbaabbaa)*,[179] which Paul renders as 'father', meaning that the *pneumatic* recognizes himself or herself as God's child (8.15-16).[180]

---

177. H 273.1, T 80.6, τῷ μὲν πεποιηκότι γνώριμον ἀεί.

178. The Galatians received Paul as a christ when he was there (Gal. 4.14). In virtues, actions, in death and resurrection, Christ is the *exemplum*, and, by identification, so is Paul.

179. See M. Smith 1980.

180. Rom. 8.15 reads: οὐ γὰρ ἐλάβετε πνεῦμα δουλείας πάλιν εἰς φόβον ἀλλὰ ἐλάβετε πνεῦμα υἱοθεσίας ἐν ᾧ κράζομεν, αββα ὁ πατήρ. Something is amiss here. *Pneuma douleias* is preposterous. The immediate logic requires *douleias* to follow *phobon*, 'you did not receive the *pneuma* [to fall] back into the fear of slavery, but [you received] the *pneuma* of sonship', a possible anacoluthon. But the rhetoric of the phrase may demand a different reading. It may be possible to see here an elliptic chiasm with *phobos* stressing the alternatives: 'you did not receive the *pneuma* of slavery [to fall] back into fear, but [you received] the *pneuma* of sonship *again for fear*', i.e. 'unto fear of God'. What Paul could say here is that the new relationship with God changes also the nature of *phobos*, from the abject (and abjured) one of slavery to *hamartia* to the numinous (and manumitting) one of awe for God. *Pneuma douleias*, the *pneuma* of slavery, exists only rhetorically, as a pointer to the πνεῦμα υἱοθεσίας, the only one with ontological status. Similarly, the old, 'backward', abrogated *phobos*, has a counterpart in a new, 'forward', exculpating fear. *Pneuma douleias* and slavery to *hamartia* are, in the new order, inconceivable categories. Such a reading may be hermeneutically and structurally verified by Rom. 11.23: the Jews, the original branches, now cut, should they reform, would be grafted again. Gal. 5.1 gives the drab, straightforward reading: 'Christ now set us

Patēr as a form of address to and a fond designation of a benevolent ruler is common not only in the Greek and Roman political culture, but also in the Septuagint. (This, of course, is not only a Mediterranean topos but a virtually universal one.) In Sthenidas (frg. 1.2), what unambiguously defines God and king is the fatherly disposition, *patrikē diathesis*. (Interpreting the meaning of the Homeric epithet 'father of Gods and father of humans', applied to God, is the focus of Sthenidas' fragment.) The identification of God and ruler with a father is routine in political treatises of Hellenistic and Roman times, particularly in those elaborating monarchic doctrines, but it can be traced to the Classical period.[181] When Paul interprets the inarticulate cry *abba* (Rom. 8.15; Gal. 4.6) as a sign of *pneuma*-inspired filial recognition, he makes a political statement. When he refers to God as *patros hēmōn*, our father, in the greetings of his letters, he is using 'father' as a political title: God as the ruler of the Christian commonwealth. In the openings of Paul's letters, formulas such as 'our father' (πατρὸς ἡμῶν)[182] and 'father of our lord' (πατὴρ τοῦ κυρίου ἡμῶν)[183] (or 'father of mercies', πατὴρ τῶν οἰκτιρμῶν)[184] function in the same way as do the titles of Hellenistic kings or Roman emperors in the dedications preserved in papyri and inscriptions.[185] 'Father' is a politically charged word, and it is meant to be understood politically. This is made explicit in the openings of the Letters to the Thessalonians, where the *ekklēsia*, the community, is said to belong to God the father. The Hellenistic political literature gives resonance to a Pauline term that otherwise fails to have its full impact on the modern reader.

free, do not submit again to the yoke of slavery', μὴ πάλιν ζυγῷ δουλείας. The ecstatic context, extolling the *pneuma*, also warrants the double *phobos* reading. A similar passage (2 Cor. 6.14–7.1), that invokes God's paternity for the believers (6.18) in heavily political terms, ends with a reiteration of the fear of God (7.1). The expression fear of God, φόβος θεοῦ, is common in the LXX, and Paul quotes Ps. 35.2 in Rom. 3.8. (For the categories of the meanings of *phobos* in Paul see discussion in Chapter 4, section on Ps.-Zaleucus, frg. 13.)

181. See Chapter 5, section on Sthenidas, frg. 1.2.

182. Rom. 1.7; 1 Cor. 1.3; 2 Cor. 1.2; Gal. 1.3; Phil. 1.2; 1 Thess. 1.3; 2 Thess. 1.2; Phlm. 3.

183. 2 Cor. 1.3.

184. 2 Cor. 1.3.

185. 'Father' was actually used for the emperor Claudius: *Pater patriae* (P. Lond. 1178.10, of 194 CE; MM *s.v.* πατήρ 498b). It is no less significant that the title appears in an early Christian letter to a provincial bishop (P. Amh. 1.3.2.16, of 264-282 CE, according to Harnack [against Deissmann]; MM *s.v.* πατήρ 498b).

Romans 8.18-26 displays a highly charged pneumatic language: secret disclosure, (ἀποκάλυψις) (8.19), rapt expectation (ἀπεκδέχεται) (8.19, 23), agonizing suffering, inarticulate groaning (8.26). The spirit pleads, cries. The *crescendo* of feeling reaches its paroxysm in the intense agitation of an oxymoron: 'eager awaiting with long-bearing patience' (ὑπομονὴ ἀπεκδεχόμεθα) (8.24), part of an excursus on hope (8.24-25). The essence of hope is magnificently described here, in apophatic language, as absence: 'Hope present is no hope, for who hopes for what he sees?' (8.24). Romans 8.27, a difficult verse, is the distillate of Paul's understanding of *pneuma*: 'He who examines the minds of those who have the spirit knows what the spirit is all about—that it is from God and that its possession makes one holy'. The power that acts in the Christian is foolproof. This leads directly to the *summa* of Paul's theory of type (8.29): that those upon whom God gazes (προγινώσκω-προορίζω; the two verbs used here have the same range of meaning and intensify each other), *con*form with the image of God's son, who is the model (πρωτότοκον) for many.[186]

8.31-39. This section ends with a renewed proclamation of sonship and the supreme expression of the father's love: he handed over his son to death for us (8.32). And in the same breath, just like Ps.-Ecphantus, Paul reasons, 'Who shall bring any charge against God's elect?' (8.33)[187] And the explication: God is he who judges (θεὸς ὁ δικαιῶν) (8.34). God's elect experience a judgment transformed by Christ's intercession (8.33-34, cf. 1 Cor. 11.32). The passage includes yet another fragment of an early *credo* (8.34): 'Jesus Christ who died, who was raised, who is at the right hand of God, who pleads [ἐντυγχάνει] for us'. This last function is particularly interesting, since it may form the basis of the notion of being found just, being exonerated of the charges, as in a court trial, and this is exactly what God determines about those who follow the Christ-model. Once one is an imitator of Christ, nothing can separate one from Christ's (or God's) love, for the source of the bond is

186. Such effusions were also encountered in the *basileia* group of writings. Ps.-Ecphantus elaborates upon calling and foreknowledge. Gaze is a 'pneumatic' mark in Diotogenes. Ps.-Archytas, of the *polis* group, speaks of differentiation of human souls, the *eikōn* notion, first-born as paradigm of imitation.

187. This is another Hellenistic *locus*. The legitimate ruler is *theophilēs*, loved by God, and is obeyed by the ruled. No one loved by God can be hated by human beings, writes Ps.-Ecphantus (frg. 1.4.3, esp. H 274.14-16, T 81.4-6).

suffering (8.35-36). Being a Christ-type reverses one's prior status as victim (8.36) and transforms the pneumatic into 'supervictor'. The meaning of suffering is reinterpreted as triumph (8.37). No cosmic force, life and death included, can loosen the bond of love between the pneumatics and God (8.38).

Romans 9.1–11.36: The World at Large and the Reign of God

In this part of the letter, *basileia* has pride of place, together with its principle, *dikaiosunē theou*.

9.1-18. How about the Jews? What is their status (9.1-18; see also 11.1-36)? Jews are out of the political scheme of God insofar as they are Jews. Does this mean that the *logos* of God is ineffective (9.6)? Or that there is *adikia* in God (9.14)? Or that his will, *boulēma*, can fail (9.19)? This periodic hypophora (suggestive of an apology?) might seem to raise the issue of the nature of God. The rhetoric of the reply, however, is one of politics, not metaphysics. Paul is not concerned here with God but with people. In answering these questions Paul sets the foundations of his *polis*. On the other hand, what appears to be a polemic is actually diatribal vituperation, barely disguised mockery. Paul appeals to *suneidēsis*, political conscience (9.1, cf. 13.5; 2.5), here authenticated by *pneuma* (9.1). The oath formula, 'By Christ I say the truth, I lie not' (Ἀλήθειαν λέγω ἐν Χριστῷ, οὐ ψεύδομαι) is alarming rhetoric. In irony-laden rhetorical style, Paul says that he would rather be an untouchable outlaw (ἀνάθεμα, i.e. dedicated to [another] God,[188]), were this to help the Israelites. The Jews are his kin, but *kata sarka* only (9.3). Their claim on Christ is solely *kata sarka* (9.5), which is very little indeed, for this means 'under *hamartia*'—that is, as humans only. I have no doubt that Paul earnestly desires the participation of the Jews in Christ's community. He is not about to make concessions, however. The Jews will have to enter the compact on his terms, the terms of *euangelion*, and not on ancient fame (cf. 9.4-5). Paul knows that attracting the Jews into the Christ-system will not be easy, and he is ridden with disquiet.[189]

188. Barrett (1957: 176) reads, plausibly, 'Separated by a curse—*anathema*—from Christ'; Paul's 'wish' is rendered unlikely by the grammatical construction.

189. The seeming impetus of James Dunn's significant and extensive writings is the desire to show that Paul, in his discourse on *pistis* and *dikaiosunē* and in his criticism of the law, does not denounce Judaism insofar as 'moral self-righteous-

In a distinctive style that mixes the midrash of the rabbis with the allegory of Greek philosophers and grammarians, Paul shows that the true Israel is not of *sarx* but of promise (ἐπαγγελία) (9.8). Birthright does not guarantee election (ἐκλογή) (9.10-13, cf. Gen. 25.23). Midrash is essentially exposition, didactic or homiletic, of a scriptural text. Allegory is a transformation of the Homeric text intended to make poetry conform with reasoned argument.[190] What midrash and allegory have in common is the fancifulness of the approach. Paul does not so much comment on the scriptural text as use it to harmonize God's *logos* with the apparent contradiction that not all Israel is Israel (9.6), that is, that not all Jews are members of the new *polis*. God's *logos*, his design, his reason, must be defended against suspicion of inconsistency or failure. So Paul appeals to Old Testament logia (Gen. 21.12; 18.10), not to explain the scriptural text but to defend God's *modus operandi*. When the gods fail in the Homeric 'scripture', the philosopher and the scholiast are quick to provide an enlightening reading. So it is with Paul, as he fends of suspicion. When it is said that Abraham had children, real offspring are not meant, but rather the dual destiny of humanity, with some of the initial seed lost to the sarkic grip and some entitled to God's inheritance. The opposition between 'children of *sarx*' (τέκνα τῆς σαρκός) and 'children of God' (τέκνα τοῦ θεοῦ) effectively accounts for the political exclusion of some Jews from the new commonwealth and explains the seeming discrepancy between this and the promise made

ness or system of religious merit' (*ap.* Cosgrove 1996: 368); for further critique of the view of first-century Judaism as a religion of performance see Nebe 1992: 147), but because of its covenantal exclusiveness, nationalist presumption and racial pride (see Dunn 1992: 11, 14); in other words not as a moral and theological system but because of its political stance. Paul's critique of the Jews is directed, according to Dunn, not at the validated content but at the segregated form of their teachings. Dunn seems to think that it is not in the *ethos* but in the *polis* that the Jews fail. Although I agree that it is the political exclusiveness of the Jews that troubles Paul, for it represents a fateful threat to his very work, I also think that this exclusiveness is strictly connected with, indeed the cause of, the invalidity of the teaching as well. The Jews' nationalism makes them both impervious to Paul's *euangelion* and defiant of the political integration he seeks. Ultimately, it is not Jewish doctrinal solvency that Paul is interested in but the Jews' acceptance of the *universality* of *his euangelion*. (As Jewett so poignantly infers from Käsemann, for Paul *nomos* and *euangelion* 'are mutually exclusive antitheses' [1994: 40].)

190. Allegorical reading is particularly popular with the Stoics, and especially with the Homeric scholiasts of the first century CE. See *DB* 171a; *OCD* 46a.

by God to the true Israel. Like all allegorical interpretation, Paul's explanation is far from adequate, but the distinction sarkic–pneumatic is elucidated and the defense rests its case.[191] (To be frank, Paul himself realizes the exposition is less than satisfactory and, in what follows, resorts to the tried-and-true adage that God's actions are inscrutable and that no amount of human effort can compete with his will.)

The inflammatory rhetoric carries through to the end of the section. There is no *adikia*, injustice, in God's court (9.14).[192] No *erga* (9.12, cf. also 9.32), no strength of will, and no length of exertion for the law (ἄρα οὖν [two hyperordinating conjunctions!] οὐ τοῦ θέλοντος οὐδὲ τοῦ τρέχοντος) (9.16) can make one a member of Israel, grant citizenship in this *polis*, but only God's favor (ἀλλὰ τοῦ ἐλεῶντος θεοῦ) (9.16)—and then only if God so wishes (θέλει) (9.18). Τρέχων (*trechōn*) (lit. 'running', in 9.16[193]), part of the assonant series *thelontos-trechontos-eleontos*, is a modified-tense snippet of the biblical expression ὁδὸν ἐντολῶν σου ἔδραμον (Ps. 119.32; LXX 118.32), 'I run the way of your commandments'. Paul throws in this tidbit and expects the rest to be understood. Thus does the critique receive a clear referent. Even if the subtlety is lost on the hearer, the ridicule is preserved by the athletic terminology:[194] no frantic running[195] but God's will win the prize.[196]

191. This entire section (Rom. 9.6-13) not only uses allegory but draws its terms from a Gnostic-inspired environment (not unlike, for example, that of Ps.-Ecphantus in frg. 3.3: *logos, sperma, tekna, sarx, phaulos*), while the content is a tame, well-known biblical story. Romans 9 is throughout an epitome of ambiguity, of *double entendre*. By Paul's times, mystery religions, secret coteries, initiatory rites—a whole callow playground had been patented to tranquilize human misery, and Paul, if he wants credibility, cannot but present his religion in the same terms. In Paul, τελειόω and cognates express initiation, perfection. Wisdom, σοφία, a secret and hidden wisdom, θεοῦ σοφία ἐν μυστηρίῳ, is revealed to the initiated, τέλειοι (1 Cor. 2.6-7, cf. Phil. 3.15); be perfect in thinking and childish in evil (1 Cor. 14.20). This enduring perfection is ἀγάπη, love (1 Cor. 13.10). Glossolalia is also a *mustērion* (1 Cor. 14.2).

192. One of the means of averting *adikia*, says Ps.-Zaleucus (frg. 6) is association with good men. God is the good (cf. 8.28; 12.2; 16.19), nothing more contrary to *adikia*.

193. Black (1973: 133) notes that *trechō*, run, for moral striving is Stoic language. Paul's preference for athletics-inspired terms obviously is a good diatribal technique. People have always liked sports jargon.

194. A similar race metaphor, in which Israel fails to win the course but its falling behind is the Gentiles' chance to overtake it, appears in 11.7-11, as identified and discussed by Stowers 1994: 304-306.

9.19-29. If this is so—if no one can resist God's will—what legitimacy can there be in finding fault with any human? (9.19).[197] In answer, Paul produces a theory of end (9.19-29), a teleology[198] that makes use of metaphorical language (potter, clay, lump of clay, pot-making, pottery) and that draws on Hellenistic sapiental literature. This theory makes the end of all and every thing the will of God (9.18, 23; see esp. 9.20-23). It eliminates the Jew-gentile distinction and replaces it with election (9.24). All humans are vessels—some to hold God's wrath, some God's favor (9.22-23). The view that the same object, action or being can have contrary ends according to whom it serves or whose slave it is, is a Pauline topos. In 9.21, a *skeuos* ('vessel', 'receptacle') is designed either for honorable or for dishonorable use; again in 9.23, a *skeuos*'s use is either for life or for ruin. This use of antithetical predicates for the same subject is a Pauline mark[199] and helps him effectively dramatize the fine line between salvation and destruction. It is God's will, however, that defines the vessel's use, not its suitability, as in Plato.[200] Paul positions his God against the philosophy that inspires his language.[201]

195. A similar danger of purposeless running is averted by Paul in Galatians when he receives approval for his *euangelion* from the Jerusalem leaders (Gal. 2.2, 6-7).

196. In 9.17 Paul indicates the scriptural source (Exod. 9.16) behind his name-power theory, ὄνομα-δύναμις, a leitmotif of Pauline literature, a theory charged with mystical and magical overtones, Hellenistic in appeal.

197. τί ἔτι μέμφεται; τῷ γὰρ βουλήματι αὐτοῦ τίς ἀνθέστηκεν; (Rom. 9.19).

198. Philosophical, esp. Aristotelian teleology, is congruent with Bultmann's understanding of Pauline eschatology: historical presence, process, inside the individual. Bultmann 'demythologizes' the utopian eschatology of Jewish Apocalyptic or Hellenistic Gnosticism of the New Testament and speaks for the historical presence of eschatology, presence understood as a process, which unfolds within the individual (see esp. Bultmann 1964b, 1941 article).

199. E.g. *sōma* in 8.10-13, *phronēma* in 8.5-8, *euangelion* in Phil. 1.28b, *stauros* in Phil. 3.18-20.

200. Suitability for intended use, the sole criterion of excellence, beauty, and rightness (ἀρετή κάλος, ὀρθότης) is the reason for the vessel's creation (*Republic* 601d).

201. *Skeuos*, 'receptacle'—the body or, metonymically, the soul as vessel—is a metaphor that belongs to the vocabulary of initiation. The identification of *skeuos* with *sōma* is a philosophical *locus*; further, this identification is often developed through an interplay of the language of mysticism and of morals, such as can be glimpsed here, in 9.21-23 and the parallel text in Phil. 3.19-21. In Phil. 3.19-21, Paul distinguishes between those whose God is the belly and glory in their shame, those thinking of things mundane, ὧν ὁ θεὸς ἡ κοιλία καὶ ἡ δόξα ἐν τῇ αἰσχύνῃ

9.30–10.4. What is the nature of the contract on which the *polis* is founded (9.30-33)? The will of God is balanced with human *pistis* (as against works, 9.32); the relation *dikaiosunē theou–dikaiosunē pisteōs* holds the *polis* together. This same formula, however, is also the crux of the system, the stumbling-stone (πρόσκομμα) and the scandal (σκάνδαλον) (9.32-33) for the Jews. The Jews think themselves in and find themselves out: here, Paul almost mocks the subtle deception inherent in a principle of justice based on the law only (cf. 9.31). The *dikaiosunē* of Jewish *nomos* is at odds with the *dikaiosunē* of *pistis*, a global law that belongs to all (9.30-31). Paul continues with a critique of the Jews' *dikaiosunē* (10.1-4) in a section laden with scriptural allusions and references (10.1-11). Again, Paul begins by claiming, rhetorically, his concern for the Jews. He has the interests of the Jews in his heart and in his prayers—that is, in mind and in speech. (Paul sticks to this mind-speech reference system throughout the section, and it becomes the axis of the formula of release that he proposes in 10.9.) Paul's dissimulation is only poorly disguised, however. The Jews are not 'us' but 'them'; Paul's good will and entreaties are 'for them' (ὑπὲρ αὐτῶν) (10.1). Paul concedes the Jews' zeal (ζῆλος) for God (10.2). What is wrong with the Jews, says Paul, is not that they do not have zeal for God, but that this zeal is not informed by knowledge that *dikaiosunē* is God's alone (10.2-3).[202] They lack knowledge (ἐπίγνωσις) of God's justice (θεοῦ δικαιοσύνη); they do not put themselves under the law of God, but follow an idiosyncratic kind of justice (ἰδία δικαιοσύνη) (10.3).[203] The former not only takes precedence over the latter, it is its

αὐτῶν, οἱ τὰ ἐπίγεια φρονοῦντες (3.19), whose end is destruction, ὧν τὸ τέλος ἀπώλεια (3.19), and those who are citizens of the city of God, ἡμῶν γὰρ τὸ πολίτευμα ἐν οὐρανοῖς (3.20), whose bodies will be changed by a savior into glorious bodies, formed like his own, σύμμορφον τῷ σώματι τῆς δόξης αὐτοῦ (3.21), a savior whose power subjects everything to himself. Those enslaved by appetites are miserable and expunged. Ps.-Charondas (frg. 3), too, transfers religious initiation language to morals, possibly a characteristically Pythagorean feature (cf. Plato, *Gorgias* 493a-c). Other major cases of the use of initiatory terminology to moral context in Paul: the warning against being initiated in desires (Gal. 5.16); or the identification of the immoral with the uninitiated in the language of mysteries of 2 Cor. 4.4-9.

202. A similarly negative zeal is stirred among the Galatians by Paul's enemies, a zeal which is for no good, ζηλοῦσιν ὑμᾶς οὐ καλῶς (Gal. 4.17).

203. See Chapter 5, Diotogenes, frg. 1.2.2. Diotogenes' king in his capacity as judge who administers both public law and private law, ξυνός (or κοινός) and ἴδιος

demise (10.3-6). One living under the law is bound to the justice of the law, but the law, because of *parakoē*, is the paradoxical instrument of *hamartia* (7.12; 10.5). What they miss is that the end of law (τέλος νόμου[204]) is Christ and that his is a universal justice for all who have *pistis* (10.4).[205] Paul apparently means to make the law, a system of political (not solely religious) right, the good of everyone, not just of an elite; he can do so only if the ruler is universal as well. Paul's Christ/king (10.4) resonates with Plato's philosopher-king, with Aristotle's absolute king (*pambasileus*)[206] and with the Hellenistic Pythagorean king.

10.5-13. Sōtēria is the result of *dikaiosunē pisteōs* (10.5-11). The justice of the law (δικαιοσύνη νόμου) is for anyone who practices it (ὁ ποιήσας αὐτά) (10.5). The justice of Paul's legislator, however, is an

νόμος, emulates God's rule of the cosmos. As a magistrate of public law, the king effects the unity of the state; as dispenser of judgment in private affairs, the king brings about harmony among his subjects. Justice and law, *dikaiosunē* and *nomos*, are also indispensable for him as *euergetēs*, benefactor, who treats his people well and benefits them. This use reflects the changes in the legal vocabulary since Classical times. For Aristotle the contrast *koinos–idios* law distinguished natural law from state law. During the Hellenistic monarchies, *nomos koinos* was the king's law, the constitution of the kingdom; *idios nomos* or *logos* was the private law, the tradition of individual *poleis*, operative on local matters only. The *nomos empsuchos* of Hellenistic political treatises presses the king's authority to its logical limit and makes him the administrator of the natural law itself, effectively identifying king and God.

204. Peripatetic vocabulary, since the meaning is: the cause of law, the reason why law came into being in the first place, the natural end of the process of law.

205. For a succinct review of the *telos* controversy, see Jewett 1994: 40-42. He distinguishes between the *telos*=end (European Lutheran and Roman Catholic), *telos*=goal, fulfillment (Calvinist), and *telos*=both goal and termination. Though Jewett finds the third approach 'the least defensible from the point of view of exegetical method' (41), it is congruent with Aristotle. We recall that the notion of end, τέλος, is essential to Aristotle's thought, a part of his general philosophy of nature. 'Natural' is a teleological movement, a process leading toward the end proper to each thing, the raison d'être of each thing in nature. Hence the notion that the end is more natural than the beginning, or, in other words, that the end is the cause of the beginning. This is the λόγος, the rational purpose, the end, or the final cause. When Paul says that τέλος γὰρ νόμου Χριστὸς εἰς δικαιοσύνην παντὶ τῷ πιστεύοντι, the Aristotelian reading suggests that *Christos* (and *dikaiosunē pisteōs*) is the resolution and the superseder of the law. Thus *telos* may mean both 'termination' of the law, as Käsemann insists, and its goal.

206. *Politics* 3.1285b33.

expression of *pistis*. Paul exchanges the justice of the law, the *dikaio-sunē* of *nomos*, a matter of convention (10.5), for the *dikaiosunē* of *pistis*, a question of necessity (τὸ ῥῆμα; the sense here is practically one of objective necessity), of heart and mouth (10.8), of mind and discourse. The traditional formula, 'obedience to the law', is changed to *hupakoē pisteōs*, 'obedience of *pistis*' (1.5). This is the engine of the Christian *polis*.

Now, Paul delivers the formula of release: 'If you profess in speech that Jesus is your master, and have *pistis* in your mind that God caused him to rise up from the dead, you shall have *sōtēria*' (10.9).[207] This is a two-part, thought–language and *dikaiosunē pisteōs–sōtēria* formula: the mind, through *pistis*, knows the justice of God; the mouth, through language, proclaims one's *sōtēria* (10.10).[208] In other words, one speaks a new language, that of salvation, and has a new knowledge, that of God's will. This is the proper context within which to understand the need for a new language, as also the 'offense criterion' for the formation of the new language. Underlying this dynamic is the *parakoē–hupakoē* antinomy, the cause of fall–salvation. *Hupakoē* is knowledge, understanding, 'hearing' (see also 16.17-20), tantamount to *pistis*. To know is to hear (10.14). *Pistis* and knowledge are identified with one another. Their source and object is God's *dikaiosunē* (10.11). To express this, to recognize the rule of Christ, is to speak the language of

207. ὅτι ἐὰν ὁμολογήσῃς ἐν τῷ στόματί σου κύριον Ἰησοῦν καὶ πιστεύσῃς ἐν τῇ καρδίᾳ σου ὅτι ὁ θεὸς αὐτὸν ἤγειρεν ἐκ νεκρῶν, σωθήσῃ (Rom. 10.9). I agree with Barrett that the formula '*Iesous kurios*' belongs to the oldest stratum of Christianity (see 1957: 200-201 for possible origins). The *kurios–doulos* relation becomes the expression of a political system. Paul moves from the cultic into the civic.

208. The dual formula mouth confesses/heart believes, apparently echoing a Septuagintal quotation (Deut. 30.14), appears to be a Hellenistic formula. It is used by Hellenistic Pythagoreans and by others of Paul's contemporaries. Ps.-Zaleucus (frg. 1) makes it a matter of necessity that the citizens be convinced and believe, πεπεῖσθαι χρὴ καὶ νομίζειν, that the gods exist. Dio Chrysostom, who also knows the Hellenistic Pythagorean thesis that the earthly king is a copy of Zeus and that God is the leader of the world-state (this is also Stoic), emphasizes the store of debt the king owes the divine in very similar words: '[the ruler] will give first and foremost place to the divine not only confessing but also believing that there are gods, so that he too may have worthy administrators under him' (πρῶτόν γε καὶ μάλιστα θεραπεύσει τὸ θεῖον, οὐχ ὁμολογῶν μόνον, ἀλλὰ καὶ πεπεισμένος εἶναι θεούς, ἵνα δὴ καὶ αὐτὸς ἔχῃ τοὺς κατ᾽ ἀξίαν ἄρχοντας) (3.51). Dio makes a seamless transition from the religious motif to the political one.

The Political Paul

sōtēria, a new language (10.12-13). To declare the dominion of Christ is to eliminate any difference between Jew and Greek (10.12, cf. 3.22)—that is, to realize the Hellenistic ideal. To invoke this ruler (ἐπικαλεῖν αὐτόν) (10.12), to speak his name (τὸ ὄνομα κυρίου) (10.13), is to be saved. The (magical) power of the name is effective, however, only if one calls upon it with *pistis*—that is, if one knows and trusts God's *dikaiosunē*.

The Classical relation between *dikaiosunē* and *nomos* is transformed by Paul. *Nomos* is deconstructed and supplanted by *pistis*. The citizen is no longer under the *nomos* but under *pistis*. *Pistis* becomes a political term, connected with *dikaiosunē*. Unlike *nomos* (ethnic, conventional, human law), *pistis* is a universal, natural or divine, law. Its personification is Christ. *Pistis* is operative within the constitutional domain described by the *euaggelion*, a universal polity that makes no national, cultural, social or gender distinctions. Paul was not interested in practical jurisprudence or positive law as the Jews or the Romans understood them, but in the general theory of right and in justice (*dikaiosunē*) as the Greeks conceived it—natural, universal, divine law. Even so, like the Greeks, Paul seeks the application of this universal, divine law to the actual human political community.

10.14-21. How is the new language made comprehensible to its hearers? Paul's answer is solidly within the Greek and Hellenistic tradition: education, *paideia*, new knowledge (10.14-15, 17).[209] To know one must hear.[210] The fine rhetorical climax in 10.14-15 is *locus* of this

209. Ps.-Archytas (frg. 5c)—and also Diotogenes, in the *basileia* group—clamor for political education of the citizens so that the constitution would reflect in their mores and not just in public inscriptions. Most authors of the Classical tradition were consummately concerned with developing systems of education suited to the constitutions they favored, education which alone could guarantee the stability of the state. (See, e.g., Aristotle, *Politics* 5.1310a12-14; according to him, the endurance of a constitution depends on habit, customs, *ethea*, and these are slow in taking root [7.1334b6-13].) First-century writers such as Philo and Dio Chrysostom, on either side of Paul's active period, fully agreed with this. Paul's insistence on *hupakoē*, a call for learning, fits the framework.

210. Finney (1984, 1993) demonstrated that the cultural cliché that opposes the Hebrew word-hearing religion to the Greek image-seeing one is a fallacy. Perhaps the Greek–Hebrew split is better illustrated by the 'hear to know'–'hear to do' dichotomy, but this requires further reflection. The hearing–obedience nexus is arguably Hebrew, the rhetoric that proposes it is Greek.

sentiment: 'How are [people] to call upon him of whom they have not heard; and how are they to hear without someone to herald him; and how could there be envoys should they not be sent?' For Paul, listening, hearing, paying heed is the equivalent of *paideia*, Aristotle's habit-forming'. What Paul is producing here is a metaphysics of hearing and deafness, a theory of Christian *paideia*.[211] This new knowledge in effect consists of a new language, a Christ-language (ῥῆμα Χριστοῦ) (10.17).

To hear one must chance upon a messenger (κηρύσσοντος) (10.14). This herald must be sent (ἀποσταλῶσιν) (10.15), that is, must have the authority to disseminate the message (and Paul is such a one; 10.15; 1 Cor. 1.17). The telling-hearing axis describes both *parakoē* and *hupakoē*, the very dichotomy between Adam and Christ.[212] *Parakoē* is opacity to discourse, revolt against what is heard. It is equivalent to the *sarkic* (see 7.17). *Parakoē*, which refers to both pagans and Jews, describes a failure of reason, either because of lechery or because of hardness of heart, of uninhibited libido or excessive superego. It finds its direct counterpart in the Pauline political construct of the *doulos*. 'You', the Christians (as opposed to 'them', the deceivers) have *hupakoē* (16.19).

Now Paul again turns to his polemical leitmotif: How about the Jews? (This time, how about the Jews vis-à-vis this new knowledge and new language [10.16, 18-21; 11.1-36]?) That Paul is not in dialogue with the Jews but *is* at pains to build his *polis*, which will stand or fall according to whether the Jews participate in it, becomes clear in this discussion. If the Jews do not join, Paul's claim that his mission is to 'Jew and Greek alike' fails—and the succeeding contention, that he speaks to men and women,[213] free and slave, with no distinction,

211. Hearing–deafness (together with seeing–blindness) are sometimes paired by Isaiah (Isa. 29.18; 35.5; 42.18, 19; 43.8), yet note the surprisingly minimal relevance of the hearing–deafness motif in the Hebrew Bible.

212. See also sections on Rom. 5.12-21 and 16.17-20 for further discussion of this motif.

213. The male–female conflicting symmetry remains ambiguous throughout ancient thought; nothing matches the eccentric Platonic position in *Republic* 4.445b-5.457b, where women are equal with men; Hellenism mediates the gap by the large number of cults presided over by goddesses and, in general, by the increasing role of women in various religious practices and cults. In Paul, women form an essential part of Christian ideology. This trait, however, must not be exaggerated. Paul is not and cannot be gender-blind or effectively aware of the consequences of the patriarchal prerogative that imbues his world.

becomes questionable. In other words, the entire Pauline edifice is in danger of tumbling.

Many have not yet heard this language (10.16). Israel, however, heard (10.18) but did not understand (10.19-20). This, adds Paul, is because Israel resists persuasion and indulges in rejection (10.21), which is the same as saying that it is proud of itself, with no inclination to share its God or its messiah with others. Paul regards this as unconscionable sabotage of his own project, which is an effort to internationalize the Jews' heritage.

To clarify the distinction between ethnic Israel and 'true' Israel, Paul proceeds (11.1-36) to tell a 'mystery' (τὸ μυστέριον) (11.25), which, like most such self-styled revelations, is a rhetorical technique to explain God's paradoxical actions under the pretext of showing God's inscrutability.[214] A proleptic quality forms the core of such *mustēria*, for disclosure always follows closely on the tracks of the declaration of secrecy. Despite his perorations on the unfathomable mind of God (11.33-35), Paul offers revealing readings of this mind: that the fall of the Jews is a means for the salvation of Gentiles (11.11-24); that the *plērōma* of the Jews (their inclusion in the full number) is most beneficial (11.12, 25);[215] that the power of God changes things *kata phusin* (i.e. changes nature) and favors things *para phusin* (i.e. works against nature) (11.17-24);[216] that the inducement to 'disobedience' (i.e. *not* hearing, metaphysical deafness) which God effects can show his *charis* (11.28-32). Being privy to the mind of God is initiatory routine. An obscure, purportedly secret discourse on God is part and parcel of the philosophical language of the times. Neopythagoreans, Neoplatonists and Stoics all indulge in it. It is to Paul's credit that he does so only very seldom, and then mostly as a pretext to reaffirm or resolve major themes. Paul's appeal to secret knowledge is the equivalent of Plato's appeal to myth: to explain things that are too vexing or of a different order of logic. (It is difficult to determine, after all, what the ontological

214. In Greek thought the rhetoric of myth expresses the aporia of reason.

215. Is this 'full number' concept a numerical speculation? Or rather a presence, an inclusion? It is no mystical cipher, after all, but a condition of political life. The number is mystical only insofar as it is critical mass for political genesis. R. Stuhlmann's (1983) inspired expression is *eschatologische Mass*. See also Volf 1990; Scott 1993.

216. This is the giveaway of the principle of Christian language as well. It also reads like a direct strike at the Aristotelian principle of *phusis*. See below.

status of Paul's disclosures here is, whether this mystical language is symbolic and largely pro forma or whether Paul means to posit an actual, existing reality.)

11.1-10. The assault on Israel (11.1-10) begins with the 'I'm one of them' trope. Paul's Jewish talent for contradiction and Greek passion for inquiry combine in a rhetorical tour de force. Are obstinacy and the spirit of controversy (10.18-21) really the reasons Israel did not understand the good news, the new language? No, says Paul. Paul's discounting human proclivity and ethnic bias is the most striking feature of *dikaiosunē theou*, the core of Paul's discourse later in this section of the Letter. In the style of a hierophant, Paul tells about a division of Israel into an elect (ἐκλογή) (11.6), or remnant (λεῖμμα) (11.5), and the rest (οἱ λοιποί) (11.7). The criterion of election is God's *charis* (11.5-6), as against *erga* (11.6). (The contorted manuscript tradition of Romans 11 suggests how controversial this item of Pauline philosophy was.) Again working in a Classical and Hellenistic vein, Paul gives contemplation preeminence over activity. Paul further clarifies, in a remarkable way, the notion of *charis*. Not only 'the remnant', (*leimma*, the chosen Jews) (11.5) but also the hardened 'rest', (*hoi loipoi*, the obstinate Jews) have been so designated by God (11.7-10). *Charis* is the result of God's *dikaiosunē*; the decision, the sentence, is the expression of his justice.

11.11-24. This section discusses the special place of the Jews in the new world-order. Paul presents a perplexing idea: Israel's fall (παράπτωμα) (11.11-12) is the salvation, *sōtēria*, of the Gentiles (11.11). But while Israel's diminution (ἥττημα) is the Gentiles' increase, Israel's *plērōma* (πλήρωμα), its 'complete number', brings untold abundance (11.12). This is obscure, and Paul, aware of the obscurity, appeals to his apostleship for credibility (11.13). Paul's rousing the jealousy (παραζηλώσω) (11.11, 14) of the Jews, his sarkic kin (11.14), is the very means for saving them.[217] *Zēlos* (ζῆλος) belongs to the spirited, affective register

---

217. Diotogenes (frg. 1.2.1) places the king in the class of professionals, no different from such experts as the pilot, the charioteer, or the physician. Their mark of success is the preservation of the ship, chariot or the sick, respectively. The objective of the king's expertise is the salvation of his subjects' lives. *Sōzein*, *sōtēria* are, with Hellenistic kings, the central feature of the political leader. Paul applies whatever strategies are necessary to save people (Rom. 11.11; 1 Cor. 1.21; 10.33).

of the soul, and is active desire for emulation.[218] The Jews' envy, in other words, can cause a change of mind. In language reminiscent of initiatory practices, Paul discloses that the Jews' loss is the gain for the cosmos, their turnabout is death's loss, literally 'life [snatched] from the dead' (11.15).[219] Both syntactically and semantically, the dead (*nekroi*), those who reject Paul's mysteries, are the ultimate losers.

With the help of a complex simile (11.17-24) Paul further elaborates on the notion of *plērōma*. The text's ambiguity and difficulty may reflect scribal confusion. Essentially, however, it says that, while the *plērōma* could suffer lapses and fluctuations, it is a determined, constant number, a mystic Israel (cf. 11.25-26). This is a *mustērion*, warns Paul, and no one can boast of understanding it (11.25). But both the philosophically derived language of the argument and the contextualization of the argument by scriptural references clarify the point. Thus, asks Paul, if the branches 'by nature' of a wild olive tree could be grafted 'against nature' onto a cultivated olive tree, how much more could those who are 'by nature' branches of the latter be grafted onto their own tree (11.24)?[220] Paul 'corrects' Aristotle's theory of *phusis*. God can oppose that which is natural (*kata phusin*, the Jews, i.e. those lacking *pistis*). He may favor that which is contrary to nature (*para phusin*, the Gentiles, those possessing *pistis*) (11.20-24).[221] This is a philosophical expression of the idea, dear to Paul, of the superiority of *pistis* to *erga*. *Plērōma* is the correlative, one pole of a metaphysical

---

218. In Ps.-Ecphantus, the king, like God, inspires one, ζᾶλος, to emulation of his own nature (H 277.9-10, T 82.21).

219. εἰ γὰρ ἡ ἀποβολὴ αὐτῶν καταλλαγὴ κόσμου, τίς ἡ πρόσλημψις εἰ μὴ ζωὴ ἐκ νεκρῶν (Rom. 11.15). This *apobolē–proslēmpsis*, rejection–acceptance by God is another example of the contrasting sets of parallels common in Paul.

220. Horticulturally minded commentators are appalled at the cross-breeding process proposed by Paul. Normally a cutting from the *kallielaios*, the cultivated olive tree, is grafted on the *agrielaios*, the wild olive, to improve the stock. Although evidence for the practice suggested by Paul was found elsewhere (e.g. Philo, see Michel 1955: 275; Str-B: III, 291, *ap.* Black 1973:145), the point is not husbandry. I take this as an example of Pauline language reversal, an intentional dichotomy between the *modus operandi* of the divine power and the common philosophical distinction *kata phusin–para phusin*. This logically leads to the doxology of 11.33-36.

221. In 11.22 *chrēstotēs*, kindness of God is opposed to ἀποτομία, severity, a pun on its more common root meaning, cutting off.

binary the other term of which is the kenotic act of Christ in Philippians.[222] Hierarchically, the latter comes first.

11.25-36. The Jews, enemies of the *euangelion*, cannot, however, be dismissed for they hold sureties from God: election (ἐκλογή), gifts (χαρίσματα), call (κλῆσις) (11.28-29). Not only that, their hostility to *euangelion* is 'for you' (δι᾽ ὑμᾶς) (11.28): the *ethnē* (Greeks) share in God's *charis* because of the disobedience of the Jews (11.30), but *charis* to the *ethnē* will also encompass the Jews (11.31). The idea is that the Jews' failings made God render disobedience universal, so that his *charis* might reach all (11.32).[223] (As idiosyncratic as this approach is, it is required by the conditions of Hellenistic life. For Paul, *charis* displaces chance and fate—*Heimarmenē*, the cruel Hellenistic divinity—but, like *Heimarmenē*, *charis* cannot be avoided, coerced or contested.) *Charis* and *pistis* are, for Paul, the split equivalent of the philosophical Greek *aretē*, now unachievable by human effort alone. *Charis* is *aretē* coming from an outside source. *Pistis* is the other face of *aretē*, the individual aspect. Ever since Plato, *dikaiosunē* (the idea of the right, justice, virtue par excellence) has created the conditions for *aretē*. *Dikaiosunē* defines a society, that society in which the individual can fully reach his potential for *aretē*. *Dikaiosunē* is the answer to the seminal question, 'How ought we to live?' The meaning of the one depends on the meaning of the other. As complex a notion as *aretē* is, it is apparent that, for Paul, it does not go far enough in expressing this relation.[224] He replaces it with what he perceives to be a more appro-

---

222. The duality empty–full, the endless process that it engenders, is not only a fundamental notion of ancient medical thinking, but also describes the mechanism of desire as represented by Pausanias in Plato's *Symposium*, and constitutes an important theme in the *Gorgias*.

223. It is Hellenistic thought that first conceives of a brotherhood of humankind. Hellenistic Pythagoreanism makes every being a part of the universal harmony. For more detailed discussion of this doctrine see Chapter 5, section on Ps.-Ecphantus, frg. 1.1.

224. The term *aretē* is used rarely in Paul and is almost unknown in the canonical writings. On the one hand, it describes the ideal of the establishment; its reputation, grounded only too deeply in prevalent philosophical thought, makes it unserviceable. Paul uses it in Philippians (4.8), but only in a list of Stoic virtues—as *a* virtue, not as the concept of virtue. The polemic dimension of Paul's—and early Christians'—lexicon must be emphasized. On the other hand, for Paul, *aretē* doesn't reach far enough. A quality enabling one to live well, a philosophical

priate term for his system of thought: *pistis*. *Dikaiosunē pisteōs* becomes
the foundation of Paul's human political society. *Pistis* is the only way
to conceive of an *aretē* that can be part of a binomial, the other term of
which is a *dikaiosunē* fully consigned to God. *Dikaiosunē pisteōs* and
dikaiosunē theou are the two sides of the same coin, Paul's unified
politics.

*Romans 12.1–16.23: Upholding the Roman Empire
and Making It Last*

Paul's teleological reflection (12.1-8) confronts the issues of the human
end (12.1-3) and the end of the *polis* (12.4-5), and then continues by
examining the necessaries for a happy life. Platonic-Aristotelian thinking, as transmitted by Hellenistic Pythagoreanism and spread by popular
philosophy, is manifest throughout.

12.1-8. Any Christ-like individual has a *telos*. The end of the body,
sōma, is to be offered (παραστῆσαι) as a living sacrifice (θυσίαν
ζῶσαν) to God; it is to be a λογικὴ λατρεία (*logikē latreia*) 'rational
worship' (12.1).[225] (Incidentally, this verse is another test for the distinction and opposition between *sōma* and *sarx*.) What Paul is saying is
relatively simple and Classical (and consistent with his views in Rom.
1.24-32): flee from passions; return to reason; allow your soul its natural
hierarchy, its control by the rational. This way perception of God will
be truthful. How he says this, however, is baroque and Hellenistic. In
fact, this remarkable passage illustrates the genre of Hellenistic popular
philosophy very well. One of its main features is the mixing of dissimilar
discursive techniques—in this case, the vocabulary of religion with that
of philosophy, the language of intellectual contemplation with that of
civic obligation. The rarely used *latreia* had meant plain menial labor,
usually for wages, but by Hellenistic times, and particularly in that
Hellenistic document known as the LXX,[226] it had also acquired the

exigency, it fails the popular Hellenistic expectation of the same in the afterlife.
    225. Schlier observes that the exhortation is in the exact language of adjuration:
διὰ τῶν οἰκτριμῶν τοῦ θεοῦ, by the mercies of God (1958: 178-80, *ap.* Käsemann
1969d: 190). The passage abounds in cultic terminology and language of sacrifice.
    226. That this may be a septuagintal echo or even quotation does not discount the
force of the Hellenistic influence. Writes Talbert (1978: 1631, referring to Meeks,
Ginzberg and Jeremias): 'Although there is persistent rabbinic tradition that Moses

quasi-technical sense of cultic worship. In Hellenistic literature, *latreia* refers to the form of devotion that involves sacrifices or offerings to the divinity.[227] While it keeps this meaning in Paul, its implied sense of the *doulos*'s service to God makes it extremely well suited to describe the relationship between the Christian and God, the 'work' characteristic of the Christian *polis*. (*Latreuō*, the verb, has precisely this function in Phil. 3.3. In Rom. 1.9 it defines the work of Paul himself: he is a *pneumatic* servant of God.) In Rom. 12.1, *latreia* is not used metaphorically, but literally.[228] As a concept, *latreia* relates to *sōma* as the rational aspects of existence relate to the physical. *Logikē latreia* differs from other kinds of *latreia* in that it is worship that comes from knowledge—a peculiarly rational kind of service to God. *Logikē latreia* is an excellent example of late Hellenistic taste and culture: the use of unlikely intellectual material and eclectic semantic spheres to create florid, seemingly oxymoronic constructs like: 'rational worship'.[229] Exegetes and translators have attempted to solve the riddle of this difficult ex-

did not die but ascended to heaven, the native home for the view of Moses' bodily rapture was probably Hellenistic Judaism.' I read this to mean that even if certain topics formed the object of rabbinical utterances, since they can be traced back to the Hebrew Scriptures, it is their root in the Greek and Roman environment that accounts for their use and popularity in Jewish and Christian Hellenistic and Roman authors. For example, even though the Suffering Servant appears in Isaiah, the effectiveness of such a motif in Jewish communities of the diaspora and in Greek and Roman communities comes from its being a topos in pagan mythology, especially the treatment Heracles receives in Cynic and Stoic literature, or the employment of *theioi andres* or immortals in portraying political rulers. Likewise, even though Moses is said not to have died in the Scriptures, it is Aeneas and Romulus who inspire his portrayal in the works of Philo and Josephus.

227. Michel 1955, *ap.* Black 1973: 151.

228. Contra *TDNT*, *s.v. latreia*.

229. Casel 1924 in an article on λογικὴ θυσία argues that 'rational sacrifice'—the translation 'spiritual worship' in Käsemann (1969d: 190) both misdirects and obfuscates the issue—was part of the polemic of the Hellenistic enlightenment against the 'irrational' cultic offerings of the folk religions; it was then modified in a spiritualizing sense by Hellenistic mysticism in order to qualify the *oratio infusa* of the praise rendered to the Godhead as true divine worship by the individual endowed with *pneuma* as representative of the whole creation. See, for example, *Corpus Hermeticum* (Nock-Festugière 13.19.21) where a hymn of praise to God is called *logikē thusia* (Barrett 1957: 231). 1 Peter, whose author obviously knew this tradition actually has πνευματικὴ θυσία (2.5). (A metaphor used in 1 Pet. 2.2—'rational milk'—has the same fanciful quality.)

pression by translating *logikē* as 'spiritual', but this is dubious and does not resolve the problem. Paul's term for 'spiritual' is *pneumatikos*. *Logikē*, by contrast, covers the semantic field of 'logical', 'rational', 'intellectual', 'argumentative', 'discursive'. It describes the rational soul, *nous*. The coupling of *logikē* with *latreia* produces a Hellenistic chimera.[230] On the one hand, when connected to *sōma*, it suggests a thought-desire system, the rational-irrational formula characteristic of Pauline psychology. It *defines* the *sōma*. On the other, it refers to duty and accountability, that is, a mode of living that gains one access to heaven on the basis of service, just as in the life of the *polis*.[231] (It may be appropriate to notice here that Paul's statements could have been intended to be read at multiple levels. Intelligible on all those levels, they were supposed to offer the superficial reader an adequate meaning while providing the initiate with the satisfaction of discovering deeper truths.)

Going further from *sōma*, Paul turns to the *nous*.[232] The mind, reason,

---

230. Paul creates another such phantasmagoria in 1 Cor. 14.9: μὴ εὔσημον λόγον, 'unintelligible reason'. And *4 Macc.* 1.1 has another famous one: *eusebēs logismos*, 'pious reasoning'.

231. Diotogenes' *logikē epithumia* superbly illustrates the priority of *Realpolitik* considerations over the tenets of Classical psychology, the pre-eminence of immediate practicality over venerable doctrine. It is, furthermore, enlightening as an example of Hellenistic indulgence in ironical self-contradiction, the pleasure it takes in philosophical slapstick and playful fondness for equivocation. Craving and reason can be coupled in Diotogenes; body worship can have its source in the intellect in Paul. Paul must, like the other Hellenistic practical philosophers, mediate between the severe rational consistency of the Classical view of the world and the Hellenistic need to compromise in the face of emotions engendered by human fallibility. (See Chapter 5, section on Diotogenes, frg. 2.1, for further discussion.) Ps.-Zaleucus (frg. 8) links together reason and salvation. In Plato (*Crito* 51b) the same phrase (παρ' ἀνθρώποις νοῦν ἔχουσι καὶ σωθησομένοις) ends before 'salvation', an enlightening demonstration of what changes with Hellenism. It has only recently begun to be noticed that, in Hellenistic times, philosophical argument is a technique for social and political therapeutics, a means for achieving emotional balance and health. The twisted, composite philosophical metaphors that permeate Hellenism are an expression of medical dialectics, a modality of coming to terms with a wrenching and bewildering world. For an outstanding discussion of the complex range of Hellenistic ethics and politics and the realm of human emotions, see Nussbaum 1996.

232. While the role of educating the soul about God is given to the *nous* in the Classical philosophers, late Hellenistic thinkers confer this role on *pneuma*. (See

nous must disengage itself from this αἰών (*aiōn*, 'age'), must not be configured like this age, but must be changed, must discern the will of God, the good, the noble, the perfect (12.2).[233] The antithesis *schēma–morphē* ('conformed'–'transformed') is Platonic. Paul opposes outer, transitory change to inner, real conversion.[234] Practical reason (φρονεῖν) must know its proper limits;[235] its criterion must be the thinking of the wise, that is, the reasonable, prudent individual (σωφρονεῖν), who alone is the source of moral *aretai*.[236] *Sōphronein* is a salient term of Classical and, later, popular Hellenistic philosophy.[237] In Paul this is not just an ethical prescription but a political necessity, a prerequisite of the fellowship's endurance.[238] Paul's exhortation (in 12.3) of the members of the

Ps.-Ecphantus, frgs. 1.2 and 2.) Although Paul is a major exponent of pneumatic thought, here it is the *nous* that discloses God's will. Paul makes both *nous* and *pneuma* channels of access to God. His pneumatology retains the rational.

233. καὶ μὴ συσχηματίζεσθε τῷ αἰῶνι τούτῳ, ἀλλὰ μεταμορφοῦσθε τῇ ἀνακαινώσει τοῦ νοὸς εἰς τὸ δοκιμάζειν ὑμᾶς τί τὸ θέλεμα τοῦ θεοῦ, τὸ ἀγαθὸν καὶ εὐάρεστον καὶ τέλειον (Rom. 12.2). As Meeks insightfully argues (1986: 13), radical newness, as demanded in Rom. 12.2, is couched in terms of traditional moral rhetoric. This is a characteristic of Paul, the conservative radical.

On impermanence of human productions see Chapter 4, section on Hippodamos, frg. 4. We have already seen (in Chapter 5, Ps.-Ecphantus section, and above, section on Rom. 5.7), the importance of *agathos* in both Classical and Hellenistic philosophy and in Paul. See also Rom. 2.10; 3.8; 7.18-19; 14.16. Here (12.2) it is the attribute of God's will and is describing those who undergo an inner transformation by way of a mind transmutation.

234. See Black 1973: 151 and the references there.

235. For *phronēsis* as generator of cohesion and cooperation see Chapter 5, section on Ps.-Ecphantus.

236. Moxnes recognizes that *sōphronein* is used by Paul 'in a more classical (i.e. *political*) sense, as an antithesis to hybris' (1995: 221; my emphasis). On *sōphrosunē* see North's 1966 study.

237. This is recognized even by such staunch defenders of the Jewish Paul as Käsemann. He comments, rather ludicrously, that 'it indicates that this concept, like that of "spiritual worship", is not completely unknown even to Gentiles' (1969d: 192). *Sōphrosunē* is an Aristotelian quality (e.g. *Nicomachean Ethics* 3.1117b23); it covers a large range, from sound thinking to temperate feeling. The political foundations of prudence have been recognized throughout Western political philosophy. It is the core of, for example, Machiavelli's political theory in *Il principe*. See Garver 1987; Aron 1994.

238. Ps.-Charondas (frg. 8) urges each citizen to be prudent rather than rash, σωφρονεῖν μᾶλλον ἢ φρονεῖν. Paul urges the senior members of *ekklēsia* to avoid condescension.

community (ἀδελφοί, *adelphoi*, practically his term for the *ekklēsia*'s citizens [12.1]), not to be overbearing (*huperphronein*), but to be wise,[239] leads to the notion of membership in the body of Christ (12.4-5), the well-known political metaphor.[240ᶜ] Ὑπερφρονεῖν (*huperphronein*) is opposed to σωφρονεῖν (*sōphronein*), while both are shown to be forms of φρονεῖν (*phronein*), in a complex paronomasia and homophony. This word-play precedes yet another politically significant passage: *pistis*, just like *dikaiosunē* in the Classical philosophers and Hellenistic Pythagorean writers, is distributed by God according to a certain measure (ἑκάστῳ ὡς ὁ θεὸς ἐμέρισεν μέτρον πίστεως) (12.3c; see esp. 12.6).[241]

In characteristic Aristotelian style Paul moves (12.4-8) from the individual to the *polis*, from ethics to politics. Like Aristotle,[242] Paul connects one's proper end with the collective end, the good of one with that of the many, ethics with politics. This relation is made plain in the list of admonitions in 12.9-21. The idea of Christ as the body of which the people are members, connects again with the idea of the *polis*. As in one body there are many limbs (τὰ μέλη, *ta melē*), each with its own function (*praxis*) (12.4), so we, the many (*hoi polloi*), are one physical body (*sōma*) in Christ, but are limbs (*ta melē*) in relation to one another (12.5).[243] The body-and-limbs motif is present not only in Paul (12.4-5; 1 Cor. 12.12-27) but also in Ephesians and Colossians, documents of the Pauline school of thought. The political substratum of this parable, evident in the body-limbs topos of Mediterranean political culture,[244]

239. ἐν ὑμῖν μὴ ὑπερφρονεῖν παρ' ὃ δεῖ ἀλλὰ φρονεῖν εἰς τὸ σωφρονεῖν (Rom. 12.3).

240. E.P. Sanders calls this 'the language of participation' (1977: 453).

241. Insists Aristotle: the proportional is a mean and the just is proportional, τὸ γὰρ ἀνάλογον μέσον, τὸ δὲ δίκαιον ἀνάλογον (*Nicomachean Ethics* 5.1131b12). In Rom. 12.3, 'the mean relative to us' of *aretē* becomes, *mirabile dictu*, the measure of *pistis* granted by God, unequal but appropriate in each. In 1 Cor. 3.5 *pistis* is assigned by the lord, ἑκάστῳ ὡς ὁ κύριος ἔδωκεν. See discussion on Rom. 12.6.

242. *Nicomachean Ethics* 1.1094a28-29, 1.1094b7-12, 10.1181b12-24.

243. Note that 'parts' (*merē*) is the name Aristotle gives his full citizens in the ideal state—as opposed to 'necessary conditions' (*hoi ouk aneu*) (*Politics* 7.1328a 22-24; 7.1328b2-3, *passim*). Lexically different, the two notions are semantically similar. (See, e.g., Plato's τὰ τοῦ σώματος μέλη καὶ μέρη, the limbs and parts of the body [*Laws* 7.795e] harmonized by dancing, component of education.)

244. This is an adaptation of Menenius Agrippa's parable, in Livy's recounting of the events about the strife in Rome between the Senate and the *plebs* (*History of Rome* 2.33, year 494 BCE). Menenius Agrippa used the example of the belly and the

confirms the political meaning that Paul gives it. The body and its members (or the upper and lower parts of the soul) are common terms of political description; they belong to the repertoire of political concepts.[245] Here, in his talk about *sōma*, Paul expresses a concrete, physical reality—social and political in content—of the *polis* type. Body and body-politic stand in close relationship. Moreover, Paul preserves the *psuchē–polis* analogy, the mark of Greek political philosophy, and is ever-watchful against psychological transgressions caused by desires, the origin of political *stasis*.

Incidentally, both Plato and Aristotle make the analogy between *polis* and *psuchē*. Paul, however, though his psychology shares many elements with the *Republic* and the *Politics*, ubiquitously prefers the simpler body–state analogy. Paul's abandoning of the *polis–psuchē* similarity in favor of the body–state, *sōma–ekklēsia* synonymity, could have been mediated by the Hellenistic Pythagorean pseudepigrapha, which used both political similes.[246] Paul's preferred analogy not only tells us something about what was in fashion in late Hellenistic and Roman times— the era's more mechanical, less sophisticated, more ascetically focused view of the world—but, more important, it reiterates the critical, foundational role that the body of Jesus plays in Paul's political system.[247]

members in his speech to the seceding plebeians on Mons Sacer, a little hill outside Rome near the river Anio, and succeeded in convincing them to return to Rome. Every child knew this story. Its roots are Greek, with variations in Xenophon, Polyaenus and Aesop. It is also encountered in Cicero and Roman historiography. (See Ogilvie 1965: I, 312-13.) About the same time as Paul, Seneca thinks that the humans are the *socii* and the *membra* of the circumscribing universe, which is one and God (*Letters* 92.30). (Incidentally, this instance of political use of *socii* significantly weakens Sampley's 1980 legal *societas* construct. See also note below, for Rom. 15.25-26.)

245. Ps.-Archytas (frg. 5e) compares the state with a body, *sōma*, a family, an army, in that these entities are well organized when free (T 35.14), i.e. when they have within themselves, and not without, the cause of their salvation (T 35.11-12). Later in the same passage, Ps.-Archytas reiterates and unifies some of the major themes of his discourse: the necessity for the interiorization of the law in the morals and the customs of the citizens, for this process alone renders them complete, and the notion of distributive justice, for the law disburses to each according to one's own worth (T 35.21-24).

246. See, e.g., Ps.-Archytas, frg. 5e.

247. The importance that the image of the body has in Paul's mission, as envoy of Christ, is outstanding: in Gal. 6.17 he speaks about carrying on his body the mark or tattoos of Jesus; in the same letter, he reproduces before the Galatians' very

The natural end of *polis* is to be a Christian *polis*. Each of its members functions in this society according to *charis* (*kata charin*) (12.6), a variable. That is, each member does what he or she does according to the measure of *pistis* alloted him/her by God (ἑκάστῳ ὡς ὁ θεὸς ἐμέρισεν μέτρον πίστεως, 12.3): prophecy (in proportion to *pistis*: κατὰ τὴν ἀναλογίαν τῆς πίστεως, 12.6), service, teaching, exhortation, giving, leadership, compassion (προφητεία, διακονία, διδάσκων, παρα-καλῶν, μεταδιδούς, προϊστάμενος, ἐλεῶν, 12.6-8). Distributive justice is a result of God's *dikaiosunē* and is disbursed in proportion (*kat' analogian*) to *pistis*. The *analogia* theory is one of the most conspicuous Pauline borrowings from the Hellenistic Pythagoreans.[248]

eyes Christ's crucifixion (Gal. 3.1, cf. 2 Cor. 4.10; Phil. 3.10). He even evokes the scent of Jesus, 2 Cor. 2.15. See M.M. Mitchell 1992.) The importance of psychological factors for his politics, however, cannot be underrated. The role that desires, *epithumiai* of the *sarx*, play as a threat to the society he establishes is incessantly recalled, e.g., Rom. 1.24; 6.12; 7.7-8; 13.14; 1 Cor. 10.6; Gal. 5.16-24.

Moral degeneration has often been perceived in the West as a political risk. The ancient view revolved around the theory of the *psuchē*; it attributed the decline of political and moral excellence to the fixation with the disreputable ranges of the soul, the regions of *hubris* and lust. This is also the case in Paul, for example Rom. 1.18-32. The shift from psychology to somatology (the *sōma* receives its boost from the Hellenistic philosophers' internalizing of political participation), endows the body with new significance and extends to it moral status. This is prevalent in Paul. Essentially, the body first appears in a biblical writing with Paul. The Old Testament does not know it; it refers to creation as 'flesh and blood', and usually binds it to the spirit. In Paul's Jewish environment (rabbinic Judaism, Qumran), 'flesh' is mostly the designation for the realm of physical existence. The body has an ambiguous presence in the afterworld. Bodily resurrection is at best a national, not a universal, occurrence (in the Old Testament, esp. in Isa. 26.19 and Dan. 12.2); of the Hellenistic texts in the Apocrypha, only 2 Maccabees shows a belief in it, associated with political martyrdom. Sadducees and Essenes reject it; the Pharisees expect it for the righteous only (Josephus, *War* 2.119-66). Hellenistic and early Christian influences ring clear in later Jewish writings (*2 Enoch, 2 Baruch, 4 Ezra*). (See *DB s.v.* body, flesh, resurrection.) I am very skeptical about Stead's (1994: 87) linking the distinctive Old Testament anthropology with Paul's resurrection of the body. Be that as it may, resurrection of the body would have been incomprehensible to Paul's Gentile audience were it not prepared for it by the Hellenistic milieu's increasing focus on the body.

248. Aristotle's primary 'particular' justice is 'distributive justice' and consists in an award in geometrical proportion to civic merit (e.g., *Nicomachean Ethics* 5.1129a1-1131b24; *Politics* 3.1280a7-25). Plato speaks of equality by geometrical proportion in *Gorgias* 507e, cf. 483e, 488c; *Republic* 8.558c; *Laws* 6.756e-757e. In

The *charismata* ('gifts') define not merely a religious but also a political community. Yet all—prophet as well as nurse—are part of the same political body and all are informed by *pistis*. This fact throws light on the notion of *erga* as well. As used by Paul, the term does not simply mean 'works', but rather activity lacking in *pistis*.[249] Paul does not condemn work, but work done without *pistis* (12.6-8). (As Paul uses *pistis*, it is his invention, and its meaning is not easy to grasp. I think his contemporaries had as much trouble with it as we do.) The hierarchy of the *ekklēsia*[250] goes something like this: cult leaders ('ramblers', i.e. prac-

the last text Plato posits two kinds of equality, one of the 'old type' city and of the legislator, τὴν μέτρῳ ἴσην καὶ σταθμῷ καὶ ἀριθμῷ (757b), equality by measure, weight and number, an arithmetical equality, and one of the 'new city' and of God, Διὸς γὰρ δὴ κρίσις ἐστί (757b), the truly political equality, i.e. justice. Political justice, τὸ δίκαιον, is the equality given to unequals, in each case according to nature, τὸ κατὰ φύσιν ἴσον ἀνίσοις ἑκάστοτε δοθέν (757d); giving more to the greater and less to the smaller in proportion to each one's nature, μέτρια διδοῦσα πρὸς τὴν αὐτῶν φύσιν ἑκατέρῳ (757c). Political justice, proportional justice, rewards nature, it is not a simple bestowal of civic honor. The weight shifts from a matter of convention to a universal principle, from the visible to the invisible, from without to within, as it also does from a citizen's service to an individual's worth, from dilettantism to professionalism. Politically, the move is from law to justice, from *nomos* to *dikaiosunē*, from the particular, limited, ethnic, to the general, universal, natural. The geometrical proportion is great among both gods and human beings, ἡ ἰσότης ἡ γεωμετρικὴ καὶ ἐν θεοῖς καὶ ἐν ἀνθρώποις μέγα δύναται (*Gorgias* 508a). (See also A. Delatte 1922: 99-102, 111.)

The connection between Paul and Classical thinking is Hellenistic Pythagoreanism. For Ps.-Archytas (frg. 3a-b) the justice of nature is proportional justice, justice κατ᾽ ἀναλογίαν, justice that apportions to each according to his worth (33.23-25). The similarity of Ps.-Archytas's text to Rom. 12.6 goes even further in making the *kat' analogia* principle dependent upon the varying individual capacity for the good, a political not a moral relativity (33.25-27). This also corresponds to Callicratidas's treatment of analogy as natural principle of proportional justice (frg 3). The contribution of the Aristotelian tradition of *iustitia distributiva* to the Pauline *dikaiosunē* has been recognized recently by Nebe (1992: 134).

249. It is evident that the age of *pistis* begins with Christ. It is a concept intelligible only with the raising form the dead, Christianity's 'noble lie', or rather, 'good story', ψεῦδος γενναῖον (Plato, *Republic* 3.414d-415b).

250. In Paul's community leadership is indicated by προΐστημι, 'lead', 'care', 'preside', more specifically προϊστάμενος (Rom. 12.8), προϊστάμενοι (1 Thess. 5.12; see also 1 Tim. 3.4, 12; 5.17), and suggests the *collegium*, the club like environment in which early Christianity functioned. (For further discussion see Chapter 5, section on Sthenidas, frg. 1.2.) In Paul the term refers, in both instances,

titioners of prophecy, a revealingly Hellenistic breed of 'rational servants of God', illustrating the logic of irrational behavior), cult officers,
cult instructors, solicitors, givers, managers, social workers. It descends
from an exemplary pneumatic faculty, prophecy, to exemplary '*sōmata*',
attending to needs of the body.[251] This passage gives a priceless inside
view of the organization and activity of the early Christian *ekklēsia*.
While *ekklēsia* could be loosely read as identical to *polis*, particularly in
Christianity, here, as in the Greek world, it is technically speaking the
assembly of the *polis*, the supreme power in a democratic *politeia*.[252]
The *charismata* define the magistrates of the Christian state.

Paul deals next with practical matters affecting the *polis* in general
(12.9–13.7).[253]

to an *ekklēsia* activity or function. Note that in Romans the *proistamenos* must care
'with zeal', ἐν σπουδῇ, another reverberation of Sthenidas' text. In 1 Thess. 5.12,
proistamenoi, the leaders ἐν κυρίῳ, in the lord, stand between κοπιῶντας (not
unlike *hupēretai*, servants) and νουθετοῦντας, toilers and instructors (an equivalent
of *didaskaloi*). For ample examples of more or less official uses of the term, see
MM *s.v.* προΐστημι 541a-b.

251. The perplexity and the lack of analysis of the relationships among the
various classes within the *ekklēsia* are due primarily to the neglect in compre-
hending the political nature of this organization. See Käsemann 1969d: 193.

252. For Aristotle, the political definition of the constitution issues in a *politeia*,
'polity'. The teleological definition arrives at a middle class type of constitution
(*Politics* 3.1278b5-1280a6, 4.1290a30-1294b2; 3.1288a32-b6, 4.1295a25-1296b11).
This is a useful framework for reading Paul. Paul, too, prefers a composite constitution, one that mixes democracy with theocracy, *polis* and absolute monarchy. I
call it *doulocracy*, a kingdom of cheerful slaves. Teleologically, Paul's constitution
centers on the Christ-class.

253. Rom. 12.1–15.13 is often given as the best example of epideictic rhetoric in
a paraenesis (Reid 1992: 262). See Karris 1977: 95-98 for a review of the debate on
the paraenesis in Rom. 12–15.

Stowers reads Rom. 12–15 as a sketch of an ethic of community based on the
principle of *pistis* as adaptability (1994, ch. 11); he stops at the level of ethics. I
think it is a political charter based on *dikaiosunē pisteōs*, the gravitational force of
the *polis*. I agree with Käsemann here (1969d: 188-89, 1969b: 196-97), who refers
to 'ethics' in Romans always in quotation marks; the New Testament possesses
only in a very small degree 'an "ethic" in our sense, i.e. a system of morality
developing logically out of a single nucleus' (1969d: 188).

Although Paul lacks a formal plan of exposition, I do think that Nygren (1949:
412) is right to identify a structural plan, even if not ethical but political. This
section is major evidence that Paul does not follow Jewish and ethical but Greek
and political models. There is nothing here of the 'casuistry' (Käsemann 1969d:

12.9-21. Paul starts this section with a moral disquisition, a concise manual on moral excellence. As has been noted, Paul, like Aristotle, connects the individual's proper end with the collective end, the good of the individual with that of the many, ethics with politics. The relation of the ethical to the political is made plain in the list of admonitions in Rom. 12.9-21. For all its monotony, Paul is driven incessantly to disburse practical recommendations. It is not here that Paul's real interests lie; but duty comes first, and he delivers. The paraenesis has a menu-like character. Advice on the good life is the leitmotif of much contemporary ethical thought and a theme of most Pauline letters.[254] Such lists are an intrinsic, even if not the most exciting, part of any itinerant philosopher's work, and Paul—who, after all, lives off his speeches—never tires of responding to the moral apprehensions of the individual.

The essence of Paul's ethics is simple: hate the evil and stick to the good (12.9), or, somewhat more profoundly, 'clobber' the evil with the good (12.21). Paul assumes that what good and evil are is known by *suneidesis*, conscience, a universal. Deeper inquiry into this—the more interesting question—falls outside the scope of Paul's 'anxiety ethics'. Some of the rules Paul lists are commonplace, common-sense Hellenistic injunctions: be not idle, be steadfast in affliction, cultivate hospitality, rejoice with those who rejoice, cry with those who cry, consider what all human beings call good (12.17). To follow the prudent, the sage, the one with practical knowledge is an idea that goes back to Classical times. Some of Paul's admonitions are Hellenistic Pythagorean or Stoic in flavor, but Pauline in emphasis: be of one mind (a political precept under an ethical guise, 12.16), be like the lowly (ταπεινοί, 12.16), praise the persecutor (12.14). Some are of common Jewish and Near Eastern store: love each other like brothers, rejoice in hope, be constant in prayer, give alms. (Greek practical advice is conjoined with Oriental patriotic injunction.) Some prescriptions reveal strains of Jewish and mystery-religion traditions: live by *pneuma*, be slaves of God. And some injunctions may come from a Q-type tradition: do not do evil for evil, do not avenge yourself but leave it to 'the wrath'.

Behind the ethical exhortations lies a political concern. All these ethical *sententiae* have a politically inspired overall topic: *agapē*, 'love'.

188, 190; 1969b: 197) expected from even remote Jewish influence.

254. It takes the form of *sententiae* loosely connected, *Stichwort*-like (see Black 1973: 153-54).

Paul exhibits a careworn concern for unity and agreement within his communities and often speaks against division and strife. In the end, the good (12.9), as in Ps.-Ecphantus (frg. 3.2), is an element of the political. Likewise, certain of Paul's ethical formulations echo ideas encountered in Hippodamos (and in Aristotle): warnings against social iniquity and even economic surfeit, and the dangers to sociality and social stability that they present. Inherent in the political structure that Paul is creating is the requirement to provide for and attend to the social needs of its members (e.g., Rom. 12.13; 2 Cor. 8.3).

As we have already seen (in chapter 3), *koinōnia* is the center of Paul's political system. (For the Greeks, *koinon* is the form of the *polis*, a bond, a ligature, both political and aesthetic, the city as political association and as artistic beauty, harmonious on both accounts. The latter aspect of the Pauline *koinos* has so far been ignored.) The term is used by Paul[255] as by Classical Greek thinkers,[256] to designate a political society. Paul often uses *koinōnoi* as the name for the citizens of his community.[257] In Rom. 12.13 the term κοινωνοῦντες (*koinōnountes*) has a different meaning. Paul's is the first attested use of *koinōnia* for charitable contribution.[258] In this last use of the term, one hears an echo of Ps.-Charondas (frg. 10), who urges the creation of a system of charity and social assistance.[259] The usage is consistent with the social vocabulary of the *polis*.[260] It suggests the solidarity and generosity that are the very fiber of the *polis*'s social fabric. The main focus of the famous Pauline collection to Jerusalem, most likely a project originating with Paul and based on the tradition of temple contribution, is to help bring unity between the Greek and Jewish *ekklēsiai*.[261]

In Rom. 12.16, a passage remarkable for the use of the *phroneō*

255. 1 Cor. 1.9, cf. 1 Cor. 10.16; Phil. 1.5; 2.1 [cf. 2 Cor. 13.13]; 3.10; Phlm. 6, cf. 17; see also Gal. 6.6.

256. E.g. Thucydides 3.10; Plato, *Symposium* 182c, *Republic* 5.466c; Aristotle, *Politics* 1.1252a7.

257. E.g. 1 Cor. 10.18; 2 Cor. 1.7; 8.23.

258. See Rom. 15.26; 2 Cor. 8.4; 9.13; Gal. 6.6; see also 1 Tim. 6.18.

259. This idea is encountered in the Classical political thinkers and the Hellenistic Pythagoreans. See Chapter 4, section on Ps.-Charondas, and Chapter 5, section on Ps.-Ecphantus (frg. 4).

260. A 140 CE papyrus uses the revealing expression κατὰ κοινωνίαν, 'belonging in common'.

261. Rom. 12.13 (verb); 15.26; 2 Cor. 8.4; 9.13. See also Georgi 1992; Verbrugge 1992.

semantic group,[262] Paul urges the community, 'Be of the same mind toward each other' (τὸ αὐτὸ εἰς ἀλλήλους φρονοῦντες), that is, to live in harmony, a use of *phroneō* consistent with another Hellenistic Pythagorean, Ps.-Ecphantus. For Ps.-Ecphantus, *phronēsis* is the cause of bonding and unity,[263] an ancient Pythagorean motif; it appears in Plato's *Philebus*, where intelligence and wisdom, *nous* and *phronēsis*, order and govern the universe (28d). *Phronēsis* is instrumental to fellowship and sociality. Paul warns against misdirected use of *phroneō* that may lead to discord in a diverse community: 'Do not think proud thoughts [μὴ τὰ ὑψηλὰ φρονοῦντες], but associate with the humble; do not think that you are wise [μὴ γίνεσθε φρόνιμοι παρ᾽ ἑαυτοῖς]' (Rom. 12.16). Romans 12.17 continues the idea: 'Take thought for what is noble in the sight of all people' (προνοούμενοι καλὰ ἐνώπιον πάντων ἀνθρώπων). *Phroneō* (as well as *[pro]noeō*) is a community-building vector not least because it connotes prudence and self-restraint. Paul presses the meaning further to suggest humility.

13.1-7.[264] Paul's genius was to create of a parallel state that posed no immediate threat to the existing political structure, the Roman state.[265] By Paul's time there was already a longstanding tradition, running from Polybius to Cicero to the Augustan poets, that the Roman common-wealth should be the model for an ideal state.

In Romans 13, Paul makes his defense of Roman government. All political power is from God (οὐ γὰρ ἔστιν ἐξουσία εἰ μὴ ὑπὸ θεοῦ) (13.1). This holds true for the authorities in place (13.1). Subjection is owed him who rules as a ruler (ἐξουσίαις ὑπερεχούσαις); that is, with God's sanction (13.1).[266] (*Exousiai* are Roman magistrates; Josephus,

262. See also Rom. 8.6, 7; 12.3.

263. H 279.16-17, T 84.5-6.

264. The prodigious literature generated by Rom. 13 has been surveyed by Riekkinen 1980.

265. As Moxnes observes, Paul not only counsels his communities to avoid conflict with society (1995: 215, cf. Malherbe 1987, esp. 95-107), but also works within 'the given structures of the Roman Empire' (216). That Romans 13 is steeped in Hellenistic political terminology and refers to state and city officials and administrative offices has long been observed (see esp. Strobel 1956, 1964, Unnik 1975; *ap*. Moxnes 214 nn. 23 and 24).

266. Note the difference from Thrasymachus's argument: to rule as a ruler meant as a professional, as an expert in the art of politics. In Paul the degree in political sciences is conferred by God.

for example, calls the Roman procurators of Judea by this name.[267])
Therefore, opposition to rulers is opposition to God, and those guilty of
it will stand trial (κρίμα λήμψονται) (13.2).[268] Paul makes resistance to
governing authorities a violation of divine order. Good and evil (defined
in 14.20-21) are described, and their sphere is shown to be not ethical
but political. The ruler is the *diakonos*, the servant of God. God is the
source of imperial authority;[269] the ruler defends the good (τὸ ἀγαθόν)
and the doer of good; he is the instrument of God's wrath (ἔκδικος εἰς
ὀργήν) against the bad (τὸ κακόν) and the evil-doer (13.3-4). The
function of the *diakonos* is also clarified. He is the magistrate and
executive power: he hands down the verdict (κρίμα), and holds the
sword (μάχαιρα). The concept of power that Paul espouses here is
Oriental and Hellenistic. Does this mean that it is completely divorced
from Classical Greek political thinking? At first glance, it might seem
so. But one must not forget Aristotle's fondness for a *pambasileus*
autocracy.[270] I am not claiming that Classical political thinkers spoke in
favor of despotic government. And, given the role theocracy plays in
the system Paul espouses, Paul's theory of political power necessarily
differs from that of the Classical philosophers. But, even here, Paul
resembles the Classical writers in his outstanding interest in political
thinking, beyond the narrower concern with ethics. Paul shows that
even absolute control of power does not exclude political reflection.

Paul's exhortation to obedience to the establishment (13.1-2) has made
many a critic wonder. It is, however, not only consistent with Hellenistic
political thinking but, to Paul's mind, the very framework for his politi-

267. *War* 2.350 (*ap.* Barrett 1957: 245).
268. A similar point is made by Ps.-Zaleucus, frg. 8, who links salvation to
obedience to laws and government officials.
269. As God bestows political power on the human ruler, so can God bring ruin
upon the whole political structure. 1 Thess. 5.3 suggests that the entire Roman
power, *pax Augustana* itself, represented by its slogan εἰρήνη καὶ ἀσφάλεια, 'peace
and security', is easily overthrown by Christ's coming. Thessalonians is, however,
Paul's uniquely eschatological document.
270. It is also worth recalling that both Plato and Aristotle flirted with actual
despots. Plato courted Dionysius I, *stratēgos autokratōr* and *archōn* (cf. Rom. 13.3)
of Sicily, though he gained only personal humiliation in reward. And Aristotle, the
great theorizer of the political game and the advocate, in his depiction of the ideal
city, of a system of power in which ruler and ruled take turns, praised Hermeias, the
monarch of Atarnaeus, as Godlike—for which Aristotle was sent into exile in 322
BCE.

cal vision. Ps.-Zaleucus (frg. 8) ties salvation to obedience to laws and
officials (ἄρχοντες).[271] In the same vein, Ps.-Charondas (frg. 9a) urges
good will toward and obedience and veneration of the magistrates, who
oversee the city's hearth and the salvation of citizens (ἄρχοντες γὰρ
ἑστιουχοῦσι πόλεως καὶ πολιτῶν σωτηρίας). *Archontes* (sing. *archōn*)
is the Greek word used to translate the Latin *consul* and *praefectus* (a
governor of an imperial province), as numerous inscriptions attest. In
the two notorious passages in which Paul speaks about the established
political powers (Rom. 13.3; 1 Cor. 2.6), however, *archontes* is a generic name for rulers, authorities or officials. To them is owed obedience
as appointees of God and defenders of the laws (Rom. 13.1-4). Payment
of taxes is due to them as contractors for God (λειτουργοὶ θεοῦ)
(13.6).[272] Paul's vocal approval of taxation (13.6-7) is perhaps his most
overt consent to the existing political regime. Paul understood the
political advantages of Christianity and used them to strengthen the
Roman political system, which he admired and endorsed.[273] Echoing the

271. A Classical Pythagorean concept, known from Aristoxenus (in Iamblichus,
On Pythagorean Life 196, 224; *ap.* A. Delatte 1922: 192 n. 2). The Pythagorean
akousma 'Do not pluck a crown', interpreted in the Hellenistic sources as 'Do not
transgress a city's laws, which is her crown', is applied by Thom (1994: 11) to
Rom. 13.1-7; 1 Tim. 2.1-2; Tit. 3.1.

272. *Leitourgoi* are public officials who carry out public works for the state
(Barrett 1957: 247). They are also farming lucrative contracts from the government.
That rulers are subservient to God is a new idea with Hellenistic political writers
(see Chapter 5, section on Sthenidas, frg. 1.2). At the same time the notion that their
authority is from God, that they are God's stand-ins, is a major principle of Hellenistic political theory, be it Greek or Jewish. The divine privilege inherent in kingship is central to the *basileia* group of Hellenistic Pythagorean writings (Ecphantus,
Diotogenes and Sthenidas). In Hellenistic Judaism, canonical Daniel, a political
treatise in its own right, expresses this idea in no uncertain terms (Dan. 2.21, 37-
38). Rabbinic Judaism retains the notion of divine sanction for rulers: Rome is
appointed by God despite its having destroyed the Temple and having slain pious
Jews (Str–B: III, 303-304, *ap.* Black 1973: 160).

Elliott's (1994: 217-26) suggestion that Paul speaks here about a particularly
volatile episode of abusive tax collection is unconvincing and even pathetic. His
reductive approach transforms a major Pauline political statement about government into a narrow issue of fleeting significance.

273. Paul's deftness in manipulating the system by working against its self-
negating proclivities is so successful as to camouflage his own wit when castigating
its representatives. Throughout Rom. 13.1-7, the irony is veiled (to incomprehen-
sion) as a political stereotype. 'Fear the governing officials' may sound as an

political dogma of imperial Rome,[274] Paul declares that all political power is from God (13.1). But, in enjoining his hearers to obey the divinely sanctioned government, Paul is also reiterating Hellenistic Pythagorean political thought. Diotogenes (frg. 2.2.1), for example, stated nearly the same thing in his theory of the divine right of monarchy: leadership is from God (ᾧ δέδωκεν ὁ θεὸς αὐτῷ τὰν ἀγεμονίαν).[275]

That the king is imitator of God is a Hellenistic Pythagorean cliché. Imitation necessarily implies lower standing. When Sthenidas (frg. 1.2) calls the king *huperetēs*, servant, however, he is expressing a less common idea. In Rom. 13.4, 6, the ruler is unequivocally presented as God's *diakonos* in executing justice and his *leitourgos* in collecting taxes. The remarkable thing about this well-known yet insufficiently understood passage is that it is not a *religious* assessment of political power (an expression of religious servitude of the king to God prevalent in the ancient Near East), but a social and economic one. Sthenidas and Paul are both giving voice to a novel idea: the monarch as God's

irreproachable advice to the authorities' ear but, these are, unbeknown to themselves, slaves to God as well (13.1). (On the other hand, add the disputed Ephesians and Colossians in an apparent gloss on Rom. 13.1-7, these authorities are of an abject kind: they are masters κατὰ σάρκα [Eph. 6.5; Col. 3.22]. The model of slavery is that to Christ, ἐκ ψυχῆς [Eph. 6.6], and the fear is of the *kurios*, the heavenly master [Col. 3.22].) Paul must have laughed when writing τῷ τὸν φόβον τὸν φόβον, (show) fear to whom fear (is owed) (Rom. 13.7). Such admonitions function perfectly well at two levels, the Roman establishment and the divine government, and actually the interplay is so flawless that the distinction becomes lost. The meaning remains ambiguous even in 1 Cor. 2.6-8, where the secret and hidden wisdom of God, θεοῦ σοφίαν ἐν μυστηρίῳ τὴν ἀποκεκρυμμένην (2.7)—divulged by Paul—eludes the rulers (2.8), who are doomed to pass away (2.6). The emphasis on *aiōn* points also toward cosmic rulers. Be that as it may, it is the ruler not the system that would go, the master not the household that fails. There is no sense of theologically rooted political violence in Paul. This is a major distinction between Paul and the Judaism of his time. Nothing is more foreign to him than insurgent radicalism. Vigilante action is conspicuously missing. There is no culture of religious violence in the Pauline literature.

274. It is encountered in Philo, Seneca, Aelius Aristide, Dio Chrysostom, Pliny the Younger or Themistius; it is found also in Tertullian and Eusebius, to name but a few. See Chapter 5, section on Diotogenes, frg. 2.2.1.

275. *Kreitton*, of the Thrasymachus source, a tenet of political power, is, in Ps.-Ecphantus, a divine entitlement of the God-elected king. Similarly, in Rom. 13.1-7, Paul finds in the judicial office of the ruler the clearest divine imprint.

servant. The notion that the king is the lackey of God—and thus the unequivocal indication of the king's subordinate office—is seldom seen in ancient political reflection before the first century CE.[276] From then on, however, the notion of the king as the servant of God is encountered increasingly frequently, and it will go on to become a central idea in the monarchic theories of Byzantine and medieval times.[277]

Paul's use of πράσσοντι (*prassonti*) in 13.4, where he speaks of the ruler as the executor of God's rage on the scofflaw, also belongs to the political field. In Ps.-Charondas (frg. 2) *prattein* is used absolutely, in a political sense.[278] The political meaning, although not the most common, is encountered both in Plato, where it means to manage state affairs, to take part in government,[279] and in Aristotle, who uses it to refer to men engaged in public affairs and in politics.[280] In the absolute sense, without any addition, as in Ps.-Charondas, the term appears in Xenophon,[281] in Plato,[282] and in Demosthenes.[283] Paul's use of the term is consistent throughout and is entirely congruous with this configuration. Used eight times in the Letter to the Romans, it never just means 'do [something]'. It always figures in a direct or implied legal or political context: actions violating God's decrees and incurring death (Rom. 1.32, used twice, cf. Gal. 5.21); actions attracting God's judgment (Rom. 2.1-3, used twice); 'doing' the law (2.25); actions that escape one's understanding and are committed as a result of *akrasia*, weakness of the will, but which confirm the good of the law (7.15-19, used twice); and, finally, here (13.4), where the word denotes actions leading to civil or criminal lawsuits and

276. Paul's title *doulos Christou*, slave of Christ, or the reference to Christ as *doulos* in Phil. 2.7, are of the same order of reasoning. See Chapter 5, section on Sthenidas, frg. 1.2, for further discussion.

277. See L. Delatte 1942: 281, Dvornik 1966. In Paul, the value that informs the Christian *polis* is, above all, *tapeinophrosunē*, humility (Phil. 2.3), the slave's condition.

278. A. Delatte 1922: 195 n. 1.

279. τὰ πολιτικὰ πράττειν...πράττειν τὰ πολιτικὰ πράγματα (*Apology* 31d). Also in *Symposium* 216a, τὰ δ' Ἀθηναίων πράττω.

280. [οἱ] τὰ κοινὰ πράττουσι καὶ πολιτευομένοις (*Politics*, e.g., 7.1324b1).

281. 'of qualified statesmen', ἱκανωτάτω λέγειν τε καὶ πράττειν (*Memorabilia* 1.2.15, cf. 4.2.1, 42).

282. 'the government', [οἱ] ἐν ταῖς πόλεσι πράττειν (*Protagoras* 317a).

283. '[T]o take part in politics and to govern', πολιτεύεσθαι καὶ πράττειν (*On the Crown* 18.45). See LSJ *s.v.* πράσσω 1460b.

punishable by the official authorities.[284] Paul must be seen through the
Hellenistic political looking-glass.[285]

The necessity of subjection (ἀνάγκη ὑποτάσσεσθαι) (13.5) may point
to Hellenistic fatalism. In Paul, however, this *anankē* of submission is
assessed wholly positively:[286] it steers one clear of God's anger and is
demanded by *suneidesis*, conscience, knowledge of the good.[287] Political
anankē is determined by God's *dikaiosunē* and by human psychology
(see 12.5). The individual's act of conscience, *suneidēsis*, refers to
subjection to rulers or to submission to the law of the *polis*, a political
conscience demanded by membership in the state (13.5; 2.15). Applying the Pythagorean theory of musical harmony to politics, Ps.-Ecphantus
writes that each being is intimately linked to the universe and is
compelled into its movement and that, because of this, common order
and individual security are affirmed.[288] This is the force of *anankē*. In
Rom. 13.5, Paul argues that this power compels submission to political

284. Or, in other letters, actions done as the master's envoy (1 Cor. 9.17), or
πράσσειν τὰ ἴδια, 'mind your own business', with the sense of doing what is right
for the community (1 Thess. 4.11), or the generic, supreme, ardent exhortation, 'do
what you saw me doing' (as a founder of your community and a propagator of the
euangelion, as an envoy of Christ) (Phil. 4.9).

285. The notion that the magistrate is an executor of God's wrath (13.4) points to
a technical expression of Roman law: *ius gladii*. It meant 'the power to punish
criminal individuals' (*Digesta Iustiniani* 2.1.3). The authority extended to the death
penalty. This right belonged to the Roman emperor; he could delegate it to the
legati, the governors of provinces, and to the prefects in Rome (A. Berger 1953:
529a; Barrett 1957: 247).

286. In 8.5 the same verb, *hupotassein*, is used to indicate submission to God's
law; in 13.1, the subjection is to authorities. In 1 Cor. Paul applies it to mastery
over the *pneuma* (14.32), the subservience of women (14.34) and subjection to
leaders of the house-church (16.16). Apparently, Paul uses it in the technical sense
of a formal, mandatory subjection to a legitimate authority. It describes an explicit
relationship of subordination, of the kind that makes a political association
effective. This subjection implies no oppression and ruthlessness but order and
concord. *Hupotassein* differs from the much more common *hupakouein*, obedience,
in that the latter lacks the formality and decorum of the first.

287. Lietzmann 1933 paraphrases the verse: 'not only because of the wrath, but
out of conviction'. At the other end, Käsemann reads it: 'in the knowledge of the
binding summons of God addressed to you' (1969b: 213). I cannot agree either with
the moral load of the first or with the theological burden of the latter. The term is
taken from the philosophical lexicon.

288. See Chapter 5, section on Ps.-Ecphantus, frg. 1.1.

authority. The mechanisms at work within this *ananke* are *orge* and *suneidesis*, God's anger and human conscience. For both Paul and Ps.-Ecphantus, the state is the epitome of order and of justice, of public and individual salvation.[289]

From this point, Paul continues with matters particular to the Christian *polis* (13.8–15.13): first psychological (love, 13.8-10; pneumatic psyche, 13.11-14) and then political (attitude toward the new members of the compact, 14.1-16); essence of Christian polity, 14.17–15.13.

Excursus: A Note on Moxnes, Winter and Elliott

Halvor Moxnes has, in two studies (1988, 1995), argued for Paul's concern for the unity of the *polis*, inquiring into the political aspect of Pauline thinking. In his 1995 article Moxnes draws an excellent parallel between Paul and Dio Chrysostom that underlines the political content of Rom. 12.1–13.7. Moxnes investigates the critique of the honor culture within the Hellenistic city as a threat to the unity of the *polis*. While the benefaction system was a central feature of the Hellenistic city culture and its life, a number of Hellenistic authors are keenly aware of the conflict and difficulty inherent in the concept and delivery of benefaction, especially the feature of pursuit of recognition that motivates it. As Dio shows (*Discourses* 44, 66), renown is the result of being a benefactor (εὐεργέτης) and of undertaking public services (λειτουργίαι). But the rivalry that this fashion induces imperils the very structure it strives to enhance. Dio's criticism goes beyond fame-hunting and extends to the political system that invites and cultivates it, the Hellenistic city and its citizens. Dio's views of honor are colored by the intensity of his own involvement in politics; he considers that competitive, discord-causing lust for repute should not animate the city elite, but the reward of mutual love and friendship. For Dio a *polis* is a genuine *polis* if it is united and harmonious: 'truly Hellenic' means 'free from turmoil, and stable...refraining from discord and confusion and conflict with one another' (44.10).

Moxnes argues that in Rom. 12.3-16 Paul continues the Hellenistic 'honor discourse'; this is shown, according to Moxnes, by the larger context provided by Rom. 13.1-7, which brings in the 'honor culture' of Roman society; Rom. 12 and Rom. 13 are set in counterpoise, thinks Moxnes, the small, peripheral Christian community to the Roman government, the 'inner room' to the forum (1995: 214); according to Moxnes, the quest for honor within the Christian community is contrasted with the accepted norms of fame-seeking in the world at large (218). The point that for the common good of the city concord and harmony must prevail over discord and disunity, emphasized by Moxnes (229) and abundantly illustrated by both Paul and Dio, is well taken, though Moxnes thinks it Stoic (230). The source of this is Hellenistic, it is true, but found primarily in the writings called Hellenistic Pythagorean.

---

289. See concluding remarks on Ps.-Ecphantus, Chapter 5.

My critique of Moxnes's analysis is that the confusions in his study come from his insistence that Paul works in a reduced, limited, ancillary *polis*, not seeing that for Paul the community is the *polis*, the real, great, grand *polis*. Still, Moxnes rightly observes that in Rom. 12.3-16 Paul elaborates upon 'the Hellenistic discussion of concord versus conflict in the city...' (220), and that in this passage Paul 'uses a pattern of Hellenistic exhortation about the "proper" life in the polis' (223). For Paul, the Christian community is not merely a part, a fragment, a marginal section, of the Greek *polis*; it is not its humble relative, existing at the edge of the *polis* and consciously inferior to it, but is the *polis* itself. In 12.1–13.7 Paul transfers the language of the Hellenistic *polis* to his Christian community, not only because he conceives of it in the same way, but also because his *polis* is alone genuine and is meant to replace the former one.

Furthermore, Moxnes is oblivious to the crucial political significance of μέτρον πίστεως in Rom. 12.3c, about which he has nothing to say in his exegesis of Rom. 12.3-16 (see 223). (Incidentally, Moxnes mentions a 'reversal motif' [230], according to which, in contrast with honor culture, humility becomes an ideal, and he sees it as rooted in Jewish Hellenism. Debasement as producing glory is a Greek Hellenistic motif found in the Hermetic literature, the Gnostic material and the Greek Hellenistic novels.)

Another of the very few scholars to pay attention to Paul's political thinking is Winter 1994. Arguing, against Meeks, that the early Christians were not 'ambivalent' toward the city, Winter compares some New Testament and especially Pauline injunctions with Greco-Roman civic activities. His study is useful insofar as it integrates the Christians into the *politeia*, understood as the domain of public life in general. Winter, however, focuses on the Christians in the context of benefactions, and by doing so makes the Christians' participation in the Greek and Roman civic life implausible while he oversimplifies their involvement in it. Equally importantly, Winter does not see that the Christian attachment to the *polis* refers primarily to the Christian *polis*, and that the social and public endeavors apply to this, more restrictive *polis*, even while it replicates the Greek model.

Elliott's 1994 study on the politics of Paul, attempts to make Paul not only palatable but even pertinent to liberation theology. The provocative work is packed with contradictions and is better suited to a discourse on oppression and liberation, a modern political theme, than to one on the Pauline political concerns.

13.8-14. Agapē, love, love of the other (ὁ γὰρ ἀγαπῶν τὸν ἕτερον) (13.8), the overarching principle of the Christian *polis*, is understood as absence of wrongdoing against one's neighbor (ἡ ἀγάπη τῷ πλησίον κακὸν οὐκ ἐργάζεται) (13.10, cf. 13.8).[290] The exhortation to love—so common in the earliest Christian material from Paul to the Gospel of John, so often attributed to Jesus and so overblown by later ecstatics and

290. 'Owe no one anything', with which the logion begins (13.8), recalls Cephalus's anxiety in *Republic* 1.330d-331b. See note for 5.6, above.

theologians—is essentially common-sense, practical advice for social tolerance, a basic rule for communal living.[291] 'Love each other' means 'display that social character that makes life together bearable'. It is political in content, and Paul's thinking here is the near-equivalent of Aristotle's dictum that 'a human being is by nature a being intended to live in a *polis*' (*Politics* 1.1253a3). For Paul, too, the human is a gregarious being whose capacities can only be fully realized by sharing in the life of a *polis*, a Christian *polis*. The human political faculty is expressed by *agapē*.[292] *Agapē* is the *plērōma*, the fullness, of law (13.10, cf. 13.8).[293] Paul's concept of *agapē* is consonant with Ps.-Ecphantus's *eukosmia*, good government of the world.[294] It is also contiguous with Aristotle's *philia*, civic or political friendship (πολιτικὴ φιλία), also called political partnership (πολιτικὴ κοινωνία), the foundation of the state.[295] *Agapē* is what makes the Christian fellowship possible.

Paul uses charged metaphors characteristic of pneumatic language (knowing the appointed time, waking from sleep, nearing salvation, lateness of night, day drawing near, putting off the works of darkness, clothing in armor of light, 13.11-13[296]). He then gives what looks like

291. As Zola put it in *Nana*, 'Religion tolerates weaknesses quite well if propriety is observed' (my tr.).

292. *Agapē* is at the center of community life in 1 Cor. 13. It becomes a defining ritual, a love-feast in Jude 12. *Agapē* is a Septuagintal term, without a technical meaning (see *DB* 593b-94a). The concept acquires a political charge in Jewish writings at the time of Jewish political rebellion and national dissolution in the first century (see Jewett 1994: 80-86).

293. Barclay notes that πληροῦν is never used in Jewish sources, either in Hebrew (מלא) or Greek in connection to the Law. Paul describes Jewish observance of the Law with φυλάσσω, ποιέω, πράσσω (1991: 138-39, *ap*. Boyarin 1994: 140-41). Stresses Boyarin (in connection with Gal. 5.14): 'Jews do the Law, but Christians fulfill the Law...the very notion of fulfillment *is a Hellenistically inspired Pauline innovation in theology*' (141, author's emphasis).

294. See Chapter 5, section on Ps.-Ecphantus, frg. 1.4.3.

295. *Politics* 4.1295b21-25. For a discussion of the importance of *philia* as foundation of a political society see Chapter 4, section on Damippos. See also Chapter 2, section on Aristotle's Ethics, and Chapter 5, section on Ps.-Ecphantus.

296. Hans Jonas reveals that these expressions are leitmotifs of Gnosticism (in his still standard 1963 [first edition 1958] treatise on Gnostic religion). Scores of studies on either the Valentinian or Sethian varieties of Gnosticism revealed by the later Nag Hammadi finds (J.M. Robinson 1977), further confirmed his conclusions. See, e.g., Layton 1980, Pagels 1975, Segal 1982, Stroumsa 1984, Burkert 1987, Pearson 1990, Maccoby 1991.

disproportionately trivial advice: no Bacchic parties, no drunkenness,[297] no sex, no orgies, no strife, no envy (13.13). The importance of the psychological in Pauline politics cannot, however, be underrated. Paul incessantly recalls that desires, *epithumiai* of the *sarx*, constitute a threat to the society he establishes.[298] The point Paul is arriving at, here, is a major one: abandon the sarkic and its drives; the time is nigh to put on Christ (13.14)[299]—that is, to become a Christ-type, a christ, a citizen of the new *polis*. What looks like trivia is actually a *logos-sophia* reflection, of possible Platonic source (via Gnosticism), an 'intelligible light' meditation.[300] The exhortations describe a pneumatic psyche, one that wards off impulses and the dread of death.

14.1–15.13. In his (and his tradition's) customary way, Paul shifts from the psychological to the political.[301] Paul has to teach his people political culture. The *ekklēsia* is dynamic, recruiting newcomers all the time, which exerts continual pressure on the group structure. Individual vanity sometimes trumps social identity. Old members may be versed in fine points of reasoning; new members may be weak in *pistis* (14.1, cf. 1 Cor. 3.2-4). Each and every member of the association, however, is a household slave (οἰκέτης, *oiketēs*) of a master (κύριος, *kurios*) (14.4). While Paul often notes, or even stresses, differences between the con-stituents of the community, parity, based on the notion of equality inherent in true justice, is always the more dominant theme. Among

---

297. Corruption of human nature by 'drunkenness' is a staple of Gnostic Hellen-istic language. It functions importantly even in a Hellenistic Pythagorean text, Ps.-Ecphantus frg. 3.3.

298. E.g., Rom. 1.24; 6.12; 7.7-8; 13.14; 1 Cor. 10.6; Gal. 5.16-24.

299. Paul refers back, as in the previous passage, to Rom. 5.6-8.

300. Stead sees in Rom. 13.12-13 a *logos-sophia* reflection of Platonism (1994: 140, 155).

301. Karris 1977: 97-98 is emphatic that Rom. 14.1–15.13 'has no specific referent within the Roman community'. Here Paul 'sums up [his] missionary theology and paraenesis' (98). Dibelius's 1953 authoritative conviction that paraenesis is general and not applicable to particular situations is challenged, yet resorted to. Karris maintains the perceptive view that Paul is here 'concerned to show how an estab-lished community can maintain its unity despite differences of opinion' (1977: 92). It is the theological exclusivism of his views that I find unsatisfactory. For a critique of Karris, see Donfried 1977: 127-32; for Karris's refutation, 1977: 149-51. Don-fried introduces the social and political in the framework of Romans; unfortunately he reduces it to the historical situation of the Jewish community in Rome.

Hellenistic Pythagorean writings, Damippos's text can be appealed to as intertext, as cultural referent for the major idea of equality-within-hierarchy that informs Paul's political theory. And, here again, Aristotle hovers in the background of the views Paul expresses. One is not to judge the *oiketēs*, for the *oiketēs* does not belong to one; a household slave is responsible only to the master (14.4). This is yet another reference to God's exclusive magistracy and the political master–slave political relationship.

In whatever one does—which days one reckons special (14.5), what one eats or when one fasts (14.6), in life as well as in death (14.7-8)—one belongs to one's master, one is Christ's. Once God has taken hold (προσελάβετο) (14.3), one becomes a citizen of the Christian commonwealth, equal to everyone else, and can be judged by the tribunal of God alone (βῆμα τοῦ θεοῦ) (14.10; see 14.10-12).

The food metaphor, a favorite of Paul's, feeds this whole section: no food is defiling (lit. inferior, vulgar, κοινόν) in and of itself; however, if a member of the fellowship thinks it unclean, then the rest should defer to him (14.14), for no one should be a cause for scandal (σκάνδαλον) (14.13) in the community. Essentially, however, insists Paul, finding food objectionable is only inappropriate discourse, misused language (cf. 14.16). (This might be regarded as a prize attack on Jewish obsession with ceremonial purity.[302]) One must live according to 'love' (κατὰ ἀγάπην περιπατεῖν) (14.15), that is, according to the principle that makes social living possible, a logos of the *polis*, a political principle (14.15, 20). It is *agapē* that holds the community together. It is a terrible thing to have the good (*to agathon*) spoken of as evil (βλασφημείσθω) (14.16) because one uses this good against a brother, a fellow citizen.[303] Ps.-Ecphantus (frg. 3.2) likewise emphasized the relativity of human good. Elsewhere (frg. 1.3), Ps.-Ecphantus makes judging God's privilege and opposes the imperfection of human justice to God's judgment.[304]

302. *Koinon* is a cornerstone of the Greek political vocabulary; τὸ κοινόν designates the state and the government as well as the common rights of the citizens (see LSJ *s.v.* κοινός 968b). Paul is concerned here, however, with the Jewish application of the term, and warns against its destructive force (see BAGD *s.v.* κοινός 439a).

303. Augustine will center his most original psychology of sin around precisely such statements: that perverse pursuit of good makes one evil (*City of God* 12.8; 13.5; 14.4, 13; 19.21).

304. This is extensively treated by Paul in Romans 2 and 14 (Rom. 2.1, 3, 12, 16; 14.3, 4, 5, 10, 13, 22, cf. 1 Cor. 3.32; 10.29).

For the notion of wholesale transfer of *dikaiosunē* to God, Ps.-Ecphantus's and

To read this section of Romans accurately, one must always keep in mind that Paul's ethics are ancillary to his politics. The stability of his communities takes precedence over moral dicta. When Paul urges the citizens of his *ekklēsiai* to refrain from offending one another, warns them about the deficiencies inherent in human nature and prods them to assist one another,[305] he does so primarily to reduce the threat of dissent in his congregations and to ensure their durability. Behind the reason-ableness of the injunctions lies the political motive: any challenge to the stability of the political association must be defused.

Mixing abstractions with plain examples, Paul continues his incursion into political principles. The state whose ruler is God, where the *basileia* is of God (βασιλεία τοῦ θεοῦ) (14.17), rests on these pillars: *dikaiosunē*, *eirēnē* (εἰρήνη, peace) and *chara* (χαρά, joy) in a spirit called holy.[306] Its foremost feature, *dikaiosunē theou*, Paul's political-trans-cendental imprint, has as its companions political *eirēnē*, Pythagorean harmony, and moral *chara*, of a purely pneumatic nature (Rom. 14.17).

Slavery to Christ is pleasing (εὐάρεστος) to God and is sanctioned (δόκιμος) by the people (14.18). *Eirēnē* and reciprocal edification (τὰ τῆς οἰκοδομῆς τῆς εἰς ἀλλήλους) are the way (14.19).[307] Finally, good and evil are defined politically. Evil (*to kakon*), that which is malignant, is to make another stumble, to destroy (καταλύειν)[308] the work of God (14.20). Good (*to kalon*), that which is beneficial, is to prevent another from stumbling (πρόσκομμα) (14.20, 21).[309] Good and bad are as much

---

Paul's ultimate source is Aristotle's analysis of the difficulty of being just (*Nicomachean Ethics* 5.1137a1-35).

305. See e.g., Rom. 2.1-3; 14.4, 10; 1 Cor. 4.5; 5.12 (being non-judgmental); Rom. 14.1, 13; 15.1; 1 Cor. 8.9; 9.22; 1 Thess. 5.14 (showing leniency towards the weak); Rom. 7.15, 23; Gal. 5.16–6.10 (considering human fallibility); Rom. 15.1-2, 7; Gal. 6.2 (engaging in mutual assistance), to mention just a few examples.

306. I.e. sent by a clean spirit and not by some deceptive spirit, mocking God, as in Euripides' *Alcestis* 1125: κέρτομος θεοῦ χαρά. Euripides voices here the urgent apprehension of participants in magical séances.

307. Black recognizes in this description 'the ideal community compactly built together by the Gospel and its exponents...a central Pauline thought' (1973: 169). *Oikodomē* is understood as *ecclesia Christi*, the Christian *polis*, by Peterson 1941 (*ap.* Black 1973: 169).

308. καταλύειν is the opposite of *oikodomē*; see Rienecker 1980 Rom. 4.20 *s.v.* καταλύω.

309. As suggested by Ps.-Ecphantus (frg. 3.1, H 276.11-19, T 82.7-14), one's *agathon* is not diminished because of public life compromise (e.g., Rom. 14.16);

principles of politics as of ethics. Their definitions arise from considerations of civic order. What is good for the state is good; what is bad is
what makes the state falter. How much better than someone else's *pistis*
your *pistis* is, is between you and God (14.22) and must not be used to
confound another.

The centrality of *pistis* is then reiterated: 'Everything that is not from
pistis is *hamartia* (πᾶν δὲ ὃ οὐκ ἐκ πίστεως ἁμαρτία ἐστίν) (14.23).[310]
Pistis is once again affirmed as the ground of the political system. Those
at home in the Christian *polis*, the strong ones (οἱ δυνατοί) owe a debt
to the newer ones, the weak (οἱ ἀδυνατοί), for the good (*to agathon*),
for the newer members' edification and the upbuilding (*oikodomē*) of
the community (15.1-2).[311] The old teachings were fine as far as they

one's personal goodness is not affected if one pursues the collective good (e.g.,
15.2). Not eating meat or drinking wine is a Classical Pythagorean tenet. Black
notes, in a circuitous phrase, that 'Judaism was probably not uninfluenced in this
connection by Pythagorean practices' (1973: 170).

310. Rom. 14.17-23 recalls Aristotle's definition of virtue as a mean between
excess and deficiency and his claims that the mean is formal cause of virtue, that
being excessively good is of dubious benefit for the *polis*. The relative superiority
of an individual's *pistis* is, at most, something between the individual and God
(14.22). But even this is an offhand concession, since it does not attract any extra-
pneuma, which it would if it were of any significance, in accord with the
proportional reward according to *pistis*.

311. Karris 1977 demolishes Minear's 1971 (so also Black 1973: 171) identification of 'the weak' with the Jewish Christians and of 'the strong' with the Gentile
Christians. He takes the link between 15.1-6 and 7-13 to be 'the love that should
not please itself (Rom. 15.1-3)' (94). It is the 'love' that, as I see it, is the bond of
the political nexus. The debate on 'the strong' and 'the weak' is an enduring one.
For Käsemann the strong are 'a majority in the community'. He sharply points out
that 'The dialectic shows that a fundamental motif of Paul's is handled here, which
was carefully considered. If a person is not an isolable being, he has neighbors as
well as masters and must have a concern for fellowship' (1980: 381). Nygren
(1949: 441-51), quite implausibly, finds here an address to a practical issue in the
church in Rome, the attitude towards food offered to the idols, and parallels it to
1 Cor. 8. Some form of abstinence is favored by most commentators.

I am inclined to read the strong and weak opposition in the sense of 1 Cor. 3.1-5,
in which the pneumatic and the sarkic are contrasted, the 'meat' and the 'milk', i.e.
strong and weak, are types of revelations, and the point is strife and dissension. The
weak would thus be newcomers into the community, people whose sarkic attachment is still tight, and whose incorporation in the community is the duty of those
strongly within. (The old Platonic distinction between the strong and the weak, the
view that the weak contrived justice to curb the power of the strong—*Republic*

went (15.4). Now, (practical) wisdom (*phronein*) is 'by the model of Christ Jesus' (*kata Christon Iēsoun*) (15.5).³¹² He has taken his followers, 'you', as his partners (προσελάβετο ὑμᾶς) (15.7), in confirmation of the promise (εἰς τὸ βεβαιῶσαι τὰς ἐπαγγελίας) (15.8).³¹³ The discourse ends on a exalted and enraptured note, and with the wish that all be included in the *plērōma* of joy and peace, that all be beneficiaries of the power of the spirit called holy (15.13).

15.14-33.³¹⁴ Paul closes the treatise (15.14-21) as he began it: self-referentially. Paul's boldness in address comes from his *charis* (15.15), his public service (λειτουργός) for Christ Jesus to the nations (τὰ ἔθνη) (15.16). The nature of the *leitourgia* is then specified: it is the office of a hierophant, a priest of the good tidings of God (ἱερουργοῦντα τὸ εὐαγγέλιον τοῦ Θεοῦ) (15.16, cf. Phil. 1.12),³¹⁵ in which function Paul makes the offering of the nations acceptable to God (Rom. 15.16).³¹⁶ He

2.359a-b, a basic political topos—also deserves attention in this context.)
Damippos (see Chapter 4) may also be invoked in the context of the weak-strong dilemma. In his parallelism of universe, humanity, and state, Damippos (and also Ps.-Archytas) follows, even if with a certain reluctance, his Classical sources, in suggesting that to agree and to be sovereign belong to both the weak and the strong. In Damippos *kratos* and *homonoia* seem to designate the participation of all citizens in political *aretē*, *aretē* which for Plato and Aristotle is justice and law, *dikaiosunē* and *nomos*.

312. *Phronein* becomes, in Paul, an equivalent for political concord, e.g., Rom. 15.5, φρονεῖν ἐν ἀλλήλοις, to live in harmony with each other. Ps.-Charondas (frg. 8) advises: each citizen should be prudent rather than rash, σωφρονεῖν μᾶλλον ἢ φρονεῖν. It is, obviously, the advice Paul gives the older members of *ekklēsia*: avoid arrogance. In Paul this is much more than a moral injunction, it is a political exigency, a condition of the community's stability. Paul and the Pythagorean Hellenistic thinker use identical language.

313. In Paul, as in Ps.-Archytas (frg. 5a), *bebaios* and its verbal cognates characterize the ideal constitution, *euangelion* (Phil. 1.7), and its synonyms: e.g., the divine promise, *epangelia* (Rom. 4.16; 15.8).

314. A note on the manuscript tradition: A Latin recension of the third century (thus predating the Vulgate) circulated without 15.1–16.24. Instead, 14.15-23 and 16.25-27 (the doxology), were positioned as the last chapters of the epistle. See C.H. Dodd (1932: xv-xvii) for possible explanations (circular letter, Marcion, orthodox editors, copyists, papyrus-roll deterioration).

315. 'God of Good Tidings' is an epithet of Jupiter, e.g., Aristides, *Orations* 53.

316. Paul likes to cast himself, in the Hellenistic Pythagorean manner, as both *exemplum* and *nomos empsuchos*, after the model of Christ. See discussion in Chapter 5, section on Diotogenes, frg. 2.2.6.

boasts that he has accomplished this service well (15.17). The means, however—Paul's speech, action, the power of his signs and miracles, and the power of the *pneuma* (15.18-19, cf. 1.16)[317]—were of Christ himself.[318] The agency of the shift from *hamartia* to *dikaiosunē* is the *euangelion*, discursively or magically used by Christ's envoys to win the obedience of the *ethnē* from Jerusalem to Illyricum (Rom. 15.18-19); the *euangelion* takes on the meaning of the new commonwealth's constitution. Obedient to instruction, the Christians have made a radical change of allegiance, from *hamartia* to *dikaiosunē* (6.17). Paul's ambition was to go where Christ was not yet named, so that he would not build on another's foundation (ἵνα μὴ ἐπ᾽ ἀλλότριον θεμέλιον οἰκοδομῶ) (15.20). I do not think this means only that Paul is avoiding interfering with another's missionary territory.[319] Paul is a *sophos architektōn* (1 Cor. 3.10). Paul's Christian society, like the ideal states of Plato or Aristotle, has its best chance if it starts *tabula rasa*, with people that have not been contaminated by an imperfect or contradictory Christ message, with people who will obey Paul (or, rather, the *euangelion* he brings them), just as Plato's guardians obey their philosopher-ruler or Aristotle's citizens their legislator.

Speaking about present circumstances and future plans (15.22-31), Paul notes that Rome is a pretty packed place. Greece, too (see 15.26), is becoming an overcrowded missionary ground (essentially, Paul is being pushed out by the envoys of the Jerusalem church), and he seems to have finished his foundation work there (15.23). Paul plans to move to Spain and to stop in Rome (15.24, 28-29). First, however, he is to go

---

317. λόγῳ καὶ ἔργῳ, ἐν δυνάμει σημείων καὶ τεράτων, ἐν δυνάμει πνεύματος (Rom. 15.18-19). Ps.-Zaleucus (frg. 5) assumes that there is only a precarious line between the exorcist and the philosopher, and that, while speech acts upon desires, magical actions are also advised. Paul insists repeatedly that he not only speaks, brings rhetorical arguments, he also, like Ps.-Zaleucus's exorcist, demonstrates (the power of) the *pneuma* and the power of God, δύναμις θεοῦ. We may seem quacks, says Paul in perfect elliptic style, yet we are true, ὡς πλάνοι καὶ ἀληθεῖς (2 Cor. 6.8).

318. The question of the legitimacy of apostles was developed in the discussion of *tupos didachēs*, Rom. 6.17.

319. This approach cannot be easily discounted, however. It is Paul's political genius to avoid conflict not only with the imperial power, but also with the Jerusalem church authority. He bypasses the latter by moving away from its territorial control and jurisdiction. See also Klein 1977.

to Jerusalem with assistance from Macedonia and Achaia (15.25-26).[320] *Diakonia, diakonos, diakoneō* are difficult terms (see also 16.1). They refer to an office, an agent or an action that offers service. Here, Paul is a *diakonos*, manager of a corporation, *ekklēsia*, an agency that collects and disburses contributions for various causes. These terms suggest a network of services characteristic of both a socialized structure and an interdependent organization of Christian groups. *Diakonos* is a term of human political life. Ps.-Ecphantus observed that God governs alone, without *diakonoi* and *hupēretai* (H 277.5-6, T 82.17-18). The *diakonoi* are major players in the Pauline *ekklēsia*. *Leitourgia*, a technical term in Greek[321] and Hellenistic *poleis*, comes from the same sphere of civic service. It is a public service, mostly a costly privilege, but very important to the *polis*. The verb *eudokeō* (εὐδόκεσαν Rom. 15.26), used in the construction with an infinitive (here ποιήσασθαι) and describing the act by which Macedonia and Achaia offered this contribution, appears from the first century onwards in legal documents with the meaning to consent, to approve, to agree.[322] What has been consented to is here called a *koinōnia*, a charity, a sharing, something characteristic of an organized society.[323] Since the *ethnē* share in (ἐκοινώνησαν) the Jews' pneumatic quality,[324] the *ethnē* are also obliged (ὀφείλουσιν) to render *leitourgia*, service, to their sarkic aspect (15.27). Here, 'sarkic' (logically, material need) is an interesting, intentional *Fehlleistung*, a 'slip' the underlying message of which is apparent. While Paul is performing

---

320. πορεύομαι εἰς Ἰερουσαλήμ διακονῶν τοῖς ἁγίοις. εὐδόκησαν γὰρ Μακεδονία καὶ Ἀχαία κοινωνίαν τινὰ ποιήσασθαι... (Rom. 15.25-26). For *koinōnia* as contribution, see Rom. 12.13.

321. See e.g., Aristotle *Politics* 4.1291a.

322. See LSJ and MM *s.v.* εὐδοκέω. The verb, a compound of δοκέω, does recall the introductory formula of official documents of Greek *poleis*: ἔδοξε τῇ βουλῇ καὶ τῷ δήμῳ, 'it pleased the Council and the people'.

323. An interesting approach to *koinōnia* is taken by Sampley 1980, who sees in some of the occurrences of this term (esp. in Galatians and Philippians) the equivalent of *societas*, a legal contractual term common in the Roman law. While he makes a convincing case for Galatians (Gal. 2.9), the attempt for Philippians founders. Sampley does not see the technical use of the term in the structure of Romans and calls it 'sententious' (96).

324. Paul is an accomplished rhetorician. What he is saying here is 'the Jerusalem followers of Christ'. From the way Paul describes them it is evident that he emphasizes the Jewishness of these Jewish Christians. His feelings toward the Jerusalem church parallel those in his address to the Jews in Rom. 9.1-18.

this service to those—the Jewish Christians—who have strong claims to the copyright of Christianity, and while he seems to encourage their practice, which he affirms out of the need for Christian unity, he actually disagrees with the Christianity the Jews represent. 'Sarkic' cannot be taken as a flattering term in Paul, no matter how construed. He bends to what common opinion perceives as source of apostolic authority—he cannot break away without high personal risk and loss of apostolic credentials—but his relation with Jerusalem is strained and causes him anguish. This pandering to Jerusalem's sarkics is glorified bribery. Paul's political genius teaches him, however, that the maintenance of his ideal state is worth any compromise. His definition of civic good, not unlike that of Plato, Aristotle or Cicero before him, is political unity. When the job is done, the 'harvest' (καρπός) sealed in the coffers, Paul will travel on (15.28). In Rome, Paul will show himself in the *plērōma* of Christ's eulogy (ἐν πληρώματι εὐλογίας Χριστοῦ) (15.29), that is, as one who derives his authority from Christ himself, even as a member of his entourage. But that visit will depend on the success of the current task, described in agonistic terms (15.30). Back in Judea, the threat is double: he must escape (ῥυσθῶ)[325] the unbelievers (ἀπειθοῦντες, i.e. the Pharisees he betrayed, the powerful party to which he elsewhere boasts that he belonged), and he must have his service (*diakonia*) accepted in Jerusalem by a no less hostile, if ostensibly friendly, party (15.31).

16.1-16.[326] Romans is Paul's political tract. To it he appends greetings to Jews, Greeks and Romans, male and female, in Rome (16.1-16),[327]

---

325. The verbal form used, ῥυσθῶ, is nearly homophonic with χριστῷ. Paul's name for 'Christian' is ἐν Χριστῷ, a formula appearing 62 times in Paul's genuine letters.

326. That most of this chapter is genuinely Pauline is accepted by the weightiest part of recent scholarship, e.g., Barrett 1957, Donfried 1977, Cranfield 1975–79, Gamble 1977, Käsemann 1980: 390 (who, however, disputes that it was originally part of Romans).

327. These greetings are to outstanding individuals, because of position or because Paul is fond of them or because they are his collaborators, as well as to leaders of Christian groups. For a linguistic analysis of the names, see Wiefel (1977: 112-13) and Donfried 1977.

Note that φίλημα, the kiss exchanged between the members of the fellowship is a Pauline ritual, Rom. 16.16; 1 Cor. 16.20; 2 Cor. 13.12, cf. 1 Thess. 5.26. The importance of women on this list is noteworthy. The title and pre-eminence of Junia— foremost among apostles—is striking (Rom. 16.3).

and includes a commendatory note[328] about Phoebe, a woman *diakonos* at Kenchreae (Corinth's port on the Saronic Gulf) and a patron (προστάσις) of Paul (16.1-2).[329]

Romans 16.5 offers a momentous insight into Pauline politics. Paul associates *oikos* with *ekklēsia* (cf. 1 Cor. 16.19; Phlm. 2; also Col. 4.15; 1 Tim. 3.4). He makes no technical distinction between household rule and political constitution. In this, Paul echoes Callicratidas, who in opposition to Aristotle, makes no distinction between political rule and household rule, *archē politikē* and *archē oikonomikē*.[330] (Callicratidas also proposes the world, *kosmos*, as the example of political and household rule.) It is taken as obvious that Paul is talking about house churches. What should be also observed, however, is Paul's merging of two central Greek political organs, family and assembly. This is precisely the essence of Paul's political thinking: the human political unit, at once household and state, is only a part of the larger picture that includes— and does not just imitate—the government of the cosmos.

Why did Paul write the letter to Rome? With people from all over the *orbis terrae* flocking to the *caput mundi*, Rome must have been swarming with partnerships that met under the name of Christ. Numerous Christian clusters, gathering in household assemblies (ἐκκλησία κατ᾽ οἶκον, 16.5), were probably held together by ethnic and geographical provenance, and most likely had sundry founders and assorted charters. Christ-associations in Rome must have presented an utterly fragmented landscape, a fractured mosaic with nothing like a coherent design. The problem with the Christian community in Rome was that *there was no community*. In writing Romans, Paul's central concern was to give the Romans unity, to bind them together in a harmonious *ekklēsia* with a coherent constitution, Paul's *euangelion*. There is no indication that Paul has specific doctrinal or behavioral violations in mind, and indeed there could be little reason for Paul to take issue with any detail of

328. προσδέξησθε (Rom. 16.2, cf. Phil. 2.29), the prodding that the Romans accept her, is a term used in diplomatic correspondence for receiving a messenger (M.M. Mitchell 1992).

329. *Diakonos* belongs to the names of civic offices often adopted by the *collegia*. Of these, Paul also uses *episkopos* and *prostatēs* (=*patronus*). For discussion of *collegia* and their connection with Paul's communities, see Chapter 5, section on Sthenidas, frg. 1.2.

330. Also, for Callicratidas ἀρχὴ πολιτική applies to monarchy, while in Aristotle it referred to democracy (Moraux 1957: 85).

doctrine, or with explicit violations of conduct, due to misinterpretation or corruption of the properly delivered *euangelion*. Paul probably knew little of what was going on inside the various groups. The general picture was, however, clear and simple: extensive organizational fragmentation and a difficult Jewish Christian minority in some associations.

In Romans, Paul is not initiating a community, as he has often done elsewhere. Instead, he means to bring together diverse existing groups and make them live in concord and harmony, to form a Christ-*polis* ruled by Paul's *euangelion*. This was a formidable initiative in which Paul could have engaged only at the full maturity of his apostleship. To reach many separate entities he needed—and he certainly relied on—a great deal of help. Paul's envoys must have infiltrated at least the most important of the local assemblies. They must have attracted to Paul's cause some of the most prominent and respected members of the various household associations. He had to have the confidence of many parties, the support of members trusted by the individual communities and the assistance of followers of status. Paul's letter is the rallying banner of this networking campaign and power game.

Paul might have seen himself as Solon or Cleisthenes in Athens, Moses in Egypt or—why not?—even Alexander. He is taking the *phulai*, tribal communities kept together by topography, place of origin and local benefactors, and unites them in a single organization under a political platform stressing the eradication of factions. Disparate tribes become one state, with all the members sharing in the same *polis*, the *ekklēsia*, and showing allegiance to the same constitution, the *euangelion* of Paul. The 'common ancestry' of the 'house' is replaced by common citizenship in a Christ-*polis*. Rome has the same importance in Paul's plans for universal Christianity as does his insistence that the Jews join the compact.[331] By preventing nascent Christian cells from going their own, separate ways or, worse, waging terminal war against each other, Paul is saving Roman Christianity.

As I have emphasized throughout, Paul simultaneously and constantly has two conceptual vistas within his compass: *polis* and *basileia*, human community and universal kingship. In relation to the first, he is well served by the fusion between household and city effected by the Hellenistic Pythagorean political thinkers; Paul assigns to this unity the name *ekklēsia* and makes the community an equality-within-hier-

---

331. Seifrid (1992: 207-208) arrives at a similar conclusion.

archy.[332] For the *basileia* portion of his scheme, he appropriates Hellenistic monarchical ideas—later translated into Roman terms and designs—and ascribes them to God. He thus produces an *ekklēsia-polis* that is a unit both of the Roman empire and of the divine *basileia*.

The relation between the Pauline *ekklēsia* and the Roman political system is a hysteron-proteron relation. The *ekklēsiai* begin as distinct and dissimilar (and cautious and secretive) political entities, sub-systems of the Roman organism, in apparent concord with it but aiming to make Rome itself a constituent of a larger, universal empire. Paul works with small communities, tightly knit internally and tightly linked externally, and makes them Rome's imperative, its critical, vital quintessence. Christianity draws on the resources and energies of the *polis*, a political model exciting intense allegiance and fierce affection, a collective and public framework for genuine personal feeling. Its 'household God' is, however, the very same ruler of the universe. The *ekklēsia*—relatively small, mostly provincial and of limited influence and power—is nevertheless vibrant, robust and disciplined, and, in this sense, impregnable. Rome, whose gods dominate every city, has always maintained a certain distinction between itself—the empire—and God's universal dominion, between its laws and divine law. This makes Rome vulnerable, and its pantheon keeps expanding to include more and more provincial gods. It is only a matter of time before Christ[333] becomes its battle God. The awesome power of Rome—its infrastructure, administrative organization, legal principles, political institutions—becomes subservient to the Christian *polis*, its backbone.

The distinction between the *ekklēsia* and Rome's political system is not one of disruption or polarization but of continuity and affinity. The Christian *poleis* do not stand against the culture and politics of Rome in a private versus public, personal versus collective or casual and familiar versus official and ceremonial relation. The relationship is much more that of local forces to a global force. Christianity, as it developed through the genius of people like Paul, took advantage of both *polis* and

---

332. Even if the pneumatic aspect determines the offices in the Pauline compact, generating an equality of sorts, Paul hardly ignores the hierarchical structure of the *ekklēsia*, and cannot conceive of *ekklēsia* in other terms than those he draws from the *polis*.

333. Included in Septimius Severus' *Septizonium* (or *Septizodium*, 203 CE) on the Palatine in Rome, the celebrated monument (destroyed by Sixtus V in the sixteenth century) at the head of the Via Appia.

imperium. By vision and collusion, by tapping into contemporary Hellenistic political speculation and biding its time, Christianity reached a critical speciation point, a momentous state. The combined energy of a large number of diverse events led to widely diffused transformation, a new mode of operation of the world.

16.17-20. Before taking leave, Paul summarizes the main point of his thesis, in the form of a final political warning: 'Watch out for those who cause divisions and scandals [τὰς διχοστασίας καὶ τὰ σκάνδαλα] contrary to the system [διδαχή] you learned [from me]' (16.17). 'Their smooth speech [χρηστολογία[334]] and eloquence [εὐλογία] deceive the minds [lit. hearts] of the guileless' (16.18). This is a capital political transgression. Though Paul does not use *stasis*—the Aristotelian term for the rhetoric of factionalism—its flagship terminology is otherwise all there.[335] Paul warns against *dichostasiai*, 'dissensions' (Rom. 16.17; 1 Cor. 3.3 t.r.; Gal. 5.20), as well as against the *philoneikos*, 'contentious' (1 Cor. 11.16).[336]

The dissenters' offense is that they are not *douloi* of Christ but *douloi* of drives (κοιλία) (Rom. 16.18, cf. Phil. 3.19). In opposition to 'them' (the deceivers), 'you' understand (ὑπακοή) (16.19). In the very opening of Romans, Paul states his mission to bring the obedience of faith (ὑπακοὴ πίστεως) to the nations (τὰ ἔθνη) (Rom. 1.5). This is also precisely how he ends the letter. *Hupakoē* is a difficult word, and its significance depends on the unit of meaning within which it functions. The common rendering, 'obedience', is problematic, legitimate only insofar as 'obedience' means making sense of something heard, understanding and accepting it. That is, *hupakoē* has a dual sense (contained in ὑπακούω, from which it derives) that has to do both with hearing and with responding accordingly. Paul is well served by this ambiguity and appeals to its entire range of signification. The term implies a relationship, and whether it concerns physical submission or intellectual assent it is based on reasoned consideration and willing compliance. It describes a relation, one involving empathy and reciprocal interest, a partnership

---

334. A play on words? *Chrēstologia*, 'Christ-babble'.

335. See the excellent study of M.M. Mitchell 1991.

336. *Dichostasia* (dissention, sedition) and *philoneikos* (contentious) have a long tradition in the political lexicon of the Greek and Hellenistic world, from Theognis (sixth century BCE) to the LXX (1 Macc. 3.29) and Plutarch. See LSJ *s.v.* διχοστασία, φιλόνεικος.

that determines a state of completion consistent with an individual's
proper end. As such it is thoroughly consistent with Aristotle's ruler–
ruled axis.[337] Both obedience and disobedience take place on a cosmic
scale—in God's kingdom. Obedience gives one the power of God to
crush 'Satan' (16.19-20). It is also the factor that alters the relation
between the wise and the foolish and makes it reversible (e.g., 1.22;
16.19; 1 Cor. 1.27; 3.19). *Hupakoē* is the mover of *pistis*, its efficient
cause. The relation it articulates is political in nature. 'They' are of
Satan; 'you' are of the God of peace (16.20). Satan is not a theological
or an ethical concept, but a political one: the metaphor for division and
rebellion.

   Doulos, introduced in 1.1 as one of Paul's personal credentials, arches
over the entire argumentative space of the letter. Its most complex use
is at the close of the letter, in 16.18. In a typical manner, Paul operates a
sharp distinction between the old and new meanings of the word: from
a base, despicable station to that of the willing, self-conscious citizen.
In 16.18-20, *douloi* of Christ are presented as the antithesis of the
douloi of passions. The difference is between understanding and urges,
self-examination and instinct, knowledge and libertinism—ultimately,
between a solid, well-founded, permanent constitution and ephemeral,
narcissistic, incoherent desire.

16.21-23. The epistle finally concludes with greetings from the community where Paul resides—co-workers, fellow Jews, his secretary, his
host, the assembly, the city treasurer (συνεργοί, συγγενεῖς, γράψας,
ξένος, ἐκκλησία, οἰκονόμος τῆς πόλεως). The use of the word *polis*
here (16.23) is especially to be noticed in view of its rarity in Paul. He
employs it twice in the known corpus when he has to indicate official
titles, as here and when he refers to the ἐθνάρχης (*ethnarchēs*) of the
city of Damascus in 2 Cor. 11.32, and once in a generic but exhaustive
list of dangers with which he was confronted by people and places
(2 Cor. 11.26). Paul offers no single suitable replacement but deliberately produces a list of periphrases, such as 'we', 'you', 'Israel', 'body
of Christ', *ekklēsia* and, above all, 'in Christ'. The sections of Paul's
letters in which he conveys greetings to and from various people illustrate Christianity's internationalism and its complex structure. They
show Christianity as a well-organized social and political phenomenon,

---

   337. See Aristotle, *Politics* 1.1259b22-1260a2, for the relation statesman or master
and state or household.

well aware of its importance. Particularly revealing is the overlap of Christian and Roman institutional functions. Some people are proudly identified as public functionaries in the municipal political system. These titled individuals are not just a gauge of the movement's success. They legitimize, even as they are legitimized by, Christianity. Christianity's incorporation of public officials shows its success in adjusting to and adopting the political body within which it develops. It is not the titled person but the title itself that is important, and Paul's recitation of such titles is a mimetic technique indicative of Christianity's concerted, consistent efforts at duplicating the institutions of the empire. Christianity moves toward replicating the *imperium*, the Roman government.[338]

Summation

What Paul produces in Romans is a grand discourse, theologically intricate and stylistically complex. Its formal structure, however, follows the model of Classical political tracts such as Plato's *Republic* and Aristotle's *Politics*, whose framework includes a critical review of the present state of affairs and a speculative proposal for a better, ideal state. In Paul as in the Classical philosophers, the political has a counterpart in the psychological dimension, the soul, with the political program unfolding in parallel and in symbiosis with a strategy for the reordering of the flawed soul. Content-wise, Paul develops a theory that displays the influence of Hellenistic Pythagorean political philosophy. On the one hand, Paul stresses the human *polis*-type organizational pattern of the communities he establishes; on the other, he focuses on the divine *basileia*, the blueprint and goal of the *ekklēsia*. The pivotal concept in each of the two configurations is *dikaiosunē*. The eminently political charge that *dikaiosunē* carries is given a unique sweep by having it qualified by *pistis* in the case of the *polis* and by *theos* in the case of *basileia*. Christ—the equivalent of the *nomos empsuchos* of the Hellenistic authors, the law that is the end of the law—operates the connection and makes possible the exchange between the two realms. The Christian *ekklēsia*, just like the Hellenistic *polis* that inspired it, retains a considerable degree of autonomy even as it submits to a central, higher authority. At the same time, Paul's Christian *polis* is not only not in

338. The farewell, Rom. 16.24, is dubiously Pauline (Käsemann 1980: 401-407). Rom. 16.25-27 is a non-Pauline gloss; this doxology may be of Marcionite authorship (Zuntz 1953, *ap*. Barrett 1957: 12).

opposition to Rome, it is actually supportive of Rome, the empire that makes the Christian *polis* feasible and that Paul's Christian *ekklesiai* will convert. In the end, the fates of the Christ-*polis* and of Rome overlap and become identified, just as, at the very end, the human *polis* collapses into the divine *basileia*.[339]

Paul upbuilds *ekklesiai*, and in so doing he works alongside Rome. Paul did not subvert the great Roman political and social institutions, he bolstered them. Paul cultivated disciples, he did not enlist the discontent. Paul encouraged participation in the system, he did not breed malefaction. (The subversive element, and there is one, is visible only in Christianity's long-term effects. There is a subversive—but not discontinuous—shift to a Christian political world, the transformed Rome.)

From Plato and Aristotle on, the political essence of the human race was recognized: the human being is complete only in the community. And this community is not only not separated from the world at large, it exists in it, and may, *pari passu*, transform it. In Paul there is no discontinuity within world history but a continuity toward a shift, the conversion of the political power structure to a Christ-world, to Christianity. Paul aspires to the *basileia* of God but he works in the world, within communities organized as *poleis*. The way I see things, the *basileia* of God is simultaneous with, and the prototype of, the community as *polis*. It is not just a promise and an expectation, but the very power at work in the present. Human community, the *polis*, is a limited but critical aspect of this present divine rule. It looks heavenward to the divine *basileia*, but it operates within the confines of the Roman government. The *polis* Paul fathers rests on a new polity. *Pistis* is the bond of the *polis*. While the demand implied by *pistis* is radical for the individual and verges on an otherworldly incomprehensibility, it is not destabilizing and is of this world in practical, public and social terms. The individual is subsumed in the universal via the collective order, a political organism. The *pistis* world has its own *dikaiosunē*, and thus it admits

339. The world already has an impeccable model of order in the divine; if only a proper power (a philosopher, a king, Christ) could be found to bring earthly disorder into conformity with the divine blueprint. For the ancient political philosophers (as for their later emulators) politics and piety are inseparable, a *totum*. They pursue the attainment of a divine truth and perfection in the human world. This is why politics, which is concerned, essentially, with no more than the concord among the citizens and the order within society, is found in proximity with metaphysics and theology.

the political. It is because of this that a *pistis* world can be constructed, a world in which, in time, the reliance on *pistis* will be vindicated. The new features of this *polis* are the good old ones: stability, concord and harmony, the Greek political ideals. In Paul, the reality of citizenship in the *basileia* of God is mediated by another reality, that of citizenship in a *polis*, the *ekklēsia* of Christ.

Hellenism by its very definition is a deeply syncretistic cultural universe, and Paul's thought straddles Hellenism, from the Jewish end to the Greek end. Establishing influences among the overlapping, interpenetrating milieux of Hellenism is a difficult but necessary task. I have made it my enterprise to track a little-studied and largely disregarded aspect of Paul's thought, the political aspect. Its investigation is the more imperative since contemporary scholarship has given so much attention to the Hellenistic roots of Paul's ethics, rhetoric and literary genres, while leaving out the political component, so central to Greek and Hellenistic thinking. In venturing to begin to fill the gap, I limited myself to what looked to be the most promising sources—the Hellenistic Pythagoreans, a much-discounted bunch whose contributions to carrying on the spirit of the Classical Greek masters and to political speculation ought not, however, to be ignored.

Juxtaposing my work on Paul with my work on Classical and later Greek political theory made me recognize an overlap in certain key themes and terminology, and I began to see that certain patternings of ideas in Paul were reminiscent of configurations of ideas in Classical and Hellenistic political theory. These patterns and terminologies were often being interpreted by others in ways that made them discontinuous with the cultural milieu in which Paul's Letters were written, alienating Paul from his context and its antecedents. Granted, my research has located no quotations from earlier political theorists embedded in Paul's works, but many terms and ideas have unquestionably retained their meanings from the Classical writings, through Hellenistic political theory, to Paul. The vocabulary is consistent, the lines of thought are the same. However indirect the communication of Greek and Hellenistic political ideas to Paul, Paul shares the same, or at least very similar, language and concepts with these political writings. Even what is new in Paul can only be interpreted if certain conceptual continuities hold. The consistency of the political reading of Paul itself gives testimony to this interrelatedness, to Paul's somehow being heir to this tradition of political philosophy.

When one examines the evidence this way, it can be seen that Paul takes a lot from Greek and Hellenistic Pythagorean political meditation, both in concept and in point of detail. First and foremost, he uses *dikaiosunē*, which becomes the Pole Star of his philosophical and theological constellation in Romans. Its consideration leads, in Paul, to other notions that are directly or indirectly political: *nomos, ekklēsia, euangelion, hamartia, sōtēria, koinōnia, pistis, charis, agapē*, Jews and Greeks, humanity. Like Plato and Aristotle, Paul links politics with psychology and verifies that the inquiry into one necessarily involves the other. Paul appears particularly interested in the two pivotal facets of Hellenistic Pythagorean political reasoning, the *polis* and the *basileia*, the human and the divine elements of political speculation in late Hellenistic and Roman times. Such essentially Pauline motifs as the importance of unwritten, divine or natural, laws; the opposition *nomos–dikaiosunē*; and the role of an incarnate law, the end of all law, all come from the same environment that fed the Hellenistic thinkers. The political grounding of *sōtēria*, whether as achieved by imitation of a model, a ruler, or as obtained through participation in an organized corporation, as a member of the state, is another place where Paul owes a debt to the Hellenistic Pythagoreans; so are his doctrine of *eikōn* as both imitation and foreknowledge, his notion of *logikē latreia* and his use of the body as political metaphor. The *oikos-polis* fusion, operated by Hellenistic Pythagorean thought, is essential for Paul's idea of *ekklēsia*. And impressive demonstration of Hellenistic Pythagorean influence on Paul can be found in the concept of analogic, or distributive, justice. Other, less significant points of contact such as the *Logos* cure for *hamartia*, the view of sonship, the immunity of God's elect and the *kairos* belief, to name just a few, are discussed elsewhere in this work and are too numerous to review here. This summation means only to recall the vigor of the contextual evidence for a parallelism, between Hellenistic Pythagorean political theory and Paul's approach to building a new *polis* and conceptualizing a new order for the world.

Chapter 9

CONCLUSION: A COLLOQUY ON *DIKAIOSUNĒ*

Scholarship is merely a branch of fantastic literature.
Jorge Luis Borges

There is a near-universal assumption that *dikaiosunē* is pivotal in the letter to Rome.[1] Here, I position myself in relation to a select sample of the most important figures in Pauline studies, entering into dialogue with some of the best-known, prevailing critical readings of Pauline *dikaiosunē*. I limit myself, however, to a relatively small number of modern interpreters of Paul. Given the vast pool of scholarly research on Romans, the choice was necessarily aleatoric and preferential, my preferences based on certain authors' innovative approaches, authoritative voices, their diversity of background and rhetorical power. In no way is what follows remotely intended to suggest a comprehensive vista of commanding commentators on *dikaiosunē* in Romans.[2] Nor do I mean this to be a contentious debate with the authors to whom I refer. Rather, by means of dialogue with these writers, I review the main issues this study raises, indicating how even hard-core theological and 'Jewish Paul' views stand in need of or, indeed, suggest the political approach, and how some original, inspiring views that ignore Paul's politics do so at a cost to their effectiveness and persuasiveness. The novel feeling that the points I make may arouse is due primarily to the

1. Seifrid devotes an entire book 'to the question of whether or not Paul's arguments for a forensic *justification* may be regarded as 'central' to Paul's thought' (1992: 46), a question to which he responds affirmatively (1992: 255-70): 'Paul developed the application of the idea beyond its original sphere of significance and used it to address entirely new problems' (255). Addressing the issue of the origin and function of Paul's arguments regarding a forensic, juridical justification, is inevitable since the time of Baur (1992: 255).

2. The bibliography, which lists only cited works that are primarily or significantly concerned with this concept, may still convey the ominous sense of what this would have had to include.

context in which I place Paul, the off-centeredness of my focus and my resolution to pursue a reading of Paul from an infrequently accessed angle.

The *Paulusbild* produced by Paul's earliest interpreters[3] shows Paul in essentially two hypostases: the suffering Paul (i.e. Paul the martyr, along the lines of the portrait Paul draws of himself in Philippians) and the missionary Paul (whose arguments are best depicted in Romans).[4] The foundation of Paul's particular apostleship is keenly understood by Clement of Rome: '[Paul] taught *dikaiosunē* to the whole world' (δικαιοσύνην διδάξας ὅλον τὸν κόσμον) (*1 Clem.* 5.7). Paul engages in political metaphysics. It is because *dikaiosunē* is the essence of God and of God's office that the world is possible, that a universal society can be built and can endure. It is precisely this *dikaiosunē* that gives sense to and authorizes Paul's missionary activity to the Greeks. If in Plato *dikaiosunē* makes the individual one and the *polis* possible, in Paul *dikaiosunē* makes humanity equal and the whole world one, a metaphysical but also a political undertaking.[5] The notion that Jews and Greeks have equal standing before God (Rom. 3.29-30, cf. 15.8-9[6]) is the grounding of Paul's particular apostleship. *Dikaiosunē*, as justice, as *impartiality* (Rom. 3.22, cf. 10.12), is no Jewish concept.

That *dikaiosunē* is the core of the Pauline message, at least in the letter to Rome, has been a staple of commentaries on Paul ever since Augustine.[7] Theological interpreters have commonly seen Paul's use of *dikaiosunē* as deriving from his anti-Jewish polemic about the law. In this view, Paul's emphasis on 'justification' (as *dikaiosunē* is theologically translated) results from an early and short-lived dispute with the Jews.[8] While Paul's use of *dikaiosunē* may grow out of an initial

3.   Pseudo-Pauline epistles (Colossians, Ephesians); Acts; *1 Clement*; pastoral (or deutero-Pauline) epistles (1–2 Timothy; Titus); 2 Peter; Ignatius of Antioch; Polycarp of Smyrna. I omit portrayals in Jewish Christianity and Gnosticism.

4.   See Furnish 1994: 4-7.

5.   Perhaps nowhere do the political and the metaphysical overlap more intimately than in the 'body of Christ' doctrine in 1 Cor. 12.4–13.13.

6.   Where Paul 'Hellenistically' reads passages from the LXX.

7.   This century, many voices (Wrede 1907 [German edition 1904] and Schweitzer 1968 [German edition 1931] to Stendahl 1963, E.P. Sanders 1977, and Beker 1984 [German edition 1980]) questioned this centrality.

8.   Stendahl (together with the tradition he represents and the school he fosters) calls this a false problem, a passing difficulty. To it salvation history is opposed (1963: 209, 211).

argument against Judaism, however, *dikaiosunē* is neither a secondary nor an obsolete part of Pauline thought. It is part of a much larger project that aims to include in one common universe not only all people but God as well.

Dikaiosunē, God's distributive justice, his impartiality, is what is new, and it dwarfs the law although it does not wholly dispose of it.[9] *Dikaiosunē theou* nullifies the claim to election associated with Jewish law. Christ as *telos* of the law (Rom. 10.4) makes the law part of the soteriological and eschatological process; it is Christ who is the law's raison d'être; the law existed to arrive at Christ. Paul's citation of the Hebrew scriptures often serves either to remind the well-disposed Jews of eschatological history or to refute the hostile ones with scriptural proof.[10] Paul the apostle's difficulty has a profoundly political foundation: how to preserve a new societal order deemed to be universal and all-inclusive without seeing it divided from the start. The union Paul projects stands or falls on the Jews' acceptance of the fellowship.[11] Therefrom the quandary and the emergency: therefrom the lip service paid to the law.

What Paul needs are the Jews, not their law.[12] Paul's overtures to the Jews are heartfelt and deep-seated. But the Jews' admission into the constitution is never *because* of law. Somehow, for Paul, securing the

---

9.   One of the more radical views on Paul's understanding of the law is held by D.A. Campbell, according to whom the *nomos* paradigm is used antithetically to *pistis*, to negatively express *pistis*, without any internal logic or content of its own (1992a: 102). On the other hand, the notion, still held by some scholars, that Paul's attachment to the Torah is 'unshakable' (Meyer 1980: 67), wobbly as it is, well describes the compass of the controversy.

10.   From whatever perspective one looks at this issue, it becomes obvious, time and again, that the law is disavowed. Thus, for example, even from the point of view of Paul as a partner in and revisionist of the wisdom tradition, as evinced in 1 Cor. 1.18–3.4 (esp. 1 Cor. 2.6-16), Paul appears to dismiss the law as the *locus revelationis* of god's wisdom and makes that the cross. See Theis 1991 ch. 3, *ap.* Furnish 1993: 727.

11.   The notion that Paul speaks from within Judaism, owed mainly to E.P. Sanders 1977 and quite significant in recent scholarship (see especially the authority and verve with which Segal 1990 espouses it; equally so Boyarin 1994), is an extreme reading of Paul's courting of the Jews.

12.   E.P. Sanders rejects the view of an anti-Jewish feeling in Paul. Paul's chief interest is the creation of culturally, socially, and gender mixed communities (1983: 209).

critical number of Greeks will automatically draw the Jews in.[13] This is actually a mode of *coercing* the participation of the Jews, a way of forcing them into the compact. They will be drawn into it by the mystery of divine intervention, by some magical *opus operatum*. But his patience with the law wears thin, and visibly so. He is constrained to spend time with it because of the 'Jewish imperative', but as far as he is concerned the law deserves no attention. Hence Paul's conceptual obscurity and stylistic prolixity.[14]

It must be observed here that even the theological party of modern scholarship acknowledges the problematic nature of Paul's theological statements and finds that 'he deals more in images and metaphors than in concepts, seldom states his presuppositions, and shows little concern for strict consistency'.[15] Flights of fancy and expository fervor also characterize the Hellenistic Pythagorean style. Obscurity of method is almost the perquisite of the one who endeavors to make a baffling, impenetrable message intelligible. It is the Greeks' contention that knowledge is possible, that the world can be understood and chaos can be disciplined, if only the proper lever can be found. Paul is in firm control of truth; his effort to express this truth shows, however, in its exposition.[16] This is why he constitutes himself an *exemplum*, as the only adequate form of discourse. Moses and Demosthenes found stuttering an impediment and fought against it. Paul seeks it. Smooth, coherent speech is unyielding; the impairment, the slip, the flaw are irresistible

---

13. Rom. 9–11, esp. 11.25; 1 Thess. 2.15-16; Gal. 3.10.

14. Hübner 1984 explains conflicting views of the law in Paul in terms of Paul's development of his theology of *dikaiosunē*. His view of the law is the result not the cause of his understanding of *dikaiosunē*.

15. Furnish 1994: 16.

16. A famous example is the tension between Romans 7 and 8. Luther (and most Protestant scholarship, as against many Catholic theologians—a recent example is Lambrecht 1992) resolved it by observing that the believer is at once pneumatic and sarkic (Rom. 7.18; 8.9, cf. Phil. 3.3; Gal. 4.14) and phrased it in the acclaimed formula *simul iustus et peccator*. As Seifrid puts it, the death and resurrection of Christ 'overcame, but have not yet eliminated the judicial and ontological conditions of the old order' (1992: 242). The stress is between soteriological and epistemological fulfillment and eschatological and ontological incompleteness. This is the strain between Christ and christ, the tension *within* the idea of type, where the model is ahead of the epigones. The example had been set, the idea enunciated—Christ died and was resurrected, salvation occurred—yet *eschaton* is not realized and being not transformed.

expressions of a rhetoric of difficult meaning. Paul acts out in address and deportment, in stutter and the thorn in the flesh, the content of his gospel.

Paul rides with the Greeks in a Roman world.[17] Rome acquired an empire on the training, discipline, and genius in war of its military. Greece, since Plato and especially after Aristotle, rested its claim to the world on right, which it understood politically. This is precisely how Paul saw Christianity in its beginning: as providing the concepts and rhetoric for a conquest based on right, on superior values. Christianity would provide the authority, the *imperium*; the might of Rome was to be its backing force. The essence of this right is *dikaiosunē*, not a concept of law but its source, ultimately the law's undoer. What Paul wants is nothing less than a universal state under the sovereignty of God. This means wresting the control from written law and legal ruler and giving it to *pistis* and Christ. Christ is for Paul the embodiment of eternal and divine law, the sole legitimate law. This law rests on the *euangelion*. (If only, thinks Paul, he can get the emperor to promulgate it!)[18]

Dikaiosunē is the pre-eminent political *aretē* in all Classical and Hellenistic political tracts. In my political analysis of the Hellenistic Pythagoreans and of Paul, I identify two strata of political theorizing: *polis* and *basileia*. The first applies to the political community of human beings; the second to the political society that has the godlike king or God as its leader. The first is a democratic constitution; the second a

17. The Greek *polis*, in its Athenian form, was a local community which governed itself through the *ekklēsia*, the Assembly. Paul, in the mode of Alexander and of Rome universalizes this institution. The Christ-types constitute the *ekklēsia*. Paul makes Christ the head of his *ekklēsia*. It is not, however, a Hellenistic or Roman bureaucracy of jurists. In a sense Paul turns back the tide towards the non-professional as ruler, but unlike Athens, opens membership to women and non-Greeks. Hence, the riotous interest of the mob in metaphysics (the daily business of the Byzantine *polis*) as recorded, for example, by the Cappadocian fathers in connection with the widespread speculation on the Trinitarian issues. (E.g. 'every marketplace must buzz with their talking; and every dinner party be worried to death with silly talk and boredom; and every festival...and all the women's apartments...' [Gregory of Nazianzus, *First Theological Oration* 2, Hardy and Richardson tr., 129].) Also, the centuries of dilettante philosophy started by the wild writings of the apologists and continued by preposterous treatises of the church fathers.

18. For an excellent discussion of civil and canon law and the issues of legality and legitimacy relevant to this theme, see Fasolt 1995.

monarchical one. Although there is no distinction within the concept of *dikaiosunē* in the Classical and Hellenistic Pythagorean writings, the increasing chasm between the human and the divine would demand a split in the idea of *dikaiosunē* as well. And not only that: conversely, a unified *dikaiosunē* would point to the unity of the two spheres, a concord between the human and the divine realms. This phenomenon is nowhere more perfectly illustrated than in Paul's dual *dikaiosunē theou* and *pisteōs*. To each of the two tiers of the Hellenistic political formula Paul applies a different *dikaiosunē*. *Dikaiosunē theou* describes the higher, divine governance of the *polis*. *Dikaiosunē pisteōs* refers to the lower one. (Since this latter *dikaiosunē* is god-dependent, however, God again has the dominant role, though human beings have a certain degree of political autonomy, at least nominally.) *Dikaiosunē theou*, the justice that belongs to God only (subjective genitive), when distributed by the divine judge (*genitivus auctoris*), takes the form of *dikaiosunē pisteos*, the justice of the one who has *pistis* (i.e. the one persuaded by Christ), the justice operative in the Christ-*polis*. *Dikaiosunē* is dispensed, according to the political principle of *analogia*, as *pistis* (Rom. 12.6).[19] Paul can speak in the same breath of *dikaiosunē theou* and *dikaiosunē pisteōs* because their essence is the same. This complex, double *dikaiosunē* is Paul's key to a grand unified political theory. He heals the split and clarifies the relationship between humans and God.

Much has been made in Pauline scholarship of the notorious 'now but not yet'. Insofar as this is a valid category (and most commentators think so), it applies to *pistis* as well. It is imperative to observe that *pistis* is both gift *and* reward.) As a reward, its critical characteristic is that it is deserved by and suitable to the individual on whom it is bestowed. It is not a benevolence but a tribute, the recognition of (a degree of) distinction, not a charity. (It is in this sense that *charis* must also be decoded, as the temper of a just reward. What is the nature of this worth? Acceptance of Christ, acknowledgment of the *euangelion*, the cognizance of the transcendental. It is true, however, that this quality was instigated in men by God, for Christ is God's offering to wicked humanity, which has no merit aside from its misery (cf. Rom. 3.5: 'our injustice serves to

---

19. In the Hebrew Scriptures God's attributes are: power, loving kindness and loyalty (*hesed*), righteousness or faithfulness (*emet*), affection, anger, holiness (Stead 1994: 97, quoting Eichrodt). God's righteousness appears primarily in his watchful care for his people—as their creator and protector (Stead 1994: 98). This is clearly not Paul's *dikaiosunē*. His is the Greek justice.

show the justice of God'). That human dejection calls for the intervention of the *Logos* is also a Hellenistic Pythagorean idea, as we see in
Ps.-Ecphantus. It looks, therefore, as if we have reached a circular argument. What is one's own has been given, and one's gift of *pistis* is the
prize for one's *pistis*. This difficulty is eased if we notice the dialectical
tension between *pistis* as gift and *pistis* as merited. As a gift, *pistis* is of
the same category as *telos*, purpose of being, the notion that one is born
for an end. In the Classical tradition, the greatest good is to be born for
political society (though not all achieve it), to take Aristotle's formula.
In Christianity, one is born for *pistis*.[20] In Hellenistic times *telos* receives
an additional component—God's foreknowledge—and this muddies the
waters. For though one strives, *dikaiosunē* is ultimately a gift from God.
God's foreknowledge in Paul (Rom. 8.29; 11.2, cf. Rom. 8.30; 1 Cor.
2.7), recalls the monarchic mysticism of Ps.-Ecphantus. *Pistis* is citizenship in the political-transcendental state. Because of this, Paul can also
say that *dikaiosunē* is a favor, a gift (e.g., Rom. 3.25, 26; 2 Cor. 5.21)
and call *charis* a present, as well (e.g., Rom. 3.24). *Dikaiosunē pisteōs*
remains an expression of the nature of a political compact; it describes
the type of constitution in the Christ-*polis*. The character of the *basileia
theou* is *dikaiosunē*, pneumatic peace and joy, *chara* (Rom. 14.17).
Foreknown *pistis* is, however, no less a merit and the rewards for it are
pneumatic qualities and hierarchical ranking. This active, positive aspect
of *pistis* has been missed by many a theologian, most of all by Augustine. It is restored to its appropriate meaning by the political context
from which it derives and in which it functions.

The semantic province of *pistis* in Paul's letters is often misunder-
stood, even by scholars with considerable familiarity with the Classical
philosophical background.[21] First Clement offers an important insight

---

20. This has memorably been put by Tertullian: 'O testimonium animae natu-
raliter Christianae', Oh evidence of a soul naturally Christian (*Apologeticus* 17.6).

21. See, e.g., Stead: 'In Christian usage the Greek word *pistis* is influenced by
the associations of Hebrew words deriving from the verbal stem *'mn*, with the root
meaning of "firmness" or "constancy"; but the Greek word itself derives from the
verbal stem *pith-*, with the meaning "to persuade". The noun *pistis* thus has the two
meanings of "firm assurance" and "that which gives firm assurance…" (1994: 110).
Stead is misleading. Paul follows primarily the Greek derivation. *Pistis* is trust, a
trust, achieved by persuasion, by knowledge and discourse. Greek writers used
pistis to indicate a justifiable assurance, or an axiom from which true conclusions
can be drawn, or indeed the demonstration itself. *Pistis* presupposes facing an
epistemological problem (Stead 1994: 111). Very quickly, by the time of the

for elucidating the meaning of *pistis* in Paul. Andreas Lindemann, a most careful student of Clement's extant letters, notes—although he does not develop this point—that, in *1 Clement*, *pistis* cannot mean 'faith' (which is what majority opinion takes it to mean in Paul) since Clement treats *pistis* as parallel to 'trust' and 'humility'.[22] I am inclined to think, with Lindemann, that Clement, in continuity with Paul, must have had a more trustworthy reading of *pistis* than some would like to admit. *Pistis* as 'trust' is consistent with the political reading of Paul that I propose. God's justice, *dikaiosunē theou*, is counterbalanced by the Christian's trust, *pistis*, the basis of all the rights and privileges of citizenship in the body politic. For Paul's believer, *pistis* is essentially an act of imitation, trust in God's *dikaiosunē*.[23]

In what follows, and as a conclusion to this study, I engage a few prominent scholars reputed for their preoccupation with Pauline *dikaiosunē*, in order to place in clearer relief the meaning of the term as it has unfolded in this investigation.

Käsemann

Ernst Käsemann, a scholar of profound insight and formidable vision, is, unfortunately, of scant use for any thesis that is not suffused by the theological. Yet his support for a political discourse, a theme he never addresses as such, must be enrolled, if only by way of observing his willingness to depart from the theological approach or his hesitation about using it in certain relevant cases.

Of the many works Käsemann produced on the subject of *dikaiosunē*, few are more challenging, more condensed and more intense than his 1961 'Gottesgerechtigkeit bei Paulus'.[24] To summarize Käsemann's

deutero-Pauline writings (1 Tim. 4.1; Tit. 1.13), *pistis* has already become the content of a belief or some authorized statement of what should be believed, a *regula fidei* (Stead 1994: 110). This concept is alien to Paul.

22. Lindemann 1992: 31.

23. *Pistis* is also a major concept in the Pythagorean system. Πίστις, 'loyalty', together with ἀπάθεια, 'detachment', and σεμνότης, 'dignity', are the features of the Pythagorean life (Aristoxenus in Iamblichus, *On Pythagorean Life* 234; A. Delatte 1922: 87). In this sense, in Paul, *pistis*, i.e. loyalty, is the rule of life in the Christian society.

24. Also in the collection *Exegetische Versuche und Besinnungen* (1965: 181-93) and, in English, in *New Testament Questions of Today* (1969a: 168-82), here referred to as 1969c. Käsemann turns Paul's thought into vast, unfathomable depth

complex and compressed argument, he understands *dikaiosunē theou* as a unified concept, objective and subjective genitive at once; elsewhere, however, he calls it *genitivus auctoris*, to emphasize the soteriological sense of the phrase (1971a: 77 n. 27). Käsemann refers to it as a power, God's saving power, and he takes it as deriving from Jewish apocalyptic and has Paul associating it with god's covenant-establishment and covenant-faithfulness.[25] Käsemann mounts this argument against Rudolf

theology addressed to communities whose Christianity was, as Käsemann puts it, 'only skin-deep' (1969d: 188).
  25. Stuhlmacher sought to verify and elaborate this point in 1965. In 1989 (English edition 1994) Stuhlmacher produces his own commentary on Romans where he expounds his view of *dikaiosunē theou*. This phrase is peculiar to Paul, and to Romans (cf. 2 Cor. 5.21). To weaken the Pauline ownership of it, Stuhlmacher brings as textual evidence Mt. 6.33, Jas 1.20 and (possibly) 2 Pet. 1.1 and traces it to Old Testament and early Judaism (1994: 29-30). Stuhlmacher believes that the Jewish-Christians already understood, before Paul, *dikaiosunē theou* 'to refer at the same time both to God's own salvific activity (Rom. 3.25f.) and to its effect in the form of righteousness which is allotted to those who, in faith, confess Christ (2 Cor. 5.21)' (31). This dual meaning, he thinks, was derived from deutero-Isaiah's talk both about God's own righteousness (Isa. 1.27-28 [deutero-Isaiah?]; 45.8, 23-24; 49.4; 50.8-9; 51.6, 8) and about the righteousness that proceeds from God (Isa. 54.17). Though Stuhlmacher posits for Paul an apocalyptic view of history and creation, and an imminent and nearing *eschaton*, and thus ties Paul tightly to Jewish apocalypticism, he cannot fail to notice that *dikaiosunē theou* is already a major force in the present life of Paul's Christian community. That this changes matters radically does not seem to bother Stuhlmacher. That *dikaiosunē theou* is the essential operative factor in the Christian society as Paul constitutes it, is the very proof that the concept comes from sources other than apocalypticism.
  Stuhlmacher, wisely, does not pronounce himself for (Luther's) objective genitive, righteousness which is valid before God, or for a subjective genitive, God's own juridical and salvific activity, but makes *dikaiosunē* dependent on the context (30-31). He would, however, favor reading it as subjective genitive (along with Schlatter 1895 [third German edition; English 1995]), Käsemann, Kertelge 1967 and Fitzmyer 1993, commentators flying flags of many colors).
  I contend that God's *dikaiosunē*, while admittedly salvific, is above all the attribute of his ruling power. He is the ruler as judge, dispensing distributive justice (Rom. 12.3), justice in proportion to *pistis* (Rom. 12.6); and he does so through the instrument of *charis*. *Dikaiosunē* of God, a political idiom of Greek origin, describes God's justice, lawfulness or impartiality, the political, constitutional or subject genitive. It is trait and endeavor, attribute and activity, and refers to God as alone perfectly qualified to rule and alone legitimate ruler. It also describes the manner of his government, the only ideal state. That other *dikaiosunē*, the one just before God, the soteriological or objective genitive, is the *dikaiosunē* of *pistis*; it is

Bultmann, who makes it an anthropological concept and who emphasizes the forensic-eschatological meaning of *dikaiosunē* and its use by Paul to describe the present reality of God's free gift of grace.[26] Käsemann describes Pauline anthropology itself as 'crystallized cosmology' (29), because he is convinced that Paul views human existence in terms of its 'need to participate in creatureliness' (21). Although Käsemann's placing the argument back in the context of eschatological Judaism is disputable, his stressing the inseparability of the human-divine link is compelling.

For Käsemann, *dikaiosunē theou* is the whole of Paul's preaching and theology *in nuce*; it is Paul's signature and sets him apart from the rest of the New Testament. This central theme is also the central *problem* of Pauline theology. The first difficulty pertains to the reading of the genitive, which could be taken either as subjective (God's *dikaiosunē*) or objective—the *dikaiosunē* that applies to us, bestowed, however, by God (supported by Phil. 3.9; Rom. 2.13; 5.17 and maintained by the Luther party). The 'gift' aspect of *dikaiosunē theou* presents another difficulty. Mostly already present and effective in humanity (2 Cor. 9.9-10; Phil. 1.11—'fruit of *dikaiosunē theou*'), it is also hope and future boon (Gal. 5.5). The 'dialectic of having and not quite having' (1969c: 170), Paul's 'double eschatology', extends to the condition of being a Christian (Rom. 4; Gal. 3.6; Phil. 3.12).[27] The dialectic arises from

dikaiosunē instilled by God but fully and exclusively belonging to the human person, the *pistis* in the very *dikaiosunē* of God.

Stuhlmacher's methodical fervor to certify Paul inoculated by the thought of his Judean elders turns Paul into a wretched author of dim-witted midrashim, commentator on selected (especially the prophetic) books of the Old Testament, and a docile follower of Jewish apocalyptic doctrines. The Paul Stuhlmacher paints is a slavish devotee of drab prophetic visions, whose study-room diligence is relieved only by sporadic half-crazed outbursts.

26. Bultmann 1951: 270-87. A recent similar interpretation is found in Seifrid: justification by faith in Romans means 'forensic justification in relation to Gentile believers' (1992: 255).

Bultmann argues that Paul's theology 'is not a speculative system' concerned with god 'as He is in Himself'. Paul's interest is centered rather on 'God as He is significant for man' and on 'man's responsibility and man's salvation', with the consequence that 'every assertion about God [or Christ] is simultaneously an assertion about man and vice-versa'. 'Paul's theology is, at the same time, anthropology' and 'Paul's christology is simultaneously soteriology' (1951: 190-91, quoted in Furnish 1989b: 334).

27. Dieter Georgi remarked that eschatology is an anchronism in the account of

Paul's confrontation with legalism and enthusiasm. The gift, then, has an asymptotic geometry, and it takes the grasp of God's invisible hand to resolve the dilemma.

Besides viewing *dikaiosunē theou* as god's saving power and deriving it from apocalyptic Judaism,[28] Käsemann understands it as a unified concept. He concentrates on discovering the privileged center, where Paul can bond present and future eschatology. Käsemann's celebrated formula is *Gabe* **und** *Aufgabe*, 'to reckon one just' *and* 'to make one just'.[29] He connects gift (δωρεά) with service (δουλεία), freedom and obedience, as well as the ethical and the mystical, the juridical and the sacramental.[30]

My research helps modify this approach. *Dikaiosunē theou* means that God alone, uniquely just, 'counts one just' by administering justice according to the principles of true justice. For 'making one just', Paul

primitive Christianity, an interpretive category of later scholars valorizing early Christianity as opposed to its subsequent forms (*ap.* Wilken 1995: 375.)

28. Käsemann contends that the phrase *dikaiosunē theou* was not invented by Paul, but cites as evidence (1969c: 172) two texts that succeed him (Matthew and James), a foreign idiom and concept (Old Testament, Qumran), and a dubious rendering of a Jewish Hellenistic document (*Testament of Dan*). The *Testament of Dan* is part of the *Testaments of the Twelve Patriarchs*, written in Greek, c. second century BCE. The text reads 'desert all *adikia* and join the *dikaiosunē* of the *nomos* of god' (*T. Dan* 6.11); in Käsemann (1969c: 172 n. 2, who quotes Oepke 1953) *nomos* vanishes. A more interesting work (not mentioned by Käsemann) is the apocryphal Baruch, a Greek text of around early first century CE, where Jerusalem is urged to rejoice at the returning captives: περιβαλοῦ τὴν διπλοΐδα τῆς παρὰ τοῦ θεοῦ δικαιοσύνης, drape around you a double clock of the *dikaiosunē* that comes from God (5.2); and, a bit later, Israel will be led by God δικαιοσύνη τῇ παρ' αὐτοῦ, with his *dikaiosunē* (5.9). Throughout, Baruch contrasts God's *dikaiosunē* to human wretchedness (1.15; 2.6; 4.13). Most telling is that the phrase appears nowhere in the voluminous Septuagint (except, in a certain sense, in Baruch) and this should suggest its alienness from the spirit of the Old Testament. Baruch is yet another proof of the interest in politics, centered on *dikaiosunē*, that informed late Hellenistic times.

29. Schoeps had already translated δικαιοῦν in Rom. 4.5 not only as 'rendering someone just' but also as a *verbum causativum*, 'to insure vindication for someone' (1961: 29). Seifrid 1992, the author of one of the most recent studies on *dikaiosunē*, disagrees with Käsemann on all three counts: that *dikaiosunē theou* is a unified concept, that it is God's saving power, and that it derives from apocalyptic Judaism.

30. Barrett sees two aspects in *dikaiosunē theou*, a *justitia passiva*—the quality of being right, and a *justitia activa*, the activity of doing right (1957: 73).

uses another technical term, *dikaiosunē pisteōs*, which I read 'to make
one just by *pistis*'—that is, the individual is rendered just on the basis
of his trust. It is not *dikaiosunē theou* but *dikaiosunē* that has a dual
facet within a unique concept. One aspect, *dikaiosunē theou* (which Paul
takes from the Hellenistic Pythagorean environment) applies directly,
exclusively and indelibly to God's supreme judicatory power. The other,
dikaiosunē pisteōs (a Pauline original, but nevertheless a development
of many Hellenistic sources, Jewish and Greek) refers to 'person-in-
God', the individual who has *pistis*, faith which is itself bestowed by
God.

It is *dikaiosunē pisteōs*, not *dikaiosunē theou*, that is God's saving
power, a metaphysical, mystical force, disbursed by God and incorporated by an individual, but according to *analogia*, the criterion of political justice. (What constitutes merit is known to God alone, and it takes
the name of *charis*.) I agree with those scholars who think that *theologically* speaking, *dikaiosunē* is 'a [not *the*] central Pauline theme'.[31]
In Paul's *political* formulation, it is, however, *the* main theme, as it is in
all Greek (and Greek-inspired) political reflection.

Käsemann insists that in the Old Testament and Judaism *dikaiosunē* is
no personal ethical quality (as it is where?) but a relationship (as opposed
to where?). Aristotle's definition of *dikaiosunē* is, we recall, perfect
excellence displayed toward another,[32] a social virtue,[33] an element of

---

31. Seifrid 1992: 270. Hays already decentralized *dikaiosunē* in his 1988 study.
Significantly more nuanced, E.P. Sanders (1977, 1983) denies that *dikaiosunē* by
faith is the center of Pauline theology, as most Protestant European scholarship
assumes. According to him, Paul's entire interest in *pistis* and *nomos* was to
elucidate the conditions for acceptance in the Christian *koinōnia*. In the process,
Sanders appears to deal a blow to the anti-Jewish motif in Pauline studies: *pistis*
alone is required for the Gentiles; the polemic against *nomos* in Paul is against
Jewish Christians only and not against Jews in general, as it is usually thought. I
think, however, that Sanders's argument does not place him outside the anti-Jewish
approach. Paul may be talking to Christian Jews, but he wants all Jews to become
Christians. The point is that *pistis* alone is required of everyone, Jew and Greek,
hence the Law is irrelevant.

Beker 1984, one of the most interesting contemporary scholars, replaces
dikaiosunē pisteōs with apocalyptic triumph (of Calvinist inspiration) as the center
of Pauline theology. He maintains that Paul's interpretation of the gospel cannot be
hierarchically structured, with one primary metaphor dominating all others (1984:
260). Although difficult or even impossible, the distinction between theology and
politics in Paul may help reassess the question of centrality of *dikaiosunē* in Paul.

32. *Nicomachean Ethics* 5.1129b30-32, 1130a3.

state.[34] The Stoics call it 'the science of giving every man his due'.[35] Unlike the juridical centering of the term, which makes *dikaiosunē* a gift pure and simple (as in Bultmann 1951), for Käsemann *dikaiosunē* as salvific is a gift 'as precipitate' (1969c: 172). Gift and giver are never separate. *Dikaiosunē theou* is no property of the divine nature, a product of Greek theology, a view that contravenes the tradition of the Old Testament and later Judaism, where it is 'faithfulness in the context of the community' (174). The gift bestowed in justification 'is never at any time separable from its Giver'; 'it partakes of the character of power [*Macht*], in so far as God himself enters the arena and remains in the arena with it' (174). What Käsemann does is consciously to refuse to see the split between the two facets of *dikaiosunē*; he is deliberate in his rejection of the fact that the split preserves a political entity alongside the realm formed by the large, hugging arms of theology. *Dikaiosunē pisteōs* allows for a human community governed by political principles; *dikaiosunē theou* for a universal empire. While full life is the feature of the first, even if communally understood, and while a certain amount of apprehension is there (it acquires intensity only at the level of theological speculation), the second brings individual certainty in a depersonalized, fantasy world. It is only when the integrity of *dikaiosunē* is restored that the two spheres collapse, the lower being absorbed into the higher. Paul, however, while enticed by the brilliant postmortem certainty (another Greek peculiarity if I ever saw one), prefers to keep the two worlds in safe orbits, beyond the enticement of final merger—not in a fragile balance, but at a healthy distance. Pauline eschatology is a waiting game of imprecise duration and no imminent end. There is no millenarian expectation in Romans, no cataclysmic social upheaval, no

33. *Politics* 3.1283a39.
34. *Politics* 1.1253a37.
For Plato *dikaiosunē*, that which is proper, the right thing, is internal order. Thrasymachus calls justice 'the good of the other', with the qualification that 'the other' is the ruler (*Republic* 1.344c).
35. SVF 3.63.27, cf. 3.30.22, 3.65.24, etc. See also Dodd 1932: 10. The Roman jurists defined *iustitia* in the same way: 'a constant and perpetual desire to render every one his due' (Justinian's *Institutes*, 1.1., *Digesta* 1.1); see A. Berger 1953 *s.v. iustitia*.
The distinction between the Greek δικαιοσύνη and the Hebrew צדקה, צדק is that while the Greeks think of *dikaiosunē* as an abstract standard of justice, the Hebrews conceive it as vindication of the wronged—see Dodd 1932: 10; I consider these distinctions oversimplifying clichés. See also discussion of Dunn, below.

political or cultural critique. (Rome itself does have a part to play in the Pauline eschatology, which is its transformation into a Christian state.[36])

Paul's disinterest, or let us say his mild interest, in eschatology may come from his distaste for the obsession with the 'when' of it.[37] Such obsession leads to fantastic tales of dubious taste, while Paul is not interested in the fable about the future but in its spirit: the first means interest in the preservation and repetition of life in its old, passé forms; the latter access to a new, vital form. What Paul envisions is the re-orientation of reality toward 'the higher' and an involvement of the individual in the common good. Salvation is in a state of political suspension, guaranteed but not achieved. The *polis*—a *polis* defined by *dikaiosunē pisteōs* and constituted on the *euangelion*—is the guarantee of salvation. The guarantor is god's *dikaiosunē*. The soteriological polity Paul creates gives the human person purpose while *in praesenti*. Paul can provide no panacea to disease and distress; he can, however, offer a solidly organized society with an effective social system.

Salvation, then, is already operative *hic et nunc* in Paul; even more, it is an essential component of the 'ontopoeic', the making of the present, the creating of the political. The bustling life of the *polis* counter-balances the eschatological indecision. The eschatological waffling is overcome by life in the *polis* and the services it requires. On a global scale, earth is no transient world. In Paul, political destitution and want of *pistis* are of the same logical order. What is destroyed at *eschaton* is the colony of those lacking *pistis*, because they form no political configuration.

Käsemann accepts that the 'mystical' conception of Christ is congruent with Hellenistic mysticism, but, he insists, it is so linguistically only and not in content (175). Christ rules over us via our hearts. But the very concept of Power that is so central to Käsemann's reading of Paul cannot be understood outside a political context. '[T]he Power who establishes his lordship…urges us on to break through to a service

---

36. Tertullian thought of Rome as 'the one thing that stands between us and the end of the world' (*ap.* Glover 1933: 120-22). He might have meant it in more than one sense.

37. 2 Thessalonians itself, Paul's only consistent apocalyptic statement, warns against the very apocalyptic realization. It defers the end indefinitely by the usual means of a *mustērion* (2.7). It emboldens to productive activity and good deeds, social and political actions. It exhorts to circumvention of messianic chatter and to excision from the group structure of the visionary idler.

which is perpetually being renewed and to a future which is always open' (175); Käsemann uses political vocabulary and concepts *malgré soi*. Once on this path, he can well see (against Bultmann 1957: 43-45) that 'Paul's theology and his philosophy of history' (1969c: 176) do not so much concern the individual. What changes, above all, in the new *polis* is the ruler.

Käsemann reiterates: gift is power; Christ is lord (176); righteousness is the possibility of access to God and possession of the lord is 'hope against hope'.[38] *Dikaiosunē*, read by Käsemann as the Old Testament and Judaic god's covenant-faithfulness, is understood as saving action and as salvation (177). Christ, the new Adam, is the bringer of the new covenant and new creation to a far-extended Israel. *Dikaiosunē theou* is proof (*endeixis*)[39] of the divine faithfulness not just to Israel but to the whole creation. The Pauline doctrine of justification, Käsemann agrees further, 'is distinguished from the Jewish one by the fact that in it the antithesis of faith and works is associated with the other antithesis between present justification and justification which is still to come (or even, still in the balance)' (178). Käsemann underscores that it is Christ who separates Pauline theology from Jewish tradition, and he ascertains that the trail-blazing Pauline notion, that *dikaiosunē theou* extends to the ungodly, represents 'unprecedented radicalization and universalization of the promise' (178)—that is, I would claim, a political expression and effect.

Given Käsemann's devotion to theology and the Jewish Paul, it is interesting to see his approach faltering in cases in which a political perspective makes for the far more attractive solution. Thus, it is in the context of the most clearly expressed notion of distributive justice in the Christian *polis* that Käsemann is unconvincing, at the very moment he astutely notes the unfair treatment of Rom. 12.3-8. Käsemann himself notes the 'astonishingly infrequent interest' in the question of the relationship between the various functions within the Christian community, 'to which hitherto no really satisfying solution has been offered' (193). He insists that '[w]e have to ask what is the relationship between the activity of the prophets, deacons, teachers, ethical instructors, distributors of alms, those who 'preside' and perhaps of those who tend

38. The way Käsemann conceives of it is rather a forlorn hope; I would call it actualized uncertainty, a form of torture, a kind of Iron Maiden of Nürnberg.

39. Proof in a juridical sense, too, acknowledges Käsemann (with Kümmel 1952).

the sick, and what is sometimes found quite senselessly lumped together in our Bibles under the general heading of 'Christian duties'' (193).[40] The perplexity or the indifference of commentators about the relationship among the various classes within the *ekklēsia* is primarily due, I think, to their failure to comprehend the political nature of this organization. Given the fact that 'the accumulating participles of the first group may well indicate that the reference here is not to officially installed office-bearers' (194),[41] Käsemann is not fully convinced that the functions designate officials in the structure of the *ekklēsia*, but he is confident that these titles refer to functions in Paul's Christian fellowship: '[T]here can be no doubt that nevertheless representative functions of the Christian community are being described here' (194).[42] Käsemann admits the smooth flow from 12.6-8 to 12.9-11,[43] which he also takes to indicate the fluent move from the *charismata* 'which give leadership to the community and are most striking in terms of its internal life, to those charismatic modes of life which characterize Christian existence both in the community and in the world' (195). This is a remarkable observation. Käsemann essentially agrees that the political *charismata*, at the level of each Christian *polis*, form a continuum with those on the grander scale of the world at large (for Paul this is the Roman empire). He does suggest a 'unified perspective' (195) for the church as a whole. But he insists that 'either the conception of office is wholly untenable because it presupposes the differentiation of the private and the public sphere, or it is valid for every Christian activity because of *charismata* of the individual being is at all times and in all places a duty to the Lord of the world' (194). In no other place is Paul's use of the view of Hellenistic political thinking more manifest and hermeneutically sound. The political centrality of *dikaiosunē*, both at the community and the universal level; the workings of *dikaiosunē* according to *analogia*; the magistracy-like offices bestowed in proportion to service (to Christ-*pistis* in Paul): all these point to Paul's sources in the Hellenistic and the political.

40. It is Lagrange 1950 who speaks of *duties* and not of specific functions within the Christian *polis*.

41. Following Kühl (1913: 428) and Brunner (1948: 87).

42. Following Jülicher (1917: 312).

43. He rightly accuses A.B. Macdonald (1934: 18) of near-sightedness for thinking that in Rom. 12.3-8 Paul can speak of the assembly for worship while in the following verses he can refer to daily life and this without any transition (1969d: 194 n. 26).

In another example, Käsemann, who believes that Rom. 13.1-7 illustrates the nature of Pauline paraenesis, which works not by subordination but by coordination, 'by association of ideas and not by logic' (1969b: 199),[44] does not see the perfect logical continuity with Romans 12 and the overt political treatment of the Christian community exhibited there.[45] Käsemann takes 13.1-7 as an alien growth, a foreign parasite, 'a self-contained passage which, as such, cannot be directly associated either with the command to love one's enemy in 12.20f. or with the epitomizing demand for love in 13.8-10, or with the eschatological conclusion of the general exhortation in 13.11ff.; much less it can be said to receive its relevance and its theme from any of these' (199). It is not my purpose to undertake a separate refutation of this approach: my entire study provides it. The consummate crusade Paul conducts for political unity gives meaning to the *agapē* injunctions. Rome provides the political cadre for the Christian takeover and Paul's mission. Rome is even endowed with eschatological force, for its *telos* is to become Christian. (As such, it *does*—against Käsemann—'point beyond itself to the End' [199].) It is no matter of indifference but part of the transformational process itself. It is included in soteriology: Rome itself is saved. This has been amply argued.[46] Paul makes the Roman empire coextensive, temporally and spatially, with Christianity. The constant in this extension-duration formula is *pistis*. What is eternal is God's rule.

The symmetry introduced by *dikaiosunē* between the human political world and the divine, and the determination that the latter has in inducing *charis* in the first, are so strong that Käsemann is compelled to acknowledge a parallelism between the earthly political authority and god's power, but he expresses it in terms 'of the Christian's worship of God in the secularity of the world' (199). The two worlds have a unity

44. 'Principles of Interpretation of Romans 13', published originally in 1961, ET 1969, henceforth 1969b.

45. Moxnes 1995, in an excellent essay, emphasizes the continuity. See also Chapter 8, section on Rom. 13.1-7.

46. The connection between Paul and Hellenistic Jewish apocalyptic is also of a political order. It has in common, for example with Daniel, a political configuration. He may be said to be a follower of Daniel's 'four monarchies', doctrine (8.22), a theory that could have been read in Paul's time as referring to Rome as the last empire. The endurance of this doctrine is best illustrated by the claim made by the German king to be emperor of the Roman Empire, a stance based on the Medieval political elaborations of the Daniel tradition (see Fasolt 1996).

of purpose expressed in a similarity of structure. After presenting the *status quaestionis*, Käsemann makes the outlandish yet telling remark, 'We might say that Paul was the first to revive the importance of the usage and phraseology customary in Hellenistic officialdom, by employing them in the service of his theology' (204). That Paul is anchored in the cultural tradition of Hellenistic politics is affirmed (see also 212), but in a way that, inexplicably, severs Paul from his very social environment and speculative context.

Let us take one more example: Käsemann's treatment of Rom. 3.21–4.25, the dual-*dikaiosunē* passage. Käsemann's view of *dikaiosunē* has been already discussed, but a few more observations are in order. The difficulty of 3.21-26 is attributed to the 'heaping up of non-Pauline terms and liturgical motifs' (1980: 92).[47] Such a dismissive statement should alert one to Käsemann's attempt at evasion. In his critique of the Roman Catholic approach to 3.21-26, Käsemann emphasizes that, in Paul, 'only the Judge can posit salvation, and, as the forensic expression indicates, establish his right to his creation with the power of grace. Mankind's justification is the actuality of God's right to his creation as this reveals itself as saving power...a truth which transcends the individual and is directed toward a new world' (93). There is nothing in this important statement with which I cannot fully agree. My entire viewpoint embraces it. Yet there is something missing here: the political structuring of men's *dikaiosunē pisteōs*. God, no doubt, works on a global scale, includes all creation. God's *dikaiosunē* has a counterpart, the *dikaiosunē* of *pistis*, characteristic of humanity; and just as divine *dikaiosunē* is the principle of the universal government of God, the other *dikaiosunē* is activated and active in a political environment, the human *polis*.[48] Käsemann is absolutely right when he says, 'The

47. *Commentary on Romans*, the fourth edition, 1980 (first German edition 1974).

48. Segal 1990 and Seifrid 1992 assume that *dikaiosunē pisteōs* developed early, as a result of Paul's conversion, which they understand as faith in Christ. Hengel 1974 and Räisänen 1983, however, think that it is late, a result of Paul's association with a Torah-critical group. This is the result of placing excessive weight on the conversion account, which, as told by Acts 9.3-8, I regard as fictional. The story is probably based on 1 Cor. 15.8, cf. 9.1. Even Acts attributes the account to secondary sources, 'men' (9.7), Ananias (9.10), Barnabas (9.27). I think that both Segal and Seifrid are too late in their location of 'early'. Conversion (as illustrated by the Christian practice of baptism—the final act of a long

righteousness of God manifests itself as the righteousness of faith' (94). As I see it, this manifestation is, of its essence, the political. Theology needs the support of practical philosophy. It is the theory of *dikaiosunē* that straddles theology and politics. And *dikaiosunē* is a Greek doctrine.

Again, it is instructive to see how in the political passages Käsemann acknowledges that something exceptional is going on: 'Paul does not use the vocabulary of Jewish apocalyptic here', concedes Käsemann (94), and, in general, says Käsemann, there is little Rabbinic tradition followed by Paul here (see 95). In connection with 3.27-31, Käsemann notes that '[g]race is simultaneously judgment because it fundamentally sets even a religious person in the place of the godless' (102). While this is true, *charis* is allotted according to the formula of distributive justice (even if the principles of its distribution remain arcane), and this draws even this mysterious and unexaminable concept into the sphere of the political. *Charis* is the procedural format that the *dikaiosunē* of God takes.

Käsemann interprets the relation between *pistis* and *dikaiosunē* in the light of Old Testament and Jewish thought: 'an eschatological act of the Judge at the last day which takes place proleptically in the present' (112). The problem here, as I see it, is that in focusing on God as judge one is exaggerating the distinctiveness of one of the divinity's functions while at the same time diminishing God. God is not just the independent judiciary; he is also the legislator and the executive. The divine is judge among other roles. The emphasis in Paul, as in Hellenistic political theory, falls on rule, on God's commanding authority, on his governing might, on God as king (and vice versa). When things are seen from this perspective, the Jewish, judicial connection gives way to the Greek, political one.

I understand *dikaiosunē pisteōs* as an offshoot of the political *dikaiosunē* of Classical and Hellenistic thought. It is god's rule 'trickling down'—an exercise in divinity *via* the political. In Paul, because of the unconsummated eschatology and the ontological duality of human being and of creation at large, *dikaiosunē* pure and simple is unserviceable. Its

catechumenical process, or, as in the case of philosophical conversions—the result of a piecemeal change of conviction) comes late, at the conclusion of a process of change. (Even the mystical Rabbis' illumination is a process preceded by lengthy preparations.) Paul's conversion is only the dramatization, at the terminus point, of his *metanoia*. By that time, *dikaiosunē pisteōs* must have already joined *dikaiosunē theou* to form the grand theory of *dikaiosunē* in Paul.

very coherence in the political tradition makes it impractical. *Dikaiosunē* (the political) joins *pistis* (of *pneumatic* and divine origin, the Christ factor) to produce *dikaiosunē pisteōs*, the principle of the Christian *polis*.

Nowhere do I find more support for my thesis than in the theological discussion of the doctrine of *dikaiosunē* by Käsemann. In 'Justification and Salvation History in the Epistle to the Romans',[49] Käsemann undertakes the most lucid discussion on justification and salvation history that I have encountered. As improbable as it may sound, Käsemann's theological reading of *dikaiosunē* closely parallels my political one. 'Friends and opponents must be tested against the question whether they only feel able to talk about the *lordship of Christ* [italics added] as a mythological, mystical or metaphysical figure of speech', writes Käsemann (77 n. 27), and he thus sets the issue in terms consistent with politics. The notion of lordship—its concreteness and reality—and the presence and factuality of Christ are consistent with the notion of rulership and royal power characteristic of Hellenistic Pythagorean political theory. Christ's statesmanship is presupposed by Käsemann's test of truth. While *dikaiosunē* begins as polemic, 'a fighting doctrine against Judaism' (70), Käsemann rejects any suggestion of its contingency or datedness. Paul may have first enrolled *dikaiosunē* in the fight against the Jewish appropriation of God, against 'the community of 'good' people which turns God's promises into their own privileges and God's commandments into the instruments of self-sanctification' (72), and that Paul appeals to *dikaiosunē* in his argument against Judaism is highly significant. He opposes Jewish nomistic exclusiveness with Greek *dikaiosunē*. Paul invents neither the term nor its content. He uses a powerful concept, one that he draws from the Classical/Hellenistic political sphere. He attacks *nomos* with *dikaiosunē*, law with justice, legalism with right, particularism with universality. Even if the Jews are the original target, it is not Judaism that Paul assaults but any form of nationalism and privileged status, any attempt to claim special standing. The purpose of his entire missionary activity is to create a community that would ignore ethnic distinctions and overcome cultural conceit—a community in which Jew, Greek and barbarian, slave and master, man and woman, wise and fool could live in concord and harmony. This is

49. An article (actually the text of a US conference tour) published in his 1969 collection *Paulinische Perspektiven* and which appeared in English in 1971, henceforth Käsemann 1971a.

one of the meanings of his *euangelion*, as expressed in the beginning of Romans (1.5). Paul's purpose and his means are political.[50] The other meaning of *euangelion*, connected with this (as demonstrated by their proximity), is the history of Christ (1.3-4). *Dikaiosunē*, writes Käsemann, is christology and the product of the cross: 'The Pauline doctrine of justification is entirely and solely Christology, a Christology, indeed, won from Jesus' cross and hence an offensive Christology' (73). This is that manifestation of *dikaiosunē* that Paul calls *dikaiosunē pisteos*, a human and terrestrial *dikaiosunē*.

Käsemann, unfortunately, is drawn into the salvation history of Augustine, who defines it as the battlefield between the *civitas dei* and the *civitas terrena* (67). For Paul, *dikaiosunē* illustrates the concomitance, the getting along, of the two *civitates*, celestial and human. Käsemann is wonderful in his observation that *dikaiosunē* does not begin with the individual, for, if that were the case, the 'cosmic horizons of Rom. 1.18–3.20, 5.12ff., 8.18ff. and especially chs. 9–11, would be incomprehensible' (74). The horizon of this political identity goes beyond humanity, to a cosmic vista. In fact, the human *polis* is a case of god's *basileia*. Declares Käsemann, 'Paul's doctrine of justification is about God's *basileia*...God's *basileia* seizes territory wherever we are and will be entirely human... Paul's doctrine of justification means that under the sign of Christ, God becomes Cosmocrator, not merely the Lord of the believing individual or the God of a cult' (75). Paul does not look upward, from a human or individual vantage point, but downward, from God's purview. *Dikaiosunē* describes god's rule, yet it has also a human thrust, one informed by *pistis* and exemplified by Christ. Käsemann systematically grounds this doctrine in the apocalyptic. Yet is not the apocalyptic simply politics with a cataclysmic end? And Käsemann further undermines this distinction by giving Paul's apocalyptic a locus in the present. In the 'apocalyptic scheme of two successive ages' (67),

---

50. We recall the importance which the 'body of Christ' motif has for the political Paul. Even on this, Käsemann's insight is supportive of a political reading. Noting that what the theologoumenon stresses is solidarity he comments: 'the multiplicity of gifts, possibilities and demonstrations is threatening to break up the unity of the church. The task of the paraenesis is hence to give the theological reason for the unity in the midst of multiplicity, to put that unity into practical effect and to preserve it. The watchword is solidarity, not uniformity. Paul finds it important for the church to remain polyform. Only in this way can it pervade the world...' (1971b: 118-19).

history as a contrast between Adam and Christ ages 'is transferred to the present' (67). It is this 'transferral' that changes everything and effectively distances Paul from apocalypticism. Paul is working in history, in the unfolding present. Adam's reign is over, Christ's begins; this is a continuum without cataclysmic consequences. And Christ's reign is over people—living, active people already organized in a vast political system, but one that already shows signs of decrepitude and self-destruction and that needs to be placed on a solid, permanent foundation based on a new type of citizenship. 'Paul really does talk [in Rom. 4.12-14, 9.6-8] about continuity in time and space and does not yet understand the sonship of Abraham in the metaphorical sense which was adopted later' (68). It is precisely this lack of the metaphorical that my approach to *dikaiosunē* emphasizes. It is this continuity that demands the inclusion of the Jews in Paul's political plans. The sacred is not some privileged space and time; it is lodged and wedged in history. Käsemann, too, is categorical about this: 'The eschatological is neither suprahistory nor the inner aspect of historicity; it is power which changes the old world into a new one and which becomes incarnate in the earthly sphere' (68). This change, however, can only be accomplished with political instruments, and Paul's use of *dikaiosunē* testifies to his understanding of the matter. This is why, as I see it, the earthly, historical *dikaiosunē* is so important for Paul (even if the celestial, eternal one is its model, its aim, and above all, its source). The history of *pistis*, as illustrated by Abraham, is connected with a physical, visible incarnation. *Pistis* is exemplified and exists in history. Faith, says Käsemann, 'has its concrete place and particular time' (69); *dikaiosunē* is 'the key to salvation history, just as, conversely, salvation history forms the historical depth and cosmic breadth of the event of justification' (75). It is *dikaiosunē*, however, that circumscribes history; it is the political model that, in Paul, provides the frame for history.[51]

51. In an original approach, E.P. Sanders 1977 considers participation, not *dikaiosunē*, the key to Pauline eschatology. (Incidentally, he bypasses apocalyptic Judaism in favor of Tannaitic Judaism. Seifrid 1992 finds all this erroneous and Sanders's inaccurate reading of Judaism leading to a bad reading of Paul.) I would claim that Käsemann inadequately joins together, under *dikaiosunē theou*, two ideas that are separate, but belong together as Pauline *dikaiosunē*, while E.P. Sanders splits and opposes two notions which derive from the same conceptual sphere: the political. Participation and *dikaiosunē* are the two essential constituents of the *polis*, citizenship and justice. In Paul's case, participation is joining in Christ's typology; *dikaiosunē* is God's prerogative.

Dunn

In an outstanding lecture given at Oxford in 1991 and polemically entitled 'The Justice of God: A Renewed Perspective on Justification by Faith',[52] James Dunn reviews some of the major themes of his work. He shows that with Luther the justice-of-god belief was superseded by justification by faith, and that its subsequent application to Paul was detrimental to ascertaining the meaning the apostle gave to both. In this timely critique of the prevalent contemporary scholarly approach to Paul, Dunn cautions against certain distortions introduced by the 'Reformation spectacles' (1992: 12) used to look at Paul. I see as no accident that the radical shift in emphasis from *dikaiosunē theou* to *dikaiosunē pisteōs* coincides with the movement from a theocratic, pontifical church and a feudal state to a middle-class, democratic church and a capitalist state; it is a latter-day move from *basileia* to *polis*. Dunn is in no way sympathetic to the Greek Paul. He actually insists that 'Paul's understanding of justification is Jewish and Old Testament through and through' (15-16). Nevertheless, his approach supports my view of Pauline *dikaiosunē*.

Dunn[53] refocuses the force of *dikaiosunē pisteōs* as primarily a social, not an individual, phenomenon, the result of Paul's concern with giving the Gentiles the same rights to election as the Jews (4-5). As I read it, *dikaiosunē pisteōs* is the prodigious leveler, the sweeping political equalizer. Dunn himself highlights the social and political impetus of this *dikaiosunē*. He notes that πάντες in phrases such as 'for all who believe' (Rom. 3.22; 4.11; 10.4), 'to all Abraham's descendants' (4.16), 'you are all god's sons' (Gal. 3.26)—Paul's leitmotif in Romans and Galatians—'meant primarily "all, that is, Gentiles as well as Jews"', and not, as it is often preferred, 'every single individual' (9). Justification by faith is Paul's answer to the Jews' claim of national privilege to election, the chief concept and medium of Paul's missionary (i.e. political) enterprise. Dunn cunningly conceives justification by faith as a corollary of Jewish monotheism, for if God is one, then he is God of the Gentiles

52. Published in 1992; this is the work referred to in this section unless otherwise indicated.
53. In the tradition of Wrede 1907 and Schweitzer 1968 (first English edition 1931), against the pervading existentialism of Bultmann, and in concert with Stendahl 1976.

also; otherwise, other gods must be assumed (12). Not only that, I add, but God is universal ruler, and *dikaiosunē pisteōs* is the human political equivalent of his justice. Dunn intuits not only the *basileia* positioning of God's *dikaiosunē* but also the political meaning built into *dikaiosunē pisteōs*, yet he does not see their Classical and Hellenistic political sources. Dunn plainly and unavoidably understands that justification by faith is 'a banner raised by Paul' against all Jewish racial, cultural and religious nationalism (15), yet he follows the misleading lead of Hermann Cremer, for whom *Rechtfertigung* is a Hebrew 'concept of *relation*', something expressed 'in one's relationships as a social being',[54] *as opposed to* the Greco-Roman understanding of justice as individual and autonomous and measured against the notion of ideal justice. This is a classic example of obfuscation. Paul uses the term and the concept *dikaiosunē*, a relation, profoundly Greek and Hellenistic, and the core of both personal psychological integrity and social political unity. As I have often shown, *dikaiosunē* is the foundation of both the individual and the state. Dunn himself acknowledges the 'corporate and social implications' of the doctrine (21) but ties it to the biblical heritage.

It is common to link the affirmation that righteousness, a Semitic term derived from the verbal root צדק, is not some universal abstraction against which everyone is measured to determine moral purity with the assumption that this is how a modern reader would understand it; righteousness is considered to be a personal gauge of ethical rectitude. Cautionary statements about this modern misunderstanding, ridiculous to begin with, look even more so when used as basis for arguing the Hebrew parentage of *dikaiosunē* in Paul.[55] The argument is made that

54. Cremer 1900: 34-38, *ap.* Dunn 16.

55. Many modern theories of justice, products of a culture of pluralism and themselves claiming historical ground in the Reformation, with its consequence of political liberalism, have critiqued the assumption of universal ethical yardsticks for the good. John Rawls's (1971, 1985) theory of justice, to mention only one of the most distinguished approaches, takes as its point of departure the very question 'how is social unity to be understood, given that there can be no public agreement on the rational good, and a plurality of opposing and incommensurable conceptions must be taken as givens?' (1985: 249, *ap.* Bayer 1996: 46). Incidentally, Rawls's definition of justice is congruous with Aristotle's: 'the way in which the major social institutions distribute rights and duties and determine the division of advantages from social cooperation. By major institutions I understand the political constitution and the principal economic and social arrangements' (1971: 7, *ap.* Bayer 1996: 47).

the Semitic concept, traced back to the covenant between God and man, is amply attested in the Old Testament, the Qumran documents, Jewish apocalyptic writings and so on, that it essentially indicates a relationship between people or between people and God and it should not be taken ethically.[56] I have already observed[57] that if *dikaiosunē* is rendered in English as 'righteousness', the Hebrew Scriptures together with the Rabbis' commentaries are immediately called to mind, but that if it is translated as 'justice', the Classical and Hellenistic political treatises come to the fore, and that no listener of Paul—Greek, Roman, Hellenized Jew or barbarian—would ever, on hearing the word *dikaiosunē*, have recalled a Hebrew scripture or a Hebrew sage. *Dikaiosunē*, as I have repeatedly shown, is the political principle *par excellence* and expresses the essence of a human association as well as the compact between people and God (a particular case of the harmonious leadership of the universe) in Classical Greek and Hellenistic thought. Not only that, but, since psychological individuality is read politically, *dikaiosunē* also describes the undivided human self. It is a relationship, a partnership and a cooperation, based on accord, concord and unity and has little to do with ethical standards per se.

Dunn interprets *dikaiosunē theou* in a covenantal way and reads it as 'God's meeting of the claims of his covenant relationship...with emphasis on the latter' (1988: 41). The issue splitting Catholic and Protestant scholarly approaches is whether *dikaiosunē theou* should be read as subjective genitive or objective genitive, a state or an action, and also whether the verb δικαιόω (*dikaioō*) means that God *makes* someone right or *counts* someone just. Though I find the covenantal sense disputable and prefer instead the more historically intelligible political justice that dominates Classical and Hellenistic political theory, I agree with Dunn's important point that the language of *dikaiosunē* is 'the language of relationship' (1992: 12)—I would add, the language of a euphonious, that is, political relationship—and with the resulting realization (which Dunn shares with Käsemann) that either view pushes 'unjustifiably for an either-or answer' when the relationship 'is something dynamic' between the perfect divine and the defective people, a partnership (which, according to Dunn, will unfold at *eschaton*) (17).

Dikaiosunē appears to be a matrix that lends itself to historical and

---

56. E.P. Sanders 1977, 1983; Dunn; Kuyper 1977 are only a few of the scholars who argue on these assumptions.
57. See Chapter 4, Review of Main Themes.

theological manipulation, and as such, undergoes many an avatar while, at the same time, disclosing its very own political essence. Paul split it not only to show its applications to disjunctive human and divine material but also to indicate the unique axis to which it belongs, the tight alliance between two different compacts, drawn together by an intrinsic unity. The rift that Paul dug to separate model from epigone, divine from human, was actually intended to show that, in a state of grace, the political model that describes any genuine human association can have an existence of its own, as if independent of the divine yet continuously infused by the divine—that the human association is complete only when integrated in the universal. Paul never meant to exaggerate the separation. His interpreters, however, have seized on it to initiate divisions, just what Paul meant to avert. As Dunn discovers, the pull of the full *dikaiosunē* is compelling. Only whole can it be adequately understood. The human and divine 'parts' of *dikaiosunē*, the activity of justice and justice itself, are irresistibly drawn together by its origin in Classical and Hellenistic political theory.

Stowers

I find it astonishing that an original scholar like Stanley Stowers, who considered the Letter to the Romans any number of times and who drew out the rhetorical, ethical and literary influences on it, never gives so much as a hint regarding its political sources. This neglect comes at a price. In 1994, Stowers produced a comfortingly striking, pleasingly revisionist reading of Romans that emphasizes the Greco-Roman 'cultural codes and interrelated texts' (16).[58] It focuses, unfortunately, on literary, ethical and rhetorical models, mostly of Stoic import, and thus misses the structural meaning and the hermeneutic of the text: that Romans is a discourse on *dikaiosunē*, a political work and not a piece of literary moral rhetoric.

Stowers properly argues that most scholarly tradition[59] has interpreted Romans in an anachronistic fashion fundamentally different from how readers in Paul's time would have understood it, and he endeavors to place Romans within the sociocultural, historical and rhetorical contexts of Paul's world. The historical method he uses is solid and

58. *A Rereading of Romans: Justice, Jews, and Gentiles*. This is Stowers's work referred to throughout this section unless otherwise indicated.

59. Räisänen 1983; S.K. Williams 1980; Hays 1989; Gaston 1987 exempted.

responsible; restoring the historical context to Paul is the salutary trend of the last decade.

The emphasis on the Greco-Roman philosophical and moral material and the near-exclusion of the Jewish Hellenistic references clearly show Stowers's allegiance. Reliance on the Stoic moral system produces the 'self-mastery' approach to Romans, which, while passable, is not adequate. 'Self-mastery' is actually an expression of *dikaiosunē*—its psychological component—and is rooted in Platonic-Aristotelian thought.

Even more instructive is how Stowers reads some crucial *dikaiosunē* passages. For example, he makes Rom. 3.21–4.2 the bearer of the message of 'adaptability' (adaptability as a result of 'the messiah who delayed' thesis), the concept Stowers regards as key for understanding the letter. Stowers comes up with the intriguing 'delayed Messiah' concept to explain how Paul theorizes the nonarrival of *eschaton*. This passage is a crucial *dikaiosunē* construct. Here Paul integrates *dikaiosunē* 's political and metaphysical components, yet Stowers reads this, one of the finest efforts of Pauline thinking, as the result of perplexity, an *aporia*. I have serious doubts about this reading. Messianic considerations seem marginal in Paul. Paul is on firm Classical and Hellenistic territory; whatever the exact hour of reckoning, Paul is establishing a secure society. What is important for him, what forms the foundation of the community, is the *exemplum* of Christ. The rest is political history. What is significant, however, is that Stowers badly needs a concept to cover the political structure of Paul's activity, and instead of going to the obvious one, *dikaiosunē*, he falls not only into theological elucubration but even into lugubrious apocalyptic theology.[60]

Stowers, perfectly confident that *pistis Iēsou* and *dikaiosunē theou*

---

60. It is entertaining how voracious appetite for rhetoric can sometimes produce unintended jocular effects. Vexed by Paul's disregard for defining *dikaiosunē theou*, Aletti (1992: 360) explains this silence as rhetorically motivated. Aletti, perplexed by the juxtaposition *euangelion-dikaiosunē theou* (how can pure grace go alongside retributive divine justice?) explains it, rhetorically, in that Paul shows how it happens, the modality by which God executes his justice, and thus 'the how' (*le comment*) defines it (373). The 'modality' is steeped, for Aletti, in biblical and Jewish concepts brought to final fruition by the gospel (374). Classical rhetoric principles are used to justify Paul's Judaism! Stuhlmacher (1994: 13) even expresses the incredible idea that Paul learned Hellenistic rhetoric at the foot of Gamaliel in Jerusalem, thus adding fancy to fiction. There is nothing puzzling in this juxtaposition. Justice-*dikaiosunē* is perfectly germane to an *euangelion*-type constitution.

are subjective genitives, relocates the center of Pauline thought outside the individual—a 'Western fixation', as he calls it (194)—to the meaning of Christ's *pistis* and to the divine *dikaiosunē*. This is an apt redress, yet Stowers fails to see the importance of Christ-typology and God-governance in producing a new political society. Despite the letter's unconditional theocentrism,[61] Romans is equally potently *pistis*-centric, and *dikaiosunē* works on two tiers. Romans 3.21-26 is generally taken as the keynote text for understanding *dikaiosunē theou*. Stowers understands it as a plan, God's shrewd plan to save the people from his anger (196), the contrivance of a human-loving ogre. *Dikaiosunē theou* is, I contend, no novel plan but an appeal to long-established political principles. The criterion of worth, however, is a new excellence, a new good, Christ. Man, infused with *hamartia*, lost his capacity to rule himself and his world. Christ changes that. The *pistis* of man, his trust in Christ, changes him, restores order and direction in and around himself and extends these beyond life, to death. 'Jew' and 'Gentile' become meaningless locutions. The force of 3.26 is momentous: 'It is now, at the present critical season, at this historical time [ἐν τῷ νῦν καιρῷ], that, through the *exemplum* of Christ's *pistis* [ἐκ πίστεως Ἰησοῦ], to everyone who follows it, God disburses justice [δικαιοῦντα], according to the principles of *dikaiosunē* that he alone can properly apply [τῆς δικαιοσύνης αὐτοῦ...εἰς τὸ εἶναι αὐτὸν δίκαιον]'.

Stowers is doubtless right when he emphasizes context and cultural codes for meaning, even when general, sweeping statements are made (202-203). He takes Rom. 3.21–4.25 as the climax of the argument in 1.18–3.21, saying that, while first Paul argued '*that* God by his nature must treat Gentiles equally, 3.21–4.2 announces *how* God has now in fact acted impartially towards Gentiles and thus made known his righteousness' (203, Stowers's emphasis). Stowers tirelessly reminds the reader that Paul considers and addresses the Gentile, yet he consistently engages in an odd apologia for the apostle's Jewish heritage. He roots Paul in a theory of grace and punishment of presumed Jewish origin that, however, does not apply to the Gentiles. Stowers, for all his unconventional approach to Paul, comes to the Gentiles via the Jews. I cannot accept this as Paul's itinerary. The Jews are the afterthought; their position and plight, the law-talk, are reflections of Paul's preeminent interest in the Gentiles. The Jews are his (metaphorical) thorn in the flesh, his antagonists.

---

61. Emphasized by Hays 1989 and endorsed by Stowers (195).

I assume that, since Paul talks about the law, the Jews of the Letter to the Romans are not only Jewish Christians but Jews in general. Paul does not distinguish between groups of Jews. One either embraces Christ or one does not, and, if one does, one either does so Paul's way or one is out. As much as Paul integrates Jews and Gentiles alike in his system, he equally excludes Jews and Gentiles who do not follow his *euangelion*. Any other distinctions are academic, although it is Paul himself who allows us a glimpse into early Christianity by so often addressing what he perceives to be aberrations. Paul has no interest in classifications and degrees. Christ showed the way. *Pistis* removes distinctions. *Dikaiosunē* rules. Paul rarely debates and argues; he sets straight and explains. He could be called a *paidagōgos*, although he did not like the term and thought of himself as more than an educator—as, in fact, a *patēr* (1 Cor. 4.15). Interestingly, Paul also treats *didaskalia* and *didaskō* with a certain ambiguity (Rom. 2.20; Gal. 1.12, cf. Rom. 15.4); as an office, it comes in third place (1 Cor. 12.28, cf. Rom. 12.7 and 1 Cor. 14.6).[62] Yet, for Paul as for Ps.-Archytas, listening, hearing, paying heed is the equivalent of *paideia* (the 'habit-forming'), and he insists on its necessity throughout. Paul's rhetoric is the rhetoric of teaching, of pronouncement, not that of controversy or contention.

When Stowers asks the question, 'What of the Jewish relation to Christ's faithfulness?' (205), he is forced to acknowledge that there is not much in Romans to answer this question, since Paul addresses the Gentile situation and Israel comes in only incidentally (205). Stowers notes that Paul does not assimilate Judaism and Christ; this because, thinks Stowers,[63] Israel continues to live by the law, while '[r]ighteous life in the law also somehow seems to proceed from Christ's faithfulness' (205). This muddying of waters, this fudging on the Jews in deference to certain strains of modern scholarship, is characteristic of Stowers. Stowers can even suggest that the promises are not the same for both groups (205). I cannot agree with this.

Further, Stowers's 'messiah who delayed' hypothesis, though interesting, is unconvincing. It essentially consists in the notion of 'Jesus' willingness to postpone the time of messianic reckoning by dying'

---

62. See also Chapter 4, section on Callicratidas, and Chapter 5, section on Sthenidas. Perhaps, also, as used by Plutarch (*Aratus* 48, *Galba* 17), with the meaning 'political leader'.

63. With a current fashionable in Pauline studies today and best represented by E.P. Sanders and A. Segal.

(214), a way of forcing God's hand to spare all repenting humanity, not just the faithful Jews. Christ's messianic duties are to be properly assumed on his return. Jesus' initial mission, according to this scenario, was to overthrow the perfidious Jews and the Roman oppressors (214). I think Stowers's theory is preposterous. It almost sounds like an attempt to tie Paul with the Essenes, whose doctrines, especially the ones about the wicked, collaborationist Jews and the polluted, oppressive Romans, the messiah-who-delayed myth espouses. Whatever its theological drift, Stowers needs this story to make sense of what I call the political factor of Paul's thought. Stowers himself notes that Paul's understanding of Christ as worldly ruler, warrior and judge, a traditional view also common in Hellenistic Judaism and derived, I contend, from a Hellenistic political *Weltanschauung*, 'has been an embarrassment to theologians and biblical scholars who marginalize such beliefs by attributing them to quotations of primitive traditions' (214). That Jesus chose a startling end—a political end, one may also observe—must have puzzled Paul, thinks Stowers, who explained Christ's heavenly lull as the occasion for an interim period of repentance. This sounds to me more like nineteenth-century neo-Protestant sectarian apocalyptic theology, or 'Jews for Jesus' street-corner rationalizations, than anything Pauline.

Paul thinks that Christ signifies not only a salvation paradigm but also a political one. In view of my analysis, the political dimension of Paul's eschatological thinking cannot easily be discounted. Stowers is not far from this point of view when he notes that what 'makes the [messiah who delayed] hypothesis so compelling is…that it seamlessly integrates ethics and Christology in Paul's thought' (219).[64] The way I see it, the myth of the 'messiah who delayed' is a tortured way of saying, 'Let's get organized, build up communities, name office-holders, gather in assemblies, all according to the blueprint of God's rule of the world and united by a *pistis* in—and like—that of Christ'. Stowers

---

64. It is true that since Paul addresses the human aspect of *dikaiosunē,* the one that is operative in the *polis*, he naturally begins with ethics. This is consistent with the Classical tradition. Even more, since all that remained of the Platonic-Aristotelian soul in the popular philosophy of the early Empire is its middle component, the rational-irrational, which forms the domain of ethics, one is not surprised to discover that part of the Pauline thought displays an intense preoccupation with morals; for morals are of the most immediate and greatest benefit for the Christian citizen.

makes much of the idea of loss of power and status associated with the myth.[65] The point is not surrender of power, however, but the disclosure of a (anti-heroic) process for its increase. Paul's communities, his *poleis*, are nuclei of precisely such a process. The salvation of the Gentiles is not a second thought, as posited by the point of view that ties Paul's theology with Judaism, but rather an exigency required by centuries of Hellenization of the world (and of the Mediterranean worldview). The importance *dikaiosunē* has in Romans demands that we give attention to the political constituent of Paul's thinking.

Sampley

Finally, I must refer to the thesis of Paul Sampley (1980),[66] which superficially resembles my own. According to Sampley, Paul adapts an association model common in his time, a 'partnership whereby individuals bind together in pursuit of a shared interest or goal' (x), the consensual *societas*, a routine partnership contract of Roman law.[67] The unique character of *societates* in Roman law came from their making the social status of the equal partners irrelevant, allowing even a slave, a person of no legal standing, to enter a *societas* as full *socius* (17). The *societas* began as a domestic, family-based association for the purpose of inheritance (12, 17), and this origin is retained in the brotherly or quasi-brotherly terminology used for the contractual parties (17, 20 n. 31). In Paul the *societas* is a partnership in Christ, the *socii* bound by the *euangelion* and by the mission of spreading it.

Nowhere do I see Paul entrusting his commission to others (cf. 1 Cor. 9.17). Of course, Paul has *sunergoi* ('co-workers'),[68] but these consti-

---

65. And, inevitably, of Phil. 2.5-11; here, the unnamed hero [ὅς] spurns his current fame and, by derring-do, a personal act involving descent, abasement and death, returns to a higher than previous station. The net result is not loss but enhancement of status. He does force God's hand, but not as Stowers thinks. The problem with preexistence is that it is counter-climactic. The God may be massacred but will make it back. This is why Paul is wary of this image of Christ and its production, or appropriation, in Philippians is still an enigma.

66. *Pauline Partnership in Christ: Christian Community and Commitment in Light of Roman Law*, referred to throughout this section.

67. It does not, however, unlike the modern corporation, have any legal personality or corporate identity (16).

68. Rom. 16.3, 21; 1 Cor. 3.9; 16.16; 2 Cor. 1.24; 6.1; 8.23; Phil. 2.25; 4.3; 1 Thess. 3.2.

tute a limited circle and the rapport is of a special nature. 1 Corinthians 3.9 makes the relationship clear: the apostles ('we') are *sunergoi theou*; 'you' are God's field and God's building. Few are chosen and commissioned as apostles; this is God's prerogative and cannot be arrogated by human beings.[69]

Societas has an imprecise analogue in the Greek *koinōnia* (12, 45 n. 26).[70] The rather ambiguous evidence[71] for the meaning of *koinōnia* as a legally binding, reciprocal and voluntary partnership or association with a shared goal or concern, mostly economic in character, is a problem for Sampley's view. Sampley himself acknowledges that '[n]ot every appearance of *koinōnia* is equivalent to the Latin *societas*' (29). One convincing case, however is Gal. 2.9, where a *koinōnia* is entered by the giving of the right hand, an act often associated in Hellenistic texts with a formal, binding agreement. And Paul does form a *societas* with the Jerusalem pillars for the purpose of partitioning the missionary territory (26-36). That the Christian community may be rooted in a 'brotherhood' compact of the type of Aristotle's *oikos*—that is, that it establishes a pseudo-family-like position between the partners—is of importance, but this points not to *societas* but to *polis*. *Oikos*, after all, is the foundation of the *polis*.

Sampley reads *koinōnia* in Phil. 4.10-20 as a technical, legal *societas* between Paul and the Philippians (60-71). The emphasis is thus on partnership. Sampley thinks that partnership would have made the Philippians understand better the nature of their relationship with Christ: 'They joined with Paul as equal partners in living and preaching the gospel. Paul became their representative, and periodically they sent him support for his evangelistic endeavors in their behalf' (61). The most obvious problem with this approach is that Paul serves no one but Christ and that he accepts no payment for his teaching. Also, equality in the Christ-*polis* is qualified by a pneumatic hierarchy. I think that the reading 'association', 'fellowship', 'community' is more appropriate. Paul appears as lawgiver and statesman, bearer of the *euangelion*. The

69. Rom. 1.1 (κλητὸς ἀπόστολος ἀφωρισμένος); 1 Cor. 9.17 (οἰκονομίαν πεπίστευμαι); 2 Cor. 1.21-22 (ὁ δὲ βεβαιῶν ἡμᾶς σὺν ὑμῖν εἰς Χριστὸν καὶ χρίσας ἡμᾶς θεός, ὁ καὶ σφραγισάμενος ἡμᾶς καὶ δοὺς τὸν ἀρραβῶνα τοῦ πνεύματος ἐν ταῖς καρδίαις ἡμῶν); Gal. 2.7 (πεπίστευμαι τὸ εὐαγγέλιον).

70. *Koinōnia* will be used, however, in Byzantine Greek to describe any contractual type society (Fleury 1963: 45, *ap.* Sampley 45 n. 26).

71. See J.W. Jones 1956: 163, *ap.* Sampley 18 n. 7.

reading I prefer is political, not economic. Significantly, as he moves on with his analysis, Sampley comes increasingly closer to the political meaning of *koinōnia*. *Auto phronein* ('being of the same mind'), which Sampley takes as a feature of *societas* (62-70), is a political injunction to unity and cooperation. The same is the case with *sumpsuchoi* (see 71). *Tapeinophrosunē* ('humility'), which he presents as basic to *societas* (66), is actually the quality that most uniquely describes the member- ship in the Christ-*polis*; its sense is best rendered by the now-proverbial expression 'to carry the cross'. In Philippians, Paul does not present a *societas Christi*, as Sampley thinks, but a *polis Christi*, with its members not *socii* but *politai*. Paul does not need to use a concept of Roman law to make his point, for he has one that is much closer and more comprehensible to his Greek addressees, one that pervades their political culture. Sampley agrees that in Romans, *koinōnia* and the ver- bal forms and *auto phronein* cannot refer to *societas*; he calls these uses 'sententious', their purpose being 'to describe how the believers should care for one another. [They are] dislodged from [the] original social matrix' (96). In recognizing that in Romans Paul refers to something other than *societas*, Sampley hits the point even as he misses it.

Summary

Even some scholars who approach Paul from Jewish perspectives (e.g., Käsemann and Dunn) arrive at assessments that cohere with my read- ing. Theological understanding of Paul is compatible with the political thrust that I identify in Paul and that I see as coming from political philosophy. In the case of Stowers, who operates with Hellenistic assumptions, disregard for the political component of Paul's Greek environment makes him run, against himself, to the Jewish Paul and forces him to produce an unlikely construct (the messiah who delayed). Sampley is important because he recognizes a link between the *ekklesiai* and the environment in which Christianity developed, but his thesis is problematic because of its reductive view of the community- building process in which Paul engaged.

My own study has focused on the Hellenistic Greek Paul. I have seldom referred here to the Hellenistic Jewish Paul, and even less to the Jewish Paul, not because these aspects of Paul are unimportant but be- cause they fall outside the limits I set for my study. My topic, it must not be forgotten, is Paul's political thought and its context, not his theology and its background. This approach admittedly has its own asymmetry. I necessarily spotlight Hellenistic and Greek traits. The subject matter imposes the method and tools of analysis. My argument is a rhetorical strategy for investigating a vector of Pauline hermeneutics.

The method I use is positive—that is, I try to move the inquiry forward. The question of direct evidence leads too easily to a dead-end. The negative approach, the one that denies influence because direct evidence is not found, freezes the field and allows for no advance of investigation. Undemonstrability of direct evidence cannot warrant assumption of influence, but neither does it prove absence of influence.[72] Rather, in the absence of direct evidence, the burden of proof rests on affinity of concept and analogy of lexis. The assumption is that little is accidental and even less coincidental. Almost everything is the product of a context, of what critical theories call an intertext or a sociolect. Nothing is created *ex vacuo*, and the similar articulates continuities even as it demarcates difference. My thesis subscribes to the critical view that regards Paul as a member of his political, social and cultural environment, that sees him as the result of a milieu.

In claiming influence, I had first to show that there is significant resemblance between Paul's thought and Hellenistic political theories, that there is nothing else in the Pauline background that can explain the similarities, and that given the circulation and endurance of these theories it is not likely that Paul arrived at quite similar ways of thinking independently of them. Next, I provided a political reading of the Letter to the Romans and examined the relation between Paul's reliance on his sources and his own originality.

Plato and Aristotle set down the principles of political philosophy as active political citizens. Their political philosophy *was* politics. When the Hellenistic Pythagoreans wrote their treatises the political reality was primarily autocratic and political institutions were a topic of academic debate. The Hellenistic Pythagoreans' productions are, after all, scholarly studies of sorts, trite but not unintelligent (and sometimes even elegant) commentaries on political philosophy. In fact, the more the application of philosophical political norms was disintegrating, the more the literature about politics seemed to grow, almost as if the scholarly prolife-

---

72. These observations are based on Sandbach 1985, who provides the example of the negative approach, on the critique of Sandbach made by Hahm in 1991, and on Sakezles's 1996 application of Hahm's methodological corrections.

ration were trying to cover up the loss. Politics withdrew into discourse. The Hellenistic Pythagoreans set the foundations for Paul's dual *dikaio-sunē* in their dual configurations of *polis* and *basileia*. It is against this setting that Paul himself enters the scene. Approached from the point of view of political philosophy, Paul offers what in many ways is a quite traditional political perspective.

Paul has little patience for scholarship, however.[73] He is an active man, a man of *erga* and *pistis*. He belongs to no formal philosophical school, has no political accreditation, holds no provincial magistracy. His only asset—*political* asset, that is—is Christ, a Christ that becomes an efficient force once it becomes exemplary, is enfolded in history, deserts its comfortable celestial niche, disenfranchises itself, descends and is fleshed out in humiliation, and, above all, dies and is resurrected. As such, Christ provides a model that is as tangible as it is ideal, and the assurance of salvation is opened to a host of christ-like saviors. This mass, once made aware of its status, had to be organized and the bases set for its indefinite earthly renewal. It had to be put to work upholding the empire.

Paul only rarely sounds the trumpet of the apocalypticists;[74] Paul is not an apostle of the end but a missionary of duration. His missionary activity devalues the eschatological perspective.[75] Paul founds, builds, establishes, cements and firms up; he does not demolish and destroy. He forges communities, *ekklēsiai*—*poleis*—and readies them for *sōtēria*. Salvation is integrated, embedded into the political. The political is saved, too. *Sōtēria* works only through the *polis*.

There could be nothing so reckless as to dispute that Paul does

---

73. Otto Pfleiderer, at the turn of the century, is the precursor of an entire school (Räisänen 1983 is a more recent example) that affirms that Paul's missionary success came at the expense of theoretical depth (see Furnish 1994: 14 n. 28).

74. The apocalyptic imagery is sparse and cliched in Paul. Among the occasional instances, see 1 Cor. 15.52, cf. 1 Thess. 4.16; 1 Cor. 3.13, cf. 2 Thess. 1.8; Rom. 2.15; 8.18-19. In general, the eschatological judgment is his stick.

75. Räisänen, following Pfleiderer 1906, writes: 'Paul was foremost a missionary, man of practical religion' (1983: 267). It may be mentioned, in passing, that even Jesus' eschatology is questioned by an increasing number of outspoken scholars, of a Bultmannian persuasion, such as Borg 1986, J.M. Robinson 1991, Patterson 1995. The great philosophical expounder of this approach was Nietzsche (e.g., *Antichrist* #34). See Eddy 1996: 456, 468-69 for an insightful review of the issue.

theology. What this study proposes is that there is a political component in all of Paul's thinking, that even Pauline theology contains a political center. This thesis takes *dikaiosunē* as central to Paul's thinking in Romans. Since commentators tend to agree with this, there are constellations of readings that make it their nucleus. Such being the case, the centrality of *dikaiosunē* posited in my analysis, even if it results in an extreme reading, makes my approach coherent and consistent with prevailing points of view. Thus I, too, participate in the common scholarly heritage of Pauline interpretation.[76]

76. A claim that echoes Käsemann's position in the German debate on justification: 'I still participate in our common heritage' (1971a: 76 n. 27).

BIBLIOGRAPHY

The following bibliography is limited to cited works only. Ancient authors are omitted if the reference is to standard editions such as: Loeb Classical Library; Scriptorum Classicorum Bibliotheca Oxoniensis; Collection des Universités de France, L'Association Guillaume Budé; and Bibliotheca Scriptorum Graecorum et Romanorum Teubneriana.

Aalders, G.J.D.
    1968   *Die Theorie der gemischten Verfassung im Altertum* (Amsterdam: Hakkert).
    1975   *Political Thought in Hellenistic Times* (Amsterdam: Hakkert).
Adcock, F.E.
    1927   'Early Greek Codemakers', *Cambridge Historical Journal* 2.2: 95-109.
Akurgal, E.
    1993   *Archeo* 105.11: 3a-c.
Aletti, J.-N.
    1990   'La Présence d'un modèle rhétorique en Romains. Son rôle et son importance', *Bib* 71: 1-24
    1992   'Comment Paul voit la justice de Dieu en Rm. Enjeux d'une absence de définition', *Bib* 73: 359-75.
Althaus, P.
    1959   *Der Brief and die Römer* (Göttingen: Vandenhoeck & Ruprecht, 9th edn).
Anderson, G.
    1986   *Philostratus: Biography and Belles Lettres in the Third Century A.D.* (London: Croom Helm).
    1993   *The Second Sophistic: A Cultural Phenomenon in the Roman Empire* (London: Routledge).
    1994   *Sage, Saint, and Sophist: Holy Men and Their Associates in the Early Roman Empire* (London: Routledge).
André, J.-M.
    1987   'Les Écoles philosophiques aux deux premiers siècles de l'Empire', *ANRW* II.36.1: 5-77.
Aristotle
    1958   *The Politics* (ed. and trans. E. Barker; London: Oxford University Press).
    1988   *The Nicomachean Ethics* (trans. and introduction by D. Ross; rev. J.L. Ackrill and J.O. Urmson; Oxford: Oxford University Press).
Aron, R.
    1994   *In Defense of Political Reason: Essays* (ed. Daniel J. Mahoney; Lanham, MD: Rowman & Littlefield).

Astin, A.E.
    1967   *Scipio Aemilanus* (Oxford: Clarendon Press).
Augustine
    1984   *City of God* (trans. H. Bettenson; Introduction by J. O'Meara; Harmonds-
                worth: Penguin Books).
Aune, D.E. (ed.)
    1987   *The New Testament in Its Literary Environment* (Library of Early
                Christianity, 9; Philadelphia: Westminster Press).
    1988   *Greco-Roman Literature and the New Testament: Select Forms and
                Genres* (SBLSBS, 21; Atlanta: Scholars Press).
    1991   'Romans as a Logos Protreptikos in the Context of Ancient Religious and
                Philosophical Propaganda', in Donfried 1991: 278-96.
Balch, D.L.
    1981   *Let Wives Be Submissive: The Domestic Code in 1 Peter* (SBLMS, 26;
                Atlanta: Scholars Press).
    1990   'The Areopagus Speech: An Appeal to the Stoic Historian Posidonius
                Against Later Stoics and the Epicureans', in D.L. Balch, E. Ferguson, and
                W.A. Meeks (eds.), *Greeks, Romans and Christians: Essays in Honor of
                Abraham J. Malherbe* (Minneapolis: Augsburg–Fortress): 80-98.
    1992   'Neopythagorean Moralists and the New Testament Household Codes',
                ANRW II.26.1: 380-411.
Ball, W.E.B.
    1901   *St. Paul and the Roman Law* (Edinburgh: T. & T. Clark).
Banks, R.
    1994   *Paul's Idea of Community: The Early House Churches in Their Cultural
                Setting* (rev. and updated edn; Peabody, MA: Hendrickson).
Barclay, J.M.G.
    1991   *Obeying the Truth: Paul's Ethics in Galatians* (Minneapolis: Fortress
                Press).
Barnes, J., M. Schofield, and R. Sorabji (eds.)
    1977   *Articles on Aristotle* (London: Gerald Duckworth).
Barr, J.
    1961   *The Semantics of Biblical Language* (Oxford: Oxford University Press).
Barraclough, R.
    1984   'Philo's Politics: Roman Rule and Hellenistic Judaism', *ANRW* II.21.1:
                417-553.
Barker, E.
    1958   'Introduction', to Aristotle, *The Politics* (1958 edn).
Barrett, C.K.
    1957   *A Commentary on the Epistle to the Romans* (BNTC; London: A. & C.
                Black).
Barthes, R.
    1974   *S/Z* (New York: Hill & Wang).
Baur, F.C.
    1873–75   *Paul, the Apostle of Jesus Christ: His Life and Works, His Epistles and
                Teachings. A Contribution to a Critical History of Primitive Christianity*
                (trans. A. Menzies; London: Williams & Norgate).

Bayer, R.C.
 1996   'Christian Ethics and *A Theory of Justice*', *JAAR* 64: 45-60.
Beker, J.C.
 1984   *Paul the Apostle: The Triumph of God in Life and Thought* (Philadelphia:
             Fortress Press, 2nd edn).
 1988   'Paul's Theology: Consistent or Inconsistent?' *NTS* 34: 364-77.
Berger, A.
 1953   *Encyclopedic Dictionary of Roman Law* (Philadelphia: American
             Philosophical Society).

Berger, K.
 1976   'Volksversammlung und Gemeinde Gottes: Zu den Anfängen der christ-
             lischen Verwendung von "Ekklesia" ', *ZTK* 73: 167-207.
 1984   'Hellenistische Gattungen im Neuen Testament', *ANRW* II.25.2: 1031-32,
             1831-85.

Betz, H.D.
 1975a   'The Literary Composition and Function of Paul's Letter to the
             Galatians', *NTS* 21: 353-79.
 1975b   *Paul's Apology, 2 Cor 10–13, and the Socratic Tradition* (ed. W. Wuellner;
             Berkeley: The Center for Hermeneutical Studies in Hellenistic and
             Modern Culture).
 1977   *Paul's Concept of Freedom in the Context of Hellenistic Discussions
             About the Possibilities of Human Freedom* (ed. W. Wuellner; Berkeley:
             The Center for Hermeneutical Studies in Hellenistic and Modern Culture).
 1979   *Galatians: A Commentary on Paul's Letter to the Churches in Galatia*
             (Hermeneia; Philadelphia: Fortress Press).
 1990a   'Humanisierung des Menschen: Delphi, Plato, Paulus', in *idem, Hellenis-
             mus und Urchristentum: Gesammelte Aufsätze* (Tübingen: Mohr Siebeck):
             120-34.
 1990b   'Neues Testament und griechisch-hellenistische Überlieferung', in *idem,
             Hellenismus und Urchristentum: Gesammelte Aufsätze* (Tübingen: Mohr
             Siebeck): 262-69.
 1991   'Christianity as Religion: Paul's Attempt at Definition in Romans', *JR* 71:
             315-44.

Bickel, E.
 1924   'Neupythagoreische Kosmologie bei den Römern. Zu Manilius und
             Plinius *nat. hist.*', *Philologus* 79: 355-69.

Bieber, M.
 1961   *The Sculpture of the Hellenistic Age* (rev. edn; New York: Columbia
             University Press).

Black, M.
 1973   *Romans* (NCB; London: Marshall, Morgan & Scott).
Blair, C.
 1983   'Nietzsche's Lecture Notes on Rhetoric', *Philosophy and Rhetoric* 16.2:
             94-129.

Bloom, H.
 1975   *A Map of Misreading* (Oxford: Oxford University Press).
Boers, H.
 1994   *The Justification of the Gentiles: Paul's Letters to the Galatians and
             Romans* (Peabody, MA: Hendrickson).

Bonitz, H.
1955   *Index Aristotelicus* (Graz: Akademische Druck- und Verlagsanstalt, 2nd edn).
Borg, M.J.
1986   'A Temperate Case for a Non-Eschatological Jesus', *Forum* 2.3, (September): 81-102.
Bornkamm, G.
1971   *Paul* (trans. D.M.G. Stalker; New York: Harper & Row).
1977   'The Letter to the Romans as Paul's Last Will and Testament', in Donfried (ed.) 1977: 17-31.
Bousset, W.
1907   *Hauptprobleme der Gnosis* (Göttingen: Vandenhoeck & Ruprecht).
1970   *Kyrios Christos: A History of Belief in Christ from the Beginnings of Christianity to Irenaeus* (trans. J.E. Steely; Nashville: Abingdon Press).
Boyarin, D.
1994   *A Radical Jew: Paul and the Politics of Identity* (Berkeley: University of California Press).
Brandis, C.G.
1905   'Ἐκκλησία', PW V: 2163-2200.
Branick, V.P.
1989   *The House Church in the Writings of Paul* (Wilmington, DE: Michael Glazier).
Brunner, E.
1948   *Der Römerbrief* (Bibelhilfe für die Gemeinde, Eine volkstümliche Einführung, Neutestamentlische Reihe, 9; Stuttgart: J.G. Oncken).
Bréhier, É.
1908   *Les Idées philosophiques et religieuses de Philon d'Alexandrie* (Paris: A. Picard et fils).
Bultmann, R.
1910   *Der Stil der paulinische Predigt und die kynisch-stoische Diatribe* (Göttingen: Vandenhoeck & Ruprecht).
1951   *Theology of the New Testament* (trans. K. Grobel; New York: Charles Scribner's Sons).
1955   'Points of Contact and Conflict', in *Essays, Philosophical and Theological* (trans. J.C.G. Greig; New York: Macmillan): 133-50.
1957   *History and Eschatology: The Presence of Eternity* (New York: Harper & Brothers).
1964a   'Δικαιοσύνη θεοῦ', *JBL* 83: 12-16.
1964b   'The Primitive Christian Kerygma and the Historical Jesus', in C.E. Braaten and R.A. Harrisville (eds. and trans.), *The Historical Jesus and the Kerygmatic Christ: Essays on the New Quest of the Historical Jesus* (New York: Abingdon Press): 15-42
1969   'The Significance of the Historical Jesus for the Theology of Paul', in R.W. Funk (ed. and trans.), *Faith and Understanding* (trans. L.P. Smith; New York: Harper & Row): 220-46.
Burkert, W.
1961   'Hellenistische Pseudopythagorica', *Philologus* 105: 16-43; 226-46.
1962   *Weisheit und Wissenschaft: Studien zu Pythagoras, Philolaos und Platon*

(Erlanger Beiträge zur Sprach- und Kunstwissenschaft, 10; Nürnberg: Hans Carl).

1972   'Zur geistesgeschichtlichen Einordung einiger Pseudopythagorica', in K. von Fritz (ed.), *Pseudepigrapha I. Pseudopythagorica—Lettres de Platon. Littérature pseudépigraphique juive* (Entretiens sur l'antiquité classique, 18; Vandoeuvres: Fondation Hardt): 23-55.

1987   *Ancient Mystery Cults: Nag Hammadi, Gnosticism & Early Christianity* (Cambridge, MA: Harvard University Press).

1995   'Greek Poleis and Civic Cults: Some Further Thoughts', in M.H. Hansen, and K. Raaflaub (eds.), *Studies in the Ancient Greek Polis* (Historia: Einzelschriften, 95; Papers from the Copenhagen Polis Centre, 2; Stuttgart: Franz Steiner): 201-10.

Cadbury, H.J.

1979   'Roman Law and the Trial of Paul', in F.J. Foakes Jackson and K. Lakes (eds.), *The Acts of the Apostles* (Grand Rapids: Baker Book House): 297-338.

Campbell, D.A.

1992a   'The Meaning of *Pistis* and *Nomos* in Paul: A Linguistic and Structural Perspective', *JBL* 111: 91-103.

1992b   *The Rhetoric of Righteousness in Romans 3:21-26* (JSNTSup, 65; Sheffield: Sheffield Academic Press).

1994   'Romans 1:17: A *Crux Interpretum* for the πίστις Χριστοῦ Debate', *JBL* 113: 265-85.

Campbell, R.A.

1994   *The Elders: Seniority Within Earliest Christianity* (Studies of the New Testament and Its World; Edinburgh: T. & T. Clark).

Carcopino, J.

1943   *La Basilique pythagoricienne de la Porte Majeure* (Paris: L'Artisan du livre, 9th edn).

Casel, O.

1924   'Die λογικὴ θυσία der antiken Mystik in christlisch-liturgischer Umdeutung', *Jarbuch für Liturgiewissenschaft* 4: 37-47.

Cavarero, A.

1990   *Nonostante Platone: Figure femminili nella filosofia antica* (Rome: Editori Riuniti).

Chadwick, H.

1967   *The Early Church* (Harmondsworth: Penguin Books).

Chesnut, G.F.

1978   'The Ruler and the Logos in Neopythagorean, Middle Platonic, and Late Stoic Political Philosophy', *ANRW* II.16.2: 1310-32.

Chow, J.K.

1992   *Patronage and Power: A Study of Social Networks in Corinth* (JSNTSup, 75; Sheffield: JSOT Press).

Clarke, A.D.

1993   *Secular and Christian Leadership in Corinth: A Socio-Historical and Exegetical Study of 1 Corinthians 1–6* (AGJU, 18; Leiden: E.J. Brill).

Clemente, G.
1972   'Il patronato nei collegia dell'impero romano', *Studi classici e orientali* 21: 142-229.

Cochrane, C.N.
1957   *Christianity and Classical Culture: A Study of Thought and Action from Augustus to Augustine* (New York: Oxford University Press).

Collange, J.-F.
1973   *L'Épitre de Saint Paul aux Philippiens* (Neuchâtel: Delachaux & Niestlé).

Conzelmann, H.
1965   'Paulus und die Weisheit', *NTS* 12: 231-44.
1966   'Luke's Place in the Development of Early Christianity', in L.E. Keck and J.L. Martin (eds.), *Studies in Luke–Acts: Essays Presented in Honor of Paul Schubert* (Nashville: Abingdon Press): 298-316.

Corbett, E.P.J.
1965   *Classical Rhetoric* (New York: Oxford University Press).

Cosgrove, C.H.
1996   Review of Boers 1994, *JBL* 115: 368-70.

Coulter, J.A.
1976   *The Literary Microcosm: Theories of Interpretation of the Later Neo-platonists* (Columbia Studies in the Classical Tradition, 2; Leiden: E.J. Brill).

Cranfield, C.E.B.
1975–79   *A Critical and Exegetical Commentary on the Epistle to the Romans* (Edinburgh: T. & T. Clark).

Crawford, M.H. (ed.)
1985   *L'impero romano e le strutture economiche e sociali delle provincie romane* (Como: New Press).

Cremer, H.
1900   *Die paulinische Rechtfertigungslehre im Zusammenhange ihrer geschicht-lichen Voraussetzungen* (Gütersloh: C. Bertelsmann, 2nd edn).

Dahl, N.A.
1951–52   'Two Notes on Romans 5', *ST* 5: 37-48.

Dahl, N.O.
1984   *Practical Reason, Aristotle, and Weakness of the Will* (Minneapolis: University of Minnesota Press).

Danker, F.W.
1960   'The Mirror Metaphor in 1 Cor 13:2 and 2 Cor 3:18', *CTM* 3: 428-29.

Davies, J.K.
1984   'Cultural, Social and Economic Features of the Hellenistic World', in CAH VII.1: 257-320.

Defourny, P.
1977   'Contemplation in Aristotle's Ethics', in Barnes 1977: 104-12.

Deissmann, G.A.
1901   *Bible Studies: Contributions Mostly from Papyri and Inscriptions to the History of the Language, the Literature, and the Religion of Hellenistic Judaism and of Primitive Christianity* (trans. A. Grieve; Edinburgh: T. & T. Clark).

1926   *Paul: A Study in Social and Religious History* (trans. W.E. Wilson; London: Hodder & Stoughton).

1927   *Light from the Ancient East: The New Testament Illustrated by Recently Discovered Texts of the Greaco-Roman World* (trans. L.R.M. Strachan; London: Hodder & Stoughton).

Delatte, A.

1915   *Études sur la littérature pythagoricienne* (Bibliothèque de l'École des Hautes Etudes. Sciences historiques et de philologie, 217; Paris: Champion).

1922   *Essais sur la politique pythagoricienne* (Bibliothèque de la Faculté de Philosophie et Lettres de l'Université de Liège, 29; Liège: H. Vaillant-Carmanne).

Delatte, L.

1942   *Les Traités de la royauté d'Ecphante, Diotogène et Sthénidas* (Bibliothèque de la Faculté de Philosophie et Lettres de l'Université de Liège, 97; Liège: Faculté de philosophie et lettres).

Deleuze, G.

1983   *Nietzsche and Philosophy* (trans. H. Tomlinson; New York: Columbia University Press).

Detienne, M.

1963   *De La Pensée religieuse à la pensée philosophique: la notion de 'daimon' dans le pythagorisme ancien* (Bibliothèque de la Faculté de Philosophie et Lettres de l'Université de Liège, 165; Paris: Les Belles Lettres).

Dibelius, M.

1937   *An die Philipper* (HNT, 2; Tübingen: Mohr Siebeck).

1953   *Paul* (ed. and rev. W.G. Kümmel; trans. F. Clarke; Philadelphia: Westminster Press).

Dodd, B.

1995   'Romans 1:17: A *Crux Interpretum* for the πίστις Χριστοῦ Debate?' *JBL* 114: 470-73.

Dodd, C.H.

1932   *The Epistle of Paul to the Romans* (MNTC; New York: Harper & Brothers).

1935   *The Bible and the Greeks* (London: Hodder & Stoughton).

Donfried, K.P.

1977   'A Short Note on Romans 16', in Donfried (ed.) 1977a: 32-49.

Donfried, K.P. (ed.)

1977   *The Romans Debate* (Minneapolis: Augsburg).

1991   *The Romans Debate* (rev. and expanded edn.; Peabody, MA: Hendrickson).

Dornseiff, F.

1929   'Σωτήρ', PW III.A.1: 1213-1221.

Downing, G.F.

1992   *Cynics and Christian Origins* (Edinburgh: T. & T. Clark).

Dunn, J.D.G.

1988   *Romans 1–8* (WBC, 38a; Dallas: Word Books).

1990   *Jesus, Paul and the Law: Studies in Mark and Galatians* (Louisville, KY: Westminster / John Knox Press).

1992   'The Justice of God: A Renewed Perspective on Justification by Faith',
            JTS 43: 1-22.
1993   'Echoes of Intra-Jewish Polemic in Paul's Letter to the Galatians', *JBL*
            112: 459-77.

Dupont, J.
1955   'Le Problème de la structure littéraire de l'Épitre aux Romains', *RB* 62:
            365-97.

Dvornik, F.
1966   *Early Christian and Byzantine Political Philosophy: Origins and Back-
            ground* (Washington: Dumbarton Oaks).

Eddy, P.R.
1996   'Jesus as Diotogenes? Reflections on the Cynic Jesus Thesis', *JBL* 115:
            449-69.

Ehrenberg, V.
1969   *The Greek State* (London: Methuen).

Eichrodt, W.
1961-67   *Theology of the Old Testament* (trans. J.A. Baker; Philadelphia: West-
            minster Press).

Elliott, N.
1990   *The Rhetoric of Romans: Argumentative Constraint and Strategy and
            Paul's Dialogue with Judaism* (JSNTSup, 45; Sheffield: Sheffield Aca-
            demic Press).
1994   *Liberating Paul: The Justice of God and the Politics of the Apostle*
            (Maryknoll, NY: Orbis Books).

Erskine, A.
1990   *The Hellenistic Stoa* (Ithaca, NY: Cornell University Press).

Fasolt, C.
1995   'Visions of Order in the Canonists and Civilians', in T.A. Brady, Jr, H.A.
            Oberman and J.D. Tracy (eds.), *Handbook of European History 1400–
            1600: Late Middle Ages, Renaissance and Reformation* (Leiden: E.J.
            Brill): 31-59.
1996   'A Question of Right: Hermann Conring's New Discourse on the Roman-
            German Emperor', unpublished paper.

Fee, G.D.
1993   Review of Yorke 1991, *JBL* 112: 357-58.

Feld, H.
1973   'Paulus als Politiker', in H. Feld, *et al.* (eds.), *Dogma und Politik* (Mainz:
            Matthias Grünewald): 9-34.

Ferrero, L.
1955   *Storia del pitagorismo nel mondo romano dalle origini alla fine della
            repubblica* (Università di Torino, Facolta di lettere e filosophia; Turin:
            Fondazione Parini-Chirio).

Festugière, A.J.
1932a   'La Division corps-âme-esprit de I Thessal. 5.23 et la philosophie
            grecque', in Festugière 1932b: 196-220.
1932b   *L'Idéal religieux des grecs and l'evangile* (Paris: Librairie Lecoffre).
1936   *Contemplation et vie contemplative selon Platon* (Paris: J. Vrin).

Feuillet, A.
1950   'Le Plan salvifique de Dieu d'après l'Épitre aux Romains: essai sur la structure littéraire de l'Épitre et sa significance théologique', *RB* 57: 336-87, 489-529.
1959–60   'La Citation de Habacuc 2.4 et les huits premiers chapîtres de l'Épitre aux Romains', *NTS* 6: 52-80.

Fiedler, P.
1986   'Haustafel', *RAC* 13: 1063-73.

Finley, M.I.
1983   *Politics in the Ancient World* (Cambridge: Cambridge University Press).

Finney, P.C.
1984   'Topos Hieros und christlicher Sakralbau in vorkonstantinischer Überlieferung', *Boreas* 7: 193-225.
1993   'The Rabbi and the Coin Portrait (Mark 12:15b, 16): Rigorism Manqué', *JBL* 112(4): 629-44.

Fitzmyer, J.A.
1993   *Romans: A New Translation with Introduction and Commentary* (New York: Doubleday).

Fleury, J.
1963   'Une Société de fait dans l'église apostolique (Phil. 4:10 à 22)', in *Mélanges Philippe Meylan*. II. *Histoire du droit* (Lausanne: Impr. centrale de Lausanne): 41-59.

Flynn, B.
1992   *Political Philosophy at the Closure of Metaphysics* (Atlantic Highlands, NJ: Humanities).

Fossum, J.
1985   *The Name of God and the Angel of the Lord: Samaritan and Jewish Concepts of Intermediation and the Origin of Gnosticism* (WUNT, 36; Tübingen: Mohr Siebeck).

Foucart, P.F.
1975   *Des Associations religieuses chez les Grecs: thiases, éranes, orgeons, avec le texte des incriptions relatives à ces associations* (New York: Arno Press).

Fowler, B.H.
1989   *The Hellenistic Aesthetic* (Madison, WI: University of Wisconsin Press).

Fraser, P.M.
1972   *Ptolomaic Alexandria* (3 vols.; Oxford: Clarendon Press).

Friedländer, L.
1921–23   *Darstellungen aus der Sittengeschichte Roms, in der Zeit von August bis zum Ausgang der Antonine* (ed. G. Wissowa; Leipzig: Hirzel).

Fritz, K. von, and E. Knapp
1977   'The Development of Aristotle's Political Philosophy and the Concept of Nature', in Barnes 1977, II: 113-34.

Furnish, V.P.
1989a   'The Jesus–Paul Debate: From Baur to Bultmann', in A.J.M. Wedderburn (ed.), *Paul and Jesus: Collected Essays* (JSNTSup, 37; Sheffield: JSOT Press, rev. edn): 17-50.
1989b   'Pauline Studies', in E.J. Epp and G.W. MacRae (eds.), *The New Testa-*

ment and Its Modern Interpreters (SBLBMI, 3; Philadelphia: Fortress Press): 321-50.

1993   Review of Theis 1991, *JBL* 112: 726-28.
1994   'On Putting Paul in His Place', *JBL* 113: 3-17.
Gabba, E.
1994   'Roma nel mondo ellenistico', in B. Virgilio (ed.), *Aspetti e problemi dell'ellenismo: atti del Convegno di Studi, Pisa 6-7 novembre 1992* (Studi ellenistici, 4; Biblioteca di studi antichi, 73; Pisa: Giardini): 37-45.
Gadamer, H.-G.
1975   *Truth and Method* (trans. G. Barden and J. Cumming; New York: Seabury).
Gager, J.G.
1975   *Kingdom and Community: The Social World of Early Christianity* (Englewood Cliffs, NJ: Prentice–Hall).
Gagnon, R.A.J.
1993   'Heart of Wax and a Teaching That Stamps: τύπος διδαχῆς (Rom 6:17b) Once More', *JBL* 112: 667-87.
Gamble, H.
1977   *The Textual History of the Letter to the Romans: A Study in Textual and Literary Criticism* (Grand Rapids: Eerdmans).
Garver, E.
1987   *Machiavelli and the History of Prudence* (Madison: University of Wisconsin Press).
Gaston, L.
1981–82   'Israel's Enemies in Pauline Theology', *NTS* 28: 400-23.
1987   *Paul and the Torah* (Vancouver: University of British Columbia Press).
Gauthier, P.
1984   'Les Cités hellénistiques: épigraphie et histoire des institutions et des régimes politiques', in ΠΡΑΚΤΙΚΑ ΤΟΥ Η' ΔΙΕΘΝΟΥΣ ΣΥΝΕΔΡΙΟΥ ΕΛΛΗΝΙΚΗΣ ΚΑΙ ΛΑΤΙΝΙΚΗΣ ΕΠΙΓΡΑΦΙΚΗΣ, ΑΘΗΝΑ, *3—9 ΟΚΤΩΒΡΙΟΥ, 1982, ΤΟΜΟΣ Α'* Acts of the 8th International Congress of Greek and Latin Epigraphy, Athens, 1982 (Athens: Hypourgeio Politismou kai Epistēmōn): 82-107.
Georgi, D.
1992   *Remembering the Poor: The History of Paul's Collection for Jerusalem* (Nashville: Abingdon Press).
Giardina, A.
1998a   'Schiavi per natura', *Archeo* 160(14/6), June: 32-39.
1998b   'Simili, anzi diversi', *Archeo* 161(14/7), July: 38-45.
1998c   'Figli della leggenda', *Archeo* 162(14/8), August: 38-45.
Gielen, M.
1990   *Tradition und Theologie neutestamentlicher Haustafelethik: Ein Beitrag zur Frage einer christlichen Auseinandersetzung mit gesellschaftlichen Normen* (BBB, 75; Frankfurt am Main: Anton Hain).
Gilman, S.L., C. Blair, and D.J. Parent (eds. and trans.)
1989   *Friedrich Nietzsche on Rhetoric and Language* (New York: Oxford University Press).
Giuliano, A.
1965   *La cultura artistica delle province della Grecia in età romana: Epirus,*

Macedonia, Achaia, 146 a.C.–267 d.C. (Studia archaeologica, 6; Rome: 'L'Erma' di Bretschneider).

Glover, T.R.
1933   *The World of New Testament* (Cambridge: Cambridge University Press).

Gnilka, J.
1976   *Der Philipperbrief* (Freiburg: Herder).

Goguel, M.
1904   *L'Apôtre Paul et Jésus-Christ* (Paris: Fischbacher).

Gooch, P.W.
1987   *Partial Knowledge: Philosophical Studies in Paul* (Notre Dame: University of Notre Dame Press).

Goodenough, E.R.
1928   'The Political Philosophy of Hellenistic Kingship', *Yale Classical Studies* 1: 55-102.
1938   *The Politics of Philo Judaeus: Practice and Theory* (New Haven: Yale University Press).

Gottschalk, H.B.
1987   'Aristotelian Philosophy in the Roman World from the Time of Cicero to the End of the Second Century AD', *ANRW* II.36.2: 1079-174.

Grant, R.M.
1980   'Dietary Laws Among Pythagoreans, Jews, and Christians', *HTR* 73: 299-310.

Gruen, E.S.
1984   *The Hellenistic World and the Coming of Rome* (Berkeley: University of California Press).
1993   'The Polis in the Hellenistic World', in R.M. Rosen, and J. Farrell (eds.), *Nomodeiktes: Greek Studies in Honor of Martin Ostwald* (Ann Arbor: University of Michigan Press): 339-54.

Gruppe, O.F.
1840   *Über die Fragmente des Archytas und der älteren Pythagoreer* (Berlin: C. Eichler).

Guerra, A.J.
1995   *Romans and the Apologetic Tradition: The Purpose, Genre and Audience of Paul's Letter* (SNTSMS, 81; Cambridge: Cambridge University Press).

Guthrie, W.K.C.
1977   *The Sophists* (Cambridge: Cambridge University Press).

Hadas, M., and M. Smith
1965   *Heroes and Gods: Spiritual Biographies in Antiquity* (New York: Harper & Row).

Hahm, D.E.
1991   'Aristotle and the Stoics: A Methodological Crux', *Archiv für Geschichte der Philosophie* 73: 297-311.

Hands, A.R.
1968   *Charities and Social Aid in Greece and Rome* (Ithaca, NY: Cornell University Press).

Hansen, M.H.
1987   *The Athenian Assembly: In the Age of Demosthenes* (Oxford: Basil Blackwell).

The Political Paul

Harnack, A. v.
1908   *The Mission and Expansion of Christianity in the First Three Centuries*
             (trans. J. Moffatt; London: Williams & Norgate).
Harris, B.F.
1980   'Bithynia: Roman Sovereignty and the Survival of Hellenism', *ANRW*
             II.7.2: 857-901.
Harvey, F.D.
1965   'Two Kinds of Equality', *Classica et Mediaevalia* 26: 101-46.
Hatch, E.
1957   *The Influence of Greek Ideas on Christianity* (Foreword by F.C. Grant;
             1888 Hibbert Lectures; New York: Harper & Brothers).
1972   *The Organization of the Early Christian Churches* (1880 Bampton
             Lectures; New York: B. Franklin).
Hauck, F.
1908   'Die Freundschaft bei den Griechen und im Neuen Testament', in N.
             Bonwetsch, *et al.* (eds.), *Theologische Studien. Theodor Zahn zum 70*
             (Leipzig: Deichert): 211-28.
Hays, R.B.
1989   *Echoes of Scripture in the Letters of Paul* (New Haven: Yale University
             Press).
Heckel, T.K.
1993   *Der innere Mensch: Die paulinische Verarbeitung eines platonische*
             Motivs (WUNT, 2/53; Tübingen: Mohr Siebeck).
Heinemann, I.
1932   *Philons griechische und jüdische Bildung: Kulturvergleichende Unter-*
             suchungen zu Philons Darstellung der jüdischen Gesetze (Breslau: M. &
             H. Marcus).
Heitmüller, W.
1912   'Zum Problem Paulus und Jesus', *ZNW* 13: 320-37.
Helm, R.
1902   'Lucian und die Philosophenschulen', *Neue Jahrbuch für das klassische*
             Altertum 9: 351-69.
Hemmerdinger, B.
1972   'Un Elément pythagoricien dans le Pater', *ZNW* 63: 121.
Hendrix, L.H.
1992   'Benefactor/Patronage Networks in the Urban Environment: Evidence
             from Thessalonica', in M.L. White (ed.), *Social Networks in the Early*
             Christian Environment: Issues and Methods for Social History (SBLSS,
             56; Atlanta: Scholars Press): 39-58.
Hengel, M.
1974   *Judaism and Hellenism: Studies in Their Encounter in Palestine During*
             the Early Hellenistic Period (trans. J. Bowden; Philadelphia: Fortress
             Press).
Hennecke, E., and W. Schneemelcher (eds.)
1963   *New Testament Apocrypha* (ed. and trans. R.M. Wilson; Philadelphia:
             Westminster Press).
Herzog, H.G.
1937   'Nutrix', PW XVII.2: 1495.

Hock, R.F.
1978   'Paul's Tentmaking and the Problem of His Social Class', *JBL* 97: 555-64.
1980   *The Social Context of Paul's Ministry: Tentmaking and Apostleship* (Philadelphia: Fortress Press).
Hodgson, R.
1989   'Valerius Maximus and the Social World of the New Testament', *CBQ* 51: 683-93.
Hogarth, D.G.
1897   *Philip and Alexander of Macedon: Two Essays in Biography* (New York: Charles Scribner's Sons).
Höistad, R.
1948   *Cynic Hero and Cynic King: Studies in the Cynic Conception of Man* (Lund: Carl Bloms Boktryckeri).
Holmberg, B.
1978   *Paul and Power: The Structure of Authority in the Primitive Church as Reflected in the Pauline Epistles* (Philadelphia: Fortress Press).
Holtzmann, H.J.
1911   *Lehrbuch der neutestamentlichen Theologie* (ed. A. Jülicher and W. Bauer; Tübingen: Mohr Siebeck, 2nd edn).
Horsley, R.A. (ed.)
1997   *Paul and Empire: Religion and Power in Roman Imperial Society* (Harrisburg, PA: Trinity Press International).
Hübner, H.
1984   *Law in Paul's Thought: A Contribution to the Development of Pauline Theology* (trans. J.C.G. Grieg; Edinburgh: T. & T. Clark).
Hudson, S.D.
1988   'Review of Norman O. Dahl, *Practical Reason, Aristotle, and Weakness of the Will*', *International Studies in Philosophy* 20(1): 71-72.
Huffmann, C.A.
1985   'The Authenticity of Archytas Fr. 1', *ClQ* 35: 344-48.
Hugedé, N.
1957   *La Métaphore du miroir dans les Épitres de Saint Paul aux Corinthiens* (Neuchâtel: Delachaux & Niestlé).
1966   *Saint Paul et la culture grecque* (Geneva: Labor et Fides).
Jaeger, W.
1943–45   *Paideia: The Ideals of Greek Culture* (trans. G. Highet; New York: Oxford University Press).
1969   *Early Christianity and Greek Paideia* (London: Oxford University Press).
Jervell, J.
1977   'The Letter to Jerusalem', in Donfried (ed.) 1977: 61-74.
Jewett, R.
1971   *Paul's Anthropological Terms: A Study of Their Use in Conflict Settings* (AGJU, 10; Leiden: E.J. Brill).
1986   'Following the Argument of Romans', *WW* 6: 382-89.
1994   *Paul the Apostle to America: Cultural Trends and Pauline Scholarship* (Louisville, KY: Westminster / John Knox Press).

Jonas, H.
1963   *The Gnostic Religion: The Message of the Alien God and the Beginnings of Christianity* (Boston: Beacon Press, 2nd edn).
Jones, A.H.M.
1940   *The Greek City: From Alexander to Justinian* (Oxford: Clarendon Press).
Jones, C.P.
1986   *Culture and Society in Lucian* (Cambridge, MA: Harvard University Press).
Jones, J.W.
1956   *The Law and Legal Theory of the Greeks: An Introduction* (Oxford: Clarendon Press).
Judge, E.A.
1960–61   'The Early Christians as a Scholastic Community', *JRH* 1: 4-15, 125-37.
1960   *The Social Pattern of Christian Groups in the First Century* (London: Tyndale Press).
1968   'Paul's Boasting in Relation to Contemporary Professional Practice', *Australian Biblical Review* 16: 37-50.
1972   'St. Paul and Classical Society', *JAC* 15: 19-36.
1980   'The Social Identity of the First Christians: A Question of Method in Religious History', *JRH* 11: 201-17.
Jülicher, A.
1917   *Die Schriften des Neuen Testaments.* II. *Der Brief an die Römer* (Tübingen: Mohr Siebeck, 3rd edn).
Kaerst, J.
1901   *Geschichte des Hellenismus* (Darmstadt: Wissenschaftliche Buchgesellschaft).
Käsemann, E.
1969a   *New Testament Questions of Today* (trans. W.J. Montague; Philadelphia: Fortress Press).
1969b   'Principles of Interpretation of Romans 13', in Käsemann 1969a: 196-216.
1969c   ' "The Righteousness of God" in Paul', in Käsemann 1969a: 168-82.
1969d   'Worship and Everyday Life: A Note on Romans 12', in Käsemann 1969a: 188-95.
1971a   'Justification and Salvation History in the Epistle to the Romans', in Käsemann 1971c: 60-78.
1971b   'The Theological Problem Presented by the Motif of the Body of Christ', in Käsemann 1971c: 102-21.
1971c   *Perspectives on Paul* (M. Kohl; Philadelphia: Fortress Press).
1980   *Commentary on Romans* (trans. and ed. G.W. Bromiley; Grand Rapids: Eerdmans.)
Karris, R.J.
1977   'Romans 14:1–15:13 and the Occasion of Romans', in Donfried (ed.) 1977: 75-99.
Keck, L.E.
1989   ' "Jesus" in Romans', *JBL* 108: 443-60.
Kenny, A.
1977   'Aristotle on Happiness', in Barnes 1977: 25-32.

Kertelge, K.
1967   *'Rechtfertigung' bei Paulus: Studien zur Struktur und zum Bedeutungs-gehalt des paulinischen Rechtfertigungsbegriffs* (NTAbh NS, 3; Münster: Aschendorff).

Klein, G.
1977   'Paul's Purpose in Writing the Epistle to the Romans', in Donfried (ed.) 1977: 32-49.

Koester, H.
1965   'Paul and Hellenism', in J.P. Hyatt (ed.), *The Bible in Modern Scholarship* (Nashville: Abingdon Press): 187-95.
1982   *Introduction to the New Testament*, II. *History, Culture, and Religion of the Hellenistic Age* (Philadelphia: Fortress Press).

Kristeller, P.O.
1985   'Thomas More as a Renaissance Humanist', in *Studies in Renaissance Thought and Letters, 1956–1985* (Rome: Edizioni di storia e letteratura): 473-87.

Kühl, E.
1913   *Der Brief des Paulus an die Römer* (Leipzig: Quelle & Meyer).

Kümmel, W.G.
1929   *Römer 7 und die Bekehrung des Paulus* (Leipzig: J.C. Hinrichs).
1952   'Πάρεσις und ἔνδειξις', *ZTK* 49: 154-67.
1964   'Jesus und Paulus', *NTS* 10: 163-81.
1972   *The New Testament: The History of the Investigation and Its Problems* (trans. S.M. Gilmour, and H.C. Kee; Nashville: Abingdon Press.).
1975   *Introduction to the New Testament* (trans. H.C. Kee; Nashville: Abingdon Press).

Kuhn, K.G.
1931   'Rm 6, 7', *ZNW* 30: 305-10

Kuyper, L.J.
1977   'Righteousness and Salvation', *SJT* 30: 233-52.

Lagrange, M.-J.
1950   *Saint Paul, Épitre aux Romains* (Paris: Librairie Lecoffre, 6th edn).

Lambrecht, J.
1992   *The Wretched 'I' and Its Liberation: Paul in Romans 7 and 8* (Louvain Theological and Pastoral Monographs, 14; Leuven: Peeters).

Lampe, P.
1989   *Die stadrömischen Christen in den ersten beiden Jahrhunderten: Untersuchungen zur Sozialgeschichte* (Tübingen: Mohr Siebeck, 2nd edn).

Larsen, J.A.O.
1973   'Demokratia', *Classical Philology* 68: 45-46.

Layton, B. (ed.)
1980   *The Rediscovery of Gnosticism: Proceedings of the International Conference on Gnosticism at Yale, New Haven, Connecticut, March 28-31, 1978* (Studies in the History of Religions, Supplements to Numen, 41; Leiden: E.J. Brill).

Leenhardt, F.J.
1957   *L'Épitre de St. Paul aux Romains* (Neuchâtel: Delachaux & Niestlé).

Lefkowitz, M.R., and M.B. Fant (eds.)
1982   *Women's Life in Greece and Rome* (Baltimore: The Johns Hopkins University Press).

Le Gall, J.
1990   'Le Serment à l'empereur: une base méconnue de la tyrannie impériale sous le Haut-Empire', in Nicolet 1990: 165-80.

Levine, L.I.
1996   'The Nature and Origin of the Palestinian Synagogue Reconsidered', *JBL* 115: 425-48.

Lévy, E.
1990   'La Cité grecque: invention moderne ou réalité antique', in Nicolet 1990: 53-67.

Lévy, I.
1927   *La Légende de Pythagore de Grèce en Palestine* (Bibliothèque de l'École des Hautes Etudes, Sciences historiques et philologiques, 250; Paris: Champion).

Lietzmann, H.
1933   *An die Römer: Einfürung in die Textgeschichte der Paulusbriefe* (HNT, 8; Tübingen: Mohr Siebeck, 4th edn).

Lindemann, A.
1992   *Die Clemensbriefe* (HNT, 17; Tübingen: Mohr Siebeck).

Linton, O.
1959   'Ekklesia I: Bedeutungsgeschichtlich', *RAC* 4: 905-21.

Lohmeyer, E.
1961   *Kyrios Jesus. Eine Untersuchung zu Phil 2,5-11* (Darmstadt: Wissenschaftliche Buchgesellschaft, 2nd edn).

Long, A.A., and D.N. Sedley (eds.)
1987   *The Hellenistic Philosophers* (Cambridge: Cambridge University Press).

Lyall, F.
1969   'Roman Law in the Writings of Paul. Adoption', *JBL* 88: 458-66.
1984   *Slaves, Citizens, Sons: Legal Metaphors in the Epistles* (Grand Rapids: Zondervan).

Maccoby, H.
1991   *Paul and Hellenism* (Valley Forge, PA: Trinity Press International).

Macdonald, A.B.
1934   *Christian Worship in the Primitive Church* (Edinburgh: T. & T. Clark).

MacDonald, M.Y.
1988   *The Pauline Churches: A Socio-Historical Study of Institutionalization in the Pauline and Deutero-Pauline Writings* (SNTSMS, 60; Cambridge: Cambridge University Press).

MacMullen, R.
1974   *Roman Social Relations: 50 B.C. to A.D. 284* (New Haven: Yale University Press).
1975   *Enemies of the Roman Order: Treason, Unrest, and Alienation in the Empire* (Cambridge, MA: Harvard University Press).
1991   'Hellenizing the Romans (2nd Century B.C.)', *Historia* 40: 419-38.

Malherbe, A.J.
1968   'The Beasts at Ephesus', *JBL* 87: 71-80.

1970	' "Gentle as a Nurse": The Cynic Background of 1 Thess 2', *NovT* 12: 203-17.
1983	*Social Aspects of Early Christianity* (Philadelphia: Fortress Press, 2nd edn).
1987	*Paul and the Thessalonians: The Philosophic Tradition of Pastoral Care* (Philadelphia: Fortress Press).
1988	*Ancient Epistolary Theorists* (SBLSBS, 19; Atlanta: SBL).
1989	*Paul and the Popular Philosophers* (Minneapolis: Fortress Press).
1991	' "Seneca" on Paul as Letter Writer', in B. Pearson (ed.), *The Future of Early Christianity: Essays in Honor of Helmut Koester* (Minneapolis: Fortress Press): 414-21.
1992	'Hellenistic Moralists and the New Testament', *ANRW* II.26.1: 267-333.

Manning, C.E.

1994	'School Philosophy and Popular Philosophy in the Roman Empire', *ANRW* II.36.7: 4995-5026.

Mansfeld, J.

1992	*Heresiography in Context: Hippolytus' Elenchos as a Source for Greek Philosophy* (Philosophia Antiqua, 56; Leiden: E.J. Brill).

Manson, T.W.

1977	'St. Paul's Letter to the Romans—and Others', in Donfried (ed.) 1977: 1-16.

Marcovich, M.

1964	'Pythagorica', *Philologus* 108: 29-44.

Marrou, H.-I.

1938	*Saint Augustin et la fin de la culture antique* (Bibliothèque des Ecoles Françaises d'Athènes et de Rome; Paris: E. de Boccard).
1956	*A History of Education in Antiquity* (trans. G. Lamb; New York: Sheed & Ward).
1960	*Clement d'Alexandrie: Le Pédagogue* (SC, 70; Paris: Cerf).

Martin, D.B.

1990	*Slavery as Salvation: The Metaphor of Slavery in Pauline Christianity* (New Haven: Yale University Press).

Maurer, C.

1964	'Σύνοιδα-συνείδησις', *TDNT*, VII: 898-919.

Mayhew, R.

1996	'Aristotle on Civic Friendship', unpublished paper. Presented to the Society for Ancient Greek Philosophy (SAGP) at the Central American Philosophical Association, Chicago, April.

McKeon, R. (ed. and introduced by)

1941	*The Basic Works of Aristotle* (New York: Random House).

Meeks, W.A. (ed.)

1972	*The Writings of St. Paul: A Norton Critical Edition. Annotated Text Criticism* (New York: W.W. Norton).

Meeks, W.A.

1983	*The First Urban Christians: The Social World of the Apostle Paul* (New Haven: Yale University Press).
1986	*The Moral World of the First Christians* (Philadelphia: Westminster Press).

Merkel, H.
1991   *Die Pastoralbriefe* (NTD, 9.1; Göttingen: Vandenhoeck & Ruprecht).
Meyer, P.W.
1980   'Romans 10:4 and the "end" of the Law', in J.L. Crenshaw and S.
            Sandmel (eds.), *The Divine Helmsman: Studies on God's Control of
            Human Events, Presented to Lou H. Silberman* (New York: Ktav): 61-72.
Michaelis, W.
1935   *Der Brief des Paulus an die Philipper* (Leipzig: J.C. Hinrichs).
Michel, O.
1955   *Der Brief an die Römer* (MeyerK; Göttingen: Vandenhoeck & Ruprecht,
            10th edn).
Minear, P.
1971   *The Obedience of Faith* (SBT, 2/19; London: SCM Press).
Mingay, J.
1987   'How Should a Philosopher Live? Two Aristotelian Views', *History of
            Political Thought* 8: 21-32.
Mitchell, A.C., SJ
1992   'The Social Function of Friendship in Acts 2.44-47 and 4.32-37', *JBL*
            111: 255-72.
Mitchell, M.M.
1991   *Paul and the Rhetoric of Reconciliation: An Exegetical Investigation of
            the Language and Composition of 1 Corinthians* (HUT, 28; Tübingen:
            Mohr Siebeck).
1992   'New Testament Envoys in the Context of Greco-Roman Diplomatic and
            Epistolary Conventions: The Example of Timothy and Titus', *JBL* 111:
            641-62.
Moores, J.D.
1995   *Wrestling with Rationality in Paul: Romans 1–8 in a New Perspective*
            (SNTSMS, 82; Cambridge: Cambridge University Press).
Moraux, P.
1957   *À La Recherche de l'Aristotle perdu. Le Dialogue sur la Justice* (Leuven:
            Publications Universitaires de Louvain).
1973   *Der Aristotelismus bei den Griechen von Andronikos bis Alexander von
            Aphrodisias. I. Die Renaissance des Aristotelismus im I. Jh. v. Chr.*
            (Peripatoi, 5; Berlin: W. de Gruyter).
1984   *Der Aristotelismus bei den Griechen von Andronikos bis Alexander von
            Aphrodisias. II. Der Aristotelismus im I. und II. Jh. n. Chr.* (Peripatoi, 6;
            Berlin: W. de Gruyter).
Morgenthaler, R.
1958   *Statistik des neutestamentlischen Wortschatzes* (Zürich: Gotthelf).
Moxnes, H.
1988   'Honor and Righteousness in Romans', *JSNT* 32: 61-77.
1995   'The Quest for Honor and the Unity of the Community in Romans 12 and
            in the Orations of Dio Chrysostom', in T. Engberg-Pedersen (ed.), *Paul in
            His Hellenistic Context* (Minneapolis: Augsburg-Fortress): 203-30.
Muehl, M.
1929   'Die Gesetze des Zaleukos und Charondas', *Klio* 22: 105-24, 432-63.

Mueller, I.

    1992   'Heterodoxy and Doxography in Hippolytus' Refutation of All Heresies', *ANRW* II.36.6: 4309-74.

Munck, J.

    1959   *Paul and the Salvation of Mankind* (trans. F. Clarke; Richmond, VA: John Knox Press).

Murphy-O'Connor, J.

    1992   *The Holy Land: An Archaeological Guide from Earliest Times to 1700* (Oxford: Oxford University Press, 3rd edn).

    1997   *Paul: A Critical Life* (Oxford: Oxford University Press).

Nebe, G.

    1992   'Righteousness in Paul' (trans. P. Cathey), in H.G. Reventlow and Y. Hoffman (eds.), *Justice and Righteousness: Biblical Themes and Their Influence* (JSOTSup, 137; Sheffield: Sheffield Academic Press): 131-53.

Nettleship, R.L.

    1929   *Lectures on the Republic of Plato* (ed. L. Charnwood; London: Macmillan).

Netzer, E.

    1998   'Sotto il palazzo di Erode', *Archeo* 161(14/7), July: 32-37.

Newsome, J.D.

    1992   *Greeks, Romans, Jews: Currents of Culture and Belief in the New Testament World* (Valley Forge, PA: Trinity Press International).

Neyrey, J.H.

    1990   *Paul, in Other Words: A Cultural Reading of His Letters* (Louisville, KY: Westminster / John Knox Press).

Nicolet, C. (ed.)

    1990   *Du Pouvoir dans l'Antiquité: mots et réalités* (Hautes études du monde gréco-romain/Cahiers du Centre Gustave Glotz, 16; Geneva: Librairie Droz).

Nietzsche, F.

    1967   *On the Genealogy of Morals* (trans. W. Kaufmann and R.J. Hollingdale; New York: Random House).

    1986   'The Antichrist', in W. Kaufmann (ed. and trans.), *The Portable Nietzsche* (Harmondsworth: Penguin Books).

Nilsson, M.P.

    1951–60   *Opuscula Selecta* (Lund: C.W.K. Gleerup).

Nock, A.D.

    1938   *St. Paul* (New York: Harper & Brothers).

    1951   'Soter and Euergetes', in S.E. Johnson (ed.), *The Joy of Study: Papers on New Testament and Related Subjects Presented to Honor Frederick Clifton Grant* (New York: Macmillan): 127-48.

    1972   *Essays on Religion and the Ancient World* (ed. Z. Stewart; Cambridge, MA: Harvard University Press).

North, H.

    1966   *Sophrosyne: Self-Knowledge and Self-Restraint in Greek Literature* (Cornell Studies in Classical Philology, 35; Ithaca, NY: Cornell University Press).

Nussbaum, M.C.
1994   *The Therapy of Desire: Theory and Practice in Hellenistic Ethics* (The Martin Classical Lectures; Princeton, NJ: Princeton University Press).

Nygren, A.
1949   *Commentary on Romans* (trans. C.C. Rasmussen; Philadelphia: Fortress).

Oepke, A.
1953   'Δικαιοσύνη θεοῦ bei Paulus in neuer Beleuchtung', *TLZ* 78: 258-63.

Ogilvie, R.M.
1965   *A Commentary on Livy*, Books 1-5 (Oxford: Clarendon Press).

Owens, E.J.
1991   *The City in the Greek and Roman World* (London: Routledge).

Pagels, E.
1975   *The Gnostic Paul: Gnostic Exegesis of the Pauline Letters* (Philadelphia: Fortress Press).

Pascher, J.
1931   ʽΗ βασιλικὴ ὁδός, *Der Königsweg zu Wiedergeburt und Vergottung bei Philon von Alexandreia* (Studien zur Geschichte und Kultur des Altertums, 17.3-4; Paderborn: F. Schoningh).

Patterson, S.J.
1995   'The End of Apocalypse: Rethinking the Eschatological Jesus', *TTod* 52: 29-48.

Pearson, B.A.
1990   *Gnosticism, Judaism, and Egyptian Christianity* (Minneapolis: Fortress Press).

Penna, R.
1984   *L'ambiente storico-culturale delle origini cristiane. Una documentazione ragionata* (La Bibbia nella storia, 7: Bologna: Centro Editoriale Dehoniano).

Peterson, E.
1941   '῎Εργον in der Bedeutung "Bau" bei Paulus', *Bib* 22: 439-41.

Pfister, F.
1930   *Die Religion der Griechen und Römer mit einer Einführung in die vergleichende Religionswissenschaft. Darstellung und Literaturbericht (1918-1929/30)* (Jahresbericht über die Fortschritte der klassischen Altertumswissenschaft, 229; Leipzig: O.R. Reisland).

Pfleiderer, O.
1906   *Christian Origins* (New York: Huebsch).

Pierce, C.A.
1955   *Conscience in the New Testament: A Study of Syneidēsis in the New Testament, in Light of Its Sources and with Particular Reference to St. Paul, with Some Observations Regarding Its Pastoral Relevance Today* (SBT, 15; London: SCM Press).

Plato
1937   *The Dialogues* (trans. B. Jowett; introduction by R. Demos; New York: Random House).
1971   *The Republic* (trans. with introduction and notes by F.M. Cornford; London: Oxford University Press).

Plezia, M.
1949   *De commentariis isagogicis* (Archiwum Filologiczne, 23; Cracow: Polska
            Akademia Umiejetnosci).
1969–70   'Die Geburtsurkunden des Hellenismus', *Eos* 58: 51-62.
Pomeroy, S.B.
1975   *Goddesses, Whores, Wives, and Slaves: Women in Classical Antiquity*
            (New York: Schocken Books).
Porter, S.E.
1990   'Romans 13:1-7 as Pauline Political Rhetoric', *FN* 3: 115-37.
Praechter, K.
1891   'Metopos, Theages und Archytas bei Stobaeus', *Philologus* 50: 49-57.
Préaux, C.
1976   'L'Image du roi de l'époque hellénistique', in F. Bossier, *et al.* (eds.),
            *Images of Man in Ancient and Medieval Thought: studia Gerardo
            Verbeke ab amicis et collegis dicata* (Leuven: Leuven University Press):
            53-75.
1978   *Le Monde hellénistique. La Grèce et l'Orient de la mort d'Alexandre à la
            conquête romaine de la Grèce (323-146 av. J.C.)* (Nouvelle Clio.
            L'Histoire et ses problèmes, 6 and 6 bis; Paris: Presses Universitaires de
            France).
Rawls, J.
1971   *A Theory of Justice* (Cambridge, MA: Harvard University Press).
Reid, M.L.
1992   'A Rhetorical Analysis of Romans 1:1–5:21 with Attention Given to the
            Rhetorical Function of 5:1-21', *Perspectives in Religious Studies* 19: 255-
            72.
Reitzenstein, R.
1904   *Poimandres. Studien zur griechisch-ägyptischen und frühchristlischen
            Literatur* (Leipzig: Teubner).
1917   *Die Göttin Psyche in der hellenistische und frühchristlische Literatur*
            (Sitzungsberichte der Heidelberger Akademie er Wissenschaften,
            philosophish-historisch Klasse, 10; Heidelberg: Carl Winter).
1921   *Das Iranische Erlösungsmysterium: Religionsgeschichtliche Untersuch-
            ungen* (Bonn: Marcus & Weber).
1978   *Hellenistic Mystery-Religions: Their Basic Ideas and Significance* (trans.
            J.E. Steely; PTMS, 15; Pittsburgh: Pickwick Press).
Rengstorf, K.H.
1964   'Ἁμαρτωλός', *TDNT*, I: 325-28.
Riekkinen, V.
1980   *Römer 13: Aufzeichnung und Weiterführung der exegetischen Diskussion*
            (Helsinki: Annales Academiae Scientiarum Fennicae).
Rienecker, F.
1980   *A Linguistic Key to the Greek New Testament* (trans. and ed. C.L. Rogers;
            Grand Rapids: Zondervan).
Riffaterre, M.
1978   *Semiotics of Poetry* (Bloomington: Indiana University Press).
Robinson, J.M.
1991   'The Q Trajectory: Between John and Matthew Via Jesus', in B.A.

Pearson (ed.), *The Future of Early Christianity: Essays in Honor of Helmut Koester* (Minneapolis: Fortress Press): 173-94.

Robinson, J.M. (gen. ed.)

1977   *The Nag Hammadi Library in English* (trans. Members of the Coptic Gnostic Library Project of the Institute for Antiquity and Christianity; San Francisco: Harper & Row).

Robinson, R.

1977   'Aristotle on Akrasia', in Barnes 1977: 79-91.

Ross, D.

1988   'Introduction', to Aristotle, *The Nicomachean Ethics* (1988 edn).

Rostovtzeff, M.

1927   *Mystic Italy* (New York: H. Holt).

1941   *The Social and Economic History of the Hellenistic World* (Oxford: Clarendon Press).

1957   *The Social and Economic History of the Roman Empire* (rev. P.M. Fraser; Oxford: Clarendon Press, 2nd edn).

Räisänen, H.

1983   *Paul and the Law* (Tübingen: Mohr Siebeck).

Sakezles, P.

1996   'Aristotle and Chrysippus on the Physiology of Human Action', unpublished paper. Presented to the Society for Ancient Greek Philosophy (SAGP) at the Central American Philosophical Association, Chicago, 26 April 1996.

Sampley, J.P.

1980   *Pauline Partnership in Christ: Christian Community and Commitment in Light of Roman Law* (Philadelphia: Fortress Press).

Sandbach, F.H.

1985   *Aristotle and the Stoics* (Cambridge Philological Society Supplements, 10; Cambridge: Cambridge Philological Society).

Sanders, E.P.

1977   *Paul and Palestinian Judaism: A Comparison of Patterns of Religion* (Philadelphia: Fortress Press).

1983   *Paul, the Law, and the Jewish People* (Philadelphia: Fortress Press).

1991   *Paul* (Past Masters; Oxford: Oxford University Press).

Sanders, J.T.

1993   *Schismatics, Sectarians, Dissidents, Deviants: The First One Hundred Years of Jewish-Christian Relations* (Valley Forge, PA: Trinity Press International).

Sandys, J.E.

1925   *A Companion to Latin Studies* (Cambridge: Cambridge University Press, 3rd edn).

Savage, T.B.

1995   *Power Through Weakness: Paul's Understanding of the Christian Ministry in 2 Corinthians* (Cambridge: Cambridge University Press).

Saïd, S.

1994   'The City in Greek Novel', in J. Tatum (ed.), *The Search for the Ancient Novel* (Baltimore: The Johns Hopkins University Press): 216-36.

Schiavo, A.L.
1993   *Charites. Il segno della distinzione* (Naples: Bibliopolis).
Schlatter, A.
1995   *Romans: The Righteousness of God* (trans. S.S. Schatzmann; Peabody, MA: Hendrickson).
Schlier, H.
1958   *Die Zeit der Kirche: Exegetische Aufsatze und Vortrage* (Freiburg: Herder, 2nd edn).
Schoeps, H.J.
1961   *Paul: The Theology of the Apostle in the Light of Jewish Religious History* (trans. H. Knight; Philadelphia: Westminster Press).
Schreiner, T.R.
1993   Review of Winger 1992, *JBL* 112: 724-26.
Schüssler Fiorenza, E.
1983   *In Memory of Her: A Feminist Theological Reconstruction of Christian Origins* (New York: Crossroads).
Schweitzer, A.
1968   *The Mysticism of Paul the Apostle* (trans. W. Montgomery; preface by F.C. Burkitt; New York: Seabury).
Scott, J.M.
1993   'Paul's Use of Deuteronomic Tradition', *JBL* 112: 645-65.
Scroggs, R.
1963   'Romans VI.7 ὁ γὰρ ἀποθανών δεδικαίωται ἀπὸ τῆς ἁμαρτίας', *NTS* 10: 104-108.
1976   'Paul as Rhetorician: Two Homilies in Romans 1–11', in R. Hamerton-Kelly and R. Scroggs (eds.), *Jews, Greeks and Christians: Religious Cultures in Late Antiquity. Essays in Honor of William David Davies* (Leiden: E.J. Brill): 271-99.
1980   'Sociological Interpretation of the New Testament: The Current State of Research', *NTS* 26: 164-79.
Seeley, D.
1994   *Deconstructing the New Testament* (Biblical Interpretation, 5; Leiden: E.J. Brill).
Segal, A.F.
1977   *Two Powers in Heaven: Early Rabbinic Reports About Christianity and Gnosticism* (SJLA, 25; Leiden: E.J. Brill).
1982   'Ruler of This World: Attitudes About Mediator Figures and the Importance of Sociology for Self-Definition', in E.P. Sanders (ed.), *Jewish and Christian Self-Definition: Aspects of Judaism in the Graeco-Roman Period*, II (Philadelphia: Fortress Press): 245-68.
1990   *Paul the Convert: The Apostolate and Apostasy of Saul the Pharisee* (New Haven: Yale University Press).
Seifrid, M.
1992   *Justification by Faith: The Origin and Development of a Central Pauline Theme* (NovTSup, 68; Leiden: E.J. Brill).
Siegert, F.
1985   *Argumentation bei Paulus gezeigt an Röm 9–11* (WUNT, 34; Tübingen: Mohr Siebeck).

Smith, J.Z.
1990   *Drudgery Divine: On the Comparison of Early Christianities and the Religions of Late Antiquity* (Chicago: University of Chicago Press).
Smith, M.
1958   'The Description of the Essenes in Josephus and the Philosophumena', *HUCA* 29: 273-14.
1973   *Clement of Alexandria and the Secret Gospel of Mark* (Cambridge, MA: Harvard University Press).
1980   'Pauline Worship as Seen by Pagans', *HTR* 73: 241-49.
Smith, W.
1858   *Dictionary of Greek and Roman Biography and Mythology* (London: Walton & Maberly).
Smyth, H.W.
1920   *Greek Grammar* (Cambridge, MA: Harvard University Press).
Stacey, W.D.
1956   *The Pauline View of Man in Relation to Its Judaic and Hellenistic Background* (London: Macmillan).
Stählin, G.
1964   'ἴσος, ἰσότης, ἰσότιμος', *TDNT*, III: 343-55.
Stahr, A.
1858   'Aristoteles', in W. Smith (ed.), *Dictionary of Greek and Roman Biography and Mythology*, I (London: Walton & Maberly, John Murray): 317a-44a.
Stambaugh, J.E., and D.L. Balch
1986   *The New Testament in Its Social Environment* (Library of Early Christianity, 2; Philadelphia: Westminster Press).
Stead, C.
1994   *Philosophy in Christian Antiquity* (Cambridge: Cambridge University Press).
Stendahl, K.
1963   'The Apostle Paul and the Introspective Conscience of the West', *HTR* 56: 199-215.
1976   *Paul Among Jews and Gentiles and Other Essays* (Philadelphia: Fortress Press).
Stern, E.
1994   *Dor-Ruler of the Seas: Twelve Years of Excavations at the Israelite-Phoenician Harbor Town on the Carmel Coast* (Jerusalem: Israel Exploration Society).
Stirewalt, M.L.
1977   'The Form and Function of the Greek Letter-Essay', in Donfried (ed.) 1977: 175-206.
1993   *Studies in Ancient Greek Epistolography* (SBLRBS, 27; Atlanta: Scholars Press).
Stobaeus, J.
1884–1912 *Anthologium* (ed. K. Wachsmuth and O. Hense; Berlin: Weidmann).
Stowers, S. K.
1981   *The Diatribe and Paul's Letter to the Romans* (SBLDS, 57; Chico, CA: Scholars Press).

1984a   'Paul's Dialogue with a Fellow Jew in Romans 3:1-9', *CBQ* 46: 707-22.
1984b   'Social Status, Public Speaking and Private Teaching: The Circumstances of Paul's Preaching Activity', *NovT* 26: 59-82.
1986   *Letter Writing in Greco-Roman Antiquity* (Philadelphia: Westminster Press).
1988   'The Diatribe', in D.E. Aune (ed.), *Greco-Roman Literature and the New Testament: Select Forms and Genres* (SBL, 21; Atlanta: Scholars Press): 71-83.
1994   *A Rereading of Romans: Justice, Jews, and Gentiles* (New Haven: Yale University Press).

Strasburger, H.
1965   'Poseidonius on Problems of the Roman Empire', *JRS* 55: 40-53.

Strobel, A.
1956   'Zum Verständnis von Röm 13', *ZNW* 47: 67-93.
1964   'Furcht, wem Furcht gebührt', *ZNW* 55: 58-62.

Stroumsa, G.A.G.
1984   *Another Seed: Studies in Gnostic Mythology* (NHS, 24; Leiden: E.J. Brill).

Stuhlmacher, P.
1965   *Gerechtigkeit Gottes bei Paulus* (FRLANT, 87; Göttingen: Vandenhoeck & Ruprecht).
1994   *Paul's Letter to the Romans: A Commentary* (trans. S.J. Hafemann; Louisville, KY: Westminster / John Knox Press).

Stuhlmann, R.
1983   *Das eschatologische Mass im Neuen Testament* (FRLANT, 132; Göttingen: Vandenhoeck & Ruprecht).

Talbert, C.H.
1978   'Biographies of Philosophers and Rulers as Instruments of Religious Propaganda in Mediterranean Antiquity', *ANRW* II.16.2: 1619-51.

Tarn, W.W.
1952   *Hellenistic Civilization* (rev. G.T. Griffith; Cambridge: Cambridge University Press, 3rd edn).

Taylor, A.E.
1927   *Plato: The Man and His Work* (New York: The Dial Press Inc).

Tessitore, A.
1988–89 'Aristotle's Political Presentation of Socrates in the *Nicomachean Ethics*', *Int* 16: 27-42.

Theiler, W.
1925   'A. Rostagni: *Il Verbo di Pitagora*', review, *Gnomon* 1: 146-54.
1926   'R. Harder: *Ocellus Lucanus*', review, *Gnomon* 2: 585-97.

Theis, J.
1991   *Paulus als Weisheistlehrer: Der Gekreuzigte und die Weisheit Gottes in 1 Kor 1–4* (Biblische Untersuchungen, 22; Regensburg: Pustet).

Theissen, G.
1982   *The Social Setting of Pauline Christianity: Essays on Corinth* (trans. J.H. Schutz; Philadelphia: Fortress Press).
1992   *Social Reality and the Early Christians: Theology, Ethics, and the World of the New Testament* (trans. M. Kohl; Minneapolis: Fortress Press).

Thesleff, H.
1961   *An Introduction to the Pythagorean Writings of the Hellenistic Period*
            (Acta Academiae Aboensis, Series A Humaniora, 24/3; Åbo: Åbo
            Akademi).
1965   *The Pythagorean Texts of the Hellenistic Period* (Acta Academiae
            Aboensis, Series A Humaniora, 30/1; Åbo: Åbo Akademi).
1972   'On the Problem of the Doric Pseudo-Pythagorica. An Alternative Theory
            of Date and Purpose', in K. von Fritz (ed.), *Pseudepigrapha*. I. *Pseudo-
            pythagorica-Lettres de Platon. Littérature pseudépigraphique juive* (Entre-
            tiens sur l'antiquité classique, 18; Vandoeuvres: Fondation Hardt): 57-87.

Thom, J.C.
1994   ' "Don't Walk on the Highways": The Pythagorean *Akousmata* and Early
            Christian Literature', *JBL* 113: 93-112.

Thrall, M.E.
1967   'The Pauline Use of συνείδησις', *NTS* 14: 118-25.

Tomson, P.J.
1990   *Paul and the Jewish Law: Halakha in the Letters of the Apostle to the
            Gentiles* (CRINT, 3/1; Minneapolis: Fortress Press).

Torjesen, K.
1995   *When Women Were Priests: Women's Leadership in the Early Church
            and the Scandal of Their Subordination in the Rise of Christianity* (San
            Francisco: HarperSanFrancisco).

Tufi, S.R.
1993   'Il mondo di San Paolo', *Archeo* 105(11): 60-111.

Unnik, W.C. van
1962   *Tarsus or Jerusalem? The City of Paul's Youth* (London: Epworth Press).
1975   'Lob und Strafe durch die Obrigkeit Hellenistisches zu Röm 13:3-4', in
            E.E. Ellis (ed.), *Jesus und Paulus: Festschrift für W.G. Kümmel* (Göttin-
            gen: Vandenhoeck & Ruprecht): 334-43.

Verbrugge, V.D.
1992   *Paul's Style of Church Leadership Illustrated by His Instructions to the
            Corinthians on the Collection* (San Francisco: Mellen Research Univer-
            sity Press).

Volf, J.M.G.
1990   *Paul and Perseverance: Staying in and Falling Away* (WUNT, 2.37;
            Tübingen: Mohr Siebeck).

Waerden, B.L. van der
1979   *Die Pythagoreer: Religiöse Bruderschaft und Schule der Wissenschaft*
            (Die Bibliothek der alten Welt; Zürich: Artemis).

Walbank, F.W.
1982   *The Hellenistic World* (Cambridge, MA: Harvard University Press).

Waltzing, J.-P.
1895–1900   *Étude historique sur les corporations professionelles chez les Romains
            jusqu'à la chute de l'Empire d'Occident* (4 vols.; Leuven: Peeters).

Watson, F.
1986   *Paul, Judaism and the Gentiles: A Sociological Approach* (SNTSMS, 56;
            Cambridge: Cambridge University Press).

Weiss, B.
1899   *Der Brief an die Römer* (Göttingen: Vandenhoeck & Ruprecht).
Weiss, J.
1897   'Beiträge zur paulinischen Rhetorik', in C.R. Gregory and A. Harnack
            (eds.), *Theologische Studien. Herrn Professor D. Bernard Weiss zu seinen
            70. Geburtstag* (Göttingen: Vandenhoeck & Ruprecht): 165-247.
Welborn, L.L.
1987   'On the Discord in Corinth: 1 Corinthians 1–4 and Ancient Politics', *JBL*
            106.1: 85-111.
1997   *Politics and Rhetoric in the Corinthian Epistles* (Macon, GA: Mercer
            University Press).
Wendland, P.
1895   'Philo und die kynisch-stoische Diatribe', in P. Wendland and O. Kern
            (eds.), *Beiträge zur Geschichte der griechischen Philosophie und
            Religion* (Berlin: Reimer): 1-63.
1907   *Die hellenistisch-römische Kultur in ihren Beziehungen zu Judentum und
            Christentum* (HNT, 1.2; Tübingen: Mohr Siebeck).
1912   *Die urchristlischen Literaturformen* (HNT, 1.3; Tübingen: Mohr Siebeck).
Wendt, H.H.
1894   'Die Lehre des Paulus verglichen mit der Lehre Jesu', *ZTK* 4: 1-78.
Wetter, G.P.
1915   *Phōs (φῶς). Eine Untersuchung über hellenistiche Frömmigkeit: zugleigh
            ein Beitrag zum Verständnis des Manichäismus* (Skrifter utgivna av K.
            Humanistika Vetenskapssamfundet i Uppsala, 17.1; Uppsala: Akademiska
            Bokhandeln).
White, L.M., and L.O Yarbrough (eds.)
1995   *The Social World of the First Christians: Essays in Honor of Wayne A.
            Meeks* (Minneapolis: Augsburg–Fortress).
Wick, P.
1994   *Der Philipperbrief: der formale Aufbau des Briefs als Schlüssel zum
            Verständnis seines Inhalts* (BWANT, 135; Stuttgart: W. Kohlhammer).
Wiefel, W.
1977   'The Jewish Community in Ancient Rome and the Origins of Roman
            Christianity', in Donfried (ed.) 1977: 100-19.
Wigtil, D.N.
1982   'The Ideology of the Greek "Res Gestae" ', *ANRW* II.30.1: 624-38.
Wilhelm, F.
1915   'Die Oeconomica der Neupythagoreer Bryson, Kallikratidas, Periktione,
            Phintys', *Rheinisches Museum für Philologie* 70: 161-223.
Wilken, R.L.
1995   Review of J.Z. Smith 1990, *JAAR* 63: 374-77.
Williams, D.J.
1999   *Paul's Metaphors: Their Context and Character* (Peabody, MA:
            Hendrickson).
Williams, S.K.
1980   'The Righteousness of God in Romans', *JBL* 99: 241-91.

Williamson, R.
    1989   *Jews in the Hellenistic World: Philo* (Cambridge: Cambridge University Press).

Winger, M.
    1993   *By What Law? The Meaning of Νόμος in the Letters of Paul* (SBLDS, 128; Atlanta: Scholars Press).

Wink, W.
    1993   *Cracking the Gnostic Code: The Powers in Gnosticism* (Atlanta: Scholars Press).

Winter, B.W.
    1994   *Seek the Welfare of the City: Christians as Benefactors and Citizens* (First-Century Christians in the Graeco-Roman World, 1; Grand Rapids: Eerdmans).

Witherington, B., III
    1994   *Paul's Narrative Thought World: The Tapestry of Tragedy and Triumph* (Louisville, KY: Westminster / John Knox Press).

Wrede, W.
    1907   *Paul* (trans. E. Lummis; London: Green).

Wuellner, W.
    1977   'Paul's Rhetoric of Argumentation in Romans: An Alternative to the Donfried–Karris Debate Over Romans', in Donfried (ed.) 1977: 152-74.
    1979   'Greek Rhetoric and Pauline Argumentation', in W.R. Schoedel and R.L. Wilken (eds.), *Early Christian Literature and the Classical Intellectual Tradition: In Honorem Robert M. Grant* (Théologie historique, 53; Paris: Beauchesne): 177-88.

Yorke, G.L.O.R.
    1991   *The Church as the Body of Christ in the Pauline Corpus: A Re-examination* (Lanham, MD: University Press of America).

Zeller, D.
    1990   *Charis bei Philon und Paulus* (Stuttgart: Katholisches Bibelwerk).

Zeller, E.
    1920–23   *Die Philosophie der Griechen in ihrer geschichtlichen Entwicklung* (3 vols.; Leipzig: O.R. Reisland).

Zuntz, G.
    1953   *The Text of the Epistles: A Disquisition Upon the Corpus Paulinum* (Schweich Lectures for 1946; London: Oxford University Press).

INDEXES

INDEX OF REFERENCES

OLD TESTAMENT

The Political Paul

CLASSICAL SOURCES

INDEX OF AUTHORS

JOURNAL FOR THE STUDY OF THE NEW TESTAMENT
SUPPLEMENT SERIES